PE: BOOKS

L   DON ORBITAL

'/   k of great passion and energy about the M25 from one of the
m   of the English sentence' John Lanchester, *Evening Standard*,
Bo   of the Year

'S   ir's prose is exquisite, his approach is a distinctively English take
o   whole strange business of psychogeography. The walk around
the   5 which is the basis for the book is no mere trope, but a way of
per   ting to the very jam of the London doughnut, by excavating
th   igh within which it is encased' Will Self, *Evening Standard*,
Bo   of the Year

'A   inating account of his heroic walk around the M25, a journey
thr   1 a new Britain of retail parks and industrial estates' JG Ballard,
Da   elegraph, Books of the Year

'A1   tant classic: part social history of the unsung lands that lie beside
the   25, and part cultural analysis of this endless terrain of science
par' golf courses, hypermarkets and speculative housing that makes
up   New Britain of 2002. A feast for admirers of Sinclair's rich and
qu   style' JG Ballard, *Guardian*, Books of the Year

'R   ling, self-indulgent, brilliant. Partly a diary, partly a ferociously
lea   l, literate and curious exploration of the plight of the nation'
St. y Telegraph

'A   solute joy. Sinclair's England is horribly recognizable, a land of
re   arks and jerry-built housing . . . he uncovers a rich history'
Th   nes

ABOUT THE AUTHOR

Iain Sinclair is the author of *Downriver* (winner of the James Tait Black Memorial Prize and the Encore Award); *Landor's Tower*; *White Chappell, Scarlet Tracings*; *Lights Out for the Territory*; *Lud Heat*; *Rodinsky's Room* (with Rachel Lichtenstein); *Radon Daughters*; and *London Orbital*. He lives in Hackney, East London.

London Orbital

A Walk around the M25

IAIN SINCLAIR

PENGUIN BOOKS

PENGUIN BOOKS

Published by the Penguin Group
Penguin Books Ltd, 80 Strand, London WC2R 0RL, England
Penguin Putnam Inc., 375 Hudson Street, New York, New York 10014, USA
Penguin Books Australia Ltd, 250 Camberwell Road,
Camberwell, Victoria 3124, Australia
Penguin Books Canada Ltd, 10 Alcorn Avenue, Toronto, Ontario, Canada M4V 3B2
Penguin Books India (P) Ltd, 11 Community Centre,
Panchsheel Park, New Delhi – 110 017, India
Penguin Books (NZ) Ltd, Cnr Rosedale and Airborne Roads,
Albany, Auckland, New Zealand
Penguin Books (South Africa) (Pty) Ltd, 24 Sturdee Avenue,
Rosebank 2196, South Africa

Penguin Books Ltd, Registered Offices: 80 Strand, London WC2R 0RL, England

www.penguin.com

First published by Granta Books 2002
Published in Penguin Books 2003
13

Copyright © Iain Sinclair, 2002
All rights reserved

Set in Monotype Bembo
Typeset by Rowland Phototypesetting Ltd, Bury St Edmunds, Suffolk
Printed in England by Clays Ltd, St Ives plc

ISBN-13: 978–0–14–101474–6
ISBN-10: 0–14–101474–1

For Renchi, and for Kevin Jackson,
shadows on the road

. . . for tho' eclipses of thought are to me a living inhumement and equal to the dread throes of suffocation, turning the valley of vision into a fen of scorpions and stripes and agonies, yet I protest, and glory in it for the sake of its evidence, of the strength of spirit that when inspir'd for art I am quite insensible to cold, hunger and bodily fatigue . . .

Samuel Palmer (letter to George Richmond)

K. Hodges (London, W8): What was your worst moment on TV?
Jeremy Paxman: Interviewing a man under the impression that he was a schizophrenic in care in the community when in fact he was an engineer who'd come on to talk about the M25.

Independent (29 September 1999)

Contents

Prejudices Declared   1

Soothing the Seething: Up the Lea Valley with
   Bill Drummond (and the Unabomber)   27

Paradise Gardens: Waltham Abbey to Shenley   79

Colne & Green Way: Abbots Langley to Staines   173

Diggers & Despots: Cutting the Corner,
   Staines to Epsom   243

Salt to Source: Epsom to Westerham. Through the Valley of
   Vision, to Dartford & the River   335

Blood & Oil: Carfax to Waltham Abbey   477

Millennium Eve   539

Acknowledgements   553

Select Bibliography   555

Index   561

Prejudices Declared

1

It started with the Dome, the Millennium Dome. An urge to walk away from the Teflon meteorite on Bugsby's Marshes. A white thing had been dropped in the mud of the Greenwich peninsula. The ripples had to stop somewhere. The city turned inside-out. Rubbish blown against the perimeter fence. A journey, a provocation. An escape. Keep moving, I told myself, until you hit tarmac, the outer circle. The point where London loses it, gives up its ghosts.

I have to admit: I was developing an unhealthy obsession with the M25, London's orbital motorway. The dull silvertop that acts as a prophylactic between driver and landscape. Was this grim necklace, opened by Margaret Thatcher on 29 October 1986, the true perimeter fence? Did this conceptual ha-ha mark the boundary of whatever could be called London? Or was it a tourniquet, sponsored by the Department of Transport and the Highways Agency, to choke the living breath from the metropolis?

Thatcher, who never grasped the concept of 'dressing down', her range going from airfixed-in-pressurised-dimethyl-ether (with solvent abuse warning on can) to carved-out-of-funerary-basalt, decided that day, or had it put to her by style consultants, that she should treat this gig as an outside broadcast, a chat from the paddock at Cheltenham, not the full Ascot furbelow. A suit, semi-formal (like Westminster Cathedral), in a sort of Aquascutum beige.

Autumn. No hat. A war footing: mufti-awkward. Argie bashing, ranting. Cromwell-fierce, hormonally stoked, she wields her small scythe, dismissing the unseen enemy, stalkers in the bushes, eco-bandits, twitchers, pennypinchers, lilylivered Liberal fifth-columnists, bedwetters, nay-sayers.

'I can't stand those who carp and criticise when they ought to be congratulating Britain on a magnificent achievement and beating the drum for Britain all over the world.' Rejoice. The military/industrial two-step. That old standard. Mrs Thatcher went on to rave over 'the Sainsbury's effect', the introduction of US mall-viruses, landscape consumerism, retail landfill.

YES was the word. Thatcher filtered in a perpetual green glow, like a Hammer Films spook. Bride of Dracula. Green meant GO. This business with ring roads had been floating around the ministries since the Thirties, since they'd noticed that cars were taking over the planet. At first, the idea had been: car as servant, parkways, elevated heaven ramps (Michael Powell's *A Matter of Life and Death*). Road-ribbons between lakes and golf courses. Orbital grooves that interconnected, working their way out from a loop around the royal bits (palaces, parliaments) to the inner suburbs, Hampstead and Holland Park. To the outer suburbs, unknowable Stanmore, Totteridge, Ponders End. To green belt nothingness, the great nowhere at the edge of Epping Forest; a territory defined by the red Italianate water towers of Victorian and Edwardian madhouses. And why stop there? Why not opt for abandoning airports and retaining huge runways that roared past Oxford, Cambridge, Winchester and Canterbury?

The snipping of the ribbon in October 1986 prefigured other ribbons, blue and white bunting that would turn the inner cities into a necrophile carnival: the spite-karma of terrorist outrages, turf wars. Irishmen, on their way home from the pub, shot, colandered, by rapid response units, for the crime of carrying unlicensed table-legs.

Newsreel paranoia is such that in the back files, even at this distance, nothing more than a face is revealed. We may know *who* is cutting the ribbon, but not where. Time has been suspended. There were, from the start, M25 myths: the woman who thought it was an oversized roundabout, the family who decided to keep going until they saw the sign for Newcastle. Archive footage doesn't let on: the location where Margaret Scissorhands, amputator of naughty thumbs, did the deed is still a secret. It wasn't at the official starting point, Junction 1, south of the Queen Elizabeth II Bridge, near Dartford. Nor was it within range of the Esso storage tanks at Purfleet, the soapy perfume of Procter and Gamble's West Thurrock factory. Nor out in the deadlands, where the blue highway loses its nerve and turns yellow for the elevated Thames crossing. A hawk-eyed swoop at the cameras on the remote north-west frontier, not too far from South Mimms service station. So it was rumoured.

A television researcher with superhuman determination, a man called John Sergeant, spent weeks on the road, living in a rented scarlet Mondeo, checking co-ordinates, chasing whispers. He narrowed the area down to a section of straight road, somewhere between Potters Bar and Junction 21 (the M1 interchange). He would interrogate newsreel clips, freeze frame, photograph the monitor; return to the motorway. Compare and contrast. He worked the hard shoulder. He scanned soft estates. He came close, but he couldn't pin it down with absolute precision.

That was left to Tony Sangwine of the Highways Agency. The film-essayist Chris Petit and I spent a morning on the road with Sangwine. The man was a visionary, a landscaper and motorway horticulturalist. He realised that taking on the orbital loop was the contemporary equivalent of getting a Capability Brown commission. Motorways were the last great public parks. Sangwine knew every weed, every salt-resistant clump of grass. He spoke lovingly of roe deer and short-tailed voles. The Highways Agency had planted more broadleaf woodland around the M25 than anywhere else in England. 'We have introduced the woodland flora you associate with ancient, semi-natural woodlands,' Sangwine boasted. 'Bluebells, dog mercury.'

Sangwine was there for the opening party, the marquee on an old airfield, the lunch that Thatcher didn't attend. She arrived in a bullet-proof car with security outriders. She snipped the ribbon and vanished. Sangwine pointed out the exact spot, an emergency phone kiosk on the northside hard shoulder, close to where the River Colne flows under the motorway, close to the padlocked shell of Napsbury Hospital.

The opening of the road was a moment of tremendous occult significance; within minutes the first circumnavigators were on the move. Simon Calder, one of nature's folding-bike men, travel editor of the *Independent*, had his thumb out. No fear of the snipper, the scissor-madame. He found the experience 'dull'. No Kerouacian epiphany, no download of spiritual gain.

No members of the general public, the great unwashed, were allowed to witness the ceremony. Corporate freebies. Big time blacktop sprayers and their guests. Plus vetted journalists, Murdoch's tame jackals. A guest list like the Dome bonanza. The first car breaks down at 11.16 a.m., precisely one minute after opening time. Within hours, it is perfectly clear that this unmagical orbit is the absolute contrary of the future Millennium Dome: the M25 instantly exceeds its expected quota of visitors, day trippers, casuals – where the flow to the Dome shrivels, week by week, until the promoters are forced to drag in school kids, the disadvantaged, confused tourists bribed with a ticket to ride the London Eye. Those who thought the down-river coda was compulsory, the price they had to pay for their ascent into the clouds.

Driving around the road was useless, as I discovered when I endured 250 miles in a day, with Chris Petit, clockwise and anticlockwise, coming in off my old favourite, the A13. And detouring into Lakeside, Thurrock. Into Theobalds Park and Heathrow. More was less, further was nowhere. In the morning, after we paid our pound and crossed the Queen Elizabeth II Bridge, we dragged, lurched, crawled on a three-lane conveyor belt, side-on to single-occupant, lightweight jacket-on-hook, cellphone voyagers. Soon these unfortunates would be penalised for their brief period of meditative calm: soothing tapes, landscape-format viewing screens.

This, according to one commuter interviewed for a television documentary, was the best of it, the highpoint of the day. The only contact with the changing seasons, the Surrey hills, canny roadside plantings. With England. This was the only respite from work stress, the on-line office, domestic responsibility. A car trip, Southend to Reigate, pushed up the heart rate but smoothed the soul; easily accessed reverie, a sensuous interplay of light and movement. Novelty that is only novelty because the route is so familiar.

On summer evenings, listening to a concert or radio play, one man admitted that he would go the long way home: West Byfleet, Staines, Uxbridge, Abbots Langley, Potters Bar. But regulations, imported from the States, will tax solitary motorists, those who refuse to share their pod, those who need this quiet time; they'll be shunted into the slow lane. Ostracised for the only reason that makes it worth running a gas-guzzling, money-burning machine.

Nobody can decide how long the road is, somewhere between 117 and 122 miles. By the time you've driven it, you don't care. You should be way out in another eco-system, another culture: Newport (Mon.), or Nottingham, or Yeovil. The journey must mean something. Not a wearied return, hobbled, to the point of origin.

It was obvious, therefore, that the best way to come to terms with this beast was to walk it. To set out, counterclockwise, from Waltham Abbey, and to complete the circuit before the (official) eve of the New Millennium.

Frosted bedroom windows, one of them cracked. Cars quilted with powdered snow. We had been talking too loudly about leaving Hackney. A fantasy, obviously, after all these years, brought on by zeros, overweening house prices. The terraced cottages of city bank clerks had declined to outside-lavatory-and-tin-bath (with scrupulously tidy garden) of honest working folk; grandparents, parents, four or five kids shoehorned into a plasterboard-improved box. By the 1960s, the Haggerston/Shoreditch fringe had been infiltrated by the abdicated middle classes (layabout communards, demi-artists); then by administrators, potential curators, first-rung medicals, single parents who spoke two languages. A few years after parturition most moved on. The school opposite was now a teachers' centre: there were more cars to catch the snowfall.

Our house didn't like quitters. It had given us shelter for more than thirty years, witnessed childbirth, seen books written and published. Casual chatter about a shift to the seaside was a compensatory gesture, a delayed midlife crisis. It didn't mean a thing. An excuse to sample oysters in Whitstable (Notting Hill prices), to swim at Walberswick (Southwold: the new Hampstead), to admire Charles Hawtrey's blue plaque in Deal (retired bookdealers, everybody I used to know).

The Bethnal Green painter Jock McFadyen who was quietly building up a bleak topography of absence, doomed snooker halls, drinking clubs on the cusp of oblivion, told me that he always felt the presence of the sea, tons of dark water, lurking behind Hackney's railway embankments and stuccoed pleasure palaces. It was only a matter of time, in his opinion, before all this trash, dirt and dust was swept away. We were amphibians in remission. On good mornings, looking out on the wet street, I was sure that he was right.

The early months of the true millennial year, 2001, had no good mornings. The house was delivering, more in sorrow than anger, its response to our treachery: the ridge from the top of my spine to my left arm was painful. The local massage man (warm office, psychology paperbacks) called the condition 'frozen shoulder'. Two years, he reckoned, if I was lucky. I'd have to train myself to write standing up, at a lectern, one-handed like Ernest Hemingway. Pre-Hailey, Idaho. Pre-shotgun. Luckily, my former bone-tweaker, a man built like a wrestler, who operated out of Purley, wrenched the shoulder back into life. 'Bag of frozen peas every half-hour,' he said. 'Work through the agony. Grab a doorknob, try a dozen kneebends.' Within a week, I was able to manage the gears on the old BMW. I could drive around that south-east quadrant of the M25; an hour to Junction 6. The 'shoulder' of the motorway, Bluewater to Brands Hatch, became my shoulder; frozen by traumatised muscles and tendons, clogged by weight of traffic.

Rain was still falling. It started around September and it hadn't stopped. Now it was turning into sleet.

Anna made the mistake. She used the word 'Brighton'. The house didn't care for it. The bedroom window, when she moved close to it, cracked into a lacework of tributaries. A map of the River Lea and its quarrelsome sibling, the Lee Navigation. With the New River breaking away, heading off in the general direction of Islington.

This was one of those London days when the light was no light, a grey hood. Trapped inside a gigantic light-bulb. You re-breathe, you use something that is already used up, exhausted. Cold cars coughed smoke. Walking was forbidden. North of the M25, on the far side of Waltham Abbey, footpaths had been closed off. Locally, the gates of Haggerston Park were padlocked; no access to the football pitches, no sylvan shortcut to Hackney Road. The authorities, in a frenzy of political correctness, removed the baa-lambs of the city farm from their paddock.

Driving along what had once been called the M16, that early section of the orbital motorway, from Waltham Abbey through the fringes of Epping Forest, south towards Purfleet and the bridge, you could see black smoke. A heavy pall over the mass graves of pigs, foot-and-mouth victims petrol-roasted in secret barbecue pits. The original outbreak had been noticed in a slaughterhouse near Brentwood. Little Warley and Great Warley, highlighted on TV's maps of shame, were conveniently off-road, with easy access to the M25 for the meat lorries, the animal transports.

Essex was plague country. Invisible airborne contagion closed the city's markets: the aisles of Smithfield were deserted. Hungry rhinoviruses fulfilled their destiny, causing blistered eruptions in the mouths and about the hoofs and teats of cattle, hogs and sheep. Sinister factory-farm sheds we had crept around on our M25 walk, protected by barking dogs, the hum of generators, were accused of malpractice.

The whole deal with the orbital motorway was called into question. The original Thatcherite pitch (civil engineering plus photogenic road-building programme being part of the Great Leader package) was anti-metropolitan; it was about protecting the suburbs. Nasty, dirty trade goods, all that was left of the north's industrial heritage, could be detoured around the city – without invading, say, Finchley; or being contaminated by the alien hordes of Hackney and Tower Hamlets. The road re-placed the working river. Seen from a distance, across a rough pasture golf course in Essex, tarmac glistened like black ice. As soon as the M25 was opened, swans lifting from the Thames at Staines mistook the bright silver surface for water; there were several nasty accidents. A report in the *Evening Standard* (February 2001) described the trauma suffered by a man, on his way to visit a retired rock star in the Surrey stockbroker belt, when a large white bird crashed on to the bonnet of his car.

The M25 shifts cargo, transports workers from Middlesex into Surrey. It carries contraband, dodgers of excise duty, grotesquely stacked humans, prepared to pay a premium for a ticket out of some Balkan hellhole. The road has become the business, while the river, emptied of everything except landfill barges and cheerless pleasure craft, is a backdrop to computer-enhanced heritage and development scams. The Thames is a false memory, constantly referred to in terms of its back story: the Globe Theatre (faked), madeover power stations, blacking factories and tanneries reinvented as luxury apartments, self-governing islands with top dollar security. You see the river but it isn't there. You hear the road but the noise is explained away as part of the general acoustic interference that assaults our ears.

The M25, from being the pet and the pride of an autocratic government, has been rapidly downgraded to a rage-inducing asteroid belt, debris bumping and farting and belching around a sealed-off city. The orbital motorway is a security collar fixed to the neck of a convicted criminal. It enforces a nocturnal quarantine.

Launched, mysteriously, as a highway to the wide world, it was soon revealed as the inspiration for tabloid headlines. YES, I AM THE M25 KILLER: *Daily Mail* (31 March 2000). M25 KILLER NOYE GUILTY OF MURDER: *Evening Standard* (14 April 2000). HOW TO SURVIVE THE M25 (We explain how to use your cut-and-keep maps): *Daily Mail* (24 January 1988).

The M25 wasn't a way of avoiding London, or a way of protecting the shires from urban corruption (socialists, non-voters); it was a convenient back lane for housebreakers, a shuttle into the excavated chalk quarries (ghosts of wartime tunnels and bunkers) now imagineered into virtual unreality shopping cities. Planet Retail. Satellite Ikea. These off-highway zones, on either side of the Dartford Crossing – Lakeside, Thurrock, and Bluewater – set up their own impenetrable micro-geographies; traffic islands, loops, dead ends that mimicked the motorway system. Bluewater looked like the entrance to the Channel Tunnel, a duty-free holding area. Water was the pitch, the selling device. A park, an idyll, a day out: a destination for those who have no good reason to travel. The old Cockney favourites, Margate, Ramsgate, Southend, Hastings, were superseded, given over to asylum seekers, banished inner-city dole bandits, workshy inadequates. Bluewater was a real outing to an unreal place. Once you've been there, in the silence, the aftershock of travel, when the skin of the car stops vibrating, you learn the awful secret: *there is no there.* The question remains: 'How many compulsory purchases do I have to make to get out?'

What else is the M25 good for? Auto-jousting: the classic road rage scenario. The Brinks-Mat alchemist (Kenneth Noye) in the Land Rover Discovery, travelling into town from his well-protected Kentish pile, arrives at the Swanley interchange at the same moment as red Rascal van-man (Stephen Cameron) and his girlfriend. A traffic light at a sliproad holding impatient motorists a beat too long. There are so many CCTV cameras on poles around the orbital motorway that this affray is pretty much an audition for *Crimewatch*, or another botched British gangland feature film.

'He stabbed me, Dan.' With a four-inch blade, which Noye happened to have about his person. Through the heart and liver. The witness, called at the trial, was piloting a white Roller.

The crime seems to be a straightforward confrontation, a matter of hierarchy, aspirational lifestyles. Noye, the wealthy Mason, with plenty of good chums on the force, the chancer who has made it into Kent, colliding with a kid from the South London suburbs in a red van. The shocked Roller-owner, a solid businessman, is there to keep a disinterested eye on the vulgar affray.

But it's not quite as simple as that. Roller-man, Alan Decabral, has substance, it's true: twenty-odd stone of it, in a red and black rugby jersey. His eyes, in press photographs, are wary, nested in pouches of angry skin. The beard is grey, hair long and unruly. Rings, bracelets, thin watch. Antiques, guns, Hell's Angels, drugs: Decabral was a fairly typical new-money Kentish rate-dodger. Everything about him – shirt, beard, biography – solicited disaster.

'The man who put road-rage killer Kenneth Noye behind bars,' according to the *Observer* (15 October 2000), 'was sitting in his son's car outside Halford's in Ashford, Kent, when a man appeared at his window and shot him once in the side of the head.'

The participants in the Swanley interchange drama, two dead and one imprisoned, drift from newspaper shorthand to full-blown figures of myth. Driving on the M25, coming over the Queen Elizabeth II Bridge, fumbling for your coin to pay the road toll, nurdling into the right lane, brings out the stories. Every cab driver has a Kenny Noye yarn: bent coppers, Masonic conspiracies, buried bullion. It is always assumed, rumoured, that the three men – killer, victim and witness – had plenty of previous, criminal connections. Three cars, three lifestyle state-ments, converging in the wrong place: one of the gates that act as circuit breakers, disturbing the energy generator that hums continually around the undisciplined body-mass of London.

The orbital motorway, opened in a spirit of jingoistic tri-umphalism, rapidly declined into a service road for toxic landfill, somewhere to shift an earlier era's mess; the rubble of asylums and hospitals, munitions factories and firing ranges. The road gave access to new Legoland housing developments. The curva-ture of the M25 was a fraud, reality was a series of badly stapled straight lines, local sprints (Potters Bar to Waltham Abbey, Upminster to Purfleet, Shoreham to Godstone), or ramps lead-ing directly into the major off-highway retail parks, Bluewater and Lakeside, Thurrock.

Any attempt to drive the circuit, or to come to terms with that journey, enforced metaphors of madness. The motorist in his helmet-on-wheels, with its petrol-burning engine, dirty exhaust plumes, faulty electronic circuits, entered into a contract with sensory derangement, diesel-induced hallucinations. He (or she) underwent the sort of voyage towards insanity, breakdown and reintegration that R.D. Laing and the antipsychiatrists of the Sixties advocated. Solitary Italianate water towers, at points of vantage around the road, on hillocks at Shenley and Claybury and Dartford, become the markers, compass points in a map of madness. Because something has vanished, because it can no longer be seen, doesn't mean that it's not there.

The M25, previously known (through brief trespass, short-hauls to Gatwick or Heathrow), was a thing to be tolerated, endured rather than experienced. The trick was to move back, step away, treat the road as a privileged entity, a metaphor of itself. Enlightenment came with distance, detachment.

At the cold turn of the year, on 1 January 1998, it began. I drove out to Enfield Chase. The area around Bull's Cross, parks behind red brick walls, garden centres, stables, eerily quiet roads, was very seductive to me. The 'story', if there was a story, had moved away from my old Whitechapel midden, from the river: developers and visible artists, explainers, exploiters, had taken care of all that. Whenever a heritage is recognised and celebrated – a moment such as the staging of an exhibition in acknowledgement of the legacy of the Whitechapel Library, Isaac Rosenberg and the circle of Yiddish poets (just as the Library is closed) – is the time to move on, move out.

Enfield was a dream; themes read about but not known, half-recalled mentions of the gardener John Tradescant, Capel Manor, E.A. Bowles at Myddelton House. Through the bare trees, you could hear the faint siren song of the road, the M25. Everything was frost-slick, glistening. Streams and rivulets caught the light. The parks and gardens were, of course, all shut; I made a note of the opening times, for another occasion.

Coming into Whitewebbs Lane, with the notion of finding a bridge over the M25, I heard a sound, a howling, that was to be one of the defining characteristics of my motorway walk: the chorus of the boarding kennels. Domestic animals are dumped, out on the fringes, where their din will cause least offence. On a working day, the yelps and snarls, the prolonged baying, would be muffled in traffic, minute-shavers hustling towards the motorway.

On Bull's Cross bridge (one of the current 264 that span the M25), you could hear it, acoustic layering; the way tyre-hum modulates as speeding vehicles move from grey to blacktop. Then the dogs and cats in their cages, riders coming out of the woods around Theobalds Park. A fragment of chat from two dog walkers who passed me on the bridge: 'In exchange for a pension, they gave him a gravel pit.'

A fox, emerging from the Western Jewish Cemetery, shot me a baleful glance and stalked into a roadside copse. White Webbs Park, on the south side of the M25, had been pleasant enough – as long as you kept to the designated walkways: PRIVATE PROPERTY, KEEP OUT, ARCHERY IN PROGRESS. This was a day for family groups, adults talking, children impatient, new mittens, new bicycles. Theobalds Park: a royal residence, landscaped by Tradescant, then the estate of a brewing family who could afford to reassemble Christopher Wren's Temple Bar at the bottom of the garden as an overambitious folly. And now? The Abbey National Centre of Excellence. A surveillance checkpoint and voice box to interrogate unlicensed visitors. I loved it. This was the true territory for the fiction that is England.

You could slither down a slope, on the north side of the road, and sit under the motorway bridge (the New River insinuates itself beside you). There's an Ice Warning box (ready to flag the next glaciation). A mosaic ramp with hexagonal panels, regular as crystal. Tough grass breaks the tiles. Feral picnickers have

been here before me, leaving punctured tins and cans of strong
lager; soggy handbags and soggier documents.

I sit, comfortably, with my back to one of the piers, munching my sandwiches and deciding that, yes, I want to walk
around the orbital motorway: in the belief that this nowhere,
this edge, is the place that will offer fresh narratives. I don't
want to be *on* the road any more than I want to walk on water;
the soft estates, the acoustic footprints, will do nicely. Dull
fields that travellers never notice. Noise and the rush of traffic,
twenty-four hours a day, has pushed 'content' back. An elaborate scheme of planting (two million trees and shrubs, mostly in
Surrey and Kent) would hide the nasty ditch with its Eddie
Stobart lorries, its smoke belchers. The M25 walk was the next
project. The form it would take and the other people who
might be persuaded to come along, to liven up the tale, was still
to be decided.

3

Those boards outside newsagents' shops, with their broken haikus, fascinate me. DIANA'S RESTING PLACE CHANGED. ROYALS URGED TO SELL BRITAIN. SPICE GIRLS 'SPLIT' FEAR. FOOT AND MOUTH ARMY MOVE IN. Anonymous poetry, urgent and anxious. Banishment of definite and indefinite articles. Present tense. Absence of lower-case lettering. It was a style to which I aspired. The city composing its own disposable legend. Royalty, crime, transport, weather. On a daily basis. Unselfconscious surrealism. Even the one-eyed got the message. Burdening yourself with a newspaper was a waste of time. Terse black-on-white newscasts told you everything you needed to know. More effective than contradictory traffic updates and fog warnings flashed from gantries above motorways.

On the final afternoon of the old millennium, the boards predicted DOME FIASCO, hours before it happened; hours before the salaried opinion-makers and big cheeses were abandoned on a cold station platform in Stratford East. Up to that point, they'd bought the New Labour spin, the shameless bullshit. The Dome, an obscene fungus on Bugsby's Marshes, empty of content, serviced by a flamboyant Underground link, had received a good or neutral press. The Jubilee Line had been shoved through (magnificent stations, no customers) while Hackney was kept in purdah, outside the system. Just because the brand name of this expensive interloper sounded regal and upbeat.

East London stayed indoors. The Acorn pub on Queensbridge Road promised: CONTINUOUS SKY. Motor traffic was forbidden to pull over, take a look at the river or the preparations for the big night. MILLENNIUM CLEARWAY. SPECIAL CONTROLS APPLY. NO STOPPING.

Helicopters droned overhead like a gangland funeral. Some of the Wapping riverside balconies made a halfhearted attempt at getting into the spirit of things by hanging YEAR 2000 banners and a few coloured balloons. A melancholy airship drifted over the News International fortress. Knots of well-wrapped folk gathered in front of the Tower Hotel, gazing hopefully upstream at the gothic spires of H. Jones's nineteenth-century bridge. Whose party was it? Had they been invited? *Where* was the action?

I wanted to stay with the story – Dome, Millennium, meridian line – but I couldn't face the orchestrated riverside jollity. The Thames resisted such vulgar and ill-considered nonsense, an evening of stage-managed spontaneity: 'rivers of fire', red, green and gold starbursts, the spinning of the new Ferris wheel, the London Eye. The Eye wasn't working, it had failed its safety check. The heavens were shrouded, rain beads hung in the heavy air.

My first notion was to try the Beckton Alp. Far enough out, down the A13, to avoid the crush; high enough to see the fire-stream as it raced, barge to barge, along the river. This manmade conical wonder, a ski slope overlooking the City Airport at Silvertown (retail park, golf driving range, Northern Sewage Outfall, arterial roads), seemed to be the ideal platform. It had everything I looked for, a privileged overview as grand as anything produced by the early London mapmakers, Anthony van den Wyngaerde or Wenceslaus Hollar. The Alp had been perfect for the solar eclipse, attracting locals and periscope-wielding enthusiasts, but it might prove bleak and damp, and difficult to reach, on the last night of the millennium.

The other obvious choice, honouring the Greenwich meridian, was Waltham Abbey. My circumnavigation of the M25 had begun and ended there; I would align myself with the fuss at the Dome, but drift to the perimeter, staying alert for distant noises, flares in the sky. I booked a table at the Shuhag Balti house (WE ONLY SERVE CHICKEN BREAST); I'd noticed the

Millennium Special menu as I'd plodded through town on the last leg of my walk.

Anna, by now, was used to my unorthodox notions of a good night out. Waltham Abbey had the edge on Beckton Alp. In light rain, we ambled out of a deserted car park.

Early evening, around seven o'clock, it didn't seem as if much was happening. We tried to get into the Welsh Harp, a quiet enough pub at the end of a day's tramp. It's a special feeling to pull off that double, abbey and pub. The great church doors of Holy Cross and St Lawrence were always locked when we made our starts, just after first light. And locked again when we returned in the dark. The presence of this sealed building, its surrounding orchards and fishponds, travelled with us. The astrological ceiling, with its zodiac symbols, deep blues, golds and whites, was a conceptual umbrella carried into the Essex countryside. The ceiling had been designed by the eccentric William Burges and put in place in the 1860s. Its theme, according to the brochures, was Time.

The guy on the door of the Welsh Harp, no bulge-eyed bouncer, let us know that the pub was off-limits, a private party. Through soft rain, we tramped the wet flags of the market square, the spokes of medieval street pattern, pedestrianised (but lacking pedestrians): the usual small-town English mix of charity shops, minicabs (Abbey Cars), insurance, junk food. As the locus for a millennial celebration, Waltham Abbey was looking pretty good. Picture-book pubs closed to strangers. Motorway fringe motels booked solid with revellers. Slithery streets. Church bells. The Lea in spate, and soon to flood the ground-floor rooms of outwardly mobile retirees. Cue: local news interview as the three-piece suite floats out of the window.

There's always a warm glow in not belonging, in being the only abstainer at a *fleadh* in Ballycastle, the only non-Iberian bull-runner in Pamplona who hasn't read Hemingway; it means that you're not responsible. You don't *have* to enjoy

yourself. It's not part of the contract to become one with the
spirit of place. You are not obliged to spew, fight, sing, dance,
wreck your car or in any other way amuse yourself. And this is
very liberating.

I felt so. I'm not sure that Anna agreed. Waltham Abbey
wasn't Hackney. It was, to a significant degree, populated
by ex-Hackney escapers who had tunnelled under the wire
years ago, at the first sign of the place going to the dogs: when
they started selling croissants, jerk chicken and putting up
notices advising you that you were walking down a cycle track.
Old-timers were nervous of nail extension parlours and hair
straightening booths that stayed open all night, doing a steady
trade with hooded youths and brothers who'd traded in black,
6-series BMWs for less conspicuous Audis. As the only way to
drive through the City of London without being pulled.

Waltham Abbey and the inhabitable pockets of Epping
Forest were white Cockney on the drift, the tectonic plate
theory. Hackney becomes Chingford. Notting Hill relocates to
Hoxton. Rafts of like-minded citizens (holding fast to their
prejudices) nudged, ever closer, to the rim of the map. It took
the M25 to stop them disappearing into Fenland mists.

Cabbies, always awkward sods, had uprooted years ago: try
finding one who didn't grow up in Bethnal Green and who
doesn't now live in Hertfordshire or Essex. Strange choice. To
commute towards the jams, to spend your days snorting diesel,
for the privilege of a Saturday shop at an out-of-town mall,
nine holes on a Sunday morning. More space – before the latest
animal husbandry disaster – to run the dog.

You wouldn't have known, from the bunting and the flashing lights through the windows of Waltham Abbey pubs, that
there was anything special about this night. The driving on
the road out, Lea Bridge Road, Hoe Street (Asian mini-marts
fully operative), Walthamstow dog track, Chingford Mount,
was unexceptional. Bumper car rules: red means go. One headlamp (full-beam) as standard. White vans, windows open, drum

'n' bass, take precedence over every other form of transport.

The police were busy elsewhere, organising their lock-ins or earning overtime at Blair's Riverside Follies. Policing this turf, at the best of times, is retrospective: sirens, three car chases, weaving in and out of sluggish traffic. The state mercenaries were funded, so it seemed, to put up blue and white decorations around murder sites. The ground was guilty, it had to be made an example of, framed off. Landscape art. East London, as I walked it, was becoming a lake of crisp cellophane, fields of wrapped flowers. Concrete bollards that sprouted nosegays. Lipstick-pink peonies, goldenrod and primrose, held in place with brown parcel tape. Commemorative cards: JUSTICE FOR HARRY.

Eventually, a lesser pub, a hangdog funeral parlour, desperate for custom, let us in. The barmaid slipped us a couple of tickets. The atmosphere was like a wake for an elderly bachelor nobody really knew or liked. They were going through the motions. It was the least they could do, but they hadn't hated him enough to start on the celebratory sweetmeats, the booze. He wasn't worth a song or a dance. Maybe the wake was for King Harold, the last Saxon king, senior stiff in the burial ground behind the abbey. They had his portrait up on the wall and they'd draped it in coloured streamers. The men hadn't arrived yet. A suspicion of women, dressed to the nines (and well beyond), perched at the bar. Kids skittered around, seeing how far they could go without getting a slap. We were the relatives who belonged to somebody else, the wrong side of the family. We smiled and nodded, paid for our drinks, slipped away before the fun started.

It isn't easy to stretch a curry pit-stop over three hours, but the Shuhag was happy to watch us try. Under ordinary circumstances, Anna keeps me out of restaurants that don't have customers. She wants the reassurance that the experience is survivable, other reckless souls are prepared to give it a bash.

Tonight, for this once-in-a-thousand-years moment, rules are relaxed. The only options are going back to the pub for a bag of pork scratchings, or home to bed.

Wine is wasted on mussel beran, chicken tikka, lamb korma, king prawn dansak, and the rest. The usual eccentric mix westerners cobble together when they order by numbers. The equivalent, I guess, of Yorkshire pudding with winkles, gravy, Spanish omelette and boiled sprouts. But, wasted or not, we kept it coming. It was turning into a great night. The waiters were friendly. The ceilings were low. A 'fully air-conditioned, Balti & Tandoori restaurant' doesn't fit easily into one of those step-down-from-the-pavement premises that are usually turned into lace-curtain tea rooms, or tourist brochure and pictorial ashtray information centres. The Shuhag and its chilled Chablis kept us in a state of non-specific wellbeing; dim red light, comfortably upholstered banquettes, unobtrusive service. A table filled with small hot dishes, replenished as soon as they disappeared.

Other diners manifested. A foursome who told us they wanted an early meal, something to line the stomach, before taking the train into town, to catch the excitement. They were astonished to hear that we'd travelled in the opposite direction, by choice. But whichever direction, in or out, we were all on the same beam, the meridian line: Waltham Abbey is one of the few places where they take notice of zero longitude, mark it with decorated pillars and a straight walk. Enough to let you feel that you're getting somewhere, before it all comes to an abrupt end: perimeter fence, strategic planting and 'Government Research Establishment' on the map.

By eleven o'clock we were moving, unsteadily, towards the church. Again, we didn't really belong, wrong clothes, and again the locals were welcoming. There was a certain powdery greyness about the anoraks and the rigorously disciplined hair, a certain sheen. Steradent and talcum powder. The god-folk were outfitted well short of *Songs of Praise*; they weren't expecting cameras. Thin-framed spectacles glinted in candle-light. Footballer-evangelical rather than ritualistic High Church; they weren't tambourine-bashers but neither did they go in for vestments and Latin and incense.

Superstitiously, I kept to the end of the row – in case I had to make a run for it. But the service, good Essex voices reverberating through that tall building with its twisted Norman columns, contained satisfyingly pagan elements. A 'Hope Tree' had been set up, to which we were invited to attach postcards, millennial wishes. We weren't, by then, in a fit state to write, but I lurched up the aisle and shoved my fractured telegram in among the pine needles.

The church was packed, the ritual unforced, the location powerful and pertinent. In such a place, the vertical view of history holds: the back story is not forgotten. The important dead are given their alcoves. Nothing disappears without trace. No part of this evening's ceremony shames the past, or forces present quietude into some gaudy exhibition that it will be unable to sustain. 'Time' is coded into the celestial zodiac, the syphilitic alabaster of the dignitaries, landowners, floating in their niches. 'Time and Eternity' is the tag line for this service. 'For the Passing of One Age and the Beginning of a New Millennium. Looking Back – Looking Forward.'

Heads down in prayer or private meditation; audible creaks as the congregation struggle to their feet, to let rip with the first hymn. Some of them are in wheelchairs. There is one black family. We have been instructed to assemble cardboard boxes which will contain millennial candles. Not easy with a fistful of palsied thumbs.

> **Parson:** *Jesus Christ is the light of the world.*
> **Congregation:** *A light no darkness can quench.*

So out of the church we straggle, smiley-touchy, in it to-gether, candles cupped against the breeze and the damp night, over the meridian flagstone and down towards the car park at the back of the abbey. Singing as we process: 'Don't carry a load in your pack/you don't need two shirts on your back.' That one wasn't written by a walker, I thought. The second shirt is to get you into the pub at the end of the day, when the first one is sweat-soaked, streaked with the colour of your cheap rucksack.

Stern, sheepy heads of the elderly; mortality shadows, so many other services to recall. The younger, louder couples, families, are clustering around the beacon, a brazier on a pole, that will be lit at midnight. Essex, England. Munitions factories. Official Secrets Act. Parkland cleaned up by the Lee Valley Authority. Exotic plantings that have survived only because they were on protected government land. The picnic grounds on the west side of Horsemill Stream are, apparently, very popular with Balkan refugees. They gather on Sunday afternoons, balalaikas and barbecued chicken.

The revelry, as we approach midnight, is coming from transistors. Subdued citizens in masks with flashing lights, wobbly antennae, stand around waiting for the heavens to crack open. Small groups have gathered in the drizzle, camp stools and folding tables, crackers, bottle of fizz, to see in the millennium: right on the line, zero longitude, listening to the distant hum of the orbital motorway, tyres on a wet road.

The millennial brazier is actually an elongated Bunsen burner, a cough of gas waiting for a spark. There's a village feel to the event; a release from corporate sponsorship. Public spectacles that only succeed in messing up the quality of everyday life by imposing road barriers, razorwire, CCTV and ubiquitous gooseberry-fool security jackets (lapel-connected to unseen controllers). The colours of the city at the end of the century: luminous custard with a drape of blue and white plastic ribbons. Smoking holes in which something has happened. Sirens. Cone islands. Chemically upbeat breakfast-time TV presenters announcing another snarl-up on the M25, slowmoving traffic between Junctions 12 and 16, an overturned lorry at Hobbs Cross; Kent disappearing underwater.

Waltham Abbey is the cathedral of the motorway. I feel as if we've just listened to Father Mapple's sermon, from the pulpit with the rope ladder in the whaling port of New Bedford, at the opening of *Moby-Dick*, before setting out on a hazardous voyage. *Yes, the world's a ship on its passage out, and not a voyage complete; and the pulpit is its prow.*

Up goes the flame, like an over-oiled chip-pan; fizzing white at the edges against the dull night. Up go the fireworks, splinters of light, coronas and diadems and pink-gold ruffs. Muffled detonations. Public and private displays. City under siege. Blitz memories. A spectacular burst, sequential and increasing in noise and circumference, has some of the old-timers believing that the munitions factory has exploded. But it's no longer there; like everything with a dark industrial history, the Royal Gunpowder Mills are in the process of being turned into a visitor centre, a heritage attraction.

Christians embrace and link arms to sing 'Auld Lang Syne'. On a portable television set, belonging to one of the picnicking families, we see the Thames, the Teflon Toadstool, the crowds; warped and rolling. We can just make out the ironed faces of the national waxworks, dutifully mouthing doggerel of the Scottish borders. What a bizarre spectacle: 'Piety' Blair (as Michael Moorcock christened him in his novel *King of the City*), Edinburgh-educated, grappling with the Germano-Highlander Elizabeth II (inspiration for the Dartford Bridge), in a rictus of homage, pantomimed ecstasy. The certain knowledge that New Labour's patronage of this awful tent was a disaster. And, worse, they are stuck with it. He can feel the laser glare of all those newspaper editors, fruit-fly celebs, who were kept hanging about on a Jubilee Line platform in the middle of the night. And who now face a nightmare journey home through the disgruntled mob.

★

Heading back down the Lea Valley, I stand on the Seward-stone Bridge over the M25, to watch the lights of the cars: two streams, gold and red. It never stops. Firework displays on the horizon. Flares and flashes reflected in the reservoirs. There was still, at this distance, something epic about the idea of London, the crenellation of bright towers.

Later, I would hear my children's accounts of their night in the thick of it, down at the river: nothing much to see, a moving stream of fire that didn't, unremarkable fireworks, trains not running or impossibly crowded. Young girls who fainted or were attacked and couldn't be got to hospital, or were turned away from police stations. Epic traverses in unsuitable shoes, further and further east, to escape the crush, the craziness. A decent party, all things considered. A subdued rave. Very average. Better next time, next millennium.

I thought of the cheery foursome from the Shuhag. If their night went as expected, the glamour of the big city, Last-Night-of-the-Proms with Catherine wheels, they were prepared, for the first time, to walk home; the full fifteen or twenty miles, they weren't sure, up the Lea Valley to Waltham Abbey. Madness. A journey no sane Londoner could be accused of attempting.

Soothing the Seething

Up the Lea Valley with Bill Drummond
(and the Unabomber)

1

27 March 1998. Greenwich peninsula. The Dome. I've been here before, many times, in all weathers, picking at the scab. I've been here with the photographer Marc Atkins. The river is always a buzz. Atkins was working then in black and white, future memories anticipated, instinctive retrievals; the darkness he tried to draw out, heavy skies reconfigured in an improvised darkroom, secret weathers. The point of the day, the walk, was to lift that grey lid, the miasma of depression that hangs over the city and its inhabitants. To wait for the moment when the sun breaks through, evening beams cartwheeling over an heroic landscape. You have to be out there all day to be sure of getting it. The remission. The pay-off that makes urban life worth enduring.

Atkins, allowed into the tent at an early stage, when there was nothing to be seen except loose cables and optimistic Zone signs, was defeated. The photographers hung back from the print journalists, they tracked each other. If Atkins stood still, the guy from the *Mirror* and the girl from the Docklands give-away froze with him. If he scratched, they scratched. He was taller than they were, he had the advantage; he didn't have to carry an aluminium ladder. But, this time, he couldn't help. The site had nothing to offer, dead ground; poisoned earth that refused to glow. Bugsby's Marshes had its own special magic: negativity. Nothingness. Zero with a skin on it. I watched the camera obscura table at the Greenwich Observatory as it scrolled in the local landscape, an invisible meridian line fired across the bows of the Dome.

Longitude was the bait for Bill Drummond (KLF activist, pop star, inventor of bands). Drummond was an interestingly complex mix of artist and anti-artist, performer and hermit, scholar, iconoclast, polemicist, prankster and well-grounded human. More than most, he honoured the past – particularly his own – even when he had to invent it. His Scottishness was important to him, although he'd lived for years in England; Corby, Liverpool, Buckinghamshire. He went north, to the island of Jura, when he decided to burn a million quid. (As a way of shaming the substance, the wads of paper, Drummond always referred to it as 'quid', never pounds. Quid gave the condemned loot an agricultural classification. Chewed and hawked tobacco. Quid was nineteenth-century slang for the vagina.) Using bundles of banknotes as peat was a transgressive act that prefigured the grotesque barbecues of farm animals, the smoke plumes that marked out the north-east corner of the M25.

Drummond was into a form of conceptual art that had mud on its boots. It was meant to *work*. You didn't just photograph it and file it away. The ashes from Jura were a register of ugliness that would be swept up and compressed into a brick. Another notion that Drummond played with, talked about, was to infiltrate this brick, bad karma, into the wall of Gilbert Scott's power station (soon to be revised as Tate Modern).

Bill's sidekick Gimpo (visionary ex-squaddie) had a very clear take on the M25. He saw it as something to be circumnavigated at the vernal equinox; pile into a van at South Mimms (everything starts there) and keep going, wired and crazy, cameras rolling. Gimpo was the inspiration and Drummond the scribe. Bill wrote about the affair in a piece entitled 'Gimpo's 25' which he published in the collection *45*. By that point, the one-time manipulator of the charts, theatre designer, was blown: he had come out in the identity he had been sliding towards for years, writer (i.e. leper, outcast). Writer and self-publisher. Double whammy. Most of us started that way – and kept quiet about it – but Drummond had triumphantly descended the evolutionary scale. He'd chucked away his chance of an appearance on *Celebrity Big Brother* to scribble in cafés, hang out in small town libraries – and plod up the Lea Valley with a pair of distressed psychogeographers.

Gimpo is the white-van man of your worst nightmares. See him parked up in South Mimms and you'd leave three or four clear bays on either side. Drummond, as he recounts, responded very positively to the idea of an orbital spin: 'Fuckin' brilliant idea, Gimpo. Can I come with you?' This was back in the days when the motorway could be seen as a video game, an arcade challenge (such things were actually marketed). Even earlier, at the outset, Thatcherite city boys re-enacted movies they'd never viewed, Monte Hellman's *Two-Lane Blacktop*, Richard C. Sarafian's *Vanishing Point*. Head-to-head, from South Mimms to South Mimms, at night: cash-splash, noise, nothing to see. Like driving down the barrel of a gun. Jogging on a treadmill.

Precise to the point of pedantry, Drummond calculates that it's 124.5 miles around the circuit. Gimpo is aiming to stick to the fast lane, the outer rim; bugger petrol consumption. His stated aim is *to find out where the M25 leads*. The demented wheelman's ambition, according to Drummond, is to 'soothe his seething'. Like extinguishing a small blaze in a frying pan by dowsing it with kerosene. The M25 is seething incarnate. Gimpo is practising sympathetic magic, treating like with like in sanity-defying doses. Nietzsche believed that 'only thoughts which come from walking have any value'. And look what happened to him, seething till his eyes popped out, conversations with horses.

The Gimpo/Drummond equinoctial circumnavigation was a primary inspiration for my M25 pilgrimage, the leisurely twelve-part walk. I liked the way Drummond responded to the Queen Elizabeth Bridge; the pleasure he derived from civil engineering, from the overview of the Purfleet diaspora, oil tanks, wilderness gardens, gleaming blue tractors waiting for export. Distribution and storage (human and otherwise) was the name of the game. Riding the high road over the Thames was the only point on the circuit where the motorway achieves the condition of vision. The rest is foot–down, fingers drumming on the wheel. But the Bridge is not, officially, part of the M25. It's where walkers are refused entry, pulled over by a cop car, told to swim for it.

Gimpo wants to be Mad Max, motorhead jester of chaos. He wants to lead an E-fuelled procession of smoking pick-up trucks, customised gas-guzzlers, Gaffa-taped camera cars, in a noise cone, a whirlwind of dead leaves and burnt rubber. A 124.5-mile, bumper-to-bumper procession: so that standing still, being held in the stream, will feel like torrential movement. The rrrr-ushh.

'The further we go, the less familiar it will all become.' That's Drummond's glorious expectation, the germ behind our walk. Gimpo's gang push it – even talking of a twenty-five-day spin, *further* – until they achieve lift-off, white van acting like a tin opener gashing the surface of the globe, letting out chthonic spectres. Drummond realises, in one of those vulture-on-the-shoulder flashes, that he is older than Tony Blair. In actuarial time, maybe. By birth certificate. But look, on TV, at those folds, those bruised pouches; look at the eyes. Nothing on earth is older than Blair. The skin job, the hair teasing, the diamond-dust orthodontics, don't help. The grin that threatens to meet itself at the back of the neck. Blair is so weary. He's tireder than a coprolite. Older than oxygen. Drummond is his direct contrary, his dark twin. Their Scots heritage aligns them with Stevenson's quarrelling cousins and potion-swallowing doctors, with James Hogg's protagonist in *The Private Memoirs and Confessions of a Justified Sinner*. Drummond is a true patriot, a grassroots football follower. He wanted to do a non-ironic recording of the national anthem, a picture of the Union Flag on the screen. With one serious prank, plotting to hang dead cows from an off-highway pylon, he was inventing eco-surrealism – in sermon form – years before Blair decided that it would be all right to do nothing, while the herds burnt, heifers were hooked and hoisted, and pigs taken out by expensively trained army marksmen.

I'm writing this at the vernal equinox 2001, wondering if Drummond and Gimpo are still out there, addicted to addiction, to counter-inertia terrorism; spinning like a blunt needle around the groove, picking up fluff. The trees are bare, the light dead. It's still raining. More and more of Hackney is being improved: that is, less and less of Hackney is available to pedestrians. The canal path is blocked so that authentic Victorian ironwork can be introduced. Public funds for private projects, hobbyism running amok. Building work has been going on for over a year, beyond my garden wall. Roads are closed off and tower blocks (that I saw going up in the Sixties) are being demolished. Alps of rubble. Dust clouds. The man from the mini-mart wants compensation. The residents of Queensbridge Road are being driven mad by the noise and the dirt. You can never establish the nature of these new alliances, council (bankrupt), state (emollient), developer (benign); Irish contractors, shit-shovellers, as ever, digging the ditches. LAINGS HOMES. Suburbs imported. Estates with no atmosphere but with clearly defined boundaries, points at which security slackens its grip, and you step out of the frame of the surveillance monitor.

2

Atkins and I waited for Bill Drummond on a bridge over the A102, alongside the Dome. When the site was no more than a few scratches in the ground, the writer Stewart Home stood here ranting about an omphalos, about Mandelson's tent being a killing zone (exhaust fumes from the Blackwall Tunnel). The ritual sacrifice of Prince Charles. Underselling his pitch, as ever. It was the day when the news of Princess Diana's death hit the headlines. Dome and crunched Mercedes were linked in popular consciousness. The route of the funeral procession, from Westminster Abbey to the M1, in real-time television, proved that surveillance footage, shots of roads, could be sold to the public. The Kennedy assassination was film, home movies marketed by Time-Life. Diana's funerary procession was drift, reverie, bouquets chucked on a glossy black bonnet. Families gathered in their living rooms, at the time of the coronation of Elizabeth II, to witness a solemn occasion; something that would never again happen in their lifetimes. Royalty doing the business, earning their corn, by taking part in durational theatre. Demigods who could die. Change the weather. Cure the sick. Bring the slaughtered flocks back to life.

Death was a spectacle, the Dome was invisible. It didn't register. Standing right up against it, we couldn't look at it. We looked across the water, at Canary Wharf, the ice-floe principality of Docklands. The original Tory scam would soon be realised: a temporary circus paid for by lottery funds, a lull (during which we were supposed to forget the shame), followed by property development. Well-connected investment cabals throwing up yet more riverside units.

Rumours were surfacing about the latest think-tank solution

to the M25. After megalomaniac schemes for expansion into eight, twelve, twenty-four lanes, ABCD rings, there was only one way to deal with the problem of the orbital highway. Shut it down. Abandon it. Pretend, in classic New Labour fashion, that it wasn't there. It never happened. Not our fault. Blame it on aeons of Tory misrule. Rebrand. Henceforth, the M25 would be a Green Way. With commissioned public sculpture. Antony Gormley, obviously. Psychogeographers and alignment freaks were already at work, proving that the Greenwich tent covered the same space as all kinds of mystically significant sites.

Drummond, hitting his final lap, had a vision. Piers Plowman in a hammock in the back of a jolting white van. 'I dream a dream where Gimpo tells me that in the future the crusties, the ravers without hope, the feral underclasses, will live on the M25 in broken-down buses, discarded containers, packing cases and anything else that can be procured for nowt and provide shelter against the rains. The M25 will be taken over, clogged up, no longer used as a thoroughfare to nowhere. It will be like one of those forgotten canals behind backstreets in Brum, stagnant and dank, fit only for dead cats and stolen shopping trolleys, until it is ripe for future heritage culturalists to proclaim its worth as a site of special historic interest.'

As with most of the walks I've undertaken with Marc Atkins, we're setting out as close as we can to six a.m. Bill Drummond will be travelling from his farmhouse near Aylesbury. He's not driving just now. One year on from the twenty-five laps of the M25, he's lost his licence. He arrives in an out-of-town minicab, red, with see-through panel in the roof and JET 421212 pasted across the windscreen. Bill is sitting next to the driver, who wears a laminated identity card. The ex-millionaire is a strategic walker and a frequent cab user, Aylesbury to London. Station to farm. A tall man, he hoiks himself out, sniffs the sour air. Green thornproof jacket, stout cords, red rucksack. Glasses attached by a no-nonsense loop. He is immediately into the narrative, attention engaged, notebook at the ready.

Bill dresses like the best sort of schoolmaster, a twitcher with a dangerous laugh. Atkins is in a long black coat with felt collar (Martin Kemp as Reggie Kray); jeans, white trainers. He bleeps. He's got a new toy, a mobile phone. His career is taking off. He's published a book of London photographs and a booklet of nudes. He has to stay in touch with potential commissioners, picture editors, galleries. Most of the incoming calls, on this outing, seem to be domestic. Brief exchanges of pleasantries, mewings. Shopping lists for future meals.

Dreadnought Street. The name takes Drummond's fancy. A nautical ghost logged in his notebook, before we double back to Greenwich, climb the hill, pay our respects to the brass rule, zero longitude marker. While I dabble with the notion of tracking the line to the M25, the true conceptualist (Bill Drummond) is determined to follow it to the ends of the earth. I'll swing west at Waltham Abbey, after a mere eighteen miles. He'll head south, France, Spain. He'll probably swim across to Africa. The guy has an evil glint when an idea takes root. Already, I can feel our narratives pulling away from each other. Will his version, sharper than my own, published in 1998 as 'Breakfast with the Unabomber', disqualify my ponderous journal?

The work Marc Atkins does is complementary. He observes the observers; he keeps his own record of journeys that are not of his choosing. The narrative he assembles is fragmentary. It doesn't have to be read in any particular order. Its intention is to freeze time; a deadpan gaze at some view, a building, a stretch of the river. Very often, I find these photographs more useful than my jottings or snapshots. In the best of Marc's prints, spurned locations come to life. He treats the reproduction of brick courses as a form of portraiture.

He'll go anywhere for a good shot. Or he would, in the past. He's much busier now and has to be booked well in advance. Drummond, I felt, was more likely to ask the hard questions.

Why the meridian line? Why stop at the M25? 'Mean time.'
'Zero longitude.' I liked those terms. They had an undefined,
Enochian attraction: science coming to the rescue of the ley
line enthusiasts who nominated Greenwich Hill as a site of
occult significance. It had been possible once to imagine currents of energy running through the Queen's House, between
the twin domes of the Naval College and on to the tower of
St Anne's at Limehouse.

The Ordnance Survey brought out a series of maps with the
prime meridian clearly marked, so that millennial cultists could
locate themselves at points along the line, when time 'changed'
on 31 December 1999. These maps are to the scale of 1:25,000.
The line is printed in green. We don't have a map. But it's
easy to see that longitude zero skims the Dome, cuts through
Bow Creek near the Generating Station and follows the pylons
up the Lea Valley. We'll stay as close as we can and make our
rendezvous with zero at Waltham Abbey.

What I didn't know was that Drummond was carrying
a copy of *The Unabomber Manifesto*, which he'd picked up the
day before at a bookshop in Camden Town. He sympathised
with the survivalist lifestyle, Thoreau hut, wild nature on
the doorstep. He knew the names of the birds and the beasts.
The Lea Valley, with its status as pretend countryside, butterfly sanctuary, deer reservation, dog track, waste disposal unit,
munitions factory, wasn't much use to him. He wanted the full-
on metropolitan experience, secret histories; lunacy he could
exploit. His underlying fear was that my outing would lead him
to 'the point where terrorism is the only option'. If you carry
the book, Bill, be prepared to use it.

3

Best Value. Someone somewhere, well away from the action, decided that this banal phrase, implying its opposite, was sexy. Best Value, with the smack of Councillor Roberts's corner-shop in Grantham, the abiding myth of Thatcherism, was dusted down and used in every public relations puff of the New Labour era. Best Value. Best buy. Making the best of it. Look on the bright side.

The spin doctors, post-literate and self-deceiving, had no use for subtlety. Best Value. They hammered the tag into their inelegant, overdesigned freebies. These glossy publications, sweetheart deals between government and private developers, political correctness in all its strident banality, existed to sell the lie. Best Value.

Government-sponsored brochures are got up to look like supermarket giveaways. Strap headlines in green. Articles flagged in blue. Colour photos. Designed not composed. That's how the planners (the strategists, the salaried soothsayers) see the Lea Valley. As an open plan supermarket with a river running through it. The valley is a natural extension of the off-highway retail parks springing up around Waltham Abbey; exploiting the ever-so-slightly-poisoned territory yielded by ordnance factories, gunpowder mills, chemical and electrical industries.

The documents put out by the Lee Valley Regional Park Authority are more impressive than any inner-city PR sheets. *Lee Valley Regional Park Plan, Part One: Strategic Policy Framework* runs to 180 pages – with charts, illustrations, maps. Statements of intent. Best Value. Whatever turns you on, the Lea Valley has got it. A media-friendly zone (close to Docklands).

A recreation zone for Essex Man (easy access to the M25). An eco-zone for butterflies, deer, asylum-seeking birds. The nice thing about no-go, Official Secrets Act government establishments is that they are very good for wildlife. Thick woods, screening the concrete bunkers and hunchbacked huts from the eyes of the curious, will provide an excellent habitat for shy fauna, for monkjacks. It's gratifying to learn that, at a period when sheep and pigs and cows, all the nursery favourites, are being taken out by snipers and bulldozed into a trench on a Cumbrian airfield, the threatened Musk Beetle is thriving and multiplying in the Lea Valley wetlands. Twenty-one species of dragonfly on a good day. The regional park is a safe haven for grass snake and common toad. The Royal Gunpowder Mills at Waltham Abbey can claim the largest heronry in Essex, a 'wildlife watchtower' with 'panoramic view'. The 175-acre site should have opened to the public in the spring of 2001, but the outbreak of foot-and-mouth led to an inevitable postponement.

The Lee Valley Regional Park was established in 1967, the year I moved to Hackney. We had slightly different agendas. The Park planners wanted to transform areas of neglect and desolation, the very qualities I was intent on searching out and exploiting. The first argument we had was over the name. I favoured (homage to Isaac Walton) the Lea spelling, where they went for the (William) Burroughs-suggestive Lee. Inspector Lee. Willie Lee. Customised paranoia: double 'e', narrowed eyes glinting behind heavy-rimmed spectacles. The area alongside the M25, between Enfield Lock and High Beach, Epping Forest, carries another echo of Burroughs: Sewardstone. 'Stone' added to the author's middle name.

The Lea/Lee puzzle is easily solved. The river is the Lea. It rises in a field near Luton, loses its identity to the Lee Navigation, the manmade canal, then reclaims it for the spill into the Thames at Bow Creek. The earlier spelling, in the River Improvement Acts of 1424 and 1430, was 'Ley', which is even better. Lea as ley, it always had that feel. A route out. A river track that walked the walker, a wet road. The Lea fed our Hackney dreaming: a water margin. On any given morning when the city was squeezing too hard, you could get your hit of rus in urbe. Hackney Marshes giving way to the woodyards of Lea Bridge Road, to Springfield Park; reservoir embankments, scrubby fields with scrubbier horses, pylons, filthy, smoking chimneys.

Without the Lea Valley, East London would be unendurable. Victoria Park, the Lea, the Thames: tame country, old brown gods. They preserve our sanity. The Lea is nicely arranged, walk as far as you like then travel back to Liverpool Street from any one of the rural halts that mark your journey. Railway shadowing river, a fantasy conjunction; together they define an Edwardian sense of excursion, pleasure, time out.

Dr Jim Lewis in his affectionate tribute, *London's Lea Valley (Britain's Best Kept Secret)*, promotes the Lea as cradle and forcing-house of the 'post-industrial revolution': water power facilitated flour mills, shipbuilding, the manufacture of porcelain; then came armaments, gunpowder, chemicals, furniture, bricks; until we arrive at Lewis's golden age, the moment when entrepreneur and investor get it together in a landscape nobody notices, or wants to protect. Settlers moved into suburbs, before there were suburbs; they cosied up to a working stream. In the same way that a wealthy Victorian brewer, picking out an estate in Enfield Chase, might marry one of his barmaids.

Everything starts in the Lea Valley, all the global franchises; electricity, TV, computers, killing machines. Forget Silicon Valley, this is Ponders End. Charles Babbage, inventor of the Difference Engine, attended the Revd Stephen Freeman's school at Enfield. As a sickly boy he was interested in ghosts. He made a pact with a friend that whoever should die first would return. Seances in a cold bedroom. No word from the corpse.

Jim Lewis tells us that, at Ponders End, Joseph Watson Swan

'demonstrated a crude form of electric lamp almost twenty years before the American Thomas Alva Edison had registered his own version'. But the Yank was a sharper operator and put in for the patent. Rather than become involved in costly legal wrangling, an early corporate monster was formed, the Ediswan Company.

John Ambrose Fleming, like a minor alchemist, joined Ediswan to investigate the causes of 'blackening on the inside of light bulbs'. Swan filled his laboratory with experimental models, lamps with an extra electrode. He became a consultant with the Marconi Wireless Telegraph Company, where he worked on improving methods for the detection of radio waves. By the turn of the century, alliances between shifting trade associations who would be given favoured status by government, lavished with defence contracts, were in place. And that place was the Lea Valley.

The military/industrial complex, demonised in the USA by Sixties radicals, was well established around Waltham Abbey before the First World War. Dr Chaim Weizmann, first president of the state of Israel, began his working life as a bio-chemist. In March 1916 he was approached by Sir Frederick Nathan, head of the Admiralty Powder Department, who was trying to cope with a serious shortage of acetone, a solvent used in the manufacture of cordite. Winston Churchill had demanded 30,000 tons of the stuff. So Weizmann, using the Nicholson gin distillery (on the site currently known as Three Mills) at Bow, obliged. Contacts were established and favours returned. Sir Arthur Balfour declared his support for the establishment of a Jewish homeland in Palestine.

Another figure championed by Jim Lewis is Sir Jules Thorn, founder of Thorn Electrical Industries, who is praised for his 'courageously entrepreneurial spirit' in importing lamps from Hungary. With a base in Angel Road, Edmonton, Thorn began flogging domestic radio receivers from a rental shop in Twickenham. He bought up the Ferguson Radio Corporation

Limited and acquired a factory in Lincoln Road, Enfield – 'on the site of a former nursery'.

Thorn's activities, his way of operating, fit quite snugly with my conceit: that the Lea Valley aspires to the condition of the supermarket (wide aisles, every product showcased in its own area, cheap and cheerful). Ex-rental TV sets heaped into pyramids, at South Mill Fields. Coffee stall alongside the Navigation beyond Tottenham Marsh. Fruit and veg at the roadside, as you approach Epping Forest.

When Ferguson decided to move into colour, Jules Thorn asked his engineers to design and develop a dual standard, large screen receiver (VHF/UVF). A junior technician was sent to the local Woolworth's to buy up their stock of plastic butter dishes. Fetishised in silicon rubber, the dishes were transformed into EHT (extra high tension) multipliers.

'Dangerous radiation levels within the receiver,' Lewis explains, 'had to be carefully and expensively screened.' This too, radiation, carcinogenic leakage, the sour aftermath of entrepreneurship, was to be a defining element in the Lea Valley. History recovered through stinks and scummy water, smoke you can taste.

On 9 December 1997, a group of former Thorn employees met, on the site that had once been the engineering laboratories of the Euro-conglomerate Thorn EMI Ferguson to witness the dedication of a plaque paying homage to the late Sir Jules. The plaque is now positioned in the foyer of the Enfield Safeway superstore.

Best Value. We, East Londoners, support the Lea, as it supports us, marking our border, shadowing the meridian line. It is enjoyed and endured by fishermen, walkers, cyclists who learn to put up with the barriers, the awkward setts beneath bridges. We pay our tithe. Sir Patrick Abercrombie's 1943 *County of London Plan* was a visionary document: 'every piece of land welded into a great regional reservation'. The Lee Valley Recreational Park. A perimeter fence around a Sioux reservation. Compulsory leisure. The Lea would lose its sub-versive, grubby culture of contraband, villainy, iffy businesses carried out beyond the fold in the map.

Way back in 1961 Lou Sherman, Lord Mayor of Hackney, got together with representatives of seventeen other local authorities, and with the support of the Duke of Edinburgh, to realise Abercrombie's vision. A levy was introduced for councils in Essex, Hertfordshire and London. Grander plans, with the passage of time, required more complex financial structures, 'partnerships'. Local authorities, UK government, Europe: more executive producers than a Dino de Laurentiis epic. The Lea Valley was a future spectacle. Water was the new oil. Housing developments required computer-enhanced riverscapes as a subliminal backdrop.

There would be funds for decontamination, a 'precept on council tax', unnoticed, except by readers of the small print. Representatives of thirty boroughs had their places on the council of the Lee Valley Regional Park Authority. Regenera-tion was the theme, the green lung. A ten-year strategic business plan: 'It firmly embraces the principles of Best Value in pursuit of enhancements of service delivery.' Management-speak for the open air supermarket. Best Value. Never know-ingly undersold. Eco-bondage. 'A unique mosaic of farmland, nature reserves, green open spaces and waterways.' The ideal brochure: god's eye maps, photographs with jagged, painterly edges, bullet points, heavy print. **Best Value**.

Ultimately, all walks contradict the lie of the land; they will be circular. An 'Outer Orbital Route' designed to 'follow the outer edge of London, a country walk with London always nearby'. The Lea, given time and investment, would stand physics on its head. It would become a sylvan alternative to the M25. With the motor car as its handmaiden. 'Consideration must be given to the needs of the motorist.' A green halo. An aureole around smoking tarmac. 'Leave the M25 at Junction 25. Follow the signs for City. At first set of traffic lights turn left signposted to Freezywater.' This is the Lee Valley Leisure Complex.

'We will make our commitment to our duty of Best Value; ensuring **clarity of objectives and customer and performance focus** at the heart of our cultural and organisational change . . . Major Capital Development will seek to achieve Best Value.'

Did we qualify – as customers? Drummond, Atkins and Sinclair? Unlikely. Elective leisure was the condition of our lives, endured through a puritanical work ethic. Drummond scribbling away, anonymously, in the cafeteria of a provincial department store. Atkins hunched in his dark room. Sinclair zigzagging around the fringes in a frantic attempt to avoid all versions of the circuit, the smooth walk that carries you back to the point of departure. We were spurners of Best Value. Drummond burnt money and gave away self-published booklets. Atkins printed more photographs than he could sell in ten lifetimes. I wrote the same book, the same life, over and over again. We wanted Worst Value. We refused cashback. We solicited bad deals, ripoffs, tat. If you explained something to us, we wouldn't touch it. We knew what Best Value meant: soap bubbles, scented bullshit. That's why our walk began at the most tainted spot on the map of London. Exorcism, the only game worth the candle.

4

Breakfast is a priority on these walks. Which is something of a problem in the desert between the neck of the Isle of Dogs at East India Dock Road and our access point to the Lee Navigation towpath at Bow Lock. The landscape is provisional. Strategic planning runs up against sulking real estate, tacky old businesses that won't fade away, inconvenience stores, revenants from Thomas Burke's Chinatown. Marine provisioners have decayed into monosodium glutamate takeaways that leave you orange-tongued, raging with thirst. Merchant marine outfitters peddle cheap camping-gear, unisex jeans, diving suits for non-swimmers.

Bill Drummond is a good walker, long-striding, easy paced. He doesn't go at it like a journalist, rushing the rush, overwhelmed by a bombardment of sense impressions. Atkins has his aches and pains, but he'll plod on for as long as it takes. Not much, as yet, to photograph. A token view across the river, back to the Dome, from the spot that featured in *EastEnders*, the hotel where Ian Beale married Melanie.

East India Dock Road, with its evocative name, has a secondary identity as the A13, my favourite early-morning drive. The A13 has got it all, New Jersey-going-on-Canvey Island: multiplex cinemas, retail parks, the Beckton Alp ski slope; flyovers like fairground rides, three salmon-pink tower blocks on Castle Green, at the edge of Dagenham; the Ford water tower and the empty paddocks where ranks of motors used to sit waiting for their transporters. The A13 drains East London's wound, carrying you up into the sky; before throwing you back among boarded-up shops and squatted terraces. All urban life aspires to this condition; flux, pastiche. A conveyor belt of discontinued industries. A peripatetic museum, horizon to horizon, available to anyone; self-curated. The wild nature graveyard in Newham. Inflatable, corn-yellow potato chips wobbling in their monster bucket outside McDonald's in Dagenham. River fret over Rainham Marshes.

Dawn on a wet road. Travelling east into the rising sun; drowned fields, mountains of landfill, ancient firing ranges. Everything smudged and rubbed. With the M25 as your destination, Purfleet and Grays as staging posts. Bridge, river, oil storage tanks. The border chain of chalk quarries occupied by Lakeside, Thurrock.

A high sierra of container units in rust colours and deep blues, chasms through which sunbeams splinter, wrecked double-decker buses with spider's-web windows. Junk yards with leashed dogs. The Beam rivulet and the sorry Ingrebourne meander through spoilt fields, beneath the elevated highway (a road on stilts).

Where a road goes informs every inch of it; there is an irritability about the section we have to cross. Why are we heading north and not swinging east, following the hint spelt out by juggernauts? The ramps that lift you on to the Queen Elizabeth II Bridge are decorated with burnt-out motors – as if joy riders from Barking and Hornchurch knew they'd reached the end of the line. Fire the evidence. Leave the orbital motorway to major league crims.

The A13 shuffle through East London is like the credits sequence of the Mafia soap, *The Sopranos*; side-of-the-eye perspective, bridges, illegitimate businesses about to be overwhelmed by the big combos. Black smoke and blue smoke. Waste disposal. A well-chewed cigar. The motorway, when you reach it, has been infected by this shoddy progress; the drivers are up for it, hard men, warriors. Hear the screech of tyres as they carve across three lanes to hit the Sandy Lane ramp without losing momentum.

To drift through low cloud, through the harp strings of the

suspension bridge, is to become a quotation; to see yourself from outside. From the Thames river path. Or the forecourt of the Ibis Hotel. A chunk of metal rattling over a concrete bandage. The toll booths on the far shore legitimise this transit. You need the ceremony of release. The motorway proper begins with mathematical nomenclature, Junction 1a, 1b. No wonder the Bluewater quarry feels like one of the Channel ports. See bemused strollers searching for someone who speaks English.

But reach the M25 through the Surrey suburbs and it's a different programme, another era. *The Good Life, Ever Decreasing Circles*. Anything with a pre-Lear Richard Briers. The motorway is perceived as a rude beast (germs from the east, asylum seekers, infected meat, rogue cargo).

The promoters, the strategists of the Lee Navigation path, hope that one day that path will carry walkers right to the Thames. They're acquiring patches of land, potential sanctuaries. But, for now, we beat against the counter-currents of the Blackwall Tunnel Approach; snarled, south-flowing traffic (one lane in the tunnel before 9.30), fraught incomers heading north. Drummond remarks on the pompous splendour of an extinguished library, white stone and weeds. The kind of building that Atkins might once have photographed (rescued), but now doesn't. I can hear his stomach grumbling. And I know it falls on me to find them a decent breakfast.

Drummond is a café man. An A13 aficionado. He spotted very early that Dagenham was the new Barcelona, the coming city of culture. Dagenham was the place to find a studio. Blight, wide pavements on which are parked gas-guzzling collectors' motors. Rusty light from the river.

There's nowhere better for the morning meditation, the crisp notebook. Strong tea, that's Bill's fuel. And plenty of it. He spends much of his life plotting in cafés, keeping one jump ahead of the trend spotters; seething, cackling. Issuing orders to abort yesterday's mad fancies.

Out here, despite the romance of a 360-degree pan – railway, gas holders, river – there's no whiff of roasted coffee, bacon-tongues crisping in a pan. The day is a London ordinary, pylon-punctured cloud base. Grey duvet flopping overhead.

Three Mills at Bromley-by-Bow is one of the showpieces of the Lee Valley Regional Park, a major photo opportunity for the heritage lobby. It's an infallible rule that anything you spot on your rambles, anywhere you nominate, will be discovered; rescued, tarted up, divided into viable units. Cycling with the painter Jock McFadyen towards the Northern Sewage Outflow, the elevated Green Way to Beckton Alp, I began to understand how the system worked. McFadyen, a perky observer, auditioner of unlikely prospects (abandoned cinemas, trashed snooker halls, drinking clubs), leapt from his French machine. He'd clocked a ruin on the wilderness promontory where the Hertford Union Canal flows into the River Lea. An islet much favoured by herons. I imagined, when McFadyen began to blaze away with his camera, that he was gathering material for a future painting. Nothing of the sort. The artist was sussing a property. These days the huge canvas is of secondary interest. Paintings are no more than blow-ups of estate agents' window displays. They're done, the best of them, with a lust for possession. Speculations that got away.

If this was Kent, you'd look for oast houses. Structures designed for a purpose, drying hops, take on a second life: women drowsy, aroused; men tilting golden liquid in a tall glass. From the car park of the Tesco superstore, we acknowledge the clocktower of Three Mills, the drying kilns. (I've done the tour, seen the flood pool, the four twenty-foot-in-diameter water-wheels; listened to the creaks and groans. I've admired the shape of the building, the bare boards. The work that is now a show, a museum piece.)

There's a café, brasserie or wine bar, with window looking out on Abbey Creek, on the junction of various streams, backwaters: Limehouse Cut, the Lea, City Mill river, Channelsea. A shuttle of silver trains over Gasworks Bridge. Industrial ghosts are loud here, but the café exists to serve media folk from the studios. And it isn't open. It used to be the bottling plant of a distillery, another kind of mill, a gin mill. Water, the flow of the Lea impounded, was a great resource. Now it comes in blue bottles, carbonated. We make do with a Tesco sandwich and a carton of something. Atkins, the veggie, takes his sugar hit from a choc bar.

The island around Three Mills will be the epicentre of a new media empire; the intoxicating sweep of the landscape stimulating concept-generating faculties. You won't actually *see* river, gas holders, exotic weeds, allotments, Bazalgette's minarets in the mustard-Gothic cathedral of sewage, but they will inform the sensibilities of the programmers. Nicholson's Gin Distillery, dark and forbidding, kept the workers anaesthetised, took the edge off middle-class anxiety. Nothing changes. The distillery peddles a different kind of fantasy, a new addiction: *Big Brother*. Prison Portakabins for jaded peepers. The TV show in which nothing happens on a twenty-four-hour feed.

Hence the Berlin effect, checkpoints, border guards, security cameras. A faint whiff of celebrity blends with the bindweed drench, the marsh gas, and that sharp smell that braking trains give off. Celebrity is fear, testosterone, oestrogen, unease. Celebrity is heat. Remove it from its natural habitat, the heart of the city (club, restaurant), and it rots, stinks. Celebrity is having a bunch of people standing around on the pavement, waiting while you eat.

At the back of Three Mills, Xerox celebrity hurts. It hurts place. The point of this area is to be obscure, a discovery any urban wanderer can make. Overgrown paths, turf islands. The imagination can reach out towards ambiguity. Find yourself by accident on the Northern Sewage Outfall path (now designated a 'Green Way') and you can follow the march of pylons, relish privileged views across West Ham; Canary Wharf glimpsed through the gravestones and memorials of the East London

Cemetery. You can make your way, with the tide of shit, towards the A13 and the Thames. Gas, electricity, water, elements that shape the grid. Polluted streams picking a route, unacknowledged, through disposable landscapes.

When I walked around Channelsea creek with Chris Petit, who was carrying a small Sony DV camera, we were tracked by a security guard with a large dog, a German shepherd. When we stopped, they stopped. Petit was very taken with a silver building like an upturned boat. It had no design features, no detail, no architect's signature; that's what Petit liked. The absence of windows. The way it stood in the middle of nothing, minding its own business.

I felt some sympathy for the dog handler. How much fun could it be following two men who appear to have all the time in the world and nothing better to do with it than to stare at a large aluminium kennel? Security is a growth industry. It's the job you get if you're running away from something. Doctors and diplomats, asylum seekers. With their mobiles. Wired to an unseen control. Putting in the hours. It used to be a glamorous career choice, celebrity hoodlums like Dave Courtney, Lennie McClean, working the door. Getting dolled up for gangland funerals. The Look: long black coat, shaved head, earring, dark glasses. But the Look crossed the line into camp, self-consciousness, when Vinnie Jones took over the franchise, designer knucklebreaker. The new villains are pimping for film deals, closeted with ghosts, while they Archer their drab CVs.

The Channelsea guards are depressed. They are the real prisoners. The fame-succubi inside the huts are being watched. Somebody loves them. Somebody wants to eavesdrop on their dim lives and tiny ambitions. Nobody gives a toss about the watchers, the hang-around-the-gate uniforms. They can't skive off. They're surrounded by a thicket of gently panning CCTV cameras. Nobody comes here. Then, for one night a week, the world switches on to see who will be expelled, made to walk the plank, the bridge that takes them back to reality, the Three Mills studio.

I like this bridge. It doesn't wobble. And it's got an ironic title: Prescott Channel. Mud, surveillance, dereliction. The best skies in London. The nightmare of the New Labour suits, the mean spectacles who blink at life like a software package, smoothed and revised. Channelsea has no use for consensus, market research, Best Value. Channelsea is off-limits.

I spent a Saturday afternoon, in the rain, observing a pair of middle-aged mudlarks, up to the elbows in liquid sewage. One of them dragged an old tin bath out into the river, at low tide. The other worked with a sieve like a grizzled prospector, Walter Huston in *The Treasure of the Sierra Madre*. They spent hours laboriously sifting shit, hoping for the odd ring or coin. And I stuck with them, watching. This was about as far as you could travel from John Prescott. He couldn't, even if it were explained to him, find anywhere to place such humans. Demographically, they had pulled it off. They didn't register.

In the past I've taken photographs of the picket fence outside *The Big Breakfast* cottage at Old Ford Lock. But I can't resist repeating myself. The messages change so quickly. Every white-painted blade is covered with names, telephone numbers. NICK CARTER IS THE FATHER OF MY BABY. TAMMY SEAMARK LIKES FREE SEX (WITH ALL SORTS). DENISE VAN OUTEN IS A BITCH. SEE YOU SOON. OR ELSE. Shorthand stalker fantasies. The cottage, which marks the end of the Lee Valley Media Zone (goodbye soaps, goodbye hysteria), has lost its edge. Dead TV. In time a blue plaque to Denise Van Outen ('lived here from 2 September 1996 to 1 Jan 1999') will appear, playing games with fuddy-duddy notions of heritage and culture. An ironic memorial to the absence of memory. An *Alice in Wonderland* makeover. Giant toadstools, paddling pools, artificial grass. You gaze over the picket fence and the surveillance cameras, the security guards, stare right back at you. The lock-keeper's cottage, beginning as a rural fantasy (sinister in Charles Dickens, jolly in H.G. Wells), ends in self-parody, colours louder than life, a cottage industry on magic mushrooms. The bricks are too bright, which isn't surprising, they're wallpaper. The security man in his little hut, guarding the pool and the synthetic grass, is too bored to bother with us, the crusty trio staring hungrily at his thermos and miniature pork pies.

Asylum seekers, border jumpers, paroled humans, those without status: they collect a uniform, lousy wages, an area to patrol, a free TV monitor playing real-time absences. In Don DeLillo's ghost story, *The Body Artist*, there's a woman who hangs on to her sanity by snacking on a 'live-streaming video feed from the edge of a two-lane blacktop'. Somewhere unknown, Finland. 'Twenty-four hours a day.' A prison fantasy, the weary body hauling itself upright to peer into a frosty window. 'She imagined that someone might masturbate to this.'

Security is (mostly) unactivated masturbation. Low arousal tapes, low definition: you watch the landscape breathe. The canal at night. Wavering reflections of sodium lamps.

The media zone of the Lee Navigation deals, as it has always dealt, with waste disposal. Junk. I wait for a time when there will be digital mudlarks rummaging through exhausted footage for images to extract, fool's gold dropped down the toilet bowls of the culture.

Hackney Marshes are pretty familiar. I had a great job once, painting white lines on the football pitches. A Forth Bridge task: start on Monday morning, under those epic skies, trolleying thick gunge, fighting the impulse to indulge in spiral patterns. Every Saturday and Sunday coarse footballers would obliterate my handiwork. Begin again.

Fat, glossy crows, cat-sized, scavenge the sward. Seagulls swoop on golf balls. They perch on crossbars, spot a knobbly egg and dive. Dozens of balls are lost in the thick grass where the Marshes slope up to Homerton Road. The walker feels small tramping towards a pylon-punctured horizon. Exposed on this broad table of land. The Friends Bridge, designed by Whitby, Bird and Partners, a way of getting across the Lea as it loops towards the Navigation, is a welcome destination.

The tough and functional steel and wood structure exposes the pretensions of the wobbly millennial effort, the spidery span that was supposed to carry pedestrians from St Paul's to the Tate Modern. This bridge works. Its scarlet paint will survive the spray-can bandits. A straight path across honest planks, pale as sand, is counterbalanced by a red steel carapace (like Dalí's fat lip sofa). The bridge understands its mythical function: to give the pilgrim, who has laboured to find it, access to a nature reserve, a slice of protected wilderness.

Back on the canal path, at the point where Eastway crosses the Navigation, we encounter one of those oracular concrete caverns. Reflected light sports in the grooves. REGGIE KRAY FOR MAYOR OF LONDON. There's a reversed swastika (with the number 23), a scarlet skull and a single bone crossed by an arrow. The panels of the wall have been finished in a sort of refined pebbledash: a beach framed for exhibition.

Under the bridge, weed-slippery skeletons of motorcycles, dredged from the filthy water, have been laid out. I've seen travellers, barechested, prudish in old trousers, diving for scrap. Ropes and hooks. Mounds of antique iron. Bicycles, prams. Immune to Weil's disease, rat bites, they submerge, time after time, in the mucilage, the electric-green scum.

The triangle of the Marshgate Recreation Ground is in the process of a rethink. Its history, summarised on a board, has been action-painted into oblivion. The newly planted patch has been christened: 'Wick Woodland'.

Along the avenue of peeling London planes, caravans have been parked. Cars. And bits of cars. An inhabited junkyard, a moveable suburb. Bureaucratic toleration pushed to its limits by the construction of waste towers, mounds of black tyres. The travellers, barred from upwardly mobile riverside pubs, anathematised by eco-planners, have found a use for this left-over arrowhead of ground. They've Balkanised it. Fouled it. Used it. They've helped to clean the Lee Navigation. And they've done it without grants or ten-year business plans. Obviously, they're doomed. They'll be moved on. Strategic planting will win the day. For now tidy citizens might wince as they pass through this corridor of filth, avert their eyes; missing the improvised beauty of the accidental – a collision between a band of traffic on its high curve, new plantings, woodchip walkways, benches on which to contemplate the scene.

The mystery of the Navigation, where the Marshes confront rows of neat canalside hutches, was best captured by Rachel Whiteread in her monochrome plates, taken on the day when the Sixties' tower blocks were blown up. Whiteread's photographs celebrate silence; small boats on the river, crowds on the banks. Tents. A revivalist mob watching vertical history crumple and disappear.

As we pass the Middlesex Filter beds (closed) and move towards the weir, close to Lea Bridge Road, by the Princess of Wales pub, I try out a *Fortean Times* myth on Bill Drummond: how two headless, skinned bears were found floating at this spot. Children reported a yeti-like sighting, in a snowstorm on the Marshes. Paw prints were discovered and photographed. There was talk of circuses, gypsies – but no animals were reported missing. The implication was that the beasts had scavenged in Epping Forest, for picnic scraps, discarded burger cartons, roots and berries. Then started to forage further afield.

The floating things looked human but on the wrong scale, evolutionary accidents. Grey-pink. Flesh like a body condom. The paws had been lopped off, leaving the sorry creatures without proper means of identification. Interspecies monsters. The heads were never recovered. They vanished into London's cabinet of curiosities, along with the skulls of Emanuel Swedenborg and John Williams (the suicided suspect in the

Ratcliffe Highway Murders), the phantom hat of gangland victim Jack McVitie.

Heads as trophies. The bears were redundant once the heads had been hacked off. Were they decorating some Leaside pub? Or were they nailed to the wall of a neo-baronial ranch in Chigwell? Did they fulfil some shamanistic requirement, bear spirits raised as guides? Heads had long been used, in London's underworld, as occult sources of power, botched voodoo displays. Instead of Dahomean carpets of skulls around the throne of a high king, the boiled poll of a smalltime informer, a rival.

East London's waterway system, dank canals, had canteens of blood-rusty cutlery in them, weapons that continued to sing about forgotten crimes. Knives that begged to confess, plea-bargain. Customised shotguns. Arsenals of suspect weaponry. The police diving team was an everyday sight on the Hackney Cut and the Lee Navigation; wet suits, air bubbles, ropes. Dark fishing after the latest bin bag floater had been hauled ashore. I've watched them, with thermoses of coffee, thick sandwiches, cranking a car from the river. Not like *Taggart*. No hardbitten dialogue, no cynical pathologist dragged from a Burns night dinner. A small team taking a blow in the sunshine.

It's more disturbing when heads start *reappearing*. I'm never happy with empty alcoves on English baroque monuments. It's too easy to picture the Jacobite heads on Temple Bar. The spikes on London Bridge. Nobody liked it when Billy Moseley's head turned up in a bundle of newspapers, in a Gents' lavatory in Islington, up on the ridge overlooking the valley of the Fleet. It was clear, from the frosted flesh, that Billy had spent time in a deepfreeze. Less clear as to why he aborted his ill-advised cryogenic experiment.

It wasn't just rubble under the marshes. There were legions of the unregistered dead. Children, animals. Foetuses. All, as I pictured it, headless. As a qualification. To preserve anonymity. Meat without eyes. Without souls.

★

I've been promising Bill and Marc a notable breakfast in the café by Springfield Park and I'm praying that it will be open. Bill, a connoisseur of cafés, knows the place. It's where he meets his early mentor, the actor (director, philosopher, madman) Ken Campbell. A Liverpool connection. Campbell lives near the park. I've passed the house, without realising that it was his, noticed the tribal masks and fetish figures in the window. Hackney Marshes is a good backdrop for this latterday pataphysician with his alarming caterpillar eyebrows. Sit down with Campbell at an outside table and you are in company with a Ben Jonson clown, a whirlwind of cataclysmic energy; you realise, caught by that stare, those white, bottletop eyes, that the man is stonecold sane. He talks tickertape but his argument is rehearsed and organised; years of improvised performances, multilayered monologues, have honed his pitch. Fast as morse – but intelligible if you give yourself up to him. He puffs a small cigar. Sucks noisily at his mug of tea. He takes his role as spirit of place very seriously.

The river, as it flows beneath the gentle rise of Springfield Park, that Middle European reservation where orthodox Jews yatter on benches, reminds Campbell of a trip he made by coracle to the source of the Lea. The river slows consciousness. I could never survive in Ken Campbell's retreat. I wouldn't write a word. I'd spend my mornings at a table in the café, skying, watching patterns of flow, oil spill psychedelia. But Campbell's a native, you feel the realpolitik of Leytonstone in everything he says.

He put on a durational, science fiction epic at Three Mills. And now he's up for a 'pidgin' *Macbeth* at the Middlesex Filter Beds. He's right. There's a sense of theatre about these abandoned industrial spaces; trenches, dark water, tumbled concrete menhirs. The experience of going up west for an overpriced musical, a rejigged Priestley, is hell. Move the National Theatre to Walthamstow Marshes.

From his days as a pop-eyed stooge for Warren Mitchell, a

bent lawyer for G.F. Newman, or anything that called for extreme physicality, Campbell graduated into a professional explainer (nutty experiments, Citroën ads). Whatever it takes to fund his own brand of spectacle and monologue, Campbell's up for it. He's not shy of self-promotion. Pidgin as a world-language is his current obsession.

With his soft black hat and his small cigars, he's a piratical, actor/manager figure. The bushy eyebrows have, unilaterally, declared their independence. He has to cope with a tangle of dogs and leads, stagy business that involves feeding them a constant stream of broken biscuits. His teeth are magnificently shipwrecked, the colour of ancient dominoes. He's performed as a duck in *Alice in Wonderland*, with Ken Dodd as a rat; he's given underwater concerts with Heathcote Williams. He wears a Dreamcatcher T-shirt. He raps through the 'Tomorrow and tomorrow' speech in pidgin to the amazement of the riverside loungers.

The café serves filter coffee and has calamari on the breakfast menu. We settle in, calling for additional rounds of tea and toast. Drummond is scribbling in his notebook. He tells us about *The Unabomber Manifesto*. 'Today,' he would write, in his account of the walk, 'I'm a born-again would-be terrorist.' From that landmine laugh, you might believe it. The look is right: sensible, corduroy, with pale-rimmed specs. What's in that rucksack? (He carries it looped over one shoulder, so that it doesn't actually qualify as a twitcher's pouch.) Bona fide terrorists are lab technicians, junior lecturers, schoolteachers with a grievance. Bill has some of that, but he's too tall, too much of a walker. He knows his wildlife. As we strolled alongside the Marshes, the reservoir embankments, he pointed out grey wagtail, dunnock. We aren't going to challenge him. Atkins knows two kinds of birds: seagulls and the ones that aren't seagulls. He's telling Drummond about his time as a Heavy Metal roadie.

★

Gradually, landscape induces confidences. The cycle gates become less of an irritation. Road bridges energise us, traffic noise plays against pastoral tedium. Ferry Hale Road, Forest Road. On my first walks up the Lea, I used to think that an old fisherman's pub, here on the fringe of Walthamstow, was truly rustic. Izaak Walton in the back bar stuffing a pike. There must have been a ferry somewhere near this clapboard ghost. A haunt of narrowboat skippers and their dogs.

The site is now distinguished by a frivolous display of marine architecture. It thinks it's on the Algarve: balconies, furled parasols, greenery dripping from window ledges, blue glass. The Heron Hospitality Centre. Even the herons are embarrassed by it, they spindle away to Tottenham Marsh. Perch, in solitude, on convenient branches, trying to pretend – which is impossible given their size, the design faults – that they're not really there. Neo-Romantic doodles, scissor-beaks and Anglepoise knees.

Drummond is gobsmacked. Hand on hip, he tries to make sense of this *latte*-coloured folly. Why would anyone position a glass and plaster box alongside a scummy lock on the high road to Walthamstow and Epping Forest? Blatant white space-ism: architects ignore the implications of where their buildings will be sited. Nothing exists beyond the frame of an idealised sketch. Invertebrate people with identikit faces lounging on an imaginary deck. There's no road, no marsh, no industry.

It's enough to get Drummond started on another of his current projects, a heart-of-darkness voyage up the Congo with Mark Manning (aka Zodiac Mindwarp). Along with the inevitable Gimpo (covert camera). The African voyage, with all its logistical problems (paranoia, corruption, disease, river-stink), is the second part of a wildly ambitious trilogy. One: a journey through Finland towards the North Pole, with an icon of Elvis Presley. Two: the Conrad revival. Three: the final (terminal) trip to the moon.

Jessie Weston's tag – 'the otherworld is not a myth, but a reality' – underwrites everything Drummond attempts. Plotting his adventures is better, much better, than carrying them out. The moon jaunt involves a swim, clutching a buoyancy barrel or life preserver, from Cuba to Cape Canaveral. The next bit is vague: blag themselves aboard Apollo-whatever, or lift off by force of will (a Georges Méliès stunt). The moon's a dead rock and also a state of mind. The secret history of popular music (which Drummond celebrates) couldn't exist without it – as a rhyme, a simile. Rhymes are dangerous things, forging connections which can never be broken. Rhymes are addictive. They clog up the memory files.

If Florida doesn't work out (troubled back story: exiled Cubans, Chicago hoods, hit men; the missing sliver of Kennedy's skull), Drummond and Manning will move on to Peru. Straight lines in the desert, clear skies. They'll take every pharmaceutical, mushroom, cactus extract, loco weed, they can get their hands on. That should do it, bring the moon down. Until they can snort its dust.

There wasn't much definition in the sky. Pylons and earthworks, water you can't see. The occasional horse hoping for a handout. I thought of Jock McFadyen's painting *Horse Lamenting the Invention of the Motor Car* (1985). A blue pantomime beast with a bandaged foreleg on a carpet of wasted turf, surrounded by a stream of toy cars. David Cohen called McFadyen 'the Stubbs of the automobile'.

The reservoir nags of the Lea Valley, scab-eyed and shaggy, are cousins to animals that live on Dublin housing estates. They stretch necks over barbed wire fences, toss at an irritation of fleas. Wet brown eyes couldn't be set further apart, without falling off. The horses have a melancholy presence, never finding a comfortable direction in which to set their too heavy heads.

Atkins is beginning to limp. This walk is a relatively gentle one, but for some reason – perhaps the monotony of the track, the uneven pebbles – it hurts the unwary.

Drummond can't decide if our expedition is asking the right questions. The land is too anonymous, no major blight, a steady stream of *I–Spy* water fowl. Fish corpses (nothing more exciting than white-bellied carp).

I think we can assume that we have penetrated the Lea Valley's recreational zone. Boats. Wet suits. Easy access to the North Circular Road, the broken link of an earlier orbital fantasy. This border is marked by a permanent pall of thick black smoke. Urban walkers perk up; we're back in the shit. The noise. The action.

The situation, at the junction of the North Circular and the Lee Valley Trading Estate, is readable. It's what we are used to, what we advocate; faux-Americana, waste disposal, spray from twelve-wheeled rigs. Powerhouse, Currys. A Mercedes franchise. Signs and signatures. Zany neon calligraphy. Warehouses parasitical on the road, on the notion of movement, easy parking. Old riverside enterprises that basked in obscurity have been forced to come to terms with brutalist tin, container units with ideas above their station. The aesthetic of the North Circular retail park favours colours that play, ironically, with notions of the pastoral: lime-green (pond weed), yellow (oil seed rape), blood-red. Road names aren't literary, they're chemical. Argon Road is a memory trace of Edmonton's contribution to the manufacture of fluorescent lamps. Light is troubled, unnatural. The scarlet scream of the furniture warehouse fights with the graded slate-greys of the road, the river and the sky.

I love it. I like frontiers. Zones that float, unobserved, over other zones. Road users have no sense of the Lee Navigation, they're goal-orientated. Going somewhere. Noticing Atkins, foot on barrier, perched in the central reservation, snapping away, drivers in their high cabs see a nuisance, an obstacle. A potential snoop. They'd be happy to run him down. Atkins sees a speedy blur, abstraction, the chimney of London Waste Ltd blasting steam.

Visible evil. Pollution from a low-level castle, remaindered Gothic. Better and better. The London Waste facility is battle-ship-grey, a colour that is supposed to make it invisible in the prevailing climate: rain, exhaust fumes, collapsed skies. The expectation is that on an average Edmonton morning, diesel fug and precipitation will disguise the 100-foot tower of the biggest incinerator in Britain.

The Waste Zone, that's one they left out of the brochure. You arrive at the edge of the city, out of sight of Canary Wharf, and you take a dump. Surgical waste, pus, poison, plague. Corruption. All the muck we spew out. It has to go somewhere. Edmonton seems a reasonable choice.

In October 2000, a group of Greenpeace protesters occupied the summit of the burning tower. Gridlock on the M25 is a modest fantasy compared to a blockage in the procedure for the destruction of clinical waste. The Edmonton furnaces dispose of 1,800 tons of putrid stuff, contaminated bandages, body tissue, dirty nappies, used hypodermic needles, every day. At the time of the protest, waste material was piling up in seven boroughs (Camden, Enfield, Barnet, Hackney, Haringey, Islington, Waltham Forest). Hackney had its own long-running dispute, black bags burst on the streets, as a consequence of the council's bankruptcy and cutbacks. Generations of bragga-doccio incompetence, a system built on institutionalised malpractice.

Waste that couldn't be shipped to Edmonton was trans-ported to landfill sites in Essex and Huntingdon. Convoys took advantage of the M25, which increasingly functioned as an asteroid belt for London's rubble, the unwanted mess of the building boom, the destruction of tower blocks, the frenzied creation of loft-living units along every waterway.

We're intrigued by London Waste Ltd and their *Edge of Darkness* estate. What was once grey belt, the grime circuit inside the green belt, is now called upon to explain itself. Before the Lee Valley Regional Park Authority, Euro slush funds and council tax tithes, it didn't matter. Reclamation was never mentioned. Fish and fowl were there to be hunted. Dirty and dangerous industries provided employment, built cottages for the workers. Now we have Best Value.

The incineration industry, and the London Waste Ltd plant at Edmonton in particular, were investigated by television journalist Richard Watson, on behalf of the *Newsnight* programme. A predictable story of fudging, economy with the truth, buck-passing and ministerial denial. Until August 2000, London Waste were guilty of mixing relatively safe bottom ash with contaminated fly ash. The end product was then used in road building, and for the manufacture of the breeze blocks out of which the plethora of dormitory estates were being assembled. Waltham Abbey and its satellites as Pompeii and Herculaneum.

The defoliant Agent Orange, 50 million litres of which had been dropped by the Americans on Vietnam, registers around 900 nanograms of dioxin to one kilogram of soil. Mixed ash from the incinerators, used on chicken runs in Newcastle, registered 9,500 nanograms. Eggs concentrated the effect. They didn't need shells. You could see right through them. Dioxins are carcinogenic. Combined with dust, when householders carry out repairs, hang paintings, drill holes in breeze blocks, they are guaranteed to keep future surgeries and hospices busy.

The Environment Agency fed the relevant minister, Michael Meacher, the usual soft soap. The firms responsible for working mixed ash into conglomerates used in surfacing new roads declined to reveal the location of their handiwork, the 12,000 tons of aggregate dropped on the landscape. Their spokesman, sweating lightly, sported a Buffalo Bill beard: frontiersman peddling a treaty to the Sioux. One major recipient of this dubious cargo was uncovered by Watson's researches: the car park of the Ford plant at Dagenham. The A13, yet again, had something to make it glow at night. A topdressing of contaminated Edmonton ash.

'No more dangerous than Guy Fawkes night,' declared Meacher to the House. When ash, removed from Edmonton, was tested, it registered dioxin levels ten times higher than the figure floated by the Environment Agency.

Walking north towards Picketts Lock, we turn our backs on the incinerators, the smoke. Frame it out, it's not there. Go with the Dufy doodle on the side of London Waste's rectangular box, the company's upbeat logo: limpid blue sky, lush grass, a pearl-grey building like a Norfolk church.

Edmonton is the Inferno and Picketts Lock the garden, the paradise park. In the past, on hot summer walks with my family, we used to come off the Navigation path for a swim at the Picketts Lock Leisure Complex. (How complex can leisure be?) This modest development, on the edge of a hacker's golf course, was an oasis. It didn't take itself too seriously and it filled the gap between the London Waste burning chimney and the Enfield Sewage Works.

The polyfilla theory of Leisure Complex placement, the old treaty between developers, land bandits, and improve-the-quality-of-life councillors, worked pretty well. Another chlorine-enhanced waterhole on ground nobody could think of any other way to exploit.

But that won't wash in these thrusting millennial times. The name Picketts Lock starts to appear in the broadsheets – and it acquires a bright new apostrophe: *Pickett's Lock*. Pickett's Lock will be reinvented as a major sports stadium (convenient access to the M25). It will be the venue for the 2005 World Athletic Championships; thereby conferring enormous benefits on the Lea Valley; tourists, media, retail spin-offs. Computer-generated graphics omit the chimney at the end of the park, the smoke pall. Nobody is bad-mannered enough to mention the fact that London Waste have put in an application to extend their site. The application has been approved by Nick

Raynsford, Minister for the Capital. It is awaiting final approval from Trade and Industry Secretary, Stephen Byers. (Poor man. It was going to get worse, much worse. Byers epitomised the New Labour attitude of glinting defiance. Fiercely tonsured and spectacled, tight-lipped, he would suffer assault by flash-bulbs, while sitting bolt-upright in the back seat of a ministerial limo. He would be attacked by forests of furry microphones at the garden gate. He would be sideswiped from Trade and Industry to Transport. Pickett's Lock to Purgatory. Official pooper-scooper. Ordered to clean up after all those years of misinformation, neglect and underinvestment. A man undone by his own spinners and fixers, he came, with every fresh appearance before the media inquisitors, to look more and more like a panicked automaton, a top-of-the-range cryogenic model of The Public Servant.)

When this matter is raised, the site's owners (Lee Valley Regional Park Authority) become quite huffy, insisting that additional incinerators will 'pose no risk' to the health of athletes or spectators. 'Better far than Los Angeles in the past and Athens in the future as venues for the Olympics,' states Peter Warren, Lee Valley's head of corporate marketing.

Lee Valley's *Strategic Business Plan (2000–2010)* is preparing the ground for change and innovation. 'The Leisure Centre is an **ageing building over 25 years old** and the whole complex is subject to emerging, modern competition.' Horror: '25 years old'! Disgusting, obscene. Tear it down. The swimming pool and poolside café might look clean and friendly to the untrained eye, but they are *older* than David Beckham. The cinema, video arcade part of the enterprise will remain.

Which is a relief. This is a rather wonderful building, with a long straight approach, a tiled, mosaic walkway. The Alhambra of Enfield. A Moorish paradise of plashing water features, ordered abstraction, glass that reflects the passing clouds. Everything leads the eye to the cinema palace, lettering that looks like the announcement of a coming attraction: WELCOME TO

LEE VALLEY. Cathedral windows catching cloud vapours, the floating dome of another burger bar.

Nothing is cramped and mean about this approach. The Pickett's Lock multiplex is one of the wonders of our walk; we begin to understand how a commercial development can be integrated into the constantly shifting, constantly revised aspect of the Lea Valley. With its strategic use of dark glass and white panels, the generous space allowed between constituent elements in the overall design, Pickett's Lock presents itself as a retreat, a respite from the journey. Buffered by the golf course, it remains hidden from the Navigation path. But, should you take the trouble to search it out, here is green water (swimming pool, ponds and basins); here is refreshment (motorway standard nosh, machine-dispensed coffee froth); here are public areas in which to sit and rest and study maps.

Pickett's Lock works best, as a concept, if you don't step inside. If you avoid the full Americana of burger reek (foot-and-mouth barbecues with optional ketchup), popcorn buckets, arcade games in which you can attack the M25 as a virtual reality circuit. UP TO TWO PLAYERS MAY RACE AT ONCE. INSERT COINS. In fact, this sideshow at Pickett's Lock represents the Best Value future for the motorway; grass it over and let would-be helldrivers take out their aggression on the machines.

This pleasing sense of being removed from the action, the imposed-from-above imperatives, that we must enjoy ourselves, take healthy (circular) walks, observe bittern and butterfly, nod sagely over ghosts of our industrial heritage, is fleeting. The builders, the earth-movers, the JCBs, will soon be rolling in; hacking up meadows to make way for another stadium, another crowd puller; more promised, but postponed pleasure.

Postponed indefinitely. New Labour couldn't face another Dome situation. Another money pit. They waited for Bad News Day, 11 September 2001. Then slipped the announcement into the small print. The Pickett's Lock athletic stadium

was aborted. No mention of London Waste. Economic consid-
erations only. The apostrophe was withdrawn like Princess Di's
royal status. Picketts Lock, now surrounded by an ever-growing
retail park with suspiciously bright roads, could go back to being
a community centre for a community of transients.

Why, I wondered, as we hit the stretch from Ponders End to
Enfield Lock, were there no other walkers? As a Best Value
attempt at drumming up clients for their recreational facilities,
the Lee Valley marketing men were not having a good
day. Most people who live for any length of time in East
London, even Notting Hill journalists with friends in Clapton,
or connections in Hoxton, claim to walk the Lea. Filter Beds,
Springfield Park Marina, Waltham Abbey, they boast of an
intimate knowledge. Any free moment, there they are, out
in the fresh air, hammering north. But the towpath stays empty.
A few dog walkers, the odd shorthaul cyclist. Where are the
professionals, the psychogeographers, note-takers who produce
guides to 'The London Loop' or the Green Way? Local
historians uncovering our industrial heritage: do they work
at night?

We're on our own, exposed; under a cradle of sagging wires
in a pylon avenue, on a red path. Marc's foot is swollen and
he's beginning to lag behind. Bill Drummond is still buzzing;
logging blackthorn blossom and brooding on his Unabomber
assignment. The Lee Navigation, keeping us company for so
many hours, provokes Drummond into a rhapsody on crashed
cars, the road movie he made with Jimmy Cauty in homage to
Chris Petit's *Radio On*.

'The film made Jimmy and I think you didn't have to be
Wim Wenders to make a road movie. So we made one and
it was dire. And that put me off the whole notion of movie
making for the rest of my life.'

On the path were rusted sculptures that should have been
milestones. They'd been sponsored and delivered, but they

didn't belong. 'Art,' I muttered. 'Watch out.' Objects that draw attention to themselves signal trouble. We were walking into an area that wanted to disguise its true identity, deflect attention from its hot core.

Drummond already had too much of this day, too many anecdotes, too many pertinent observations. That night, on the train home, he would look over his notes, 'crossing out anything descriptive'. Text is performance. The only memorial of the synapse-burn in which it is composed. 'Zero characterisation,' said Bill. Don't burden yourself with the manufacture of copy-cat reality. The more I read Drummond's short tales, the more I admired them; envied their insouciance. He'd learnt how to lie; a man sitting at a kitchen table with a mug of tea, talking about an episode that he feels compelled to relive or exorcise. Confessing his subterfuges, his strategies, he wins the confidence of the reader: trick and truth. His stories never outstay their welcome. The Drummond he reveals is the Drummond who writes. Writes himself into existence.

The Royal Small Arms Factory at Enfield Lock is an island colony, once enclosed, independent, now up for grabs. It's surrounded by water so it has to be desirable real estate. The Italianate water tower, or clock tower, will be preserved and the low, barrack buildings transformed into first-time flats, housing stock. The nature of government land, out on the perimeter, changes. Originally, work was life, work was freedom (the cobbled causeway running towards what looks like a guard tower triggers an authentic concentration camp frisson); now work is secondary, it takes place elsewhere. Sleeping quarters have become the principal industry. Compulsory leisure again. The factory revealed as a hive of non-functional balconies, satellite-dishes monitoring dead water.

Enfield Lock is imperialist. It has signed the Official Secrets Act – in blood. A scaled-down version of Netley, the Royal Victoria Military Hospital on Southampton Water. Hospitals, ordnance, living quarters: the same pitch, the same hollow grandiloquence. Public footpaths, where they cross recently acquired government land, will be 'extinguished'.

If you come east from the town of Enfield, from the station at Turkey Street, you march down Ordnance Road. This was the route the poet John Clare took, travelling in the other direction, when he walked away from the High Beach madhouse in Epping Forest. Powder-burns on privet. Suburban avenues, lacking pedestrians, with front gardens just big enough to take a parked car. Vandalised vehicles, cannibalised for spare parts, stay out on the street. There's not much rubbish, no graffiti. Military rule is still in place.

The Royal Small Arms Factory was a Victorian establishment, post-Napoleonic Wars. Private traders couldn't produce the quantity of guns required for maintaining a global empire. The cottages of Enfield Lock were built to house workers from the machine rooms and grinding mills. The River Lea was the energy source, driving two cast-iron water wheels. The name of the river and the name of the small country town on the Essex/Middlesex border came together to christen the magazine rifle familiar to generations of cadet forces, training and reserve battalions: the Lee Enfield. This multiple-round, bolt-action rifle, accurate to 600 metres, was the most famous product of the Enfield Lock factory, the brand leader. In the First War it was known as 'the soldier's friend'. The factory survived until 1987. To be replaced by what promotional material describes as 'a stylish residential village'.

The developers, Fairview, take a relaxed view of the past. 'New' is a very flexible term. ENFIELD ISLAND VILLAGE, AN EXCITING NEW VILLAGE COMMUNITY. A captured fort. A workers' colony for commuters who no longer have to live on site. The village isn't new, the community isn't new, the island isn't new. What's new is the tariff, the mortgage, the terms of the social contract. What's new is that industrial debris is suddenly 'stylish'. The Fairview panoramic drawing, removed from its hoarding, could illustrate a treatise on prison reform: a

central tower and a never-ending length of yellow brick with
mean window slits.

We've had our lunchtime drink. Marc's rested his foot,
which is now quite swollen. And Bill has grilled me on the
motivation for my orbital circuit of the M25. Why *counter-
clockwise* he wants to know. I dodge that one by moving
sideways into a discussion of J.G. Ballard and the western
approaches. I admire the way that Ballard has stayed put in
Shepperton, same house, same themes. He can hear the traffic,
he can hear the planes overhead; he has no responsibility for
either of them. Blinds drawn, brain in gear. Three hours a day
at the typewriter. Future memories, prophetic TV.

The answer to Bill's question has something to do with
Italianate towers, the only surviving markers of hospitals and
factories. Our walk is a way of winding the clock back. But I
haven't worked out the details. We haven't set eyes yet on the
M25. Like America to the Norsemen, it's still a rumour.

If you knew nothing about the Small Arms Factory, and
were wandering innocently along the towpath, you'd pick up
the message: keep going. Government Road. Private Road.
Barrier Ahead. The pub, Rifles, must be doing well; it has a car
park the size of the Ford Motor Plant at Dagenham.

Rifles isn't somewhere you'd drop into on a whim. The
black plastic awning features weaponry in white silhouette,
guns crossed like pirate bones. TRAVELLER NOT WELCOME.
'Which traveller?' I wondered. Has word of our excursion
filtered down the Lea? OVER 21's. SMART DRESS ONLY. Is it
the migratory aspect that these Enfield islanders object to? Or
the clothes? What were they expecting, red kerchiefs, broad
leather belts, moleskin waistcoats?

Whatever it is they don't like, we've got it. NO PUBLIC
RIGHT OF WAY. Footpaths, breaking towards the forest, have
been closed off. You are obliged to stick to the Lee Navigation,
the contaminated ash conglomerate of the Grey Way. Enfield
has been laid out in grids; long straight roads, railways, fortified

blocks. Do they know something we don't? Are they expecting an invasion from the forest?

Enfield Lock has an embargo on courtesy. In a canalside pub, they deny all knowledge of the old track. Who walks? 'There used to be a road,' they admit. It's been swallowed up in this new development, Enfield Island Village. 'Village' is the give-away. Village is the sweetener that converts a toxic dump into a slumber colony. You can live ten minutes from Liverpool Street Station and be in a village. With CCTV, secure parking and uniformed guards.

The hard hat mercenaries of Fairview New Homes plc are suspicious of our cameras. Hands cover faces. Earth-movers rumble straight at us. A call for instruction muttered into their lapels: 'Strangers. Travellers.'

The FIND YOUR WAY AROUND ENFIELD ISLAND VILLAGE map doesn't help. Interesting features are labelled 'Future Phase'. You'd have to be a time-traveller to make sense of it. A progression of waterways like an aerial view of Venice. YOU ARE HERE. If you're reading this notice, you're fucked. That's the message.

'Building on toxic timebomb estate must be halted,' said the London *Evening Standard* (12 January 2000). 'A report published today calls for an immediate halt to a flagship 1,300-home housing development on heavily polluted land at the former Royal Small Arms Factory, Enfield Lock.'

The drift of the piece by Stewart Payne is that the Enfield Lock scheme was the model for the decontamination of a series of other brownfield sites, worked-out sheds, shacks and bunkers that once operated alongside London's rivers and canals. A cosmetic scrape at the topsoil, a capping of the lower levels, wouldn't do.

An attitude of mind that found its apotheosis in the Millennium Dome on Greenwich peninsula was evident throughout New Labour's remapping of the outer belts, the ex-suburbs. Nobody can afford to live at the heart of the city, unless they are part of the money market (or its parasitical forms). The City of London is therefore the first Island Village; sealed off, protected, with its own security. Middle-grade workers and service industry Transit van operatives will be pushed out towards the motorway fringes. The hollow centre will then be divided up: solid industrial stock, warehouses and lofts, will go to high-income players (City, media); Georgian properties (formerly multiple-occupied) will recover their original status (and double as film sets for costume dramas); jerrybuilt estates will go to the disenfranchised underclass, junkies and asylum seekers.

Unsafe as Houses: Urban Renaissance or Toxic Timebomb (Exposing the methods and means of building Britain's homes on contaminated land). A report, commissioned by Friends of the Earth and the Enfield Lock Action Group Association, revealed that planning permission had been granted before questions about contamination had been resolved. Planning permission was, in fact, granted on the basis of information supplied by the developers. Enfield Council's chief planning officer, Martin Jarvis, stepped down from that role. He soon found a new position: as a director of Fairview Homes. He was among familiar faces. His son also worked for Fairview, as did the daughter of Richard Course, chairman of the council's environment committee.

'Should I cover my shoulders?'

I returned to Enfield Lock, to a cottage in Government Road, with the filmmakers Chris Petit and John Sergeant. We had arranged to record an interview with local activist Beth Pedder. Pedder lived on the edge of Enfield Island Village. She was one of the authors of the *Unsafe as Houses* report. Her testimony confirmed the impression I formed on the original walk with Bill Drummond and Marc Atkins: bad turf, suppressed history.

Pedder became involved with community politics when she started agitating against cars and for a school. 'Our first issues were traffic and the overloading and log jamming of our local roads, already laden with industrial traffic. We worried over the lack of health care, and the lack of a new school for an Island development of 1,300+ new homes in an area already deprived of services.'

National journalists and television companies took an interest when the exploitation of brownfield sites was advocated as the solution to the housing problem by a telephone directory-sized report from an urban task force, chaired by Lord Rogers of Riverside: *Towards an Urban Renaissance*. That's Lord Rogers as in the Richard Rogers Partnership, Dome designers by appointment to Bugsby's Marshes. Greenwich peninsula was showbiz brownfield, Peter Mandelson as Kubla Khan. Enfield Lock was left to Fairview Homes plc. They picked up the Royal Small Arms Factory makeover: land contaminated 'with an Arsenic to Zinc range of chemical substances, plus explosives, oils and tars and the by-products of five gas works'.

In 1984 the Ministry of Defence, which controlled a major parcel of land (very loosely mapped) around Waltham Abbey, on both sides of the M25, decommissioned the Royal Small Arms Factory and sold it to British Aerospace (BAe). British Aerospace got together with Trafalgar House to launch a joint venture company, Lea Valley Developments (LVD). Limited tests were carried out on the contaminated land. In 1996 LVD sold the land to the housing wing of Hillsdown Holdings, Fairview New Homes.

Pedder found herself being interviewed for *Panorama*. 'Wear black, cover your shoulders, get rid of the Pat Butcher earrings,' she was told by the media Taliban. They didn't want her coming over as a central casting hippie, a wacky-baccy anarchist of the suburbs. We didn't care what she wore. Our motives were just as suspect. Pedder's tattoos were a work of art: naked nymphs climbing out of lilies, with a few revisions and skin-graft cancellations elsewhere. Silver bracelets, rings. Black nail varnish.

None of which had anything to do with what she had to say, the seriousness of her research and the effectiveness of her pursuit of the true story. She couldn't set foot in Enfield Island Village. Conservationists, bird-watchers and tree-lovers had been chased off by the hard hats. Some had been threatened with sticks. Beth kept at it, digging for facts, writing letters to ministers, asking to see documentation. If Pedder hung on, won the day, it couldn't be long before Julia Roberts would be hired, painted tattoos and nose-stud, to battle the corporate giants in a Californian mock-up of Enfield Lock.

Beth spoke with feeling. 'We were concerned that the MOD had produced no records for this site. We would be interested to know why.' Enfield has a long tradition of enforced silence. 'It was always a very secretive site. Ex-workers said that no one was allowed outside their own area. People didn't have a clue what went on in other areas. We had one ex-worker who attested to the fact that the building she worked in was tested every month with a geiger-counter. They had large X-ray rooms and three lead-lined rooms with lead floors, lead ceilings. They had a rocket test tunnel that ran the length of the site. It had an internal railway. There were people with white coats and radiation badges who went further into the site than anyone else was allowed to go. Workers were blood-tested every month.'

The zone was known as the 'Enfield Military Complex'.

Secret State parkland. Surrounded by water. Pedder was concerned that the local developers had no experience with contaminated land on this scale. 'They didn't have any MOD records. They didn't at first acknowledge that there was much contamination, despite the fact that previous test results had shown high levels of mercury, lead, nickel, cadmium, chrome, copper, zinc. There are PCBs, high quantities of asbestos. They don't even have a complete set of maps to show where the pipes run. There was a bash and burn policy with the MOD. They either burnt their leftovers, or they made them much smaller, bashed them up and buried them. A report was done by a

Government body that expressed concern that the MOD didn't have records for a lot of these sites, sites where radiation appeared to be present.'

We drink our tea in a pleasant kitchen, in one of the workers' cottages from the old days of the Small Arms Factory. We walk out into the garden. Look across a brown canal at the new estate. Pedder talks about the stink from the London Waste site at Edmonton. 'With all incinerators, there's a five-mile circumference within which you can suffer the effects.' Smoke. Hanging clouds that never migrate. In the early days, Pedder contacted her MP, Tim Eggar. He phoned her back. 'This is business,' he said. 'There's big money involved.' When Pedder pressed her case, Eggar replied: 'Are you entirely stupid? Profit before people, that's how the world works.'

Memory is trashed. 'I was told by an ex-worker, at the time when the site was decommissioned, that MOD turned up and took away vast amounts of files. It looked like they had been ransacked, records and details scattered about the floor. They came and flooded the place. We understand the records were taken to Aylesbury. Without the MOD records we will never know. There could be anything. A lot of the substances are mobile in water. A lot of them are carcinogenic. Crown Immunity means the site was never inspected by a local authority. They weren't covered by the rules for disposing of substances. The MOD's accepted and published policy, they've admitted to it, was bash, burn, destroy.'

In the Government Road terrace, between Lee Navigation and the Small Arms canal, people have suffered the effects. Bad water. High levels of phenols. 'Some of the residents had blistered mouths and hands, terrible headaches. They were suffering nausea, dizziness, general weakness and lethargy. The children were very ill. Those that had drunk bottled water recovered.' Fairview Homes denied all responsibility.

Pedder got the phone calls. 'Can you come down? We can't breathe.' She remembers walking along Government Road. 'It was hitting you in the face and it was hurting. You couldn't see. It was like grit. That was the asbestos.' Fairview had knocked down Building 22. 'A cloud floated towards the area of Government Road. I could see the smoke. I live probably quarter of a mile away and I could see the plume of black smoke rising up and forming this massive cloud.'

We went back inside. There were other, off-the-record stories. Connections were exposed. Things suspected but unproven. Names. Pedder was very emotional. She had a heavy investment in this story. She lived here. We would stroll back to the car park, move on.

Now our goal is in sight, beyond Rammey Marsh, traffic floating above water. Site clearance (leisure, commerce, heritage) pushes the horizon back. 'A new country park is to be developed on the site of the former Royal Ordnance works,' announces the Lee Valley Regional Park Authority's *Strategic Business Plan*. 'The site is immediately to the south of the M25, adjacent to major housing developments and strategically ideal for the Authority to pursue its remit to **safeguard and expand the "Green Wedge" into London**.'

This sounds like an uncomfortable procedure. Not just 'soil amelioration' and 'imaginative and sensitive landscape design' but the effort of will to rebrand a balding and sullen interzone, the motorway's sandtrap, as a wildlife habitat, 'a vibrant waterside park'. For years, Waltham Abbey has functioned like a putting course, a splash of shaved meadow surrounded by bunkers. It was a course that had to be played with a blindfold firmly in place. Much of the territory was unlisted. 'Government Research Establishment' to the east of the Navigation, 'Sewage Works (Sludge Disposal)' to the west.

In this red desert, sound moves from margin to margin: caterpillar-wheeled vehicles, mud gobblers, chainsaws, pneumatic drills. The delirious swooshing of the M25.

The bridge support, the thin line that carries all this traffic, is pale blue. The space beneath the bridge expands into a concrete cathedral, doors thrown open to light and landscape. Water transport gives way to road; the old loading bays are empty, a few pleasure boats and converted narrow boats are tied up against the east bank. Reflected light shivers on pale walls. Overhead, there is the constant thupp-thupp-thupp of the motorway. After heavy rain, the ground is puddled and boggy. Travellers haven't settled here. The evidence is all of migration: extinguished fires, industrial-strength lager cans, aerosol messages.

Bill Drummond leads the rush up the embankment. The M25, after miles of walking the ditch, is a symbol of freedom. The Amazon. A slithery, ice-silver road in the sky. I have a moment of panic. Drummond's bulging knapsack is still unexplained, no spare sweaters, no rain kit, no cameras. Is it possible? *Could he?* This obsession with the Unabomber. Are we going to find ourselves on the *Six O'Clock News*: TERRORIST OUTRAGE ON MOTORWAY? Bill spends time in a tower in Northern Ireland. Red Hand of Ulster? Scots Prod? A fanatic certainly. Capable of anything.

After a sharp climb, a fence hop, slipping on gravel and thin wet grass, Drummond reaches the roadside. He vaults the low barrier and performs a Calvinist version of the papal kiss. He puts his lips to tarmac, tastes the vibration of the orbiting traffic. Destination not detonation. I'm relieved and disappointed.

Sitting on the crash barrier, feet dangling on the sand-coloured hard shoulder, we are buffeted by backdraught: the road is a blur. Clockwise: Waltham Abbey and the forest. Anticlockwise: Paradise. A chocolate-brown notice: PARADISE WILDLIFE PARK. A Lascaux sketch of stag's horns, an arrow. A shamanic invitation to the country of parks and gardens and paradises. Lee Valley Park.

Cars are streaming into the sunset, brake-lights bloody. Drummond wants to walk straight off down the road, west. A truck swerves and honks. I have to grab him, persuade him that

I don't intend to stay, dodging lorries in the half-dark, on the metal skin of the M25. That would be blasphemous. I'm going to stick to the countryside, as near as I can to the loop, straining to catch the hymn of traffic, hot diesel winds.

We'll finish the day at the abbey, the grave of King Harold, but first we look back towards London. Sunshafts over a jagged horizon, towers and chimneys, unregistered ground. The mix as it always is: off-highway Americana, secret estates (Royal Gunpowder Mills, Small Arms Factory) rebranding themselves. British Aerospace. Waltham Point ('New 48 Acre Industrial Park') developed by the Kier Group and Norwich Union. Earthworks. Noise. Feeder roads that glow in the dark.

Beyond Waltham Abbey, proper countryside kicks in: the foot-and-mouth ribbons begin. The amphetamine buzz of the motorway changes everything: warehouses instead of shops, dormitory estates instead of hospitals. A road is a road is a road. When the M25 went underground, near Amesbury Bank on the northern edge of Epping Forest, they laid out a cricket pitch on the roof of the tunnel.

The road at night is a joy. You want to imagine it from space, a jewelled belt. As a thing of spirit, it works. As a vision, it inspires. There is only one flaw, you can't use it. Shift from observer to client and the conceit falls apart. Follow the signs for LONDON ORBITAL in your car and consciousness takes a dive. The M25 has been conceived as an endurance test, a reason for staying at home. Aversion therapy. Attempt the full circuit and you'll never drive again.

Paradise Gardens

Waltham Abbey to Shenley

1

Looking back over my files, the excursions to the parks and gardens of Enfield Chase, I notice soft green photographs overlaid with current images (April 2001) of smoke and blight. Footpaths and designated country walks are now ribboned off, reckless hikers face £5,000 fines. The word of the moment is 'contiguous'. Hireling academics and anonymous spokespersons, sweating under studio lights, don't like the taste of it, this awkward term they have been instructed to employ. To be contiguous is to be served with a death warrant. Animals (pre-supermarket cellophane) face the bullet if they live in a bad neighbourhood. Reading the future by computer prediction, wanting to get shot of the whole business before a June election, government-sponsored boffins have decided to take out potential disease carriers (any unlanguaged, non-voting quadruped with a cold), and then to start again; or, better yet, turn the countryside into a memorial park. Recreation for visitors, the banning of country sports. Go and stay there, but don't leave the hotel, that seems to be the message.

Channel 4 News takes a perverse pleasure in its nightly apocalypse franchise, the parade of liars and shifty scientists; merciless footage of fauna carnage, pyre smoke. More upside-down cows, bigger pits; fleecy lambkins cuddled by hooded executioners in gloves and white overalls. Held up to the camera for a tearjerk CU, before being dropped off at the big shed; the killing floor of upturned, expectant faces; shine-in-the-dark eyes.

By the spring of 2001, barred from the motorway orbit, I was trying to exorcise the embargoed Dome (£80 a minute to the taxpayer) by carrying out a series of walks, from Greenwich peninsula to various motorway interchanges. Heading south-east towards Swanley, you get a good sense of how one zone (generous proportions of Blackheath, grim bus shelters of Shooters Hill) gives way to another; small architectural revisions causing major shifts in the psychic balance. Complacency to rage within 200 yards: out of ribbon-development, the poly-filled Tudorbethan avenues of New Eltham, into the heritage Kentish village of Chislehurst (rain, caves closed, footpaths for-bidden). Vehicles change from silver, mercury bubbles tucked away in car ports to four-wheel-drive cruisers with gentleman farmer aspirations.

The Swanley interchange is the spiral gate where South London lowlifes go head-to-head with drug barons and cur-rency dealers. But, just now, according to the *Evening Standard* bulletin boards, the motorway, like the country paths of the Green Loop, is verboten. OFFICIAL: STAY OFF THE M25 IN RUSH HOUR.

This is too bizarre. It's been rumoured for some time that New Labour want to downgrade (re-evaluate) the M25, turn it into the equivalent of a defeated candidate for Mayor of London or Mo Mowlam. Leakages have been hissing for months, penal-ties for single-occupant vehicles, but this announcement is still a surprise. A motorway, built to solve the problems of flow and congestion, has now become the problem. Success has killed it. The M25 is too popular, people use it indiscriminately: thieves on away days, touring the bosky suburbs; sexual service in-dustries taking advantage of the excellent parking facilities and discreet greenery of the Royal Horticultural Society's gardens at Wisley; walkers, random inner-city strollers trying to define the point where London abdicates.

So let's celebrate the first non-motoring motorway, the 'girdle' imagined by altruistic planners in the Twenties, Thirties and Forties. The road is tired, it can't take the stress of traffic; 170,000 vehicles a day going nowhere, wearing away the tarmac mantle. The solution is obvious: steer clear of the road at times when the road is most needed. Without traffic, the M25 is a marvel, a delight to the senses. Leaflets have been printed for distribution to travellers at service stations, channel ports and airports: KEEP OFF. Detour around the road that takes you around London. The Highways Agency understands that future autobahns will be virtual rather than actual. In time, the clapped-out circuit will be covered with Barratt homes, Fairview Estates, Laing's flagpoles; 120 miles of housing stock, pedestrianised.

Once the M25 was redefined as a special-needs case, a privileged unfortunate soon to be granted heritage status, it was time to deal with contiguous countryside. The road that was no longer a road was sandwiched by fields that were no longer fields (golf courses, boarding kennels, pig sheds, reinvented woodland). The next step was obvious: downsize the green belt, slip the corset. Brownfield was the preferred option, trashed land nobody had any use for, armament factories, bone yards, gas works, could be computer-swiped into paradise pastures.

The first intimations that green belt was no longer acceptable in think-tank circles came when books started to appear promoting 'blue sky' fantasies. What is said is always the opposite of what is to be done. I was nervous when I read Bob Gilbert's *The Green London Way*, an eco-excursionist book put out by those decent old leftists Lawrence and Wishart. Hand-drawn maps of a new London dreaming; anecdotes, small histories. *The London Loop* by David Sharp continued the process of opening up the suburbs, linking patches of woodland, riverside paths, tracks across chalk and greensand. These men saw London in its entirety, as a fortunate mixture of town and country, speculative development and eccentric vision, follies, palaces, water towers, footpaths that had been walked for generations. They respected the geography, the pattern of rivers and hills. Their conclusions were based on experience. They had been out there with their notebooks and cameras. They had done it.

In December 1999 the Cabinet Office issued a consultation

paper, the green belt had created an undesirable 'moat effect'. A moat or ditch or ha-ha to keep out, as architect Nicholas Hawksmoor wrote of the denizens of Whitechapel, 'filth Nastyness & Brutes'. The document was, in effect, an early warning on behalf of the developers, the mall conceptualists, the rewrite industry. Government was pure Hollywood: hype, the airbrushing of bad history; dodgy investors, a decent wedge in disgrace or retirement. A pay-off culture of bagmen and straightfaced explainers.

'Special protection for the best agricultural land would be removed, while farmers would be encouraged to launch new kinds of businesses.' *What* businesses? Barbecue pits? Landfill? Ski slopes (of carcasses) to rival Beckton? There must, said the report, be 'a general presumption in favour of market forces'. A sweeping away of fussy restrictions. 'A planning system more supportive of an enterprising countryside.' The only way the countryside could become enterprising was to cease to be countryside: to become 'off-highway', a retail resort (like Bluewater), a weekend excursion that depended on a road that we were being advised to avoid. Tony Blair's 'Performance and Innovation Unit' (a thirteen-strong team of academics and civil servants, 'overseen' by Andrew Smith, Chief Secretary to the Treasury) made the dissolution of the green belt a major element in an attempt at 'joined-up' government.

Metropolitans need this green fantasy, the forest on the horizon, the fields and farms that represent a picture book vision of a pre-Industrial Revolution past. We need the illusion of sap in the vein. We hanker after market gardens, allotments bedded out with the latest horticultural novelties. The M25 is tolerable because it moves through an extended parkland (Epping Forest, the Thames Crossing, North Downs). The green belt, futile as it is, turns London into one of Ebenezer Howard's garden cities. Howard's vision, originally published in 1898 as *Tomorrow: A Peaceful Path to Real Reform*, imagined a Utopian community, public buildings at the centre, surrounded by parks, houses with gardens, set within 'an agricultural reservation'. Such reservations, check out Milton Keynes and Welwyn Garden City, don't really work. It's too swift an enactment of something that needs to evolve, through compromise and bodge, through centuries. Lay it out overnight and you get a Mormon dormitory or an unoccupied cemetery that looks great in the catalogue.

But the green belt is on a grander scale, conceived in desperation. G.L. Pepler's 'Greater London' (published in the RIBA *Town Planning Conference – Transactions*, 1911) proposed a parkway encircling London at a ten-mile radius from Charing Cross (from the monument that marked the last stage of the funeral procession of Queen Eleanor, wife of Edward I). The parkway would act as a ring road and as the basis for a necklace of garden suburbs.

Arthur Crow, also writing in 1911, went further; he wanted to connect ten 'Cities of Health' (Barnet, Bromley, Croydon, Dartford, Epping, Epsom, Romford, Uxbridge, Waltham, Watford). They would be joined by a 'Great Ring Avenue', a fantastic Egyptian or Mayan conceit, radiant settlements as outstations to a centre given over to public buildings, places of ceremony, commerce and worship. The avenue would be 500 feet wide and eighty-eight miles in circumference.

By the time Londoners had seen their city bombed, riverside industries destroyed, they were ready to think of renewal, deportation to the end of the railway line, the jagged beginnings of farmland. Patrick Abercrombie's *Greater London Plan 1944* (published in 1945) still worked through concentric bands: the Inner Urban Ring (overcrowded, fire-damaged), the Suburban Ring (to which inner-city casualties would migrate), the green belt (ten miles beyond the edge of London), and the Outer Country Ring, which would extend to the boundary of the regional plan.

Visionary maps, in muted Ben Nicholson colours, were produced. Lovely fold-out abstractions. Proposals in soft grey, pale green, blue-silver river systems. But always with the blood circuit of ring roads, the pastoral memory rind at the edge of things, at the limits of our toleration of noise and speed and grime. There must, said William Bull (in 1901), be 'a green girdle around London's Sphere . . . a circle of green sward and trees which would remain permanently inviolate'.

Until now. The first usage of the term 'Green Belt', in a London County Council resolution of 1924, stressed the same terms: 'an inviolable rural zone around London'.

By the 1960s there was substantial 'nibbling' into that inviolable belt; Hertfordshire and Essex were targeted for housing schemes 'because spare railway capacity existed'. Surrey and Kent could look after themselves. The Lea Valley with its disused greenhouses was approved as a residential area (for those opting to quit the increasingly 'multicultural' inner cities). A 400-acre green belt site was cleared for development in 1966.

New Labour, masters of double-talk, gesture politics, non-consenting consensus, were reversing the old Tory sentimentality over Metroland and the suburbs (Edward Heath in Bexleyheath, Margaret Thatcher in Finchley, Michael Portillo in Southgate). Thatcherites hated the inner cities (Hackney, Lambeth). Their pitch was simple: turn proles into home-owning suburbanites, stakeholders, share-buyers. London would be ring-fenced into ghetto, city of surveillance, privately policed estate. New Labour went further, a two (two dozen in the case of Michael Meacher) home portfolio; town house and country house. Wilderness was abhorrent. Rough pasture must be rationalised into Best Value recreational zones, retirement homes for happy butterflies. Farm animals were dirty, smelly, unreconstructed: cull them. What was required was a vertical wedge through the landscape (the Lee Valley Regional Plan), a designated hierarchy (media, recreation, development). What was not required was an holistic vision, any talk of belts or girdles or circuits. What was lost was the old dream of paradise gardens.

2

Enfield Chase tucks neatly into the north-east corner, where the A10 (the Great Cambridge Road) meets the pale blue horizontal of the M25. My Nicholson's *Greater London Street Atlas* is a well-travelled, one-and-a-half-kilo wad of overannotated pulp. The white blank of Enfield Chase is dressed with parks, enclosures, gardens, woodland walks: Clay Hill, White Webbs Park, Forty Hill (Museum), Capel Manor, Trent Park. Greenness slips under the motorway, Rorschach blots mopping up the grey.

On the eastern slope of the Lea Valley is Epping Forest; the people's forest, festooned with burger cartons, silver cans, ghosts of prisoners, runaways, pastoral melancholics (cop killer Harry Roberts, poets John Clare, Alfred Tennyson, Edward Thomas). On the west is the old forest of Middlesex, Enfield Chase. The broad, marshy floodplain of the Lea is a natural boundary.

The royal family were the first suburbanites, recognising that London was only tolerable if you could run second (third, fourth, fifth) homes in the country, in easy commuting distance. And, if that proved expensive, or you became bored by your own furnishings, you could always land on a neighbour and bankrupt him. The first circle around London, precursor to the orbital highway, was the property portfolio of royal palaces: Greenwich and Eltham in Kent, Havering in Essex, Hampton Court in Middlesex, Nonsuch, Richmond and Oatlands in Surrey. As with the M25 – the 'missing' service station on the west side – there was a gap in the chain. Theobalds Park, just north of Enfield Chase, was not in royal hands. It belonged to a servant of the crown, master of the Secret State: William Cecil,

Lord Burleigh. His son Robert, Earl of Salisbury, handed the place over to James I (taking Hatfield House, twinned with Welwyn Garden City, in exchange).

Green is seductive. There's something unnatural about its chemistry. Nature, bent and abused, is grey. We're happy with the grey variables: silver to sludge. Stand on a footbridge over the M25, anywhere between Junction 26 on the edge of Epping Forest and the Junction 25 exit for Enfield, and you'll watch traffic through tattered sails of greenery, roadside plantings, overripe saplings fed on diesel. The context of the valley is revealed: mud paddocks bulldozed for future development, new systems of access roads, sour yellow Wimpey boxes for first-time buyers; low, wooded hills; the persistent chlorophyll of Enfield Chase and environs. Captured estates. Garden centres. Pubs that offer Thai, Chinese and Indian lunches, while hanging on to their fustian titles: The King and Tinker, The Pied Bull, The Volunteer, The Woodbine.

We dream of a green paradise. The solution to Gimpo's teasing riddle – 'to find out where the M25 leads' – is here. After the circuits of madness, pilgrims must claim their reward: the secret garden. Residual desire is articulated in street names. Paradise Road and Paradise Row are both located in Waltham Abbey.

Going east from Waltham Cross, a confederacy of country houses and secure estates straddles the motorway. Theobalds Park, to the north of the road, is modest about its royal pedigree. If you drive along its boundaries you will be scanned by surveillance cameras, quizzed by interrogators at unmanned checkpoints. Walkers are suspect. The site reveals nothing that might provoke unwelcome attention. History declines into romantic fiction.

Philippa Gregory in her novel *Earthly Joys* (1998) nominates the gardener John Tradescant as her hero, a familiar generic trope. Tradescant is best known as a Lambeth figure, keeper of 'Tradescant's Ark', a proto-museum and grand cabinet of curiosities, storehouse of plants, bones and anthropological swag. He is celebrated in the present Museum of Garden History in St Mary's Church, alongside Lambeth Palace.

But Gregory is more interested in the young man, the tanned, strong-shouldered son of the soil. Tradescant is the gardener at Theobalds Palace. The relationship with his patron, the hunchbacked, avian figure of Robert Cecil is composed as a straightfaced version of a *Fast Show* homoerotic playlet, enacted by Charlie Higson and Paul Whitehouse. '*Any early vegetables?*' *his lordship asked.* '*Asparagus? They say His Majesty loves asparagus.*'

Earthly Joys become earthy joys as Tradescant drops his breeches for the Duke of Buckingham. 'The pain when it came to him was sharp like a pain of deep agonising desire, a pain that he welcomed, that he wanted to wash through him. And then it changed and became a deep pleasure and a terror to him, a feeling of submission and penetration and leaping desire and deep satisfaction. John thought he understood the passionate grief and lust of a woman who can take a man inside her.'

Gregory's romance limns the period when Theobalds Park passed from Cecil to James I. A property to complete the circuit of royal residences. Known variously as Cullynges, Tongs, Thebaudes, Tibbolds, the palace was built by Lord Burleigh in 1560. The attraction of the estate was its distance from London and the court, a single day's ride; enclosed forest could be domesticated, organised into gardens, walks, rides, hierarchies of contemplation. Cecil's son ceded the palace to the Scottish interloper, James I. James's grandson Charles II gifted the estate to the turncoat General Monck, Duke of Albermarle. So Theobalds declined, always with a sense of favours conferred, male alliances, pay-offs to special friends. Heritage flashbacks were all that remained by the time the land was purchased by the Victorian brewer Sir Henry Meux, Bart.

Cecil, according to a contemporary *Life*, 'greatly delighted in making gardens'. Royal visits by Elizabeth cost him many thousands of pounds, but this retreat from the realpolitik of the state, the fabrication of conspiracies, justified paranoia, gave the civil servant scope to construct his paradise garden. On the forest fringe, posthumous fantasies could be played out, an Alhambra of scents, fountains, symmetries. A commissioned painting of Cecil (now in the National Portrait Gallery) places him, absurdly, on a mule: Don Quixote as Sancho Panza. Berobed, ringed, a raddled imago of power. 'Riding in his garden and walks upon his little mule was his greatest disport.'

James I, resting here at the end of his progress from Scotland, experienced a thrill of recognition. Like romantic novelist Philippa Gregory, he found the discretion of Enfield profoundly erotic. Theobalds Park, according to Gregory, 'had been laid out by Sir Robert's father in the bleak elegance of the period. Sharply defined geometric patterns of box hedging enclosed different coloured gravels and stones.'

Tradescant plotted a New Age makeover. 'He longed to take out the gravel from the enclosed shapes and plant the patterns with herbs, flowers and shrubs. He wanted to see the whole disciplined shape softened and changing every day with foliage and flowers which would bloom and wilt, grow freshly green, and then pale . . . Tradescant had a picture in his mind's eye of plants spilling over the hedges, of the thick green of the box containing wildness, fertility, even colour. It was an image that drew on the hedgerow and roadside of the wild country of England and brought that richness into the garden and imposed order upon it.'

The Earl of Salisbury entertained James I for four days at Theobalds, while the new king received the homage of the Lords of Council. Coming from the bleak north, James wanted to take possession of a house and grounds, elegantly planted, artfully laid out, on the side of London in which he was most comfortable. He commandeered Theobalds and a large portion of Enfield Chase, as a kind of dowry. A wall, ten miles in circumference, enclosed his estates.

The circuit of the wall crosses the motorway and cuts through the grounds of Capel Manor, now an horticultural college, garden centre and display of show gardens. The pleasure of walking through the grounds derives from the change of pulse, slowing of breath, coming away from the road gives you. All the usual irritants with which great gardens protect themselves are blessings: they make access difficult. Persistence is rewarded. Capel Manor, like its neighbour Myddelton House, is open to visitors on certain days, at certain times – if those times don't have to be revised, if there are no plagues or elections on the horizon.

Capel is the first estate you notice, exiting the M25, making the tricky turn into Bullsmoor Lane. Follies, Gothic ruins, are glimpsed over the wall. Ivy-covered John Piper arches floating in sparse woodland. It's only after you've bought your ticket and followed the signs that you recognise these stacks of tumbled masonry as customised fakes, commissioned from William Chambers. Rams and urns and centaur heads among pink rhododendrons. The small area of tolerated 'wilderness' is punted as a 'garden feature', introduced by William Robinson and other members of the 'Natural' school of the late nineteenth century. It doesn't feel like woodland. A two-minute stroll loops you back to a prospect of the south lawn, the Liriodendron Tree, the famous Caucasian Elm (*Zelkova carpinifolia*); the ha-ha which marked the division of the Theobalds and Capel Manor estates.

On a mound that overlooks the motorway is another folly, an open-sided, open-roofed Temple of the Winds. Voices from the gardens are distorted. Children scampering around the maze. Water. Filtered traffic whooo-whooo-whoooing under Bulls Cross Ride.

Capel Manor, promoted under the slogan 'Where the City meets the Countryside', has downgraded the paradise theme to a series of botanical rooms, conservatories with the lid lifted off. There is a garden for 'Physically Challenged People' and a garden for 'Visually Impaired People'. There is a Yellow Garden and a Blue Garden (with flowers blessed by the M25 ribbon-cutter). 'Now this is my type of garden,' said Margaret Thatcher at a photo-opportunity in 1989. *Wisteria sinensis, Brunnera macrophylla, Lirioe muscari* and *Cynara cardunculus.* 'Blue is one of the "cold" colours, providing a calm and restful feel.'

There's a lake, of course. But it's notable, in this area of springs and rivulets, riverine speculations, that Capel Manor has chosen to market non-liquid water, fake water. This season's idea is the virtual water garden (a drought fancy which only succeeded in predicting the continual rain that would raise London's water table and float off anything that wasn't firmly anchored). The concept of designers Angela Grant and Nigel Jackson was to stimulate those parts of the brain that 'think water' – without actually involving that precious resource in the exchange. Diuretic gardening: as sponsored by a 'co-operative venture' (Anglian Water, West Water, Yorkshire, Thames Water, Severn Trent). Nifty arrangements of broken slate and silver paper (gallery quality) make up the 'water conscious' garden (i.e. the garden that makes us conscious of the absence of water). A notion that is about as much use as handing a dehydrated marathon runner a photograph of a high-energy drink. Or playing a video loop of Ullswater-at-dawn on a Tunisian sand dune.

Princess Elizabeth, the future Virgin Queen, was brought from Hatfield House to Enfield Chase by her 'keeper', Sir Thomas Pope. She travelled, according to Nicholas Norden's *Progresses of Queen Elizabeth*, with 'a retinue of twelve ladies in white satin, on ambling palfreys, and twenty yeomen in green on horseback, that her grace might hunt the hart'.

The forest was a site of enchantment for a green belt monarchy; a theatre for role reversals, sexual travesty, debating schools. 'The Queen came from Theobalds to Enfield House to dinner, and she had toils set up in the park to shoot at the

buck.' The court stood for wild nature, ecology, the preservation of animals so that they could be killed for sport. The
forest, when it is enclosed and exploited, is royalist. Republican
sentiment cuts down trees. The major deforestation took
place under Cromwell and the Commonwealth. The diarist
John Evelyn described the Chase as 'a solitary desert with 3,000
deer'.

Royal physicians were rewarded with Enfield estates. Trent
Park was given by George III to his favourite quack. Elizabeth I
presented White Webbs House to her physician, Dr Hucks (or
Huicks). Huicks – and the house he occupied – came under
grave suspicion in the time of Elizabeth's successor, James.
Guido Vaux (aka Guy Fawkes) was a frequent visitor. Heretics
(Catholics) were always shunted out to the fringes, rural and
riverside suburbs, while nonconforming fundamentalists clung
to the city, plain chapels and places of assembly. Recent aristocrats, royal servants, cash-rich bureaucrats bought into the
green girdle, leaving the inner suburbs, Hackney and Hoxton,
to argumentative mechanics and tradesmen.

Vaux took White Webbs House and furnished it at his own
expense. Garnet the Jesuit stayed with him. The house was
reported, by government agents, to be filled with 'Popish
books and relics'; a fiendish warren of 'trapdoors and passages'.
What is now White Webbs Lane was once known as Rome
Lane. Terror and counter-terror lived in close proximity: the
spymaster on one side of the fence and the heretical assassin on
the other.

Walking through Enfield Chase, estate to estate, you notice
small streams, channels cut for Sir Hugh Myddelton's New
River. Myddelton was a speculator, water was a resource. By
the late Elizabethan period, medieval wells and conduits could
not adequately supply the needs of the City. Edmund Colthurst
looked to the Hertfordshire springs at Amwell and Chadwell,
near Ware. The goldsmith Myddelton exploited Colthurst's

initiative. Born in Wales in 1560, he was MP for Denbigh and jeweller to James I. The dull silver of the River Lea was converted, by labour and promotion, to gold, a personal fortune. Adventurer shares were issued and Colthurst was appointed as overseer of the work, the digging and cutting; the New River would travel forty miles in making the twenty-mile journey to London. It hugged the 100-foot contour line, falling eighteen feet in the course of its travels. It opened at Christmas in 1613. Myddelton was knighted, made a baronet. He prospered. He died in 1631, leaving versions of his name scattered through the suburbs, tracings that can still be followed into town.

But any attempt to walk the length of Myddelton's New River is a forlorn exercise. Water: known but not seen. Dishonoured water. The muddy trickle of streams that no longer pay their way, edging in embarrassment through the dog-exercising pastures of Enfield Chase. Relics of Pymmes Brook, Salmons Brook, Turkey Brook.

The New River Head on the Penton Mound in Islington has been developed by Stirling Ackroyd. A spindly fountain playing in a shallow pool. A wink at those who have chased the brook from Hertfordshire. St James Homes promote: 'a dynamic living environment'. There are still parties of intent walkers, greyheads in anoraks and trainers, straining to catch the guide's patter above the noise of the traffic. Elderly street signs, white on blue, with their brighter replacements: Myddelton Square, Amwell Street, Chadwell Street, Sadler's Wells, Merlin's Cave. Just as the reprieved statues and arches of the old city migrate to the green belt, so the names of the source places, the springs, are planted in a townscape: pastoral aspirations. Lloyds Dairy in Amwell Street: a black and white chequerboard display for bottles of contour-banded yellow milk, heavy with cream. Simulations. Heritage nudges with a true heritage: Welsh cows, draymen and dairymen from the west. Thick-necked bottles are clotted to give the lie to Cockney rumours of Welshers (from Cardiganshire) watering their milk.

The Metropolitan Water Board (privatised, defunct) have left a sepulchral, marbled wreath behind them, a text nobody bothers to read: ERECTED BY THE METROPOLITAN WATER BOARD ON THE SITE OF THE NEW RIVER HEAD. On the corner of River Street is a peeling signboard: *The Village Buttery*. Cream, milk, butter, pseudo-apothecaries: the village within the city, the small green oasis of Wilmington Square Gardens.

Following the New River, north, up Colebrooke Row, brings you to the cottage Charles Lamb shared with his sister Mary. Restored, white-painted, plants on window sill. The cottage dates from 1760. The Lambs lived here from 1823 to 1826. The New River, already tired, drudges past the front of the house. My children, when they were told the story of Mary Lamb murdering her mother, preferred to walk on the other side of the road. What is curious is how the Lambs, taking up a rustic retreat in Enfield, followed the river out. Water remains, in my fancy, a messenger substance, linking reservoir with source; a dream hinge between city heat and Arcadian potentiality.

Lamb has been heritaged as one of the treasures of Enfield. Contemporary reports were ambiguous. 'Charles Lamb quite delighted with his retirement. He does not fear the solitude of the situation, though he seems to be almost without an acquaintance, and dreads rather than seeks visitors.'

With Mary Lamb's health deteriorating, brother and sister shifted from house to house, lodging to lodging: The Poplars in Chase Side to Bay Cottage, Church Street, Edmonton. Lamb was buried in All Saints Church.

Enfield lacked culture. Enfield was not Islington. Food was dull. The chief bookseller, Lamb informed Mary Shelley, 'deals in prose versions of the melodrama, with plates of ghosts and murders and other subterranean passages'. The fraudulent antiquarianism in which the Chase specialised: the plaster devils of Capel Manor.

Back on my New River trail, I tried to photograph the

heritage plaque on Colebrooke Cottages. Two women brushed past. 'He's sharp as a pin. Got all his marbles, only he can't talk.'

Myddelton is memorialised by a statue, facing south, at the sharp end of the little park that divides Upper Street and Essex Road, Islington. The water speculator on his high plinth is a carry-on conquistador, back turned to the lowlife scramblings of park bench, bushes. Palm trees surround the base. Myddelton has hacked his way through a Douanier Rousseau jungle, climbed a small hill to stare over unconquered lands; his eyeline will carry him to Cleopatra's Needle and the Thames. Stone putti with pockmarked skins kneel in the shrubs, flanking a dish of rusty water. Myddelton's right hand keeps his cloak clear of the muck; while his left hand clutches a map or charter.

Sir Hugh Myddelton, fortune secure, built himself a house and laid out gardens in the neighbourhood of Forty Hall, near Enfield. The New River flowed through the grounds. Forty Hall was later acquired by H.C. Bowles, described by James Thorne in his *Handbook to the Environs of London* as 'the fortunate possessor of shares in the New River company'. Into these suburban reservations was gathered the cultural ballast of London: a portion of ballustrading from Christopher Wren's church of St Benet (demolished in 1867), a Portland stone Grecian temple from the Duke of Chandos's house in Edgware, twelve stone balls from the front of Burlington House, Piccadilly. Scattered throughout the Chase were jigsaw mementoes of a lost London.

Bowles, on a site adjoining Forty Hall, once known as Bowling Green, built Myddelton House. Here all the elements that defined Enfield Chase came together: accumulated wealth, green politics, architectural salvage from the City, royal courtiers working their connections, paradise gardens. Myddelton House, glorying in the name of the original water promoter, is presently the headquarters of the Lee Valley Regional Park Authority. On those days, and at those hours, when the grounds are open to the public, you can creep up to the high windows of this comfortable property and see computers, coffee machines, filing cabinets, the steel-grey trappings of bureaucracy. But, unless you have business with LVRPA, you can't go in. You must shuffle across the gravel to wonder at the heritage of the notable botanist E.A. Bowles.

Philippa Gregory and her sorority got it right. The Bowles story and the story of the garden do play like an historical romance. It *is* a romance. At the Capel Manor garden centre, massed copies of Joan Hessayon's *Capel Bells* are offered for sale. An Edwardian lady with parasol drifting across lawns. Beneath the heavy relief lettering of the author's name, a tapestry of fuchsias, the eponymous 'Capel Bells'. Prosperity on a stalk: 'They look like petals, I grant you, but those of us in the know refer to them as sepals . . . Blooms increase on a mathematical progression. Damned clever little things.'

Capel Bells is a grand read, pre-optioned television: Cookson heroine battling to establish herself in society, knockabout sub-plot of Cockney chancers, horticulture, discovery of unknown father, sail off into sunset with the inheritor of this magical country house. It's like finger-licking your way through a seed catalogue with racy bits, headset history on a guided tour of the grounds.

The gravity of Hessayon's novel pulls towards the notion of Arcadia as an achievable condition, the contrary of urban struggle. 'Charlotte had boarded the train at Liverpool Street station in the sooty air of the City, deafened by the cries of unhappy children, the whine of beggars, the scolding of irritated mothers and the bellows of station staff. Fifteen miles north of this cacophony, the outer reaches of Enfield were a paradise of leafy trees and empty roads. She had not seen a single motor car.'

Paradise. That word again. A.R. Hope-Moncrieff in his book on Essex calls up the spirit of William Morris. 'Morris also played in a suburban garden, and was mainly brought up in the next parish, on the edge of Epping Forest, that was an Earthly Paradise for his youth.' Paradise Road, Waltham Abbey. Paradise Wildlife Park, just north of Junction 25, on the orbital motorway.

'Strangely, for a young woman known for her down-to-earth attitudes, she felt an almost mystical affinity with Capel Manor,' writes Hessayon of her heroine, Charlotte Blair (a working girl who has the temerity to rent a substantial Essex property). 'She had no idea what exactly she craved, but felt certain that a few months living in the old house in Enfield would solve the mystery and give her peace.'

The romance, bastard progeny of Malory and Spenser, is the proper form for describing this territory. The structure is formal, fixed rules that shock us into enlightenment: a still pool in a woodland glade, an artist who captures essence with a few swift brush strokes. The owner of Capel Manor goes into business with a Tokyo firm in anticipation of global capitalism. All the scams and development pitches of the Lea Valley are here in outline. Future shadows creep across rigorously managed lawns. 'Of course we couldn't live on a pound a week. What a thing to say! Popple will buy you a nursery ... I believe the area is full of nurseries. The Lea Valley. That's true, isn't it?'

Of course it is. As true as the hero's chum Buffy who comes up with a wizard scheme 'to make a fortune by building homes in the suburbs'. The first paradise of the car. Nobody demands an orbital highway. The only routes follow the rivers, north/south, follow ancient trackways. Great estates are always one day's ride from the centre. The suburbs wait on the railway. They swallow up dozy market towns, places of retreat: Enfield, Waltham Abbey, Chigwell, Edmonton. Then polyfill the bits in between.

In Joan Hessayon's romance, characters represent the categories of invader who will come to occupy the fringes of the old forest. Essex man and woman in embryo. The Covent

Garden entrepreneur. The flower girl with push. The ambitious Big House servant with an unhealthy passion for fuchsias. The bent solicitor with a nubile daughter. Jack-the-Lad from the Rookeries with an eye for horseflesh. Plants are currency. Gorgeous swathes of scent and colour. Bearded iris for toffs and auricula ('gold-laced polyanthus') for the working man.

'I dare say people whose hobby is growing auriculas would not be received in the neighbourhood, although I doubt if that was the reason Lady Meux wasn't received,' remarks the catty Charlotte.

Hessayon's romance doesn't simply predict coming social trends, it inducts historic personages into the narrative. There is Lady Meux, Valerie, chatelaine of Theobalds Park – who is not (as a widow) received in Upper Lea Valley society. Her husband, the brewer, picked up the former royal palace and brought his much younger wife with him. Valerie had served behind the bar at Meux's Horseshoe Tavern, on the site of the Dominion Theatre, Tottenham Court Road. Hessayon sketches her as a game widow who entertains unmarried men and makes very imaginative use of an indoor swimming pool.

But the dominant figure in this patchwork of country houses is E.A. 'Gussie' Bowles of Myddleton (sic) House. Bowles drops in at Capel Manor, accompanied by the formidable garden-planner and author Gertrude Jekyll (venturing north from her Surrey patch). Gussie, a confirmed bachelor, is rather sharp with women and amateur horticulturalists. Jekyll is one of the chaps.

E.A. Bowles was a gift to writers of fiction. The family were Huguenot (original name Garnault). They purchased a block of shares in the New River Company, enough to provide them with a controlling interest. In 1724, according to Bryan Hewitt (*The Crocus King: E.A. Bowles of Myddelton House*), Michael Garnault acquired 'an estate with an Elizabethan house called Bowling Green House at Bulls Cross in north Enfield. By coincidence a loopway of the New River cut through the garden.' This loopway had, it was said, been created to prevent the destruction of a Tudor yew hedge.

Henry Carrington Bowles married into the Garnault family in 1799. A swamp cypress was planted to celebrate the nuptials. When Anne Garnault, the last of the line, died, the Bulls Cross property passed to the Bowles family. A new house, white Suffolk brick, was built in 1818. And was eventually inherited by Henry Carrington Bowles Treacher, on condition that he assumed the Bowles surname and coat of arms. E.A. Bowles was Treacher's fourth son.

The process of drift, centre to margin, is very evident at Myddleton House. Huguenots, frequently associated with Spitalfields, the streets around Nicholas Hawksmoor's Christ Church, remove themselves to an area of play country. They become more English than the English (aping the parodic squirearchy of the royals). A great chum of Gussie Bowles is Thomas Hanbury, one of the Quaker brewers of Brick Lane (hops to the city, profit to the suburbs). Bowles stays with Hanbury in his fourteenth-century palace (with terraced gardens) at La Mortola. Quaker wealth comes with responsibility: schools for the children of workers, grace and favour cottages. Gussie is also keen on good works, socialising with the lads of Enfield, 'Bowles Boys'.

Gussie fits out his garden with York stone slabs from Clerkenwell. He collects one of those strange, ovenlike, igloo-block shelters that once stood on the old London Bridge. (These structures trace a psychogeographic progress across London, from Guy's Hospital to Victoria Park in Hackney, to Myddleton House in Enfield. Memory nudges, displacements that weave across an indifferent landscape, as invisible as the New River.)

Bowles rescues the Enfield Market Cross and a diamond-shaped pillar known as 'the Irishman's shirt'. Cargo-cult plunder dresses his gardens: a portion of the New River, antiquarian oddities from London, exotic blooms from European plant-hunting expeditions. Myddleton House is a museum of false starts and wilfully perverse hints. Gussie lays out 'The Lunatic Asylum', an area of the garden that includes a contorted hazel known as 'Harry Lauder's Walking Stick'. Flora can be as zany as fauna. The grounds of Myddleton House are revealed as a microcosm of the Lea Valley/Enfield Chase Arcadia: captured river, a market cross, tulip terraces, beds of gold and white and silver; a reservation for the outpatients of the botanical world.

Beyond Bulls Cross, moving west along the hard shoulder of the M25, from Potters Bar towards Abbots Langley, we learn how the old estates were broken up and rebranded as asylums, retreats, drying-out clinics, holding pens for troublesome inner-city aliens. Looking at my map, before the walk began, I logged: Shenley, Harperbury, Napsbury, Leavesden and, a little to the south (North Circular rather than M25), Friern Barnet.

E.A. Bowles kept gas and electricity out of Myddleton House until 1954. As he got older little quirks of character were refined into fullblown eccentricity. He wore spectacles with a single lens (the left). He put his finger through the empty socket and twirled. He was a member of an all-male dining club, the Garden Society, that admitted only one woman, the Queen Mother (royals are hermaphrodite).

Garden books were produced, small controversies aired: Bowles wasn't keen on the fad for rock gardens. (The estate of his greatest rival was acquired by a later millionaire gardener, George Harrison, the former Beatle.) Life centred on masculine Christianity, the Jesus Church at Enfield. Boys who attended the church were encouraged to spend weekends messing about in the grounds of Myddleton House, clearing the pond, or doing a bit of weeding. 'For this they wore bathing costumes, Gussie's being of Edwardian vintage with blue and white rings reaching down to his ankles,' reports Bryan Hewitt. 'A straw hat with his college ribbons completed the outfit (it was the same hat in which the boys picked strawberries).'

The boys were taken on excursions to Brighton. They were

given the job of lifting and sorting crocuses. They enjoyed themselves, fishing and playing cricket on the lawns. There is a photograph, something like a Latigue, of a card school dressed in Edwardian bathing costumes. One boy, the nearest to the camera, has stuck out his tongue. Another favourite, Fred, did an impression of Gussie with a watering can. He fell into the river. 'He squelched off to the house,' Hewitt writes, 'where Gussie gave him a bath and dry clothes. He reappeared dressed in a pair of Gussie's flannel trousers, a Norfolk jacket and a trilby with the brim turned down and proceeded to shamble about giving a hilarious imitation of Gussie who joined in the fun.'

Bowles Boys served on the Western Front in the First War. Gussie wrote to them with news of the harvest and the 'burning hot days in July', he sent food parcels. Many were wounded, crippled, killed. The honoured dead of the Hertfordshire Yeomanry, the Royal Field Artillery, the Middlesex Regiment and the Royal Fusiliers.

The residue of what Bowles attempted, a life given over to the creation of a garden, remains. It works in a way that Capel Manor, with its strategic planting, its demonstrations, never will. Capel Manor debates a Princess Diana memorial garden, the form it should take: a place of remembrance beside an orbital motorway. Myddleton House has a more direct royal connection. The foreword to Bryan Hewitt's book is written by the grandson of E.A. Bowles's brother. 'I think of my Great Great Uncle Gussie often as I walk around our small Wiltshire garden,' writes Brigadier Andrew Parker Bowles, OBE (horseman, courtier and former husband of the royal mistress, Camilla). 'If, as I suspect, my uncle is looking back from "across the wide river" he will be amazed to discover that his name is still revered and his works much admired.'

3

Bill Drummond – green weatherproof, thick blue jersey, specs on string, spiky hair – eased himself out of his Aylesbury cab. I was waiting with Marc Atkins beside the (closed) doors of the Church of the Holy Cross and St Lawrence at Waltham Abbey.

Bill has the look of a man interrupted: he's been thinking about another project, talking/not talking, skidding across a dark landscape, and now he's expelled. Damp air. Another early start. A walk across Enfield Chase to the National Institute for Medical Research at Mill Hill. Why?

Dumb instinct – on my part. Which is always the best method. It's a slight detour, in terms of our orbital circuit, but Waltham Abbey to Mill Hill, across the Chase, favours the lie of the land; the way the rivers go, the direction of the foot-paths. I reckon we can knock this one off, through parks, woodland, farm roads, and arrive at the hospital in time for the lunchtime lecture. At 1.30 p.m., in the Fletcher Hall, German conceptualist Jochen Gerz (associate of Joseph Beuys and Reiner Ruthenbeck) is going to address the whitecoats on the subject of 'Works in Public Spaces'.

I don't like deadlines. They put a damper on the urge to digress. Shouldn't we expect the unexpected? But the hospital block on the summit of Mill Hill is a real marker, generator of paranoid imaginings. I'm always uneasy when covert research, generously funded, starts to cosy up to subversive art. There's something awkward about the relationship. To access the art manifestation (conceptual corridor, lunchtime lecture) you have to blag your way into the Pentagon, into Langley. Surveillance swipe, signature in book, electronic barrier, phone call to a higher authority.

I turned up, the first time, to see a show, 'Cityscapes', by the photographer Effie Paleologou. 10 February 1998. I love Effie's work, her nightstalker's liminal meditations. A young Greek woman, living in East London, she starts at the railway station, moving away, making the familiar unfamiliar, playing with scale and expectation, discovering the City as theatre: curtains, alcoves, trees sculpted with artificial light. Upper-deck revellers in red buses, the revel burnt out of them. Effie looks for risk (surreal anecdotes) but purges it from her prints, which are infinitely calm, balanced, resilient.

Effie's show was described on the handout from the Medical Research Council ('research undertaken in diverse fields, including neurophysiology, molecular structure, developmental biology and mycobacteriology') as 'the first manifestation' of a visual arts programme. 'Large format colour photographs depict nocturnal landscapes in which the ephemeral and fugitive is captured within the stark industrial shapes of the city . . . Selected photographs provoke a dialogue with the striking architecture of the Institute and play with the notional intro-duction of the city into the pastoral.'

I walked to Mill Hill from Hackney. A mild day, a pleasant tramp through Golders Green. At 12.50 p.m., I found myself with my nose pressed to the glass of the Villa Dei Fiori ('Fully Air Conditioned'). One couple in the place. Slatted blinds and white linen (like a Californian hospital, face-lifts, tummy tucks, Mozart). Celebrity photographs with sprawling encomia: Ernie Wise, Christopher Lee.

I bought a chocolate-bar and an apple at the mini-mart. A notice fixed to the top shelf: SORRY NO READING. Hi-gloss, washable magazines. I thought that was the whole point of the transaction. Looking and simulating. Not reading.

Golders Green retains its identity as a civic centre. You can have a pee, buy a rich Viennese pastry, find an urn for your ashes. Near the station, the little barbershop offers showbiz trims. 'To Tony Thanks For A Perfect Cut'. More celebrity snaps: David Janssen, Johnny

The suburbs begin with the Cremat
about 60 cars'. I search out Sigmund Freu
across a buttercup meadow to admire the
red brick, hill town monastery with its cloisters
moved on and out, stepping up the pace to na
seemed to be an exclusively Japanese enclave; sat   .s,
silence. JAPAN HOMES announced the estate agent. White
houses, red roof tiles, net curtains. Avenues of pollarded trees.
No shops, no dogs. Bankrupt, discredited Hackney can't afford
planning officers or planning restrictions; our borough is a
building site. Dust is the taste. Noise is the norm: power-drills,
chainsaws. Not a leaf can be moved in Kyoto-by-Finchley
Road. Not a pebble can be revised. If you talk on the street
you face banishment to Hendon or Palmers Green.

The whole, deeply suspect business of *hiking* through this
complex labyrinth of crescents and circuses and dead ends is
dreamlike. De Chirico without the squares and fountains. The
Crematorium is the liveliest joint in town, folk gathering
to chat in the car park, strollers among the colonnades, nicely
kept gardens.

Once you cross the North Circular Road you enter a different territory. You're greeted by an ecstatic sculpture, a strong
woman, naked, with an upraised sword. *La Délivrance* by
Emile Guillaume. This is a traffic stopper and even better if
you're on foot. A *Health & Efficiency* nude, tiptoe, on a stone
beach ball, lifting Excalibur instead of a tennis racket.

Passing through Mill Hill viaduct, and starting to climb the
hill itself, is dropping into mild-mannered English science
fiction; the village that is too much a village, the big house set
back from the road. Captured land. Barrack blocks (remember
the Mill Hill bomb?). Cult centres. A heavily protected laboratory. WARNING GUARD DOGS ON PATROL. MOD PROPERTY
PRIVATE NO PUBLIC RIGHT OF WAY. UNAUTHORISED ACCESS
FORBIDDEN. KEEP OUT! Chainlink fence. Lights on poles.

de Mill Hill East station, I see a man, encountered
rlier in the day near the North Circular Road. He was sweating hard, the sweat dried on him, in a suit. Glaswegian. Searching for London. Uncertain as to the direction in which to strike out. Now he was trying to blag his way on to a train. 'The staff don't want to take you. The train will be held. Police have been sent for.'

'Ya alus pick onna feckin homeless,' he shouts, walking off, back to Scotland.

Deep inside the National Institute for Medical Research, Effie's photographs dress a corridor. Nocturnal streets, Whitechapel, Bethnal Green, franchising paradox. Novelties to be nodded at on the way to the buffet. Beyond her dimly lit arcade, fields and greenery are always visible. Land dropping away towards the South Herts Golf Course, Dollis Brook and the beginnings of Enfield Chase. Caught, as ever with Effie's work, between sodium flare and green window, I listened to the dry morse of a table-tennis ball bouncing from a well-sprung table. The rattle of cups.

Tuesday 28 April 1998. Bill and I decide, independently, in one swoop, to touch the Harold stone at the back of the abbey. Marc is moaning about his swollen foot and his twisted hip, the aftermath of our tramp up the Lea Valley. But he's got the energy to pitch Bill with plans for books, exhibitions, trips to Northern Ireland. Bill has strange tales of Jimmy Savile – always a good topic – in Aylesbury, at the hospital. An anchorite in a shellsuit. A life of conspicuous charity and public secrets, bolt-holes, cigars, self-mythologising.

I use a couple of photocopied pages from a comic strip as my guide, for the walk from Waltham Cross to Theobalds Park. The story I'm working with is the preamble to a text by Neil Gaiman, illustrated by Michael Zulli: *Sweeney Todd: The Demon Barber of Fleet Street*. These days graphic novelists operate with expensive cameras (just like painters of the Hockney lineage).

Before laying out a narrative, they will rehearse what they later draw: the envisioned version (dream), the enacted version (logged and recorded), the public version (smoothed, idealised).

I'd collaborated with one of the most respected artists in this field, Dave McKean, on books and films. Dave told me that he had taken part in the original Gaiman outing. He couldn't remember exactly where they'd gone, somewhere north of the M25, by car. These boys, designer leather jackets and bright shoes, don't do a lot of walking. They were looking for a gate, a gate to the City of London. It had gone missing from Fleet Street; hence, the connection with the mythic Sweeney Todd. Real heads, hacked off, were displayed on this gate: warning or trophy. The underlying story is occult. The barber, with his priapic pole, his 'anything-for-the-weekend-sir?', is an urban prankster. 'Was your old man a barber?' is a line of dialogue that reverberates through London pulps and chapbooks until it achieves definitive utterance in the Nicolas Roeg/Donald Cammell film, *Performance*.

Alan Moore and Neil Gaiman, more than any of their peers, have exported contemporary deconstructions of the Gothic. The footnote, the scholarly apparatus of the graphic novel, is the only place where speculations derived from obscure poets, outer-rim science, antiquarian folklore, can frolic and inter-breed. The great modernist push, the collage, the cut-up, finds a commercial outlet. *Batman* reworked. Mary Shelley revisited. Blake. De Quincey. Orwell. The world its own Xerox. Originality as quotation.

Gaiman's story laid out the experience that anyone, follow-ing the trail from Waltham Cross, up Monarch's Way to Theobalds Grove and Theobalds Lane, might enjoy: watercress beds, a park with a picturesque ruin, a flinty section of wall. 'Ah!' cry the unwary. 'We've found it.' The gate. A transported chunk of London real estate.

'WE CAN ALWAYS TAKE PHOTOGRAPHS FROM THE ROAD,' announces the Gaiman character, filling his bubble. 'WE

HEADED FOR JUNCTION 25 OF THE M25, SIXTEEN MILES
NORTH OF THE CITY OF LONDON.'

I felt the presence of Gaiman, nosing about the Cedars
Public Park, six years ahead of us, dowsing for bad memories.
The folly in the park is a trap. Some excursionists go no further,
believing that they've found the object of their quest, the Fleet
Street gate. 'MM. THAT WAS EASIER THAN I THOUGHT . . .'

But the phantom Gaiman has only achieved the periphery of
the haunted wood, a triple-arched gateway to the mysteries.
There are difficult decisions still to be taken. The graphic
novelist delivers a snappy summary of the gate's history. 'IT
WAS AT THE ENTRANCE TO FLEET STREET – PROBABLY
ORIGINALLY ERECTED BY THE KNIGHTS TEMPLAR IN THE
TWELFTH CENTURY . . . IT WAS REPAIRED FOR ANNE
BOLEYN'S CORONATION . . . BUT ANYWAY, CHRISTOPHER
WREN BUILT THIS INCARNATION IN THE EARLY 1670S . . .'

A convenient tea lady serves burgers and puts the seekers
right. 'TEMPLE BAR'S IN THEOBALD'S PARK. OVER THERE.
NOT IN CEDAR PARK. OF COURSE THEY WAS ONCE THE
SAME PLACE, BUT NOW THERE'S THE A10 IN THE MIDDLE.'

An off-highway day, sky like porridge. My colour shots,
Drummond slouching, hands in pockets, are soft: grey road,
grey sky. The graphic novella of our walk towards Theobalds
Park contrasts with Michael Zulli's monochrome panels (in
cinemascope or church window format). His couple also keep
their hands buried deep in their jeans, but they have hair,
shoulder-length. Dark glasses for the Gaiman figure. Who
smokes. They drive across the A10. We stand on the verge,
waiting for a gap in the morning traffic.

They miss the signs at the edge of the wood. TESCO COUN-
TRY CLUB. THEOBALDS PARK, ABBEY NATIONAL CENTRE
OF EXCELLENCE. The royal palace, the hunting lodge, the
gardens laid out by John Tradescant, having passed through
the hands of the brewer, Meux, are now in the keeping of a
supermarket chain (the source of Lady Shirley Porter's wealth)

and a building society. The gate is spiked. Drummond examines the sign and roars with laughter. Through another set of padlocked gates we can see the New River, heading towards London. NO SWIMMING.

Atkins has his camera out faster than the lads in the comic strip. FALLING MASONRY: an alien structure banged down across the full double-page spread. A turn in the track, the entrance to Lady Meux's estate (furnished with gate-keepers in Joan Hessayon's romance), and here is Temple Bar. Christopher Wren's Fleet Street gate, slightly distressed, rescued and reassembled, lifted beyond the pull of the M25. The brewer Meux made various improvements, extensions, rooms in which to entertain his guests.

It's still impressive, this Essex captive. There has been talk recently of finding a couple of million quid to knock it down, carry it back to dress a portion of river frontage, around St Paul's. Much better to extend it, stretch it, slap it over the M25. You can hear the wind, the traffic sirocco, howling through the gap, rattling the corrugated sheets. Temple Bar is reinstated as an energy gate, a switch, a consciousness junction.

Marc scoots around the masonry, finding ways to circumvent the fence, keep it out of shot. Surveillance cameras swivel, not much interested in his antics. From the woods, bird noises that Drummond can identify, if you ask him: garden warbler, blackcap, lesser spotted woodpecker.

A certain unease. 'IT'S SITTING HERE IN THE MIDDLE OF NOWHERE LIKE AN UNEXPLODED BOMB,' thinks the Gaiman character. His pal, Mike, goes over the fence. As does Marc, factoring images, cramming his camera with potential light-sculptures to be brought back to his London studio. History leaks.

Wren rebuilding London after the Great Fire of 1666 designs a triumphal arch for Fleet Street: Temple Bar (completed 1672). Fire and water (Fleet River) are both invoked by this structure. A gate through which the traffic of the city will flow.

A gate aligned with other gates, with Lud Gate, with the effigies of King Lud and his sons.

John Collet's painting (*c.* 1760) presents the western prospect of Temple Bar. Narrower and taller in aspect. Lacking the wings that Meux used to unbalance the original design, lacking the stone balustrades. Lacking royal figures in the alcoves on either side of the window above the gate. Perspective is worked, so that Fleet Street gives Temple Bar its wings. There is meaning in this placement. It harks back to the Roman model, the imperium. It's fated to become a traffic hazard, an absurdity in such a narrow thoroughfare. Displaced, fenced in, misaligned, it has become a provocation, Gothic furniture. The unwieldy backdrop for a Sweeney Todd musical. 'History out of context,' as Gaiman has it.

The best we can do is turn it over to Marc, in the expectation that his tunnel vision, his gift for excluding the unnecessary, will release the arch, or place it in his catalogue of archetypes. With the collection of obelisks, doorways, church towers, graveyard statuary. Temple Bar, removed from its location, is also removed from time. Its energies are released.

A quick hit of the M25 from Bulls Cross Bridge; the confirmation that the metal river still flows. A photo opportunity at the dogs' home. Drummond caressing a black, plaster bulldog: DO NOT ATTEMPT TO STROKE DOGS. Surveillance cameras on poles. Severed heads. A cacophony of yelps and snarls, pooch to German shepherd, as we slouch along the edge of the Whitewebbs Lane rat run. A country track has been overwhelmed by shorthaul motorway users. Pedestrians, heading for Enfield Chase, are squeezed between a mesh fence and a screen of thorns.

It's damp, it's green and it's English. And Drummond, the displaced Scot, cackles over it. This obstacle course of negatives: DO NOT ATTEMPT ... NO SWIMMING ... NO HORSE RIDING ... NO STOPPING ... KEEP OFF ... KEEP OUT.

Drummond is upbeat. He recommends ornithological text-books as tools for the replenishment of language. 'Yaffle' is a recent favourite: the sound of the green woodpecker. We yaffle. We do the *I–Spy* country walk. We eye-swipe bluebell carpets, ex-squirrels. Bill holds a dead shrew in his hand, so that Atkins can photograph it (looking like a moustache that has just fallen off).

Tackier properties, shacks with bits of farm machinery, chicken coops, have handpainted notices (white gloss on hard-board): BEWARE BAD DOG. They can't afford the animal. They're saving up for a pit bull recording. Ironwork gates, all curls and commas, are deceptive. Slow down and the dogs, which usually operate in pairs, will have you. Lean-ribbed black ones with slavering fangs. If their tails haven't been docked, they wag.

Detached houses on the edge of the motorway are a shop-ping mall for thieves with wheels. A nice run out from Dalston or Canning Town, straight up the M11. Hoist a bit of garden statuary, an urn, carry it back to its place of origin.

Once we achieve the path through White Webbs Park, skirting the golf course, heading south-west, it gets easier. We don't bother with the map. Green patch leads to green patch. Clay Hill to Trent Park. Drummond identifies an Aylesbury duck by its orange beak.

Permitted pedestrianism is still a source of pleasure, old woodland, meadows, brooks. The obelisk in Trent Park is a memorial to the Duke of Kent. Royalty continues to leave markers on the outer suburbs. WATCH OUT THERE'S A PLANT THIEF ABOUT.

What I love about this 'empty' quarter of London (if it is London) is the way that, out of nowhere, supervised parkland, suburban clutter, you suddenly find yourself on a long, straight stretch of country road. It's dreamlike: telegraph poles, hedges, a red farmhouse tucked under a line of low hills. You're still carrying the weight of the city, the density of talk and noise and interference, quick-twitch nerves that keep you from being run down; but you let it go, bleed away. Momentary transcendence. Soft warm air. Birdsong. And, in the distance, over the horizon, the mortality whisper of the orbital motorway.

In this hallucinatory half-country, we come across a building that is difficult to interpret, easy to admire: a white cube, its windows blinded with hardboard. The boards have been cut to fit their apertures. The shadow of a downward pointing security light throws an elongated cone across the white wall. The building, an assembly of smooth, chalky blocks, reminds me of Rachel Whiteread's *Ghost*. Lacking discernible narrative, this structure is an unrequired art work. In a gallery it would solicit cultural comparisons, validation. Out here we can do nothing, beyond registering its presence, the displacement it achieves. The way it offers itself as a memory-flash, between the Trent Park obelisk and the hospital on the hill.

By now, we're beginning to look at our watches. We stride out. I can't remember if the Jochen Gerz lecture is at one or at one-thirty. But that doesn't stop us logging the drift. Twin urns on a gatepost. TRENT PARK CEMETERY. ANOTHER SERVICE PROVIDED BY ISLINGTON COUNCIL. A stretch-limo, self-consciously mirror polished, outside Il Vesuvio *Trattoria Italiana*. Nothing like playing up to racial stereotypes.

Cockfosters. New Barnet. Cherry blossom hamlets. Drummond gives a sympathetic nod to Barnet FC, a team who will soon be appearing on his beloved Non-League circuit. (I picked up a nice piece of football/motorway ephemera. A booklet entitled *Inside the M25: The Football Programmes*. A road map linking future nowheres, dormitories, slumped industrial huddles, by the colours of their football programmes: Beckenham Town, Chingford, Boreham Wood, Erith & Belvedere, Rainham Town, Ford United. Glories of the Delphian, Spartan, Aeolian, Corinthian Leagues. Dagenham linked with deepest Surrey. Harrow with hop fields. Dockside with Dorking.) Bill Drummond's green anorak comes into his own as he waxes lyrical on the Aylesbury FC experience, the windy terraces, the pies, the purity of kick and rush, the yaffling of the mob.

The steep green roof of the National Institute for Medical Research, a fearsome complex (known to its inmates as 'the benzene ring'), catches the midday sun. It dominates the summit of Mill Hill. Coming on it, from the north, the Folly Farm side, we experience the difficulties that made the planners hesitate when they decided to move the Institute (as an out-station) from the Hampstead Laboratories in 1937.

The ground was boggy, the gradient severe. But Mill Hill was obscure, sensitive research could be conducted without attracting unwelcome attention. Government scientists would enjoy the benefits of country life – tennis, cricket, bracing walks – while staying within an easy commute (underground, mainline, Great North Road) of civilisation. The Hampstead Labs were known for their experiments on animals.

The design of the building, a broad Y frontage, masking an hexagonal spread, was by Maxwell Ayrton. The man respons-ible for the now defunct Wembley Stadium. Monsters of the imperium lording it over North London's gentle slopes. The twin-towered arena with its energy-sapping turf (demo-cratic spectacle) and the forbidding cliff (brick-and-glass) of the Research Institute with its bright copper roof.

From the Ridgeway, the Institute offered its public face; dark bricks weathered to a muddy red, narrow windows. The Institute was definitively institutional, government approved, government sponsored. From the rear, the fields: the Big House, the asylum of popular imagination. Where ugly things happen unseen.

The sensitive nature of the research undertaken in the soft corridors, the cells of this building, explained the level of security. ALF, video libertarians, subversives: armies of un-reason at the gates. Art is the palliative. Pick up the MRC brochure, *Research Opportunities*, and it promises: 'visits to the theatre, ballet and concerts'. Pick up the Millennium Edition of MRC essays and the booklet concludes with a nightshot, a snoop-snap: gold windows, a deep blue sky worthy of Effie Paleologou.

Acquired Immunodeficiency Syndrome. Brainmash on a glass slide. Up on the hill, gazing out of the restaurant over the fields and small farms – John Constable heathland floating to margin – you wonder if this is the site of incubation, foot-and-mouth, or the place where the virus will be snuffed. Hot cubicles, rooms with double-doors and security locks. Meshed windows. Browse the official literature and you fall into a J.G. Ballard reverie. Pieter Nieuwkoop 'elegantly demonstrated that sandwiches of cells of two poles recreated equatorial-like tissue'. A Ballardian tropic, jungle flies fat with meat, housed in a secure compound. Infected quacks, pushing the limits of theory, experimenting on themselves. Tennis courts, easily available narcotics. An island of greenery, secluded mansions, cult centres, business parks, surrounded by fast-flowing arterial traffic.

'It was the hippy era. Young men in the US forces, and students throughout the universities of the world were experimenting with drugs that changed their perceptions of the world. And in the rather splendidly placed new laboratories under the high roof of the National Institute for Medical Research at Mill Hill, (Mike) Gaze used electrical recording to show that if impressions coming from the outer world become too disturbing, the brain can respond by modifying itself.' So wrote Geoff Raisman in his essay 'Unravelling the Workings of the Brain'.

The scientists Gaze and Keating established that 'nerve fibres arising from the back of the eye form a pathway that sends an image of the world to the brain. The image fits with what we expect.' But what happens if expectations are confounded? Gaze showed that the brain is capable of configuring chaos, re-establishing order. The community of scholars playing dice with reality can, with proper adjustment, reconvene that reality. The ratty trio out there, scuttling and jogging and sweating up the slope, can be made to appear as standard citizens; interested parties on their way to a lecture by a German artist.

James Lovelock worked in Mill Hill for twenty years before writing *The Gaia Hypothesis*. Zhores Medvedev, exiled from the Soviet Union in 1973, studied the mechanism of ageing. 'He was,' according to a brief biographical sketch in one of the Institute's publications, 'the first to report a major nuclear disaster, and its cover up, that occurred in the Urals in 1957. Later he recorded the aftermath of the Chernobyl accident.' Mill Hill absorbs traumatised intelligence, shock waves of what-if; solo artists and team players chasing endgame consequences.

I sense X-ray spectres and affronted animal entities breaking away from Mill Hill's determinist gravity. There's too much stuff in the literature about dog distemper, pig farm viruses, snail vectors, 'minced tissue of infected animals', *in vivo* research, 'transgenic' experimentation. Too many flashbacks, memory shards: King George VI and his munificently hatted consort performing the official opening ceremony in 1950. George, the chainsmoker, was not by then much of a photo opportunity for things medical. Wasted, death-printed; white knuckles on a well-polished black top hat. Funeral wear. Queen Elizabeth, gracious, glacier-slow, accepts the flowers.

Mill Hill is a memory device. Tom Bliss, the current head of the Division of Neuropathology, worked on methods of demonstrating how the brain's network of nerve cells (the road map) stores memories. The building becomes a brain, nervous activity in the hippocampus, boosting the efficiency of our chemical transmitters. Using thesis research, drugs will be developed to enhance memory, to hold time.

But there are other methods, walks, landscape meditations, looped journeys. We were there on the morning of 28 April, in a lather, panting through the formalities, reaching the lecture hall – where Effie is sitting one row behind us – in time for Gerz's talk. Drummond's account, should he give it, would sheer away from mine. Marc's considered prints would contradict my snapshots. The memory of the memory slips. We invent. New memories, unaccountable to mundane documentation, are shaped. The dream anticipates the neurotic narrative.

Gerz is relaxed. He's done this before. Being foreign is a good scam. An English conceptualist couldn't manage the gravitas, the heavyweight back story. Foreign lets you play for time in the Q & A session: Gerz answers questions, asked by another German, in English. He translates, retranslates. Like W.G. Sebald, he exploits the melancholy of not-belonging, making fabulous. White spaces, broad margins, grey photographs of empty libraries. He can do smooth English or indifferent English, claiming the benefit of a certain ambiguity of expression. He disagrees, so he says, with all polemic statements about public art. Discussion of practical issues – the wheeze, how you pull off a project – brings him to life.

Antifascist monuments spearing the karma have given Gerz his fame. Names signed on a column in Harburg, which sank slowly into the earth. Doctored war memorials in France. Cobblestones lifted and inscribed with the names of vanished synagogues. Unappeased memories. Civic corruption exposed or ridiculed. There is always, if you concentrate, a solution. Something to be done. Gerz lives a long way from Hoxton (domestic trivia, personal distress, reconfigured trash). If you can sell it, if a sharp suit can sell it for you, it's no good. Simple rule. The best of the English conceptualists aren't conceptualists, they work with memory; work *on* memory, infection. The sculptor Brian Catling got it right: leave your show in a skip, let the audience walk away with whatever they want, the unfranchised version.

Drummond is engaged by this performance. Gerz has got the look right: blue, buttoned to the neck, with (Beuys-copyright) poacher's waistcoat, pockets for pens. He's scholarly and fiercely quiet: 'I'm not normally giving lectures. I'm not alone to talk.' Thin spectacles. 'The contemporary only is contemporary.' He speaks of the object, the painting that qualifies for museum residence, as 'baroque'. Mill Hill is imperialist baroque. It is fixed in time. Alongside Wembley Stadium. Prewar optimism. Post-war austerity. Football, science: the New Elizabethan World. *Eagle* comic, helmed by an ex-Revd, with its sliced-through sections of technological wonders. The hippie researcher blasting in the attic. Beagles in the basement. Off-duty technicians getting their culture hit in the lecture hall.

A woman challenges Gerz. Drummond has his hand up, but she's younger and prettier. She wants to know about monuments for other life forms, for animals. 'What we call language,' says the conceptualist, 'is a one-way road.' There have been poems to fruit trees but no fruit tree has ever written a poem to us. 'Reality not ethics.' Drummond likes the message, but Atkins (the vegan) is visibly annoyed.

'It wasn't any more fountains, fountains was the good thing,' Gerz announces. 'Parks – that's a crazy place to put art.' Drummond, who envisions (but does not always enact) subversive gestures in the street and alongside motorways (dead cows from pylons, lager distribution to vagrants, cash barbecues), can buy the antipastoral thesis. If they let you put it there, if they pay you for it, walk out. Dead fountains, erased obelisks, vandalised public statuary achieve meaning only when they are ignored, when they have become anonymous.

The message, according to Gerz, never changes: 'half makes sense, half is baroque'. There is memory and there is the object, the diary, the book of photographs, the video tape. Gerz, a polemicist, operates through the questionnaire (realising, I suspect, that the person who sets the questions sets the script). Democratic dialogue is revealed as a tool of the benevolent demagogue. 'I'm looking for viewers, I'm looking for artists,' he says. Which describes the fix very neatly. In a perfect world

(a world that behaved according to the freaks of my imagination), I'd walk away. Atkins and Drummond, separately, would
deliver their accounts of this excursion. I'd sit in the pub, read
them over, edit them: twin voices, contrapuntal contradictions.

A six-and-a-half-hour walk for one hour in the company
of a German conceptualist, an account of acts undertaken in
other countries to honour memory. 'Even if they didn't have
dead people, they had an obelisk.' The Research Institute is
the right place to receive this message. 'Photographs,' Gerz
concludes, 'are always healing.'

There were no more walks with Drummond. Mill Hill
earthed all that, the hunger, the predatory attention. Atkins
took part in several Drummond projects, recording signs,
shooting portraits. Drummond is a collector of images. He
spent the money left over from the glory days, the small change
that he didn't burn, on a print by Richard Long. He found it in
a gallery at the end of a day's psychogeographical hiking (the
shape of his own name walked into the landscape). But photographs do not heal, they hurt. They hold time. They obstruct
the flow of memory. Drummond put the Long print up for
sale. He printed leaflets. The concept: burn the cash and bury it
at the Icelandic location depicted in the artist's print.

One year after our attendance at the Gerz lecture, on 10 May
2000, a set of 'specially commissioned photographs', portraits of
scientists, was exhibited at the National Institute for Medical
Research at Mill Hill. Fifty years of achievement: discoveries of
the structure of viruses, antibodies; 'mechanisms for the control
of gene transcription; the gene for sex determination'. The
photographer, the healer, had 'exhibited extensively, including
London, Paris, Rome, Amsterdam and New York'. His work
was 'published regularly in books and magazines worldwide'.
Name? Marc Atkins.

4

We drove out of London, using a section of the M25 (Junction 15 to Junction 12) as a slowmoving travelator, for the culture-switch (M4 to M3). Sun going down behind Wraysbury Reservoir. Sword-shaped flashes from the windscreens of oncoming traffic. Gravel pits, lagoons, reservoirs: factored from aeroplanes climbing into the clouds, out of Heathrow. Grounded motors in fidgety lines; crawling like invalid carriages as they creep up on a supermarket check-out at Tesco's, Mare Street.

Anna doesn't care. Just so long as she's leaving London. Even if it's only for a few hours, an art show in Selborne; a mile or two outside Alton, Hampshire. Gilbert White's Selborne. Curate White (1720–93) was born in the village. He refused richer livings to remain in his birthplace. He kept a 'Garden Kalendar' and later a 'Naturalist's Diary'. In 1767 he published his *Natural History and Antiquities of Selborne*. That book, in various disguises, has been a staple of secondhand booktrade ever since.

One of the first and most civilised customers of my dealing days, an elderly Jewish gentleman called Mark, who lived in Sandringham Road, Dalston (aka 'The Front Line'), in a book-crammed flat, put me on to Gilbert White. He loved White and Jane Austen (house heritaged in an Alton suburb); Hazlitt, Lamb, De Quincey. Whenever he found one of their books on a stall, in Camden Passage or Farringdon Road, in Cecil Court, he would buy it. And, if possible, talk to the vendor about the author. If Mark got a day off work, he took a bus into the countryside. He would visit Austen's house or walk through the fields around Selborne.

I helped Mark clear his room when he moved into sheltered accommodation in Green Lanes, Finsbury Park. There must have been two dozen copies of White's *Selborne*, in all shapes and conditions. Illustrated. Pocket-sized. Distressed. Uncut. Mark's England, playing against the streets in which he lived, was conjured from these precious volumes. But now, at his daughter's insistence, he was forced to choose: one copy per title.

Selborne had a mystique. A connection with a set of multiple-occupation houses at the back of Ridley Road Market, Dalston. We drove into the village on a mild spring evening (25 April 1998), found somewhere to park, and set off to look for the Mouth & Foot Painting Artists' Gallery.

That title wasn't an obvious crowd pleaser. Better then, previrus, but still capable of triggering unhappy associations. The gallery was easy to find, the crowd spilt out onto the village street. I recognised a few faces, old friends from Dublin and Hackney. The show we had come to see had been hung for one night only. 'Michael & Mary Dreaming: 21 paintings celebrating a journey along the Michael ley-line from Norfolk to St Michael's Mount in Cornwall.' The artist was Laurence ('Renchi') Bicknell. Leaflets offered a selective CV. 'Born 1946. Previous exhibitions include Combined Show at the Whitechapel Gallery (1974), One Man Show at the Amwell Gallery (1974), and the original 8 paintings from this series at the "Shamanism of Intent" exhibition at the Goldmark Gallery, Uppingham (1991). Renchi has been running The Little Green Dragon bookshop (with Vanessa) for the last 15 years and since selling the bookshop in October 1997 he and Vanessa are both working at Lord Mayor Treloar College as House-parents.'

I knew most of this story. I'd met Renchi in Dublin, when I was (officially) a student and he was a transient, a presence, a painter. A runaway. There was a certain romance attached to this: *Caporal*-blue workman's jacket, handpainted shoes. Hair combed with a fork. Youth. Enthusiasm. Talk. Connections,

back in England, with the *New Departures* mob, Michael
Horovitz and Pete Brown. Adventures on the road which, in
telling, grooved into myth. Restlessness, the quest. *Petit mal*
seizures.

Renchi laboured under an impossible burden. Laid on him
by his peers. *Be* the painter. Americans with trust funds
syphoned the production line. Public-school Englishmen with
jobs in the City commissioned portraits. *Be* the Rimbaud
genius. Burn out. Nominate your Abyssinia. Disappear.

Into Hackney. Communal houses. Paintings that were endlessly revised, toshed over, abandoned. Sacred sites visited and
recalled. Dissatisfaction. A plump ginger cat. An infant in dun-
garees. Window open on a wild garden. Paintbrush in mouth,
cigarette. Unshaved. Multicolour cardigan. The romance
wearing thin, overexposed in 8mm diary movies. Exploited.

I'd been involved with the Whitechapel Show and the
Shamanism jamboree at the Goldmark Gallery. But I hadn't
seen much of Renchi in the years between these events. He'd
left London for Hampshire and we'd stayed put. Running a
bookshop took most of his time and energy. I had also been
peddling books, secondhand, used, rediscovered. A relentless
circuit of dawn markets, days at the wheel, up and down the
country, cleaning, pricing, stalling out. We both survived, by
the skin of it. What Renchi and Vanessa had left over went, as I
read it (from a distance), into the spiritual quest, communality,
networks of likeminded associates. Earth magic. Ceremonies of
appeasement and rapture. What I had in the tank was saved for
operating a small press and scratching at road notes, quotations
from obscure books, that might one day be shaped into a viable
structure.

I circled the Selborne gallery, following the drift of Renchi's
journey. The hang was chronological: '24 days of walking and
further days of exploring a network of lines coming alive'.
Yellows, golds, blues. The work was unshowy, without tricks
or painterly effects; quiet ego. The sense was meditative,

respectful of place, of geology: crumbs of chalk or flakes of stone were sometimes pressed into the margins. If you insisted on a genealogy you could think of Cecil Collins or Ken Kiff. But that might be a false note. There was, at one level, a real, blistery narrative to these walks; chorographic mappings attendant on the soar, the flash of revelation. The pull into light. And if Renchi steered, at times, towards a Glastonbury orthodoxy of angelic orders, stars, wells (panels that might pass as New Age greetings cards), there were also plenty of hard miles and English downland weather.

This was no stroll. Or mere record of snatched days, outings from the bookshop. Ivan, Renchi's fit and chunky son, accompanied him on the final stages, through Somerset and Cornwall. When they took a break on Dartmoor, Ivan filled his dad's rucksack with rocks.

Chorography, not topography. Paul Devereux, in his book *Re-Visioning the Earth*, makes that distinction. The ancient Greeks, he tells us, 'had two senses of place, *chora* and *topos*'. Quoting Eugene Victor Walter, Devereux sees spiritual tourism as 'a complex but organic mode of active observation'. This was Renchi's methodology, arrived at after many years of trial and error, false starts. The chorographer was hungry for place: 'place as expressively potent, place as experience, place as a trigger to memory, imagination, and mythic presence'.

The feel of this Selborne event, the friendliness of the crowd, was resolutely non-metropolitan. Paintings that had been executed over a seven-year period, a journey of around 350 miles (as the crow flies), with backtracking, exhibited for one night only. In a specialist gallery in a Hampshire village. The opening *was* the event. The following morning the paintings would vanish (they would subsequently be shown at The Miracles Room, Isle of Avon Foundation, Glastonbury). You wait twenty-four years for a solo show from Renchi and then it's gone in the blink of an eye.

Leaving, as a prompt, a small blue book with tipped-in

colour reductions, bright stamp-sized panels accompanied by a textual gloss. Picture and legend facing each other, so that the journey can be re-experienced. It's a nice form.

Leafing through the blue book, moving with the crowd, I make connections. Circuits, haloes, spirals, starbelts: Blake's Dante orbits or the overlapping spheres of 'Milton's track'. Zones that cluster around the 'Mundane Egg' (or 'Shell'). The world through which the spiritual Milton journeys. Wheels. Rings.

'The sphere of the north heavens aligned to the Pole star touches into spheres of Earth and Sky,' Renchi writes. Clumps and mounds and ridges and globes. 'Vortex energy centred . . . serpentine lanes.' Here is the road as a hot and angry tongue, cars like sunset coals. 'The pilgrim following Faustus and Faustus confronting Mephistopheles.'

So I am drawn in, at last, to greet the painter. My response to his work, chat. Renchi as Paradise Pilgrim. The poet Aaron Williamson, who met him for the first time at the 'Shamanism of Intent' weekend in Uppingham, was walking through Hampshire. Coming into Selborne in the twilight, he chances on this show. A special night. Dublin faces, who haven't seen each other in years, reconvene; pick up conversations, left mid-sentence in 1965.

I tell Renchi about my notion of a walk around the M25. He is, instantly, up for it. As the next project. A scheme brokered at the perfect moment. It's mad enough. It's inevitable.

On his return from Glastonbury, the second showing of the paintings, Renchi writes:

Being in Glastonbury for a week was brilliant and gave time to explore the old 'Paradise Line' which was followed by pilgrims . . . and has been obscured by housing and factories . . . At this time of year it was a great joy to walk round the small fields with apple trees in blossom and cows and calves and sheep and lambs grazing beneath. I am still very excited about the M25 post modernist mosaic and I enlisted some interesting leads . . . about a vibrational device that is being distributed to people in circle around London and a special music played to them at timed intervals! (More on this when we meet.) Also another site of interest near Cockfosters/New Trent – Camelot fields??

We'll return to Waltham Abbey and wing it from there.

5

Here it begins, the walk proper. No detours. No digressions. We decided to take Waltham Abbey as our starting point, the grave of King Harold, and to shadow the motorway (within audible range whenever possible) in an anticlockwise direction. We wanted, quite simply, to get around: always carrying on from where we left off at the finish of the previous excursion. From now on the road would be our focus, our guide. We'd snatch days whenever we could (when Renchi's shifts permitted) and get it done before the millennial eve.

On 30 September 1998, we stalked into town. Renchi had been working until 10.40 on the previous night – but he arrived in Hackney by eight a.m. He read the weather as: rain trousers, heavy blue sweater, furry cap with ear-flaps. He spoke of sweat lodge ceremonies based on the number four: sixteen poles, four dances a day for four days.

He is fifty-two years old, grizzled, with a tidy silver beard, a naked scalp. He walks with his wife, every morning. The same circuit. Spurning novelty, giving the mind time to settle; noticing the unnoticeable, tiny shifts in season and climate. The work he does, as a house-parent at Mayor Treloar's College, is physically demanding; manhandling wheelchairs, sharing the enthusiasms, sulks and piss-takes of a group of teenagers. 'An enabling education,' it says in the brochure. Renchi, I imagine, would be good at this.

New Age gypsies, who have been tracking me, town to town through Hertfordshire and Essex, on a counterpilgrimage, have arrived in Waltham Abbey. PSYCHIC FARE (Town Hall, Highbridge Street, Waltham Abbey). A signboard attached to the fence outside a property that doesn't register on my

Nicholson's map. An absence. There's nothing there, but you can't come in: 'Government Research Establishment'.

A day of locked gates. The abbey was off-limits, a funeral. So we wandered through the orchard, the monastic reservation, circumnavigating drained fish ponds. Nobody knows quite what to do with these green spaces: they're not enclosed, but access isn't free. They don't belong to the town and locals don't make much use of them as places for contemplation or dog walking. They're suspended. Visitors can't crack the behaviour code: are you a temporary believer or a confirmed sceptic? A residue of retreat, monasticism, is still present in whatever remains of the original layout; measured avenues, monuments to the godly or powerful, warm red bricks. But, play the empathy game as much as you will, you can't escape the song of the road, the mantra of transit. A perpetual cycle of auto-prayer.

From the gardens we see traffic stall as the funeral procession arrives, led by a gleaming black stretch-limo.

Behind the abbey, we hit the meridian line. The local authorities are keen on this abstraction. They want to give it a physical form. The abbey church with its astrological ceiling is working a number with Time and Movement, the Clockwork of the Heavens, the colonisation of zero longitude.

We've fallen for it before and we fall for it again. The meridian walk through Cornmill Meadow. I've noticed granite pillars lying on the ground, aligned with church, with Greenwich, with zero. I've imagined cultists taking zero for their symbol. But now stones, which might have been ignored as glacial detritus, have been erected as markers for a permitted zero longitude pathway. The copywriters of the Lee Valley Park are keen 'to develop a strategy through which Vision can be made a reality'.

It's a typically English conceit, the millennial mile. Begin with a grey omphalos on a base of stones and shells, a sun-crowned archetypal figure with a letterbox navel (into which requests, questions for the oracle, can be posted). This south-facing man/pillar is like something Renchi might have drawn, in the days when he was supposed to be studying anthropology or comparative religion. (We subsequently discover that the granite blocks once formed part of London Bridge.)

A line runs down the pillar, an apparent crack, marking zero longitude, its long flight across the Southern Ocean. We can see where we are and see what our journey should be, through Suffolk and Norfolk, to the edge of the Wash.

Renchi scoops up a feather, a section of bright orange rubber (an inner tube), a pebble.

The walk we are offered, strategic planting designed to flatter a diminishing perspective, is very seductive: the distant prospect, at the end of a closely mown avenue, of another pillar. It carries us away from the M25, but it's irresistible. A grassed extension of the Lea. A spirit-path that runs in parallel with the Navigation, the Cornmill Stream.

We identify (or Renchi does and I note it) the call of jay and green woodpecker. But, just as we adjust to the rhythm of the green avenue, it ends; it runs up against another perimeter fence, the earthworks of the Government Research Establishment.

This site – 'Access for All' – is the showpiece real estate of the Lee Valley Regional Park Development. One hundred and seventy-five acres of land ('one of the most secret places in England') have been thrown open to the public. It's a great day out. I was there for the postponed (foot-and-mouth) launch on 17 May 2001. And I came straight back, the following weekend, for a family picnic. A haunt of timid deer, a nesting habitat for herons, now available to ticket-buyers for the first time in 300 years. A Paradise Park formerly known as the Royal Gunpowder Mills.

Labourers, searched at the gates for flammable materials, encouraged to work at an easy pace, had lived (and died) here for generations. But the secret didn't travel. Enclose the wildest wood in the parish, cut your own canals, build a city of sheds, blow up houses, rebuild them, stage underwater detonations, and keep it all under wraps. That mixture of timidity, diluted patriotism and an absence of curiosity, leaves great tranches of Britain unmapped; purpose and practice undisclosed. We respect secrecy. It's for our own good, in the end. One day, when the research and development has moved elsewhere, the abandoned colony will be turned over to the heritage industry. Wild nature, thriving in an exclusion zone, will be promoted and paraded.

The plantation of alder buckthorn through which you can tour, in a carriage tugged by a tractor (areas forbidden to walkers), is glossed as the most effective forestry for producing charcoal. Charcoal, saltpetre, sulphur: gunpowder ingredients. History is the resource. Come off the highway, using the drive-in McDonald's as your marker; ease over the speed bumps, the sleeping-policemen, and through the new, yellow-brick estate which is being built right up against the fence of the Gun-powder Mills. Pad over the oozy foot-and-mouth cushion and enter this decommissioned nowhere.

There are promotional films (with bangs and flares), inter-active games, charts, rescued nitroglycerine trucks – along with helpful guides in scarlet polo-shirts, local-history buffs (as ever) peddling sepia postcards of trams and trains, beekeepers from Enfield with pots of liquid honey.

The story is astonishing. The seventeenth-century watermill that evolves into a factory of death: Trafalgar, Waterloo, Barnes Wallis and his bouncing bomb (you've seen the movie). Primitive technology shifts from fireworks and loud noises to stealth planes, non-nuclear explosives and propellants, Gulf War gizmos and guidance systems. Research that is still embar-goed. 'Access for All', yes, but hard information stays in the files. Post-mortem reports from the Forties will be locked away for years.

From eighteenth-century cottages, through Incorporating Mills, to plantation-style bungalows and anonymous, low-level barrack blocks. The sheds, factories and storage facilities, clustered around Queen Meads, are a village without a war memorial, a cricket pitch. The invariable mix of domestic and sinister: pink, electrical junction boxes on the sides of detached Tudorbethan properties, in which covert research took place. 'Climactic Test Cubicles' were constructed in 1951: microclimates suitable for activities that were both jokey and fantastic. A device known as the 'Master Slave Manipulator' is photographed as it pours out a cup of tea for a gentleman in spectacles (with loud plaid tie). This performance is located within the 'X-Ray Bay' (1968).

The deserted sheds, on an overcast afternoon in early summer, present a melancholy spectacle. Suppressed noise. The clumsy architecture of asbestos, plasterboard, concrete. Slippery decks and verandahs. There are visible wounds, gaps where heavy machinery has been removed. In a restored gallery you come across a display case filled with weapons of war: death kit. Lee Enfield rifles. 'Stock, magazine, bolt,' mutters a Cadet Force veteran. Grenades. Bayonets. Machine guns. Antiquated ordnance playing the memory game, busking for sentiment.

Around the walls are hung photographs – from the Gunpowder Mills, from Woolwich, the Midlands – women working in armament factories; women in time of war. Elegant black and white prints. (Men, when you see them, reserved occupations, are sickly, done in, diminished by this army of powerful females.) The presiding mode is dignified surrealism: groups sitting around tables, in poses made familiar by Dutch domestic interiors, by Victorian moral fables, but they're not weaving, working looms, carding wool, they are filling cartridge belts. In massive sheds (white light from an open door), women with covered hair stand among gleaming shells, an iron harvest. Women, hanging from overhead cranes, float above meadows of lethal toys. Women pose in groups, their uniforms hardworn, functional rather than fetishised.

A pattern of waterways confirms a formal geometry. Fat carp, protected from fishermen, glide through sunken powder boats. The skeletons of these craft are better preserved under-water. Grey ribs beneath the heavy green. Hooped bridges facilitate curved deck canopies (above leather-covered boards). Drained canals, running away from a brick tower, lead the walker towards the woods: a set, blending the pastoral with the industrial, that calls up bleaker Polish and East German settings.

The architecture of disclosed ruins is Neo-Mayan: traverses, blast-deflection walls, railway lines. The Gunpowder Press House with its powered water-wheel, its ivy-covered ramparts, has (according to the brochure) 'become an icon'. An icon of what? Transition? Erasure? When the mills went up in a spectacular explosion in May 1861, one worker threw him-self, blazing, into the pond – and survived. Another man was spotted, lying in the long grass, by the flames rising from his clothes. He died.

The drift through these woods, jolting over rough tracks, induces reverie: angular shapes among the dense branches, sites that are still forbidden. Elements of the megalithic, primitive mounds and encirclements, disguise Crimean War technology. Ziggurat walls, slanted, necrophile, guard a woodland clearing; a village green, known as 'The Burning Ground', on which discarded explosives were destroyed. It would be impossible, from this catalogue of post-industrial relics, to work your way back to any culture. This is all that's left, monuments returned to nature, photographs in a reclaimed shed.

We breakfasted in an Italian place that looked out on Waltham Cross. There is a cross, a nibbled Gaudí pillar, a monument marking the funeral procession of Queen Eleanor of Castile, wife of Edward I. Her body (she died while travelling to Scotland to join the king) was brought back from Harby,

Nottinghamshire, for burial at Westminster Abbey. Crosses were erected to witness every stage of this journey.

Webbed-in with protective nets, restored, cleaned to an ivory sheen, the Eleanor Cross is more like a radio mast than an item of funerary sculpture. It's the focal point of this prolapsed market town: red litter bins, benches for drunks, a pedestrianised precinct (that repels walkers). The original effigies from the Cross, the work of Alexander Abyndome, are now housed in Cheshunt Public Library.

Renchi likes it. He whips out a sketchbook and settles, crosslegged, on a white stone bollard. GOLDSTEIN (FINANCIAL ADVISERS). COFFEE HOUSE: DOLCI, CAFFE, PASTA. FISHPONDS BUDGET SHOWROOMS.

There's a background buzz of barely suppressed aggression underwriting Renchi's Ruskinian seizure: civic architecture has got it badly wrong. A semi-circle of scarlet metal benches attracts other transients, strong lager fanciers who have made contact with some of the local barechest boys. A breakfast brew. A bit of a domestic is in progress; raised voices, repetitive insults escalating towards resolution. You can see the coffeeshop women pausing mid-sip, cappuccino moustaches. There's quite a clique of these ladies in Waltham Cross, with the Italian place as their obvious hangout. Walnut-coloured leisure wives, still steaming from tanning beds. Metallic blondes with vivid nails. Very trim in fiercely pressed jeans.

A doppelganger manifests at Renchi's shoulder. It's Renchi himself, ten years older, ten years frostier in the beard. A messenger from the future steps up, loaded plastic bags in hand, nautical cap on head, to adjudicate the drawing. Renchi talks about going beyond preservation (the photograph); he wants more of an exchange with the recorded object. Sketching frees the hand. We listen, sympathetically, to our Ancient Mariner: another paroled artist who has wandered abroad and found his place.

He sets us on our way: charity shops, post-mortem clothes,

financial services, stalls stacked with cheap tat. Waltham Cross has a boutique favoured by Victoria Adams (Mrs Beckham, Posh Spice). Tarty with class (the price tag grants respectability to the diamanté thong). Victoria is a local. Visit Waltham Cross and her otherness comes into focus. All the women in the coffee-bar have that hard sheen, the laminate of non-specific celebrity. Interspecies. They look as good as the photographs in the magazines. Their faces are stiff, moving like heavy paper. You can acquire, if you concentrate, follow the regime, a toxicology of fame. A fame cosmetic. Like whacking up the colour balance. Achieving alien status: part ennui, part peevishness, part camera flirtation.

Posh Spice, an odd label for a person, suits this location. It reminds me of the Indian restaurant at Waltham Abbey on millennial eve: exotic, dusky, dangerously perfumed. Victoria Beckham is the future Eleanor Cross. The name of a dumpy, longlived Germanic royal inherited by a whippet-ribbed starveling. Who shops. Who is famous for shopping. Who arrives, incognito, at a modest boutique on the Essex/Herts border: and makes sure that her visit is widely reported.

We don't spend much time in Cedars Park, or at Temple Bar, we want to get back to the road; to attempt the north side of the M25, a network of paths and rides that go west towards Potters Bar. This area, just outside the motorway, is a blank: woods, stables, kennels.

The gates of the Western Jewish Cemetery are locked, even though we have arrived within the advertised opening hours. WHEN GATES/ARE CLOSED/ALSATIANS/ARE ON PATROL. What I'm pursuing is the burial place of the Spitalfields scholar and hermit, David Rodinsky. A long quest has been resolved by artist and archivist Rachel Lichtenstein. The haunting story of a locked room, a vanished man, has been grounded. Rachel found a death certificate, the suburban hospital where Rodinsky died, a grave with a metal name-plate. The grave,

Rachel said, was near Waltham Abbey. I guessed, since I had passed this place so many times, that the beginning of my new project, the M25 walk, might overlap with my previous one, the Rodinsky story. Time after time, urban obsessions would be resolved at the very point where London lost heat, lost heart, gave up its clotted identity.

The lodge-keeper, skull covered, put us right. This had been an insensitive blunder on my part, the intrusion at the cemetery gates. Today was Yom Kippur, the Day of Atonement; a time for abstinence and prayers of repentance. (Rachel told me that she finished work on her part of the Rodinsky book at 2.30 a.m., on the morning before Yom Kippur.)

The structure of our walk is elegiac: discontinued rituals, closed shrines. The funeral service, the emptied pond. The horse-trough near Theobalds Grove station filled with flower petals. Fenced off monuments and gates that are not gates.

We sit for a time under the Bulls Cross Bridge, watching the tide of traffic, the hallucinatory rush. Listening to the shift in the tyre sounds as the road surface changes, the thunderous amplification of the bridge. Renchi sprawls on hexagonal tiles, white road-dirt in the grooves of his boots.

I read him a quotation from Paul Devereux that seems pertinent: 'One of the key entoptics is the spiral-tunnel-vortex, which heralds a shift from merely observing the entoptic and iconic imagery to participating in it. There is a sense of the self's becoming mobile, leaving the body, and rushing down a tunnel or being sucked into the eye of the spiral or vortex . . . It is with this specific entoptic that the out-of-body or spirit-flight is associated. This entoptic tunnel could be the neurological blueprint for the straight line on the shamanic landscapes.'

The markings on the motorway are shamanic. Noise takes us out of ourselves into a dispersing landscape. Giddy, we enter movement. We could do the whole thing here, on the ramp. We could dream it.

Renchi has his own tale to tell. His father, Peter Bicknell, a

Cambridge architect and academic, accumulated a notable collection of travel journals, records of walks and alpine excursions. Limited editions, rarities, manuscripts. When Renchi visited his mother, he would rummage through the library, searching out topographical information relevant to our orbital pilgrimage. Our shambling progress around the M25 could be seen as a parodic reprise of the material that interested Peter Bicknell. Welfare State ghosts on the tramp, in the footsteps of gentleman botanists, muscular Christians.

A Hampshire psychic told Renchi that his father's library held a great clue. She described a room she had never seen. He should search the stacks, second shelf down, third book from the left, such and such a page.

He left at once for Cambridge. He found the volume. It was just as she had pictured it. A handwritten journal, a journey.

'What did it reveal?' I asked.

'Nothing,' Renchi said. 'Absolutely nothing.' A trek through the North of England, in search of nothing in particular. And not locating it. A record kept for the sake of keeping a record. A singularity that awaited a singular readership.

The tracks, around Temple House, are clear enough on the map. Bull Cross Ride, Old Park Ride. What I didn't realise was that 'Ride' meant just that. It was an order. Get in the saddle or bugger off. We trudged for a mile or so before we hit the gate. No warning. Entry denied. We should have taken the hint when we passed Gunsite Stud and Hanging Plantation. Off-motorway green belt is jealous of its status. Here are city-subsidised farms, stables, country that doesn't have to acknowledge its rowdy southern neighbour. The M25 is a sewer of potential bandits, rustlers, burger-munching trippers carrying the virus of the slums. It's border country and the borderers know on which side of the motorway unlicensed pedestrians belong.

★

Traffic snarls, the air is scented. Our route, from Whitewebbs Road into Cattlegate Road, under the Crews Hill railway bridge and up the slope towards the M25 (between Waltham Abbey and Potters Bar), shivers with ambiguity. It's a rat run, the end of the liberties of Enfield Chase, but it is also a retail paradise. Horticultural retail. Instant gardens. Statuary. Sheds. Bedd⸺ plants. Gravel. Compost. Dutch juggernauts unloading t⸺ tired plants.

Teased⸺ ⸺ion, by painted decking, water features and shiverin⸺ ⸺adequate T-shirts, householders demand flatpac⸺ ⸺an be assembled by a gang of self-pro⸺ ⸺ey skive off for a round of golf. Ga⸺ ⸺atching celebrities take exotic hol⸺ ⸺d in which we float and seek ou⸺ ⸺ narcoleptics in a period of mi⸺ ⸺ransport systems, failing sch⸺ soil, snorting the night pe⸺ ⸺eal us.

⸺ ⸺logues, pubic thatches (in⸺ ⸺arketed as 'The Con-ten⸺ copy is a lubricious con⸺ ⸺ctacular, moody . . . with dar⸺ ⸺eaves. *Briza media*: delightful Co⸺ ⸺rembling heart-shaped flower spikele⸺ ⸺dense tuft-forming sedge. *Imperata cylindrica*: tall sword-like green leaves which turn blood red from tips.'

The TV garden is an extension of the house. You can still find allotments, salvaged from unexploitable buffer zones, but they are weirdly anachronistic. Strip-system allocations, fenced in and worked by elderly, all-weather gentlemen. A good example can be seen near the Sewardstone Road bridge, between cemetery and motorway, in Waltham Abbey. A solitary ancient leaning on his hoe, shuffling backwards and forwards to his shed. The villein with his small corner of England. That never changes, though such sites are threatened. They have to hide away, hope that they've been forgotten.

Crews Hill services the patio-lounge fantasist. Horticulture is discussed in terms of plant furniture, colour schemes, architectural bamboos. There are flirty plants and flighty plants, stylish plants, bimbo plants and 'as seen on television' plants. A banana tree ('special offer for readers of *Good Housekeeping*') is pitched as a lifestyle accessory. 'A definite "it" plant. In fact if *Hello!* magazine were to interview their first celebrity plant it would probably be this one.'

Blues and purples and mauves. Lavender and ceanothus. The drench of suburbia. Intoxicated bees reeling from flower to flower, a great year for Enfield honey. Lipsticky and dripping thick over fingers and plate rims. The hum of the pastoral, the beehive in the English garden: as depicted on the label of a honey jar.

Crews Hill, representing the final flourish of the Lea Valley/Enfield Chase tradition (as heritaged in Joan Hessayon's novel *Capel Bells*), has come to an arrangement with the motorway. Walk back towards the old town of Enfield and you'll find the glasshouses; you'll understand Hessayon's thesis, the way that gardeners from the big estates began to trade in plants. An escape from patronage, servitude, the tied cottage: the realisation that plants were a commodity. This astonishing parade of drive-in retail opportunities, part Sunday excursion, part car boot sale, operates on the cusp of what has gone (*genius loci*) and that which is coming: Americana.

Try this for a roadside menu: Garrick Furniture Design, Antique Fires (of Enfield), Four Seasons Pottery, Crews Hill Art & Crafts (Hang Ups), Fernleigh Landscapes, Monty's Furniture, Three Counties Garden & Leisure Buildings, The Quilting Bee, Enfield Bird Centre, Macbar Army Surplus. Cash & Carry Winter Pansy's (sic). These are not garden centres (for those you need to go to Suffolk, Oxfordshire), these are garden suburbs. Listen to the names of the kids who are running amok among the bedding plants: 'Get down from that, Brandon. Leave him alone, Harrison.'

As we slog uphill, Renchi delights in the display of slug-repelling, crushed shell mounds, bark-chip puddles, grey slabs (made to look like York stone). We negotiate fibreglass rockeries that would horrify Gussie Bowles, boulders so light you can lift them as easily as Steve Reeves in *Hercules Conquers Atlantis*. There are regiments of gum-coloured statues: hounds, hedgehogs, bunnies, ducks; loosely classical nudes, lions cubbed from Landseer, water-spitting gargoyles, Egyptian cat-gods tamed and domesticated. You can smell the bird house, the deceased lizards. You can purchase a hairy spider, a bag of snakes or a tray of delightful scorpions. Sniff the resin, the hot-house biodiversity. Compost that doesn't smell like shit, but a blend of roasted coffee and turf from Galway. There are enough customised sheds and cabins and pinewood studios to house all of Jack Straw's asylum seekers.

The fetid concentration of this botanical stew stays with us. I am sticky with spray, perfume-processed for the next stage of our walk. I'm sure that the Crews Hill herbal affects drivers on the motorway. They open car windows, take their foot off the gas, smile. Easy country. No red cones. They're on one of the original sections of the road, the gently weaving passage where the M25 defined itself, discovered its identity. And now, in the September evening, at the golden hour, they pick up an hallucinatory hint of paradise gardens on the outskirts of Potters Bar.

Escaping Crews Hill, going under the M25, is a woeful experience for pedestrians; we face the oncoming traffic. A constant stream, both ways, clusters of five or six cars, nose to tail in barely controlled frustration: metal projectiles time-warped on to a drovers' track, Cattlegate Road. In the intervals between the blam-blam-blam, Renchi hears a woodpecker in the twilight woods. There are long stretches without verges on which to walk. We are conscious of being nothing more than columns of vulnerable meat, obstacles made hazardous by the glare of the sinking sun.

Moving west in the direction of Potters Bar, looking across the valley to the hamlet of Cuffley, we feel a nudge in our perception of space/time. Renchi relates this to certain devices in children's fiction, the way a network of green lanes can sidle alongside the densest clots of population. The walker 'goes back', forgets himself (or herself). A pre-visionary condition, in which it is possible to let go of the present and access an older narrative, a secret garden or enchanted wood.

By his reading, the tunnel under the motorway is a gate of memory. Concrete walls become screens on which are projected phantasmagoric tree shapes. But reaching the tunnel, coming up against the wall – cut to fit the slope of the motorway escarpment – we find that the concrete is no casual wash. The wall is made with deep grooves, like a sheet of corrugated paper. The effect is of something wrapped and hidden, a stone curtain. Motorway sounds reverberate and shake the tunnel. Nothing to be seen, everything to be imagined.

Grand houses dispose themselves along a golden road: IT mansions and cult centres (probably sponsored by George Harrison). White fences, gravel drives. Ironwork gates on which CCTV cameras replace heraldic beasts. JAIN ESTATE. Millionaire mendicants, spiritual conglomerates, multinational god franchises: they absorb this liminal landscape. The sign, Jain Estate, made me think of Allen Ginsberg's photographs: Shambu Bharti Baba on the sepia cover of *Indian Journals* and the poet himself, pole in hand, naked and hairy, beside the Sea of Japan. Elective ecumenicism. The state of being Jain, adapting a dualistic sixth-century religion, the liberation of the soul through asceticism, to twentieth-century trauma, by the act of removing one's clothes. I pictured the rooms of this Hertfordshire retreat as luxurious caves occupied by nude men. By stepping aside from the world, they had somehow acquired a very nice chunk of it in which to practise their austere rituals.

The evening road to Potters Bar is an enchantment. As we walk over Hooke Hill and through Fir Wood, the sun is setting at the end of a tunnel of shadowy greenery. An image I would see many times during the course of our circuit, Renchi with pack on back striding down a long straight road. The cars have gone. The road comes into its own. A solid stream in which we wade.

Swallowed in suburban modesty, banks of blue hydrangeas, we acknowledge that Potters is one bar we won't cross. Potter's forest gate: the old name. A railway town at the end of the line from Moorgate. Property values are beginning to climb as city folk appreciate the connection. It plays two ways. Once we've located the station we're out of it, back home.

6

17 November 1998, we're back in Potters Bar. The logistics of the walk become more complicated as we move away from the Lea Valley and its convenient rail system. Now we're into a two-car relay. We meet at our destination. It's an awkward choice, but we have to decide in advance where we'll stop at the end of the day. We pick Abbots Langley, which is pretty much the top left corner of the circle. We are convinced that the M25 orbit has corners and that those corners are important. They force us to take decisions: north or south, east or west, inside or outside?

Choice made, one car left in the grounds of a mental hospital (defunct and in turnaround), we travel back in the second car to the point where the previous walk finished. Therefore, we experience the motorway. Our status changes. I drive. It's not a section of the road that I know. Renchi points out the usual towers on hills, buildings that might be monasteries or schools or madhouses. He talks of a meteor shower he witnessed on the previous night. A cold morning, the car windows are frosted and have to be scraped.

Leaving the car in an underground car park, near the station in Potters Bar, it takes us a mile or so to adjust: the road on which we were recently travelling is our event horizon. We won't be happy until we place ourselves in a steady relation to the acoustic footprints that define our pilgrimage.

Renchi is fur-capped, mufflered, gloved. The sky is pink; the sun, as it climbs above the suburban avenue of Laurel Fields, disseminates a red-gold beam. Potters Bar is not a bad place to leave behind. On the chainlink fence of the Elm Court Youth and Community Centre: PSYCHIC FAYRE. HERE. NOV 19TH.

These boys are tracking us, using us as Judas goats. They're on our trail.

We feel, plodding down Mutton Lane, that we're working the crease, the fold between cultures, Essex and Hertfordshire. Out of an exhausted shopping precinct (Blockbuster Video, burger bar, hairdresser) we chance on a spanking new civic centre, bright bricks, big windows. The still green surface of an empty swimming pool seen from a cold street.

The best way out – Potters Bar doesn't give up easily – is to follow a fast-flowing stream that seems to carry us in the 'wrong' direction. Mimmshall Brook? Is that the A1 or the M25? Who cares? When you find a landscape of this quality you don't let it go. The fields are frosted, distance is soft. From a motorway bridge we can read the road signs: the A1, heading south to the M25 interchange. On a novocaine winter morning, the motorway sleeve is suspended like a Chinese scroll painting. Wooden fence. Bare trees. Electricity poles.

Time for breakfast. The South Mimms service station is our target. Welcome Break (the new name for Trusthouse Forte's motorway catering) have been allocated the northern arc of the M25, licence to create an oasis of weirdness: a soft sell to road-bruised civilians. People talk affectionately about South Mimms (without the motorway it would be as obscure as its neighbours, Welham Green, Bentley Heath, London Colney). South Mimms was the first (for a long time the only) pit stop on the circuit. City boys with loud shirts and floppy hair (pre-Hugh Grant) used South Mimms as a garage, the starting flag for a lap around London.

One of the mysteries of the M25 (as it might be pitched by Carlton TV) is the 'badly mutilated' body of a woman, discovered near the South Mimms service station in 1990. The woman is still unidentified. Her age was put by the pathologist as 'somewhere between 30 and 50'. She was 5 foot 5 inches tall, with short dark hair and grey/blue eyes. She was buried in an unmarked grave as 'Jane Doe'.

News of this coincidence, nameless victim and recently completed service station, coming a few years after Peter Ackroyd's novel *Hawksmoor*, with its ritual sacrifices, dead children secreted in the foundations of London churches, provoked all kinds of rumours. Bill Drummond and Gimpo, scratching away the earth at the side of the road, near this site, to hide the plaque commemorating their spring equinox drive, seemed to be responding to the same imperative. If vampires are buried at crossroads, stake through the heart, to trap and confuse unresting spirits, then what torment did the South Mimms inhumation represent? A poor soul pitched against interlinked spirals, under and over, the multi-choice channels at Junction 23 of the M25.

Appeasing savage dogs at the gates of scattered properties, we creep up on the service area by way of the Forte Posthouse Motel, a Southern Californian Mission-style, white-walled pastiche, with awnings and arches. You could call the look: Epping Forest pueblo. A good set on which to remake *The Magnificent Seven*. An effect that's tricky to pull off without the weather, the desert. The Posthouse Motel is the bright-windowed fortress of an alien culture. They're not in the hot pillow trade, catering for lazy afternoons, sticky liaisons, leg-overs for the entrepreneurial classes of Potters Bar, Hatfield and Barnet. They're touting for power brunches, coffee-and-croissant bull sessions: conference facilities in the 'theatre style' with a seating capacity of 170, or 'classroom style' for eighty-five, or 'banquet style' for 120, or 'boardroom style' for forty. Between arse-kicking and number-crunching, laminated badge-wearers can make use of an indoor swimming pool, a sauna solarium, jacuzzi spa and gym.

But they can't, just now, drop into the service station to pick up a newspaper, magazine, CD or fast-food snack. South Mimms is a burnt-out shell. UNSAFE STRUCTURE. NO UN-AUTHORISED PERSONNEL BEYOND THIS POINT. Our breakfast is in ruins. Someone has torched the gaff. WELCOME LODGE

FULLY OPEN. Says the sign. But it's only open as a rest area, a parking site; somewhere to piss in the bushes. Fire-blackened struts poke over a blue and white fence, the exoskeleton of a pleasure dome.

If you've been on the road long enough to let your personal grooming slip, you can always book in for a shave and trim. THE HAIR BUS. A customised chara in the lorry park. MEN'S HAIRDRESSING SALON. Truckers with gently protuberant T-shirts are settled on their thrones, catching up with the gossip, while clippers snap and shears buzz. The mobile barber came out on spec, one day, and launched a new career. Nothing pleasanter than a tool around the motorway for a No. 1 crop, before a Full English breakfast in South Mimms.

Service industries are the sort that always mushroom around army posts: barbers, junk food, fancy motel, bunkhouse. Looking down the line of high trucks is like peeping in at the bay windows of a suburban street with a cavalier attitude to net curtains. Fat men shave or change their shirts, spray themselves with industrial-strength deodorants. Lorry girls repair their faces. Some of them, minimally skirted, swing down from the cabs; pick up new patrons for the run north. Juggernauts block the slip roads. Brakes hiss. Radiators steam. Road dirt is sluiced.

We find a truckers' caff, which is cheaper, better, more efficient than any of the service stations. As much coffee as you can drink, elevated screens pumping out colour TV, time to study the maps.

When, much later, Chris Petit and I, driving around the motorway for two days at a stretch, return to South Mimms, the service area has been revamped: as an air terminal. Clean, tactfully lit, unendurable. Everything is designed to get you out of there within minutes of finding a table. Crematorium muzak. Food that isn't. Photo-booths that offer portraits in the style of Van Gogh, Renoir, Dega (sic). Concessions on the point of collapse. A major hike to locate the Gents. No alcoves or areas in which to retreat. You sit on the edge of a hard chair, waiting for your flight to be called. It's not day or night. You're completely disorientated. You can't remember if you're supposed to be travelling east or west. And then, to boost the paranoia, two genetically modified cops, one of each sex, waddle up to the burger bar. They're wearing blue protective vests and they're packing guns at the hips. We get the message and take off for the safety of Purfleet.

On another occasion, after filming with Petit, we found ourselves in a major traffic jam. In the South Mimms car park. Gridlock. No question of reaching the road, the A1 was at a standstill. It began here. Too many supplicants for motorway hospitality, too many tourist coaches. Too many admirers of the service station rock garden. North London devastated – *because too many drivers were trying to get off the road at the same time.*

Returned to base in Hackney, I received a letter from the poet and visionary Aidan Andrew Dun (author of *Vale Royal*). 'How far round are you on your orbital pilgrimage? You probably know this but when HMS *Belfast* was moored just up from Tower Bridge its monstrous gun-turret was trained on a service-station somewhere in the north-western sector of the M25, demonstrating a range of twenty-something miles. Dunno what this means. Perhaps some omen of war on the forecourt!'

Worse than that, Aidan. Worse than the blockades and the motorway slowdowns. HMS *Belfast* was a crucial element in architect Theo Crosby's attempt at rewiring the Celtic Christian alignments of London (as proposed by Elizabeth Gordon in her inspirational 1914 publication, *Prehistoric London: Its Mounds and Circles*). Crosby, in a promotional booklet for his Battle of Britain monument (designed with Michael Sandle), worked everything from a point that seemed to have little significance in 1987. By whatever prophetic or occult arts, Crosby chose to launch the psychogeographic redefinition of London's fields of force from the line of zero longitude (which he called the 'Turner Axis'). His Speer-derived monument would be sited around Cuckold's Point in Rotherhithe (the starting place for an historic pilgrimage to the Horn Fair in Charlton). It was, in fact, a precise equivalent (west for east) of the dead ground on which the Millennium Dome would be built (as an unconscious tribute to the spirit of Crosby).

The Turner Axis, starting on Greenwich Hill, spurned the ancient ley (the Hawksmoor line through the domes of the Naval College to St Anne's, Limehouse), and passed through Cuckold's Point to HMS *Belfast* and St Paul's Cathedral (where it met the 'Canaletto Axis'). The guns of the battleship were trained on the only (at that time) service station on the orbital motorway. The arc of fire represents another of London's invisible threads of influence. In that curvature, the fall of a shell, can be seen one span of a grander dome: river to margin.

'The place is unimportant,' writes Crosby. 'So is the alignment and the orientation, the magic rules of the past that governed the disposal of buildings and particularly monuments. They are the cardinal points, the directions of the equinox, the midsummer sunrise, the turning of year, the evocation of growth, the stopping of time.'

Before it was a service station, South Mimms (Myms) was a hilltop village with church and notable funerary monument for the Austen family: a double plinth (the upper element decorated with a five-skull panel and crossed bones) topped by an inverted pear.

'Pear. No, light-bulb. No, pear,' says Renchi.

The stone pear has a vestigial stem growing from its bulb. It sucks light from dim fields. It gives nothing out. A provocative sculpture shielded from the curiosity of the vulgar by a curtain of spindly, ivy-covered trees. The pear, according to J.C. Cooper's *An Illustrated Encyclopaedia of Traditional Symbols*, stood for 'hope; good health'. To the Christian it represented 'the love of Christ for mankind'. What then of the inverted pear?

The pear with pedicel growing from rounded bottom, not slender neck?

As we head across country in the direction of Shenley, navigating fields of winter cabbage, hopping brooks, appreciating the high, quilted clouds, seeing nobody, I try to explain my notion of our walk as a fugue. This improvisation would make more sense when I read Ian Hacking's excellent account of epic, seemingly random pedestrian journeys undertaken by French labourers in the late nineteenth century. *Mad Travelers (Reflections on the Reality of Transient Mental Illnesses)* offered one perfectly reasonable 'explanation' of our orbital pilgrimage: an hysterical fugue – attended by the sort of minor epileptic seizures (electrical storms in the consciousness) Renchi suffered in Dublin.

Albert Dadas, a gas fitter from Bordeaux, is the pivotal figure in Hacking's narrative. An ambitious provincial doctor, Philippe Tissie, interested himself in Dadas and wrote up the case; thereby inducting the *fugueur* into a Conradian tale (weather, brooding topography, fatalism). Dadas, a compulsive masturbator, would simply walk out of his quotidian life; the domestic routines, the duties he performed to his employers' satisfaction. There was no obvious motive, no trauma to be left behind. The journeys were a willed forgetting. They were like Aboriginal songlines, enacted dreamings: Bordeaux to Moscow, to Constantinople, Algiers.

Tissie's account of the Dadas phenomenon launched a fashion, the roads of Europe were cluttered with amnesiac pilgrims, temporary vagrants. The fugue would pass. The middle classes, metropolitans, took up the craze. Long-distance walking spread like a virus. You didn't walk to forget, you walked to forget the walk. You carried on, often for months, years, until it was appropriate to return to your previous life.

I found the term *fugueur* more attractive than the now over-worked *flâneur*. *Fugueur* had the smack of a swear word, a bloody-minded Tommy muttering over his tobacco tin in the

Flanders trenches. *Fugueur* was the right job description for our walk, our once-a-month episodes of transient mental illness. Madness as a voyage. The increasing lunacy of city life (in my case) and country life (in Renchi's) forced us to take to the road. The joy of these days out lay in the heightened experience of present tense actuality, the way that we bypassed, for a brief space of time, the illusionism of the spin doctors, media operators and salaried liars. The fugue is both drift *and* fracture. The story of the trip can only be recovered by some form of hypnosis, the memory prompt of the journal or the photo-album. Documentary evidence of things that may never have happened. The fugue is a psychic commando course – Albert Dadas, bloody-footed, stomped seventy kilometres a day – that makes the parallel life, as gas fitter, hospital carer, or literary hack, endurable.

Mad walking has its key image: Van Gogh's *The Painter on the Road to Tarascon* (1888). (Along with Francis Bacon's obsessive reworking of this vanished painting.) Van Gogh's original was burnt in the Second World War when the Kaiser Friedrich Museum at Magdeburg was destroyed.

A straw-hatted man, burdened with the implements of his trade, spins around to face the viewer. The artist as a version of Bunyan's pilgrim. 'A rough sketch I made of myself,' Vincent wrote to his brother Theo, 'laden with boxes, props, and canvas on the sunny road.' The road shimmers. He is tracked by a distorted shadow. This is precisely the spirit of the *fugueur*. Dadas met Tissie for the first time in 1886.

Another group of Van Gogh walkers is closer to our project: *Prisoners Exercising (After Gustave Doré)*. Completed in the asylum at Saint-Rémy-de-Provence in February 1890. Stooped convicts (or madmen) process in a slow circle, a chain that mimes our penitential motorway orbit. No end and no beginning. Humans dwarfed by high brick walls. A reworking of Doré's *London*, flooded with colour. The prisoner who turns towards the viewer, showing his face, is Van Gogh.

Contemporary medical opinion associated epilepsy with marathon expeditions, French workmen on their motiveless walkabouts. Numerous doctoral theses (Birnbaum, Evensen, Leroy, Doiteau, etc.) diagnosed Van Gogh as an epileptic. Other authorities (Jaspers, Westerman Holsttijn, Riese, Prinzhorn) preferred schizophrenia. Notions such as 'episodic twilight states' were floated. Stertz wrote of 'phasic hallucinatory psychosis'. Delirium, sun-seizures, fits of melancholy that couldn't be walked out or worked out. Leading inevitably to the 'Maison de Santé', the asylum. Voluntary confinement.

In the advertisement, the prospectus for the madhouse at Saint-Rémy-de-Provence, is a drawing of the hospital and its grounds. From the viewpoint of the Alpilles at the foot of Mont Gaussier, you can see an Italianate tower with surrounding low-level buildings, sharp hill. And this is very much the prospect that confronts us as we advance on Shenley. The asylum as a retreat, in the countryside, a few miles out of town. The tower on the hill was one of the features Renchi pointed out on our drive from Abbots Langley. On Nicholson's map, checked over breakfast in South Mimms, Shenley Hospital is revealed as a substantial estate, a colony of the disturbed, black blocks, a church and a social club. We recall Chris Oakley, once an associate of R.D. Laing and David Cooper, telling us at the time of Renchi's exhibition in Selborne that Cooper had run an experimental unit at Shenley. The psychiatrists, if we had the right place, joining the inmates on their hallucinogenic voyages.

In twentieth-century representations of the fugue, the walker disappears from the walk. Landscape artists Richard Long and Hamish Fulton erase the trauma, along with the figure of the troubled pedestrian. Minor interventions are tactfully recorded; a few stones rearranged, twigs bent. The walker becomes a control freak, compulsively logging distances, directions, treading abstractions into the Ordnance Survey map. Scripting minimalist asides, copywriting haikus.

Renchi's recent paintings merge walker and landscape. Chorographic overviews, diaries. In earlier times, the brush-strokes were looser, the paint thicker. Walks were shorter, paintings fiercer. As the fugues extended – London to Swansea, Hopton-on-Sea to St Michael's Mount – the records were calmer; there was more of a narrative element, transit across landscape remembered in chalk, flint, granite, slate. Canvases, left behind in Ireland, mouldered in damp outhouses.

Shenley Hall, a pompous white property, with fountain and porch and pedigree, has made the usual transition from seat of landed gentry to hangout for corporate man. The house has become the image, the emblem in the brochure. WELCOME TO SHENLEY HALL. ROADRUNNER, ROAD TECH COMPUTER SYSTEMS. Perfect! Motors lined up on gravel like some house party or shooting weekend from the Edwardian era. The panoply of autogeddon on parade: four-wheel drive, off-road (M25 to B5378), executive Rover, rep-saloon, white van. If the company expands – and they're operating in the right area – they'll have to acquire a couple of home farms as parking spaces.

While I stop to photograph a stone eagle on the gatepost ('victory; pride; authority; solar power; omniscience'), Renchi falls into conversation with two villagers: a ruddy-faced military gentleman in a plaid cap and good tweed jacket (pens in pocket) and his partner, a lady in green anorak, headscarf, woollen gloves. Being walkers themselves, they are interested in our outing. They don't much like what's happening to Shenley, but they are realists. Things change. The daily circuit of the territory takes more out of them, but they'll go on making it.

Shenley Manor, it appears, once belonged to the wealthy Raphael family. One brother kept the stud farm and bred a Derby winner. The other brother owned the land on which the hospital was built. The asylum was an investment, nothing more than that. A way of maximising return on holdings, keeping the house and the life that went with it. The old couple put us on the right track, the hospital is on Black Lion Hill.

At the crossroads with Radlett Lane, Renchi stops (as if taking part in some boundary marking ceremony) to piss against the bark of a magnificent pine tree. The water tower of Shenley hospital is our guide, its grey roof a pyramid, above triple windows and an absurd balcony. These towers, the compass needles of our walk, survive (thanks to preservation orders) when all the other buildings are gutted and built over.

Shenley Hospital is one of a number of isolated developments (asylums, pumping stations) in the Vale of St Albans which were granted green belt status. Reservoirs of madness. The village of Shenley is green belt, South Mimms is not.

Green belt or not, Shenley Hospital, active until a couple of months before our arrival, has vanished, replaced by a housing development, the bright new units of a Crest Homes estate. The back story of the asylum has been totally erased, apart from the baleful presence of the water tower. How do they explain that monster to first-time buyers? They've started by fixing a working clock on its side, so that the brick stack can be renamed: The Shenley Crest Clocktower.

We are stunned by this disappearing act. We've seen the old photographs, Shenley was like a benign concentration camp. Thirties architecture, industrial/pastoral units: a processing plant for mental hygiene. The scale was epic. Vast dormitories. Kitchens. Bath-houses. Estates within estates, radiating out from that water tower. Asylums have their hierarchies, their degrees of compliance. They have their dark places and their gardens. Within a few months, Shenley had been eradicated.

Nicholson's *Greater London Street Atlas* was promoting another fiction, a detailed plan of something that wasn't there. The Shenley vanishing act counterbalanced the recovery of the Royal Gunpowder Mills at Waltham Abbey: history heritaged for anyone with the price of a ticket. You could buy the book, the souvenir pencil. At Shenley there was only the estate office. The JCBs. The screech of earth-moving machinery.

CREST HOMES. The Pavilions, Shenley. A glossy brochure with a mendacious cover illustration: yellow-brick units. 'Photograph depicts a completed Crest development in Camberley Surrey.' Military personnel, junior officer class: regulation issue. Nice title, 'The Pavilions', with its suggestion of John Major's reworking of Orwell, the England of warm beer, bicycling spinsters, the sound of willow thwacking leather. The Far Pavilions. A retreat to the hills. A mock Surrey, Guildford or Dorking, Abinger Hammer, with lawns and trees and cricket squares. An escape from the heat and dirt of the city. Eight hundred yards from the M25.

Where were the former citizens of Shenley, the inmates? Turned loose into the countryside? Tipped into the hedgerows? Or abandoned to 'care in the community' when there were no communities left? Shenley had been a retreat, a zone of healing, as well as a place to tidy away the casualties of urban life.

History is being revised on a daily basis, through the northern quadrant of the motorway, by copywriters employed by the developers. 'The historic village of Shenley combines excellent local interest with outstanding travel convenience.' Much is made of the 'pleasant undulating countryside' and the 'fine views northward over the historic city of St Albans'. To qualify as 'historic' you need green belt development permissions, new estates across a bowling-green from an old church. History is an extra zero on your property prices.

The story of the historic village can be outlined in a paragraph: 'ideal for those who love the "great outdoors" . . . pleasant walks . . . a traditional walled garden dating back to the 17th century; tennis courts . . . and, of course, the Shenley Cricket Centre, the origins of which lie with the great cricketer WG Grace . . . four golf courses within easy driving distance and both Borehamwood and St Albans offering a choice of indoor sports centres and health clubs.'

Pleasant. Traditional. Convenient. Those are the terms to hammer home. The convenience of the golf course was the reason why Tom Cruise and Nicole Kidman took a house here while they underwent the Stanley Kubrick endurance test, making *Eyes Wide Shut*. Stanley himself, being chauffeured at a steady forty mph, from his St Albans hideaway, around the loop to the studio. Pinewood, Elstree, Borehamwood, Denham: image factories and their green belt backlots, shadowing the motorway, shadowing the chain of mental hospitals.

We find it difficult to escape the Crest Homes development; the units are red brick, rather than the muted yellow of the Camberley illustration. The homes, for the most part, are unoccupied; ghosts press on every window. The surviving components of the hospital – water tower, church – have a niggling poignancy. In time they will adapt, be seen as 'historic', but for the moment they are too much themselves. The church with its low tower, narrow windows, red, pantiled roof is Bavarian. There's a path, hidden between slanting earth banks that runs into the basement, a secret door. It's easy to imagine all kinds of unpleasant compromises between obedience, stern care and obligatory ritual.

We left the Crest colony (which replaced the previous colony of the mad with a grid of nicely finished units, pressing too close against each other), and moved on to the mansion, once known as Shenley Manor. The mansion commands fine views of Watling Chase, Coombe Wood, Swanley Park. It looks like one of those hotels to which politicians or jaded executives go for strategy sessions (the strategy being to lig as much booze-sauna-TV porn-golf as can be packed into a hoggish weekend). Swanley Manor is ready to take on the Hamiltons, Jonathan Aitken and a bunch of Saudi money men with their massage parlour-maids. It's white, discreet, lawned, planted. Bowed, pillared, balconied. There are heraldic shields, verdigris domes, weather vanes. Behind dark yew hedges there is a maze that isn't a maze, a hidden meadow with erased patterns in the grass; disguised exits that shift as we attempt to locate them. Swanley Manor cries out for Peter Greenaway.

No plutocrat is in residence. No megalomaniac or software czar lives here. No Branson or Maxwell. If they did, we'd never have got up the drive. Renchi, with his silver beard, red scarf and ear-flapped, cross-country ski cap, might be a Russian commando on a recce. The first of the Mongol horde to reach the gates. A fleeing Chechen.

Grace Avenue climbs, padded in leaf-fall from a spreading oak, towards the house on the hill. PRIVATE ROAD, RESIDENTS ONLY (white on blue). SHENLEY MANOR (gold on green). 'Restored Late Georgian Houses', Town & Country (green on cream). ALL SOLD (white on red).

This house, before it was parcelled up into executive apartments, was known as Porters Mansion. Yes, we've picked up another leaflet. 'For centuries this house and its surrounding estate were a dominant feature of the local landscape and witness to many changes not least its encirclement by Shenley Hospital in the 1930's . . . The Mansion has had a fascinating history.' *Has had*. Present perfect. History, once again, put in its place. The future used up.

Porters, as an estate, dates from the thirteenth century. Farms were added, plantings undertaken. Royal courtiers, self-made men of business, politicians, naval officers: the usual mix of exploiters and improvers acquired house and land. Sir Richard Coxe. John Mason (distiller of Greenwich and Deptford). Viscount Howe, First Lord of the Admiralty and victor of the Battle of Brest. Howe was known to his men, so the pamphlet claims, as 'Black Dick'. 'Solid as a rock and just as silent.'

And so on, from the Marchioness of Sligo to Luke White, to Colonel Henry White, Samuel Clarke Jervoise, William Joseph Myers, James Harris Sanders. Sanders met his wife Mary in New Orleans. She undertook good works for orphans and the poor of the village, she improved the garden. The author Ann Bridge was one of eight children. *Portrait of My Mother* is set at Porters.

After the gardening Mrs Sanders came Michael Paul Grace. It is rumoured that W.G. Grace laid out the cricket square. The ground is still there, we visited it, just beyond the walled garden. A green sanctuary. Cecil Frank Raphael, who bought the estate in 1902, built the pavilion. His son John captained Surrey – and died in the First World War in 1917.

During the war, part of the estate was used as an airfield. It was known, to avoid confusion with the field at Kenley (to the north), as London Colney Aerodrome. The sheds and huts on the east of Black Lion Hill were the base for 56 and 54 Squadrons. Temporary hangars known as 'Besseneau', wooden frames and canvas covers, were still in use in the Forties. In this empty landscape, the floodplain of the M25, with its scattered villages, hospital colonies, sewage plants and rescued mansions, there are always characteristic features: war debris and immaculately tended cricket squares. Bunkers, concrete ziggurats: overgrown, bird-occupied, or converted into piggeries.

Many of the young men at the London Colney base didn't survive the training period. They are buried in the graveyard of the small roadside church of St Botolph's. The last of the Royal Flying Corps sheds, known as 'The Hangar', were incorporated into one of the local asylums, Harperbury Hospital.

In 1924 Raphael sold Porters Park to the Middlesex County Council, who used the site to build Shenley Hospital. Patients arrived, sectioned, drugged, or by their own volition, from Harrow, Wembley, Acton, Willesden. The hospital, at its peak, housed 2,000 of them. It's hard, seeing the photographs of the place in its Thirties pomp, not to think of other experiments in social engineering, eugenics. This is a camp, a colony, a plant to process non-conformity, to tidy away girls who got into trouble, drinkers, ranters; those who gave too vivid an expression to the overwhelming melancholy of urban life. Shenley, with its blocks, its wards, didn't belong on the outskirts of London. To achieve its benevolent aims, the colony needed alps and forests, not 'pleasant undulating countryside'.

Shenley mixed (Rudolf) Steinerist notions of garden cures, plant magic, sympathetic colours, with the flipside: control, mind-experiments, coercion.

The site was chosen for its location, near the Middlesex border, a short drive (or march) from Radlett station. Madhouses belonged on the periphery. Instability might infect healthy working people. Out here, in the clean air, the virus was contained. The plan, according to the Middlesex County Council, was 'to build a new mental hospital and a Colony for Mental Defectives'. In other words, transportation. Far Pavilions. A Tasmania established at the rim of London. The contract for the building work was given to John Laing. A firm that would, in the future, be one of the major motorway contractors; responsible for the Dartford to Swanley section of the M25 (1974–7). Laing would also develop significant off-highway estates. (Laings had a discreet colony of their own, not far from here, with a number of fine cricket pitches.)

Another Laing, Ronnie, the charismatic Glaswegian anti-psychiatrist, was to make his mark on Shenley. The 'Villa' system, taking patients away from huge wards (and a recreation hall that seated 1,000 people) to 'family' units of between twenty and forty-five members, fitted nicely with the Laingian ethic. The grounded ocean liner of the Thirties, with its rigid hierarchies, became a flotilla of pirate craft, ships of fools with crazed or inspired captains.

Clancy Sigal, a successful screenwriter and novelist, an American exile in Sixties London, became a patient of Laing and left a fictional account of those years. His novel *Zone of the Interior* was suppressed in England. The Sigal character is in awe of Last, a lightly disguised version of Laing.

My thirty-odd years of ignorance and spiritual flabbiness, he said, had been the Tao's way of preparing me for the final, self-healing Voyage.

'Where to?' I asked.

'Schizophrenia,' he replied.

Sigal sees the asylum for what it is: 'a rural caesura . . . a gateway'. He knows that it can only be reached by a transit through the 'semi-industrial suburbs of Ealing, Southall and Hayes'. The cure begins with a drive 'past Heathrow airport, tiny streams and beacons in the scrub fields . . . to golf courses, cows and stockbroker villas . . . small meadows, citified villages, the outer spokes of London's huge wheel'.

The original design of Shenley was constructed around a central axis, male and female accommodation were separated; patients were not allowed to stray beyond their 'airing courts'. By the time R.D. Laing and David Cooper arrived, patients were being encouraged to work on the construction of new buildings. They helped in the gardens. Staff and patients came together for dances and coach trips to 'places of interest'.

Sigal's novel suggests that beneath these liberal gestures nothing had changed. The intake was still made up of 'post-Edwardian spinsters banished from their families for an unmarried pregnancy; the deaf and the dumb; undetected autistics and mild subnormals; alcoholics and homosexuals – or simply homeless men and women who lost their kin and had nowhere else to go'.

A battle was being fought between opposed concepts of architecture: the grid and the skin hutch, the rational colony with its avenues and the yurt of the shaman. Sigal draws up a plan for 'an all-male community on the edge of London' and presents it to Last (Laing). 'Laid out like a medieval town, it was governed by a nuclear core of Perfectii, or Brothers, who studied and prayed in a shedlike temple far apart from the un-Elect (women, children, cats and dogs). Girding this inner sanctum was a ring of mobile prefab huts inhabited by the mad and broken down – i.e., patients who might also be any of us. Unlike the wives and families of the Perfectii, who were segregated in an Outer Zone where they contentedly raised chickens and bees to make the community self-sufficient, the mad always had free access to the Nuclear Brothers.'

The psychedelic Sixties were awash with such plans, derived from misreadings of Buckminster Fuller, mythical accounts of life at Black Mountain College in North Carolina (under the rectorship of Charles Olson), libertarian communes in San Francisco. Sigal shifts between the asylum, with its forcing-chambers, its concentric geometry, its gardens, and the city (the generator). The hut of derangement can only be constructed at the heart of the labyrinth.

I prepared my launching pad: a London version of a Siberian shaman's hutch . . . At each of the tent's corners, to signify the Zodiac elements, I deposited a jar of Thames River water, a box of Swan matches, a plastic bag of earth from St. James Park and a toy balloon I had to keep inflating. After a brief purifying ceremony, I invited Willie Last, who took one look and said quietly, 'That's pretty mad, Sid.' With this blessing, I knew I was in business.

Renchi, when he completed his circuit of the M25, hoped to devise similar ceremonies: sand paintings in the chalk tunnels under Epsom Downs, songlines drawn on flyovers, cave art inscribed in earth colours on the grooved walls of underpasses. Reasserted alignments.

But there are significant differences between the two men. Sigal, the New Yorker, the hip Jewish screenwriter, has a weakness for one-liners. Socialism and comedy, that's his schtick. The magic of the city is something he recognises, but it is always absurd: the visionary is a beggar and a clown. Whatever strange rituals he is prompted to undertake, they will always come out like a quotation from a Thirties B-movie.

In the small dark hours of the night, when the others were too stoned or sleepy to notice, I crept out of the manor to lope the quiet empty streets of south London. From Crystal Palace to New Cross, from Catford to Woolwich, I heel-and-toed it to escape the thing that was chewing me up. All night and into the next morning, up to twenty miles a day, I tramped, a 1960s Werewolf of London dreading only the bright sunlight.

Another fugue. Another mad traveller. We were discovering a useful genealogy: gas fitters, painters, novelists. Through the suburbs at night, the motorway verges by day, we were there; heel-and-toeing it, sucking water from a plastic bottle, trying to find some way to unravel the syntax of London.

A stroll around the paths and levels of the estate at Shenley (aka Watling Chase Community Forest) restores us. The autumn colours of an English fashion shoot by Lord Litchfield. A stout wooden bench facing an orchard of pruned apple trees. Among the ninety-odd varieties of apples grown here is the Seabrook Pearl, which is unique to Shenley.

We find the estate office and are given permission to explore the walled garden. The estate is in that limbo between memories of privilege (forelock-touching gardeners) and community art (in its remedial aspect). I take a photograph of Renchi stretched out beneath a set of sculpted steps on which is printed: NO/REST/FOR THE/WICKED.

Catching an obliging volunteer in the estate office, we are given permission to photocopy some of the old maps of Porters Park. The house was at one time occupied by an architect far better known than W.T. Curtis (who was responsible for the design of the Italianate water tower and hospital). The volunteer couldn't remember the name. He rummaged among his papers until he found the relevant passage. Nicholas Hawksmoor. Had we heard of him?

Porters Park, mansion and grounds, had once been in the keeping of Hawksmoor. I knew I'd read somewhere that Hawksmoor had taken a house, out from London, a day's ride to the north. But it came as a shock to stumble across it on the second day of our orbital walk. I couldn't disassociate the man from his chain of East London churches, from city and river. Hawksmoor kept houses in Greenwich and Westminster, but this was his retreat; symbol of achievement and status.

At the end of his career, after Christ Church, Spitalfields, St Anne's, Limehouse, and St Mary Woolnoth, Hawksmoor came to Shenley. He gave advice on the planning of restoration work at St Albans Abbey. There is a Hawksmoor drawing of the north face. He corresponded with the Bishop of London: 'By the help of the magic of Archdeacon Stubbs I have erected the Ancient Temple of St. Albans in brass, which heretofore was only in stone . . . I have put into the landscape the famed site of Verulam, destroyed by Boudicea, there is also the lake and the situation of the new town which has arisen . . . We can but support this vulnerable pile from being martyred by the neglect of a slothful generation.'

Succeeding Wren as Surveyor of Works at Westminster Abbey, Hawksmoor moved from Greenwich in 1730, but retained his country manor. He died at Westminster, aged seventy-five, but expressed the wish to have his body returned to Shenley. For a number of years, the precise whereabouts of the grave was forgotten. The architect's reputation drifted into obscurity. His riverine churches were locked, dark. Then, according to the notes our informant was reading, the burial place was rediscovered in 1830.

We could search for Nicholas Hawksmoor's grave in the little church of St Botolph. Apart from a beehive hut on the village green, with the inscription 'Do well, be vigilant and fear not', St Botolph's is the only Shenley curiosity thought worthy of mention in *The New Shell Guide to England*. The church was on our route to the motorway.

The beehive hut recommended in the guide turned out to be a lock-up for miscreants, known locally as 'The Cage'. Offenders were held overnight before being taken to Barnet to face the magistrate. There were, in fact, two inscriptions, placed over the windows. 'Be sober, be vigilant' and 'Do well and fear naught'.

Emerging from the woods that surrounded Hawksmoor's mansion, we hit Black Lion Hill. The road ran directly down towards the M25. Off to the east, just back from our path, was a site marked on my map as 'Old Church (redundant)'.

The burial ground which stood above the church was accessible, weathered gravestones in a carpet of autumn leaves. There were monuments to the airmen of Shenley who had died during their training period. But there was no sign of a memorial to England's greatest architect of the Baroque.

The church, flint with brick dressings, was of course closed. It wasn't a church, but a set of private flats. The drive was a gravel crescent. Renchi rang the bell; using the voice box was like trying to contact the dead. I took a photograph. Renchi with his archaic headgear: the frontispiece to Blake's *Jerusalem*. 'Los as he Entered the Door of Death.' Renchi with hand outstretched for the buzzer is a ringer for Blake's pilgrim, as he approaches the door, the Gothic arch. Renchi with burden. Renchi with solar disk. 'Los took his globe of fire to search the interiors of Albions's/Bosom . . .'

Blake wrote to Hayley (23 October 1804): 'I was again enlightened with the light I enjoyed in my youth, and which has for exactly twenty years been closed from me as by a door.' Renchi as artist/seeker. Los, according to the catalogue of the millennial Blake exhibition at the Tate, is 'artist–poet–architect, *alter ego* of Blake himself, in the guise of a London nightwatchman'.

We made a circuit of the church grounds, stepping over children's bicycles, fingering letters on tumbled tombs. At the back of the building, near a barbecue pit, we found it. A stone slab with a diagonal crack, a covering of yellow-gold beech leaves. A shallow earthenware dish filled with water. A circular mirror of clouds. The rectangular, slate-grey lid, which had been awkwardly set on a rim of bricks, was as unspectacular as a deepfreeze unit. A safe. A lead box. No pyramids, no decorative motifs, no Masonic symbols.

Three weeks before his death, Hawksmoor was busy with plans for Castle Howard: 'I may be employed in Some Shape or other if I shall be alive in Building the Bridge.' His own monument in the Shenley church is, as Kerry Downes writes, 'characteristically erudite'.

PMSL. Piae memoriae sacer locus. 'The formula appears to be unique.' My remembered Latin was rough but we're in the territory of sacred places and pious memories. St Botolph's was certainly a sacred place. Hawksmoor's grave, along with Temple Bar, were the beacons of our walk; heavily freighted memorials that had been allowed to pull away from the centre.

NICHOLAUS HAWKSMOOR, ARCHITECTUS. We waited. Behind us, the red tower on the hill. Across an open field, a few hundred yards to the north, the continuing rush and fret of the orbital motorway.

7

There is a set of twenty-four cards called Myriorama (or, Endless Landscape), based on a 'novelty' published in Leipzig in the 1830s. Lay out the cards in any order – one long straight line or 12×2, 4×6, 3×8 – and you achieve 'a perfectly harmonious landscape'. A landscape of symbols: road, lake (or river), low hills, distant village, travellers on a highway. Time frozen at the edge of extinction. Something of Breughel, something of Christian Rosencreuz: hermetic-cabbalist hieroglyphs. The scale of these pocket-Polaroids induces vertigo. The black birds hanging above the rocks are too big. Why should eagles or vultures be found at the outskirts of a pretty German town? Why is the solitary horseman blowing a bugle? Everything tugs and tosses. Two youths cling, terrified, to a lifting kite. A decorated hot air balloon drifts in one direction; the sails of a three-master billow, as it surges, in the other. There is an obelisk like a war memorial with an unreadable inscription. Two walkers, rucksack-burdened, debate a signpost.

The thing you can't do with the twenty-four cards is arrange them in a circle. The pattern fractures, the road breaks; the drawings are revealed as cigarette cards from a prophetic tarot pack to which the key has been lost. The trick that puzzles Renchi is: how to iron out the M25 circuit. How to convert the orbital motorway into a device made from straight lines, simple contraries: north/south, clay/gravel, water/tarmac.

We pore over maps; it doesn't help. Renchi, in cap and red scarf, photographed on a traffic island in Shenley Lane, with a church (a copy of King's College Chapel, Cambridge) behind him, on the far side of the motorway, is a contemporary transcription of a Leipzig card. The obvious solution is to take the direction the ink-drawn figure nominates, to strike west. We're confused, crossing familiar ground without retracing our steps. The cardboard landscape is endless, the elements archetypal, but they shift, they change their story.

We sit at an outside table, a mill house pub beside the River Ver (closed for refurbishment), and drink the last of our plastic water; we scratch at the linings of our pockets, in search of that elusive Polo mint. Somebody has set fire to a bungalow. White plasterboard and asbestos panels on a wintry pyre.

Renchi has been reading Foucault, *Madness and Civilization*. A fitting complement to this stage of our walk. Asylums haunt the motorway like abandoned forts, the kind of defensive ring once found on the Thames below Tilbury. Hospital colonies are black mandalas of madness: circles set around a central axis, depictions of an unstable brain chemistry. Shenley is a hilltop encampment, Cadbury or Maiden Castle; Napsbury is a winged creature. The fantastic sigils of the madhouse architects dominate the map, the docile north-west quadrant of our journey.

The hospitals at Harperbury and Shenley are separated by a few fields; coming away from our inspection of the motorway fringe, we choose the long way around, by Harper Lane. NO A & E (white on blue). Motorway casualties must look elsewhere. Limbs hacked off by agricultural machinery will have to be left on ice. Foucault suits Harperbury; a Francophile poetic hits the spot.

There is a long straight avenue, pollarded limes, flanked by huts and severe brick blocks with windows set in mansard roofs. Light is declining, a pinkish glow in the grey membrane, trees like witches' brooms. Go back into reverie, into black and white, and this is a film by Georges Franju, his first feature, *La Tête contre les murs* (1958). The critic Raymond Durgnat, summarising the plot, wrote of 'a delinquent adolescent' whose 'sadism against his father has a *visionary* quality, and accordingly, he seems insane'. To avoid scandal the boy is placed in an asylum in which a doctor who punishes irrational behaviour is in conflict with a younger colleague who inclines towards a more progressive treatment of those given into his care. Charles Aznavour in his first substantial screen part plays an epileptic.

With hindsight, the film's polemic (based on a novel published in 1934) can seem too naked, a simplistic argument between fashions in psychiatric practice. What survives is Franju's sense of geometry, his ability to articulate the shapes and movements that define place. Sociology matters less than the layout of the buildings, the choice of location.

Durgnat quotes Franju: 'I shot *La Tête* in the Psychiatric Hospital of Dury, with a quite unbelievable courtyard. Dead in the centre was a phallic tree with four benches grouped around it . . . We lived as a community in their community. We hardly emerged from it . . . If we'd slept in the asylum, we'd still be there.'

In the courtyard inmates describe small circles, heads against the wall; the plodding, eyes-on-gravel prisoners of Van Gogh. Ian Hacking writes about an unmarried shepherd who was committed to an asylum in 1857, suffering from severe seizures. 'Before or after an attack he would compulsively pace up and down, or in circles, always clockwise. He had an obsessive conviction that he should put the whole world, and the heavens and angels, in his head, or in his heart.' His autopsy revealed atrophy of the brain, especially of the right hemisphere. Leashed, he walked the pain, lacking balance, a tight circuit around nothing. His epic peregrination, the few yards of a hospital ward, is a doomed attempt to recover memory. Movement provokes memory. Photographs from a dozen journeys over the same ground refuse to cohere: the result is never that 'perfectly harmonious landscape'. The result is: monuments without inscriptions, twisted signposts.

Durgnat correctly interpreted Franju's film as a pitiless equation: 'The pattern has the finality of an Euclidean Q.E.D., its rigid reversal and angularity evokes helplessness, despair, a stiffening fear, a tightrope-walk over the abyss of madness-by-contagion . . . Poetry and geometry meet amidst these land-scapes whose greyness is as charged and nuanced as the sky before thunder. In shot after shot, the white walls of the asylum enclose windows and open doors, or other apertures, through which black-branched trees and skies seem, not just a glimpse of freedom, but themselves subjected to the enclosing architecture.'

Harperbury has sunk into the half-life of discontinued surveil-lance, decanted buildings, bored curation. The developers haven't yet moved in, although the patients have leaked away. Nobody questions us. Nobody takes any interest in our ramble through their property. We find an office with a blow-heater, a woman drinking tea. Some account of the hospital's history has been published, but it isn't available. We give our names and addresses and receive a promise that information will be sent to us in due course. But we understand this will never happen. The energy has gone from the place. The hut that once belonged to the Shenley airfield has infected the other buildings; they're demob happy. The war's over and the future hasn't begun.

It's getting dark as we walk down Smug Oak Lane towards the complex symmetry of the junction that marries the surging streams of the M25 and the M1. A site of magical resonance: triangular field, wood, torrential traffic-rush. The layering of access roads, tributaries, slipstreams, fires memory sensors, pro-vokes narrative. We feel as though we are eavesdropping on a thousand private conversations, sharing monologues and weary daydreams.

Renchi explains how Foucault tracks the asylum back to the pesthouse, the hospital for lepers which had to be built out-side the gates of the city. 'In 1348,' Foucault wrote, 'the great leprosarium of Saint Albans contained only three patients; the hospital of Romenal in Kent was abandoned twenty-four years later, for lack of lepers.'

Perhaps we were misreading the transition from closed communities of the hurt and drug-damaged (lepers of the cosmetic city) to Barratt estates designed as novelties: protected enclaves with no memory. Perhaps there now existed a shortfall in derangement. Madness, visionary seizure, nonconformist rage belonged in another era – with the cinema of romantic individualism, bad boys, naughty girls provoked by the dull-minded orthodoxies of life under the nuclear umbrella. Jean Seberg sleepwalking through Robert Rossen's *Lilith*. Jack Nicholson collecting an Oscar for deploying the most sinister grin (this side of Tony Blair) in *One Flew Over the Cuckoo's Nest*. Madness as performance. It was over.

Sets were being struck. Foucault's leper houses, part of (or in close proximity to) monastic institutions, became hospitals, prisons, prophylactic domes; isolation bred cruelty, until cruelty gave way to dialogue, the sanctioned shaman who interpreted dreams. Ships of Fools, sailing the rivers, putting out to sea, take on the guise of a fleet of Eddie Stobart lorries floating above the Dartford Bridge on a misty spring morning. Shenley, Harperbury and Napsbury were islands of the damned. From which the damned had vanished.

'In the margins of the community,' Foucault wrote, 'at the gates of cities, there stretched wastelands which sickness had ceased to haunt but had left sterile and uninhabitable.' We were moving through just such a zone. The mad had departed, leaving the hospitals functionless, inert. The remaining clerks and doctors were depressed. Central government had no interest in these sites. They were statistics to be manipulated, real estate to be turned to profit. Sweetheart deals with developers saw the great Victorian parks, with their dark histories, their infamous architecture, pillaged, revamped, repackaged in a matter of months. With little or no public debate, no accountability.

'Celebrities flock to Chigwell,' screamed the property pages. This was the Chigwell 'made famous by the BBC's hit comedy *Birds of a Feather*'. Repton Park, 'with its Georgian-style villas and uniformed concierge service', is wowing 'snooker players and actors from *EastEnders*', who are attracted by 'the right combination of prestige and seclusion'. Crest Homes are the developers (note the tell-tale water tower in the illustration of this former asylum).

What Crest have done is lose the name and history of Claybury Mental Hospital. So much of the East End, so many real East Enders, were decanted into this hilltop settlement. The sister of the Whitechapel hermit David Rodinsky died in Claybury. The water tower is an aid to navigation seen by motorists coming into London on the M11, by orbital traffickers on the North Circular. Claybury was a city in exile, forcible re-immigration. If they spoke in these long wards they spoke in tongues.

When I was undertaking a series of walks that traced markings on Rodinsky's battered copy of the *London A–Z*, I arrived at Claybury on the day when bulldozers were moving in. Georgian wasn't the word I'd have used to describe the blocks I could see through the iron gate. But developers believe that a strategic change of name will wipe the slate: from Claybury Hospital to Repton Park. Claybury was once a manor house, a hall. That story fades and the name of the great English landscape-gardener, Humphry Repton, is invoked. Repton Park. Flashed into brochures and websites as a subconscious prompt: instant aristocracy. The improving of estates was Humphry's scam; nothing could be more picturesque than an old madhouse. Repton Park is Crest Nicholson's *Northanger Abbey*, pastiche Gothic: spooks, incestuous bondings, mad monks, secret passages recalibrated as pretty parkland. Prestige and seclusion. In skips outside the gates of Claybury, men in yellow hard hats were burning the hospital records.

Repton kept his own work notes in 'red books', which always featured watercolour sketches showing the estates he had redesigned in 'before' and 'after' condition. Crest Nicholson favour the tactful dissolve: the tower remains, minatory blocks morph into detached villas, lawns and cricket squares are tidied up.

Crest Nicholson are working their way around the loop on a '35 minutes from Liverpool Street' arc. Claybury, Warley Hospital in Brentwood (aka Clements Park), Shenley. What they like is the floating colony, the space station landscaped by Humphry Repton or Lancelot Brown. A stylish no-place that is everyplace. No attachment to the local, an easy commute to the centre. The ideal Crest Homes estate defies history and computer-enhances geography.

'It is not on the way to anywhere and is a real enclave,' said Sarah Jones, sales and marketing director. 'You drive off the main road and down a spine road before reaching the entrance gates. There is a real sense of arrival.' A sense not shared, not in that way, by the displaced of Whitechapel. Without a trace of irony, property journalist David Spittles puffs Repton Park as 'one of the most sought-after addresses in the South-East'.

As for the ecosystem, developer and hospital planner have much in common. Crest's 'masterplan' is to create 'a total living environment'. An independent community with chapel, recreation hall, gymnasium, swimming pool, park – alongside 'the original Victorian water tower and cricket pitch'. The only difference is the quality of the silence: by day, the Crest Homes estate is deserted (no sign of children); you feel the eyes tracking you, the soft hum of surveillance cameras. The silence of the asylum was the silence of repression. Language interdicted. To speak was to confess.

Evening in Harperbury is a sombre business. The status of the hospital is unresolved. It feels very much as if those who have been released from their confinement are about to make a down-payment on a more sophisticated version of the very thing from which they have taken hundreds of years to escape. Now there will be a public/private partnership: they must pay for their own prison. The only healing passage is the motorway fugue, the journey between this nowhere and the place of business. The road is the relieving dream.

Walking under the M1 and on to Chequers Lane carried us east towards Abbots Langley. And Renchi's car. Somehow, even though it looked simple when scrutinising the map under a light-pole, we became disorientated. The virus was getting to us; worse than the ulcers and terminal sniffles of foot-and-mouth, the memory haemorrhages of the Shenley Ridge hospital trail. We avoided footpaths and stuck to the road, dazzled by headlights.

We were spinning, blindfolded, around a Foucault wasteland, a bell jar of ill-defined territory caught between the north/south pull of the M1 and the curve of the M25, as it turned towards Heathrow and the Thames. We felt the presence of water, the River Gade and the Grand Union Canal (ahead of us), and the Colne (which we had left behind). We were entering the gravitation field of Watford. That might have been the source of our directional difficulties: I couldn't convince myself that Watford belonged *inside* the M25. It was too exotic for that: the family-friendly football club with the Italian millionaire manager, the multimillionaire figurehead, sparkly pub pianist Elton John (the former Reg Dwight). Watford was the testing ground for the multi-storey car park. In fact, Watford was to car parks what Chartres was to cathedrals. Watford's automobile stacking experiments had an advocate as obsessed with their strange beauty as Monet had been with the light-filled windows of the great French cathedral.

J.G. Ballard came to Watford to make a television document-ary called *Crash!* which preceded his notorious auto(mobile)-erotic novel by two years. 'There are an enormous number of multi-storey car parks in Watford,' he told me when I inter-viewed him for a book on the Cronenberg film of his 1973 novel. 'It's the Mecca of the multi-storey car park. And they're quite ornate, some of them. They played a special role in *The*

Atrocity Exhibition. They were iconic structures. I was interested in the gauge of the psychoarchitectonics. The multi-storey car park and its canted floors, as a depository for cars, seemed to let one into a new dimension. They obviously decided to beautify these structures. They covered them in strange trellises. It was a *bizarre* time.'

Picturing Ballard's haunted concrete temples, I brooded on why they made me uncomfortable. It doesn't matter how high you climb, how many tight bends you sweat around, how narrowly you avoid leaving paintwork on a pillar, the trip to the top deck of a multi-storey car park is a voyage under-ground. Space-time is reversed. There's no sound like the trapped screech of anxiously cornering tyres. They reverberate even when there is no vehicle on the ramp. The secret interiors of these post-human fortresses solicit conspiracy, acts of sexual transgression. Illicit exchanges between dealers. Movement fuzzes on the monitor, drivers swim from their vehicles.

I used to meet a publishers' rep in a car park in Watford, when he wanted to sell proof copies and other promotional gimmicks that would never reach the bookshops. Watford was the perfect location; obscure but not quite inconvenient for London or the garden city satellites. I drove there often, with-out really knowing where it was. The route wasn't worth com-mitting to memory. Ballard, describing a multi-storey car park in *The Atrocity Exhibition*, enthused over 'inclined floors . . . forever meeting the events of time and space at an invisible angle'.

That's what was throwing us, we weren't in a car. Watford only made sense if you drove. The rest of the ground, captured in a bell jar, was being squeezed of air. We couldn't take de-cisions, so our best option was to walk faster. In the twilight, by full-beam headlights, you couldn't tell a Theological College from a Rehabilitation Centre. From a terminated asylum.

The novelists of the early Sixties got it right with their titles. Sylvia Plath's *The Bell Jar*, published in 1963, activates a metaphor that describes not only the airlessness of the 'queer, sultry summer, the summer they electrocuted the Rosenbergs', but also the landscape in which an asylum should be located.

'The air of the bell jar wadded around me and I couldn't stir.' *Wadded* is spot-on for the top left corner of the M25 circuit; punchdrunk, throat choked with feathers. The neurosis is in the weather, alternately speedy and sluggish micro-climates. Fast roads, slow rivers; traffic grudging to a halt. Fingers drumming on wheels. Harassed women who light up the first cigarette of the day, before checking their lipstick. The comfort-dummy of the cellphone.

Plath's novel, originally published under the pseudonym 'Victoria Lucas', was reissued by Faber in 1966, with a spiral cover illustration that looked as if it had been lifted by Bridget Riley from the credits of Hitchcock's *Spellbound*. The intended effect, I presume, was to gaze into or out of (according to temperament) a bell jar. Concentric black lines refocusing, forming hallucinatory Maltese cross patterns, left the viewer nauseous and shaky.

A fiction that in many ways anticipated *The Bell Jar* – sensitive, high-achieving young woman cracking up, retreating to an institution that is of course more eccentric, more difficult than the outside world – appeared in 1961. And again the title could be interpreted as referring to territory on the fold of the map: Jennifer Dawson's *The Ha-Ha*. Dawson's metaphor of the moat or ditch (to keep out animals or imprison inmates) was expressed in heritaged, country house language. Archaic (if charming) terminology for the corner into which we were digging ourselves.

A turn in the road, a gateway, a set of buildings, an arrangement of trees that seemed almost familiar: morning impressions compared with the evening return. The discovery of an arranged meeting place, early in the day, coming in from the motorway, is a very different thing to our arrival after a day's walk. In walking, Potters Bar connects with Abbots Langley (lost apostrophes, both); we have followed a preordained narrative and not skipped from first sentence to conclusion.

Without Renchi's white car (I only do cars by their colour), I wouldn't have known that this was the hospital where we had parked. The buildings have an uncomfortable Victorian look – grass you can't walk, regimented flower beds, gymnasium that doubles as chapel: uniform design for hospital, barracks, Borstal, public school.

At Leavesden Hospital, unauthored depression vectors the clammy ground. Abbots Langley (bestowed by Edward the Confessor upon the abbot of St Albans) was always sequestered territory: the pastoral care of the church devolving to apparently enlightened provisions of the state. By removing incapacitated and antisocial elements from the city and exposing them (in 'airing courts') to country breezes, it was fondly supposed that troubled memories would fade, useful skills could be acquired.

'The country, by the gentleness and variety of its landscapes,' Foucault wrote, 'wins melancholics from their single obsession "by taking them away from the places that might revive the memory of their sufferings".' The country, or this remnant of it, was therefore a kind of amnesia, and the asylum a place of forgetting. Urban loci – churches, pubs, markets – were always provokers of pain. The narrative burden of the generations was overwhelming. Out here on the motorway rim there were no memories. Nothing had happened. All accounts of incarceration, all voyages towards recovery, begin with that journey: the cart, the ambulance, the distance between home and the walled nowhere.

Colne & Green Way

Abbots Langley to Staines

1

8 February 1999. Meeting at the railway station at Denham (Renchi has vague memories of having edited a film here, the beginning and end of his career in art house cinema), we ticket one car and drive the other back; a short, liberating burst of M25 motorway. To Abbots Langley. And the Leavesden Hospital.

It's early enough to experience the sense of motoring-as-freedom, the open road, that Abercrombie and the other visionaries of the *County of London Plan* espoused. They saw: city centres with monumental civic buildings surrounded by rubble; then suburbs, garden satellites, to be reached by an interlinked series of parkland drives. We were skimming around the lip of a dish, climbing through lightly wooded countryside, sleepy villages, the fantasy England of J. Arthur Rank and his film studios. This excessively domesticated landscape had never recovered from its exploitation in hundreds of undistinguished films. It sulked about its status as generic woodland: highwaymen, beauty-spot ladies with scooped necklines, farcical campers, middle-aged medical students whooping it up. Dirk Bogarde, Leslie Phillips, Diana Dors, Joan Collins, Kenneth More, the Mills family, Virginia McKenna, Dickie Attenborough.

Back at Leavesden Hospital in Abbots Langley, there were signs that the developers were moving in. We could still park undisturbed in the grounds, but that wouldn't last. Since our last visit I'd read up on the history of this estate; I'd looked at maps and plans, drawings by the original architects John Giles and Biven of Craven Street, London – who produced the successful application in March 1868. Giles delivered a layout of separated (and segregated) units, an E tipped on its back, with a single extended building as its spine. The E is not only the code-breakers' friend, the commonest letter in any document, it is also the most common element in the architecture of social containment. Around the motorway there are numerous E-shaped blocks, scoring madness. Sounding, when pronounced, like a cackle of mocking laughter: 'E-e-e-e-e.'

Leavesden was set up to deal with rigorously enforced categories of incapacity: the mentally handicapped, imbeciles (who couldn't look after themselves), and idiots who were deemed to be 'deeply defective'. The hospital was organised around rules laid down in the 1845 Act 'for the Regulation and Care and Treatment of Lunatics'.

Curved paths and tactful plantings disguise the nature and extent of the hospital colony. We are parked on the drive, near the entrance gates. Visitors would see a chapel, an administrative building with a clocktower, the darker blocks with their narrow 'airing courts' would be hidden.

London was divided, as if by a rope stretched from Poplar to Paddington. Those who lived south of that line, if they were thought to be in need of care and treatment, were removed to Caterham in Surrey, to St Lawrence's Hospital. Those who lived to the north of the Poplar/Paddington line were dispatched to Leavesden.

The notions of the Victorian committee men who drew up the rules for the treatment of lunatics (and the designs for the hospitals that would hold them) were very much like the projections of present developers. Hospital estates should be 'not less than twenty acres in extent'. Hospitals should be sited 'within a radius of twenty miles of Charing Cross'. But twenty miles was often too far for friends and families of the Leavesden inmates. One visit a month was permitted, but rarely taken up.

The 'quiet and harmless' imbecile who could be trained to undertake simple tasks was the ideal. Women were put to the picking and coiling of hair. Their bed linen was made by patients at Colney Hatch (later Friern Barnet, later still another development site). Mats and baskets were woven by prisoners in Coldbath Fields, Clerkenwell. Clothing was coarse. It was taken away at night, locked in another room, to be re-sorted and claimed the next morning: a cumbersome proceeding that resulted in garments going missing or finishing on inmates of a different shape and size. Men slept in their work shirts. Women were given Turkish baths, to counter the 'biliousness' conse-quent upon poor diet, lack of exercise.

When there is only the Italianate water tower left, the coldness of the water, drawn up through chalk or clay or sand, seeps like a shadow across the tame lawns. Water was always a hinge for magicians, a means of switching modes of conscious-ness. Water was universal memory. The hospitals belonged to water, to underground reservoirs. Water for treatment. Water for hygiene. Water for sanitation. It wasn't until the 1920s that patients at Leavesden were, if they earned the privilege, allowed to use toilet paper rather than cut-up squares of railway timetables.

Patients were watchers, never participants. They watched the staff play cricket. They moved about the grounds on lines of tolerance, keeping off the grass, forbidden to wander. They were rounded up for weekly dances. They attended film pre-sentations in the early days of cinema – until the projector was banished as a fire risk. They witnessed films that were juddery snatches of reality; a train coming into a station, a hosepipe on a lawn. They saw frantic comedies that parodied their own convulsive movements. The films were silent. There was no musical accompaniment. They were marched into concert parties performed by the staff. That was the world of the hospital: warder and patient, subject and object, performer and milk-eyed witness. Patients were encouraged to achieve the Buddhist sense of clinging to nothing, disembodiment, no desires: strange ceremonies were put before them but they must react without excitement or hysteria. Their days were slow circuits of obedience, repetitive tasks, brief exposure to the weather. Leavesden was a monastery policed by non-initiates, uniformed citizens who must make their own entertainment – sport, music, theatre – like colonialists in a distant outpost of Empire.

In 1884 the Medical Superintendent, Dr Case, decreed that 'the use of tobacco was absolutely necessary in the treatment of the insane'. Smoking was encouraged. Clay pipes were issued. After 1905, wooden pipes were permitted. Smoke soothed. The fiddly rituals of the smoker gave a shape to the day. Tobacco was a form of shamanic magic. The sweat lodge of the Turkish bath. Blue smoke curling upwards in the long wards. An interior fug that made them nostalgic for London's autumnal peasoupers.

The hospital accurately reflected society. By 1913 new categories of infirmity were recognised as suitable grounds for certification. The 'feeble-minded' (any nuisance, drunk, women suffering post-natal depression) could be banished to Leavesden or Caterham. 'Moral imbeciles' were also rounded up in a programme of culling that would eugenically cleanse the national blood stock. Anti-social behaviour – inappropriate pregnancies, adultery, radicalism, riot – could see the offender put away, signed for by GP, magistrate, or their own disaffected relatives.

In time, libertarian theories were introduced. Patients worked on a farm – until that was sold for development. The piggery lasted until 1973, when it was deemed to be no longer commercial. 'Harmless' inmates were taken, in a long crocodile, for walks into the local countryside. They went to Bedmond by way of East Lane, past the home farm and the burial ground. East Lane was thought to be relatively free of traffic. There was one obvious drawback to the continuance of that walk. Leavesden and Bedmond are on different sides of the M25. East Lane tunnels under the motorway.

More enlightened attitudes prevailed. Inspections identified mismanagement, the cruelties that are always found in closed systems. Smaller units replaced the huge wards. Old people were given some dignity by exchanges with younger children, in which they became surrogate grandparents. Names replaced numbers on the dormitories. The sexes were allowed a measure of free association. The number of patients fell.

Leavesden, in the Thatcherite Eighties, had to be put on a proper business footing. Management consultants arrived. The NHS was under pressure to realise its principal asset, land. New Labour redefined Tory asset-stripping as a kind of mysterious life-enhancing policy that was too complex, too sensitive, to be revealed to the voters. Victorian hulks didn't belong in the green belt. Best Value. There were skirmishes over planning permission at Napsbury, but the directive stood: sell to the highest bidder. A measure of heritage would be retained, water towers, cricket pitches. Turn expediency into a boast: we will set the last inmates free. If there is no society, how can there be any social inadequates? Let them take up residence in Watford hostels.

But the citizens of the motorway corridor don't like that word, hostel. Hostel hisses. Hostel suggests hospital, hospice. Dying rooms, cancer clubs. Hostel speaks of charity, pilgrims. Asylum seekers. Benefit scroungers. Watford, with its street of hostels, could become another Margate, another King's Cross. Junkies without proper medication. Thieves. Bandits. Tarts. Gyppos. Loonies.

Foucault understands very well how a place that 'was formerly a visible fortress of order has now become the castle of our conscience'. The fugue, the search for a site of redemption, can very easily turn into a counter-pilgrimage. Madmen find themselves confined alongside the holy relics which they have travelled so far to honour. When the shrine is converted into a ward, the mad traveller (according to Foucault's interpretation) will be classified as just another 'ritual exile'. He doesn't belong to city or countryside: that is his curse and his privilege, to be always moving, to be at home nowhere and everywhere.

The sky was a miracle of pink, stippled over the early blue. Renchi was stocking-capped against the strong diagonals of the cloud streets. A placard on the hospital wall: DEVELOPMENT OPPORTUNITY/FOR SALE/ALL ENQUIRIES/WEATHERALL/ GREENE & SMITH.

Glints from bowed windows, net curtains. The occasional electric milk float. Nothing else moving around the streets of Abbots Langley, as we make our way towards the conjunction of the River Gade and the Grand Union Canal. River systems nudging out from Chiltern chalk towards the Thames.

There is a residual strangeness in these aborted villages; settlements are unsettled, restless, dozing alongside the muffled millrace of the motorway. The original layout of streets, around the manor house and the church of St Lawrence, has been warped to accommodate hospital colonies, their farms, the Leavesden Aerodrome. The North Orbital Road drags everything towards the hungry M-numbers, M25 and M1. Watford is ballast to the south.

Even the speculative builders are confused. Should they run up identical units, pebbledash kennels that grow in the night like serpents' teeth? Or should they go for that post-Voysey, Arts and Crafts look? Gabled, mock-beamed, doors decorated with stained glass sunsets? Hedges, shrubs, evergreens. These avenues don't smell like Hackney. Without the shops, fast food outlets, cigarette packets chucked out of cars, cartons and wrappings and newspapers, claim forms and parking tickets, final demands and chewing gum, paving slabs are free of the soft, bright mulch of the city. They don't rock when you put your weight on them. No sparkling puddles of glass punched out of bus stops, crystals from trashed windscreens. No vomit skids, no steaming canine excreta. Out here cars sit serenely on wide pavements, each in its own space – within meticulously observed demarcation lines. Gallows Hill Lane is like a funeral procession held at traffic lights that will never change.

One car is obviously a collector's piece. It's white, but nothing like the white of Renchi's well-used vehicle. The white of aspiration, of burnt-out film frames. It would never make it around the tight spirals of a Watford multi-storey car park. It's long and low and lean, with fins and exoskeletal ribs; fat, white-wall tyres, girder-sized bumpers, tinted windows, banks of rear lights like a Spielberg spaceship. Lefthand drive. The lightning-flash trim is supposed to suggest that, even parked on a pavement in a deadbeat suburb, this mother is flying. A gas-guzzling, highway-devouring passion wagon. Head-on, the blunt bonnet with its sharks' fin decorations, chrome-nipples, pseudo propellers on front bumpers, predatory radiator grille, is pure bombast. The Detroit recipe: carved fat, metal on steroids. But this is nothing more than a trophy, going nowhere, wheels sunk into grooves on the pavement. An anachronistic art work with its nose pointing at a motorway it will never ride.

Access to the canal is easy, we're on a footpath that will take us south, back to Denham; we're walking a line that's parallel with the M25 – but we're separated by the soft tissue of golf courses, woods and fields. We might have been tempted, later in the day, to make a detour for Merlin's Wood and Merlin's Spring, but we prefer just now to push on, in the general direction of Watford and breakfast.

The canal path is perfectly pleasant, still water reflecting a brightening sky; a shaggy rim of winter trees, smoke climbing straight from the thin chimneys of moored narrow boats. The walk becomes a stroll. We're never entirely comfortable about travelling through territory that is happy to have our company. (Blairite motto: *Everything that is not forbidden is compulsory*.)

The Grand Union Canal is no longer a commercial artery, working water. It's deeper into its transformation than the Lee Valley Navigation. The spectre of quango-approved recreation, leisure lakes, hangs over us. We can smell bacon fizzing in the pan. A crisp morning with a taste of snow in the air.

The Gade ox-bows with the canal; if we're given a choice, we take the river. In its day, the Grand Union was a wonder, eight canals connected in a network that linked Birmingham with Nottingham, Oxford and London. Wide locks were built to take seventy-ton barges.

The bridges are a feature. They're numbered. We're at 162 and climbing. The Earl of Essex, who graciously allowed the Grand Junction Canal Company to cut a navigation through his park, commissioned an ornamental stone bridge to ameliorate the vulgarity of the venture. By designing an elegantly minimalist structure, with stone balustrades, heraldic capstone, symmetrical foot tunnels, he turned the canal into a pond, Palladian whimsy, a Chatsworth or Stowe of the (future) motorway fringe.

Before we reach this minor architectural feature, there are lesser spans to negotiate, bridges that have been customised to come into line with the prevailing post-hippie ethos of the narrow boats. Woodsmoke and the herb. Bright flowers in painted mugs. Bicycles. They haven't cycled off to fetch the milk, but they've fired the day's first spliff. These psychedelic barges are Notting Hill squats, batik-draped tents, Hendrix hutches of thirty years ago, now migrated (in my cultural tectonic plate theory) ten or twelves miles along the canal to the west. The stretch of water, from Watford to Uxbridge, is a floating Ladbroke Grove, a flooded Westbourne Park Road. They leave their boots out on deck. They have cats and books and guitars. They turn the arches of the nearest bridge into a Westway; extravagant murals of crows, purple seas and a black ship of fools. I LIVE HERE scrawled in chalk over a scarlet beach.

The canal is an interloper in what was once a landscape of private parks, perched on a synclinal basin of chalk strata. The evidence of country mansions, captured and downgraded, is visible on all sides. Pheasant woods and copses with their well-tended roads, their gates and surveillance systems. The Grand Union Canal was a Faustian contract, which allowed ruffians into the garden. Locks for road tolls, riverside pubs for service stations. Industrial cargoes on the move, without much noise, without devastating fossil fuel reserves. Between the Midlands and London. Cassiobury Park on the outskirts of Watford, with its golf course, bowling green, paddling pool and watercress beds, was once part of the Earl of Essex's estate.

The Navigation was a conduit for runaways, disappearances, the adoption of new identities. Alongside one of the bridges, a notice in a plastic envelope has been pinned to the wall: MISS- ING. We're used to pet solicitation, pen portraits of dogs and cats. Snapshots taped to trees in parks and suburbs. Rewards offered. This is different. 'Man aged 57, silver-grey short wavy hair, slightly built 5ft 5in tall, last seen in Gadebridge (Hemel Hempstead) 9:30 am Tues 26th January 1999.'

The head of the man, smiling, has been cut from another photograph and enlarged. White, open-neck shirt. A segment of striped sofa, a wallpaper border of roses. The smile is hesitant. What's the occasion? Who took the photograph? Who *kept* it? Is this a working man or a member of the middle classes relax- ing at the weekend? He's clean-shaven. The hair is short, care- lessly chopped. The visible right ear is a flesh oyster, a boxer's ear. The jaw's firm, there are no teeth on show. The nose might once have been broken. But somebody is still looking for this unnamed man who was last seen in Gadebridge.

Canals, creeping out of town by the dimmest and dirtiest ways, brought harm into the countryside. Canals were places of suicide. They were convenient for the disposal of bodies. The literary trajectory runs from Dickens to Alex Trocchi and the Northern working-class novelists of the Sixties – who favoured the urban Gothic of dying industries and wild nature, aban- doned paths and gloomy basins. In *Our Mutual Friend* Dickens uses the canal system as a clogged drain, silted with recrimina- tion, self-lacerating guilt and fantasies of revenge. Walkers hustle beside dark water, pursued by ghosts and whispering demons.

Bradley walked out of the Lock-house. Catching up from the table a piece of bread, and taking his Bargeman's bundle under his arm, Riderhood immediately followed him. Bradley turned towards London. Riderhood caught him up, and walked at his side. The two men trudged on, side by side, in silence, full three miles. Suddenly, Bradley turned to retrace his course. Instantly Riderhood turned likewise, and they went back side by side.

And so on.

After an hour or more, Bradley abruptly got up again, and again went out, but this time turned the other way. Riderhood was close after him, caught him up in a few paces, and walked at his side.

The bitter schoolteacher, Bradley Headstone, and the bounty-hunting riverman, the fisher of bodies, who doubles as a Lock-keeper. They walk their fugues: stop, turn, retreat, begin again. Until they plunge together into the weir, Riderhood gripped by Headstone: 'girdled still with Bradley's iron ring, and the rivets of the iron ring held tight'.

Watford, though I've never thought of it that way, is a place of water, the River Colne closing on the Gade, the sweep of the Grand Union Canal; there are basins and barges and docks that facilitate waterborne traffic. Road signs direct us towards the promise of a necklace of 'Springs'. Watford is Hertfordshire's biggest town, a hilltop settlement known for its breweries and printing works. Or that's what the brochure would have you believe. Our impressions, coming in on foot, are less focused.

There are no shops, no cafés. A Tesco megastore dominates the canal, exploiting water as a picturesque backdrop, rather than a way of transporting potential customers. A spray-bandit has revised the British Waterways sign that forbids swimming ('danger of contracting waterborne disease'): ANGER for DANGER. A Nottingham narrow boat offering TAROT readings is moored alongside the railway bridge.

We decide that it is time to come away from the canal, to head into Watford in search of breakfast. We tramp, obediently, towards the 'centre' of a town that has no centre, just a collision of random bits and pieces representing different eras, abandoned speculations. Renchi returned a few weeks later to a house in a quiet Watford street. He attended a Hindu fire-ceremony. Fire and water. Music. Candles and food. A welcome for this stranger.

When it seems as if the road we are walking will never be anything but a featureless stretch of low-energy commerce, linked by roundabouts, we spot a Grimms' Fairy Tale cottage, a misplaced quotation. The frontage is an exercise in marquetry that has got seriously out of hand: rectangular panels assembled from sawn logs. A sharp gable. Leaded windows, red tiles, Jacobean chimneys and cluster of TV aerials. There's no explanation for this oddity, a forester's retreat (from the time of the Earl of Essex).

Our situation improves, a side street (burst rubbish bags, threadless tyres, prams, shoes, mattresses) skews towards a container park: a zone of hauliers, mud, spare parts and rogue apostrophes. Good to see the Christian name of Dickens's drowned schoolteacher: BRADLEY. SKIP HIRE, WASTE DISPOSAL.

Find a razorwire fence, gold-on-red signs, contradictory arrows, outdated phone numbers, and you'll find a proper breakfast. MUNCHIES CAFE (steaming cup logo), OPEN 7AM—4AM.

Some of the best British conspiracies were hatched here, in greasy caffs; men with coloured cellphones, anorak over pinstripe, elbows on red Formica. Andrew Morton's ghosted biography of Diana, republican propaganda, was chopped and stirred and cooked from tape-recordings made with Diana's deepthroat go-between in a workmen's café in Ruislip (convenient for the M40, Junction 16 of the M25, and our car park at Denham).

You don't have to be an Aboriginal to track MUNCHIES by its teasing, wafting bacon trail. Deep-fried pig overrules diesel and rubber, chemical spills. The gated Portakabin fortress is a place where you pay cash money to get rid of things. Cities need covert dumps where ex-motors are cannibalised, chained dogs hurl themselves against chainlink fences. Watford, protected by its towers of parked cars (the M25's equivalent of those sea forts at the mouth of the Thames Estuary), took care of a measure of London's off-highway business; it acted as a buffer between the capital and rude territories to the north. All-Day Breakfast shacks on dirt paddocks where unwanted and unsightly rubbish can be disposed of, crushed, buried.

R.J. & H. HAULAGE LTD., SPECIALISTS IN SKIP HIRE AND ALL TYPES OF WASTE DISPOSAL will facilitate any little difficulties in the general area of removal, disappearance, eradication of material that has served its time. Obsolete consumer durables are not really so durable after all. R.J. & H. HAULAGE can see you right for 'soft and sharp sand, ballast, peashingle, hardcore, crazy paving, crushed concrete'. They are happy to engage in post-industrial collaging: they smash, trample, piledrive, squeeze, stretch, tear, hack, chop and jack-hammer anything you want to bung in a skip. They're inventive. Alchemists of the scrap yard. Shape-shifters. Streets fold into their bright yellow receptacles to re-emerge as jigsawed garden walkways, toxic rubble on which you can lay mile after mile of tarmac.

Our breakfast, in the *Mad Max* kingdom of these war lords of waste, is a treat. A caravan, an awning, white plastic tables. Strip-lighting on the strobe. A large lady with big gold rings in her ears. And a face as featureless as a satellite dish. Eggs in their dozens, ready to break into the pan. Pink and yellow notices

with handwritten specialities of the house: TOASTED SAND-
WICH VARIOUS FILLING FROM £1.50. In France this vehicle
would have appeared in half a dozen movies. In California it
would (as a replica) have its own gag-a-minute TV series.

We swill our mugs of near-coffee, lick our plates and con-
gratulate ourselves on being somewhere we'll never find again;
a morning epiphany among stacked containers, long sheds. The
best of England: close to a canal path, close to allotments, close
to a football stadium, faces deep into a (£2.50) 'big breakfast' in
a culture that only does breakfasts. On a circuit where, all too
often, microwave pubs won't serve you after 2 p.m. and can't
offer anything more appetising than saltlick potato shavings
dipped in mouth-numbing additives.

Soft rain patters on the plastic awning. We're inside and
outside at the same time. In town and hidden away. Tinned
tomatoes bloody Renchi's mouth as he articulates the anxiety
we share: we're pulling too far from the motorway. Like the
Colne, we need to move west.

After Batchworth, the Colne stays outside the Grand Union
Canal, wandering south through industrial estates and sewage
farms towards a scatter of small lakes. Using the Colne, we
re-establish contact with the road. But nothing is happening
up there, a sluggish section where traffic snarls towards the
mess that lies ahead, the M40, the M4 and Heathrow. Solitary
drivers are hunched into themselves, coming down from the
buzz. Tapping like speed-freaks. Waiting for the horror.

The Munchies caravan sets us up for the next section of the
canal. A yellow morning, quite cold. Evergreens and alders
reflected on the canal's glassy surface. Narrow boats are moored,
nose-to-tail, streetwise, downwardly immobile. They're moving at about the same speed as the lines of cars on the motorway – which is to say, they move as the earth moves. They
are where they are and they know where they are. They stick
and they drift. This is the last vestige of the old hippie dream:

self-sufficiency (of a sort), a stove, a bicycle, dope. Living on water, you connect with water. And water things. Dreams. Clouds above and below. The long thin boats are like beds with lids. Removed from their original, cargo-shifting purpose, aligned on a north/south axis, they are freed from orbital madness, the clusters and roundabouts of fear and confusion that make up the scattered outstations of London.

On the M25, fixed in their lanes, trying to make sense of flashing overhead signs and warnings, smoking, finger-drumming, jumping radio bands, jabbering into cellphones, the motorists are out of time, out of place. Between Junctions 16 and 17, there is nothing on the map, nothing on the ground. A frosted whiteness. Refuse tips, gravel pits – if you want them. If you know they're here. The orbital motorway, on its western flank, in the long morning rush hour, is where claustrophobia and agoraphobia are indistinguishable. Tensed travellers, sweating in their metal pods, discover the inside of the outside. Nerves are stretched. Memories of the miles they've driven, to arrive at this compulsory stasis, melt into exhaust fumes.

Renchi and I return to our discussion of the figures who took up residence just beyond the circuit of the motorway: culture heroes pinned to the wall by centrifugal forces. It happened before the M25 was imagined, let alone constructed. Blind John Milton in Chalfont St Giles, escaping the plague, composing *Paradise Lost*. Bill Drummond, near Aylesbury, forever brooding on a move to the city, shuttling between writerly retreat and urban conspiracies; looking for an excuse to get out on the road for another conceptual/missionary journey. Roald Dahl in his garden shed at Great Missenden, board across knees, fan-heater going full tilt, as he cranks out another juvenile revenge saga. Russian roulette fantasies from Graham Greene, the head-master's son in Berkhamsted.

I proposed Arthur Machen, the ultimate city wanderer and fabulist, who retired to the contented obscurity of Amersham.

'Machen, as an artist, had many deficiencies,' wrote Wesley

D. Sweetser, 'not least of which was his psychological obsession to write on every possible occasion.' That, unfortunately, is the nature of the contract. Amersham is as good a place as any other (as good as Lawrence, Kansas) to try to forget the signature in blood. The long wait for that knock on the door. The smiling stranger in black.

Judging by the names of the narrow boats, I'm sure we could have tapped at portholes and come up with a suitcase of Machen paperbacks. ARCTURUS. SORCERESS. VISCOUNT SASCHA, INTERNATIONAL PHYSIOTHERAPIST (BY SPECIAL APPOINTMENT TO THE PRESIDENT OF THE USA). Really? Which one? Kennedy's spine? Nixon's retracted turtleneck and hunched shoulders? Clinton's cigar? Sascha's barge is five or six miles from Heathrow, and next to nothing from Northolt, the military aerodrome where royals and celebs fly in. I'll buy it: the vision of Slick Willie rocking the boat, while the Viscount dances along his backbone.

As we leave Watford, communes of narrow boats give way to solitary pirate craft, hulks. The sort of cheerful but slightly squalid domesticity that Machen cultivated in Amersham. Nautical rubbish, sheets of polythene, black bags spread on the bank. Use one of the tyres hung around the gunnel as potential life-preservers and you'll sink like a stone. This isn't a boat, it's a kennel nailed to a dismasted fishing smack: all deficiencies covered with green tarpaulin. There's a second, peeling Dunkirk veteran with odd-sized windows, which looks as if it's held together with gaffa tape and unfounded optimism. Somebody started to daub the wheelhouse with a can or two of knocked-off battleship-grey. Inspiration ran out with the paint. Which has started to devour the wood. The vessel is low in the water, but still afloat. As a precaution, the skipper has shifted his household goods on to the towpath: a red, simulated-leather armchair, a duvet, overcoats and pyjamas, a disconnected deepfreeze unit filled with melting TV dinners, roadkill and industrial-strength lager.

The Colne has been our companion over a good stretch of country. We've followed it south from its adolescence among the hospital colonies. The river's name connects with the harshest of asylums, Colney Hatch. Nut hatch. Booby hatch. Freak farm.

Too much towpath walking was depressing us, we decided to leave the Grand Union and to climb the slope to Harefield. After our tour of the Crest Homes, we were ready for a hospital that was still operative. A hacksaw and catgut operation. The perfect place for a change of heart. We fancied paying our respects to Magdi Yacoub and the Eric Morecambe Department of Cardiology. The metaphor was right: we panted uphill, thirsting for transfusions of the imagination. A fresh start.

2

The ascent of Mountain Pleasant: neat, detached houses, humped road unspooling like a roll of grey felt. Nobody. Nothing. Not a car. Renchi slumps on a bench in Harefield village to attend to his feet. A sharp-sided obelisk alongside a duck pond, a memory needle. The date '1914', the faded names. This is a village that is still a village. Formula patented in popular fiction: Enid Blyton, Richmal Crompton, P.G. Wodehouse, Agatha Christie. The exportable paradigm of a fantasy England (copyright acquired by offshore asset strippers). A strategic site above a river valley; crossroads, chapel, choice of pubs for different political or religious factions. A green, a pond. The big house that became Harefield Hospital.

There is still a post office, a shop where Renchi buys plasters for his blistered toes. Red brick, slate, well-maintained pointing. The King's Arms (beer supplied by Benskins of Watford) is multicultural, multitemporal: Tudor beams, cod-Georgian lamps, Chelsea hanging baskets (sophisticated displays of spiky red grasses, winter pansies). Real Ales and Fine Ales. Curry Night every Tuesday. Where there might once have been a wooden signpost with distances to other villages, a strip of tin has been wired to a lamp-standard: POLICE, HAREFIELD HOSPITAL. We pick our way along the wooded perimeter of the estate: MEDIPARC.

We're excited about finding a hospital that is still in business. After struggling through the Thatcher and neo-Thatcher (Blair Which) years, Harefield is under pressure to 'utilise' its potential by selling off land acquired at the time of the Great War from an Australian benefactor, Charles Arthur Moresby Billyard-Leake.

History, at this altitude, plays as a sequence of rapid dissolves. Ivy-covered Edwardian country house with French shutters (billowing canopies, rose garden). Wooden huts filled with Aussie soldiers, the casualties of Gallipoli. Futurist operating theatres in which body parts can be swapped or customised.

ROYAL BROMPTON & HAREFIELD: NHS TRUST. We wander, unchallenged, through the grounds. It is no easy task to rescue the Harefield narrative from the present assembly of buildings. Vehicles in the 'Spaces Reserved For Permit Holders' are not as flashy as the showroom specimens in the IT manors of the motorway fringe. Those cars are part of an employment-and-benefits package, status toys in silver and grey. Silvergrey. A new coinage. There is, at the turn of the Millennium, a colour which is not a colour; a varnish that simulates light-shock. That modifies shape (curve, comma): until the sprayed vehicle becomes an energy parenthesis, a crisply outlined bracket around . . . nothing.

Harefield cars – red, blue, white, GB stickers – belong with the brick frontage; metal-framed, Fifties windows, exposed drainpipes, tight entrance hall. The reception area speaks of benign bureaucracy, the Welfare State. This building would be comfortable anywhere in the western corridor, Western Avenue to Ruislip, Hatfield to Welwyn Garden City. It says: laboratory as office, office as ward. It says: hierarchies of command, paperwork, chitties, storerooms. It says: white coats and brown coats. It says: numbered parking bays, employment for life, team spirit, works outings, cricket. Harefield looks like a film studio from the industrial era, everything on site. A British studio working on cobwebby Gothic (Frankenstein transplants, graverobbers with stage Irish accents, Byronic doctors distinguished by their height).

That's the only choice for British cinema: hospital as low comedy, farts and gropes, or hospital as base for sinister experiments. In Harefield these tendencies came together. Cardiology units were sponsored by TV comics who had themselves

suffered heart attacks. They were also utilised as sets by surviving production companies. The patronage of Sir John Mills
and Eric Morecambe was enhanced by facility fees earned by
the hospital's appearance in *Carry On* films, BBC documentaries; and by Russell Grant 'reliving his childhood' for *Down
Your Way*.

'One never knew,' according to a Harefield surgeon, 'when
a team of actors, cameras and technicians would invade . . . On
one occasion caravans were parked all around the roundabout
outside the front door and even the switchboard was moved
and signs changed.' *Carry On* nurses in 'the highest heels
imaginable' were confused with real workers going about their
duties.

The hospital/studio is a very British fantasy. Authority figures, naughty nurses. Blood fears: contamination, infection by
aliens. Farce and horror. Everything contained within a closed
set: tame countryside, autumn woods fringing the motorway. Our paranoia over the machinations of the Secret State
(silent complicity) can be burlesqued in *Avengers* television. The
journeymen of British cinema can earn a crust by playing out
simplistic ethical dilemmas on authentic stages, found within
a few minutes' drive of the studios. Not for Rank the dark
poetics of Franju; the asylum that is itself the metaphor. Rank
peddled post-Shavian paradox. They wrote (rewrote) scripts
that were like business plans. Then identified a suitable (and
economic) location in which to photograph exteriors that
would validate their fiction.

Director Basil Dearden came to Harefield to make *Life for
Ruth* in 1962. A blood story: the father who won't, on religious
grounds, permit a transfusion for his dying daughter. Patrick
(*The Prisoner*) McGoohan is the doctor and Michael Craig
the fundamentalist father. Otto Heller, who shot *The Ipcress
File*, was DP. Secondhand blood, given up or sold as a Third
World commodity, is the coming theme. Deeper fears surface
only when Harefield followed the Gothic visionaries of Bray

and started to exchange hearts, to use captive animals for quick-fit spare parts.

Later Harefield 'co-productions' would include Bryan Forbes's *The Raging Moon*, in which his wife, Nanette Newman, and the endemically malign Malcolm McDowell 'give rousing performances in a moving tale of love in a home for the handicapped'. Sentimental fables authenticated by a realistic backdrop gave way to dramatised documentaries. Harefield as itself. In 1974 the BBC filmed *Cross Your Heart and Hope to Live*.

Taped to the window of the next building we approach is a handwritten note: DEAR DONORS WE HAVE CLOSED. THANK YOU. Closed? Like a Mare Street kebab house, where Euro-approximate spelling turns 'doner' into 'donor'. The notice conjures up grotesque images: *Carry On* clowns – Bernard Bresslaw, Kenneth Connor, Charles Hawtrey, Jack Douglas – standing in line, lumps of dripping meat in their hands, hearts, lights, liver. I saw a performance of ghost dancers, white nudes, male and female figures plastered in kaolin, walking through the exhibits in the Victoria and Albert Museum. I fantasised the statues of Harefield, white gods and goddesses painted like a butcher's chart, searching for someone to accept their posthumous donations. Hearts beating in closed fists.

Our tour of the grounds discloses a mansion, stable blocks, gardens that would once have belonged to leisured gentry; huts, sheds, bungalows that could have been transported from an outback cattle station. A heliport. A Buckminster Fuller structure, a pyramid, mysteriously known as the 'Playdrome'. Another colony has grown up in the grounds of a private park, committee-inspired geometry imposed on a lazy English landscape. Thanks to its history, the direct transition from family home to wartime hospital, Harefield escaped the Italianate water tower. Because there is nothing to preserve under the heritage label, the enterprise might survive.

There is a building known as 'The Mansion'; it replaced an

older house called Rythes (or Ryes). In 1704 the property which stood in 170 acres of land was sold by John Stanyon to John Cooke, who bought it as part of a marriage settlement for his son George. George Cooke, a lawyer, Knight of the Inner Temple, became Chief Prothonotary of the Court of Common Pleas and Lord of the Manor of Hayes.

It was Cooke who demolished and replaced the old house. The usual programme of improvements, extensions, was initiated: a square building with thirty rooms, a cast-lead roof, columned portico and many, many windows. There was as much glass as plaster, whiteness muted by a veil of creepers. White is a memory colour, the colour of the dead, black's negative. The Mansion passed through the influence of its various patrons, each one revising and amending, until it was bought by the Australian Arthur Billyard-Leake.

The relation of road to estate to village doesn't change. Nineteenth-century maps present the same village green, two pubs (King's Arms and Cricketers), parish church. But Harefield Park changes dramatically; once mansion, stables, coach house were surrounded by woods, farms. There were lakes, streams, mature trees (oak, horse chestnut, a great cedar of Lebanon). Then, decade by decade, trees were felled, parkland was lost to hospital, nurses' home, occupational therapy, laundry, record office. The Mediparc is a J.G. Ballard version of the pastoral. Information brokering, fibre-optic transactions, in place of the acres of enclosed, seigneurial countryside. The more apparently opened up an estate, the fewer its freedoms. Security operatives and surveillance cameras replace bailiffs, gamekeepers and man-traps.

Accounts by local historians speak of Harefield as blessed, one of the earth's bright places. It might be the situation, looking west over the valley of the Colne, but the PR is justified. (We spoke of the name Hare-Field. Of Foucault's ships of fools, hippie narrow boats on the Grand Union Canal. Of how sailors could never use the word 'hare'. It was considered an unlucky thing. An ancient prohibition, unexplained, that came with the craft. Hares and boats didn't mix. Hare was a burrower, a chthonic spirit. Boxer, dancer, trickster. Hare was a companion of witches. His foot was a specific against sorcery. The term 'hare' is hidden in 'heart'. Hare *is* heart, a lunar spirit. Mad in March. Mad with good heart.)

Harefield holds firm to a particular narrative. The back story has not been deleted, but entrusted to one of their own – Mary Shepherd, former senior thoracic surgical registrar at Harefield and Hunterian Professor at the Royal College of Surgeons. Shepherd's *Heart of Harefield (The Story of a Hospital)* is an insider's legend: anecdotal, properly sourced and attributed, humane. Copies of the book, approved history, can be purchased on site.

The Harefield tourist pauses to flick through the illustrations, checking monochrome prints against present reality. This publication, while looking like a National Trust calendar, performs a useful service: it tells patients what they can expect, it grounds them in the privilege of place. The journey to Harefield, knowing that some trauma, insults to the immune system, devastation to body chakras, lies ahead, is a time of stress. Shepherd's narrative prepares future victims, guiding them through the levels of anaesthesia. The expedition to the house on the hill is made in fearful expectation, dread of the consultant's verdict. The trees of the long avenue become obstacles around which mental anchors are cast, slowing the car, postponing this awful moment.

Harefield Park is mapped with pain. Fifty thousand wounded Australians were treated during the First World War. Many are buried in the village church. The soldiers, walking out, visiting pubs, making friends with local children, left a print on the territory. Convalescence is the slow release of pain-memories, the shifting of horror from sand and hot rock to damp English greenery.

Therapeutic rituals are initiated, to reassert normality, life before war, home life. Cricket, always. Cricket on a rough meadow. Photographs of cricket. A nurse, in full uniform, hands spread wide, is behind the wicket. The batsman, in military cap, heavy serge jacket, keeps his eye on the ball. Playing in the Aussie spirit that marries technical correctness with bloody-minded determination, he does his best to move his front foot into line. But it's not possible. He doesn't have a front foot, or leg. It's been amputated, just below the knee. The man in the bush hat, fielding dangerously close in, at – ouch! – short-leg, is watching the bowler, not the batsman. His right arm is in a sling. No worries, mate, they'll stuff any eleven Englishmen. By lunchtime on the third day.

Harefield doctors liked their cricket and weren't too bothered about cars. Cricket was part of the ethos. The Welshman Dr Kenneth Stokes, Medical Director between 1940 and 1959, was quite happy to share his house and his car, a 'plucky little bus', with the Matron, Beatrice Shaw. He relaid the cricket square that the Aussies marked out in the First War and he built a pavilion. Matches were arranged, the team travelling by van, against the Uxbridge Electricity Works and the Chalfonts Epileptic Colony.

After the days of Stokes, Harefield was seen as less of a village, more of a suburb, 'an extension of London'. Sir Thomas Holmes Sellors spoke of the difficulties of a hospital 'built without the city walls'. Nurses, willing to banish themselves to the countryside, were scarce. Relatives and friends of patients found the journey to Harefield long and difficult. Cars were important. Nurses drove to Ruislip to visit cinemas and restaurants. The sense of Harefield as a private estate, protected by the river valley, cushioned by golf courses (Moor Park, Sandy Lodge, Northwood, Haste Hill) and other Mediparcs (Mount Vernon and the Radium Institute Hospital), was threatened. Everything was changed by the coming of the motorway.

The M25 was a blue-grey pulmonary artery; oxygen and nutrients carried to the cells (cars, units of housing). The liberties of the old park were terminated. The wild cats, a free-ranging tribe with about seventy members, were rationalised: inoculated, neutered, hunted. The last cat was shot in 1986.

Now the work force is migratory. 'Everybody has a car.' Cars surround the buildings. Twenty-five acres of the north park have to be sold. The cricket-loving Dr Stokes, who doted on his 'decrepit and bird spattered' Ruby Austin 7, didn't indulge in serious commutes. On 9 July 1959, he took a run down to the village. Sitting in his tin box, he suffered a heart attack and died at the wheel.

Recovering heart patients, where it was appropriate, were encouraged to walk, a few steps across the ward, a tottering excursion to the corridor, before the release into the grounds: until they were clocking up fifteen or twenty miles a week (the winter distance of one of our orbital walks).

We are superstitious about major surgery. The place where it happens, this Aztec ripping of a heart from the cavity of the chest, fills us with dread. I wouldn't say as much to Renchi but the fear clings: they'll keep us, they won't let us out. We'll have to pay, in flesh, for our casual tourism, this unsanctioned stroll around the Tenochtitlán of the Colne Valley.

On a 1542 map, made for the Spanish viceroy Antonio de Mendoza, the city of Tenochtitlán is symbolised by an eagle, wings spread, perched on a cactus. The omen guided the Aztecs to the site of their capital. One of the Harefield photographs I take of Renchi has him standing in front of a building with a one-armed clock. On the roof is an eagle with spread wings. The coach house. The clock never moves, it's a painting.

The eagle was a significant symbol for the first occupant of The Mansion, Sir George Cooke. The 'Eagle Room' was the most important room in the house. If the hare is a lunar creature, the eagle is the sun. In alchemy the eagle is the liberated spirit released from the *prima materia*. Zeus commands an eagle to devour a portion of the liver of Prometheus, the fire thief. Each night the liver renews itself, so that the torment can recommence on the following day. The outline of the myth is well known but we forget the reason for the withdrawal from humanity of the gift of fire: Prometheus tricked the gods when he divided a sacrificed ox. He arranged flesh, entrails, edible matter to one side and left the bones on the other, under a coat of succulent white fat. Prometheus, chained, suffers his punishment for an eternity, until Hercules slays the eagle and sets him free.

Reading about the procedures that took place in Harefield, the technical advances, doesn't help. My heart thumps loudly, standing in for the mechanism of the clock that freezes time. As a metaphor the heart is too assertive; several of the Harefield administrators died, at work, of heart attacks. This is not surprising; the layout of the hospital, with its 'oxygen storage' sheds, its intricate system of paths and walkways, its sealed chambers, becomes a pictogram of the heart. I think of my father and grandfather dying suddenly, out of the blue, when their hearts gave out. At home, in a chair, after a shopping expedition; on the pavement, outside the house, after an uphill walk.

Because we have come here from the canal, with the motorway as our sound-strip, running at the edge of the frame, we see Harefield in terms of the drowned, of roadkill; a deepfreeze waiting for spare parts. Magdi Yacoub is the Egyptian virtuoso. Fate-defying surgical feats extend life beyond all reasonable expectation. Changes of heart. The 'Domino Procedure' during which hearts are shunted, person to person, in a frantic game of pass the parcel. Patients would, under certain circumstances, undergo full heart/lung transplants, even when their hearts were healthy, because combined transplants have proved more successful. The 'spare' heart would then be utilised in a second transplant operation.

In 1987 the first 'triple' (heart/lung/liver) was carried out at Harefield. A heart/lung transplant in 1983 cost around £25,000. Roughly the sum expended in servicing the *empty* Millennium Dome for one day (essential maintenance, security, utility bills, insurance, PR). The dead Dome ticks away, New Labour's tell-tale heart, at £13 a minute, while Harefield fights to stay in the game. Hospitals, it has been declared, must become 'self-governing', part of a Trust within the NHS. They are obliged to provide a service that will attract the right clients, the ones who can pay. Income will then rise and hospitals will have 'the freedom (within limits) to borrow money'.

We don't know it, but this is another of our obituary circuits; Harefield is doomed. The news-spinners waited for 11 September 2001 before making their announcement: the hospital would close, it would be moved into town. Much more convenient. Valuable real estate could be released on to a market desperate for housing. A done deal.

Time whirls in tight vortices: ghosts of the big house, rose garden, sun-dial, are slow to decay; they are overwhelmed by the clamour of the Australian convalescents in their huts, the mortal theatre of transplant surgery. Lost lives. There are tales of patients, during that period when consciousness is lost, when they sink into meat-memory, blood forced around the body, functions taken over by machines; reveries of floating, becoming one with the orbital sunstream, the cars on the road. Rib cages split like broken toast-racks. For a short time there is no heart in the cavity. Arteries are outlined with radio-opaque fluid: a night map of the M25. After coronary artery bypass grafts, the graftee is confused, suffering from double vision, speech and thought out of synch. They've been given the wrong script. When the recovering patient *can* speak, when the tube has been removed from the trachea, he admits that several days have been 'lost'. They've gone. They've entered the ecosphere of the parkland. Or so, walking slowly across the damp lawns, we imagine.

★

Among the unsolicited items that turned up in Jiffy bags, at the time when I was writing my book about the M25 walks, was a VHS tape with the label *The Nine Lives of Tomas Katz*. My agent (who sent it) had very little information to impart: 'German subtitles'. There was no letter of explanation, no production notes. They had been mislaid. I wasn't in a rush to play this one: an Ashes series was just beginning, there were video logs from my own road trips.

Muggy heat in the centre of London, unconvinced breezes (diesel backdrafts) in West Thurrock. I returned, exhilarated, from a trip to Purfleet. The photographer Effie Paleologou, seven months pregnant, was banged up in a cabin-sized room in the Ibis Hotel. Accompanied by a friend who could help with the hauling of equipment, she was undertaking a twenty-four-hour conceptual project: one minute of tape shot every hour, on the hour. Plus: three exposures (playing safe with F-stops) on her still camera. Behind this exercise, surveillance as art, lay Don DeLillo's ghost story, *The Body Artist*.

She spent hours at the computer screen looking at a live-streaming video feed from the edge of a two-lane road in a city in Finland. It was the middle of the night in Kotka, Finland, and she watched the screen. It was interesting to her because it was happening now, as she sat here, and because it happened twenty-four hours a day, facelessly, cars entering and leaving Kotka, or just the empty road in the dead times. The dead times were best.

West Thurrock (the view over the Queen Elizabeth Bridge) was a seductive area to film. Visiting Effie had the added advantage of a run down the A13. The wobbly yellow chips outside McDonald's at the Warner Centre, Dagenham. The Ford water tower. Container stacking yards, pylons. All my old favourites.

Effie's high window, double-glazed, looked across a glinting paddock of cars waiting for export, the Purfleet refineries and storage tanks. Purfleet was the fabled site of Dracula's abbey,

Carfax. Distribution of blood has now become distribution of (Esso) petrol.

After watching the afternoon's video diary – Lakeside, Ibis Hotel, A13 – I was ready to sample at least three of *The Nine Lives of Tomas Katz*. Katz was a good name, the name of the Brick Lane string shop, the last Hasidic enterprise in Bangla-town; the place where I had first seen the work of Rachel Lichtenstein.

The VHS, with its unexplained German subtitles, is credited, script and direction, to Ben Hopkins. It opens on the M25, a (sha)manic hitchhiker appears from nowhere (a hole in the ground), to wave down a passing London cab. Disbelief duti-fully suspended, I let the tape run. There's a tradition of road crazies, asylum escapees picking up unlikely lifts. Our cabbie is no Ralph Meeker. He's a fat man. The hitchhiker, dressed in a long coat hung with bones, looks like an English Civil War veteran, a Digger on his way to St George's Hill, near Wey-bridge. He's a dream-catcher, a shape-shifter. He summons the cabbie's recurrent nightmare, a post-operative trauma involving the Happy Eater creature, a giant pink bug dripping the blood of the cabbie's cannibalised child. The source of the dream, so the visionary explains, is the cabbie's new heart – which was borrowed from a pig. 'A baboon,' the sweating driver insists. 'It was a baboon.'

On the level of myth, road and heart were always interlinked. The orbital (going nowhere, being everywhere) motorway sweeps up London's lucid dreaming. Harefield, with its reserve blood stocks, and Purfleet (with its vampiric traces) confirm the heart as metaphor. Blood is an international commodity, the base trade. Drained arms for asylum seekers and junkies, quality stock laid down by the wealthy. Pre-donation is the advised policy. Leaflets are distributed at all luxuriously appointed private hospitals, suggesting that 'many people who have to undergo major elective surgery . . . now choose to deposit **their**

own blood. This removes the risk of infection . . . Blood can be stored in our blood bank.'

Surgical procedures affect the way we picture the M25; 'clotting' in Harefield is twinned with sluggish traffic, stalled cars in the Heathrow corridor. Emergency lights flash. Cardiac arrest. The heart has its quadrants, dividing London into four unequal quarters. When they opened the skull of Ian Hacking's mad walker, the man who paced his neurotic circuits, trying to fit 'heavens and angels' into the bowl of bone, they were searching for a road map, a physical explanation. Landfill sites in Essex (gunpowder mills, foot-and-mouth burning pits) damage the fragile balance. Road rage in Swanley. Disorientation in Surrey. The man who went blind but kept on driving along the hard shoulder. We have to learn to walk the damage, repair the hurt.

Out on the road a forensic vocabulary is brought into play. Highway patrols talk of 'foxtrot fatals'. Planners mourn 'severed communities', 'undrained cohesion'. 'Bypass' is a term common to both sets of initiates. Artery, flow, circuit. Cardiac teams deal with the heart as a malfunctioning machine. Drivers, enduring the grind between Junctions 10 and 17 of the M25, slide through layers of anaesthesia: from panic to yawning detachment, from waking dreams and hallucinations to blackout. Helicopters that ferry roadkill hearts, urgent meat, are now being proposed as the only solution to motorway jams. A rapid response unit will move in on any 'blockage', freeing circulation, bringing respite to coronary candidates in their sweating pods.

Ben Hopkins wrote the script for *Thomas Katz* in Essex, 'over a long, hot weekend, in a rather strange mood of delirium'. He saw the M25 as 'a doughnut', a cholesterol hoop; the jammy outside of nothing. A sugar tunnel. A caul between motorist and the external (always moving) world.

Looked at from above, traced in red (to represent the paths

we have walked), the M25 defines London as a hammered and misshapen heart. Atria and ventricles. The four compartments, divided by the journey from Dome to Waltham Abbey (completed), and Dome to Clacket Lane (still to come). And by the River Thames. The contractions of the city squeeze the muscle, drive the blood on its circuit.

The city is only inhabitable if it exploits (as part of its placement on earth) the notion of circuits, orbits, spirals. The early visions of Utopians called up rational designs, the circle within the circle. 'One symbol of original perfection is the circle,' wrote Eric Neumann in *The Origins and History of Consciousness*. 'Allied to it are the sphere, the egg and the rotundum – the "round" of alchemy . . . Circle, sphere, and round are all aspects of the self-contained, which is without beginning and end, in its preworldly perfection it is prior to any process, eternal, for in its roundness there is no before and no after, no time, and there is no above and no below, no space.'

It was easy, given the talk of hearts, the labyrinthine wanderings through Harefield Park, to elevate our sweaty stroll into a Blakean pilgrimage: the twisting Mount Pleasant road, from river valley to park, became Blake's envisioning of Dante, *The Ascent of the Mountain of Purgatory*. Studying Blake's drawings in the big Tate Britain exhibition (in November 2000), I couldn't help reading the Dante spirals as models for a celestial M25. Dante and Virgil, in the second circle of Hell, on a cliff (or motorway bridge), watch the tumbled bodies of the Lustful as they swim, nose-to-tail, up a gridlocked whirlwind.

The problem is that our heart/road metaphors are clogging up: language overload. Blake's vortex of steroidal sinners (sunlight glinting on a never-ending procession) is a depiction of word-jam, logorrhea; nothing is, everything is a simile. A psychotic condition. Impossible to transcribe: how all the London visionaries insisted on the necessity of a system of concentric circles.

Ford Madox Hueffer (later Ford) published an extraordinary

essay, 'The Future in London', in 1909. Ford recognised that roads were 'the chief feature of a city's life'. Without its roads, London was a dry sponge. 'If I can walk along roads that I like I am happy, alert, energetic, and as much of a man as I can be.' The wellbeing of the man and the wellbeing of the city were linked, freedom of movement, walks were the key to the good life. Ford looked back to a period when it was not unusual to stroll from Fleet Street to Hampstead, Westminster to Richmond; for dinner, conversation, a moonlit return. Victorian clerks, as Dickens frequently demonstrated, hiked to the City from Camden, Holloway or Walworth.

Ford isn't another sentimental antiquarian (he *is*, but only as a convenient pose), he has a take on London that pre-empts Abercrombie and trounces the feeble private/public ditherings of New Labour with its clapped-out, expensive and dangerous transport systems. Ford, the huffing, puffing Edwardian, has a radical solution to deliver:

I should make travelling free, smooth, and luxurious. Along the railways I should set motor-ways, and, between hedges, moving platforms for pedestrians and those who need exercise. I should clean out the Thames and set upon it huge, swift, and fine express launches. Who would put up with this bottom of a basin that London is if, being as near their work and their pleasant pleasures, they could inhabit a residential London that crowned the hill tops and scattered along the beaches of the sea?

Not content with reviving the river, building motorways over tired railways, turning footpaths into open-air gymnasia, Ford lays out the first great vision of the M25: as a single sweep in a series of ever-expanding circles.

Let us consider now my outer ring of the Future . . . With one leg of my compasses set in Threadneedle Street, with the other I describe a great circle, the pencil starting at Oxford. (Roughly speaking, Oxford is sixty miles from London, and in my non-stop, monorail expresses, this should be a matter of half-an-hour, about as long as it takes you now to go from Hammersmith to the City.) It takes in, this circle, Winchester, the delightful country round Petersfield, Chichester, all the coast to Brighton, Hastings, Dover, all Essex, and round again by way of Cambridge and Oxford. Think of the cathedrals, the castles, the woods, the chases, the downs, and the headlands! You would not sleep in Kensington if you might as well at Lewes . . .

It is on the road, this change. It has got to come. All south-eastern England is just London.

Walking the South Downs, Ford remembered Holland Park; marooned in town, he dreamt of drowsy Wealden villages. Abercrombie echoed Ford. The *County of London Plan* of 1943 spoke of an 'age of mobility', avenues and radials linking parkways, eroding the distinction between town and country. 'Also included is a parkway leading from the centre of London to Crystal Palace and its nearby hills, and thence, by existing and proposed roads, to the Downs and the coast.'

The visionaries of the inner city thought in terms of circuits, contour lines. Bernard Kops, poet and playwright, grew up in Stepney Green. The natural transit for him was Whitechapel to Soho (labyrinth to labyrinth), immigrant household to the liberties of Bohemia. Divided loyalties, a hand to mouth existence as jobbing writer (bookdealing, junk), left Kops in Belmont Hospital (a bus trip from the end of the Northern Line). 'I thought,' he wrote, 'neurotics were the first prophets of true sanity. "After all, if you reject the world of today you must be sane. Draw a circle anywhere in London and you'll have a cross section as neurotic as us."'

By the late Sixties, many of the orthodox Jews of White-chapel – their behaviour interpreted as eccentric – were tidied away to hospitals in what is now the southern arc of the M25. Kops in Belmont. David Rodinsky in Long Grove Hospital, Epsom. Wards like meeting rooms, soup-kitchens;

like the wide pavements of Whitechapel Road and Mile End.

Kops appreciated his pastoral retreat, the slowing of city time. 'I wrote constantly and wandered the grounds. The prolonged contact with earth helped me. But beyond the gates was London. The great filthy disease called a city.'

He had to return. He accepted the help of a fellow patient who gave him the fare to Oxford Circus.

I stood there not knowing what to do. I wanted to run but was embarrassed, so I stood buffeted by the lifeless mass of people screaming my head off inside, with my hand over my eyes unable to move. Hell! There was a band tightening around my head. Oxford Circus was a narrow ledge in endlessness. On either side was a deep abyss. I walked as if on a tightrope, thinking that the traffic would chase me up the walls or that the people would come at me with knives, tear me to ribbons.

The Circus at the centre of the centre is where the skull splits, the bands do indeed tighten until the pain is unbearable. Gerald Kersh, another Jewish writer, born in the suburbs, understood perfectly the centrifugal forces that hold the city together: Soho, or any other ghetto, is a maze within a maze. And there is no escape. In *Night and the City* (1938), Kersh lays it out:

He saw London as a kind of Inferno – a series of concentric areas with Piccadilly Circus as the ultimate centre. The shape of a human face, like a key, touched a series of springs beneath his consciousness, and set in motion a complicated mechanism of comparative memory which, juggling with permutations and combinations of a thousand observations, could deliver an immediate and reasonably accurate estimate of the qualities behind that face and the circle to which it belonged.

The image of the Inferno is a constant in the literature of London. Poets, hacks, lively journeymen, they all return to this sense of entrapment, the heart as a labyrinth. Maureen Duffy in her wonderfully strange 1975 novel, *Capital*, anticipates Michael Moorcock's *Mother London*. The person who undertakes research into the city's history, minutiae and odd particulars, will become unbalanced. Identification with London's biography is too intense. The familiar mental bonds tighten. Duffy (in character) writes:

I suddenly saw the city as a series of anonymous concentric rings each further and further from the centre point which is always I or in childhood me: department, faculty, college, university, city, each increasing the depth of anonymity and isolation, wrapping the gauze layers tighter and tighter until all sound and sensation are padded away. Only the eyes are left free to blink and water as they stare at a world that they can't make meaning of by themselves.

Peter Ackroyd, completing his magnum opus, *London: The Biography*, suffers a heart attack. Typescript on desk. Quadruple bypass. Biography of city: autobiography of city writer. *Resurgam.*

Breaking away from the motorway, Renchi and I spent a day in London. I guided him around a few of my favourite loci: the remnant of the City's Roman walls, lanes and passageways near St Paul's, Fountain Court and the Temple Church. The Round Church, consecrated on 10 February 1185, was built on the model of the Church of the Holy Sepulchre in Jerusalem. The building, found within the collegiate enclosure of the Inner Temple (cloisters, courts, gardens, Oxbridge name boards), is a respite from the east/west fluster of Fleet Street. The traffic chaos that was already being felt at the time of the demolition of Temple Bar. The Temple Church, in plan, resembles a stubby thermometer: an elongated chancel with the mercury bulb at the west end. The church has no parish and is not subject to the authority of the Bishop of London.

We come to the Round Church with firm but undefined expectations. There is, inevitably, some talk of the Templars, the way London divides into enclosures, cities within cities; the survival of this spirit in the area around Smithfield. It is the effigies of the sleeping knights, within a circle of six pillars, to which we are drawn. The status of the knights is a matter of debate; Templar or Templar associate, it is unresolved. Here are William Marshal, Earl of Pembroke, and his sons, Gilbert and William the younger. Hands on sword pommels, shields at the ready, feet (in some cases) resting on heraldic beasts. The circuitry is still active. It's easy to promote these rafts of the dead as the original circle from which all the other rings of energy drift out. Memory and meaning have a form. The church is both accessible and private, known but not over-whelmed with fake narrative. It has presence in place of the strident absence of the Millennium Dome, the money-eating tent. We see the mandala of the fixed effigies, within the circumference of Purbeck marble pillars, as an earthing device for the M25; a validation of the motorway as a symbol of wholeness, without end or beginning.

Renchi sits on a stone bench to ponder the complex geo-metry of triangles within the nave, pillar to pillar; window, column, arch. How does the circular nave relate to the rest of the building? The Round Church to the Inner Temple? The Inner Temple to the other Inns of Court? The Inns of Court to the heart of London?

Edward Clarkson, in *Illustrations and Account of the Temple Church*, published in 1838, outlined his notion of the mystical significance of the six free-standing four-faced columns. David Lewer and Robert Dark, in *The Temple Church in London* (1997), explain Clarkson's theory. When the columns were taken 'together with twelve columns of the aisle walls, within which are seven minor columns, the 42 columns of the tri-forium arranged in groups of seven, he concluded that this was no accident but had direct links with sacred numbers that can

be traced back to Egyptian masonry, Jewish cabalists, Pythagor-
ians, Gnostics, the Romans and the Druids'.

The cross-legged knights were repositioned more than once.
The fact that they are unbearded has to be taken as evidence
that they were not Knights Templar. They may or may not
have been crusaders. The effigies are made from Sussex marble,
Reigate stone, Purbeck marble. What we project, as we drift
around the knights, around the church, is the emblematic force
of the figures as the true patrons of our journey. They seem to
be sleepwalkers, laid on boards, frozen in mid-stride. They died
on their travels and were brought back, rotting, to this place;
the sanctity of the enclosure.

Our London wanderings follow contrails of previous excursions. Fleet Street, Farringdon Road, Smithfield. The church of
St Bartholomew-the-Great with its dim interior, incense, its
flattened circuit. A walk around the pillars, the stone forest of
London's most numinous church, is a re-dedication of our
motorway trance. This, at last, was the paradigm, the contem-
plative circuit that would make our 120-mile slog tautologous.

I knew that a circle of alchemists, among whom David Dee
(kinsman of Dr John Dee and rector of St Bartholomew's) had
been a prominent member, were associated with Bartholomew
Close. I explored the Close, photographing fig trees, dirty lab
coats hanging on pegs; the film was lost. I guided Renchi
around the church, monument to monument, in search of one
name: Dr Francis Anthony (1549–1623).

The monuments, Elizabethan and Jacobean, were like stage
sets in alabaster. Posed groups that presented an idealised, three-
dimensional portrait of a life. Francis Anthony was on the north
wall. If the nave is a model of the M25, then Francis Anthony
must be lodged in Waltham Abbey. His epitaph was composed
by his son John.

> Religion, virtue and thy skil did raise
> A threefold pillar to thy lasting Fame

Though poisonous envye ever sought to blame
Or hyde the fruits of thy intention
Yet shall they all commend that high desygne
Of purest gold to make a medicine
That feel thy helpe by that thy rare invention.

Anthony discovered and marketed 'Aurum Potabile', a gold extract which, when dissolved, was a cure-all for the credulous. The doctor's fortune was made. He bought property near the church. He wrote a defence of his potion and dedicated it to Michael Maier. Maier, author of *Arcana Arcanissima*, was a considerable figure in hermetic circles in Europe. He had been court physician to Rudolph II in Prague. Joy Hancox in her book *The Byrom Collection (Renaissance Thought, the Royal Society and the Building of the Globe Theatre)* quotes Elias Ashmole on Maier, saying that he came to England that he might 'so understand our English Tongue, as to translate Norton's *Ordinall* into Latin verse!'

Hancox tells us that 'Maier visited Anthony in Bartholomew's Close and also met Robert Fludd'. One of the illustrations she publishes from Maier's *Atalanta Fugiens* shows 'a philosopher pointing with dividers to a geometrical figure which consists of two circles, a square, a triangle and, at the heart of the pattern, a man and a woman . . . It is entitled "Monas or the One", a clear reference to John Dee.'

We were close to the 'heart of the pattern', but it would only become clear when we moved back, out to the road. Part of John Anthony's epitaph for his father was clarified by the design that went with it. 'A threefold pillar to thy lasting Fame.' The three pillars carved on the monument are crowned by a chaplet of roses, a Rosicrucian emblem for our orbital pilgrimage. As we turn away from the monument to the church itself, we find the arrangement repeated, made actual in the galleries. Stuart monument mirrors Norman stone. The first and last three-line elements of Anthony's coded epitaph play against the middle line, the reflecting surface. The message is revealed by reading the capital letters (RAFT), against the neutral line's 'Or'. And then the reversed capitals of the second triplet: TOY. We had our instruction: RAFT Or TOY.

Church and priory, dedicated to the flayed St Bartholomew, maintain a connection with the hospital. In 1609 William Harvey became a physician at St Bartholomew's Hospital. In 1615 he was appointed to the Lumleian lectureship of the college. His first published work was *An Anatomical Exercise Concerning the Motion of the Heart and Blood* (1649). From the manuscript notes for Harvey's lectures in 1615, it is clear that he had already decided that blood can pass from arteries to veins; that the heart was a muscle, its valves served to prevent flow in a reverse direction. While the heart beats there is 'a perpetual motion of the blood in a circle'.

With the blood banks of Harefield, the distribution depot of Count Dracula at Carfax, the discoveries of William Harvey, our project was in imminent danger of cardiac arrest. Circulation: blood and the road. An orbital motorway contracting London's hammered heart. It was time to get back to water, the Grand Union Canal.

Coming away from Harefield, we collected the car at Denham, drove back to Abbots Langley: a day's walk undone in a few minutes of motorway transit. Trying to shake Renchi's hand, on parting at the Leavesden Hospital, in the chill twilight, is like reaching out for a glove of air. We fade, the handshake remains: one of those Masonic symbols found on sooty gravestones in obscure London burial grounds.

3

In the south-west corner, I'm as far as I'm going to be from Hackney. By the end of the day there'll be almost as much driving as walking. 3 March 1999: Staines station. Another of our two-car relays. The plan is to take the motorway back to Denham, leave one car there and begin the walk – which will carry us, along with the Colne, through an impossibly clotted landscape, to the green-brown barrier of the Thames.

It's a 5.30 a.m. start in Albion Drive. And Marc Atkins doesn't make it. Seduced by the promise of motorway junctions, Heathrow, reservoirs, the whole J.G. Ballard psychoclimate, Marc was about to rejoin the tour. He did a lot of book jackets but didn't, so far as I know, read novels. He made a few exceptions: Ballard's *Crash* was one of them. If he mentioned *Crash* it was by way of a hint that I might learn to fashion shorter, crisper sentences. I might experiment for once and try for narrative, pages that could be turned without a forklift truck. Night roads. Sex. Driving. He was fed up with pedestrianism: of concept, prose, action.

I hung on as long as I could. I tried Marc's mobile. It was off. Always protective of his private space, mysterious in his shifting alliances, Marc had gone to ground. Self-tagged (cellphone, fax, video), the system only worked when it was switched on. I had to make the rendezvous with Renchi, who swam through currents of plural time, but was never late for a meet at the start of one of our walks.

The thing that pissed me off about Marc's failure to show was that he would have captured some great images of this drive through the Heathrow hinterlands. There was a full moon. A morning of high, wild clouds, fast changes. Planes skimmed the

road. You couldn't help being drawn into the tremble, the jet
roar, the throb of traffic streaming in every direction. M4, M25,
A4, A30; slip roads, link roads, trunk roads, deleted coach roads.
Two hundred thousand vehicles a day used the section of the
M25 between Junctions 13 and 14. Ballard was absolutely right:
if you set aside human interference (aka life), London was a
mausoleum. Kensal Green Cemetery with the walls knocked
down. Pompous monuments, redundant public buildings, trash
commerce, heritage tags. Oxford Street was a souk. Charing
Cross Road a gutter.

The city, in its Victorian overcoat, the muck of centuries
on its waistcoat, bored Ballard. He promoted this new place,
the rim. The 'local' was finished as a concept. Go with the drift,
with detachment. The watcher on the balcony. Areas around
airports were ecumenical. They were the same everywhere:
storage units, hangars, satellite hotels, car hire companies, apolo-
getic farmland as a mop-up apron for Concorde disasters. If you
see the soul of the city as existing in its architecture, its transport systems, its commerce and media hot spots, then Ballard's
championship of the suburbs is justified. But they're not really
suburbs if they don't feed on the centre. The Heathrow corridor
has declared its unilateral independence, that's what makes
it exciting. The abdication of responsibility and duty; glossy
goods, ennui, scratched light.

London for Michael Moorcock, Ballard's *New Worlds* editor
and colleague, lived in memory and human traffic. That was the
heart of the argument between two veteran writers. However
dim and dirty the buildings, however sleazy the political games,
Moorcock would identify a special spirit: the London mob. The
outsider, the dope fiend, the alien. Sentiment, delivered with
such gusto, such knowledge of the streets and moves, coheres
and remains a powerful motor for fiction. But Moorcock,
despite the many licences he inherited over the years, doesn't
drive. Doesn't want to drive. This early morning spin down the
Colnbrook Bypass is not for him. In earlier times, well insured

(for the sake of the kids), he dealt with car-cramps and the dullness of the suburbs, by climbing on to the roof, feeling the wind in his hair; riding out of London like one of his Viking champions.

Staines railway station was a country affair – with too much action, too many parked cars. A decorous brick building with uncertainly heritaged globe lights, corporate logos, warnings, prohibitions, ticketing machines.

Renchi, muddy boots in hand, is waiting alongside a wide-screen hoarding: ULTRA EFFECTIVE/SMOKING KILLS. In his stocking cap and libertarian red scarf, he's a Digger, a travelling saint of the 1640s. The Silk Cut illustration is a beauty: a turnip-head archer, a scarecrow shaman in a ploughed field. The scarecrow is nailed to a spindly cross, straw feet don't touch the ground. Gloved hand on drawstring. Slit-eyes watchful. A crow killer guarding the painted landscape that Renchi is about to enter. Archer as straw man. Archer crucified. The prophecy of Staines: don't make them breathe your smoke.

We drive back to Denham, another station, deeper country-side. DENHAM TWINNED WITH SHARK BAY WESTERN AUS-TRALIA. In 1939 J. Arthur Rank (the Yorkshire Methodist who leased his name as a rhyming slang term for the act of self-pleasuring) bought Denham Studios, the largest in Britain, from Alexander Korda, after Korda failed to duplicate the international success of *The Private Life of Henry VIII* (1933). The Prudential Assurance Company had lent him the money to build Denham Studios. A none too prudent investment. Korda folded.

Rank (dim product, sharp management) developed a production and distribution base. They went global, acquiring a quarter share in the US company Universal, which gave them the distribution rights to glitzy Hollywood product. They purchased off-highway real estate, Pinewood, Denham. They took over the Odeon chain of suburban cinemas and the Gaumont

British circuit (which included, as part of the package, Michael Balcon's Ealing Studios). Rank, a late flowering of the Dissenter tradition that had once flourished in the Chiltern and Hertfordshire villages, was also a forerunner of coming multinational capitalism. The old tracks and paths that, for a few years during and after the English Civil War, allowed tinkers, visionary herdsmen, disaffected mechanics to roam, preach, discuss, debate became the super highways of petrol/burger culture.

In the Denham bun shop, Renchi can hardly keep his eyes open, far less make a decision on what kind of cake or biscuit to munch. He was working until eleven o'clock on the previous evening, drinking too much coffee, plotting the day's walk. The bun shop has a kind of Christmas shrine to the Death of Cinema; red paper spotted with snow, green plastic garlands, framed photos of Patrick Mower and 'the girl who used to do high kicks on *The Generation Game*'. White suits. Pink flesh burnt by the shock of flash photography at some long forgotten première. Teeth for the camera. Twinned with Shark Bay. 'I'm still me. I'm still here.' The immortality of non-recognition on the wall of an early-morning bakery near a suburban railway station.

We follow the Colne to Uxbridge. Renchi has borrowed a pocket recorder. We've talked a lot about sound but never cracked it. Long, rambling conversations about how to keep a useful record of what was said. 'Um, ah, like, you know, yeah, like . . . right.' There would be interrogations of persons met on the road. But no walkers are out and about, no dogs. It's early and the light is so recessive that my colour prints look like sepia. Steam from the flat roofs of narrow boats. A weak sun caught in a thatch of spindly trees. Lakes, islands. It's easy to imagine ourselves on Mark Twain's 'river road'; we drop to our knees, use that heavy sky to conjure up the Mississippi. (Think: Robert Frank. *Mississippi River, Baton Rouge, Louisiana*.)

Sound is elusive. No slap of tide, no river romance of clicks and creaks. Our own muted footfalls on worn turf, on trampled mud, splashing through spring puddles.

South. Under the arch of a brick bridge: REPUBLIC NOW. There is no way of accurately recalling Renchi's monologue (even from notes taken at the time). The recorder of course is unused. Cameras can log, sketch, record graffiti, make clumsy portraits. Sound is an element. Like the canal, the motorway. We don't have the skill, the eavesdropping genius of composer/guitarist Bruce Gilbert (once of Wire). Bruce skulks in pub corners, on station platforms, at obscure locations, *sampling*; gathering material to construct a sound field. He is an X-ray of Gene Hackman in Coppola's *The Conversation*. From units of sound you can make a world, re-edit the past. Put it on a loop. Bruce long ago cracked the thing we were still struggling with: he learnt how to 'play the gaps'.

Renchi's riverbank monologue moves ahead of him, like one of those men with red flags who preceded the first cars: 'Father's library . . . Stukeley, arcane researches . . . Heathrow as a kind of Avebury . . . keep the pattern in our heads as we enter that territory.' In 1723 the antiquary William Stukeley investigated the earthwork known as Shasbury, or Schapsbury or Fern Hill, and pronounced it 'Caesar's Camp'. A ditch, earth ramparts. An enclosure, sixty feet square, with points of access at north and south. A diagonal path running through it, to other access points in east and west. Figures, perhaps surveyors, in the foreground. Holding chains. A coach pulled by six horses.

The canal's a soporific. Pylons, lagoons. We push closer to the M25. The strip of tolerated country between road and water is scruffier, fewer estates, more poultry farms. By the time we pass West Drayton, hippies and freebooters are disputing the right to scavenge with travellers, scrap-metal pirates, unlicensed Irishmen. You have to tread carefully when you walk these lanes with a camera in your hands. In every off-road junk yard, somebody is watching. Big dogs on small chains.

We see distant Western Avenue, the A40, as a target, a beacon of hope. At Uxbridge we climb up to the road: a taster, a sighting. Electricity Sub-Station: DANGER OF DEATH KEEP OUT. Western Avenue sounds better than it plays; a sluggish trawl of family saloons, company cars, white vans, middleweight haulage shaking itself free of London. Ribbon-development dystopia: before the motorway, Iver Heath, the woods of Langley Park and the descent into Slough.

Uxbridge (aka Wixebrug, Uxebregg) exploits its position, where the Colne and the Grand Union Canal meet Western Avenue. Victorian trade routes. The smoke-coughing trucks that took over from the narrow boats are themselves doomed to oblivion, breakers' yards between river and motorway embankment. Uxbridge has cornered the market in liminal architecture. (It's here and not here. Visible, but you don't see it.) The Battle of Britain was directed from Uxbridge, so the guidebook says, by the late Air Marshal Lord Dowding. 'The town is perhaps noteworthy for its selection of modern and futuristic buildings in a variety of competing styles.'

The buildings along Western Avenue don't want to be there; they'd prefer Satellite City. Or Las Vegas. Phoenix, Arizona, with Scunthorpe weather. They'd like to be closer to Heathrow's lingua franca. Mediterranean green glass. Low level units with a certain lazy elegance. *Super-Cannes* functionalism interspersed with Fifties grot. The heritaged emblems of an old riverside pub, The Swan & Bottle, have been banished by their corporate operators, Chef & Brewer, to the top of a wooden pole. That stares insolently at the slick shoebox of: X (The Document Company XEROX). The Xerox building is designed to look like office machinery, a shredder or printer. The windows are an enigmatic blue-green. Like chlorine. Xerox, Western Avenue, is a swimming pool on its side; from which, by some miracle of gravity, water doesn't spill. That's the concept: intelligent water. X marks the spot. Uxbridge is made from Xs. Lines of cancelled typescript. Fields planted with barbed wire.

The Xerox building duplicates itself; come back tomorrow and there'll be another one, and another. And another. X started out as a narrow four-storey column, then multiplied in the night. Horizontal 'lanes' of aqueous green glass play with notions of flow and drift, the river captured and tamed. The front elevation, serene as it is, gives me the bends: it's like looking down from the high board on to an Olympic swimming pool. Sun-sparkling lanes and dividing ropes which, in this case, convert into metaphors of a clean white road. Motorway and canal system seamlessly linked.

Traffic is at a standstill. The bridge over the river, with its red brick parapet, is a sad relic. Workers and drones, in thrall to the glass beehives, plod down Slough Road, towards the UXBRIDGE sign. They have their own, end-of-the-Metropolitan Line style; viz., baggy blousons or black puffa jackets worn over lightweight grey suits, brightly polished shoes. They are bareheaded, ballasted by oversize silver attaché cases. That is, male and female. Trouser suits, short hair. The women carry a second bag, slung from the shoulder, for personal effects. The attaché cases are the kind that turn up on the TV news, left in cabs by Secret State bagmen. 'Just popped into Blockbusters to pick up a video and it was gone.' The invasion plans. The list of informers.

Downtown Uxbridge is not a place to tease out an acceptable breakfast. We return to the canal path, head south towards Cowley. Now the green-glass buildings are lower, but they spread over a wider area (Terry Farrell's Aztec MI6 temple at Vauxhall squashed flat). Cowley is where Mediparc pretensions devolve into muck yards and low-rent trading estates.

TRIMITE (*The* Printmakers – for Industry). A collection of metal drums in green and various shades of blue; industrial conceptualism. Seven of the drums – one letter on each – spell out the brand name, TRIMITE. They've executed this conceit in the style of the popular (with exiles) yeast extract paste: Marmite ('contains 31 servings'). Red and yellow on a beef-brown background. Fantasies of squat jars with tight lids, all those B vitamins, have me salivating.

Experience proves: where there's a trading estate and a canal, there's a caff, a caravan with serving hatch, a tea stall. It's a risk worth taking, to detour from our path – fearing that once we come inside the fence we won't be allowed back to the waterside. More vans than cars. Flat-roofed hutches bodged in asbestos. Print and salvage seem to be the principal trades (along with appearing in deleted TV cop shows).

PINKY & PERKY'S CAFETERIA (PHONE OR FAX ORDERS WELCOME). Grinning pig's head motif, transfer lettering on every window. The clientele (early shift) is demographically mixed. Suits (jackets slung over seats) laying down grease before the office opens. Working men with spider tattoos, oil scored into the pores of large hands. They seem happy to share this space, which is clean (yellow Formica, red bucket-chairs). The all-day breakfast floats on my hub cap of a plate like a relief map of London and the Thames Valley. Greensand, oolite, chalk. The bubble and squeak of Enfield Chase, bacon ridges of the Chilterns, rubbery fried egg of the Dome, sausage of the North Downs, bean swamp of Dagenham and Purfleet.

The Cowley Lock and the Cowley Peachey Junction have a particular interest for me. As far as the Grand Union Canal is concerned, Cowley marks the end of a twenty-seven-mile 'pound' and the start of the ascent to the Colne Valley and the Chiltern Hills. In more leisurely times, the *Paddington Packet* used to ply the fifteen-mile, lock-free stretch between Cowley and Paddington, pulled by four horses.

The anarchist and libertarian graffiti of the Colne Valley shares the concrete with dopers and slackers and sticky adolescents.

I was ere smokin weed
I was ere   but now
I'm not round the corner
Smoking pot I'm writing this
To prove a point but uter shit
Without a joint

In another hand, the critical riposte: YOU SUCK COCK. Princess Di is memorialised by twin hearts and a question mark. A great red cock, Basquiat-hot, spurts blood. A fleshy light-house tower floating on a savage sea. WHEN WAS THE LAST TIME . . .

Low clouds part, rain in the air. Sunbeams scintillate on ruffled water. The smooth curve of a brick bridge, the Cowley moorings. There is none of the jaunty Notting Hill communal-ism here, decanted Sixties street warrens. The agenda is quieter, more serious. Boat people keep their heads down, mind their own business – which is often survival (the new subversion). One of the true British poets of the last half-century lived in Cowley, tactfully removed from the scene, carrying out his researches, a rate of production (a bibliography of 'about four hundred' items) that would shame any of our logophile novel-ists. Booklets flow from the grizzled (and exiled) Bill Griffiths with the regularity of newsprint. He avoids publication dates on many of his self-produced chapbooks. There'd be no point. He revises, reissues, amends, sticks on a new cover. Bill's poems require time codes like video tape. He brings out more editions, so it seems, than the *Evening Standard*.

I wrote to Bill, when he was staying in London, cataloguing the Eric Mottram archive (a monster task), and asked about his time in Cowley.

Now, as to the Grand Union, *he replied*, I can tell you much or little. It was one of the last canals to be built, unifying the country's canal system into an Orion-like configuration (now the Kennet Avon is reopened, it literally spans from Thames to Severn Estuary as well as north to south). North of Uxbridge I am not too sure about; the settlement tends to get thicker around Uxbridge itself, and I was based at Cowley, about 2–3 miles south of Uxbridge, where there is a lock, a couple of bridges and a few coveted residential moorings. Near there too is the 'Slough Arm', an extra limb of water, which I used in 'Rabbit Hunt' and which is notable for the banks of refuse from Central London deposited there in the early C20th.

This 'Rabbit Hunt' was a good place to start thinking about Bill. Rabbits and boats again. Griffiths's work atomises, splits off into discrete files or songs; his poems are many-voiced, resolutely non-hierarchic. You learn to navigate the tributaries, while waiting to be carried back to the main stream. He's a musician who deploys subtle and shocking rhythms.

The critic Kevin Jackson, visiting Griffiths at Seaham on the Durham coast, locates the poet as existing in 'about the most cheerless Spartan dwelling I've seen since I stopped hanging around with graduate students'. In other words, a beached narrow boat. A terraced cabin in a sea-coal settlement, a few miles south of Sunderland. The only incongruous item in this brick coaster was a grand piano. Griffiths, Jackson reveals, is a virtuoso. 'He tells me he's been playing since the age of three and, just before I left to catch my train, underwrites the claim by running effortlessly through a complex little piece by Bartok, LOVE and HATE rippling along the keyboard so swiftly that they begin to blur.'

Fading Hell's Angel tattoos on the cuticle-chomped digits of a softly spoken man: LOVE/HATE. Bill wheezes, enjoys a roll-up. Beneath all that scholarship – stately build disguised under lumberjack shirt and baseball cap – is a man of the river. Dr Griffiths fits very comfortably into the ruled margins of the Cowley moorings. A boat dweller who hunts rabbits.

'The Rabbit Hunt' comes from *The Book of the Boat*, which, in standard Griffiths fashion, appears in various undated editions. The original would seem to be the Writers Forum version in blue covers, with repro-holograph text, line drawings, stapled sheets. An attractive variant was issued from Seaham by the poet's own Amra Press: spiral bound with hand-coloured drawings. *The Book of the Boat* celebrates an odyssey, a serpentine voyage from Cowley through London's canal system to the Thames at Bow Creek, and around the Essex coast to Brightlingsea.

As someone who has survived a number of rackety voyages in that direction, with percussionist and sound-pirate Paul Burwell, and other less competent skippers, I can vouch for the accuracy – and wit – of Bill's base account. Place gets at poet. The structure has to encompass sea shanty, camp-fire yarn, hero tale; the hiss and spit of masterless men, rogue spirits who passed through Cowley. In the upheaval of the English Civil War, discharged soldiers, freelance prophets, took to the roads. There were meetings, debates; chapbooks and pamphlets were produced and distributed. Dissent worked its way around the western fringes of the capital; Enfield, Iver, Kingston, Weybridge, Cobham. Griffiths's associates, his tribal connections (from Hell's Angels to the narrow boat survivalists), are aligned with traditions of independence, the freedom to roam and rant. In the shadow of grandiose civil engineering projects, scavengers camp out like seventeenth-century Diggers. In his letter, Bill spoke of 'a family with houseboat and own view onto waste land near Heathrow'.

Mythologically astute, Griffiths begins *The Book of the Boat* with a passage through the Blisworth Tunnel (or birth canal); a 'ballad' he calls it. Once boats had to be 'legged' through the second longest tunnel open to navigation (3,057 yards beneath Blisworth Hill). Now travestied water folk queue up to chug down the dark bore. Griffiths has fun with those who sentimentalise history, closet antiquarians who think a voyage into the past is a matter of wearing the right hat.

All folk-fakery is a bare-arsed bane. and lace & bonnets &
                                    [waistcoats are a
    shame. awful to tell as th'opening time came near. they most
                                    [dressed up in quaint
Victorian gear.
To match these ghouls was not an easy task. we settled for
                                    [lots of balloons &
    pirate masks. soon the boat was trimmed with bobbing skulls.

Disposing of this tame carnival, the narrator goes off on a
'Rabbit Hunt'. Stuart has the gun and is 'speechlessly quiet: &
mute of eye'. Barry is 'a guy who knows about holes & rabbits'.
What a revelation the hunt is: 'snow set in the sky', 'a good
deal of slow introduction'. It is late afternoon before this half-
wild bunch move off into the real and actual landscape. Don't
they know about the superstitions, rabbits and boats? The hare-
fields of the heart hospital? The necessary appeasement of lunar
gods? Ancient gravity that will put lead in their boots?

They drink: 'like unpacked astronauts'. It's 'beer, beer, beer,
lovely luring beer' as they stand in 'a magic circle', hallucinating rabbits who will never hop into their pot.

    I stare. & I crunch. but and I weave. all around the waste-way.
    after him. (I like to keep the gun in front). I'm no nearer a catch.
    than is Alf: Why not the geese? (I ask).

Geese or swans, sheep, chickens, dogs, cats: anything with
flesh. They must live, but the hunt is a chance to walk out in
company, to drink, and know the country.

    Alf walks by the Colne: I take the upper plateau still. I see one
                                    [rabbit.
    I whistle for him. I catch the boots I found on the tip. and give
                                    [up: go home.

Nothing shot, no kill. Hare and heart safe. The voyage begins.

The reading and knowing and experiencing of Bill Griffiths's work, over a quarter of a century, has bred a firm conviction in me, a trust: how these plural voices move and operate. The right place and the right response, reports from Whitechapel prefabs, tribal rucks. ('The real war was Essex! One of them blasted w/- a shotgun//on Chelsea Bridge, Levi I remember and one other. They had//a caravan on the North Circular and their speaking and planning//was well OK, sunshiny.') And then the canny recyclings of M.R. James, Christopher Smart and less-known witnesses, journal keepers and correspondents. Everything is ghost. Lurid and swift, in pulse and being. Cowley, by its secret melancholy, its sprawling mess (backing on to waste mounds and dead water) was a place worth looking at; the knowledge that Bill Griffiths had lived here for a time (before the loss of his boat in a fire) made it special.

What is shocking, if not surprising, given the tight politics of the poetry franchise, the indifference of the world at large to language and imagination, is how inadequately Bill Griffiths's work is known. He hasn't, it's true, solicited attention. The trajectory of life and career from biker youth, through a period as 'guest worker' in Germany, to the burning boat and the decamping to County Durham, remains a private matter; the ordinary accidents, as he would have it, of a life lived. Griffiths received the support of Professor Eric Mottram and the ever-enthusiastic polemicist Jeff Nuttall, but the broadsheets were otherwise engaged, proud of their bottomless ignorance. A collection that appeared from Paladin was very soon pulped and forgotten. The hundreds of chapbooks, the leatherbound volumes, the hand-coloured variants, pass around a small band of enthusiasts. This is a craftsman, a scholar capable of reinvigorating the language; a master of the weights and units of breath.

Reading the selection of Griffiths's poetry that Clive Bush

gathered for the anthology *Worlds of New Measure* (1997), I began to superimpose those radical songs ('Troops, curfews, and reason') on to the Colne Valley, our march towards Heathrow. *Thirteen Thoughts as though Woken at Dawn by 150 Policemen in Riot Gear with Helicopter and Film Back-up . . . Wandsworth ('a turbulent river/an offer of valium') . . . Star Fish Jail . . . The Hawksmoor Mausoleum.*

Was it legitimate to read that decade of samizdat publication (1965–75), poetry wars, readings above pubs or in disestablished chapels, as in any way analogous to the outpourings of the Dissenters (Levellers, Diggers, Ranters) in the years after the English Civil War (1646–56)? Much of the dissenting rhetoric, a country on the cusp of republicanism, had the same primitive, biblical, improvisatory meld of speech. Paragraphs were urgent and energised. With knowledge of coming defeat? Accepted truths were interrogated. Earth magic and antinomianism argued a rationale for independence, the overthrow of a Leviathan state of priests and landowners and kings.

It was my contention, a small conceit to toy with as we moved south towards the 'impounded' market gardens and common land of Hounslow Heath and Harmondsworth, the lost village of Heathrow, that the group of London-based poets who read (under Mottram's patronage), at King's College in the Strand, represented a recrudescence of the Dissenting tradition. Griffiths, obviously, sampled the original texts and lived by their spirit. Allen Fisher ('I am in the garden of a coming English Revolution' . . . 'Met hunter/hungry on Sydenham Common' . . . 'should people of low and mean condition/cause offence by stake removal/they will be openly whipped near unto the place') is interested in process and prophecy, the erosion of liberties and *above all* the corruption of language. In his 'Letter to Eric Mottram' (from *Stane, Place Book III*), Fisher is concerned about how the 'sacred hierarchy' dissolves into 'stockbroker belts'. City dwellers are restless, unplaced, knowing that 'the airport is now 60 minutes away'.

Echoes of dissent, and the promptings of unappeased voices, are always there. Barry MacSweeney, electively possessed by Shelley and Chatterton, experienced in the blather and compromise of union meetings, wrote a book called *Ranter*. He worked at a desk alongside Basil Bunting in a newspaper office, keeping a none-too-fastidious record of shipping on the Tyne.

> *Ranter. Call him Leveller, Lollard,*
> *his various modes*
> *Whispering sedition, libel,*
> *love lockets of memory*
> *coaxed from his memory box.*

Bunting would be an exemplar, the dissenting poet, avoiding fuss, handing out good advice to those who came close to him: 'Cut, cut, cut.' His name is recorded on a plain stone in the burial ground alongside the Quaker meeting house at Brigflatts; near the place where George Fox preached on one of his journeys through the north.

At Packet Boat Lane, we came away from the tow path, twitchy to make contact with a road that went over the motorway, where a (disused) branch of the Grand Union Canal passed under it. The tarmac had broken up into sticky black granules, like a porridge made from coal. Tough spikes of grass pushed through the mantle. I lay, curved to the camber, to take a photograph; and would, if I could, have swum away to the west. The sounds of the road, as the M25 approached the tangled interchange with the M4, were compulsive; as complex and as many-voiced as a Bill Griffiths poem. A sound that was its own score.

4

We lost the Colne at Cowley and now, at West Drayton, we bid farewell to the eastward swerving Grand Union Canal. Off-highway territory is cake-sliced into discrete bands; the natural flow, of water and footpath, is to the south, the Thames, but the Money requires a series of difficult-to-negotiate horizontal barriers. Railway (out of Paddington). M4. A4 (Bath Road). The inscrutable geometry of Heathrow's terminals, runways, hangars and car parks. How are we going to walk through that lot?

Our first step must be to the west, in the direction of the vertical blue band of the M25 (colour co-ordinated on my Nicholson with its mate the Colne). River and road define the westerly limits of London Airport's piracy. The land-grab that will never be satisfied. Terminals 5, 6, 7: it's not enough. Flight-zone must be bigger than the city it serves. In five years, so the planners tell us, there will be four-hour intervals (on good days) between leaving the centre of London and being called for your flight. (Such optimistic forecasts were soon overtaken by events: four hours might get you down the Euston Road, invalid carriages sailing past the window of your cab, limping backpackers leaving you in their wake. Heathrow *was* the holiday. You'd be lucky to get out of there in a week, patted down by security, papers checked, sleep on a bench. The full asylum-seeker experience for the price of a bucket-shop ticket.) Check-in queues will stretch back to that model Concorde on its traffic island, to the M4. Severed communities, such as Harmondsworth, are under threat; in time, West Drayton itself will be swallowed.

A theatre of catastrophe in which all the global disasters play:

heightened security, longer waits. More time for comfort-blanket shopping malls, bad coffee. Flight after flight of Third World drug mules, snacked to the eyeballs on coke-flavoured condoms. More desert parking lots for unwanted aircraft. Why not use the M25, stack 'em nose-to-tail, Colnbrook to Leather-head?

'Who needs West Drayton?' you say. But you're wrong. West Drayton is the gateway to the Green Path, a site of some significance for psychogeographers, dowsers, Zodiac concept-ualists (of the K.E. Maltwood tendency).

None of these great themes was immediately obvious, as we picked our way through the urban sprawl. You could, if you pushed it, remark the Railway Arms, with its balconies and verandah; a colonial outpost fallen into disuse when travellers became commuters. The rest was a standard extrusion of hair-dressers, charity caves, fast food. The difference is – thinking back to the sleepwalking hamlets of the Colne Valley – a slip-stream energy derived from railway/motorway/canal systems. West Drayton is the frontier, the first whiff of the (wild) West. Bicycle shops are a nostalgic recollection of the days when H.G. Wells's clerks took to the country roads. Tidy suburbs, brave in their pretensions, bleed into raw-elbowed commerce.

For a pound I snaffle a copy of Simon Winchester's *The Surgeon of Crowthorne* (on the strength of its puff as 'A Tale of Murder, Madness and the Love of Words'). The cover illustra-tion (Broadmoor Special Hospital) showcases, under an operatic sky, the most extreme version of the asylums we've been track-ing around the M25. A prison for no-hopers with no date for release. Winchester runs with the ambivalence of that term: *asylum*. He quotes Johnson's *Dictionary*: 'A place out of which he that has fled to it, may not be taken.' Sanctuary, refuge; trap.

An ordinary house, in an ordinary village, in a prettily rural royal county just beyond the boundaries of London.

We have to orientate ourselves for the push south, over the M4. I like the look of a church set at the head of something called The Avenue. The church tower, if we blag our way inside, will offer a view across lagoons and gravel pits to the Tower Arms Hotel on the far side of the M25.

Lurking-with-intent, in the vicinity of a fifteenth-century church, parts of which have a thirteenth-century pedigree, when coated in the dust and dirt of a seven-mile yomp down the canal, tends to arouse a degree of suspicion in proper citizens. The solitary communicant (female) is not so bad; the parents dropping off their kids (from gleaming metro-country motors) are less happy. To the point of making the phone call. Hitting the emergency button. We have cameras and ruck-sacks. We're indigents or asylum seekers, possibly paedophiles. John Piper-tendency terrorists. The 'church as sanctuary' deal has been discontinued, charity begins in Station Road, West Drayton, with the musty books and racks of dead clothes. Charity is a corporate enterprise, cold calls, junk mail, celebrity auctions. It's where skimmers like Lord Archer get their start.

We persevere, follow the communicant, gain access. St Martin's is the parish church of West Drayton. A square-towered building lodged in a small, well-kept burial ground, alongside a turreted sixteenth-century gatehouse. A good day on the hoof should include: (1) a section of river or canal, (2) a Formica-table breakfast, (3) a motorway bridge, (4) a discontinued madhouse, (5) a pub, (6) a mound, (7) a wrap of London weather (monochrome to sunburst), (8) one major surprise. So far, so good.

Being *inside* a church, after the locked doors of the northern quadrant, is a minor shock: the 800-year franchise works its spatial and temporal magic, the narrow building detaches itself from its surroundings, the bluster of West Drayton.

Hats off, from custom or superstition, we creep and whisper. Cruise the usual circuit, interrogating the fabric: in expectation of some clue or sign. Or confirmation. Thicker air. Stone-dust and candle grease. Stained light. Windows designed by Burne-Jones, to the memory of the Mercers. The monumental brass of Dr James Good, the Elizabethan physician. Alabaster memorials to the De Burghs – an echo from Jane Austen (Lady Catherine de Bourgh); Fysch and his wife Easter. A 'ship' memorial to Captain Rupert Billingsley. The suspended teardrop of the pyx – in which the sacrament is reserved. This is lowered on a cord from the opening above the tower arch. A medieval survivor? A swinging lodestone from which to navigate the next stage of our journey? Not this time. The pyx is a crafted fake, based on the canopy at Dennington, Suffolk, and created by underemployed technicians at Pinewood Studios.

The item of church furniture that pricks Renchi's interest is the font. He chews his fingers, studies the leaflet, in which Theo Samuel sounds a cautionary note: 'We are aware, at St Martin's, that the beauty of the architecture and surroundings of the ancient church can contribute on the one hand to a sense of calm trust in God, but on the other to an overdependence on the achievements of the past.' The Revd Samuel wants to shake the faithful from their torpor. They must confront 'the everyday realities of life', especially the needs of 'the poor'. He invokes the tradition of St Martin of Tours.

Martin sounds like a useful guide: he was both bishop and hermit, missionary and wonderworker. According to my *Dictionary of Saints*, 'he penetrated into the remotest part of his diocese and beyond its borders, on foot, on donkey-back, or by water'.

The whiteness of the font, with its relief figures, has a grubby pink sheen – from generations of supplicating hands that have polished, but not worn away, the curious tableaux. The font dates from the fifteenth century. Beyond the standard Christian iconography, crucifixion and pietà, is a stumpy-legged man in a cowl, brandishing a chisel or poignard. Near his right hand is a large leaf. The suggestion is that this personage is the sculptor, the stone carver working on ecclesiastical tracery. The design incorporates a vine leaf to signal the fact that the donor was a vintner (of whose trade St Martin was the patron saint).

The carver's chisel, driven into the ground by a raised bone or dildo, marks the spot; the spring from which the Green Way begins.

It was another visit, months later, when I managed to get up into the tower. To see for myself how the land opened out: the path to St Mary's Church at Harmondsworth. The crop of torpedo graves. The M25 with its constant flickering movement. We had stumbled on an active, but little used, pilgrims' path. The Avenue. Heading, through a tunnel of pink blossom, towards the motorway and the site of a Benedictine priory at Harmondsworth. The sequestered principality of Heathrow.

The breeze barrelling down the long straight track – a diminishing asphalt tongue – doubled Renchi over. He leant into the wind, tugged on the straps of his rucksack like a skydiver. For the first time, since Shenley, we didn't need maps. We trusted the ground. Snow-pink excesses of municipal cherry trees. We followed our noses.

Patches of greenery, dog grass, a few trees: they are absorbed into a grander scheme. Isolate one Lombardy pine. Stand still and *listen*. Outsiders are struck by effects, shifts, that locals walking their animals, or collecting their kids from a fenced-off school, take for granted. There is a mystery at the edge of great conurbations; in the light, in places travellers have passed through for centuries.

West Drayton peters out, estates double-glazed against motorway siroccos; a tangle of tree-named streets (Laurel Lane, Rowan Avenue, The Brambles). Would you fancy 'The Brambles' as an address? End of the line. Shuddering from traffic. Fence decorated by tossed paper, ubiquitous scraps of black plastic (burst bin bags from an ecological division of household rubbish).

I'm intoxicated by this path; a squeaky gate takes us on to a footbridge over the hectic M4. The demons are not only answering our questions, they're shouting each other down in their eagerness to get in on the act. There's Junction 4, the Heathrow turn-off, with its attendant fear and rage. Primal screams. And the warped rectangle of Junction 4B (M4). The infamous Junction 15 of the M25. A cat's cradle of underpasses and flyovers, impossible decisions.

Our footbridge is a stopped wave. The sky, this morning, is dull and anxious; a dirty scum of cloud into which lamp standards twist their necks, in a feeding frenzy. Beyond the small lake, the tree line of Harmondsworth, planes are coming into Heathrow; a procession of them, drifting in slow motion, like thistledown over yellow fields.

Renchi squats on his heels, meditating. The footbridge trembles and vibrates. If it ran across the Thames between St Paul's and the Tate Modern, they'd close it down. The West Drayton bridge isn't a tourist attraction, not yet. It *ought* to be. All the powers and thrones and dominions of transport are here, angelic orders of diesel, jet fuel, crop spray, animal and human shit. Burial grounds of lost villages. The Perry Oaks Sludge Disposal Works.

The pond's surface is choppy. You can imagine fat-bellied planes blown backwards. 'Billy & Mary' have scratched a Unionist courtship poem into the metallic handrail of the bridge. A sponsored artist has laid out a giant's causeway of limestone rocks in an incomplete maze; an arrangement that sustains the Hegira, the secret track. Good agricultural land skirting grey water. The continuing alignment of filed-and-forgotten churches.

The account of how the Air Ministry (Civil Aviation Authority) acquired this land, as told by Philip Sherwood in *The History of Heathrow* (revised edition, 1993), comes to life as we move in on the erased village. It's not just nostalgia, the loss of market gardens, farms, cottages and coaching inn. Such things have their time and are doomed to removal (as images)

into local history archives – which will themselves be rationalised and dumped. Heathrow, one of a chain of small settlements to the west of Hounslow Heath, is a site with a pedigree
as old or older than London itself. (Renchi and I, on our walk
around the City walls, finished in the Museum of London,
where one of the better exhibits featured an Iron Age village; a
cluster of huts that dissolved, as you looked at them, into an
aircraft taxiing on to the runway. Rub your eyes and thatched
huts break through the tarmac. Neither description is definitive; one state of consciousness bleeds continually into another.)

Sherwood's *History* opens with an 'aerial view of Heathrow
in 1935'. What appears to be a road choked with traffic is
revealed, under magnification, as a dense hedgerow. Prime
agricultural land, divided into rectangles, squares and strips, on
the edge of an unseen city. The field where London Airport
was to be built, in an era before crop circle frenzy, is loud
with evidence of previous settlement; a square within a square,
a deep ditch, secondary paths that confirm Stukeley's 1723
drawing of 'Caesar's Camp'.

Stukeley's three figures (their chains, their cloaked supervisor) anticipate the choice of this ground as a suitable location
for General Roy's establishment of a baseline of accurately
measured length – which would act as the prelude to a trigono-
metrical survey of Great Britain. Roy spoke of 'the extraordinary levelness of the surface'. The line was drawn, with
some annoyance from coach traffic, on the 'Great Road'
(Hounslow to Staines), between King's Arbour at Heathrow
and the Poor House at Hampton Court, a distance of five
miles. Surveyors discovered that the spire of the church at
Banstead in Surrey was 'dead in line with the two ends of the
base'. The work was undertaken in June and July 1784.

The terminals of the baseline were marked with wooden
pipes and wagon wheels set in the ground; by 1791 these
decayed and were replaced by upturned cannon. A plaque at
King's Arbour records the event. The distance, as measured by

Roy, was 27404.01 feet. Captain Mudge repeated the exercise: 27404.24 feet. Finally, the Ordnance Survey Standard, as determined by Clarke, was declared at 27406.19 feet. From a pleasant suburban stroll through market gardens, heathland, river valley, the triangulation of Britain and the construction of 'a complete and accurate map' was begun.

Common land, which Cobbett in his *Rural Rides* (1853) found to be nothing but 'nasty strong dirt upon a bed of gravel . . . a sample of all that is bad and villainous', had once, thanks to abundant sources of manure (human and animal), been fertile and productive. Wagons taking produce into London returned with a ballast of horse dung.

What happened, in 1943, when the Air Ministry began to evict the people of Heathrow, to tear down farms and cottages, can be interpreted as a standard Orwellian exercise: obfuscation, emollient lies, bureaucratic steamroller, oblivion. Philip Sherwood, searching Air Ministry cabinets for photographic material to illustrate his history, stumbled on files dealing with the development and compulsory purchase of land (under wartime regulations).

Sherwood writes:

The claim has always been made that Heathrow was developed as a result of an urgent need for the RAF to have a bomber base in the London area. The files in the PRO show that there never was such a need and the airfield was regarded from the start as being a civil airport for London. The War Cabinet was deceived into giving approval for the development . . . The Defence of the Realm Act 1939 was used by the Air Ministry to requisition land and to circumvent the public enquiry that would otherwise have had to be held.

Harold Balfour (Parliamentary Under Secretary of State for Air between 1938 and 1944) is breathtaking in his arrogance. Sherwood quotes a 1973 autobiography. Balfour, by then, was Lord Balfour of Inchrye. 'Almost the last thing I did in the Air

Ministry of any importance was to hi-jack for Civil Aviation land on which London Airport stands under the noses of resistant Ministerial colleagues. If hi-jack is too strong a word I plead guilty to the lesser crime of deceiving a cabinet Committee.'

Emergency wartime powers were used to establish, by a network of dubious commercial deals, a major airport that was only fifteen miles from the centre of London. Much follows from the original deception. It was suggested that an airstrip had to be laid out for the transportation of troops to the Far East, when it was known that this would never be necessary and that, in any case, there were other airfields that could quite easily undertake the operation.

'We took the land,' Balfour boasts. 'Hiroshima killed Phase Two (troop transport). London Airport stands.'

To the innocent, those who prefer to believe that government is always right, there is nothing very shocking in this fix. It worked. An unimportant village disappeared. Fairey Aviation, who had run an aerodrome on the chosen site, were put out of business. Bullying letters with official stamps. Compensation boards that moved with Kafkaesque torpidity. The English way. Perimeter land was tolerated for several very clear purposes: to stack the mentally inadequate, to build golf courses, to board cats and dogs, to hide toxic industries, to dump landfill and to provide bunkers, research stations and safe houses for the Secret State.

The chicanery that converted a convenient strip of ground into the madness of Europe's busiest airport was an unexceptional piece of business. It had all happened before, in London, when the railway stations were built. Now it was the turn of the complacent country folk who got their living from trade with the city. Whingeing yokels. Serial sentimentalists. Couldn't they appreciate the economic benefits, the cultural connections? American hotels with room service and mini-bars, instead of crusty old coaching inns.

Perhaps the original planners had an instinct for the sacred geometry of Heathrow. Measurement and surveying were always the metaphors. Three men linked by chains. A ditched field. The pattern of early settlement revealed by aerial photography. A temple of the stars.

The brick and flint church of St Mary in Harmondsworth is notable for its Norman doorway. The church, of course, is locked. But the famous tithe barn, restored, pretty much cased in perspex, is still on show: HARMONDSWORTH INVESTMENTS, XYPLEX. Neat gravel drive. Fake gas lamp standards. Coach house as office. Tall yew hedge. The corporate spread of Surrey demands its heritage tokens. Efficiency and pedigree: old but clean. Air-conditioned Elizabethan. Tithe barn with IT power lines. Miss Marple's church and pub and village green: ten minutes from an international airport.

The Green Way slants across a recreation ground at the precise angle that keeps it in parallel with the M25. I'll forgive Balfour all his machinations for leaving us with this definitively unresolved track between worlds, topographies. To our left – kill the scream of the jumbos – is a swoop of green; a lush crop contained by low-level industrial units, the Heathrow sliproad. A curving chainlink fence with the obligatory paraphernalia: photo-voltaic scanners, surveillance towers, radio masts. We're in the sound spiral of the flight path, the drone of traffic. We're on camera, obviously, the only figures in a wide-sky landscape. There are no tall buildings, nothing that might knock the wheels from a Boeing.

When our path abandons us, without warning, on the A4 (the Colnbrook Bypass), it's disorientating. This is flags-of-all-nations hotel territory: Sheraton, Heathrow Park (aka Alamo). Stars and stripes on the highest pole. People (J.G. Ballard, Jean-Luc Godard) have discovered eroticism in the conjunction of hotel and airport. This, I suppose, would be the 'rubber insulated sex' that the judge at the first Archer trial found so distasteful. Anonymity. Processing plants through which faceless couples pass without leaving a trace. A sound-baffled cell. A power shower. Neutral ground. Oblique glimpses, through gauze, of aircraft on the runway.

The concessionary buses ('Courtesy Service') that shuttle customers into the Alamo look like ambulances. German transport to an American hotel. A hard road to cross.

Pulling west, down a vestigial trace of the old Bath Road, we recover a taste of what was lost when Heathrow (the village) turned into landfill. A run of deep-England gardens, thatched wishing wells, early season blooms, determined to ignore the incursions of an international airport. This is a notion as perverse as Derek Jarman's rock garden in the lee of the nuclear power station, the off-channel gales of Dungeness. Windows shudder, tiles are threatened. Any day now a brick of frozen shit, a lump of aircraft debris, a falling asylum seeker, will crash through the roof. But, with leaded panes, net curtains, white doors, beds of hardy perennials, carpet-sized lawns, the rustic fantasy thrives. You can't hear yourself speak, the flow of traffic is continuous and agitated. The quirkily local is asserted in the teeth of the architectural Esperanto of Heathrow's expanding purlieus.

On a bridge over a tributary of the Colne, stamped with a brightly gilded crown from the reign of William IV (1834), we watch an airbus skid over the protective fence of the Western Perimeter Road. Heathrow is its own city, a Vatican of the western suburbs. London flatters itself in insisting on the connection. The airport complex with its international hotels, storage facilities, semi-private roads, is as detached from the shabby entropy of the metropolis as is the City, the original walled settlement. They have their own rules, their own security forces, the arrogance of global capitalism. They service Moloch in whatever form he chooses to reveal himself; they facilitate drug/armament, blood/oil economies.

Negotiating Stanwell Moor Road, with the Colne and the elevated M25 to our right, we hit one of those passages where the Green Way is swallowed and overridden by furiously competing narratives. Dwarfish lighting poles, bright yellow cruciform structures (flight-path indicators) in roadside fields. Planes coming in at various heights. The vibrations shake our skeletons, loosen fillings. The madness of this pilgrimage through a landscape that challenges or defies walkers is a pure adrenalin rush. At the big roundabout, the blue and white sign – M25 – is a holy relic on our Milky Way. Renchi, resting at the verge, cross-legged, hood up, contemplates the vortex: planes, vans, airport buses. Tremendous discriminations of noise.

If you want a severed community (cut off and proud of it), try Stanwellmoor. Airport access roads on two sides, M25 and King George VI Reservoir on the others. Rabbit killers, poachers, dealers in whatever can be shaken loose from Heathrow (definitively misdirected luggage), Stanwellmoor has them all. Living in an easygoing, freebooters' paradise, under the flight path; under the tons of stored water. I like what there is of it, a couple of dozen houses and two pubs. The first is open, but won't feed us.

'Do you do food?'

'Yes, but not this week. Kitchen's closed.'

We plod on. At the roadside, in a wire cage, is a notable collection of broken plaster statuary: praying hands, decapitated madonnas, oyster shells, tortoises. Renchi fishes out a draped, classical figure – Minerva? – and poses, his large bearded face in place of her missing head. The white of the plaster has worn away, revealing runs of terracotta that look like roadkill. I dip for trophies, shoving a few amputated limbs in my rucksack for replanting in Hackney.

The Hope Inn, oxymoronic, is nicely situated on the moor's edge; a friendly, but essentially hopeless enterprise. Asserting its humanity in a place that has no use for it. Remove the Hope Inn to somewhere between Winchelsea and Dymchurch, give it a pedigree as a haunt of smugglers, and it might work. Ploughing through a ploughman's mighty roll, washed down with cider, I understand why the Industrial Revolution succeeded: ploughmen were doubled over with stomach cramps, mouths gummy and snag-toothed. The quantity of this lunchtime treat is overgenerous, a brick of orange cheese, a tub of onions and pickles on a bed of lettuce (the size of rhubarb leaves).

Rain is jabbing at the moor. It's comfortable in here; genial folk hitch themselves on to stools, nobody bothers much about two gently steaming walkers with massive packs. I stretch the break with a dried-out cigar, take it with me when we move on, down the Bonehead Ditch. Along the embankment of the King George VI Reservoir.

We agree: this is the most inspiring section we have so far encountered on our M25 orbit. The road keeps its distance. We can hear it, but we're closer to the spirit of the Colne as it wriggles across Stanwellmoor.

How could you get a car on to this path? Reservoir on one side, Bonehead Ditch on the other. And here is a burnt-out shell, on its back, scaly with rust; the kind of trophy joyriders leave in Epping Forest. With a POLICE AWARE notice.

Renchi decides to go through the fence, to climb the slope to the reservoir. Burdened with broken statuary, Nicholson's map, spare sweater and water bottle, I don't follow him. I photograph his progress – as he turns into a chalk figure, cousin to the Long Man of Wilmington. Red scarf tossed by the wind, pitched against clouds, he looks heroic. What he sees, the mystery of dark water, is not revealed – until I come back, in the summer, to do some filming. Even in my snapshots, you find something that announces: Big Subject. Thunder skies pressing on an inland sea (a Soviet-style secret); concrete fence posts dividing the unwalked reservoir fringe from the lush yellow slopes of the embankment. It's like working your way around a Dorset earthwork – and still being in sight of Heathrow. Thomas Hardy or John Cowper Powys cohabiting with J.G. Ballard and Thomas Pynchon. Land, where it is forbidden, is also preserved: the reservation reserves time, that which is unviewed becomes the ultimate view. The recognition of a dream place.

After the taboo-defying vision, the Green Way ties all the loose ends together: Colne, pylons, Staines Bypass. On the rough wall of the dual-carriageway underpass is an arrow and a strange graffito: INIT ILAND. Cockney paraphrase of Inuit? Green weed in swift-flowing water. Our track winds its way through the dormitory estates of Staines. We've made it, the town, the railway station. The car.

Ad Pontes, the Romans called it: a place of bridges, over the two rivers, Thames and Colne. There was once a stone, in a meadow beside the bridge, known as the London Stone, said to mark the western limit of the jurisdiction of the City of London over the Thames. The back story has been quietly buried, tidied away into a museum around the side of the (discontinued) town hall. A few main street pubs peddle their pedigree. Staines is best known these days as the fictional base for the comedic celebrity, Ali G. A branded look: dark aviator glasses, sock-hat, male jewellery, white as black. A voice, innit?

The market element of the Roman town is still present in a scatter of sweet stalls and a lorry dispensing fruit and veg. The museum boasts of Staines as the world capital for the manufacture of linoleum. That's about it.

A statue of Queen Victoria, a war memorial angel that everyone (including me) photographs, access to the Thames path. For the first time, since we lost sight of the Millennium Dome, we're back with the river: in all its sovereign dignity. The sun is going down behind the bridge, the familiar sludge-coloured waters, running smooth and swift, are fired. Like a petrol spill. We stand at the point where the weary Colne rushes under a footbridge and into the main stream, the Thames.

On another day, we might have plunged into the water. The Swan Hotel, with its sloping lawns, looks inviting. Reality inhibits instinct: we trudge, through evening traffic, back to the station.

The shamanic archer has vanished. In the course of our day's walk, the Silk Cut poster has been papered over. Scarecrow, smoke warning, fields: deleted.

Diggers & Despots

Cutting the Corner,
Staines to Epsom

1

Picking my way early through Shepherd's Bush: 26 May 1999. Associated as it is with stop/start journeys out of town – the grot-shock of the Green – this is not an area with which I'm comfortable. I've never walked it, other than rapid hikes through Popular Book Centres on my way down to the original Any Amount of Books in Hammersmith. I came here recently to interview J.G. Ballard for a book I was doing on Cronenberg's film of *Crash*. Ballard weekends in the borough. It's as close as he wants to come to London.

I took the wrong road, involved myself in an unnecessary detour, a swing past Fortress BBC in White City. I was looking for a side street, a right-hander off Wood Lane. The conjunction of Wormwood Scrubs Prison, Westway and the White City estates struck me as a convenient accident of civic planning. Empty-headed fools, heading for the TV studios, drive through here with their windows down, flashing conspicuous expenditure in the form of a Rolex. Masochists blabber on cellphones. East Acton to White City (desolate rat runs between Westway and the Uxbridge Road) is bandit country. I was fortunate, it was first light. The bandits were sleeping it off. And, in any case, as was obvious to the most shortsighted teenage toller: I was unreconstructed Swatch Man in a twelve-year-old motor. An ex-drug dealer BMW with one active headlamp and moss emphasising the rectangle of the sunroof.

Now that our orbital walk had crossed the river and – if you included the Lea Valley opener – reached its halfway point, I made the mistake of talking about it. A journalist (autodidact, radio producer, scriptwriter, assembler of micro-books that come in alphabetically arranged units) thought he might be able to punt a piece, written while accompanying us on the next leg of the journey. Kevin Jackson, in his day, had wallpapered most of the broadsheets: Blake, Ruskin, Humphrey Jennings, Anthony Burgess, Surrealism. You hum it, he'll play it: Alan Moore, Bill Griffiths, a photographer called Richard Heeps who chased the Greenwich Meridian Line across Cambridgeshire. Jackson tags Heeps as working 'the old Modernist Project of Making It Strange'. If there is anything stranger than camping (without coercion) in the triangulation between the Westway, Scrubs Lane and Harrow Road, I don't want to know about it.

Kevin uses his West London property as a bibliophile's crash-pad. He lives elsewhere. With his interests, the need to hit libraries on a daily basis, do jokes in Greek and Latin, eat competitive dinners, it was inevitable that he'd return to Cambridge. He acts as generous patron to the sort of troop Sandy Mackendrick assembled for *The Ladykillers*. Undiscovered geniuses of the city, free (for a time) to pursue arcane researches or compose intricately layered epics set in suburban hinterlands. The bathroom was an unrequired extra. The fridge contained a pot or two of outdated yogurt.

The bell doesn't ring. Kevin's house is posthumous, dead in the definitive way East Acton houses die: theoretical tenants come and go, you never see them. The front door is a coffin lid. This byway is a Prozac dormitory, a self-referential nexus feeding on a busy through-road. In East London it would be squatted. And the hallway decorated with hanging bicycle parts. Alongside Wood Lane you have invisible Crusoes, let go by Radio 3; decent souls enduring an exile at the limits of the possible (where the Central Line loses contact with the centre).

6.15 a.m. The figure at the upstairs window is Kevin Jackson. Dressed and ready. He's been waiting there all night. Tall, quite sturdy, with a full head of hair. Bounding downstairs and out of the door, he employs a manly handshake. I'm not convinced that Wardrobe have come up with the optimum outfit for a hike through the Surrey countryside on a warm day. If you spotted Kevin, hanging about the bus stop near TV Centre, you might guess: alpha male from *Blake's Seven* – a British lead with Californian aspirations. Wardrobe has gone with Sam Shepherd leather (improperly distressed). Combat veteran. This can perform, coupled with circular (*Dr Strangelove*) spectacles, quite effectively on a filigree-featured miniature like Tom Cruise. Kevin is no miniature; he's the proper size for an English gentleman, head and shoulders above the mob.

This overload of culture references, film titles, anecdotes, fits the man. He's lived in America, labouring on (unmade) scripts with Paul Schrader. He's worked with an Oscar-winning documentary director. He's edited and written episodes of *The Archers*. He's visited Ballard in Shepperton (*New Worlds* fan from the age of eleven). He's just back from Scotland. On his way to . . .

Kevin is the freelance's freelance. Whatever hours you burn – essays in New York, reviews in London, radio, TV, presentation, production, small press squib, large press remainder – you sink a little deeper each year. It never comes in as fast as it goes out. Success kills you. Copy is edited on the phone as you wait for the next appointment. You review your own reviews. A day on the hoof is just what Kevin needs – but he's lumbered himself with having to write as he walks. He's doing a photography course and a Latin course and he's dropping out of social anthropology. By the time we reach the M4, he'll have compiled (by alphabet) a list of British road movies, a dictionary of motorway fiction, a critique (illustrated) of Manser Associates Hilton Hotel at Heathrow (glass-fronted fridge for body parts).

Some monkey-drumming battery, or Puritan residue, keeps Kevin on the move, an exuberant neurosis of achievement. Been everywhere, read everything, but he hasn't come up with the right kit for Staines. The leather rucksack hangs too low on his back, it'll bruise the spine. He's midway through the photography course; studied the masters, penned the thesis, bought the camera. One small detail overlooked: no film stock. The gleaming jacket, authentically frontier (envelope-pushing, ass-kicking), is too heavy. It will cook him if he wears it; cripple him if he carries it. The greying hair is probably long enough to keep the sun off his scalp, but he's not hefting any water, or packing plasters. Yellow trailbreaker boots may look great at the timber line (tested in Notting Hill), they're an overreaction to the Thames path, the lazy villages of Surrey. The preppie striped shirt with button-down collar and pen in pocket is fine, if a little tight fitting for a day of swinging arms and excited conversational semaphore.

Renchi is waiting at Staines station: blue shirt tied into piratical bandanna, loose sweater, rucksack packed with maps, water, spare T-shirts. I pose the two men under the hoarding: the Silk Cut scarecrow has been replaced by a fake US Marine, a black and white BT ad. The affronted sergeant (old-timer with moustache) and jug-eared recruit, muddy from route march. The freshness and bright expectancy of our two strollers play ominously against their oversize counterparts.

From the window of the station café, I see the Marine sergeant, mouth wide in a silent scream. He is both promoting Cellnet and demonstrating how you can live without it: Just Shout. The sky, bad news for Kevin's body-armour, is an unbroken blue; of a purity that cohabits with the glassy surface of the Formica rectangles on which our plates of poached eggs and thick buttery toast rest, waiting for a break in the chat.

The café, convenient for station, town and river, is so true to itself that we award it the immortality of the unnoticed. The building is twinned with the Slough Electrical repair shop, outside which is parked a Vespa motor scooter. Bodged Bauhaus. Flat roof (with shipboard rails), metal-trim windows, narrow doorways; white paint showing signs of weathering. Light pours in, casting precise shadows across wood-panel walls. Tables are small and set close together to encourage intimacy with other all-day breakfasters. If you want democracy, the free debate of the Levellers and Ranters, this is where you'll find it. Elbow to elbow with layabouts, semi-urban casuals. Readers of yesterday's newspapers.

Kevin Jackson's account of the day's walk, published in the *Independent* (as 'Putting London in Its Place'), is very good on our induction into Staines café society. We noticed the other dilettantes, the early loungers (two skiving, one in permanent residence), but that didn't stop us pulling out the maps and associated literature. Kevin, I realise, is taking everything down in a neat notebook. Like a proper journalist. Or TV policeman. (I'm with the old-time coppers who always wrote up their notes *after* the event. Selective memories.)

We might have got away with it – if Renchi had held back on Mary Caine's *The Kingston Zodiac*, which he'd picked up on one of his visits to Glastonbury. Advancing from Waltham Abbey to Shenley, by way of Temple Bar, we were in my liminal territory, we ran with my myths: star ceilings, Rodinsky, John Clare in Epping Forest, Hawksmoor's grave. Now that we were about to cross the river into Surrey, I was adrift. Renchi would act as our guide.

Mary Caine, inspired by Mrs Katharine Maltwood's *A Guide to Glastonbury's Temple of the Stars*, had marked up the country around her base in Kingston in accordance with the configurations of a spiritual zodiac. The blue and gold ceiling of Waltham Abbey church would be reasserted as a metaphor – by a walk that carried us, initially, down the back of the Dog. 'Huge hounds guard these circles,' warned Mary Caine.

Glastonbury, mound rising out of the Somerset levels, is easy to map (and read) in terms of gigantic 'effigies'. Motorways, warehousing, ribbon development and private estates do not complicate the picture. The outlines of ancient field systems are still visible from the air. Mrs Maltwood's Dog is Gwyn Ab Nudd, 'the British Pluto'. His pedigree is Celtic and he inhabits *The High History of the Holy Graal*. The Hound is formed 'by conducting channels of water between immense artificial earthworks, and by the ancient "path" bounding Aller Wall'. Maltwood quotes a section from *The High History*. It refers to a river as 'water royal'.

With 'bounding' moors and 'water royal' (the Thames running through Windsor, where pedestrians are turned away from the riverbank), it would be easy to suppose that we were working from Maltwood's text. Such speculations are energising devices; they help us to respect a landscape. The local is taken into the archetypal: contours and canals construct patterns around churches, monastic ruins, 'historic' houses.

'It might be supposed,' Mrs Maltwood writes, 'that one could see such creatures on any map! but it would be impossible to find a *circular* traditional design of Zodiacal and other constellation figures, arranged in their proper order, and corresponding *with their respective stars*, unless they had been laid out in sequence, according to plan.'

Fold-out maps, in the 1964 reissue of Maltwood's influential book, show star-creatures. Cloud shadows drifting over a circular bowl: 'The Circle of Giant Effigies.' Why not read the M25 orbit as another such circle – and let Mary Caine's tightly packed frontispiece act as our guide to the south-west corner? Maltwood's circle is sparsely inhabited, forms swim free; Caine's zodiac is an exotic slum, an outstation of Thorpe Park. An orgy of symbols: interspecies collisions. The Lion of Chessington mounting the Doggy of Chobham Common. Rams, bulls, griffins, they're all at it.

'Kingston's Cerberus rears his head at Egham, where Holloway Sanatorium's tower on his nose is a landmark for miles,' reads Renchi. Thereby alerting our shaven-headed neighbour. There's a pair of them; one in a down-stuffed gilet, the other in flowerpot hat and blood-red spectacles. The speaker, the crophead with scimitar sideburns, has a trace of the rent boy about him (if you were casting a drama for Channel 4). Delicate/ tough and pushing it hard, to come on as a wit in Staines station café. He interrogates us, his mate does the local history. 'Payroll boys' with time on their hands.

'What do you do for a living?'

'We walk.'

'*Walk*? They're fucking tramps,' shouts the old boy, barnacled to the corner.

It has to be explained: walks, photographs – then, at some future date, a book. Kevin, who is force-feeding his notebook, breaks off to dig out a mound of my back titles from his rucksack. He travels with a portable library. He is approaching this walk (and the rest of life) as a tutorial for which he is inadequately prepared. Keep talking, reminiscing, improvising. Don't let the buggers stray anywhere near the ostensible subject.

The payroll boys are appeased: we're nutters with a project, some remote chance of a distant pay day. We need their services. The old man snorts, returns to his *Sun*.

'Bloody drug addicts!'

One breakfast under the belt, second teas and more toast on order, the lads are in good humour. A fine bright day. A light breeze from the river. The cosmological fruit machine doesn't pay out very often, *carpe diem*.

Mary Caine for the spirit, the payroll boys for the nitty-gritty: our man talks of tunnels, bunkers, mysteries. This is the list. A village, Thorpe, with the longest village green in England. Brooklands racetrack with underground workings and a ghost. St George's Hill. 'That's where Cliff Richard lives. Squatters took over a mansion where Tom Jones used to . . .' John Lennon with his white pianos and customised Rollers. St George's Hill is definitely on the agenda, the place where Gerrard Winstanley and the Diggers launched their experiment in rustic tribalism. But we won't make it, not this time, unless we get going.

Much of Staines is steel-shuttered. MADHOUSE UK: green lettering above an undisclosed business venture. Kevin has film in his camera (no reserve stock) and is blazing away. Renchi, more circumspect, continues his quiet logging: prompts for future paintings. We cross the bridge, pick up the Thames path, move out in the direction of the M25.

Shadows from overhanging greenery infect the river. The walk is shady, agreeable. Dappled sunlight. Kevin's dark glasses aren't strictly necessary. Runnymede Bridge, with its shallow span, emerges from the tree tops. It looks too slender to carry motorway traffic. My sense, when I'm driving, is that the river makes no impact on the road. Unless you know it's there, you'll miss it.

It would be better to swim. These are sacred places, where road meets river. Staines and Dartford, very different Thames crossings, are the highlights of any motorway circuit. On the Queen Elizabeth II Bridge, road dominates. The tidal Thames is unwalkable, unswimmable; impossible. Literally suspending disbelief, to drive over the broad span of water, as it opens (storage tanks and container ships) to the World Ocean, marks you. You die into what you see. You purchase vision at the expense of mortality. You relish the play of cables as they flick against riverlight. You feel younger, stronger, elevated by a section of motorway that isn't motorway: the only point in the circuit where imagination overrides the M25's compulsive reductionism.

Coming on Runnymede Bridge, white stone, is less dramatic: water shimmers, plays with sound. Here is the cathedral of the motorway: an open-sided temple of transformation. Perch on one of the broad ribs, tight under the road, and watch curved concrete sail on green water like a crescent moon. A single arch, mirrored in the dark river, becomes a cave. Light dances on the rough underlay of the M25. Passing craft set up surges that turn the reflections on the far bank into spirals of smoke. You could treat these spaces beneath the motorway as cubicles of incubation; cold bunks in which to dream of fantastic journeys.

This structure, set across the Thames, is discussed in terms of Egypt or Babylon. A water shrine in which to acknowledge and record the passage of the sun. Steps down to the river. Slopes leading up to the road. The bridge is actually two bridges, one for each carriageway of the M25. Arriving from Staines, you see a plain, functional structure, something like Waterloo Bridge; walking east from Runnymede, back towards London, you notice the decorative features, stone balusters that belong in a country park.

The harmonious linking of disparate elements, a symbolic marriage of river and road, has a simple history: in terms of civil engineering. The 1961 bridge, designed by Sir Edwin Lutyens, was incorporated into 'a graceful concrete structure' by Arup Associates and the consultant engineers, Ove Arup and Partners. Genteel Surrey rustification. The Lutyens bridge would carry the northbound traffic of the M25 and the A30; the Arup bridge the southbound carriageways of both. The new bridge was 138 metres long. The tender price was £6.4 million. And the contractor was Bovis Fairclough.

Walking from bright sunlight into this cool darkness – reflections, brilliant bars moving across ruffled water – is always exhilarating. Excursion parties break up: somebody will climb on to the arch, somebody will lounge against a pillar. Renchi, this time, puts himself in the split between the southbound carriageway and the supporting arch. Graffiti (tagged by Blade '98) is minimalist: a name becomes a labyrinth, with arrows and hearts. Tribes are invited to advance on Stonehenge for the summer solstice.

Kevin, still armoured in his heavy jacket, takes photographs. He thinks he might approach Marc Atkins, make him the subject of a dissertation. He accesses a John Boorman reference; the director mentioning the fact, in an interview, that he used to swim in the Thames near Runnymede Bridge. A Wordsworthian encounter with a shadow on the water, the Green Man.

He remembers a friend, Dr Dylan Francis. 'We were like Little and Large,' he says. Kevin is always generous, reaching for books that might help other writers. Thick fingers drum on his head as he tries to fix the wording of the pertinent quotation. Right books into right hands and the world is reconfigured. He sent me a copy of Dylan Francis's posthumous collection, *The Risk of Being Alive (Writings on Medicine, Poetry and Landscape)* – for which he had done the introduction. He highlighted: the 'incomparable conversation' of his friend, 'the swift workings of his mind'.

Francis, I discovered, was a scholar with a Double First in English from Cambridge; a philosopher, a poet, a doctor of medicine who worked in neurology and cardiology. He was connected with St Bartholomew's Hospital in Smithfield. He read voraciously and aggressively, was interested in Robert Fludd and William Harvey. He took off, whenever he could, into the Lake District or the Welsh borders; he walked his demons down: '[J.H.] Prynne under one arm & Gray's Anatomy under the other'. A Romantic sensibility, scrupulous in address, compares and contrasts landscape in terms of his own emotions, with relevant literary asides. Like all Romantics, he pushes it, language; wanting nature to behave with more sensitivity, more intelligence. The responsibility of poetic tone threatens to undo him:

From Hereford through wind and bright sunlit rain resilvering and quenching the day, reflections shivering & amazed across blurred tillage pocked with rain, pleached hedgerows, the sun barely lifting above the churned earth's rim but to be ploughed under/where outlying rains trace & retrace lines of descent . . . to Hay.

Something was wrong and walking couldn't solve it. Francis speaks frequently of 'pressure'; pressure to perform, refine, perfect. Pressure of circumstance. Being in London, in the hospital, getting away; roaming, reading, making notes for un-

defined future projects. 'I've turned this sort of "get-beside-
yourself-in-London-then-jump-into-a-car-and-drive-to-some-
where-remote-and-walk-around-by-yourself" into something
of a genre.'

Francis killed himself in December 1992. The collection
edited by Kevin Jackson opens with an essay on 'William Harvey and the "Motion in a Circle"'. This is reprinted from *Bart's
Journal* (Summer 1982). And what a useful prompt it proves:
microcosm and macrocosm, the alchemists of St Bartholomew's Close, circuits of blood that mimic the passage of the
sun. Dr Dylan Francis carrying me straight back to Dr Francis
Anthony's memorial in St Bartholomew's Church. Nagging
away, at the back of our orbital walk, were recurrent themes,
unsolved puzzles.

Paracelsus, 'the Swiss physician, alchemist, mystic and pioneer of chemotherapy' (as Francis glosses him), is the presiding
influence.

He held that:

Man and the universe had the same form and had behind them the
same reason. He likened the circle of heaven to man's skin, and dis-
cerned a pulse in the firmament, spirits in the winds, fevers in the
motions of the earth, and chiromancy in minerals.

My superstition, sympathetic to Fludd and Paracelsus, persists: the walk around London's orbital motorway is *personal*.
From Harefield to Purfleet, the rushes, surges of excitement,
are connected to an imagined – solar powered? – circulation
of blood. We can't resurrect the period when the 'objective
method' (scientific induction) co-existed with older notions of
mystical correspondences; a time (the 1620s) when John Donne
was a patient of Harvey, folding the surgeon's 'research into the
capacity of the heart and other hollow viscera' into his verse.

Dr Francis concludes his essay with reflections on Robert
Fludd's *Anatomiae Amphitheatrum* (1623). As with Blake's

cosmological epics, his forcing of humble place names into a mythic structure – and, on a humbler scale, Mary Caine's zodiacal configurations – Fludd reads topography in terms of the human body. The walk we take, from that first step, progresses by analogy:

Since, as the sun travels around the earth daily in a circle, it impresses on the winds – which contain the breath of God – a similar circular motion, this moving air is breathed by man, reaches the blood, and from the heart the spirit of life is thus carried around the body in an imitation of divine circularity.

The spaces under Runnymede Bridge, cool shadows, flicker of sunlight, wash from passing rivercraft, encourage metaphysical speculation. We should stay here, stretch out on our curved shelves. Dream. Follow the Egyptian script, the journey of the sun boat.

But that's impossible, without aborting the tour. We labour up a grassy slope, at the side of the bridge, and on to the M25. For the first time in our half-circuit, we are actually walking the motorway, and also (courtesy of Mary Caine) walking the Dog. After the oracular opulence of the space beneath the bridge, M25 reality has us rocking on our heels. Blamblamblamblam. Sssssssss. Grey bitumen (courtesy of Shell): the mantle of choice for Associated Asphalt, French Kier, W.C. French, London Roadstone, Redland Aggregates and Wimpey Asphalt. Blamblam. Ssss. Light is harsh and scouring. Air is filled with stinging particles. We walk towards Egham, inches away from speeding metal projectiles.

Standing on a thin strip of ground in the central reservation, traffic snarling on both sides, I stared through my long-focus lens at a range of facial expressions that would have fitted into a Victorian Bedlam collection: Criminal and Subnormal Physiognomies. V signs. Drooling narcolepsy. Trance. Fugue. Rage. Idiot grins. Nobody signalled their pleasure at the miracle of motoring over the Thames. They were part of a thrashing comet-tail. Mary Caine's Dog was no guardian of the mysteries. It was a ravening beast, a mastiff on a chain. On Runnymede Bridge, Cerberus claims his victims for Hades. The line of traffic advancing towards the rising sun looked like a procession of the returning dead. Every one of them, solitaries in clean shirts, smoking, checking mirrors to see if their reflections were still there, wore dark glasses.

2

In less than half a mile, the M25 spurns us, it's picking up momentum, a straight run on the junction with the M3 ('a major freeflow intersection: continuous span bridges with hollow reinforced concrete decks'). We walk Indian file, Kevin has to boom to make himself heard. You can smell the panic. 'These crazies mean it,' he realises. 'They are actually going to *walk* around the motorway.' It's true, I would be perfectly happy sticking with the hard shoulder if it got me through Surrey in a day. The treadmill experience is fine. Conversation dies, the countryside vanishes (tactfully screened and baffled).

'Economically viable, environmentally sound'. The sponsor's message. Tony Sangwine (well named), senior Highways Authority horticulturalist and expert on motorway landscaping, boasts of 'interventions'. Drought-resistant dust. Salt-tolerant, low-maintenance grasses. Plantings of hawthorn, dogwood, the Wild Service Tree. To foster the illusion: the road is a rippling brook. Sangwine is talking Dunsinane forestry, forests that move in the night (the A2/M2 road-widening scheme). Forget your National Parks, footpaths clogged with pedestrian traffic, mountain bikers and plague-ridden beasts, the M25 is the ecological fast track. Kestrels nest on gantries. The central reservation is a wildlife sanctuary, taxonomies of flora and fauna are located in land trapped between the M40/M25 interchange.

Rudely woken from hard shoulder reverie, we find ourselves in Egham. A chainlink fence, on the edge of the escarpment, is patrolled and protected by ON-SITE GUARDING LTD (LAPD-style enforcers whispering into handsets). Security, when it got its start in the East End, was run by hoods and armbreakers. Ex-Parkhurst. 'Security advisers' to banks and art galleries were old Yard men who had taken early retirement (before they were found out). Down here, among the soft estates, asylum seekers carry out the night patrols. When multinationals boast about their record in employing local inhabitants, they mean issuing them with dog leads and shiny peaked caps.

Someone is building something, right on the road. JCBs, noise, a fence. No flags as yet, so it's probably not a housing development or a motel. Renchi, perversely, takes a special interest in this hole. He sees it as a direct response to the charms of Runnymede Bridge (with its Alma-Tadema steps leading down to the river, a bathing pool for draped and languorous Roman sirens). Every time we walk the river bank, he suggests checking out the rapidly evolving building at the Egham end of the bridge.

Two years passed before we made our tour of inspection. The incongruous lighthouse that Renchi spotted from road trips and railway excursions was revealed as one of the wonders of the orbital circuit. 'SIEBEL,' it said. The vulgar security precautions of our first sighting were gone. Amazingly, there were no obvious CCTV cameras. No uniforms, no dogs. No checkpoints. Siebel, I recognised at once, was the future. *Post*-surveillance. A discretion so absolute, so understated, that criminality and vandalism were impossible concepts. Siebel was the visible manifestation of Ballard's coming Mediparc psychopathology: intelligent buildings for soberly dressed, quiet, indecently healthy people. Health is the only valid currency. Credit-rich vampires from the old capitalist empires buy new faces, fresh blood. Middle management sweats in medieval gyms. The real players, the Siebel lighthouse-keepers, have health as part of the employment package. A few feet away from the clanking, shuddering, diesel dust-storms of the motorway, Siebel immortals float through a chlorine-glass tank. Doing nothing.

Doing nothing. *Being*. That's the key. All the way down to Staines, on the car radio, I was hearing about economic disaster, global recession, the collapse of Marconi's share price. Even the biggest, most ruthless conglomerates were going belly up because they made the mistake of investing in product. Manufacture something, anything, and you're dead. Fashions change. Mobile phones will go the way of kipper ties. Play smart. Do nothing. New Labour (lessons of the Dome fiasco learnt) have it absolutely right: take soundings, soothe your critics, commission reports. Talk in colourless catch phrases: 'Best Value. Economically viable, environmentally sound.' *But do nothing*.

The ideal is a building with no function other than to carry, discreetly, the company's name. Siebel. The telescopic tower with its green-glass wings sits alongside the M25, but it is not *of* the M25. The motorway is as archaic as a Victorian railway, a fun fair ride. You can think of it in terms of traction engines, stagecoaches, ox carts. A Little England folly from the day it was built. Off-highway, faux-American science parks are now as pertinent as Legoland or some model village in the Cotswolds. Those CCTV camera-boxes, poking out of the shrubbery on stalks, are SF hardware from another era. Surveillance, the fortress estate, boastful flag poles, paranoid architecture: redundant.

Siebel understand. Siebel have created this beautiful bird of a building, a swan of the motorway: curved spine and neck, angular wings. Tinted windows through which you can see nothing very much. The car park comes on two levels and is almost deserted, eight or nine unostentatious motors – with space for sixty or eighty more. A roof park, spiky Mexican plants as a border. A ground level space beneath, more conceptual gallery than garage.

Yesterday there was nothing here. The Siebel building appeared, fully formed, from nowhere. You can't date it: elements of the Thirties, Sixties, Nineties. No irony, no pastiche. Something clinical or forensic, germ-repelling. The building doesn't impose, it insinuates: no sweat, today is your first tomorrow. A metal arm, a gesture that divides Siebel-world

from the Egham underpass, creaks. The only sound in a perfectly smooth acoustic environment. A car arrives, the arm
cranks up. A man in a lightweight suit, no papers, no case,
saunters to the entrance, the green world of indoor tree
shadows and underwater light.

Surveillance systems are unnecessary. Siebel have created
a force field. Egham, a town trading on a loose connection
with Runnymede and Magna Carta (sandstone effigy of King
John outside the yellow-awning pavement café), needs Siebel.
Siebel have put up a number of other buildings – no product
mentioned – as a rebuke to earlier, urban rim outfits that made
the mistake of hugging the railway. Businesses give the appearance of being on the verge of bankruptcy by simply having the
wrong address, being stuck in some cosy little town rather than
in the zone, the slipstream of the M25.

A car's width from the hard shoulder, anything is possible.
Siebel could be an illusion. A photo-realist hoarding. We walk
towards the central tower, the bottle-glass Panopticon. And
then we're inside – with no memory of having passed through
an automatic door. The building has no inside. There is *more*
space as you approach the great ledge of the control desk than
when you stand in the car park, looking in. The air is better,
the temperature gentler. Light dazzles from every surface.

Unlike Bishopsgate in the City, or Canary Wharf, no one
challenges your right to wander. The women at the desk are
charming; young (but not too young), elegant (but not
intimidating). They smile. They know nothing. You are welcome to see whatever you want to see, but there is no content.
Glass lifts rise and fall like water features. Strollers drift from
level to level, doing nothing; nodding, avoiding conversation,
argument, the testosterone urgency of the market. What Siebel
are peddling is: absence of attitude. Zero attrition. No cutting
edge. The right decision – which is no decision.

Road-ragged pedestrians, such as Renchi and I, are welcome
because *we do not register*. As far as the women at the desk are

concerned, we do not appear on the screen. We come from another universe and very soon we'll go back to it.

Can we make an appointment to inspect this marvellous place? Of course. But not now, not here; another tomorrow. What does Siebel produce? Who can say? Siebel *is*. A shimmering mirage. A virtual oasis on the edge of a collapsing motorway system. Siebel sibilates. A near anagram of e-libels.

I pick up a brochure. Fatter, glossier, more anodyne than an in-flight magazine. The atrium is the least resistant hotel lobby in the world. The ultimate waiting room. Blue-grey magazines can be carried, but not read. We settle ourselves in a set of criminally comfortable armchairs; leather too soft to wear, so tender it feels as if it's still alive.

Siebel, The Magazine has a man in a suit on the cover. He's not smiling, or frowning. He wears a beard that isn't a beard; it's a quotation from a film nobody can put their finger on. 'Customer satisfaction,' says the brochure. 'Seamless integration.' 'Comprehensive upgrade.' *Of what?* I want to scream. 'Solutions provider.' Siebel has solutions for questions that have not yet been asked, will never be asked.

A Sino-American businessman holds a tiny screen in his hand: 'You're always connected and always available. Some call it a revolution; others call it evolution.' Language is de-fanged, homogenised. Yellow E-tab faces leer at you. Ecstasy without frenzy. Satisfaction, whether you want it or not. 'The Siebel eRoadmap to Successful eBusiness.'

I've had enough. I'm with Georges Perec, whose novel *La Disparition* was written without the letter *e*. The commonest letter in the pack is an untrustworthy creature. A nark, a grass. They use it to crack codes. Too much tail, too much wiggle. A high-pitched sound. A petulant fly in an afternoon bedroom.

If we believe in the Siebel world, we might as well give up the walk now. But there's another option: I decide to visit J.G. Ballard at Shepperton. How does he feel about predicting, and thereby confirming, the psychogeography of Heathrow's retail/recreation fallout zone?

It was a day when the weather was so warm, the view from the slow train (M3 across golf paddocks and 'refuse transfer stations') so seductive, that any sane North European would begin to think the unthinkable: climate change. This greenery with its huddles of loud-leisure golfers, traffic breezing westward, is future desert. *The Drought*. Ballard isn't dealing in metaphors, he means it. The wise men (poets, social scientists, demagogues, Diggers, anti-psychiatrists) gathered at the Roundhouse in Camden Town in 1967, for the epochal 'Congress of the Dialectics of Liberation', all talked about one thing: Gregory Bateson's riff on melting polar ice-caps, carbon dioxide emissions, the squandering of fossil fuels. Bateson wasn't messianic. He didn't rant and rage like Stokely Carmichael. He didn't hide, junk sick, behind dark glasses, muttering apocalypse and revenge (like Emmett Grogan). He was very reasonable, steady voiced; the dark humour of an implacable logic.

So we accelerated our road building programme in the white hot technology of Old Labour. We put a necklace around London, from the Exxon/Mobile (Esso) storage tanks at Purfleet to the jumbo-park of Heathrow. We burnt the city's waste at Enfield, then fed the compacted dust back into new motorways.

Out in Shepperton, Ballard was as calm, as rational as Bateson. They were both Cambridge men who had lived abroad. Ballard was a copywriter for the Book of Revelations, the final dissolution. He skimmed technical journals, adapted their vocabulary. He was on friendly terms with scientists like Chris Evans. From such apparently innocent documents as the Siebel brochure, he factored the terminology for a sinister poetic. That's where the virus was located, in the blandest of all forms, the puff, the free-sheet, the trade launch. The Motor Show at

Earl's Court, as Ballard recognised, would prove to be a more subversive gathering than the coming together of counter-cultural magi in Camden Town. William Burroughs, a major influence on Ballard, had been saying it for years: read the financial reports from IBM, cut them against a travel book by Graham Greene, a rhapsodic paragraph of Conrad, a snapshot from Tangier.

Burroughs took a dozen lifetimes to grow into his face, that prescient skull. A dozen lifetimes to arrive at the red cabin in Lawrence, Kansas. Ballard made it to Shepperton in the 1960s. *The Drowned World*. This was never an exile. You can only achieve exilic status when you'd prefer to be somewhere else, when you acknowledge the power of the centre. For Ballard the transit out of West London was a spin to the colonies, the desert resorts of his fiction, not a banishment. The metropolis, so far as he is concerned, can sink into the swamp. The buildings are old and dirty and uninteresting and the furniture is dull. Ballard, at twenty-one, was an enthusiastic visitor to the Festival of Britain. The Skylon. The conjunction with the river. Those Swedish chairs!

Ballard's fiction, reprising and reworking its own templates, is not prophetic in a way that would be recognised by H.G. Wells or George Griffith. The tone is matter of fact. Seemingly extraordinary or perverse episodes can be traced back to images in art books, cuttings from magazines, nightcap television: trade journalism and copywriting with their hypnotic present-tense blandishments, when you microwave them, turn feral. Let out the demons. Ballard doesn't use a PC, he hammers away on a trusted portable. These are some of the books in his library (1984), as logged by interviewers from *RE/SEARCH*. *The Warren Commission Report*. *Céline: A Biography* by Patrick McCarthy. Stanley Spencer catalogue from the Royal Academy. *White Women* by Helmut Newton. *The Soft Machine* by William Burroughs. *Mountbatten* by Richard Hough. 'I don't have much to do with those literary people,' Ballard told me.

I was delighted to learn that Ballard, who previewed the target towers of Canary Wharf in *High-Rise* (1975), had come to town to check out the Millennium Dome. His account of the excursion dealt, for the most part, with the journey. East London is a mystery to him. He's read about it, but he has no desire to sample it first hand, other than through the window of a car. The Dome was nothing. He'd conjured up just this kind of hucksterist tent show (carny booths, empty car parks, toxic mutations, cyber-sell) in his early fiction. The Dome, as a concept, lagged years behind the Festival of Britain. The Dome was a marquee from a Regency pleasure park, Ranelagh or Vauxhall, visited by offcuts from a novel by William Thackeray.

Driving through the weekend-dead Isle of Dogs, under-passes, captured water, quotation architecture, was a nostalgic, back-to-the-future exercise. The septuagenarian writer, car window like a cinema screen, slides through a manifestation of short stories sold to pulp magazines at the period when his career was launched. Silvertown Airport is an epiphany, no flights, tropical vegetation splitting the quays of the deepwater docks, jet-skiers bumping over choppy water. Nothing pleases Ballard more than to walk in, unexpectedly, on one of his own sets. He is redundant, he can let go. Achieved fiction writes itself. He knows, after all these years, he has reached that point. Silvertown as a suburb of *Vermilion Sands*.

I arrived at Shepperton a couple of hours before I was due to meet Ballard at the station. *Bad Day at Black Rock*. The paper-shop was closing, Ballard told me, because Shepperton had run out of commuters. The dozy, sun-hammered town was an island settlement, between the wide blue of the motorway (M3 rushing into M25) and the meandering Thames. Ballard has reversed Edwardian polarities, he weekends in London – where the earlier inhabitants came out to their bungalows, huts, hutches, on Shepperton's two islands, to get away from the pressures of the city. A ferry at Weybridge is still operative, summoned by a bell that may be rung at quarter-hourly intervals.

Main street, Shepperton, is a carousel of estate agents (£300,000 upwards for a riverfront box) and charity caves; a library (closed on Thursday mornings), a video shop, a specialist in TV memorabilia, toys and annuals. You can do the river-bank or stroll (across a bridge over the M3) to Shepperton Green and the film studios. 'You *walked*?' said Ballard, incredulously. 'We do have buses in Shepperton.'

It was a scorcher, the midpoint in a freak heat wave. They didn't need to drain the River Ash, which passes through the studio estate. The river was my target. Three significant 'river' films had been shot here: John Huston's version of C.S. Forester's *The African Queen*; the heritage Tudor barges of *A Man for All Seasons*, stately as a Hampton Court *son et lumière*; and the notorious colonial fantasy, *Sanders of the River*. In 1935 Zoltan Korda, adapting an Edgar Wallace novel, built an East African village on the banks of the Ash, and cast Paul Robeson, a leftist Othello in a loincloth, as Bosambo, the native chief. The rest of the tribe were bussed in from Tiger Bay in Cardiff. Jomo Kenyatta, President of Kenya (1964–78), had a bit part as a grass-skirted spear-waver.

Shepperton Studios spread themselves at the foot of the earth banks that contain the Queen Mary Reservoir (the site where E-culture, motorway raves began). Taking the twenty-minute walk from Shepperton station, close to where Ballard has his house, to the security gates of the studios, I travel through the landscape of Ballard's fiction: lagoon (reservoir), motorway (Heathrow traffic defining the edge of the frame), wide-aisled supermarket (through which sleepwalking suburban adulteresses can practise their 'amiable saunter'). To be here, in bright sunshine, a small Thames-side town where nobody hurries, is to balance on a hinge. Specifics of the geography that inspired a writer seem, in their turn, to be responding to that oeuvre.

'Where else is there to go?' Ballard said. 'The past is a biological swamp, the future is a sandy desert – and the present is a
concrete playpen.'

From the shade of a balding tree, I watched Ballard's car pull
up at the station. He didn't look like any of the other early-
afternoon motorists; he was in Mediterranean mode (straw hat,
dark glasses, open-necked purple shirt). We drove to a riverside
pub and, too hot to sit outside, lounged under an overhead fan
in a comfortable, clubbish atmosphere. 'You know, I haven't
been in this place for fifteen years.' Finding somewhere to park,
Ballard reckons, is the biggest problem of contemporary life.

He's here, but he doesn't belong. I think of him as a long-
term sleeper, an intelligence operative forgotten by his pay-
masters. The periphery, according to him, is where the future
reveals itself. New Labour, he asserts, was hatched in airport
satellite-strips and gated communities. The child terrorists of
Running Wild are the result of benevolent eugenic planning;
Internet education, leavened by supervised abseiling, white-
water rafting, paragliding, will result in the spook children of
Blair and flinty Jack Straw. Ordinary hormonal adolescents
making a mess of it, spewing on pavements, dealing dope.

But it's not suburbia. Suburbia is drift-Hackney (relocated
to Chingford). Bethnal Green and Limehouse, once seen as
the epitome of urban experience (immigrant, criminous, highly
spiced), are now models of Neo-Suburbia: expensive dormitories, Barratt and Laing estates, commuters working elsewhere.
The concerned middle classes discussing equity, schools; laying
out gardens (even on roofs).

Ballard referred me to a piece he had written, 'Welcome to
the Virtual City', for *Tate* magazine:

But Shepperton, for what it's worth, is not suburbia. If it is a suburb
of anywhere, it is of London Airport, not London. And that is the
clue to my dislike of cities and my admiration for what most people

think of as a faceless dead-land of inter-urban sprawl. Hurrying back from Heathrow or a West Country weekend to their ludicrously priced homes in Fulham or Muswell Hill, they carefully avert their gaze from this nightmare terrain of dual carriageways, police cameras, science parks and executive housing, an uncentred realm bereft of civic identity, tradition or human values, a zone fit only for the alienated and footloose, those without past or future.

And that, of course, is exactly what we like about it . . . The triangle formed by the M3 and the M4, enclosing Heathrow and the River Thames, is our zone of possibility . . .

He doesn't speak badly of anybody, any named individual. It's almost a superstition, no gossip. The enemy is generic and vague: 'the literary mob', 'cities', 'dull furniture'. Like Burroughs, he might not choose to join the club, but he passes very effectively: a voice from another world, good manners. It's very decent of him to give me this riverside afternoon. He doesn't take a drink before eight o'clock. I don't need what Ballard says, I know what he says, I've read the books. What I need is the chance to pay homage, in the course of this mad orbital walk, to the man who has defined the psychic climate through which we are travelling. It's a romantic foible on my part, the impulse that once had De Quincey tramping off to the Lake District, to make a nuisance of himself in Wordsworth's cottage.

The hair is long and silvery, the skin ivory coloured. Ballard, through his long residence and his riverine hermeticism, has joined the company. He looks and behaves like a magus, like Dr John Dee: modesty of address enlivened by a proper arrogance about how his vision of the world has been confirmed. I show him the Siebel brochure, but it means nothing. He *knows*. Blake at Lambeth, Dee at Mortlake, Pope at Twicken-ham, Ballard at Shepperton: the great British tradition of expulsion, indifference. The creation of alternative universes that wrap like Russian dolls around a clapped-out core.

Ballard drove me back to the station. The streets were deserted. We passed some white, flat-roofed, vaguely Thirties properties. 'I thought of trying one of those,' he said. The paint was peeling. A failed experiment, a Utopian fantasy that had run out of puff. A warehouse, near the river, was used for shooting TV commercials. I thought of *Crash*. 'I aimlessly followed the perimeter roads to the south of the airport, feeling out the unfamiliar controls among the water reservoirs of Stanwell.'

Shepperton was sun-dappled, leafy, bleached. The Asian community, if it existed, were all out at Heathrow. The streets were as white as the Suffolk littoral, as Shenley. Ballard, when I interviewed him in Shepherd's Bush, spoke of a malaise, the death of affect. 'Rather than fearing alienation,' he said, 'people should *embrace* it. It may be the doorway to something more interesting. That's the message of my fiction. We need to explore total alienation and find what lies beyond. The secret module that underpins who we are and our imaginative remaking of ourselves that we all embrace.'

3

I don't know where we are. None of the landmarks relate to anything in my past. As a motorist, I've kept clear of this section of the M25. My world has been turned upside-down: the Thames is now at the back of me, a lost ceiling.

Renchi clips along (tales of a painter friend who offers spirit-guided walks around sacred sites; who paints, under mediumistic instruction, hundreds of canvases). Kevin sheds his jacket and puts away his notebook. We stick with the motorway.

Thorpe is undistinguished. Low-level warehouses, industrial estates: ALPHA WAY, PRIVATE ROAD. Across still-green cereal fields, I notice a spectacular Italianate tower. One of our orbital acupuncture needles. We're back on track. Through the long lens, I can make out a red brick château, crenellated parapets, too many windows. This hilltop fantasy, Renchi tells me, is the Royal Holloway College. The tower isn't Italian: it's loosely modelled on the Cloth Hall at Ypres. Belgian Gothic as interpreted by the architect William Crossland, under the patronage of patent medicine magnate Thomas Holloway.

There was of course a story, an anecdote connected with the college. A relative of Renchi's had been at Royal Holloway, briefly, studying drama. An end-of-term party. Drink taken in the cloisters. A marble hand broken from the statue of Queen Victoria, removed. This dark token was now buried in a country garden. Should it be located and returned? The college was too much of a detour, we let it go.

In deep lanes you come on parked vans. I assembled, in the course of our walk, quite a collection: men slumped over wheels, sleeping. Away from the science parks, the railside

enterprises, drivers take time out: a folded newspaper, a tat-
tooed arm hanging against warm metal, cigarette smouldering
in a two-fingered grip. Dashboard as travelling mantelpiece. An
indented tray for the tupperware lunchbox. A slot for ciggies
and plastic lighter. Family portraits: wife and baby in hospital,
girl-child and large doll in bed. Pulling away from the M25, the
puff goes out of motorists. On the road there is a communal
energy, flight chemicals, petrol fugues. Green lanes are private
dormitories, windows wide to birdsong, pesticide; a sewage
farm beyond the Junction 12 interchange ('a two-level cyclic
design, close to the 164 feet high St Ann's Hill').

In the next village, Kevin flashes his notebook. All sorts
of interesting things are happening: a group of chefs in tall
hats, white jackets and checkered trousers are hanging out with
dangerous looking schoolgirls. *Alice in Wonderland* revisited.
Among rose-red brickwork, white window frames, yew hedges,
is an American/Swiss school. With appropriate catering. Three
cooks to every pupil. Moneyed Americans and international
Swiss, when they get together, look for security, security and
security. Exclusion of undesirables. Food that doesn't knot in
your throat, explode in your belly. Thorpe Village, Eastly End,
Virginia Water: these places are perfect. Convenient for the airport. They look like Agatha Christie. Behave like Bern or Basel,
Orange County (California).

Wild girls, experimentally made up, wearing customised
chalet-school outfits, are smoking. They don't have bike sheds
in Thorpe. But they do have the Monk's Walk, which carries
us out among the grey lakes you see from the M3 (as you head
out of London, for Winchester and Southampton). Trees,
rounded like broccoli crowns, reach to the water's edge.

The sudden absence of notable features, the quietness of the
lake, is very appealing. People take up fishing as an excuse for
standing all day in just such a place, doing nothing. Our modest
view disguises an important conflux of energies: the M25
beginning to pull to the east, St Ann's Hill (with ruined chapel),

Great Foster's Hotel (talked up by Mary Caine) – and, on the horizon, another red tower, the Holloway Sanatorium.

The weight of possibility, unsecured narrative taking off in every direction, hits Kevin. He makes no complaint, but he is starting to limp. That jacket drags like a lead poncho designed by Anselm Kiefer. He knows: it's untellable. Memory is a lace doily, more hole than substance. The nature of any walk is perpetual revision, voice over voice. Get it done, certainly, then go home and read the published authorities; come back later to find whatever has vanished, whatever is in remission, whatever has erupted. Kevin has sunk into the trance state all hikers know: the initial excitement, the yarn-spinning of the Staines station café, is over. Books in the rucksack are dead weight, ballast he'd be happy to dump. The theoretical is overwhelmed by the actual. He knows what lies behind him – home, car, breakfast – but he has no idea what lies ahead. *How am I going to get out of this?*

Movie references help. Conveyor belts of gravel crunch and moan. We speak of the end of *Touch of Evil*; a bloated Orson Welles stumbling among derricks and nodding donkeys, bridges and gantries of an oil field. Black water, floating rubbish. *Get Carter*. That's closer to home. A rig for sea coal. Rattling stones on a belt. An extraction system that plays into the aerial rides and thrills of Thorpe Park.

Walking beside the perimeter fence, we smell wild animals in their enclosures. They're too bored and depressed to roar. Water sloshes against glass. Empty carriages trundle around their rickety circuit; a slow ascent, then the plunge through the water chute. Suspended excitement. A sorry piece of engineering that can only be brought to life by the screams of deliriously anxious punters.

A bridge over the M3, looking back to the junction with the M25: Renchi is busy with his camera, but Kevin has moved beyond transcription. Why would he want to prolong, to memorialise this agony? The leather jacket is hooked over a rigidly horizontal left arm, a struck flag. A trophy smuggled out of Saigon. Kevin poses dutifully; a light slick of sweat, smile contracted into a wince of discomfort, eyes on the ground. If he lifted them, he'd see where we are going, the short sharp hill – which, if he knows anything about it, will involve detours, diversions and a horrible, spine-twisting, corkscrew ascent.

'We walk and walk and walk,' Kevin wrote in his article for the *Independent*. 'By this time almost five hours have passed, and the metaphorical tenderfoot is also a literal tenderfoot. I've chosen the wrong kind of boots, the wrong kind of socks; the soles of my feet are blazing, and by the evening will erupt into a gratifyingly spectacular crop of blisters.'

Hoping to postpone the assault on the conical hill, Kevin initiates a discussion of private estates; the sort that flourish unseen among these wooded slopes. We won't go as far as to align ourselves with Charles Manson's dune buggy berserkers, but five hours on the hoof has given a certain edge to our argument. The alienation that Ballard, safely bunkered in Shepperton, recommended as a device for firing the imagination, flourishes in territory trapped between motorways (M4, M25, M3).

Look west from St Ann's Hill, beyond the restless levels of Junction 12 (of the M25), beyond Virginia Water, and you have Wentworth; land drops sharply away, property values climb into the stratosphere. CCTV estates concealed by managed stretches of ancient woodland. Nicholson's map has nothing to say: white on white, private roads in an ex-directory reservation. A golf course the size of Rutland. Wentworth is a sand trap with satellite housing, Jimmy Tarbuck and Bruce Forsyth. Razor-smooth greens walked by men whose shoes are as bright as their sweaters, men in hair-hats. More rough on their heads than down the edge of the fairway. Superglued Shredded Wheat. White teeth in collapsed mouths. Crinkly tap dancers, rheumy with showbiz nostalgia: Windmill and Winter Gardens. December-tan comics who hack out their rounds, rehearse their schtick, mourning the defeat of Margaret Thatcher. They promise to quit Britain if another Labour government is voted in. And they honour that promise. Wentworth *is* another country. With its own golfing prince, Andrew. Its Dallas ranches. Winking security. The Wentworth zodiac, should Mary Caine find the time to compute it, is made from lizards, serpents, hammerhead sharks. The divisions of the woodland are militaristic, imperial: General's Copse, Duke's Copse, King's Copse, Wellington Bridge, King George's Field. And, in any case, Lew Grade's veterans console themselves, the Conservatives might have been wiped out in successive elections, but the Thatcherite lineage is secure with Tony Blair. All that has happened is some discreet rebranding, less confrontation, better suits. Sex scandals lose their zest. Denials are issued with straighter faces.

One of New Labour's most unyielding red-tie commissars is the former student leftist Jack Straw. It was Straw who was landed with the hassle of 'The Dictator on the Golf Course': the million-pound safe house on the safest estate in the safest county in England. General Augusto Pinochet, butcher of Santiago (funded by the CIA, armed by Margaret Thatcher), liked to do his Christmas shopping in London. He would receive Lady Thatcher and other old cronies, cruise the Knightsbridge bazaars, check into a clinic for a 10,000-mile service. Chauffeured from hotel suite to Harrods, winter traffic at its busiest, the General was well placed to offer an opinion on the level of courtesy available on English roads. Ian Parker, in 'Traffic' (an essay published in *Granta*), notes that Pinochet 'praised Britain for its impeccable driving habits'. The verdict of a man who is always driven. The streets Pinochet glimpsed through a tinted window were swept of rubbish. The populace dressed well and didn't sing or shout or form ugly mobs brandishing photographs of the disappeared. It was Pinochet, after all, who instructed Thatcher in the advantages of a deregulated bus service. 'Check out downtown Santiago,' he said. 'Any time you're passing.'

It was a terrible shock to be arrested, threatened with extradition, a 'human rights' trial in Spain. Old chums, Falklands War colleagues, were outraged. Lord Lamont: 'Disgraceful!' Lady Thatcher: 'His health has been broken, the reputation of our own courts has been tarnished and vast sums of public money have been squandered on a political vendetta – so friends of Britain be warned, the same thing can happen to you.'

But the health of elderly gentlemen in good standing with the establishment is not like the health of ordinary mortals: when they are faced with public examination, it declines rapidly and demonstrates the most alarming symptoms – premature senility, dodgy ticker, the shakes. No memory and a drooling, but brave smile. Partial blindness. Sight like a one-eyed football manager: 'Sorry, missed that one. I was unwrapping a fresh stick of gum.' Released into the bosom of the family, on compassionate grounds, they stage a remarkable recovery. Alzheimer's disease can be shaken off like the common cold. Malfunctioning hearts regenerate; the miraculously restored patient, cured by love and tender care, is back on the fairway. The boardroom.

Pinochet benefited from the hospital service that is still out there in the north-west quadrant of the M25 – for those who really need it.

A medical report was issued – and leaked. Lamont fumed. The motorcade rolled to Wentworth. The dictator was boarded out in an up-market Barratt home. Newsreel crews were on hand to capture the phone call, expressing support, from Margaret Thatcher. From this point on, footage is real estate promo: wheelchair access to garden, picture windows, double-glazing to neutralise the racket from drummers beating out their protest at the limits of the security cordon.

Wentworth swallows celebrity. And takes its sheen into the immaculate grass, the dazzling windows.

The story retreats into a blizzard of newsreel clips. Police car with flashing sign: KEEP OUT. Pinochet photo-op with Baroness Thatcher.

Thatcher: 'Senator Pinochet was a staunch friend of Britain throughout the Falklands War. His reward from this government was to be held prisoner for sixteen months.'

Aerial view: convoy of cars taking Pinochet to military airbase in Lincolnshire for flight home to Chile.

Peter Schaard (friend of Pinochet): 'I have seen a deterioration in his health – more than anything else his mental health. He said that when he was back in Chile he would like to learn to read again.'

Aerial view: RAF Waddington, Lincolnshire. Barbed wire. Plane taxiing on runway. Plane taking off. Protesters drumming, Wentworth. Held back by police.

Voice-over: 'The former Chilean dictator, Augusto Pinochet, has won his fight to go home. He is on his way back to Chile this lunchtime, after attempts to have him extradited finally failed. The Home Secretary, Jack Straw, ruled this morning that he wouldn't send him to Spain to face trial. The operation to move the General out of the country this morning was quite a cloak and dagger affair. He was finally smuggled out of the Wentworth estate where he's been staying, in a police convoy, shortly after ten o'clock.'

Cloak and dagger is something we do better than most. If America wants you in the dock, as a redundant Serb, the wrong kind of Afghan, you go down. If you've got previous as a top customer for military hardware, you walk. That seems to be the rule. Noted political thinker Lord Lamont mused: 'I don't see how the world can conduct business between states if heads of government do not have immunity from prosecution. Many democratic politicians, who may find themselves held accountable – *perhaps Lady Thatcher* – for things that happened in their name, will be very uneasy about this.'

Neil Belton, in *The Good Listener* (his life of Helen Bamber), pointed out that as soon as the Conservatives were elected in 1979, horse-trading between the two heads of state, Margaret Thatcher and Augusto Pinochet, began in earnest. Diplomatic ties, damaged under old Labour, were restored in October 1980. 'Nicholas Ridley at the Foreign Office made no secret of his wish also to resume arms sales,' Belton wrote. The release of a report on the torture of a young British student, Claire Francis Wilson, was deliberately delayed, 'in order not to interfere with his [Ridley's] announcement . . . ending the ban on arms sales'.

Prince Andrew, the royal most closely associated with golf (and the Sunningdale/Wentworth/Windsor triangulation), would do the state some service, flying helicopters during the Falklands conflict. But the chummy relationship between Britain and Chile would be damaged by Pinochet's sleepover in Wentworth. What had once been considered, socially, a plumb posting – military attaché (arms rep) at the British Embassy in Santiago – was now a disaster. Retired submarine commanders, instead of being welcomed, fêted, wined and dined, found themselves in purdah at the ragged end of the world.

Winding up St Ann's Hill, by a spiral path, it became obvious that Kevin was in some discomfort. His blisters had blisters. His eyes were itching. And the leather straps of his rucksack (book bag) were cutting into his armpits. Renchi, who had moved ahead, searching out the chapel (remains of), paused at a gap in the tree line: a beacon had been established, a potential fire-basket to celebrate coronations, Armadas, millennia. Summit linked with summit across England, coast to downland, hill fort to coast. News of invasion would be relayed to the relevant forester.

We are fleas in the fur of Mary Caine's Dog. The beast is barking at Wentworth. 'A British camp defends the circle on the dog's contoured shoulder at St Anne's Hill, Chertsey,' she writes. 'Its steep terraces and woodland walks haunted by a ghostly nun executed for trysting here with her lover . . . Here the Otherworld begins – the Mysteries of Ceres, Ceredwen, Black Annis.'

Contemplating such possibilities, Renchi stretches out, full-length, on a low wall: he dreams England. Eyes shut, hands resting on belly, feeling the passage of breath, he lets the orbital miles flow into the green world, the distant lakes. It is important to halt at the right place, switch off, put the system into suspension. Spying, cataloguing, recording give way to leisurely meditation. Kevin likes the sound of that. I warn him not to take his boots off, not yet; he must wait for the pub, a couple of stiff drinks. The socks will have to be cut away with a knife.

The woods are filled with wonders. Abandoned cars are part of the ecosystem. Once you get them off the road, on to Rainham Marshes, the Green Way to Staines, the River Lea, they achieve a posthumous status as sculptural objects. Nature loves alien curves and textures. Bugs root into soft padding. Birds nest. Paint, whatever its original colour, shades towards river-bottom green. Rust predicts autumn. We stopped to admire a Wolseley whose headlamps were owl-eyes and whose side-mirrors had twisted to catch glints in the high canopy. Spiders' webs glazed missing windscreens with tough lace. A mulch of leafmould, like shredded tobacco, cushioned (insect-arm) wipers.

In a clearing, we met two builders in baseball caps. They said they were working on a round white house, a distant relative of Bexhill's De La Warr Pavilion. Someone, inspired by Erich Mendelsohn and Serge Chermayeff, had created a late Modernist barrel: DNA staircases, screen walls and a panorama of Surrey pastoral. The house was hidden, as in a fairy story, and yet its flamboyantly minimalist design shouted: 'Notice me, write me up.'

Renchi and Kevin were still talking architecture when, on the road to Chertsey, we found a pub (the Golden Grove) where we could settle ourselves in the garden, without making a public spectacle of Kevin's feet and the rituals that would be needed to keep him mobile. Pints secured (lemonade and orange juice in Renchi's case), the Golden Grove became the golden bowl. Kevin eases off his boots, abandons the formerly white socks, and stares at forensic evidence of his overambitious hike. I photograph the damage, while Renchi begs a brown plastic tub and does the Jesus thing with Kevin's wrecked phalanges and metatarsals. Tendons have contracted, skin is raw or puffed into mushroom cushions. The twenty-six bones, a hundred-plus ligaments and thirty-three muscles are outraged by mistreatment. They've carried the journalist around town, into the belly of the BBC, on and off trains, why this impetuous vagrancy? My photographs of feet in bowl are like those water-colours in Tate Britain of the deformities of war, insulted flesh stitched together, torn mouths, missing appendages. Kevin's ankles have their own imprinted tartan, ghost socks. The originals, a pulp of sweat and blood, would fit over a baby's head. Renchi, prepared for all eventualities, kits Kevin out in spares, hairy red numbers (to hide the leakage of bodily fluids).

Restored, Kevin decides to curtail the excursion and take a train from Chertsey. This is close enough to the Thames to give his day on the road a certain symmetry, river to river. Decision taken, spirits lift. Renchi consults Mary Caine. Chertsey, it seems, is under the titular protection of Sirius. 'Chertsey, anciently spelt Cerotes, Sirotes, Certesey, recalls both Ceres and Cerberus.'

I recall the white house on St Ann's Hill – which brings the other two back to their architectural jag. They have a common interest in a much-discussed private residence in Cambridge. To Kevin this house, thanks to its occupation by Mansfield Forbes (who taught English to Humphrey Jennings, the subject of one of the half-dozen books Kevin was currently working on), was a significant footnote. To Renchi, it was home.

'Finella', in the Backs, on Queens Road, was owned by Gonville and Caius College, and leased to Mansfield Forbes in 1927. Forbes, by repute a charismatic and eccentric teacher, didn't pursue publication. Outside Cambridge, the archivists of the English Faculty, purveyors of gossip, he is unknown. With

a little more effort, a frolic with Wittgenstein, a decisive encounter with Leavis, he might have made a teleplay by Alan
Bennett. His achievements in friendship are rehearsed in a
biography by Hugh Carey for the Cambridge University Press.
(Kevin duly picked up a discounted copy for £3.)

Specs held together with sticking plaster, lectures begun in
carpet slippers, a fondness for nephews, nervous breakdown:
Forbes played from an orthodox script. The healing part of his
story consisted of a love for the Scottish wilderness and a series
of epic walks. He painted and composed occasional poems.
Most of his life consisted of shrugging off the effects of a dismal
adolescence (in the same West Country public school where
Patrick White and Lindsay Anderson did time).

Hugh Carey salvages the comic turns expected of a
Cambridge man, sympathetic to Modernism. When a friend
was done for cottaging, Forbes became convinced that the vice
squad were about to raid 'Finella'. He bundled up the Paris
editions of *Ulysses* and *Lady Chatterley's Lover* in an old waterproof and chucked them into the Cam. Panic over, he stood
on Clare bridge and supervised, with a pocket torch, while a
young research student dived in the murk (without success).

The madeover house in Queens Road is generally acknowledged as Forbes's greatest achievement. I imagined that, in
the casual fashion of the time, 'Manny' (as he was known) had
built the place from scratch; a gentleman amateur like
Christopher Wren. I soon discovered that 'Finella' began life in
the more prosaic disguise of 'The Yews': 'a Victorian villa some
eighty years old of the Bayswater period, of sooty ash-grey
brick, with a sloping lawn, overhung with yew trees'. Manny
confronted 'sombre dullness' with the vigour of a TV virtuoso,
a hit squad of carpenters and fabric teasers. He made it new.
And cod-Mediterranean: yews chopped, grey brick washed
with rose-pink, woodwork and frieze in lemon-yellow.

The story came to me in teasing fragments. At the De

La Warr Pavilion in Bexhill, I bought a book on Serge Chermayeff, a self-taught architect (dancer, painter, teacher). Skimming it, I came across a reference to 'Finella'. I knew 'Finella' as the house in which Renchi had grown up. He often talked about it. Finella was supposed to be a Scottish goddess of glass; the Cambridge house traced her legend through mirrors and doors, a 'waterfall' encased in the wall of the dining room. The narrative of Renchi's childhood is interwoven with the geography of 'Finella' and its grounds. In 1973 he published a chapbook, *Relations*, in which drawings, family snapshots, were overwritten with holograph text to contrive a slender Jungian album of place, dream, antecedents. A cedar tree like an un-fleshed spine. An aerial view of the roof: 'home as centre'. A child in bed. A shared bath (mother). Sisters and father playing a game on the drawing room floor.

I visited 'Finella' once, the reception after Renchi's wedding, figures spilling out of the house, across slanting lawns. Grey photographs of a white afternoon.

The Chermayeff book placed 'Finella' in context:

If there was a modernist 'establishment' in England at the end of the 1920s, it was centred on the house 'Finella' at Cambridge, the home of Mansfield Forbes (1889–1936), a fellow of Clare College, who commissioned a young and unknown Australian architect, Raymond McGrath (1903–76), visiting England on a scholarship, to transform the interiors using a great deal of glass and other modern materials such as copper-faced plywood, 'Plymax'. The effect was novel and theatrical.

The house was widely reviewed and lavishly praised in the architectural press. Modernism – in terms of a look or a style – was promoted here, in a series of parties, gatherings, debates. Forbes and Chermayeff were much influenced by Eric Gill. Cambridge contacts got Gill the Broadcasting House commission in Portland Place. Gill was the link to the pre-1914 artistic avant-garde in London; an inheritor of Arts and Crafts theories, proselytised in the language of St Thomas Aquinas.

Chermayeff, who frequently quoted Wyndham Lewis's *The Caliph's Design* (1919), might well have challenged the other members of the 'Finella' group (Frederick Etchells, Joseph Emberton, Howard Robertson, Maxwell Fry): 'Architects, where is your vortex?'

'On Queens Road, Cambridge,' would come the reply. 'Finella' is where the new ideas cooked: Plymax, glass, pink paint. Mansfield Forbes opened his house for the exhibition of Jacob Epstein's scandalous figure, the squat (child-carrying) figure of *Genesis*. Punters rushed the lawns, clutching their shillings. For the duration of this event, Forbes slept on a rubber mat at the foot of the primitive stone-carving.

I photocopied an anecdote from the Chermayeff book: 'Barbara Chermayeff remembered "Manny" performing a fake black mass in the mirrored hall, turning off all the lights and making it up as he went along.'

This provoked Renchi, in his turn, to dredge up a memory of his mother. She was a connection of Mansfield Forbes. She spoke about Manny's prophetic dream of flight: how he saw himself floating over Finella's shallow roof. Next day came the news of his death.

Hugh Carey mentions the incident in his Forbes biography:

Manny seems to have had a natural affinity with the uncanny; friends often described him as 'fey' without the usual implication that he was also ineffective. On the night of his death a Scottish cousin, anxious about him, dreamed that he was teaching her to levitate, then himself flew out of the window at 'Finella' over the big cedar tree in the garden and out of sight.

Invented and misremembered rituals gave 'Finella' its ability to provoke dreams, communications, dialogues with the dead.

It would take an M.R. James – across the Cam in King's – to do them justice.

You can define the towns of Little England by their ability to deliver 35mm black and white film. Kevin was struggling. He'd used up his single reel on roads, bridges, ruins. And forgotten that he was supposed to procure an author portrait to go with his article. We combed Chertsey and finally came up with the goods in a shopping development that was more car park than mall. Posed among wire trolleys, I squinted at the camera. Then Kevin was on the train and out of it.

The walk had to be commemorated with a book. Naturally. Out of the Jiffy bag, with Kevin's covering letter (and Latin inscription), fell a copy of *Abraham Cowley: Selected Poems*. Cowley, a Royalist at the time of the English Civil War, an accused spy, opted for the classic upriver (Ballard) exile: in Chertsey. His bibliography included, along with a political epic (*The Civil War*), a 1643 satire called *The Puritan and the Papist*.

Chertsey wasn't fussed about literary associations. The heritage committee couldn't summon the energy to run with Cowley (wig and gigolo moustache). He escaped local interment (and possible pilgrimage status) by being buried in Westminster Abbey. In his riverine retirement, Cowley delivered *The Visions and Prophecies Concerning England*.

Nobody, other than Kevin Jackson, could have written about 'the incalculable part his [Cowley's] ghost played at various parts of our ramble, from the Payroll Boys' incomprehensible gibberish about the "Abraham Cowley Ward" of some local hospital to the Cowley Roads we encountered'. Kevin's blisters, apparently, were deflating, leaving flaps in the skin of his feet. He squeaked slightly as he hotfooted over Cambridge pavements. He was undergoing a strict physical regime (reading the training manuals, High Sierra psycho-yomping guides), in expectation of joining us on future walks.

★

In the evening light, long shadows on a dull road, we marched on Weybridge. DRIVE SLOWLY ANIMALS. I applaud a red brick semi that has taken the trouble to convert a strip of communal lawn into a paved terrace, topped with decorative balcony (so tight to the house that nobody could stand behind it). Scores of young children in yellow waistcoats (crash-helmets) push their bikes along the pavement.

The sky over Woburn Park sagged with Zeppelin cloud-socks. An hour when bad photographs work best, smearing essence: egg and ketchup colours. Well-licked breakfast plate under a glaze of washing-up liquid.

Dragonflies twitching on nettles. A blue too slight to capture. The diluted English surrealism of a twilight park: a water chute with empty plastic logs, a misplaced Epstein woman drumming robotically (visible wires trailing from her back). A Toshiba showroom designed to look like a roadside temple.

Crossing the River Wey is a big moment for Renchi. A quick turn around a Chinese church (eccentric anti-vernacular, Gothic turrets, Greek Orthodox dome) and we head for the station. Weybridge is a good place to leave for another day; suspended visions of St George's Hill, phantom Diggers camped among immaculate golf course mansions.

4

16 June 1999. Renchi talked so much about Sara H that she became a real presence in my own imaginings; I saw her work as feeding on (and ameliorating) the momentum of the M25's perpetual (stop/start) motion. Sara lived outside the orbit. In a comfortable house in a village on Salisbury Plain. A mill stream, coming off the River Avon, ran through the garden.

Sara was the one who guided Renchi (and others) around the heat-contours, the dispensations of Stonehenge. She was a painter. Her regular shows – still life, animal – sold out. The work was meticulous, unsentimental, based on close observation. Pet portraiture, had she continued with it, would have provided a decent living. The singularity of the beasts, the glint, was assiduously recorded; hyperreality as a branch of Surrealism. There was nothing soft or splashy about this work. Fruit displaced its own weight, cut a shape in the consciousness: Zurbarán, not Renoir. A memory world captured in a convex mirror.

And then, abruptly, the career was aborted. Sara, under the control of a spirit guide, struck out on an epic undertaking. She was instructed to abandon the garden produce, moggies and curs, and move into abstraction. Abstraction in which every line had a moral integrity, every curve mapped a dream motif. The manageable format of the earlier oils replaced by vast canvases – which had to be painted, fast, in a narrow, off-kitchen extension. Stacks of canvases, calling for expensive paints and brushes, were produced to order.

What were they like? Renchi struggled to describe them. He spoke of the magnitude of the task, of quantity. Technique. The Wiltshire house with its inherited furniture, lived-in rooms, creaking stairs, tight corridors, was bursting with the product of this merciless grind. Each canvas had a narrative, an interpretation that only Sara (handmaiden to her unappeased instructor) could deliver. The meaning of the series would not be revealed until *all* the paintings – three, four, five hundred – were exhibited in one place.

Coming off our walk to Weybridge, we felt that it was the right moment to break away, a trip to Salisbury Plain. By leaving the road, witnessing Sara's dream maps (a project as mad as our own), we might achieve an overview. Whatever compelled me to spend two years expiating the shame of the Millennium Dome was as fierce and inexplicable as Sara's daily ritual in her studio.

Anna was up for the outing, by train to Alton, where Renchi would meet us and drive us to Sara's house. The first breath of morning air, on the kitchen doorstep, was hot. London was sticky with pollen, obscure allergies were activated. Pass a particular building, pause at a road crossing, and the sneezing would start. The fits were not related to trees or bushes, they were triggered by memory, previous attacks, forgotten journeys.

The Nigerian mini-cab was late. It had gone to the wrong Albion. We were forced to dodge, double back; foot-down detours to avoid the sombre (Farringdon Street) march of the 'Carnival against Capitalism'. We jumped on the train as it was moving out.

Settled in an almost deserted carriage, we met a young sculptor, friend of Renchi's stepdaughter, who was also interested in witnessing Sara's work.

I've always enjoyed – pre-privatisation, pre-Hatfield and Clapham and Paddington – riding on trains. Real time cinema, floating landscapes. And now there is the bonus of linking up, seeing from a different perspective, areas we have walked through. It was important, Renchi and I agreed, to get the first circuit done: start each walk, fresh, from the point we stopped

on the previous outing. Which meant that quite significant locations – such as Royal Holloway College, Holloway
Sanatorium – demanded a supplementary visit.

A walled estate, effectively restored and policed, the Holloway Sanatorium in Virginia Water was the ultimate heritage-
asylum conversion. Discreetly positioned, within a few miles of
Windsor Castle, Eton College and the liberties of Runnymede,
the sanatorium catered to the carriage trade. Socially awkward
relatives of the well connected were boarded out: inconvenient
pregnancies, mild eccentricities, boozers, society dope fiends.
No headbangers, no drooling imbeciles, no lowlife. Marienbad
on the Bourne.

Mervyn Peake was treated with ECT in Virginia Water:
the Holloway Sanatorium as an electro-convulsive manifestation of Gormenghast. In more recent times, the poet John
Welch, undergoing remedial therapy, was given the task of
burning medical files.

Thomas Holloway, the philanthropist responsible for college
and asylum, spent £40,000 on the Belgian Gothic building.
He consulted E.W. Pugin, launched an architectural competition, and named Crossland, Salomans and Jones as the winning
firm. It wasn't charity, wealthy relatives would pay a premium
to lodge patients in a set every bit as extravagant as St Pancras
station hotel.

How many lunatics was Holloway expecting? The restored
sanatorium buildings, rebranded as 'Virginia Park', seen through
ironwork gates, are grouped like an Ivy League campus (imposing, pastiched). Big Ben tower, numerous chimneys, turrets,
archways, cloisters: Holloway Sanatorium was a magnum opus.
The architect William Crossland, pupil of George Gilbert Scott,
made a huge emotional investment in this paradise of the
slightly disturbed. Everything about his pitch was wonky.

Examine the Victorian portraits in their silver-framed
ovals. Crossland, bald and bearded, is a serious man with an
expanding forehead. Holloway, on the other hand, is quiffed

and teased; commas of luxuriant growth decorating his cheek-bones. Crossland, the artist in stone, presents himself as a solid citizen. Holloway, peddling his patent remedies, ointments possessed of a 'healing genius', photographs like a male lead out of Dickens: Pip or the youthful David Copperfield. The magic medicine, when analysed, was found to consist of yellow beeswax, lanolin and olive oil. It made Holloway's fortune, sponsored his civic benevolence: two colonies, red brick monsters, college and sanatorium. A theme park madhouse carved out of beeswax.

The final cost of the collegiate fantasy in Virginia Water rose to Millennium Dome proportions; by the time the first brick was laid by Jane Holloway, her husband had become a melancholy recluse. He died in 1883.

The architect Crossland's last major commission was the Memorial Chapel to Holloway at Sunninghill. He died in a Camden Town boarding house in 1908, leaving an estate of £29.

It took two or three attempts before we were allowed in. We chatted to security through iron gates. We were repulsed at manned lodges. But part of the remit at Virginia Park – the developers Octagon having received a contribution from English Heritage – is to allow students of architecture (and the vulgarly curious) a glimpse of this restored Victorian folly. Virginia Park had always been a high-risk development: lead had been stripped from the roof, decorated walls were damp-stained. English weather had devastated the property. But the Octagon operation wasn't one of the asset stripping (burn and bury) efforts we'd encountered along the northern section of the M25. Memory was not trashed but tactfully restored, varnished: improved. Virginia Park would combine the gravitas of the Victoria and Albert Museum with five-star facilities, acceptable to multinational transients: gym, swimming pool, state of the art plumbing, landscape gardening.

On the right day, at the right hour, cash in hand, visitors are allowed to pass through the security gates. An (achieved) asylum seeker, friendly, but nervous of writing a receipt, steps from his checkpoint-office to point out the route we should take.

If you weren't already an orthopedic waistcoat-wearer (laced like Lillie Langtry), the decor of the entrance hall at the Holloway Sanatorium would push you over the edge. If you suffered from nerves, if you were thyroid-twitchy, spots in front of the eyes, flinching from bright colours, here was shock therapy. Nothing in our approach had prepared us for this. The path was immaculate, as were the white sports clothes, white ankle-socks, trainers, baseball caps of the women who cruised the grounds: four-wheel drives, multi-geared mountain bikes (for the bowling-green flat trip to the gates). The investors in Octagon's award-winning development are looking for convenient crash-pads, close to London Airport: maximum security, modest service charges, en suite exercise equipment, *silence*.

'An enviable lifestyle on the grand scale,' says the brochure. The very pitch that was made to wealthy Victorian families with flaky relatives. 'Gracious four storey town houses.' (If you can have town houses without a town.) The message, in the promotional photographs, is confused: Japanese minimalism (one blue and white vase), US hygiene fetishism, ersatz Regency drapes, Trusthouse Forte oil paintings.

However meticulous the makeover, the back story always leaks, seeps through as an ineradicable miasma. Pain, displacement. The agony of knowing enough to know that something is wrong, a moment's remission will be followed by a renewed attack. Consciousness misplaced in long corridors. Buildings slip and shift and refuse to settle on a single identity. They have been created through the madness of money, designed by a man harried by all the demons of the Gothic imagination.

The entrance hall, restored by 'artists and craftsmen', is

insane; a Turkish bath of wild candyfloss colours, synapse-destroying detail – Celtic, Moorish, Norse. Sultan's Palace arches. Pillars dividing into lesser pillars. A bestiary of monsters: tongues, mouths, teeth, claws. If you were a tranquillised stoic, calm as a stone, you'd freak and tremble. 'I'm not going near that scarlet carpet, that staircase.' Imagery is hysterical. The eye can't settle. The part of the brain that has to unscramble visual information spins like a fruit machine.

The front door is still open, the stone floor is cool. The woman who does PR for Octagon is a helpful and reassuring presence. Knowing how we feel, she distracts us; leads the way to the hammerbeam-ceilinged dining hall.

Dark wood – inset with Arts and Crafts panels. Stained glass. A Pre-Raphaelite hall. Illuminated by low-hanging glass bowls. The heat has us coughing. Hothouse moist. Comfort pushed, until it becomes a torment.

We make admiring noises. This is a very striking set. But it is also a brain teaser. When you walk around Virginia Park you develop split-screen vision: the ceiling of the dining hall is just what you might expect in a Victorian public school, a university of the right vintage, but the body of the room has been utterly transformed. It is now a swimming pool. An attractive woman – I think of Ballard's narcoleptic Mediparc communities – does her lazy laps. The acoustic memory-track of Holloway's disturbed patients is absorbed in steady plashing, lost in tall space. Temperature has to be cranked up to preserve the fancy carpentry. The solitary swimmer, observed by the ruffians at the door, doesn't break her stroke. She cultivates a method of moving through this speckled blue medium, excluding all fear of the tons of overwrought wood, the stalactite forest that hangs above the water.

After the empty gym, the abandoned exercise bicycles, we are free to explore the development. The Grand Hall, once a rather intimidating library (not many books, portraits of worthies), now features a stage and a sheeted grand piano. The foot-pedals have been slipped into cosy white socks. The scale of the Hall would have agoraphobics cowering under the piano. It struck us, perambulating the acres of polished floor, that every phobia was humoured: you name it, we'll give it to you. A white-knuckle ride for the mentally incapacitated, the morally enfeebled.

We'd been loaned a swipe card which let us into the chapel. Octagon realised that their transients would never agree on a form of worship: there were Buddhists, Catholics, Greek Cypriots next to Turkish Cypriots, US fundamentalists, flag-worshippers and total abstainers. The chapel, once the focus (social and ethical) of the community, had been reconceptu-alised (and left out of Octagon's brochure). Patterns of coloured light from stained-glass windows played on a brilliant parquet floor. The altarpiece was curtained off, but we had been given permission to look at it. Madonna, gilt. Niches, stone vines, elaborate iconography: symbols of discontinued superstition (that the developers were superstitious enough to preserve).

A new cross-substitute had been erected in front of the altar: a basketball net (black tree, white halo panel, string bag). The floor had been polished for a purpose. The chapel was now a basketball court, divided into zones and quarters. The Jesus figure from the stained-glass window (scarlet loincloth) gazed down on the spectacle: an athlete sponsored by Nike. The saints and apostles were witnesses of a new cult: narcissism, conceptual exercise, the squeak of rubber soles on pale wood.

Going for a double-header, we walked back to Egham, to visit Royal Holloway College. Renchi was keen to exorcise the theft of Queen Victoria's hand.

We stopped in a pub, an average English summer's day (wickets were tumbling in the Test Match), then marched up the hill. The College was as strange as the Sanatorium: twin cloisters, an excess of windows, a history that overwhelms pres-ent occupants. Having entered one set of cloisters – panned around in amazement – we located the wrong statue. Victoria occupied the other court. Trying to figure out a way of getting close to the royal pedestal, without backtracking, we lost ourselves in subterranean passages, kitchens. An alarm sounded.

Had we set it off? Intruders. It went on and on ringing. Students, unconcerned, ambled into the cloisters. Corridors, staircases, walkways were deserted. We had the place to ourselves. A fenced-off rectangle of grass, a statue; red brick on all sides. An overemphatic alarm.

We found our way back out into the grounds, circled to where we hoped to discover the entrance to the second set of cloisters. By now, fire engines were arriving on the scene, bells jangling. A dementedly civilised episode: dons in ermine trim, students in black gowns, tame clergy, garden party females. Lovely dappled sunlight. Degree ceremony interrupted by this irritating bell, fire drills processed as per instruction. The whole mob have to stand, making conversation, under a tree, waiting for the all-clear – which no one in authority is prepared to sound.

A lawn sprinkler shudders and jerks. Rainbows dazzle in the stream. The blackened statue of the queen is framed in an archway, behind dignitaries and students; behind the security men who are blocking our access. Through my long lens I can see that she suffers from no deformity. The hand, if it was ever missing, has been restored. The original, buried in a Hampshire garden, can stay where it is.

Renchi almost made it, the arrival of the train at Alton; we were standing with the young artist, an awkward group, in front of the phone-in sandwich bar, as his car pulled up. Then, three or four simultaneous conversations interrupting engine noise, we were off, moving through soft countryside.

Being driven, being a guest – and then a guest of a guest – was disconcerting. The house, in the village on the edge of Salisbury Plain, was an accumulation of other houses, red brick extensions, converted stables, potting sheds with conservatory flourishes. The selling point was the mill stream. With lawns, vegetable gardens, clouds of white blossom.

The house was deserted.

The doors were open, we wandered through, and out into the grounds. Nobody challenged us, nobody was seen. Renchi, naked head wrapped in blue bandanna, was in shorts, sandals. A LEARN-SWAHILI T-shirt. He squatted on a plank bridge, a black dog beside him, hoping for a walk. Green water, reeds. Country time ebbed around us, as we sat, strolled, waited.

The day was warm. The mill stream, the moist greenery, made it bearable. Would it be possible to live in pastoral suspension – no traffic noise, no military helicopters (just then), free-flowing water, dropsical bees? Would it be feasible to paint, to produce work at the stupendous rate Sara H achieved? Why not let it all go, feet in stream, dogs sleeping in shade? A little light gardening, raspberry picking, when the sun went down.

Out of this trance came the call to lunch. Odd chairs, indoor chairs (walnut, oak, rosewood) brought outside: all shapes and sizes, around a long table. A selection of used hats are offered: shapeless fishing things with flies, broadbrim stockman, baseball, battered Panama, Van Gogh straw. The Chinese/Vietnamese sculptor, a neat person, sun specs nestled in hair, is astonished by this ritual. She declines, flinching from the notion of communal headgear. Most of the others go for it, something to keep off the midday sun.

An empty house, grounds given over to large black dogs, and then out of nowhere a mob around a long table. Who are they? We're too English to find out or to make proper introductions. It seems that an elderly male occupies the main house and that others, daughters, ex-partners, future partners, friends, associates, camp somewhere on the property. Sara paints in a cupboard.

A pike has been caught in the mill stream by a man everyone

says should be a TV gardener. The mythic monster was brought ashore in a net improvised from chicken wire. The flavour is ancient, almost meaty. It's a subversive act to taste this flesh, cool, ivory-green, rare; afterbreath of decay disguised in a creamy mayonnaise ointment. Bowls of brown potatoes from the garden. Jugs of fruit juice.

Sara is quiet. We know that the meal, however welcome and well managed, can't be allowed to stretch too far into the after-noon. It is the hospitable preliminary to the move indoors, the viewing of the paintings.

Processing through the dark cool house, Sara's early paint-ings are pointed out – lemons, dogs, prize cockerels. 'Red is always good. Red sells,' a lady with smoked glasses and rings (who hopes to promote Sara's new visionary series) tells me.

Stairs creak. Family plunder, more than a single household can store, takes up all the available space. Houses lived in for generations become museums of the familiar. There is always an attic, a space under the roof where the reserve collection, unattributed cargo, can be hidden away: universal memories, the dream-sludge of lost childhoods. One section of the Wilt-shire attic bows under the freight of Sara's dictated paintings. Her audience sit, or squat, in an outer chamber, as she carries her work through, painting by painting, several hundred of them, and each with its own narrative.

We're in the old nursery. White cupboards. Stolen light. The managed effluvia of banishment, frustration. Rest hours that spanned the eternity of a summer afternoon. We can't move. We're trapped in children's chairs, wedged. If I stand up, the chair comes with me.

The spirit guide, who arrived at a time of personal crisis for Sara, let it be known that her task was to produce twelve sequences, each sequence consisting of a hundred or more linked canvases. The room we are sitting in is too small for this news. As an audience, we shrivel: our reception of the descrip-tions Sara offers – precise, slightly robotic – shifts from shared excitement to indifferently disguised boredom. Claustrophobia. Mad, isn't it? The blue paint costs £20 a tube. The guide says that the next series will require larger canvases. Sara is rapidly depleting her financial reserves, rapidly filling the nursery with paintings that look like maps, dreamings, motorway junctions. You can't make aesthetic judgements, that one canvas is better or more achieved than another; they are produced so quickly – and wheeled into the room where we're sitting with no break in the monologue. Sometimes there is an anecdote, sometimes we're told that an area of the painting refers to a pre-birth memory, pain cluster, the resolution of a psychic drama. What appears to the casual eye as abstraction is known to the artist as the record of movement through time, a journey. Technically the paintings are difficult to transact, certain lines in certain colours have to be laid down first. The guide is firm on that point. The background is painted last – without muddying outlines already set in place. The whole process sounds agonising. But Sara doesn't complain. She answers our questions – which are hesitant. Nobody knows quite how far they can go with these revelations – sympathy, awe, bemusement? Other artists are invoked – Klee, Kandinsky, Bernard Cohen – but the comparisons aren't helpful. Sara isn't refining a style; she's a technician, a willing stenographer of the unconscious. Notions of Aboriginal art, songlines, Navaho sand paintings, are more appropriate. If Renchi is looking for a way, through his walk around the M25, to find a topography sympathetic to his romantic sensibility (part documentary record, part vision), Sara seems to have accessed that chaos map. Renchi's task is finite, 150 miles of liminal wanderings and the circuit will break down into columns: salt, sand, chalk, dirt. Accepted symbols. The white canvases of Sara, with their weavings, dark loops, are infinite. No way out: the impulse to create won't be appeased, there is no evidence for the landscapes her maps describe.

Sara's titles, delivered by her guide, are wild. She takes

dictation from the dead, the disembodied. I thought she was talking about 'bent lions', before her finger pointed out a bend in the *line*. Her colours could be aphasic, vile: neon-greens, lurid oranges she would have spurned in her former life as pet portraitist. Even now she finds herself apologising for the aesthetic shortcomings of her inflexible master.

The attic is about dispersal. Moments of inspiration become, through repetition, de-energising. An hour is as much as the audience can take. Sara, brown and fit, long skirt and sandals, must tell the *whole* story: to the last canvas. I fixate on her mouth, the voice, the strong white teeth. She is a psychic trumpet to a performance that belongs outside our motorway orbit, far from London. Sara has been told to varnish a number of the paintings and send them to the Royal Academy.

Afternoon light thins. Our concentration makes the attic room feel cold. There is a requirement to respond, to do something with this work. I try to persuade Anna that it would make a book, the trajectory from English animals, Wiltshire garden, to the never-ending and unresolvable project. But she's too canny. She knows how easy it would be to disappear into the tale, the obsession. We're starting to struggle for breath. A soft white dove, said to be 'stupid', bangs against the window. The apparition is taken for a sign. There are trains to catch. We express, inadequately, our gratitude to Sara, and we're back on the road.

London, by early evening, is under siege. Public transport isn't operating and the cab rank at Waterloo is attended by travellers moving at the wrong speed – as if they've arrived, unprepared, from a distant country. The city is muggy, close, airless.

Getting into somebody else's vehicle, abdicating responsibility, giving out an address, is usually a relief. You might pay for it – punitive damages on the clock, unprovoked monologue – but, weary from train-hours, the events of a long day, the indulgence is justified. Not advancing, being overtaken by pedestrians with Zimmer frames, is the norm. The taxi heart thumps, adding its fumes to the stickiness that glues the city streets. We pull all the usual cab stunts, U-turns, lane jumps, window-to-window exchanges with other initiates; it doesn't signify. We could run west as far as Mortlake, creep east in the direction of the Blackwall Tunnel, we would never cross the river.

The protesters have succeeded in closing the bridges. Cabbies have the best take on congestion, traffic flow: they take it personally. All other life forms (mini-cab bandits, asylum seekers, politicians, cyclists, pedestrians) have it in for honest, self-employed, home-owning, golf-whenever-possible, Hertfordshire fringe, knowledge-achieved British taxi man. Cabbies don't swear (even at the illegitimate 'thems' and 'thoses' that make their lives a misery). They've been schooled in rage management. They don't want you to smoke. They keep a clean vehicle. They take some exercise. They are married, divorced, married again. They are buying in Spain. Only to discover that everything they've grafted for is threatened by state-sponsored anarchists.

We give it up, pay the man off. Forty minutes on the clock has carried us down the ramp at Waterloo. As soon as we begin to walk, oxygen returns to the brain. I'm living out a long dormant fantasy, London without cars. I lie down in the middle of the road on Blackfriars Bridge to take a photograph of an arrowed sign saying: CITY. At the end of the bridge, the portly silhouette of Queen Victoria on her pedestal, hands intact, winks back at the Royal Holloway College effigy.

The orderly protest processions of the morning, making their way up New Bridge Street towards Ludgate Hill, are now – thanks to armed response units, Samurai snatch squads – a small riot. Provocation and response, the dance at the end of the day. Battle honours, blood on the T-shirt, lightly worn. The two groups are like characters from different movies who have become inexplicably tangled: the last Mohicans taking on robocops. Coxcomb reflected in Plexiglas visor. I know that it's my fault: I shouldn't have left town. Pike lunches and weedy mill streams are not my business.

Writers, other than those who do it for money, are about as much use in times of crisis as ghost-hunter Harry Price's curious machines (horn trumpets, boxes that record the whispers of the dead). We sit in a bar in Smithfield, relishing the riptide of energy, the necessary civic argument in which we play no part. Let the city burn for the cameras. It has happened before. This is nothing. There is worse to come. The blood on the streets is a sideshow to the café society of the meat market. They lap up tin bowls of mussels, call for Belgian beer brewed by monks. No point in trying to go home, make it a party.

5

16 July 1999. An underdeveloped Weybridge morning and the news is that Marc Atkins is back on the road. If you can fit him into frame, he dresses a dull walk. He knows how to catch the camera's eye. (You've probably noticed him doing his starved Brando impression on the cover of the Penguin Classics *Heart of Darkness*.)

The moment outside Weybridge station (infiltration of enemy territory), when Marc and Renchi come face to face, is their second encounter. Marc (hands in pockets) and Renchi (hands on hips) in front of two hoardings. NOW YOU SEE IT, NOW YOU DON'T/A DIFFERENT KIND OF STRENGTH. Marc is travelling light, black T-shirt (rolled sleeves), camera. Renchi is in a blue sweater, carrying a heavily freighted rucksack. The two men met in the Museum of London, when Renchi and I were doing the London Wall walk. Marc had been checking out an unimpressive (so he said) show of Sixties' metropolitan photographs; fashion, celebrity, urban sentimentality (Bailey, Donovan).

Over the parapet of the bridge, we watch the commuters on Weybridge station. They advance towards the yellow line – MIND THE STEP – but do not cross it. Men in dark suits, women in summer dresses. Lines of black cases set down on the platform. Who is there to talk to, on the mobile, at seven a.m.? Answering machines that won't answer.

If psychogeography is the theme, Weybridge has it – well disguised, screened by foliage, always present. According to Mary Caine's zodiac, we are abseiling out of the Dog's arse. The station, on Cobbets Hill, lies just to the north of an intriguing double bill: the former Brooklands road racing circuit (later controlled by British Aerospace) and the private estate of St George's Hill. Today, we're going to attempt the walk over St George's Hill, and on towards Cobham Heath, following in the steps of Gerrard Winstanley and the community of Diggers, in the period after the English Civil War.

Brooklands was left until the M25 pilgrimage had been completed, when we were revisiting certain sites, making a series of secondary excursions. Land in the valley of the Wey arranges itself according to the conventions of science fiction. Brooklands was Ballard, before Ballard came to Shepperton. An unashamed concrete island. The name – BROOKLANDS – has been chiselled, vertically, into the grey lip of the circuit, alongside Barnes Wallis Drive. Ghost architecture (grass invaded ramps) provokes accounts of spectral sightings: record breakers who died in the attempt, blown tyres. A spook's tour is available for those who want to tap into the crisis of sudden death.

We stood at the top of the bank and looked down into the bowl: a retail park, Marks & Spencer, Tesco. Cars massed as if for some great event: S.F. Edge's 24 Hour Run in 1907, Percy Lambert's 1913 feat, when he covered one hundred measured miles in an hour. (Lambert died, attempting to improve that record, a final spin before marriage. He is now an official Brooklands ghost.) Malcolm Campbell, John Cobb, Eric Fernihough. The photographs are necrophile, printed with posthumous light. Malcolm Campbell's shed is a clapboard coffin. Eric Fernihough, hooded and leathered like Fantomas, crouches over a Brough Superior bike, a man/machine hybrid.

The Brooklands circuit, devised in 1907 by Hugh Locke King, a wealthy landowner, was a forerunner of the M25: an oval that you travelled, flogging your vehicle to its limits, only to arrive back at the point where you started. There were frequent fatalities. The circuit, according to a leaflet put out by the Brooklands Museum, was 'a unique civil engineering achievement . . . one of the seven wonders of the modern world'. Locke King employed 1,500 labourers and craftsmen to reshape the landscape, to carve out a chunk of the Wey valley, to plant appropriate forestry around the rim. Instead of the paradise gardens of Enfield, the subtle interventions of the Highways Agency, here was a rich man's park that was resolutely of its time. A maze of concrete blocks instead of a redirected river.

The pro tem nature of the sheds and garages, the demob recklessness of the early racers, gave Brooklands the spirit of a Home Counties combat squadron. Men tinkering with machines. Improvised shelters. Cars that roared out of nowhere, spitting oil and making too much noise. Why, I thought, didn't they put the M25 on this convenient site? As a model of itself. A themed motorway. A circuit you could drive without harm or inconvenience to others. There was plenty of room to build a miniaturised Waltham Abbey, Dartford Bridge (for spectators), Swanley interchange for mock road rage duels (fought with paint guns). The retail parks, cadet versions of Bluewater and Lakeside, Thurrock, were already in place. There was even a duplicate of the Siebel building, green glass, back at the tree line; visibly invisible.

We stroll down the straight, cars skidding, slaloming around oil drums. Huge skies. In the meadow, at the end of the circuit, aircraft are parked. The 1945 Vickers Viking airliner (developed from the Wellington bomber). The Valiant (Britain's first 'V' bomber). A VC10 of the Sixties. It's an aeronautical graveyard. Some of the planes have been sliced in half.

Renchi is reading fiction that relates to areas through which we are walking: you could, in theory, string together a necklace of books, a bibliography for the motorway. Aldous Huxley's *Brave New World* is 'spot on', so he says, for the move into Surrey. Predictions of science parks, research establishments of the Thames corridor. Victorian and Edwardian novelists took the trouble to place literary contrivance in a convincing – and relevant – topography. Huxley, the fashionable author of the Twenties and Thirties, might have drifted out of favour, but

Renchi reckoned he was truer to the Siebel spirit than Orwell. Huxley, as the critic John Clute wrote, produced 'the model of pharmacological totalitarianism'. The ecology of least resistance.

An empty charabanc, clouds reflected in window panels, stood at the end of the runway. Green lettering: BICKNELL'S.

Marc, heavy dark glasses perched on brow (paparazzo), and Renchi, red shirt bandanna, advance on the security checkpoint. PRIVATE ROAD. RESIDENTS ONLY. NO PARKING. Gentle, wooded hills disclose colonial estates. Disclose silence. An absence of jingly ice-cream vans, squealing tyres, yelping dogs, raised voice, ambulance sirens.

A signboard. ST GEORGE'S HILL (white on deep green): PRIVATE ESTATE. NO PUBLIC RIGHT OF WAY. *St George's Hill Tennis Club. St George's Hill Golf Club.* VISITORS PLEASE STOP FOR SECURITY GUARDS.

We were expecting this. The payroll boys, back in the station café at Staines, alerted us to the rock star dormitory: Tom Jones, Cliff Richard, John Lennon. The sort of recreational facilities the British Raj, escaping from summer heat, always demanded. Well-defended luxury becomes an open prison. We can't come in and they can't come out. They're not here, at home, even when they are. Security, under threat of instant dismissal, will never admit to their presence.

Locals – even Weybridge has some – can work the gate. Fill a uniform. Renchi has a cunning plan. He knows a builder who jobbed on the estate, who *might* be there now. A name. An address (which he has mislaid). Renchi is very good at these chats with security. The approach to St George's Hill is orthodox Surrey: a public road that, quite suddenly, isn't. Tarmac that gleams like polished pewter. Even the pollen has been airbrushed, tweezered by hand into the kerbside.

Renchi marches forward, alone. We hang back, snapping away. A rusticated hut (small cricket pavilion) with white gate. Bushes, shrubs, poplars. A white Fiesta with checkered trim (faking at official status). Yellow flashing light: ST GEORGE'S HILL SECURITY.

A radio is playing, something bland and matutinal, in the deserted sentry box. Further on, at the final checkpoint, Renchi initiates a conversation with the bearded guard. The man looks the part (which covers most of his job description), but he's decent, a local taking what he can get in the way of casual employment. Renchi mutters about his builder friend. The guard is bored enough to let us in. The status of the road is anyway ambiguous. We're passing through, a country walk, we explain. We'll keep our eyes to ourselves. We're making for another estate, the workers' village built for employees of Whiteley's department store.

Keep moving, no detours. Heads down. No sudden, unexplained gestures. We're on camera: all the way.

This, self-evidently, was the future: what should have happened, and now won't. A county within a county; calmer, cleaner, emptier than the rest. A magnet for villainy. A refuge for villains. At a reading I met a student from Weybridge. She told me that the local beauty parlours, the hairdressers, were full of women in studio make-up speaking Russian. Nails sharp as daggers. Clanking with gold chains. Mafia wives from Moscow.

The road, as we wind up the hill, is spookier than Brooklands. Nature on its best behaviour, heathland smoother than a bowling green. Small plantations of red-barked conifers: BEWARE. GOLFERS PLAYING FROM THE LEFT.

The text Renchi has to hand is H.G. Wells's *The War of the Worlds*, which he is using as a guidebook. The 1898 fantasy – alien invasion – plays very nicely against this unpeopled estate. Where better for the Martians to put their marker than a discreet private golf course? From a real-estate point of view, the Woking landfall made sense. 'Hundreds of observers saw the flame that night and the night after; and so on for ten nights, a flame each night.' Technologically primitive

Surrey suburbanites were zapped by future war weaponry; it was a horribly unequal contest. Roaming bands of survivors took to the hills; the defeated military attempted guerrilla raids from their shelters on the North Downs. Religion was no consolation. Fundamentalist clergy wandered the back roads and river paths between Staines and Richmond, calling for divine retribution. They died raving, in the rubble, doctrine decayed into a stream of incoherent curses. No building, however innocent its function, was safe from the Heat-Rays. 'I saw the tops of the trees above the Oriental College burst into smoky red flame, and the tower of the little church beside it slide down into ruin. The pinnacle of the mosque had vanished.' Yes, Woking (heathland bastion of English values) had a mosque. But the ruthless invaders, who had travelled 140,000,000 miles with mayhem in mind, had no interest in cultural niceties. Burn, blast, batter. Convert the primitives of Ottershaw and Chertsey into meat. Liquidise them. Very perceptive, these foreign devils. With one glance, they understood that our soft estates were good for nothing but future golf courses, catteries, mediparcs and orbital motorways. Wells knew the geography of the perimeter, he had cycled for miles through country lanes and villages that would soon be swallowed by ribbon-development and retail landfill.

Orson Welles launched his career by shifting invasion paranoia to American radio in 1940. Premature anti-fascists under every bed. The youthful Orson met the literary globe-trotter, H.G. Wells, at a radio station in Texas. Both versions of *The War of the Worlds* haunted the Surrey section of our walk; the reverberation of those names, Wells and Welles, staying with us until the true wells, medicinal and salty, could be located at Epsom.

In his 1997 film, *Robinson in Space*, Patrick Keiller's narrator takes Robinson on an outing to inspect the Martians' crater, at Horsell Common, near Woking.

He told me that there are more than 100 patents in microelectronics, nanotechnology and other fields for uses of buckminsterfullerenes, the large, spherical carbon molecules discovered in cosmic dust by British and other scientists, but they are all held abroad.

The Martians destroyed most of Surrey. Five hundred tons of Mars are estimated to land on Earth each year.

Robinson's excursion party moves on – by car, unfortunately – from Woking to St George's Hill. A sacred place for dissenters. Common land was developed as a private estate in 1911. The hurt remains. There was every reason for the guards to feel uneasy, they were protecting the unprotectable. Robinson recalls the occupation of land at Wisley, near St George's Hill, by a group of eco-campaigners. This is the doctrine: off-road incursions (by British Aerospace, weapons technology, biological research facilities) celebrated by the arrival of the tribes. The worst piracies solicit attention by the freest spirits, activists. Flies drawn to the stink of rotten meat. Protesters promote chainsaw-security, tree-police. Occupation of threatened sites turns political argument into ritual theatre.

Keiller footnotes the invasion of St George's Hill:

The group was 'The Land is Ours' and the spokesman was George Monbiot, writer and Fellow of Green College, Oxford. St George's Day is April 23rd. The site was 'set-aside' land beside the disused Wisley aerodrome. On Friday the 28th, the group processed to St George's Hill and performed a play, based on the legend of St George and the Dragon, on the practice range of the golf-course.

I heard about this procession from Billy Bragg, who featured a Digger song at a Blake evening in the Festival Hall. Bragg recommended Christopher Hill's *The World Turned Upside Down (Radical Ideas during the English Revolution)*. It's easy to feel sentimental about the one period in English life when we played at being a Republic; court and courtiers were discounted.

Splinter groups, fanatics and visionaries of every stamp, took to the roads. Churches and civic buildings were used for debate: hamlet to hamlet, along the Thames from Putney to Kingston. Agitators, appointed by their fellow soldiers, argued against parliamentary orthodoxy. Levellers, Diggers, Ranters. Veterans of the Sixties are drawn to this period, the late 1640s and early 1650s: they know about splits and schisms, expulsion, denunciation. Impotence.

St George's Hill was a place of pilgrimage. Gerrard Winstanley and the Diggers camped on the common, cultivated the ground – much to the annoyance of the squirearchy. The Diggers called themselves The True Levellers, believing that land belonged to those who worked it. The first Digger commune was established by Winstanley and the others on 1 April 1649. By August, hostility from local interests drove them on to Cobham Heath. The following year, like asylum seekers, they were 'dispersed'.

Winstanley received, so he asserted, divine inspiration, while in a trance. There must be common ownership of all means of production and distribution, complete freedom of worship, compulsory education for both sexes. When the voice of God triumphed, the formal authority of the state would wither away.

In *The True Leveller Standard Advanced*, a tract published in 1649, Winstanley made his 'declaration to the powers of England and all the powers of the world, shewing the cause why the common people of England have begun and gives consent to dig up, manure and sow corn upon George Hill in Surrey; by those that have subscribed, and thousands more that give consent'.

BEWARE OF GOLFERS PLAYING FROM THE RIGHT. Slanting shadows across road and heath. Morning light, revisited months later in a Marc Atkins print, is exquisite. The lifting sun glints from dust-free windows, hidden among the trees. Roof tiles, gables, tall chimneys. Water towers disguised as Rapunzel follies. A white club house for the private golf course: imposing as a country hotel.

On St George's Hill, no two properties are the same; that's the point. This is not a Barratt asylum conversion. You get the ironwork gates, lions on pedestals, the cute names (WITS END) – but the Hill doesn't have much truck with Essex ranch-style, or faux-Mediterranean coke haven. Did Lennon (*Working Class Hero*), playing posh, remember Winstanley? A friend of mine, a schoolteacher from Leamington Spa, pitching some Utopian scheme, visited the Beatle in his den. Time was different, he recalled, for the seriously rich. Place was accidental. From the moment you stepped through the door, you were on the point of leaving. There was nowhere to hang your coat. It took an entire evening not to get the cup of coffee, offered as you searched for a chair, or cushion, or appropriate yard of floor space.

Walkers fall under immediate suspicion. Those who 'travelled the country', as Christopher Hill points out, were thought to be conveyors of intelligence, spies, plotters, heretics. A new type, the gamekeeper (suborned working man), was invented to guard against wanderers. The genial tramps of English fiction, colourful trespassers in villages curated by Richmal Crompton and P.G. Wodehouse, might be John Buchan agents in disguise. Discharged soldiers, lunatics. Joseph Salmon, a Ranter, told how, in the days of his trance, he had 'walked in unknown paths, and become a madman, a fool among men'.

Winstanley, defeated, returned to London where he had been an apprentice in the cloth trade, a freeman of the Merchant Taylors Company. He played no further part in public life. As a corn merchant, his fortunes revived. He lived in the modest obscurity that is London's greatest benefit. After the Restoration of the Stuart monarchy, he became a Quaker. He died in 1676 – by which time laws had been passed giving gamekeepers free access to the cottages of those they suspected

of being poachers. Weapons could be confiscated at will.
Dissenters were persecuted. Justices of the Peace harassed and
imprisoned vagrants. England was brought to that happy state
where those who roamed – without good reason, without pass-
ports and permissions – were liable to be defined as being out
of their wits, Tom O'Bedlams. Trance-travellers, like common
ground, suffered compulsory enclosure.

A Mercedes with darkened windows slides out from behind
spiked gates that close automatically as the car pulls away. The
long drive, in a herringbone pattern of pale brick, stretches into
a leafy distance, perspective flattered by lines of thin aspens.
Terrace, fountain. Pausing to admire the potential photo-op,
we are interrogated by a security patrol. A white Fiesta draws
up. A guard, in mirrored sunglasses, leans out. Courteous. 'Just
checking, sir.'

Nothing has changed since the first car challenged us, ten
minutes earlier. You are allowed to walk half a mile between
security shakedowns. Slow-moving Fiestas are on constant
patrol. CCTV cameras, panning restlessly, alert the monitor
jockeys. Calls come in from nervous watchers at windows:
'Walkers.' Walkers without dogs. The public aspect of this
private road, between the B374 and the B365, is being subtly
erased. In the end, it's less bother to go the long way around.

As we advance down the avenue, towards the eastern
checkpoint, smaller, ruder vehicles begin to appear. Domestics
checking in. The occasional limo, or Range Rover, carrying
uniformed children to school. We encounter the only walkers
the estate allows: young women struggling with pairs, even
packs, of leashed dogs. Accredited canine accompanists. Peripatetic toilet attendants scooping the lush verges. Leather lead
in one hand, silver shit-shovel in the other.

The map of St George's Hill, near the entrance gate, is
highly selective: the estate is creamy-white ground, no houses
are marked, roads look like rivers. Two islands of greenery

represent the only named zones: Tennis Club, Golf Club. The western entrance lets you into the golf club. The eastern entrance adjoins the tennis club. There is no other reason to be here. The notice – YOU ARE HERE – is ironic. You only see it on your way out. As the barrier closes behind you. And the guard ticks you off his list. Phones down the line with an all-points warning.

This second estate, Whiteley Village, on the west side of Seven Hills Road, makes a powerful impression on the map, on my Nicholson. In its benevolent aspect, the village (with its Home of Rest) is a Jungian mandala, circular paths contained in an outer square. We are about to enter a panopticon, all areas visible from the centre. Another ambivalent asylum of the suburbs.

The approach to the village is kinder than anything we encountered on St George's Hill, the planting is shaggier – a path vanishing into a green tunnel (one of Samuel Palmer's oval bowers). There are gates with heraldic shields: WHITE-LEY VILLAGE/PRIVATE/ELDERLY RESIDENTS/PLEASE DRIVE SLOWLY. But the gates are open.

Renchi strolling, hands cupped to support his awkward rucksack, leads the way. The taller, shavenheaded Marc (in black T-shirt, dark glasses, white trainers) is the inappropriate figure. He might be security. Earlier that morning, he told us how he'd been in the music business. A roadie at the tail-end of Heavy Metal, the cusp of Punk. He almost fitted on the Hill; delivering substances, a sessions man down on his luck. Up there, Renchi screamed offence: eco-warrior, sans-culotte. Ambling through these red brick bungalows, this play village, he comes into his own. A helper with rolled-up sleeves, a sympathetic listener: suitably rough at the edges, fuzzy in outline.

As with all Surrey estates, there is nobody to be seen. It's too early for the old folk. The bungalows are generously spread out, detached, with neat garden plots; wide, trim lawns. The design is uniform but not oppressively so. Low tiled roofs on public buildings, twisted licorice pillars. Whiteley Village plays like *The Prisoner* – but that's our own perversity; we've been schooled to be suspicious of charity, of surveillance (where it doesn't declare itself).

At the centre of the estate is a raised garden, a plinth; a near obelisk with a stone sculpture of the seated figure of 'Industry'. Industry is female, wide-skirted; a beehive (covered with bees) is cradled under her left arm. Beneath her, in profile, is a memorial to William Whiteley (1831–1907). Whiteley died in the year that Brooklands was launched as a motor racing circuit. He was a businessman, shopkeeper and philanthropist. His department store in Queensway, Bayswater, was a Victorian and Edwardian institution. A virtual high street with all its retail variety enclosed in a single spacious building; a way of experiencing Knightsbridge or Regent Street in the inner suburbs. Like Arding and Hobbs in Clapham Junction or Jones Brothers in Holloway Road. It was possible to promenade, fit out a house, purchase groceries, reading matter, take tea. The vision lasted for much of the century, gradually declining into situation comedy and shabby grandeur – until Whiteley's rebranded itself as a true mall, a shelter for: Ace of Cards, Tower Records, Elegant Nails, Poons Restaurant. Railway terminus opportunism.

William Whiteley (of Westbourne Grove) made provision for his workers; after years behind the counter (floorwalking, packing, nodding and greeting in Bayswater), they qualified for a red brick bungalow in the Mole Valley. The memorial tablet alluded to a 'munificent bequest'. Whiteley purchased the park and built cottages 'for the comfort of old age and as an encouragement to others to do likewise'.

The verdigris stain made the plutocrat's plinth look like a green fountain. Instead of being the eye of the panopticon, from which the inhabitants could be observed (and controlled), Industry and her beehive were the focal point. The spokes of the roads led attention *in* to the statue and its message: 'Blessed be the man that provideth for the sick and needy.' Charity being done, and well done, need not be inconspicuous. Retail veterans, their years of useful labour concluded, would meditate – with gratitude – on the benevolence of their patron. They would be encouraged to read his abbreviated biography, as it was carved in stone. 'Apprenticed at the age of 16 to a drapery firm in Wakefield . . . went to London to see the Great Exhibition of 1851 . . . the busy life of the Metropolis attracted him . . . ten years of thrift and constant study with a City firm . . . small business of his own at 63, Westbourne Grove . . . won himself the name of the universal provider . . . world wide reputation . . . pioneer of the great London retail stores of the 19th & 20th centuries . . . died in London . . .'

The memorial bench is a good place to spread our maps, assess their contradictions. St George's Hill buffers the M25; we have lost touch with our orbital democrat, the conveyor belt of urban dreaming. We decide to follow Winstanley and the Diggers, in the direction of Cobham Heath, rather than pay any special attention to the 'corner', where the road begins to pull to the south-east. The Royal Horticultural Society Gardens at Wisley will have to be left for another day. It wasn't, in any case, the gardens that pricked my interest, but the woodland car park (easy access to the motorway).

EVIL THAT LURKS AT THE GARDEN GATE: reported the *Evening Standard*, dressing a scare story with a photograph of cars and camper vans in a sylvan glade. The Wisley car park has become a meeting place for sex pests, weirdos, stalkers; a venue favoured by motorway prostitutes and gay cruisers. Six hundred and fifty thousand plant-fanciers visit the famous gardens every year without suspecting that the zone of car parks, each catering to a particular taste, is possessed by the Dionysiac frenzy articulated by J.G. Ballard in his 1973 novel, *Crash*. Adulterous couples favour one area of the woods, homosexuals another, transsexuals a third. Wisley Common, an undulating tract of heathland, Scots pine, birch and oak, is now a popular resort for sexual dalliance: the contemporary equivalent of the old riverside pleasure grounds, Vauxhall and Ranelagh.

The sixty-acre estate took shape as a garden in the 1870s, when it was purchased by George Wilson of Weybridge, a former Treasurer of the Royal Horticultural Society. After Wilson's death, the estate was acquired by Sir Thomas Hanbury, and given by him, in trust, to the Royal Horticultural Society: 'for the purpose of an Experimental Garden and the Encouragement and Improvement of Scientific and Practical Horticulture in all its branches'. The pattern, seen in Enfield Chase, repeats itself. A paradise garden, owned by a brewer, confirms the relationship of inner and outer, city labyrinth and bucolic suburb. Hanbury, Quaker brewmaster (Truman, Hanbury and Buxton of Brick Lane), laid out a patch of ground where stressed workers could recover their vital energies by walking among beds of exotic plants. The flavour of Wisley (as represented in the RHS booklet of 1969, picked up in one of Shepperton's many charity shops) is resolutely outer-rim M25, Surrey hill station: bright gashes of colonial colour. Evergreen azaleas, 'Temple Belle' rhododendrons. Alpine rockeries that 'Gussie' Bowles of Myddelton House would have abhorred.

Heady drenches infect the woods. Martin and Vivi Gale (in their tea-stall) are 'plagued by predatory homosexuals'. Squelchy paths are strewn with hardcore magazines. It's too convenient: lay-bys on either side of the A3, resinous paths, filtered light; a rapid escape route to the M25 (the ribbon connecting nowhere with everywhere).

A lorry driver called David Smith picked up Amanda Walker, a known prostitute, in Paddington. He drove her to Wisley, where he 'mummified' her with cling-film, before raping her. While she was still alive, he stuffed her mouth with leaves. And then he stabbed her. Her naked body was recovered from a shallow grave, found within yards of the Royal Horticultural Society gardens.

Smith, who is thought to have used the motorway system to identify and secure women for ritualistic sexual practices, was a Wisley regular. He liked to see what other couples got up to in their cars. An enterprising white-van owner used to charge drifters for watching while he had sex with underage girls. And, being a favoured resort for cruising men, the park also attracted homophobe gangs.

A vicious attack on a couple in a parked car in a quiet Surrey lane (an Austin Princess with a brown top) launched the night of violence that resulted in the unsafe conviction of the men known as the 'M25 Three'. One of the victims, Peter Hurburgh, kicked and beaten (by machete), drenched in petrol, died. The other, Alun Ely, survived: to offer a number of contradictory accounts of his ordeal.

The orbital motorway was still a novelty, operative for two years, when the assault, burglary and murder occurred in December 1988. The road solicited crime. The accused men lived in Sydenham, an easy-going culture of amateur drug dealing, car theft, fencing and serial fatherhood. It didn't seem like crime, the life. It was what everybody did. Everybody lied, everybody informed. Everybody was fitted up. Short spells on the Isle of Sheppey got your head together.

The new motorway was a route into previously inaccessible territories; you could spin Surrey, explore Kent. The expedition for which the M25 Three went down began with the theft of a Triumph Sprite – abandoned when Alun Ely's Austin Princess was commandeered. And so on, car for car, through Leatherhead and Oxted. When the police started to get heavy, the surviving motors were torched. None of the witnesses can remember their assailants: white becomes black, dreadlocks and long greasy hair are confused. Stories are subject to infinite revision, adjustments of time and place. The cars are never forgotten. A woman coming home late remarks the Union Flag logo on the Sprite. The pub musician at the White Hart, William 'Budgie' Robins, who vaguely noticed a gay man in white, paid far more attention to the motor in the car park. That yellow/brown combo, he reckoned, was 'a bit special'.

With the advent of this bright new motorway, a support belt beneath South London's sagging suburbs, criminal imagination was booted into a higher register. Street crims became upwardly mobile; they were soon thieving beyond their capacity to fence, dishing out grief where it was least appreciated. With substantial rewards from insurance companies and tabloids on the table, with the constabulary ready as ever to customise a fiction, the comfortable laissez-faire, live-and-let-live of the Sydenham, Catford, Croydon lowlife imploded.

Like a powerful magnetic field, the west/east pull of the M25 affected old alignments, the familiar runs towards Brighton and the coast. Narrative fractured. Verbals didn't stand up. Confessions wouldn't cohere. The motorway was loud with Chinese whispers. When dusk fell, villains took to their (borrowed-without-the-owner's-consent) cars. On the cruise. Tooled up with hand guns, machetes, petrol cans, monkey wrenches.

Nothing in 'The Case of the M25 Three' makes sense. Alun Ely, who admitted in court to 'careless handling of the truth', drops off his girl friend and then drives aimlessly around Croydon for hours, down to a Fina petrol station on the Brighton road – before parking up for sex with Peter Hurburgh. A man walking a dog remembers the car but doesn't know what day of the week it was. Girl friends of the accused men (Raphael Rowe, Michael Davis, Randolph Johnson) receive stolen jewellery and forget the donors. The grey sprawl of South London subtopia bleeds into Croydon: nothing is fixed, journeys overlap. Speed chilled with puff. None of the men packed into the stolen car wears a watch. Time is crosschecked by hallucinating a petrol tanker refuelling a set of red-and-green pumps in an oasis of yellow-white light, in the middle of nowhere.

Surrey declines to acknowledge these incursions. Surrey celebrates private estates, notable gardens, the E.M. Forster movie
franchise. Bandits who motor through leafy lanes sussing
properties, preying on deviants, wired to the eyeballs, don't register. They are as invisible as scuttling things in the long grass
of the central reservation. Landscape artists of the Highways
Agency have made access tunnels for badgers, there is no human
equivalent. Ratepayers see the M25 as a barrier to be defended,
villains know it as a job opportunity.

The Whiteley Village golf course, unlike the striped sward on
St George's Hill, is in use. Early. Old chaps greet us with a
wave. They're happy to debate a path to carry us over the
Mole, the A3, and into Cobham. THIS SPACE COULD BE PRO-
MOTING YOUR COMPANY LOGO: is the message on a green
hydrant.

The Mole is reedy, nettles and willowherb and field pansies
in profusion; there's no way we can wade across, we hear traffic
on the far side. A Pre-Raphaelite stream and a functional dual-
carriageway running in parallel. A neat bridge with harp-shaped
wings. A path that burrows under the road.

We pause, resting on the crash barrier, for the usual roadside
photo session. Renchi abandons his sweater. Marc's belly is
rumbling; as a vegetarian he needs to graze at regular intervals. In several hours, hacking through estates, woodland, golf
courses, roads and rivers, we haven't seen anywhere to get
a cup of tea. No cafés, no coffee stalls, not even a petrol station:
a green desert. If we don't find somewhere fast, Marc will keel
over and posterity will be denied his Surrey pastoral portfolio.

6

The effect of the road, the A3 and its Cobham junction (with spiral-shaped cochlea and semicircular canals, a diagram of the inner ear), is to deafen pedestrians. The underpass sucks out country sounds and replaces them with traffic-stream percussion; blimps and creaks and soft bombs. Then, hitting sunlight, there is no sound. We're in it, in the band – adjusting to speed, torn air, sticking fingers in our ears; we march, single file, through an unresolved, town-edge landscape. Development is on hold. We feel the volume displacement of power drills and JCBs, even when they're not operative. Avenues of red cones, red-and-white detour boards, make walking difficult.

SAINSBURY'S THIS WAY.

The others aren't convinced but I have a notion that you can eat in these places. We follow the arrow down a white fence that is just tall enough to mask the new estate (sand-coloured housing units with red tile roofs). Naked trees. CCTV masts. The superstore, demographics run through the computer, anticipates the coming, off-road expansion. The map is decorated with heaths and commons that aren't common: pony-exercising paths, discretion suitable for American Community Schools. You walk these areas under sufferance, under observation.

Our breakfast is excellent and modestly priced, on a par with a transport caff. This is what Sainsbury's has become: a place to which you can drive, to which you *must* drive. A warehouse in which to bulk buy (card-and-carry) foodstuffs that haven't quite gone off. In Surrey, the picture-window superstore is also an all-day breakfast facility. They give you a numbered flag to place on your table, so that the eating area, when it's busy, looks like a pitch-and-putt course. Nobody else has walked here, or come just for the breakfast. Fast food is a loss leader. Hugging the A3, this branch of Sainsbury's could outperform the Little Chef; a motorway pit stop attached to a larger than average impulse-shop. If you aren't shopping, if you don't have to do the consumerist assault course, the Cobham Sainsbury's is an oasis of quiet conversation, unemphatic service, managed light. English hash-jocks have never been able to work the corporate grin of retail fundamentalism. 'Have a nice day', in their shipwrecked mouths, sounds like a threat. Employment, with its funny uniforms and patronising name badges, is a form of probation; a way of demonstrating that another small town, another strip of countryside, has been captured.

If you have the model town of Sainsbury's, with its busy avenues, young mothers, kids, arguing couples, flirting singles, cruisers, slow-moving oldies (walking frames on awkward wheels), you don't need Cobham. Sainsbury's is universal (like America). In supermarket heaven, you're at home everywhere. The name sounds like Salisbury. You might bump into Edward Heath, V.S. Naipaul, Cecil Beaton. Or find John Constable sketching meadows of lettuce. The retail landscape supplies all the ingredients for a day out: butcher, baker, fishmonger, deli, confectioner, video store, florist. The acoustic environment keeps trippers in a trance state. Lulled by the scent of lilies, tulips, carnations, weary excursionists rest on the bars of their trolleys. Dazzled by cosmetic colours, the eye-damage of too-red strawberries, tomatoes, peppers as green as the deep Atlantic, sleepwalkers call up mildly erotic reveries. Their hands keep moving, making guided choices, filling the basket. Supermarkets are the last pleasure gardens, brothels of the senses.

Do we take the time to visit Painshill Landscape Garden (aka Painshill Park)? We don't know anything about the place, but here it is – and, on this rather dim section of the walk, we're ready to access the unexpected. The A3 runs down the west side of the extensive grounds and the M25 carves around to the south: Painshill (supported by the National Heritage Memorial Fund, English Heritage, the Countryside Commission and Surrey County Council) is overendowed real estate. Like so much else that we've encountered, it is dedicated to customising the past as a way of making us feel good about ourselves: we come from somewhere, we have a lineage. That which is worth preserving has been preserved. We meditate, by walking specified and guided routes, on the lessons that history can teach us. The M25 is ringed with National Trust properties, mansions, estates, hills, towers. Runnymede through Hatchlands Park to Box Hill. Brochures tell you what you should notice: 'mammals such as the dormouse, plus a nationally important bat population'. Box Hill is doubly blessed: by 'spectacular views towards the West Sussex Downs' and by its association with the Jane Austen movie franchise. Surrey is divided between the bits where Merchant/Ivory exercise their Forster options (watch out for a naked Simon Callow plunging into a woodland pool) and hillocks where one of Austen's headstrong young ladies can be beastly to her elders. For location caterers, it's west to Hardy country (Polanski, Schlesinger) or east to India (David Lean).

The ascent of Box Hill, formerly a Cockney outing (deplored by mandarin essayists like Sir Sidney Colvin), is now pictured in the National Trust brochure as a procession of mountain bikes. 'On the summit there is a visitor centre, shop with plant sales, servery and a fort (partly open to the public).'

My feeling is that anywhere with a 'servery', anywhere that is 'partly open', is to be avoided. Why let someone else nominate sites that are worth visiting? If you want a shop, you should find a shop. Sainsbury's (Cobham) has a better servery than Box Hill. The space underneath Runnymede Bridge is more exciting than the National Trust recommended Runnymede Meadows (with 'popular tea-room'). Don't take my word for it, don't bother with my list of alternative attractions – Junction

21 of the M25, the Siebel building in Egham, Hawksmoor's gravestone in Shenley; discover your own. In the finding is the experience.

Painshill, unrecommended, unknown to us, was irresistible. Acquired, designed, planted by the Honourable Charles Hamilton (1704–86), the estate consists of several hundred acres of barren heathland converted into a gallery of views, framed landscapes, to rival Stourhead or Stowe. Hamilton almost bankrupted himself in the process. An enterprise undertaken to satisfy his vanity, and to astonish his friends, is now – after two hundred years of 'seclusion' – offered to the public, as a venue for 'events'. Days are given over to Teddy Bear Trails, Santa in the Grotto and demonstrations of water wheels. The park, with its Augustan conceits, its Gothic fantasies, has been thoroughly democratised.

We're conscious, from the start of our tour, from the moment we pick up the Painshill Park Trust leaflet (and map), that we are processing through an elaborately staged masque; graded effects. The aristocrat Hamilton, youngest son of the Earl of Abercorn, travelled widely. He was influenced by 'poetic and literary sources'. Alexander Pope's Grotto at Twickenham. The fashion for chinoiserie. The lake, created above the circumfluent River Mole, looks like a faded transfer on a willow pattern plate. The South Bank bridge has the spindly quality of something borrowed from an oriental romance: a landscape in quotation marks. Dank English reality shaped to provoke memories of unread books, almost-familiar illustrations. Catherine the Great commissioned a dinner service from Josiah Wedgwood, decorated with scenes from Painshill Park. If we followed the route suggested by the official guide, pausing to appreciate the Gothic Temple, the Ruined Abbey, the Temple of Bacchus, the Turkish Tent, we would be tramping through a vista of smashed crockery. A Julian Schnabel replay of William Gilpin's watercolours, the generic views of Prosser and Wollett. Between the artifice of the Augustans and the passion of the Romantics, we were lost: day trippers in quest of easy revelations, shock effects, anything that could be satirised in a couple of sentences.

But Painshill outmanoeuvred us. There is a triangulation between the paradise gardens of Enfield Chase, Painshill (and Wisley) on the south-west corner, and Samuel Palmer's Shoreham (the Valley of Vision). A recrudescence of the pastoral in the teeth of all contrary indications. A triangle within the circle of the motorway: flashing like a hazard sign. Heaven and hell. Early visitors to Painshill referred to it as Elysium or Eden. A place to be enjoyed after death. Or through the myth of origin. A sanctuary in an unpeopled world. A doomed experiment by some remote and paternalistic deity. The Painshill leaflet stresses this theme: 'Paradise, once lost, cannot be regained in a single day . . . We are recreating an inheritance – the magic and mystery of Hamilton's garden.'

Seduced from the road, let into this estate, our duty is to record the eighteenth-century theme park experience. The decahedral temple is too white, wood as stone; the recreation of a fraud, the missing turret of a Disneyland castle. A cardboard crown from a touring production of *Richard III*. The temple is anti-Gothic, lacking creepers, dirt, dust, spiders, any trace of the North European spirit. The temple should have been located much closer to the M25, peeping out of a thicket of salt-resistant grass. It's a hut, open on all sides, arched windows acting as doors. The design of the floor points inwards to a jagged circle made from hexagonal tiles. The white orbit contains a brown centre which contains the outline of a square. The floor, as we contemplate it, becomes a theoretical dome.

Hamilton's architectural conceits, stressed by tame artists hired to make promotional sketches, demonstrate the proposition that there are always two viewpoints. The distant prospect of an exquisitely sited folly. And the view *out*, from that privileged position. Prosser, in his 1828 drawing (made at the Gothic Temple), highlights the lake, the Chinese bridge, two figures at the water's edge. Further attractions – Turkish tent, Temple of Bacchus, Gothic tower – are distant features. The drawing teaches you how and where to look. Where to walk.

Contemplating the lake, we find ourselves alongside it. No digressions, no psychogeographic detours. Each view leads, directly, to the next feature. The 'ruined abbey' is insufficiently distressed, the fake of a fake. This sort of thing was, until very recently, known as 'postmodern irony', but architecturally contrived ruins don't seem so ironic after the newsreel footage of 11 September at 'ground zero', New York; or photographs of collapsed tower blocks in Mexico City, crumpled flyovers, devastated cheap hotels. Hamilton's abbey, incompletely complete, is cheesy and nibbled. The lakeside setting is picturesque; a potential swamp waiting on winter rain.

This homage to Monk Lewis and Horace Walpole was an afterthought, built in 1772. Brick plastered over to simulate stone. Atkins is interested in brick. The jagged finish, with rodent toothmarks, reminds him of abandoned jobs of his youth, when contractors went bust or upwardly mobile Brummies ran out of readies. Contemporary excavations explain the choice of location for this one-room abbey: vaults and ducting were found beneath the floor. The abbey was built to conceal Hamilton's brick kilns. Within the illusionist scheme of Painshill, evidence of mechanical and mundane things had to be suppressed or disguised. Figures in recorded views of the estate are schematic, at ease, caught in reverie. No record of manual labour was left for posterity. Fakes faked themselves into oblivion.

The game is movement. Walkers undergo a form of aesthetic analysis as they travel from folly to folly, a strict examination of their responses to the freakish sets with which they are confronted. The interval between wonders is nicely calculated; just enough time to compose a poem of celebration. Here, on English heathland, is an eruption of weathered limestone, the aftermath of a volcanic catastrophe. The grotto is shaped from outcrops of tufa, razor-sharp stone you might find on a barren Mediterranean island. Tufa needs heat, sunlight. The sea.

The grotto, after Pope, was the ultimate challenge for the landscape conceptualist: a retreat, a back reference, a geologically impossible shrine to the Muse. But it's done as a gesture, a performance. You don't mean it. Hamilton doesn't really want to hide here. He isn't soliciting trance or fugue. He invites his guests to admire the artifice. He wants their astonishment. He plays with the laws of physics. He constructs a fantasy cave with stalactites and crystals: in order to deliver an authentically metaphysical experience. By strolling out of sunlight into a dark place, where reflected crystals glitter beneath water, the excursionist is agreeably stunned, disorientated. Amazed.

Jennifer Potter (in her 1998 book, *Secret Gardens*) commends Painshill Park for featuring her favourite grotto:

The first part is easy: a chink of natural light ahead makes the tunnel seem longer than it is. The wall to your left opens into a shimmering view of the bridge; an *oeil-de-boeuf* admits light from above, heightening the tension between earth and air, black slag below, crystals above. The gardener, meanwhile, has galloped round the outside to switch on the taps so that when you finally stumble into the main chamber, blinded by sunbeams, you see the water gushing down the walls and the lake opens up to view beyond spangly stalactites.

Pulling away from the too rapid succession of Hamilton's conceits, we zigzag through the plantation at the western extremity of the estate. Conifer avenues remind me of South Wales, the densely planted darkness of pit prop forests good for nothing except rally driving and hunting foxes with shotguns. Painshill has been invaded with pylons. One of them has the impertinence to place itself directly in front of the red brick Gothic tower.

From the woods, as we climb towards it, the four-storey stump is a Romantic allusion, a nod to Samuel Palmer's etching

The Lonely Tower. Palmer, by the time he completed this work
in 1879, was living in Furze Hill House, Reigate. His property
stood 400 feet above sea level. The Palmer scholar Raymond
Lister said that the South Downs and Kentish hills could be
seen in the distance and, 'on a clear day', Chanctonbury Ring.
Hamilton's tower, seven or so miles from Furze Hill House,
was well within range. Palmer had the habit of jotting lines of
verse on to labels which he pasted to the frames of his canvases.
Two years after *The Lonely Tower*, at a period when he blended
remembered elements of Shoreham (foreground) with Italian
hills (background), he quoted Milton's 'L'Allegro' as a form of
dedication for his watercolour *The Prospect*.

> *Straight mine eye hath caught new pleasures*
> *Whilst the landscape round it measures . . .*
> *Towers and battlements it sees*
> *Bosom'd high on tufted trees.*

The memory of stars and owls and lounging shepherds dissolves into a busy road. The A3, hurtling towards Junction 10
of the M25, is the graphic margin in our western view, a rude
invader. The democracy of speed, pod culture, ensures that
Hamilton's hillside prospect is ignored. Motorists are trained
to read signs, watch for hidden cameras, to ready themselves
for disaster: the jam, the shunt, the swerve into a service
station. They ignore landscape. It happens, but it is as featureless as television; no better, no worse. Narcoleptic resignation,
postponed pleasure.

By a fortunate chance, we're given access to the tower. It's
not the right day, but an official happens to be around and says
that, if we're quick, we can climb the circular stairs to the roof.
From the castellated summit we gaze out over three counties –
and, better yet, two motorways. The riptide where the roads
merge.

Looking down on the pylon, the path between close-packed

trees, we understand why Hamilton's paid hermit felt the need to escape. The hermitage, on the escarpment, was a rustic hut with a thatched roof. I was reminded of Jack Kerouac, fire-watching on Desolation Peak. Too much transcendence gluts the soul. Grand views, elevating prospects, shrivel the human spirit. Kerouac was reduced to writing haikus about winter flies in a medicine cabinet. Hamilton's salaried loner lasted a fortnight, his existence a spectacle, before he took off to town in search of ale.

The gate in the tree line, indicated on the map, was a chimera. Traffic on the A3 flashed between gaps in the forest screen. The road was a torrent to which we could find no access. From the battlements of the high tower, the motorway was a steel rule in an expanse of woodland, broken by a few small red patches of settlement. Shrubs and new plantings on the gradient of the roadside verge, the soft estate, struggled to disguise a sliproad. We were forced to trek back the way we had come, revisiting every highlight in Hamilton's portfolio.

Beyond the Ice House, blind children were being led down the long avenue by sighted companions. They worked in pairs. An educational game. Supervisors with clipboards lurked, benevolently attentive, checking the blindfolds. This condition of blindness was temporary, induced. There must be no cheating. Tiny guides, in sports clothes and baseball caps, grinned. Both hands cupped around the leading hand of their unsighted friend. They leant forward, tugging – as if they had a sheep on a lead. The blind ones stretched back, arms flung wide, to ward off obstacles. Progress was slow. Between them, explainer and unseeing audience, they came to understand the ambivalence of Painshill Park.

There's no help for it, we have to endure a section of road walking; Indian file, facing the oncoming traffic, pressing our body-prints into spiky hedges. A three-mile plod down the A245, through Cobham Tilt and Stoke D'Abernon (like routed

Diggers). Vernacular architecture, Surrey brick (headers, stretchers, English Rose, Contra Dutch) proselytised by Marc, are quietly extinguished as we advance on the motorway.

The M25 is an old friend, a vagrant travelling with a special visa, under instruction to keep moving, keep its eyes to itself. The earth-sculpting and planting of the soft estates around Leatherhead Common and Junction 9 is majestic; Tony Sangwine of the Highways Agency can be proud of this one. Leaning on a five-bar gate, among golden fields of corn, to view the low hills and darkening sky, we wouldn't know the motorway was there – if it wasn't for the gently humped bridge, the hum of traffic. The road is a painless intervention in a complacent landscape.

We're in a twilight mood. Emerging from the final clump of settlement, another deserted common planted with lines of dwarf trees, we recognise the sign – ELDERLY PEOPLE – as an appropriate message. There aren't any on the street. They must have taken the warning to heart and stayed indoors. If there *were* humans in this part of Surrey, they would certainly be elderly. The road is elderly. Its energies have diminished to the point where it can do nothing but trickle into the brash sweep of the M25, spin on to Chartwell, Tunbridge Wells and the coast, or risk an outing to the Bluewater shopping experience.

There's a three-mile stretch, pretty straight, between Great Bookham Common and the Leatherhead Junction; a chance to go for it, pedal to the floor. Tony Sangwine's modulated landscape planting doesn't register with these high-speed dolts. What do they care about interestingly crinkled trees chosen for their ability to peep over fences? They'll never see, as we do, the hidden spaces, the rampant ecology, weeds, wild flowers; hawthorn, dogwood, hedge-parsley, willowherb, tormentil.

A detour into Leatherhead is debated; briefly. Epsom is still the target, but there's a church I want to visit. Renchi is always up for a church, any church. He's soon bounding across roads, confronting citizens, women with bags of shopping. The

Catholic Church of Our Lady and St Peter? There is a reason
for my interest. The church has a series of panels carved by Eric
Gill, the fourteen Stations of the Cross. Gill features in a novel
I'm trying to write, as the paterfamilias of the small community
at Capel-y-ffin in the Ewyas Valley on the Welsh borders.

As we draw towards the end of the day's business, Marc's
mobile starts to trill; friends and potential commissioners activ-
ate his signature tune. 'I'm out on the M25, somewhere in
Surrey. Don't know when we'll finish.' Sounds implausible
but, this time, it's true.

A slightly disgruntled priest – Father Paddy – gives us a key.
He's pissed off with a sale sign outside the presbytery. There
should be enough elderly people to keep the church afloat,
even in Leatherhead – but, in a period of economic instability,
realisable assets have to be cashed in.

The church was built in 1923. Father Redway, 'remembered
principally as a man of holiness and poverty', secured the
patronage of Sir Edward Hulton, the Leatherhead-domiciled
newspaper magnate. Hulton agreed to guarantee the costs of
the church's construction. He also, having viewed the Stations
of the Cross at Westminster Cathedral, commissioned the Gill
panels.

Gill was responsible for more stations than British Rail. They
came off a production line: Westminster Cathedral, St Alban's
(Oxford), St Cuthbert's (Bradford), the Church of Our Lady
and St Peter (Leatherhead). The panels for Leatherhead were
cut in Gill's Ditchling studio and fixed in groups of two or
three. The last panel was finished in April 1925. Hulton died a
month later. The car, taking his body to London for burial,
paused at the church gates for a blessing.

None of us, tracking around the Stations of the Cross, is
inspired by them. Maybe that's the point: Gill didn't want the
church to be a gallery showcasing his genius. The panels were
there to do a job, provide illustration, mark out the route for
a series of devotional exercises. These low reliefs, produced in

the Twenties, long after Cubism, Vorticism, Suprematism, seem perverse in their customised antiquity. Innocence of vision is hard to fake. Primitivism, smoothed and stroked, looks coy. It's an art for believers – many of whom, astonished by the eccentricity of the stone carver, didn't want it. More accurately, it was an art for patrons. In paying for a work that demonstrated their taste, their selfless generosity, they bought a short-term immortality.

It worked. We had come here for Gill's panels: to see how an orbital journey could be mapped as an album of stone cartoons. The Passion of Christ as a graphic novel, a storyboard. Gill modelled (in the tenth panel at Westminster Cathedral) for the figure of Christ – by standing naked in front of a mirror. In the submissive curves of these low reliefs, the thrusts of staves and crosses, is a masochistic eroticism; in the gilded detail, a tinsel coarseness. The antiquarianism hasn't lasted. It doesn't offend, it's all of a piece with Paul Woodroffe's stained glass windows, his version of Holman Hunt's *Light of the World*.

The Gill project doesn't help Renchi to decide how he'll put together his own panels, a record of our journey which has to be both documentary and mythic. He sits in a pew, studying his Ordnance Survey map, plotting the best way out of here. As I click the camera, Marc (the Catholic boy) lifts his left forefinger in a parodic blessing, a mirror image of the Holman Hunt window.

Around Junction 9 the M25 is in spate. Heading north, over the motorway bridge, for our late-afternoon walk to Epsom, we pause to admire the eight lanes of moving traffic. There is no congestion, white vans and light-load heavy goods vehicles (returning to base) are snowflakes dissolving in a fast, grey stream. The central reservation is paved, without impact barriers or any form of planting; a few brave weeds push between the cracks. When the Highways Agency photograph a scene like this (for the brochure, *Towards a Balance with Nature*), they make sure that motor traffic is an out-of-focus blur; roadside flowers and grassy banks are pin sharp. Roads, the promoters suggest, are not about cars. Roads are landscape improvements, an architecture of 'managed' space. My snapshots, freezing the action, tell a different tale; a fast shutter pins each vehicle to the board. Safe distances are observed. Travellers, gunning for Gatwick, have no hold-ups to panic them, no jackknifed articulated lorries. The Leatherhead stretch, on this July evening, is leisured, a mini-autobahn, a military highway of the kind Margaret Thatcher fantasised when she cut the ribbon. The principal difference, so far as I can see, between the Thatcherite Vision of the Eighties and National Socialism in the Germany of the Thirties is that Thatcher couldn't make the trains run on time. The M25 never was an invasion route down which the master race could roll, just a three-hour fairground ride with dull views.

But here, at Junction 9, the M25 almost succeeds in living up to its statement of intent; Box Hill directly to the south, the genteel Clacket Lane Service Station (the best on the road) up ahead; swathes of unoptioned greenery, a literal green belt, downs and commons and broadleaf woods. At Dorking there is a gap in the ring of hills which protect always-timorous London. We discuss that gap, recall fantasies of future war. George T. Chesney's *The Battle of Dorking* (1871) is generally acknowledged to have launched the genre: landscape paranoia (with an undertow of viral sex horror, the Home Counties ravished by cruel Huns). The Germans (Russians, Kosovans, Martians) were coming to Surrey. 'The line of the great chalk-range was to be defended,' wrote Chesney – who looked, resolutely, back to the future. Let the suburbs spread and before you know it brutish Prussians will be advancing on Epsom, occupying Thames Ditton.

The streets reached down to Croydon and Wimbledon, which my father could remember quite country places; and people used to say that Kingston and Reigate would soon be joined to London. We thought we could go on building and multiplying for ever.

Sir George Tomkyns Chesney was a military man, a lieutenant colonel, founder of the Royal Indian Civil Engineering College at Staines. Suburban complacency brought the risk, so Chesney thought, of a weakening in moral fibre. We were unprepared for the coming hordes: tunnel-rushing aliens. Premature Euro-scepticism was a popular fictional brand. Iain Duncan Smith ghosted by H.G. Wells.

When I look at my country as it is now – its trade gone, its factories silent, its harbours empty, a prey to pauperism and decay – when I see all this, and think what Great Britain was in my youth, I ask myself whether I have really a heart or any sense of patriotism that I should have witnessed such degradation and still care to live!

Box Hill was England. The recollection of childhood, picnics, walks. Literature. John Keats, at the Burford Bridge Inn, finishing 'the last five hundred lines' of *Endymion*. George Meredith at Flint Cottage, a solitary walker, visited by Robert Louis Stevenson – and later by Leslie Stephen and his 'Sunday Tramps'. Meredith pronounced: 'I am neither German nor French, nor, unless the nation is attacked, English. I am European and Cosmopolitan – for humanity.'

But 'one of the most beautiful scenes in England' (as Chesney called it) was also one of the most vulnerable.

The shoulder of this ridge overlooking the gap is called Box Hill, from the shrubbery with which it was covered . . . The weak point was the gap; the ground at the junction of the railways and the roads immediately at the entrance of the gap formed a little valley, dotted, as I said, with buildings and gardens.

Geological trauma: the break in the 'great chalk-range which extends from beyond Aldershot in the east to the Medway'. We found in the course of our orbital circuit that the fear of invasion was still an active concern; horticulturalists were employed to screen numerous MOD properties. The M25 was London's perimeter fence. The outer suburbs were infested with bunkers, deep-shelters, airfields, tunnels, tank traps, concrete pillboxes, radar beacons, telecommunications dishes. The architecture of paranoia mushroomed around London. Private researchers, hearing about my walk, deluged me with local evidence: maps, photos, sketches, copies of letters. The main defensive rings – established in the 1890s – started about fifteen miles out from Charing Cross. I visited the once secret Royal Gunpowder Mills at Waltham Abbey and one of the government's nuclear bunkers (disguised as a farmhouse) at Kelvedon Hatch, Essex. How many more 'conversions' were there? How much more unmapped territory?

Junction 9 and its complimentary system of baffle-boards, pedestrian overpasses, had its own architectural style: pastoral/schizo. Our old green path was back (not quite wide enough for two men to pass without touching), but it ran between high fences. If Renchi stood on Marc's shoulders, he still wouldn't see over the top. On one side, the road (audible behind clean timber boards); on the other, impenetrable chain-link. Scrubby, sandy soil. No detours, no way out. Graffito with literary pretensions: YOUR SHAPE, MY EYES, THE FAN-TASTICAL, PHASES – MY HEART IS A TOOL, A DEVICE, A TOOL/A SAVIOUR.

Walking this narrow path is like patrolling forbidden ground: we don't know what we're guarding. We've lost all sense of direction. Sound is doctored. We trudge on towards a distant circle of light, the end of the green tunnel. Noise is managed. Noise is subject to 'reduction technology'. Tyres kiss sympathetic surfaces. Curtains of aspen swallow engine shrieks. Acoustic 'footsteps' are plotted by Highways Agency snoops;

spectral footfalls in country lanes; posthumous whispers down secret paths that shadow the motorway.

At Ashtead we cross the railway line. Two young lads (one Arsenal, one Spurs) are the only human figures in the landscape. They're tugging a bright red trolley which contains a yellow plastic sack. Newspapers. GUARDIAN. Are all the inhabitants of Ashtead liberal-leftists? And why do they get their papers at night? The news a day ahead of itself.

Renchi has information, somewhere at the bottom of his rucksack, on the well at Epsom. We can't go home until we've found it. The railway bridge, unlike the user-friendly span over the M25, is from another era; it bristles with spikes – if you're determined to throw yourself off, you are going to be punctured on the way.

Ashtead Common ('Camp: Remains Of') has an excess of paths, decisions to be made. We tack, north/south, east/west, until our enthusiasm flags. It's been a long day. Marc and I would be happy to hold the well over for the start of the next walk. But Renchi is hot on wells (friend of Glastonbury). Magnesium sulphate constipation remedies (taken in pints from a stone beaker) I can leave alone. I did ten years in Cheltenham. I have something of an allergy to spa towns (twinned, as in Cheltenham's case, with post-colonial residues and Secret State listening posts, high frequency huts).

Even here, deep in the woods, Renchi locates someone to interrogate, a ranger in a green jeep. We're realigned. We head off towards the snail-shell spiral of 'The Wells', sited on what's left of Epsom Common. On the map, this is a maze: take the wrong road and you'll circle aimlessly for hours. The area has ambitions to be suburban-sprawl. 'The Crescent', boasts a streetsign. 'The Greenway'.

The well on the Common was Epsom's original, the beginning of England's fashion for spas. Salts and sediments were plentiful (hence the brand name, the universal white tin,

Epsom Salts) – but the water supply was mean. At the height of Epsom's popularity (end of the sixteenth century, beginning of the seventeenth), rumours of sharp practice abounded: the well drunk dry by mid-morning was surreptitiously topped up with buckets from elsewhere.

Everybody sampled the waters, once; Pepys, Defoe, John Aubrey. Thomas Shadwell had a hit with his theatrical romp, *Epsom Wells*. The combination of bodily purging with amorous adventure, gaming houses, gluttony, was perfectly suited to the English love of 'Carry On' humour. Farts, gropes, excursions.

Many of the earliest visitors walked from London. Successful men set themselves up with country estates. John Aubrey, who wrote the first known history of Surrey in the 1670s (published 1718), carried out experiments to analyse Epsom Water. His property, Woodcote Park, was visited by Pepys in 1667. Voluntary rustification was all very well, Pepys thought, but a day trip was as much country living as he could tolerate. His diary account of an excursion to Epsom is still a model for M25 Man: arrive early, try the waters, gossip about Lord Buckhurst and Nell Gwynn, pub lunch, siesta, buy souvenir bottles, back to the pub for dinner, home. Better to invest in a coach than a burdensome house, miles from the City. Provincial novelty is all very well, but the journey is the best of it.

In 1662 a Dutch artist, William Schellinks, walked from Kingston to Epsom Common with the son of a shipping magnate he was shepherding around England. The drawing of the Old Wells that Schellinks made on 5 June reveals the true nature of the scam: a turf-roofed hut of the kind you usually encounter at the edge of Indian territory in an Anthony Mann western, a blasted heath. Coin paid, visitors were encouraged to swallow ten or fifteen pints of murky water; after which, segregated by sex, they trotted up and down until their bowels loosened. The canny employed youths to reserve a bush, warn off intruders. The tumbleweed of the Common shook with bad wind, episodes of projectile vomiting.

None of this dubious history deters Renchi. It's obvious from the Ordnance Survey map of 1866 that the well, on Oldwells Farm, is at the heart of a cosmic maze, a slice of brain coral. Well Way, if we hit it, will carry us directly to the sacred spot. And so, plodding through what seems like a translation of the less exciting areas of Hampstead Garden Suburb, it proves.

The 'new' Old Well, designed by pupils from Epsom High School, dedicated in June 1989, has a touch of the fishing leprechaun about it. Brick steps leading to a circular well – which is topped with a glass light-globe supported by four metal pillars. A grille prevents you getting at the doubtful water. Lepers and tremblers, the spleen-sick, need no longer apply. The Old Well is lost heritage. Aubrey boiled gallons of the stuff to provide himself with a tobacco-box of grey sediment that nobody wanted. We twist through painful contortions, floor to wall, trying to contrive a reasonable visual record of this place. Then we leg it for the station.

Salt to Source

Epsom to Westerham.
Through the Valley of Vision,
to Dartford & the River

1

Just beyond the Common, to the north, the map revealed a phalanx of hospitals aimed at London. The narrator of *The War of the Worlds* speaks of making 'a big detour by Epsom to reach Leatherhead' (where his wife had taken shelter from the Martian invasion). The plan was: Newhaven and out, reverse asylum seekers. But Wells's narrative carries the traumatised Surrey suburbanite back along the route Renchi and I adopted, on a late walk (from the Siebel Building and Brooklands) in the direction of Weybridge and Shepperton. At the ferry (still operative), close to where the Wey flows into the Thames, the Martians crossed into Middlesex, devastating the riverbank with their heat-ray tripods (future estate agents' cameras).

The Epsom hospital colony, serrated semi-circular outlines masked by complacent greenery, looks like a set of schematic plans for interplanetary robots. Transformer toys. Something very black and sharp lies in wait along Horton Lane – with brain-burning lasers and hot wires, knives, masks, drugs, instruments of restraint. To deal with London's damaged citizens. The hospitals become a second ghetto, wards from Whitechapel, excited aliens punished for their difference. Tidied away by misplaced benevolence.

The dissolve from spa town to prison colony was realised by the construction of the hospitals at the beginning of the twentieth century. And now, in the late summer of 1999, conversion is in full swing; the Epsom legend is being rapidly revised. Where once patients were encouraged, as therapy, to summon up and confront painful images from their past, memory is wilfully erased. Or doctored. New names, new roads and roundabouts. Smarter uniforms for the warders (aka security).

Filmmaker John Sergeant, researching a project on the M25, interviewed Dr Sidney Crown, a consultant psychotherapist – who explained how the apparent endlessness of the orbital motorway induced rage and states of trance. The road is a midden of competing archetypes. Driving is a meditational device, summoning future memories: driving is prophecy.

Dr Crown, provoked, remembered Epsom. As a very young doctor, he walked where we were walking, from the station (by paths and green ways, metal signposts) to Long Grove Road. His suitcase a dead weight. Long Grove, Horton and The Manor were dumps, Victorian asylums near the bottom of an overburdened system. The medical staff weren't ambitious or enlightened. They lived like colonial administrators; priding themselves, as Crown recalled, on the quality of their cellar, the excellence of the kitchen. The natives might be restless, there was little hope of a better posting, but the evening meal was an event: crisp linen, sparkling glass, heavy silverware, four or five courses, decent wines, brandy and cigars. The asylums were country houses in an era of revolution. Old-timers in the town deplore the wanton destruction of trees, removed to make way for the new estate roads. Horton and Long Grove, at their peak, between the wars, were a focus for Epsom society: tea dances, tennis parties.

Themes that flickered like St Elmo's fire along the northern stretch of the M25, between Waltham Abbey and Abbots Langley, found resolution here. Epsom was the pivot in our story. I felt that this was the halfway point in the walk; after Epsom, we would be heading for home. I had worked on a book with a young Jewish woman, Rachel Lichtenstein; an artist and archivist. Rachel solved one of the great mysteries of Whitechapel: the disappearance of David Rodinsky. Rodinsky lived above a decommissioned synagogue in Princelet Street. One day, in the Sixties, he vanished. The room was sealed like a shrine. When it was broken into, years later, the scattered debris of a life – books, clothes, diaries, food, records, maps –

were exposed to investigation, public gaze, incontinent theoris-
ing. The man was absorbed by the set which had contained
him. Films and vulgar speculation followed. Rachel was the
first person to treat Rodinsky as a human being, a man with a
biography and a finite lifespan.

Rachel found Rodinsky's death certificate:

> Name and Surname: David Rodinsky, no.391, DX 421235.
> When and Where: 4th of March 1969. The Grove, Horton
>   Lane, Epsom.
> Sex: male. Age: 44 yrs. Occupation: none.
> Address: 19 Princelet Street, E1.
> Cause of death: broncho-pneumonia, II epilepsy with paranoid
>   features.

She drove to Epsom. 'Epilepsy' was the convenient clinical
formulation arrived at to explain (or justify) nineteenth-century
fugue walkers, long-distance amnesiacs. It meant: restlessness,
mysterious expeditions such as those Rodinsky plotted on his
London A–Z.

Rachel, a good detective, hot on the trail, fluctuated between
rage and fugue. Anger and inspiration. Arriving in Epsom, she
met with indifference, hints at conspiracy, perimeter fences and
guard dogs. The Grove was off-limits. Long Grove Road, in all
its sinister beauty, concrete-slab walls, curtains of evergreens,
rebuffed her.

In a pub, keeping to the generic rules of crime fiction, she
fell into conversation with a 'large balding man, dressed in grey
overalls'. They were the only customers in the place. He was
a driver; for years he had delivered medical equipment to the
hospitals in Horton Lane. 'He moved closer and told me in
whispers that the Long Grove had mysteriously burned down,
along with its records, five years previously . . . He lowered his
eyebrows and told of strange goings-on, unexplained fires,
weird disappearances.' When Rachel produced her notebook,

the man backed off, retreated to the fruit machine. 'More than my job's worth,' he muttered.

Our early-morning ramble down Horton Lane confirms the atmosphere of elective paranoia that infects much of orbital fringe London. Something is happening but nobody will take responsibility for it: any formal announcement will let the cat out of the bag. Boredom has been synthesised into threat. PRIVATE PROPERTY/TRESPASSERS WILL BE PROSECUTED/ TEL. SURREY HEALTH AUTHORITIES ON 0126 445 876 FOR FURTHER INFORMATION.

Being Rachel, she pushes it; face against fence – until the dog, the slavering German shepherd, leaps at her. Being Rachel, she makes the call to the Surrey Health Authorities. 'A curt secretary answered: all records had been destroyed in the fire, she could not help.'

Without Lichtenstein's possessed pursuit, the story of Rodinsky's death would blacken in a convenient bonfire. The medical records of his sister and many of the other displaced and disturbed patients from East London, kept at Claybury (now Repton Park), were burnt in a builders' skip. Heritaged history is the new TV pornography, the ratings winner. Henry VIII's wives, Elizabeth II's suitors. The Normans, the Romans, the Vikings. Ghetto history is unrequired: we want to know about the planting of the estate, the notable figures who lived in the great house. Developers peddle an anodyne future of managed ecology, fitness regimes, security. The Long Grove ward where Rodinsky died was described to Rachel as a babble of arguing Hasids, displaced cabbalists, a city hive. Even now, when the walls are coming down, the noise won't go away.

I met Renchi at Epsom station on 5 August 1999. He was wearing a T-shirt of many colours, many signs and symbols: GIVE PEACE A CHANCE. Not the best disguise for infiltrating what remained of the hospital colony.

Out of the station, past the newsagent (*Epsom & Ewell Herald*:

POLICE DENY SOFT TOUCH WITH TRAVELLERS), we find
the route. Our footsteps in other footsteps; the pavements are
conveyor belts carrying out-of-towners away from the centre
towards the hospitals. Another green way, screened from the
business of the town. A prophylactic tunnel to the isolation
zone: carports instead of front lawns, monkey-puzzles, cedars,
yellow lines to deter opportunist parkers. The roads are
deserted. The florist is boarded over with chipboard panels.
The signpost – HORTON AND LONG GROVE HOSPITALS – is
rusted. Some of the lettering has been chipped away, in an
attempt to remove HORTON. Horton is rumoured to be the
only active building in the whole development area. Active and
therefore secret. Geography has been twisted by a Lewis
Carroll logic: if somewhere is featured on a sign, it no longer
exists. If it isn't, it does.

In captured fields, close to the hospitals, the housing is institutional vernacular: grace and favour cottages, warders (for
the use of). Clean, well-presented, lace curtained – with weed-
less, lifeless gardens, grey-brown lawns like bad wigs. Only the
military (or civilians under the rule of the Official Secrets Act)
would tolerate the particular shade of tomato-rust favoured on
this estate: two-tone, semi-detached boxes, ketchup-brown
below and porcine pink above, with a hint of pebbledash.

Long Grove Road, the hospital approach, is thickly screened
with mature chestnut and beech trees; a dull grey fence, assembled from concrete planks, is little more than six feet high.
Graffiti are dispirited, painted over. Distance stretches, the walls
are unforgiving, as you struggle towards the first checkpoint.
Hopping up and down, I manage to see into the grounds.
We're at an angle to the semi-circular design, bulk and depth
remain hidden. I'm struck by the tower on which is displayed
what appears to be a non-flashing, neon Star of David.

Renchi, red bandanna, PEACE/LOVE–ONE WORLD–STOP
ALL DE FUSSIN' T-shirt, bright blue rucksack, leans on the
barrier, trying to bond with the security operative in the red

brick gatehouse. CCTV cameras swivel, monitors freak. The loonies are at the gates, begging for admittance.

DANGER, THIS IS A MULTI-HAZARD AREA. NO UN-AUTHORISED ADMITTANCE. ALL VISITORS MUST REPORT TO RECEPTION. ALL VISITORS OR NON PASS HOLDERS PLEASE REPORT TO THE GATE-HOUSE.

Black-spike gates, voice-operated security barriers. Otherwise the site looks abandoned. The gatekeeper, brazenly cross-eyed, is straight out of *Macbeth*. Except that he's stone cold sober and won't give up any information. We move on before he can make the call. Paranoia has erected its own exclusion zone, an invisible shock-stun fence. Knowing nothing, passing innocently down the road, you'd be immediately alerted to: fried air. Rubber tyres on a bonfire of petrol-soaked rags.

By chance, we have a notion of the real story: a friend of Renchi's works here, counselling sex offenders. The other asylums – Long Grove, The Manor – have gone, given over to developers. Horton still contains, among its derelict blocks, a hard core of deviants, many of them clergymen. (The Church of England is one of the sponsors of the operation.) Development plans demand that, very soon, the unit will be closed down and relocated to somewhere remote, Scotland is suggested. This hasn't worked for asylum seekers, who would rather live anywhere than Glasgow; but a rump of tabloid sex monsters, paedophiles, rapists, might, it is thought, be a negative factor when promoting 'Quality New Homes' for Epsom.

And so it proved. In the Bad News avalanche that followed 11 September, the possible relocation of Horton Hospital was leaked. Sex criminals, who had never, visibly, been there, were now presented as a threat. Several had 'escaped'. For the continued safety and wellbeing of the citizens of Epsom, the lowlife would be removed to Knaphill in Surrey. No mention was made, in all this, of the housing development. No mention either of Knaphill's proximity to Woking and the Martian invaders. Official spokespersons alluded to 'a cage', a secure pen. The Surrey suburbanites were having none of it. Some wilderness would have to be found, ex-MOD. An island, a rock. Nobody, as yet, floated the Millennium Dome option, the unwanted tent on Greenwich peninsula.

Discretion and paranoia are bed-fellows. Hence the high level of security, the CCTV cameras. Pass holders only. A gulag that was once suitably remote and pastoral is now prime, off-highway development land. Decant the inner cities. Wipe memory. The familiar mantra. Say nothing. New Labour have become masters at having 'nobody available' for interview. They form committees, convene discussion groups, put out brochures of non-stick language. 'Management strategy based upon full consultation . . . partnership . . . service quality . . . best value'.

The Epsom hospitals, close to healing springs, were a prevision of town planner Ebenezer Howard's garden cities: quiet suburbs, independent of the metropolis, where ghetto hurt could be soothed. We are told (in such books as *Cities for a Small Country* by Richard Rogers and Anne Power) that four million extra houses will be required in the next twenty-five years, sixty per cent of them on brownfield sites.

The large red sign – PEDESTRIANS – isn't a quiet blessing (like a cycle lane); it announces the segregation of an antiquated life form. A reluctantly ceded track across the minefield of development. Goodman Price Demolition Ltd have taken over the hospital where Rodinsky died. The gate-lodge with its sharply pointed gables is out of our reach, behind silver gates. Red brick buildings and fine old trees, like a minor public school, are visible beyond the temporary board-fence.

LAND SELECTED FOR QUALITY HOMES. BRYANT HOMES. TAYWOOD HOMES. ALFRED MCALPINE HOMES (RECOGNISED FOR QUALITY).

Trenches. Heavy mud. Red cones. 'Moon boots,' says Renchi, as we approach Long Grove Hospital. We're dragging lead-soled footwear, claggy with yellow sludge.

'It's all going, nice job,' an affable Welsh labourer in a blue hard-hat tells us. Should be in work for months, before moving on to the next toy town makeover. The new estates (Laing, Barratt, Fairview, Bryant) are like TV meddling on a huge scale: the gang of cheery bodgers who steam in with decking and water features (builder's bum) to destroy a perfectly decent suburban garden. Development is an extension of the game show. Beat the clock. A golden key to the lucky winner.

Our man leans on his pick. The ditch runs for a mile or so, in a straight line, and he is the only visible worker. Yellow waistcoat (ALDERSBROOK CONST. LTD.) and battle honour tattoos. He tips us off about a hidden path into Long Grove, a link to the Country Park.

Within minutes we are in Deep England, a track meandering through old woodland, yellow-brown fields with Pony Club jumps and the occasional, solitary horse. 'Great Wood,' says the map. Great Wood it is. With an Italianate tower in every clearing. Hospital farms, rundown outbuildings.

Exploring these, we meet a young warden from the Country Park: David Seaman ponytail and Beckham (September 2001) beard. He's sorting out the merchandise for the coming season; mugs with tree prints, booklets that tell you where you are. Car parks are being developed among the burning chimneys and boiler houses of the old hospital.

He's interested in our quest and gives us a copy of *Asylum, Hospital, Haven (A History of Horton Hospital)* by Ruth Valentine. We sit at the roadside and skim this booty. Local histories, conceived, written and frequently published close to the area they describe, are labours of love: genuine enthusiasm, human sympathy, transmits itself to the outsider, the tourist passing through. Valentine, while doing a proper job in documenting Horton, finds room for anecdote, eccentric evidence, case history, abbreviated memoir. Nurses and patients are not excluded. The illustrations, formal and unpeopled or group-posed, are windows on lost time. Focus holds for an instant.

The images are dignified, a contract between model and photographer. Nurses, starched till they creak, sit on the grass in a semicircle (an unconscious reference to the standard asylum design). Patients, strapped into the science-fiction devices of the electro-therapy unit, stare out with resigned acceptance.

Valentine's narrative is a spirited apologia for the failure of benevolence, good intentions undone by institutional inertia, hierarchic regimens. Horton and the other hospitals of the Epsom gulag began as country estates and were downgraded into prisons for urban inadequates: cedars and oaks, woodland walks, Edwardian lawns that were supposed to heal and mend, were glimpsed in segments through barred windows.

The London County Council acquired the estate in 1896. The name of the vendor, on the original document, was Sir Thomas Fowell Buxton. Buxton, from a family of Whitechapel brewers and philanthropists, was an ancestor (on his mother's side) of the cultural historian Patrick Wright. In *A Journey Through Ruins* (1991), Wright honours an earlier Thomas Fowell Buxton, abolitionist, opponent of capital punishment. 'Buxton the Liberator' was the nephew of Samuel Hanbury, who had him appointed a director of the Brick Lane brewery. On 26 November 1816, Buxton made a speech at the Mansion House in which he drew the attention of the wealthy to the plight of the 'naked and hungry' of Spitalfields. His namesake, at the end of the century, cashed in land, moved to Australia: so that the wretched of the inner cities could receive a custodial sentence to sample estate life. There were no voluntary patients, no patients from the middle classes. These were members of the urban underclass brought before a magistrate and certified. The population of asylums rose as the century withered. The plan was to build twelve hospitals for twelve thousand inmates: a town with exactly the population of Epsom.

Horton Asylum opened in 1902. Only five of the proposed twelve hospitals were actually built. The architect who always seemed to pick up these gigs (after suspicious mutterings from less successful rivals) was George Thomas Hine. Hine had a standard design: he used it at Claybury. School, prison, barracks: European detail on a Soviet scale. Local, sour mustard, London-stock brick. And lots of it. A gigantic semicircular corridor – like half a cyclotron, a particle-accelerator chamber. A geometry that allowed those early forms of twentieth-century spiritual malaise – melancholia, dementia, mania – to spread like a contagion. Morphic resonance. Patients grew into the disease descriptions that were offered to them; they defined themselves in poses captured by photographers looking for genealogies of defect.

The ghosts of Victorian fiction, working-class women in white, were put away for offering visible proof of their sexuality, conceiving a child out of wedlock. Middle-class women could also be banished for trivial acts of 'rebellion'. Valentine recalls the case of Anna Wickham, sent by her husband to a private asylum in Epping (shades of John Clare) for having the audacity to attempt the publication of a volume of poetry. Females dominated the asylum population as black males were to do in the post-war years. Horton was a reservation, remote (a long and expensive journey from Central London), well-intentioned. 'Kindness, fresh air, country views, sweet reason,' wrote Valentine. These aspirations, it's true, were available: on the other side of the glass. Beyond the iron bars.

Walks were not walks. The citizens of the spa town – busy market, pubs waiting to welcome race crowds – didn't approve. There were petitions. Lord Rosebery, owner of the Derby winners of 1894, 1895, 1905, and (in his spare time) Prime Minister, attended a protest meeting, called in 1908, to oppose the building of further asylums. 'I represent a constituency of the sane,' Rosebery proclaimed.

The local press – our friends on the *Epsom and Ewell Herald* – agreed with his lordship: 'LUNATICS AT LARGE'. Gangs of the insane roamed their streets, frightening the horses. Wealthy Londoners who kept 'Derby houses' took their stables to

Newmarket – where the racing programme was expanding while Epsom's was curtailed. A naked madman escaped from one of the walking parties and terrified respectable ladies.

Processions from the hospital, shuttling from estate to town centre, hand-in-hand like something out of Breughel, were embargoed. Inmates were denied walking therapy; they were kept to 'airing courts', grim circuits of an enclosed yard. The system was more convenient, it could be fitted to a military time-table. These circuits became the treadmills that drive the Blakean geometry of London; spiral visions that find their deranged resolution in Margaret Thatcher's orbital motorway.

Fantasies of escape were uncommon. Most of the patients seemed resigned to their rural limbo, the food was better than at home. They worked, if they were able, and were paid in coin. But there were occasional attempts to breach security. A woman called Lydia Johnson had been committed for no good reason, so her sisters said, by a spiteful husband. The sisters smuggled in a dress. Lydia changed out of her asylum uniform and set off down the long avenue. Walkers were suspect. She was caught. Her sisters were banned from making future visits. One sister, Louisa, applied to have Lydia discharged into her care. The application was refused. Dr Lord told the sub-committee that Louisa must herself be insane to make such a request.

A later sibling escape plot was more successful. It wasn't just the remnants of Jewish immigration who were being tidied away in the Sixties. Other anachronistic elements of the East End were incarcerated in Long Grove: exile as punishment. Ronnie Kray, a paranoid schizophrenic gangster, a fury from the ghetto, was certified insane. Which was about as useful a procedure as sticking a 'Police Aware' notice on the burnt-out shell of a stolen vehicle on Rainham Marshes. Ronnie wasn't insane, he was insanity: a psychotic elemental, a whirlwind of malignancy. A crazy comedian with a cutlass and a court of celebrity sycophants.

Early in his career, Ronnie was banged up in Long Grove. In the psychiatric wing of Winchester Prison, he had received news from his twin of the death of their favourite aunt, Rose. They had to put him in a strait-jacket and bus him to Epsom. All the material London didn't want – aliens, slum bandits, ranters, poets – was dispersed in a southerly direction. To the colony, the walled estate.

'All the discretion and forsythia in the world will never alter the outline of the old lunatic asylums built to an identical pattern round London at the turn of the century,' wrote John Pearson (in the least-contaminated biography of the Kray Twins, *The Profession of Violence*). 'Ronnie was driven here from Winchester Prison on 20 February 1958. He was never to forget the terror of those first days.'

Kray made a radiator his best friend and thought the man in the opposite bed was a dog. 'If I got his name right he'd come and jump in my lap.' Medical reports disclosed signs of 'verbigeration and marked thought blocking'. (Verbigeration is the constant and obsessive repetition of meaningless words or phrases.) It took an old school journalist as thorough as Pearson, and a self-recorder as voracious as Ronnie Kray, to rescue medical records from the Long Grove fire. David Rodinsky was unrecorded, without papers or documents – until Rachel Lichtenstein moved away from the cluttered Princelet Street garret, that museum of false trails. No photograph of Rodinsky has ever been published. The Krays, by contrast, had every scrap of memorabilia logged and filed. Fat albums of gangland nostalgia are offered for sale. The distribution of Kray-approved relics (sanctioned by Reg from his cell in Maidstone) is one of Bethnal Green's most successful industries.

The Long Grove medics dosed Ronnie on Stematol and assigned him to Napier Ward. Sunday visiting, as Pearson pictures it, with the tribes arriving from the East End, was like Derby Day. Wards loud with argument, contraband food, kisses and rucks. Two cars, gas-guzzlers, made the trip from

Vallance Road: an electric-blue Lincoln and a black Ford. Squeezed inside were men in square-shouldered suits, black shoes gleaming like their creosote hair.

Ronnie put on his twin's camelhair coat and strolled out, like a bookie coming back from Brighton. Reg stayed in the ward. When the nurse sounded the alarm bell, it was too late. Ronnie was on his way to London. The motorised Krays succeeded where the pedestrian Johnson sisters, with their long walk to the station, failed. Ronnie had the wrong kind of craziness for Epsom.

The pharmaceutical industry is fond of the urban fringes, nice clean estates, discreet grants, none too scrupulously supervised research. The green belt propagates science fiction: from Wells's robotic invaders to the chemical controls of Aldous Huxley. When J.G. Ballard, at the start of his career, depicted drowned worlds and Devonian jungles erupting around Shepperton, he was reactivating deep-images derived from Richard Jefferies and H.G. Wells. The red Martian weed which proliferates in the Thames Valley (from *The War of the Worlds*) prefigures anxieties about genetically modified crops – and George Monbiot marching on St George's Hill.

Long Grove, Horton, The Manor, St Ebba's, West Park – linked reefs in a green sea – became, with the tacit blessing of the supervisory authorities, a testing ground for experimental procedures: *The Island of Dr Moreau*. Much was cruel, much fantastic. A captive populace inducted into a science fiction narrative. Within George Hine's crab-shaped buildings, long wards looking out on the pastoral scene, drugs known as 'liquid coshes' were developed. Before the early Fifties, only one chemical form of sedation was available: paraldehyde – which, Ruth Valentine says, 'was addictive, smelt terrible' and 'rotted your teeth'.

Chlorpromazine (Largactil) followed, introducing the range of pharmaceutical mind-benders that feature in all the ghosted memoirs by East End hardmen. At first they were dished out like Smarties at a children's party, side-effects were never considered. A tame, blank-eyed population made the smooth running of the asylum colony possible.

Electrical torture, invasive surgical procedures, brain-clamps were props in a grand guignol theatre. Insulin comas, ECT (widely used, in the late Forties, without anaesthesia), modified narcosis (week-long sleep cures), pre-frontal leucotomies: no fantasy was too extreme. The logic for these experiments was itself insane. If epilepsy and schizophrenia were incompatible, then induce epilepsy. Nightmares of the city, of immigration, poverty, families crammed into one room – image and acoustic overload – were treated with fire and blade, earthed in Epsom's tranquil parkland. David Rodinsky, removed from his books and papers, his solitude, living in a ward of strangers. Ronnie Kray befriending a radiator.

The most Wellsian of all the curious fictions imposed on the kidnapped Londoners was the Mosquito Chamber.

The unsuspecting patient is led into a room with double-doors and sealed windows. The walls are smooth. There is no fissure or crack in which a fly can conceal itself. The patient waits. And waits. The milky window a frozen panel. There is a humming in the ears, imagined tinnitus. The patient scratches at the irritation. But it is not imagined. The clean, feature-less room is loud with things that can barely be seen: swamp mosquitoes. They are released, one by one, from a specially constructed box. The patient suffers repeated bites. He remains in the room until the observers are happy his blood has been infected. He is returned to his ward – and, in due course, develops malaria fever: sweats, shivers, high temperature. Parasitic protozoa multiply, destroying his red blood cells.

The researchers are satisfied. The theory has been tested, if not proved: malarial fever, when it has passed, helps sufferers from 'general paralysis' to recover their sanity. GPI (General Paralysis of the Insane) is the result of syphilis reaching the brain. Malaria is supposed to kill the spirochaetes: in the way that decapitation could be said to cure the common cold. Malarial therapy was developed in Germany. In England, experiments were conducted at Claybury and at Horton – where the fourteen-bed isolation hospital provided the perfect research facility. The laboratory at Horton became the leading mosquito-breeding centre in the British Isles. Seventy per cent of those treated at Horton survived. Three out of every ten died.

The closure of the hospitals around the motorway fringe, which we witnessed in the course of our walk, and assumed to be a New Labour initiative, was revealed on further investigation to be another borrowed Tory policy. The story went back much further than the Mad Ribbon-cutter of Potters Bar, it reached the *fons et origo* of Maggietone philosophy: Enoch Powell. Powell, the unbending moralist who would dive into any sewer to keep a handle on power, was the motorway Mekon.

In 1961, the National Association for Mental Health invited the Conservative Minister of Health to address their Annual General Meeting. Enoch Powell, Latinist poet, was always happy to put his trenchant views to a captive audience. He announced: 'the elimination of by far the greater part of this country's mental hospitals'. No more money must be wasted on 'upgrading and reconditioning'. The insane must pull themselves together, get on their bikes or face eugenic engineering; castration or expulsion.

The move towards Barratt estates had been in place for more than forty years. Laingian anti-psychiatry (the heritage of Foucault) had some sympathy for Powell's policy. Victorian asylums had ceased to be asylums, they were mind-prisons, politically repressive, socially divisive. Smaller units, urban communes, retreats, were more useful than George Hine's minatory colonies: the architecture of fear and control. Not for the first time, extremes of left and right found common ground.

Tories enact grand gestures that always result in land sales, asset stripping, collapse of public services. New Labour loves phantom government, virtual policies, obfuscation. Talk of 'care in the community', as Ruth Valentine recalls, was denounced by the House of Commons Social Services Committee in 1985 as 'virtually meaningless'. That was the Thatcher method: the shameless lie, endlessly repeated, with furious intensity – as if passion meant truth. Blair lets it float, drift, until it's all too late; the shrug, the missionary smile, the shafting of another convenient scapegoat. The 310 patients, living in Horton in 1993, were dispersed, struck from the record. Some stayed in the grounds, tolerated in a half-life, while they waited for the developers to finish the job. As ever, the minister responsible would be elsewhere; enjoying a recuperative break in the Maldives or smoothing a crisis in Kashmir.

The hours circling Long Grove and Horton had not been wasted, we could walk away. Back down the green lanes towards the station, in quest of a late breakfast.

We found: a cheapjack clothes store, everything racked, everything one price. I bought a grey polo-shirt for £1 and put it on. Breakfast in the centre of Epsom might require 'smart casual' dress. It was that sort of town: clock tower, pubs with history, chainstore catalepsy (Boots, Burtons, Dickins & Jones, Dixons, Dolcis, Dollond & Aitchison, H. Samuel, Laura Ashley, Marks & Spencer, Next, Paperchase, Mothercare, Top Shop, Waitrose, WH Smith, Oddbins, Victoria Wines, Monsoon, Radio Rentals, Thomas Cook, Vision Express). Multi-storey car parks and a ripe undertow of horseshit among the carnations. Serious money has colonised the higher ground, the foothills of Epsom Downs; small dank pubs, near the railway, cater to traditionalists with fond memories of riot, debauched soldiery, racetrack shysters and quick-fisted travellers.

A memory technician, with a window display of cigarette cards (British regiments, cricketers) and collectible issues of *Picture Post* (Ingrid Bergman and Roberto Rossellini), peddles sentiment; the heritage Epsom of sepia postcards, railway histories. We browse. The cluttered shop is like an annex of the asylum colony. Vintage magazines are so crisp they might have been published that morning. Punters discuss the hospital railway as if it were still running. And running over the unwary. Rough sleeper Mary Tobin was killed at the Hook Road level crossing. The Long Grove Light Railway, sections of track still visible in the ground, carried building materials for contractors.

The owner of the ephemera shop recommended a café: 'Carry on past Sainsbury's, end of the High Street, Café First.' We soon faced a choice of more than twenty blends of coffee, every combination of egg and sausage, bacon, tomato; fresh orange juice in an iced glass. I go for the Ethiopian coffee: 'with cheese undertone and flavour of chocolate'. The long, narrow design of the place, the tight Formica units, gives no hint of the quality of the cuisine, the cheerful service. This has to be the best on the road (as I say every time). West Coast America for European-sized diners: germ-free, bright-coloured, a little too eager to explain itself. There is only so much I want to read about a cup of coffee.

Our tell-tale maps and bulging rucksacks involve us in conversation with a retired local couple who are happy to find fellow hikers taking refreshment. As motorists talk road numbers, convinced pedestrians talk gradients. We face a steep pull up on to the chalk. This pair, stately-round and so well-matched as to be virtually cloned, have wrecked knees and ruined feet (flattered by comfortable trainers); they have caps and tinted spectacles. Debating various routes that would carry us towards Epsom Downs, Walton on the Hill and the M25, they follow us out on to the street. The wife favours a scenic route, while the husband appreciates our whim to check on such matters as the underground tunnels, near Chalk Lane.

They wave us off, watching as we recede. When I've finished snapping the Albion, a black and white, Tudorbethan pub, they are still there, alongside the café, philosophising over the advice they've handed out. The man, prompted, scuttles after us, with several revisions. The woman, who has taken her cap off, looks very much like a younger Iris Murdoch. Self-barbered fringe. Snub nose, bright eyes. A clever child disguised as an old lady. The man, hair tufting in all directions from beneath a flat cap, might be John Bayley. They aren't, they couldn't be; but the generosity of their engagement with two strangers, their mutual affection, makes them paradigms of English eccentricity. Kindly ghosts deputed to hang about cafés, setting travellers on the right road.

2

An excursionist mood grips us, time out; after the dark residues of the asylum colony, we turned our faces to the south, to Epsom Downs. The town has become an inconvenient traffic island, a sequence of roundabouts with shopping centre and public toilets attached. It's not meant to be helpful to walkers – who came from elsewhere with bad news and germs; if you want exercise, the guide book offers the Gym in the Park and the Epsom Polo Club. Car parks (mostly short term) are everywhere. The route for the 'M25 & Epsom Hospital' is trumped by a large red and white box: TO THE HAYWAIN TRAVEL INN & CHALK LANE HOTEL.

Advice to motorists wanting the racecourse is: 'Follow the one-way system.' Advice to pedestrians: forget it. EPSOM TOWN CENTRE IS MONITORED 24 HOURS BY CCTV.

We hopped metal barriers, dodged traffic. We hit the suburbs of the suburbs. Overemphatic lakes of carnations and pinks – buttonholes for racegoers? – gave way to shady avenues where insurance brokers and IT operatives showed off their good taste in Grade II listed mansions.

'The Borough Council will seek to conserve and enhance the built heritage of the Borough; the design of new development is to make a positive contribution.'

Chalk Lane, which runs in parallel with the recommended traffic route, Ashley Road, reeks of wealth and privilege. Horse money. Stables. Easy access to the Downs. The Welsh actor/producer Stanley Baker had a house in this area: remember the racetrack heist from the film he made with Joseph Losey, *The Criminal*? Baker liked to associate with underworld faces; they enjoyed his hospitality, having him in the photographs – Soho

Rangers FC (with Eddie Richardson and train-robber Tommy Wisbey), a frost of nightclub tables. It was rumoured for years, on not much evidence (beyond the celebrity snapshots), the film roles he chose to play, that Baker funded the Great Train Robbery. His production, *Robbery*, directed by Peter Yates in 1967, gave Bruce Reynolds and the team a celebratory send-off (for their twenty-year stretches). Mythologising the headlines of 1963, Baker reinvented historical genre painting; the way Victorians like Benjamin Haydon and W.P. Frith could freeze-frame contemporary dramas and make them epic. (The noise of Frith's *Derby Day* was the event horizon for our ascent of the chalk ridge, the pull towards the Downs.)

Suspend disbelief in Stanley's terrible wig, that squirt of octopus ink, and his physicality as an actor makes him an honorary B-feature Yank. Blacklisted, or happy-to-work-in-Europe, American directors liked Baker: Joseph Losey, Robert Aldrich, Raoul Walsh, Robert Rossen. They exploited his hard stare, his displaced Celtic narcissism and melancholy; muscular baroque.

However he made his fortune, Stanley found the right place to spend it. Much came from South Africa, from the film he made with director Cy Endfield, *Zulu*. Poet and school-teacher Peter Carpenter, who grew up in the town, called the Epsom asylums 'our camps'. He reckoned they were built on the military model (Woolwich Arsenal, Netley). 'They belong,' he told me, 'in the period of the first concentration camps in the Boer War.' So it's fitting that Baker's white château was paid for by restaging the heroic but futile defence of the mission at Rorke's Drift (from 1879).

South Africa was prime landscape for producing imperialist westerns: Zulu warriors were cheaper to hire than Jews (or tent show extras) who usually played generic redskins. Baker had some interesting Old Kent Road connections in the Land of Apartheid: scrap-metal merchant (and serial company director) Charlie Richardson was trading in dubious mining rights, fraud, and political favours for Broederbonders. His ghosted

autobiography, *My Manor*, has a photograph captioned: 'Best of
Friends. Gordon Winter with General H.J. Van den Bergh,
head of the South African Secret Service, at his Pretoria farm in
1979.' Another remembrance of corporate hospitality captures
Major L.H. Nicholson, 'who helped me set up my South
African business', sharing a glass or two with Harold Macmillan
and Lord Soames. This was the period when, as Richardson
recalls, 'My brother Eddie was running around with a friend of
his, Stanley Baker, the actor. They were making *The Sands of
the Kalahari* film.'

Naughtiness, gaming, risky ventures in the colonies paid for
the copper pagoda roofs, octagonal towers, stables for potential
Derby winners. Aristocracies of blood, crime and the City set
themselves up on the edge of the racecourse; just as rock
dinosaurs, deposed politicians and coke barons bought into
bunker-land, the golf course perimeters of Surrey.

We climb through a cool woodland passage at the road's
edge; a soft, pepper-red track overhung with tough bunting,
ivy. Dappled sunlight. The noise of traffic labouring up Ashley
Road is swallowed. These paths are a teasing reminder of
revoked liberties. You can see where kids have burrowed,
pulling the skirts of the chainlink fence away from the ground.
The copse survives, giving shade to motorists, in order to disguise a network of tunnels. Where nature puts on its Ivon
Hitchens (or Samuel Palmer) act, overarching vegetation feint-
ing at the Gothic, you *know* that something is being hidden.
Beneath our feet, running all the way to the racecourse, secret
tunnels have been cut into the chalk.

MYSTERY OF TUNNELS THAT COULD HAVE BEEN ROYAL
REFUGE: London *Evening Standard* (21 November 1999). A
supporting illustration in which George VI, Queen Elizabeth
and her daughters have been superimposed on a grim brick
passageway, disappearing into darkness. The implication, the
subliminal message: Russian Revolution, Ekaterinburg.

Our beechwood copse, according to the *Standard*, was no more than the verdant roof of a subterranean city: 'one of Britain's last forgotten deep air-raid shelters, which is rumoured to have been built as a refuge for the Royal Family and their staff if wartime London had been completely destroyed'. Madmen and gangsters of the inner city to the asylum gulag, royalty to their chalk warrens; the pack was shuffled, and all the cards, joker to king, land on Epsom.

Peter Carpenter, who went to school in the town, and whose parents still live at the bottom of the hill, promised to give us the full tour: 'St Ebba's – the paupers' graveyard, isolation tower . . . Stanley Baker's house . . . Tattenham Corner (the mental patients collected the rubbish after Derby Week) . . . my old school (Dave Hemmings expelled from it) . . .' And, of course, the tunnels. Carpenter reckoned that individual tunnels were 'given London street names'. So that the buried city became a parallel world London, a memory maze. If the metropolis was destroyed, mole-people could relearn its geography and legends by tracking candlelit brick passages.

The complex, so the *Standard* revealed, had been sold at auction to 'a mystery buyer'. Agent Conrad Ritblat facilitated the deal. His representative, Stephen Bellau, claimed that a potential purchaser would have 'the chance to own somewhere very interesting in a beautiful area of land for not a great deal of money'.

Despite thorough research in the records of a number of government departments, no hard facts have been uncovered. 'All files on the bunker appear to have been lost.' A report commissioned by the now defunct Property Services Agency recommends an expenditure of £116,000 on 'beefing up perimeter security' – and mentions, in passing, the fact that the land was requisitioned on 8 February 1941. Floor plans show food stores, a marshal's post, field kitchens, lavatories, dormitories.

It's tempting to explore this area now, to go over the fence.

The new owner will obviously secure the entry to the tunnels and remove all traces of wartime and post-war occupation. We have no torches, no tools – and Peter Carpenter's local knowledge, when he leads his Epsom expedition, will give us more time to do justice to the mystery.

Crossing Ashley Road, we enter a cemetery; it's well kept, white stones bright in the morning sun, a view back over the town. Reservations of the dead are often the best parks; avenues of granite, grey-green envelopes addressed with names that have disappeared from the telephone books and trade directories. Cut flowers, little pots of chrysanthemums from garages, signifying remembrance – instead of the pebbles and black stones of a Jewish burial ground.

As we come to the crest of the hill, through paddocks and stables, we turn back to appreciate the huge sky: a dark stand of beechwood, the poplar windbreaks of the cemetery, a cordon sanitaire protecting Epsom from the white tower blocks of London. Then, soaring above it, fast-moving parachute clouds. We try to recognise familiar landmarks. We imagine groups from the hospitals, bussed up here, working to clear the rubbish after a race meeting: the confusion. Attempts at orientation. After the trip from London, ambulance or train, the years on the wards, the drugs. That is what sane people miss most: knowing where they are. *Why* doesn't matter. *When* is of no account. We have to be able to track the story back: this is where it began, that's the station, there is the river.

A racehorse, a shivering thoroughbred, is trapped in a cylinder that operates like a set of revolving doors. As we approach, the animal speeds up. It isn't going anywhere and there is nobody to supervise its drudgery. Observation, by strangers, increases momentum. The method might be economic, but the beast is going to finish up with two legs shorter than the others. If it comes across a clockwise track, it's finished; it'll never make it around the first bend. Maybe, this training programme is designed for counterclockwise courses. The horse must feel as if it's got a termite factory in one ear. The remorselessness of its tight circuits leaves us slightly seasick, hungry for the epic spaces of the Downs.

Massive displacement: crowds that aren't there. W.P. Frith's *Derby Day* painting denuded, stripped to bare canvas. History as a deserted beach. The flags and balconies of the grandstand like a marine hotel. Without prior knowledge, what would you make of this smoothed hilltop? Wide roads, lacking traffic. Combed sand runs (with inward-leaning fences). Hitching rails in the middle of nothing. A battleground? A wounded meadow? When the British regiments were defeated at Box Hill, in George Chesney's future war fantasy, they fell back on Epsom Downs. The Downs were the final ridge, before the invaders moved on to Kingston and the Thames.

BEWARE. RACEHORSES HAVE PRIORITY DURING TRAIN-ING HOURS. That's fine with us. The Downs are open to the public. Unlike the defunct and imperialist Wembley Stadium, the racecourse doesn't make you pay to visit a ruin, to watch videos and marvel at footballers' shirts in glass cases. Keep your dogs 'under strict control' and you're free to wander. The air is oxygen rich, heady. There's nothing to bet on, but we feel reckless. It's easy to understand the delirium of giving it all away, risking your mortgage on a broken-winded nag.

W.P. Frith (1819–1909) was no punter. On trips to Dorset, he was quite prepared to get into the saddle, but his one ex-perience of the hunting field was a disaster. His mount bolted. Redcoats swore at him. He jolted over ditches, hurtled across rough country, boneshaken. He vowed that in future he'd stick to the queen's highway. But the drama of Epsom Downs gave Frith his greatest triumph.

As a technician, an organiser of large human groups – Paddington Station, Ramsgate Sands – Frith was meticulous. Paintings were campaigns, crafted to whatever size or shape a patron was prepared to sponsor. He moved in society; he made money, knew everybody, wrote in a lively anecdotal style, and was popular with royalty. If Joseph Bell wanted him to produce 'an important painting, five or six feet long', the artist would oblige: for a fee of £1,500 (residuals from future engravings reserved). Frith operated in the manner of a film studio, an advertising agency. He was a materialist and a hardworking man of business.

Like his friend Dickens, he gave value for money: his canvases could be prosecuted for multiple occupation. They were picaresque slums. Even the largest compositions were claustrophobic. Aesthetic real estate. When *Derby Day* was exhibited at the Royal Academy's Summer Exhibition in 1858, a protective rail had to be put around the painting to keep the crowds back. Mobs stared at the mob. Frith reports one of the royal princes saying: 'Oh, mamma, I never saw so many people together before!'

Compositions were events, researched, pre-planned, built up from disparate elements, enacted in the studio. Painterly accidents and epiphanies of light played no part in Frith's disciplined practice. He went to Epsom for the first time in 1856. 'My first Derby had no interest for me as a race, but as giving me the opportunity of studying life and character, it is ever to be gratefully remembered.'

The artist strolled the scene with his friend Augustus Egg: he was tempted by a find-the-pea scam run by a troop that included a bogus clergyman, a Quaker and a 'fellow that thinks he looks like a farmer'. Frith didn't sketch, he trained himself to make 'mental notes'. His ability to structure epic compositions was a 'knack'. Derby Day at Epsom saw London decanted: aristocracy, thieves, the 'sporting element' and the mob. Gypsies camped on the heath. Race week was a fair, a holiday, a spectacle: there were sideshows in tents, bareknuckle boxing matches, 'nigger minstrels', pickpockets, 'carriages filled with pretty women'. Frith froze 'kaleidoscopic' chaos into a narrative that could be read as instantaneously as an advertising hoarding. By his skill in handling gradations of colour, he led the eye to a single defining episode: the acrobat and his son. In other words, Victorian sentiment. A story.

It isn't easy to work the trick in a CinemaScope format. Fluttering flags demonstrate the prevailing winds, a busy June sky presses on the Downs. The crowd divides into a dark X; leaving, in the foreground, the 'incident', the splash of white that catches our attention: kneeling man, child with back turned, broad-skirted woman. Every major character was modelled from the life: Frith found the acrobats, Joseph Bell provided the women. They were all condemned to hours in the studio – even the jockeys were made to pose, up in the stirrups, on wooden horses. The conceit is architectural, literary: a mass of anecdotage, human types, dressing a small episode of the picturesque that anticipates Picasso's Blue Period. It was an art for well-to-do English folk at a period when art was still respectable. The Prince Consort surprised Frith 'by his intimate knowledge of . . . the *conduct* of a picture'. Frith took the proffered advice, made alterations and improved his painting 'in every instance'.

While Frith laboured, his sitters talked. *Derby Day* is a madness of noise, competing voices. The achievement belongs in the register of mechanical feats, like Clifton Suspension Bridge or the *Great Eastern*. Sociable as the work pretends to be, its clutter isn't far from the hyperactivity of patricidal Richard Dadd and the Bedlam hordes of *The Fairy Feller's Master-Stroke*. (The two paintings hung side by side in the old Tate Gallery at Millbank.) But Frith's narratives have died. Warped into rhetoric. They are a lecture on social history, a prompt for costume designers. The catalogue of accurate detail condemns them to a bell jar status: like wilting fox-masks and white ferns.

Degas, using photography for his racetrack scenes, exploited the camera's capacity for roughing up an image, framing the action in an unexpected way. Humouring 'accident', he achieved a degree of formality that was far beyond Frith's range. The photographs Frith commissioned were regarded as footnotes, less useful than the costumes he kept in his studio.

The viewpoint from which he composes his scene is the viewpoint of the photographer, the same sliced segment of the grandstand. But Frith stretches the composition – like a battle-field scene – to include necessary incidents from the theatre of Derby Day. The horizontal strip could be spun, effortlessly, into a cyclorama: primitive cinema.

The source photograph, to contemporary eyes, is more inter-esting than the epic painting. Documentary reality becomes surreal: men in polished top hats standing on carts and trestles. Other figures, dejected, formally dressed, sit on the ground. Massed tadpole-heads of the crowd in the grandstands. And nothing to be seen. No race. No parade. It's over. The image defies explanation. The form is democratic: the crowd is a crowd, united. There are no discrete episodes – false lovers, ruined gamblers, rustics in smocks; there is no obligation to charm. Photography doesn't, as yet, play to an audience. It's a trade, not an art; it serves. It logs information. And, in so doing, it is making a dark trace of the world. The photographic plate exists in our present, while the contemporary/historical can-vases of William Powell Frith belong in a cabinet of curiosities. They tell us about the painter, not the place. The day, the time. The taste of high air.

LOOK RIGHT HORSES TRAVELLING AT SPEED. A flashback to black and white newsreel, Frith's famous print twitched into life: the suicide of a suffragette, Emily Davidson, throwing herself under the horses' hooves in scratched and jerky archive footage. A tragic clip by which a political campaign is mis-remembered.

Striking south, across the Downs towards the motorway, we navigate by a distant church steeple; we walk old paths, climb stiles, exchange greetings with other walkers (an elderly man in a white cap, barechested, creased naval-issue shorts, white shoes, piloting a small craft, a six-wheel buggy in which an infant is shaded by an umbrella-sail).

We're aiming for Walton-on-the-Hill. And there's a reason for this: Renchi wants to locate his grandmother's house. He remembers: the chauffeur, the drive out from London, a Surrey village and a classic Voysey/Jekyll house and garden, chosen for its proximity to a good golf course. There was a gatehouse. Granny kept, as well as the chauffeur, a nanny and a team of gardeners. The garden was what Renchi remembered most vividly: the scar on his chin, now disguised by a silvery beard, came from the Walton-on-the-Hill rockery. Long drives, pinned back against the yielding and over-padded upholstery of the car, left him queasy. A landscape too green to stomach.

By glaucous tunnels and sandy tracks, we emerge into another deserted English village. Through sun-shafted copses, Renchi has been spinning anecdotes from an episodic and unreachable past. Now, in Walton, he moves towards full-blown Proustian seizure. The past is shrivelled and chipped, but easy to map. Following faint Clarks sandal footprints, he walks the once-familiar village street. The major difference is the soundtrack: rolling motorway surf.

A Tudorbethan prefab offers: JAMES CAR HIRE. STATIONS AIRPORTS CITY AND WEST END. Nice to imagine this enterprise being run by the former chauffeur, remembered perhaps in the old lady's will. Proust was fond of chauffeurs; caps, boots, gloves.

Renchi is on the trot; he's found the gatehouse, the lane – and he's marching up the drive towards the Surrey mansion. We've had a good run, no police cars, nobody has pulled us in since we escaped from St George's Hill; but this is pushing it. Renchi, red T-shirt bandanna, ringing the bell of a stockbroker house in the burglary belt: less than half a mile from the M25. With bulging blue knapsack and cold-sweat partner.

I'm at his heels, poised for flight, camera hidden behind my back. The intensity with which Renchi has vanished into childhood – the drive from Central London, the moment of stepping from the car, the chauffeur holding the door – is palpable. Then is now. The bell chimes in the depths of the house. On one side of the button: a vaguely classical statuette, breast exposed, amphora cradled under arm. On the other, a large yellow and black notice: NO DOOR TO DOOR SALES PERSONS. WE DO NOT BUY AT THE DOOR.

Nobody at home. Good. Let's get out of here. The door opens a crack. Renchi has convinced me, we're in a warp, the dead grandmother is ever-present. On the loop.

Out of the gloomy hall, framed in the slit, catching reflected light from frosted glass panels, is a grinning leopard. A Saki beast. Above its glistening snout, a silver-haired woman. Renchi's long-buried granny. Who else would wear a Save-the-Leopard T-shirt in a Voysey house?

The old lady is a charmer. Renchi explains the case, his family's stake in this property, his freight of memories. She shouldn't do it. Slip the chain. Step outside. But she is perfectly happy to let us wander through the garden, explore the grounds.

The past shatters. The house has been split in two. The garden is a remnant of what it once was. From the woods, we can hear traffic hammering down the motorway. The views to the south, towards Box Hill, Reigate and the North Downs, have been eliminated by tactful M25 soft estates, gentle gradients with incipient forestry.

There is a touch of *Sunset Boulevard* about the swimming pool: Ganges-green sludge, loose bricks heaped in the shallow end. Abandoned garden furniture. Moulded plaster nudes posed against a high box hedge. Nothing belongs in this pool – except perhaps a crocodile. Or a human floater. A posthumous tale-teller condemned to repeat the legend of a lost life. The pool is finished. It's about to be filled in.

Before we get back on the road, the old lady invites us inside for a cup of coffee (revised, on closer examination of our dusty appearance, to lime juice). Madness! I want to tell her: 'You shouldn't do this.' Sitting in the kitchen, I feel an overwhelming urge to confess to all the crimes and insults enacted by London on suburbia. The rapes, thefts, murders. Renchi, no longer a city dweller, has no such qualms. He crunches through a plate of biscuits.

They came, the lady and her husband, from Epsom; retreating to the green fringe when demolition contractors started to cut down the trees around the hospital colony. Dances, croquet, tennis parties: the asylums were so much a part of her social life. The town, she felt, had lost its soul.

Our soul, as ever, is the M25; to which at last we have returned. There's a convenient bridge, coming out of the woods; then, sparkling beneath us like silver river-sand, the eight lanes of the motorway. Planting, at this point (between Walton Heath and Buckland Hills), is dense; a deep green gorge with nothing, so far as motorists are concerned, beyond it.

One man (with his dog, an Alsatian) leans on the parapet, chin resting on cupped hand. Tracksuit trousers, sports shirt, trainers. He pats the dog's head. This view is all he desires. The motorway has replaced the riverbank he might once have made his destination. Standing where he always stands, cars glint in the shallows, lorries cruise like pike. Lighting poles stretch into the distance: angling rods. Speed-trap cameras hook the unwary. We are those fleeting figures glimpsed by cruising motorists; lesser life forms, bridge-hugging gawpers.

Going outside the M25 is a large undertaking: we've already noted the Walton Oaks laboratories, the Hermitage and the 'Experimental Farm'. Walking won't be easy. The idea is: stay on the bank, the verge, follow the North Downs path to Merstham. And then take a train for London.

LAING. MCGEE. NO PUBLIC RIGHT OF WAY. That's better. We're back with the script. Radiant tarmac flattering the

Pilgrims Way, heading east in the general direction of Canterbury. Property held in some undeclared public/private partnership. Big construction firms. Crop modifiers. Chainlink fences topped with backward-leaning barbed wire strands. This is what we're used to, this is what we like. Something ugly enough to be worth photographing.

With a machete and a pouch of coca leaves, we could probably hack a passage through the roadside jungle. Highways Agency horticulturalists always plant to keep pedestrians out (for their own safety); thorn thickets, whiplash branches that slash at neck and eyes. We love it, hearing the race of the road, as we advance at one mile an hour. High on diesel fumes and plastic-tasting water.

Given this abandoned farm, the new drive (with ramps for lorries), screen of Scots pine and clipped yew, we're duty bound to stick our noses in, investigate. A bungalow gate-lodge with tile roof, a barrier and a surveillance camera on a tall pole. The set is now easily recognisable: it's called 'The Future'. It's what happens to liminal land, between motorway and heritage countryside. PFIZER/WALTON OAKS.

Pfizer is good. The name fizzes in the mouth like an effervescent hangover cure. Various conspiracy buffs (Chris Petit, John Sergeant) are convinced that there's a relationship between the pharmaceutical industry and the motorway corridor: convenient for Heathrow and Gatwick. Petit reckons that the more extreme forms of animal (and probably human) testing for pharmaceutical products take place in Turkey. Much less red tape. An unholy congruence of asylum seekers (finding themselves on involuntary round-trips; returned from Budapest), Swiss banks, construction firms with sweetheart contracts, poisons the off-highway biosphere. New commodities are in play. New targets. Global cigarette manufacturers, with dumped politicians as ambassadors, are targeting the Third World. Outdated medicines are repackaged in Tijuana.

★

The gate-keepers of the Pfizer estate are happy to point us in the right direction: swallowed footpaths, a hack through Bushfield Wood, a vermin-tunnel on the very edge of the motorway. Here and there, we come across hints of the Pilgrims Way; civil engineers have stuck with the flow of ancient footpaths. Sometimes we disappear into chest-high corn and have to navigate by occasional glimpses of lighting poles on the M25. The afternoon sky is as blue as the end of the world, cumulus continents broken into puff balls.

For an hour or two, we enjoy the kind of walking that guidebooks promote: *The London Loop*, *The Green London Way*, *Country Walks Around London*, *The Shell Book of British Walks*. *The Shell Book of British Walks*? That sounds a bit odd, hikes sponsored by a Dutch oil company. 'At a time when life for most of us has become more complex than ever before and more filled with possessions, it is no coincidence that so many people are turning to the simplest of all pastimes: walking.' Available at all good service stations.

The editor of *The Shell Book of British Walks* lets us know that 'a few hundred yards from the room where I am writing, there is a delightful footpath winding through woodlands and over a favourite hillside where I can see from the Surrey downland across to the Kentish hills'. We are on this fortunate man's heels, passing his garden gate, alerted to 'huge notices warning that the land off the path is private'.

I'm fond of these books with their selective maps, line drawings that try to look like woodcuts, topographic views. The walking they promote is benign: it begins at a car park, saunters, by way of a quaint church and some 'typical high downland scenery', to 'the highest point in south-east England'. Hikers are discreet, eyes averted from contemporary horrors, tutting from time to time at the excesses of developers or upwardly mobile vulgarians. These are strolls for the visually impaired, guided tours with checklists of flora, fauna, archaeological remains. The walk is an interlude of 'somewhere between an hour-and-a-half and three hours'. It's good for you. And it brings you back to the point from which you set out. To the car.

Following a commentary we have to imagine, we climb – by easy increments – on to the North Downs. The landscape drops away into a pattern of small fields, copses, hillocks, a lush bowl unimpeded by visible roads or settlements, with the South Downs as the distant, blue rim. The Weald of Kent, Box Hill. Renchi can piece it together, fit each location to a chapter of autobiography.

Above Reigate, couples are lounging on sun-bleached grass. There's no better place to 'sky', as the meteorologist Luke Howard called it; to watch clouds mass and break, adopt the shapes he named and categorised. The Pilgrims Way has become a paradise path. Walking is drifting and we're not quite easy about it; Surrey is too soft. We must be missing something.

The folds of the land are unreadable: to an East Londoner, clogged with blight. No script. No graffiti. No prohibitions. Planes do not circle continuously overhead. The only celestial markers are miles away: sky scratches, contrails, that fix Gatwick Airport.

My sense of unreality is confirmed by coming, out of nowhere, on to a small Grecian temple. Gifted to the hillside in 1909. So that pedestrians from Reigate might offer up a prayer, they are the blessed of the earth. This is a generic temple, circular, colonnaded – without content. No walls, no Vestal virgins. (Hawksmoor's mausoleum at Castle Howard – without the gravitas, the morbid stone.) The altar, at the centre of this temple, is a device – highly polished – with which travellers can align themselves: distances to notable destinations. The table becomes a pool, reflecting trees and clouds – and Renchi (as he leans in to make his readings). On the ceiling is a golden sun, bright as an egg dropped in a pan.

A uniquely ordinary English evening, warm, calm, finds us on the high ridge, moving east: water tanks, tall masts barnacled with boosters for mobile phones. The route, in its day, was a green road, favouring the lie of the land, hill forts, camps. It's not much used; the more a path receives official designation, the more it is written up in guidebooks, the more the surrounding country withdraws, protects its 'territorial security'. As a public park from which the public have been excluded.

By the time we pass through the grounds of the Royal Alexandra and Albert School, long shadows precede us. The emptiness of Deep England seems absolute: if no recreational activity is on offer, no one moves. The school serves various disadvantaged groups. Those with difficulties requiring special care. Large tin sculptures, semi-abstract (from the Kenneth Armitage/Lynn Chadwick period), have been nailed to a high brick wall. Bronze, where it has been used, has weathered to an alien green. The diminishing perspective of the evening avenue becomes a Samuel Palmer watercolour, in which silvery poplars meet in Gothic arches – and the single, symbolic pedestrian, his back to us, lurches through shadow pools. He walks on the twist; one leg, permanently bent, kicking to the east.

Merstham nests among golf courses that have been shaved to a No. 1 fuzz. Yellow balls and red balls meticulously placed on baize. The tired metaphor has been achieved, these greens really *are* a snooker table. The balls, I'm told, represent positions from which golfers of different abilities, sexes, drive off. Beyond the golf course, the streaming motorway. Then a brown hill, a white scribble of sky writing. Concealed lightboxes allow the golfers to play at night.

Without golf, the M25 would be entirely encircled by smears of oil seed rape, boarding kennels and deconstructed Victorian asylums. Golf stretches the suburban lawn into the motorway landscape; the kiddies' sandpit, the lake that is not to be fished or swum. The sanctity of the English golf course (Wodehouse and Christie again) has facilitated the latest M25 landfill scam: permission is granted to some cowboy to dig out a brownfield site, convert it to a golf course. In roll the lorries, the JCBs.

Huge pits are dug, mega-bunkers. Toxic waste is dumped. After a few months, money made, the 'developers' move on. 'Golf' has become its anagram: 'flog'. Flog the soft estates. 'Golf course landscaping' is the euphemism for black bag burial. Money in dirt.

Golf draws fringe real estate into the defensive ring. Nicely shaved fields look blameless and they have the advantage of keeping the riffraff out. Golf clubs are all about what journalist Steve Crawshaw calls 'hermetic exclusivity'. Crawshaw reported on the mysterious events that occurred at a 'golfers' Garden of Eden', near Brands Hatch (just up the Darent Valley from Samuel Palmer's Shoreham).

The property is known as the London Golf Club – but it's not in London; it's an adjunct of the infamous Swanley interchange (scene of the Kenneth Noye road rage killing). The club car park boasts the kind of motors Noye (and deceased prosecution witness Alan Decabral) favoured: alpha-male Alfas, fuck-off Ferraris, premier league Porsches, T-registration Mercs and Beamers. The course was designed by Jack Nicklaus. Members include: Sean Connery, Denis Thatcher, Gianfranco Zola, Kelvin McKenzie. A conspiracy freak's directory. Kerry Packer paid thousands in membership fees and hasn't been known to whack a ball in anger (on Kentish soil). Celebs are buying into a hall of mirrors. The famous looking at the famous. Discretion, servility (with a price tag). No guests can be signed in for a day's play. 'They can't,' as Crawshaw observes, 'even get through the gates.'

On 7 July 1999, one month before we crossed Merstham golf course, greenkeeper Steve Jones discovered the ruin of Nicklaus's 'Heritage' course: infiltrators (Saddam Hussein-sponsored asylum seekers, anti-global capitalism anarchists) crept out in the night and dug up the fairways. They drew cabbalistic diagrams with weedkiller. The letter D was burnt into the middle of a green. Why D? The general manager of the club is Daniel Loh. The damage was inflicted on the 12th green (the 12th letter of the alphabet is L). The biblical Daniel was a prophet with an apocalyptic book to his name. Daniel, in Hebrew, means: 'The Lord is my Judge.'

Among early attempts to find scapegoats, someone to pay for this outrage – 'It's a war situation' – travellers were implicated. They used to occupy the fields where the golf course was laid out. Travellers deny all knowledge, the head man says that he is very fond of the occasional round of golf.

Smart money is on an insider. An ex-member, a disgruntled barman or caddy. Detectives need to look at the psychogeography of the setting: Brands Hatch is rage culture. Town/wilderness. Motorway forced through a cutting in the hills. Dangerous roundabouts. Vibes from the other side of the bridge, from Purfleet and West Thurrock. Bandit country. Kenny Noye, the well-known Freemason, was a member. Rogue trader Nick Leeson had his membership suspended after his little difficulty in Singapore. On returning to England, sentence served (book, film and subsidiary exploitation rights flogged), he rejoined. A £10,000 reward is still on offer for evidence leading to the conviction of the Green Destroyers.

I don't much like the sound of Merstham. I don't like places I can't pronounce. Before finding the station (which has some kind of pioneer commuter status), we walk out of town on to the motorway bridge – look east to the flurry of Junctions 7 and 8 (access to M23). Highways Agency horticulturalists have obscured the pitch, trees to the edge of the road. The sun drops behind us, just as my film runs out. The final shot: half a frame of red-gold meltdown, a Fiesta speed-stretched to limo status.

3

12 August 1999. On Merstham station, Renchi looks serious: he's arranging his blue-shirt bandanna, it's going to be a long day. We aim to clear the southern stretch of the M25, leaving us free to walk the Darent Valley for our next expedition. Somewhere in the vicinity of Otford ought to do.

There is a threatening, milky haze over the town. The pattern of settlement — single street, mini-cab firms — exists to justify the railway station. Merstham is a fantasy England conjured by a distant viewer, a state-sponsored psychic: train, newspaper shop, white church with steeple. Then he ran out of inspiration, left the rest blank.

St Katharine's Church is on a slope, hidden among ilex, willow, yew. Trees feed on, and express, the early-morning melancholy of the burial ground. Clipped bushes and globes of yellow privet organise the mound into corridors for private walks. This is a necessary halt for pilgrims.

We're pleased to find an effigy of Catherine (with broken wheel) set high on the wall. The wheel, standing on its rim, could be taken as the arc of the motorway circuit that we have already covered. The second part of our story is lost.

St Catherine of Alexandria protested to the emperor Maxentius about the practice of worshipping idols. She demolished the arguments of the fifty philosophers sent to refute her. They were burnt for their failure. Catherine was beaten, imprisoned, fed by a dove; tied to a spiked wheel ('Catherine wheel') which fell to pieces. Spectators were killed by the detonated splinters. When she was beheaded, milk flowed from her neck. Her church at Merstham, with its war dead, its generations of buried villagers, is coded with the devices of martyrology (scourges, nails).

The church door is locked. A Norman chevron decorates the arch. Renchi pauses, so that I can record another of our improvisations on Blake's 'Los as he entered the Door of Death' from the *Jerusalem* frontispiece. Which is our own form of idolatry, offered to the spirit of place.

Paper boys (and girls) are the only sign of life as town gives way to broken countryside. We're trapped on another island, another microclimate of motorway-bordered land. Dwarf children (sacks on their backs) wear bright red, hooded anoraks. The houses they service are detached, 'his and hers' motors still in the driveways. Wistaria climbs over red brick towards leaded windows: the usual argument between Arts and Crafts, Tudor beams, lamps in alcoves, neo-Georgian urns. Pink hydrangeas, ferns and hollyhocks gesture at the sentiment of lost cottage gardens.

Out of this resolute disregard for the M25, the intruder at the garden gate, they promote a village life from which villagers (the rural underclass) have been expelled. Country properties to delight any estate agent in Reigate or Redhill (sold instantly on the Internet) are in fief to other places: Croydon, the City, Gatwick. The suburb is no longer a suburb, it's a denial of the motorway – on which it depends for its future survival. This is play country, a 'lifestyle' choice. Available to those with liquidity, equity reserves. The Balkanisation of the rail network, the horrors experienced by regular travellers, means that commuting is an activity for overworked, overstressed citizens who can't quite afford to be where they are. The journey isn't a respite, a convivial passage between work and home. It's the focus of the day, feared and endured. The silence of these broken hamlets is the silence of deep trauma; the slow-motion sigh of those recovering from their brush with privatised transport, their hit of motorway madness. Working from home, logging on, is no solution: being part of the global telecommunications weave, you are still in Merstham. What's here is what you have: a sequestration that takes you out of the crowd, away from noise, smell, touch. Marooned in an off-highway set, you are plunged into the monasticism that suits certain writers. It was never intended for humans. But, more and more, I sense a lack of mobility in these North Downs communities. The travel impulse has atrophied. Any contact with the territory that surrounds them is casual and unrewarding. The M25, that unmentioned cataract, is the defining reality. The road out is also the road back. A legendary presence that nobody wants to confront or confirm.

The interchange of M23 and M25 is like a postcard from Oregon, a rural fantasy. Pine woods and metalled silver streams. An absence of bears. Speed and stasis co-exist. Structural solutions in steel and concrete blend the picturesque with the functional. The interchange works best for pedestrians (crossing the M23 by Rockshaw Road); the very real fear of taking a wrong decision, hurtling off towards Gatwick instead of Maidstone, is removed. Motorists who go wrong never recover; they're sucked in among the hospitals that surround Coulsdon. Walkers are free to appreciate the art of the landscape architects: multi-levelled, dynamic. A three-barred safety fence replaces the five-barred gate as somewhere to lean, chew a stalk of grass, watch the road. A heat-singed motorway palette encourages contemplation; dark greens and burnt browns disappearing into a range of recessive silvers and blues.

Quitting this exhibit, with some reluctance, we strike out along Pilgrims Lane.

One thing there isn't, pilgrims or no pilgrims, is breakfast. Now that we have agreed a route, any possibility of rogue coffee-stalls or bacon-smelling caravans has vanished. We are on our own in country that doesn't want us. It's a strange feeling, climbing and descending, in and out of woods, views across ripe fields of corn, and being unable to get any purchase on the experience. Our walk is compromised. We're pulled between the territorial imperatives of Surrey, Kent and Greater London. The old Green Way is barely tolerated, a dog path, a route that might, if you stick with it, offer accidental epiphanies. It's more likely to lose heart, be swallowed by a disused chalk quarry, an agribiz farm, a radio mast. Some unexplained concrete structure, fenced in, and surrounded by tall trees.

The road hums. The more the motorway is screened, the more the farm tracks shudder with deflected acoustic backdraughts. Farms have a back country quality. We notice such things as a low-loader with a cannibalised helicopter, a paddock of battered racing cars. A fairytale tower in a plantation of firs. Small dogs yelp at farm gates and sometimes follow us, large dogs froth and snarl. The focus on my camera refuses to hold.

HIGH PASTURES PRIVATE. Deserted outhouses, earth churned up, animals missing – removed for slaughter? Farms that don't farm. Farms that operate as up-market scrap yards. Farms that yield to hidden clusters of houses that don't cohere as villages; the scattered outwash of Caterham.

In Woodland Way (red brick backing nervously into forest), we come across: Pilgrims Cottage (signature in concrete of GJ & CG Morley, 1986). The Morleys – husband and wife, siblings, father and son? – weren't satisfied with simply setting the plaque in a grey brick (fake granite) wall (lion couchant and carriage lamp); they reprised the name on a pokerwork board. Hung it like a Red River ranch.

Coming on Fosterdown Fort and a self-advertised 'viewing point', it would have been churlish not to stop, sit on a bench, in a clearing above the tree line, and view away. Until our eyes bleed. Down to the road. The irregular display of topiarised bushes. The litter bins. The display board that influences your viewing, by telling you what's out there. The sights (and sites) worth noticing.

Samuel Palmer's 'Valley of Vision' is our destination, the

hoped for resolution of a day's nervy pilgrimage – but in anti-cipating a coming blitz of visual sensation we have affected our approach, the long transit through the foothills. I'm having problems with focus. For some time, I've had to take my spec-tacles *off*, in order to read the small print on the map. These glasses are only good for middle-distance travelling. Another set comes into play when I venture on to the road in a car. And so, to keep to the spirit of the day (confusion), I leave the discarded spectacles on the bench by the viewing platform. We're at the next map-checking spot, four miles on, before I notice what I've done: before I picture the bench in focus so sharp I can feel every splinter.

Dropping down through the woods, to cross the M25, the picture darkens. A red circle has been painted on the smooth grey bark of a beech tree. (*Holmes shook his head gravely. 'Do you know, Watson,' said he, 'that it is one of the curses of a mind with a turn like mine that I must look at everything with reference to my own special subject. You look at these scattered houses, and you are impressed by their beauty. I look at them, and the only thought which comes to me is a feeling of their isolation, and of the impunity with which crime may be committed there.'* The Copper Beeches.)

Renchi, placing his hand within the red circle, calls up an Ulster loyalist symbol. Further on, sprayed across a slanting ash, we notice the return of a familiar logo: NF. This is the first time that River Lea (or Grand Union) graffiti have infiltrated the pleasant Surrey hills.

Next comes a tin kettle, hung by red rope, from a low branch. The kettle has been dented and punctured with bullet holes.

At the top of a lane, on the wood's edge, is a compound of caravans and tumbledown bungalows, guarded by dogs. XMAS TREES. A broad white arrow points towards a yard. Horses' heads (plaster) are nailed to the gateposts. A bright yellow RASCAL van alongside a plum-coloured pantechnicon, behind a chainlink fence. A low-loader hidden under electric-green tarpaulin. Five dogs, mixed breeds, shaggy, small, ridiculously loud, snap and yelp and snarl, back off when challenged, turn – after fifteen yards – and attack again.

A bow window, with fresh white trim, is thrown open. This combination of elongated kennel and neo-Georgian improvements is unusual. A non-travelling traveller, dealer in Xmas trees (scrap-metal, poultry, the black stuff), screams abuse. Specific threats. He's seen the camera. Luckily, he's still in bed – in vest – possibly on the job; there's a high flush to the man (between pleasure postponed and apoplexy). He asks if we'll be kind enough to wait a few moments while he slips the dog. The unleashed mongrels don't count. They nip and run. The real beasts, drooling, heads too heavy to pick from the dirt, are on chains.

We trot on, briskly, to the motorway bridge. From where I spot a tea stall sign. Renchi is adamant: we don't have the time. He's in the middle, just now, of complicated holiday season travel plans that carry him from a Wordsworth seminar in Cumbria to a New Age symposium in Portugal. He has inherited his father's Citroën.

Soft estate walking – there's no other means of reconnecting with the Pilgrims Way, on the north of the M25 – is like plunging into a river in spate. Juggernauts lurch on to Junction 6 (Sevenoaks, Dartford). We opt for the A22 (E. Grinstead, Eastbourne) – before recrossing the motorway by Flower Lane.

A police bike pulls us. No sane person would voluntarily offer themselves as roadkill. August is the optimum period for animal ironing, clogging tyre grooves with flesh and fur. Fifty thousand badgers, 100,000 foxes and at least 10 million birds: ex'd, maimed, mutilated. The Glorious Twelfth! We are walking on the day when grouse are slaughtered in the Highlands, on the Yorkshire Moors. In the south, traditionalists use the M25; a motor vehicle hurtling at seventy, eighty, ninety miles an hour. There are tunnels under the road for badgers, but nothing for humans: as we explain to the policeman. Entry to the fields is forbidden. There is no other route.

I've had meals in Shoreditch where people raved over the pheasant – before discovering that the feast was roadkill. Birds scraped from tarmac. Watercress scavenged from Chiltern pools. A room of drooling carnivores begging for the recipe, the frisson of scorched rubber across traumatised meat.

And here it is, courtesy of Jonathan Thomson:

The entire process is as follows:

- Having gathered the creature from the road, I check to ensure the condition of the bird is reasonable – I reject those which are infested with maggots or are too damaged from the impact of the collision.
- Once gathered next step is to pluck the bird – I always do this while still in the country – this is a problematic task in central London.
- A good 'hanging', from the neck with entrails intact, is essential to bring the flavour on – if this step is missed or the duration of the hanging is too short the meat does not develop a sufficiently 'gamey' flavour. The hanging process and the smell this produces stirs many adverse comments from those who live in our building; the last hanging bird was hauled down because of the strength of protest rather than the meat being sufficiently matured.
- On completion of the hanging the bird is gutted and cleaned.
- The cooking is as follows: I very slowly cook the legs in braise of white wine, game stock, onions, carrots, juniper berries and thyme. The dish is best cooked in a heavy skillet. Method is as follows: sear the legs over a high heat in butter and oil. Remove; add salt & pepper and sweat off onions, carrots and celery until softened – then add 2 crushed garlic cloves. Deglaze the pan with either white wine or calvados – ensure that all the sediment is scraped from the bottom of the pan. Replace the pheasant legs and add enough game stock to generously cover the bottom of the pan. Put into a moderate oven and cook slowly until tender. To finish: remove

the legs (keep at serving temperature), strain off the braising vegetables and reserve the liquor in a saucepan (this is optional, the
brazing vegetables can be retained). Place over a high heat and
reduce, thicken the sauce with cream.

- The breasts, which are removed from the carcass before cooking,
  are cooked very quickly and served close to rare – dependent
  on individual taste. I cook the breasts on a skittle over a medium
  heat in a little butter and olive oil. Once cooked they are sliced and
  plated – they are served with a sauce which is made from the stock
  of the boned/legged bird and sometimes finished with cream to
  thicken.
- The vegetables I like to serve with this dish are roughly mashed
  potatoes, fresh fine green beans and carrots.

It's not just a Carl Hiaasen menu of birds and hedgehogs and
foxes, it's fish. 'Impervious edges to roads,' as journalist Sanjida
O'Connell reports, 'increase the flow of water from the road
into streams – leading to a build up of sediment, increased
water temperature and pollution'. Salmon, apparently, are very
sensitive to irregular 'flash flows'. Salmon loss affects many
other species, including bears and orca whales. The chain of
interconnections is alarming: Moby-Dick threatened with
extinction by the Art Nouveau filigree of Junction 5, its run-off
into the River Darent.

Highway chemicals leech into streams. Heavy metals over-
whelm motorway-fringe wildlife. Rock salt, used in road
gritting, is toxic to many species of plant. Fish are unwell. Song
birds, sensitive to the M25's acoustic footprints, back off.
Vibrations from the constant, twenty-four-hour madness of
traffic persuades earthworms to keep their heads down; leading
to an excess of crows – and crowkill – as birds try to prise their
breakfast from unsuspected depths.

Now seriously peckish, almost ready to dispute crow-spoil, we
lengthen our stride. If we stick with the Pilgrims Way, the first

refuelling station will be Westerham; which is over the Kent border and about seven miles on. Sometimes we're in deep countryside, no settlement in sight, no trace of the road – other than a continuing sense of unreality. Tidy fields, without cattle. Well-kept B-roads linking villages and farms. A lush buffer zone, a cushion. The unseen motorway as the dominant presence.

We're always within a single field of tarmac, or admiring the pinkish-silver stream from a safe distance. The temperature is climbing. A sticky morning. Renchi abandons shirt and bandanna. We swim through a huge field of what looks like sweet corn, the feeling is Mediterranean. Like Godard's *Pierrot le Fou*. Bright, comic-book colours; greens and blues. A hazy sun. Camions jostling for position on a shimmering road. The dry morse of crickets.

It's when we sit to interrogate the map that I miss my spectacles; the act of having to take them off, or shove them up towards a vanished hairline. We're on the nursery slopes, an arable field (unoptioned golf course) giving a clear view of the motorway, the steady mid-morning traffic.

I'll go back. That's my first thought. The bench. The 'viewing point'. Which means: all that way along the edge of the quarry, the steps cut into the hillside, the travellers' bungalows. The dogs. I'll leave my rucksack, try a gentle jog – while Renchi, dressed only in shorts and boots, dries his shirts on the fence; presses his hands together, meditates on the landscape and his passage through it.

I lurch through a couple of fields, down among the corn, up the next slope, then change my mind. A degree of softness in focus is no problem. It might even be a benefit. Elective Impressionism. Anything close is still sharp. I'd rather put up with the hassle (and expense) of getting another pair of specs than endure the additional hours in Surrey. Let my Kingsland Road frames be the necessary sacrifice.

Renchi, in all probability, hasn't noticed that I've gone.

Dark blue sweater, light blue bandanna, white T-shirt: draped along the fence. Gently steaming. The pale-skinned, half-nude mendicant squats in the dirt, contemplating our assault on the Valley of Vision.

He has become, in my conceit, both a reprise and an anticipation of his great-grand-uncle, Clarence Bicknell. A physical embodiment of the Eternal Return and a tribute to the Victorian botanist (hillwalker, watercolourist, tracer of the rock-engravings of Monte Bego in the maritime Alps). Memory is homage. Engraved by time and experience, we grow to look like daguerreotypes of ancestors who have rehearsed our destiny. Except that they did it with more conviction, more innocence. Instead of hopping, boulder to boulder over black-violet sandstone and fine-grained schist, taking rubbings of Early Bronze Age rock carvings, we slide down Beckton Alp, photographing middens of urban rubbish.

Part of our task in this circumnavigation of London is to become our fathers, our grandfathers; to learn respect for obscured and obliterated lines of biography. Accessing the fugue, we parody lives that preceded our own. Reading Victorian memoirs, we come to believe that these events have not yet happened.

Renchi was showing me the book, on the day of our walk around the City's Roman walls. We were sitting in the café at the Museum of London. *A High Way to Heaven (Clarence Bicknell and the 'Vallée Des Marveilles')* by Christopher Chippindale. Marc Atkins, who had just met Renchi for the first time, was there. With his camera. I held the cover of the book close to Renchi's face and asked Marc to take the shot. It's an extraordinary double portrait: the slanted book becomes a mirror. Twin grey beards, spruce. Twin noses. Heavy eyebrows. Faces full of stalled wonder. The sloping shoulders of Clarence in his pale jacket slide into Renchi's T-shirt ('Fruit of the Loom'). On the wall of the café, above the coffee machine: SUMMER DESSERTS.

Reading about Clarence, I discover a template for Renchi; not an explanation, or psychological profile, but a concurrent stream of particles navigating a way around a similar landscape. 'Then' and 'now' are distinctions I can't make. Clarence Bicknell, the youngest son of a wealthy businessman, entered (and abandoned) the church; he travelled, settled at Bordighera on the Mediterranean coast of north-west Italy, a few miles from the French border. He took long daily walks. He explored Liguria, painting more than 3,000 watercolours of plants. He was a vegetarian and a promoter of Esperanto (attending conferences in such places as Krakow). He commissioned a house (decorated with Art Nouveau foliage and playful mottoes) on the slopes below the high Val Fontanalba – where he would carry out the extensive survey of rock-engravings by which he is best known. He shipped stones back to Cambridge. His herbarium of dried specimens was displayed at the Hanbury Institute, Genoa. He funded and stocked his own museum, the Museo Bicknell, in Bordighera.

This life, as Chippindale annotates it, was one of discreetly inflicted patronage, questing, categorising: true liberality – before the term became degraded. The busy leisure of a gentleman amateur of the best kind: rising at five a.m. to tend his garden, offering hospitality, walking the mountains, carrying out his obsessive logging of the marks on ancient rocks. 'Casa Fontanalba', his colonial chalet, was known as: 'The Cottage at the Entrance to Paradise'.

Clarence Bicknell's father, Elhanan, made his money in whale oil. Which meant epics of slaughter, boiling vats on Bugsby's Marshes; bones and blubber. A heavy stench that drifted on the east wind. You can smell it still as you emerge from the Blackwall Tunnel to drive over the exhausted tongue of land on which the New Labour visionaries chose to erect their Millennium Dome.

Bicknell's sperm oil lit the world, but Elhanan was also interested in another kind of oil, in paintings. And painters.

Clarence's mother, Lucinda (the third of Elhanan's four wives), was the daughter of Hablot Knight Browne – who produced illustrations for Charles Dickens, under the pseudonym 'Phiz'. Bicknell was comfortable with painters, as patron and as friend. His large house, in the rural suburb of Herne Hill, was close to the Ruskin property. Young John was a frequent visitor. Oils and watercolours by J.M.W. Turner dominated the Bicknell collection (which included works by Roberts, Etty, Landseer, De Wint). David Roberts was a relative. His daughter married one of Clarence's half-brothers.

A private gallery for contemporary art in the Surrey foothills. Elhanan didn't care for old masters. Turner, from whom he commissioned a number of works, was sketched by Landseer (and painted by Count d'Orsay) enjoying the hospitality of Herne Hill: *Turner in Mr Bicknell's Drawing Room*. Player and gentleman. Turner's Melvillean epic, *Whalers* (of 1845), was produced with the sperm oil magnate in mind. And painted, this dark monster rearing from a red–gold sea, six years before the publication of *Moby-Dick*. Melville devoted three chapters to pictorial representations of whales: illusions, myths, truth. He tracked the story back to a crippled beggar on Tower Hill holding up a crudely daubed board which featured a primitive summary of 'the tragic scene in which he lost his leg'. The whale narrative returns to Elhanan Bicknell, investor and col-lector – and to the London works, alongside the Thames, where he refined spermaceti.

When (in the 1840s) Turner wasn't 'at home' in Queen Anne Street, he hadn't necessarily slipped away to Mrs Booth at Margate; his other refuge was Herne Hill, with the Ruskins or the Bicknells. The Cockney lion wasn't an easy guest, some-times talking at length, charming the ladies with accounts of his sketching expeditions, sometimes mumpy and silent. With his host, Turner discussed the operation of the whaling industry, the source of that soft light that bathed the dinner table.

Bicknell is thought to have commissioned all four of Turner's whaling subjects.

The inevitable quarrel between artist and patron came over plans to engrave an edition of *The Fighting Temeraire*. Turner asked for fifty proofs, Bicknell offered eight. Taking an inventory of *Whalers*, inch by inch, as if reading a balance sheet, the Herne Hill entrepreneur discovered some fiddly detail he didn't care for – and which he intemperately rubbed out 'with Handky'. Turner, in a strop that could never be mended, was persuaded to make alterations.

They live with us, these phantoms. The collaboration between Turner and Elhanan Bicknell. Hunted whales and boiling vats on Greenwich peninsula. Definitions of the Light. Clarence, the youngest son, escaped from trade, from London, to become a rehearsal for Renchi: for the problem of finding the true path. Painting was a useful pursuit, a necessary irritant; never a profession. Questing walks. Generosity to friends and fellow townsmen. Vegetarianism. The urge to research, record. The karma of family wealth modestly dispersed – along with the difficulties (or guilts) associated with that process. The will towards good (that stumbles and blunders and is aware of its own absurdity). We repeat patterns that we can barely discern. We make old mistakes in new ways.

Clarence Bicknell, from his 'Entrance to Paradise', searched for pictures in the rocks. He sketched groups of horned figures: 'Weapons and implements'. These implements, now interpreted as 'halberds', are characteristic of the early metal age in prehistoric Europe. Triangular blades set at a right angle to their shafts: they look like flags marking holes on motorway golf courses. Pin men dancing for joy: Conan Doyle's *The Dancing Men*.

More significantly, Bicknell made a rubbing of 'Le Scale del Paradiso'. Here indeed was 'The Highway to Heaven' (the dream of a celestial autobahn). Here was the (unacknowledged) inspiration for the work Renchi produced when the M25 walk was completed. As part of a deprogramming process, he picked certain sites along the road as suitable for sand paintings, drawings with vegetable dye. In rehearsal, he sketched his designs in chalk on the road between the London Waste chimneys and Picketts Lock. The full ritual was intended for the tunnels at Epsom. Our orbital circuit was broken down into four vertical lines, like the Paradise ladders; chalk chippings were placed along one margin, small stones from a deleted burial ground along another. Drumming continued throughout the day, as Renchi laboured to complete his painting.

The Marc Atkins double portrait – Clarence and Renchi Bicknell – becomes a triptych with the addition of Clarence's sketch of a 1909 discovery in the Mediterranean Alps: *The Chief of the Tribes*. After a day, during which they had endured intermittent heavy showers, Bicknell and his companion, 'in a state of great excitement', came upon something like a stone mirror: his own bearded image, thousands of years old, softened by lichen. 'Le Sorcier' was the title the French used. Bicknell spoke of 'Devil-dancers or Witch-doctors of savage tribes'. A beard, teeth suggested by a line of dots, intense eyes under a single horizontal bar (eyebrows or a lid to prise open the skull). The 'horns' on the head become hands, digits emphasised with chalk by future portraitists, determined to capture a clear representation. A human face. An archetype. As shocking in its immediacy as the mummified body of 'Otzi the Ice-man', who was recovered (clothing and weapons intact) from the snowfield on the Italian-Austrian border.

Renchi, in the booklet that collected the paintings from his *Michael and Mary Dreaming*, the walk to Land's End, writes of: 'Son following father/and father following son/a previous time of taller trees/and different animal energies.' The son smuggles rocks into his father's rucksack.

Clarence Bicknell travelled to Ceylon at around the time that my great-grandfather, Arthur, was botanising and managing tea plantations. Arthur did not come from a wealthy family. He reveals, in a chapbook (Arthur Sinclair: *Planter and Visiting Agent in Ceylon: The Story of his Life and Times as Told by Himself*) published in Colombo in 1900, that his parents 'were descended from an old Jacobite stock, at this time still rather at a discount'. He walked to school from a 'little farm-house at King Edward, Aberdeenshire', carrying the day's ration of peat. He didn't linger. 'I ended my schooling and began my education.'

A self-taught plantsman, he was taken up by Sir John Cheape and shipped off to tea estates near Kandy. He had already laid out a garden of his own, which he rose at four a.m. to work. He was a hungry reader. 'I read indiscriminately every book in my father's house ... I read and re-read with intense delight.' He walked home from Aberdeen, 'sitting down by the wayside' to dip into whatever he had scavenged from the book stalls. Thomas De Quincey 'fascinated' him, and was soon established as his favourite author.

From other books by Arthur Sinclair, accounts of his travels, I remember pen and ink sketches of flowers, more detailed, less painterly than Clarence Bicknell's. There are photographs of plants, Chuncho chiefs in Peru, artefacts, skulls. Arthur, in his dug-out canoe, rifle across lap, is another Victorian beard. Another quirky traveller, roaming the globe, writing up journals, mythologising, making jokes.

Renchi and I won't be scrambling over the Andes or discovering rare plants. We have to make do with a few shards of broken Roman pottery in a display case at the Clacket Lane Service Station, or the etymology of the woods we are skirting ('Devil of Kent').

Pilgrims Lane, when we blunder across it, is still a buzz. A hedger (human – not one of those grinding machines) puts us right; with his hook, he pulls back a curtain of greenery to gesture at a path across the fields. The road to Westerham dips once again under the M25.

Deep in a bramble thicket that erupts from the edge of the road, Renchi makes his discovery. An antique message printed on tin. Not quite 'La Via Sacra' or 'Le Scale del Paradiso'. A plain, shit-brown rectangle with a prancing white horse: KENT. Welcome.

4

Westerham, Kent, doesn't work: not for pedestrians. Or travellers of any kind. Which is strange, because the siphon-
ing of small change from transients, heritage tourists (with an
imperialist bias), is the reason for this long shank of a town's
continued existence. Westerham is shaped like a mantrap,
narrow jaws sprung against incursions by the unwary. Primed
to snap shut with a satisfying crunch.

The predominant colour is chocolate-brown (river mud,
Gault clay, shit). Reasons for stopping, detouring, paying your
respects to sanctioned real estate, are promoted at every turn in
the road. White lettering on a red-brown field: CHARTWELL,
HEVER CASTLE, SQUERRYES COURT, QUEBEC HOUSE, THE
HIGH WEALD COUNTRY. In Victorian times, London was an
occasional destination, over the horizon. A coach operated
between the Grasshopper pub (near St Mary's Church) and
Fleet Street. Citizens of substance, men of business, travelled
in – when they had to, when it was strictly necessary. Most of
the Westerham populace never moved, before trains and
metalled roads, more than ten miles from where they were
born.

We look for shade beneath a roadside tree, sumach or medlar,
while we figure out the quickest means of escape. And, more
importantly, somewhere to eat. Dust-free cars are parked,
bumper to bumper, along Croydon Road. That name tells you
something about Westerham. If you want to head north, the
choice is: Croydon or Biggin Hill. Croydon has become a
creature of the depths, a subtopian city-state; constantly reaching out to devour the lesser hilltop developments of South
London. Croydon has trams and transplanted Docklands towers.

Croydon has company HQs, untargeted terror targets (nobody knows they're there), towers of glass and steel. Croydon has its own suburbs (which house the street-cred TV personality, former footballer, Ian Wright and his family). So Westerham, Kent's western outrider, gives its allegiance to Croydon, not London.

There are no shops, not yet. No other walkers. There is nobody for the barechested Renchi (blue bandanna, red socks) to interrogate. That eerie sound – like ice breaking – is the M25. It's always there, barely audible acoustic footsteps, a soothing whisper; a nuisance we have learnt to love. Westerham, with pretensions to a kind of Cotswold status, ignores the interference. Between red brick houses, in narrow gaps, beside pubs clinging to the rumour that James Wolfe once dropped in for a swift half, you catch the glint of transit: Eddie Stobart and his rivals jingling their petty cash, searching for a pound coin with which to pay the Dartford Tunnel toll.

We don't have outfits appropriate to the Rendezvous café-brasserie ('french, fresh, friendly'). Renchi, in truth, hasn't much of an outfit left. The Rendezvous is packed, a whirl of activity, punters being turned away. Flocks of OAP anoraks use the place as a tea room: pot of Darjeeling and a pale slice of something that is as close as the French come to seedcake. Local artists (and dressed the part) compete for space with cardiac-flushed antique dealers (with too many shirt buttons undone), and motor racing investors whose round tables clink with empty bottles, mobiles parked like six-guns. The harassed young women who run the orders are the only people under retirement age. Smoke, noise, conviviality: to counter the compulsory siesta under which the rest of the town yawns.

The popularity of the Rendezvous is soon explained: look at the competition. Coaching inns with balconies and blackboards offering specials, such as: NO FOOD, REFURBISHMENT. A 'picturesque "wood clad" pub dating from the 14th century' and named, in case you miss the point, GENERAL WOLFE

(1727–59). The Kings Arms is the High Street's flagship property: 'an elegant Georgian Coaching Inn ... for a relaxing lunch or a light snack in the bar or Town Jail'. White in appearance, white in soul. We keep walking.

Down at the George and Dragon, we gnaw through some ploughman's leftovers. Back in 1883, the George boasted of its proximity to the 'new South Eastern Railway Station'. Westerham still smelt of hops, the brewery flourished. The old 'posting house' catered 'for Gentlemen especially', offering 'Pyramids, Pool and the only Public Billiard Room' in town. Now the sporting spirit has definitively run out, replaced by dedicated afternoon boozing, history like a puddle of ullage. We grind and gum in a microclimate of stale tobacco, spilt stout and clinical depression.

Making conversation, Renchi asked the girl in the papershop (as we stocked up on chocolate bars and water), how far it was to Chartwell, Winston Churchill's country place. She couldn't do distance, miles, metres; didn't understand the concept. 'Five minutes,' she said. 'Where's your car parked?' No car. On foot, walking. She looked blank, couldn't get her mind around it. 'Five minutes,' she repeated. 'Up past the common. Follow the signs.'

Not today. Not if we're going to make Otford. Save it. Every charity shop in Kent carries a copy (bottom shelf, cardboard box) of the Pergamon Press *Churchill and Chartwell* by Robin Fedden. Robert Maxwell, as ever, doing his bit to puff Great Men (Enver Hoxha, Nicolae Ceauşescu). This publication had run through two editions and one revised edition, before the 1974 printing that I acquired in Westerham. It has to be a black propaganda exercise, the dumping of thousands of copies of book ballast – in order to con charity shop vultures into paying £11.80 (two adults, non-concessionary) to visit the place Fedden calls 'the most important country house in Europe'. Nobody but Maxwell could succeed in flogging a book with nothing but a pink chair on the cover; a pink chair with pink box (or footstool) on a strip of grass by a goldfish pond. An image that is meant, emotively, to spell out: absence. A feeble attempt at invoking the famous Churchill icon – © *Life* – which turns up here as a frontispiece. The warlord, at ease, seen from behind, pregnant with destiny, hat and a coat (no neck); sitting on a rock contemplating the swimming pool he designed and the lake beyond. It could very easily be a stand-in (as with the famous wartime broadcasts), an actor. But it is an effective summary of the man's relationship to the land, to Kent. After a good lunch, a morning – in bed – dictating memos, he liked to sit by the pond 'in a simple garden chair' feeding 'fat golden orfe'.

Churchill and Wolfe dominate Westerham; effigies, postcards, memorials in the church. Mementoes and memorabilia designed to tempt us into Quebec House or Chartwell, to remind us of a glorious past that is now largely in the keeping of Americans and Canadians. To move east along the A25, in the direction of Sevenoaks (Brasted, Sundridge), is to progress through an elongated version of Camden Passage, Islington, or the Brighton Lanes: antique shop after antique shop (with, by way of variety, the occasional up-market estate agent). The road is busy and impatient, single file traffic unable to make the adjustment after coming off the motorway. Tourist buses and old folk wrestling with maps. Chartwell, when Churchill motored down, was twenty-five miles from London, from Westminster. These days, as the girl in the newspaper shop so shrewdly recognised, distance has no meaning. Miles only matter to horses and pedestrians. We have to deal in drives measured by the hour. Units of nuisance between pit stops. Road works, accidents, congestion: a geography defined by junction numbers on the M25.

There's a narrow triangle of ground at the eastern end of this one-street town, a redoubt known as 'The Green'. It is dominated by two sculptures. They can't be called art works. They ignore each other, nervous that they might have to defend their position against legions of dead generals. The western effigy, on the higher ground, was erected in 1911; designed by Derwent Wood, heaved into place on an ornamental pedestal of Portland stone. It's as camp as they come, a *Carry On* tantrum; weapon raised more in pique than anger. Kenneth Williams, Charles Hawtrey. Major General James Wolfe repels all incomers (aliens, grockles). His sword is up, his three-cornered hat is cocked; his hose clings to slender calves. He's going to give somebody a fearful slap.

Down in the dumps, ignoring Wolfe's hysterics, Winston Churchill sags, his back to London. Oscar Nemon's monument, donated by the people of Yugoslavia in 1969, is set on a limestone block. This bronze looks like a landslide of molten biro caps. It's oozy, cloacal; a mash of boiled seaweed. Any day now it's going to collapse, slither from the plinth and clog the drains. The chocolate Churchill knots his fists, sunk in a deep throne; an old man struggling to raise himself. Straining at stool. Near this spot, he received the congratulations of the town. He stood on a cart, his family around him, to acknowledge the cheers. Now he glares, unseeing, across Tower Wood towards Chartwell. The job of these effigies is simple: alert passing trade to heritage properties where they can spend their money.

I returned to Westerham, on the Sunday after my hike with Renchi, with vague notions of retracing my steps, recovering my lost spectacles – and also locating the source of the River Darent. The Darent, anticipating the M25, heads north at Riverhead, and would give us our route, back to the Thames at Dartford. The river rises near Crockham House, in the hills above Westerham, before dropping down through the Hythe beds of the Lower Greensand. A neighbouring spring at Chartwell lent its name to Churchill's 800-acre estate – which he picked up for £5,000 in 1922.

I did the tour, beginning at Squerryes Court. I was too early for the house, but was able to walk the grounds. Gurgles and slurps. The dark mirror of the lake. The young Darent enjoying a little aristocrat patronage before slumming it in Mick Jagger's Dartford. Liquid whispers from Wealden clay infiltrate the salt marshes of Crayford and Stone: rumours of another life, big houses and gravel drives. That must be where the adolescent Mick caught the infection, his compulsion to join the nobs, metamorphose into a dandy and a gent.

Squerryes Court, privately owned, lets in temporary guests, respectful trippers. Cash customers from the suburbs, from Surrey. The Warde family (who lived here from 1731) put up an obelisk to the memory of James Wolfe. One of those damp mysterious things abandoned in an English garden – as if waiting to catch the eye of photographer Bill Brandt. A fog of heavy grain, a couple of lines of valetudinarian verse. There to be found, by those who need to find it; found and forgotten.

Wolfe, aged fourteen, was hanging around in Squerryes Court when the royal messenger (redirected from Greenwich) arrived with his commission. The route to martyrdom was preordained: the Heights of Abraham or the descent from the High Weald. Wolfe seemed sickly/heroic – like Nelson – a mode the English have always admired. Wolfe was a green ghost.

In psychogeographic terms, the man who introduced Freemasonry into the North American continent plotted a path from Westerham to Greenwich Hill. He confirmed the East London ley line celebrated by Nicholas Hawksmoor. It still runs from Wolfe's shrapnel-scarred statue, across the Isle of Dogs, to St Anne's, Limehouse. News, coming from Greenwich, is returned there: obscure Squerryes Court obelisk to much-photographed memorial (via Wolfe Close, Bromley).

Quebec House, where Wolfe lived for his first twelve years (before moving with his family to Greenwich), marks the point where Westerham runs out. Behind the house is the trickle of the young Darent, a puddle you can leap. Wolfe's former home is a spook show, a sequence of recreated sets in which we are invited to call up the shades of a vanished family. The history lesson, the reason why we are all shuffling through this undistinguished town house, outlines a biography; it 'explains' the battles and military campaigns. Muffled oars, assault by impregnable cliff, victory and death. Flags, swords and bloody linen. A memorial industry: 'statues and songs, paintings and prints'. History is sexy. House detectives, grubbers in fields, tomb raiders: we love them for their ability to make us more than we are. They connect us to a fictional back story.

Winston Churchill, so they say, looked at the street wall of Quebec House and discovered a hobby that would carry him through the years of Chartwell exile, through the glooms of Black Dog depression, the underbelly of his manic energies. In time, he would pick up his union card and become a self-employed brickie: Wendy houses, garden walls, ponds for carp. Water features drawing on Wealden springs.

Chartwell, off-highway (but lavishly signposted), anchors the south-eastern corner of our M25 circuit. Top-dollar heritage. Major attraction. When I turned up, on a dull dank morning, the car park (two levels and extensions) was almost full. Unculled livestock, the descendants of the herd of Belted Galloway cattle that Churchill acquired from his friend Sir Ian Hamilton, dressed the park; huddling together on high ground. There could be no better place to play at being a gentleman farmer (author, artist, bricklayer). Churchill bought Middle White pigs, a dairy herd. The animals, as the National Trust booklet admits, 'tended either to die of disagreeable diseases or become household pets'. Black swans were a *bonne bouche* for Kentish foxes. A dove from Bali is laid to rest beneath a sundial. Indulged poodles and pussy cats are buried under every bush.

House and grounds are a dream of benign domesticity, aristocrats playing at being ordinary English folk; country pursuits, hobbies, croquet, games with the kids. This might explain

Chartwell's popularity; suburbanites (unlanded) feel at home with the aspirations. Life as it might be after a lottery win: swimming pool, pets, rose garden, tennis court, an inconvenient kitchen in which vegetables are boiled to death. Chartwell is not impossibly grand: 'his and hers' bedrooms, certainly, but many English couples, given the space, would go for that.

There are notable views of the High Weald from the dining room. Windows down to the floor, lovely filtered light. The circular dining-tables and comfortable chairs (with arms) were commissioned from Heal's – to Churchill's specifications. The tables are unstained oak. This suburban fantasy is as fudged as William Nicholson's painting of *Breakfast at Chartwell*. In reality, the Churchills rarely took breakfast together. Winston stayed in bed till lunchtime, reading the newspapers, dictating memos to the two secretaries who were permanently on call. The sun–dappled domesticity – cat on table, bantam cock wandering in from garden, fond couple chatting over tea and toast – is a fable of the Good Life.

I stood in steady rain, Kentish mizzle, waiting for the exact hour that would let me into the house. Entry was staggered. Elderly gentlefolk of unimpeachable character guard each room, hallway, staircase. 'Fresh flowers, daily newspapers and the occasional cigar' add to the atmosphere. The *Express* has shrunk to a tabloid since Beaverbrook's day and the *Times* has lost its status as a journal of record. Who, I wondered, had the job of smoking those Havanas – until they were suitable butts? Who provided the dark rim of spittle?

A tumbler of well-watered whisky and a comforting cigar were always within reach of the Nobel Prize-winning author (who dictated with the panache of Edgar Wallace), the compulsive painter. Books were everywhere, histories, biographies, volumes and volumes about Napoleon, the occasional novel or humble classic. I noted Edmund Wilson's *To the Finland Station*: a first edition, I assumed, lacking jacket. Wilson's book was published in 1940 – when the Churchills had left Chartwell (too risky, ponds visible to bombers; too close to Biggin Hill) and the house was shut up. So how authentic was this library?

'On only one recorded occasion during the whole of Marx's thirty years' stay did he attempt to find regular employment,' wrote Wilson. 'The resistance to the idea of earning a livelihood may, at least partly, have been due to an impulse to lean over backwards in order to forestall the imputation of commercialism which was always being brought against the Jews.' Karl Marx and his sprawling family, evicted from the 'fashionable suburb' of Camberwell, occupied two rooms in Dean Street, Soho. Another heritage myth. Another potential shrine. Churchill was quite effective at commerce, without getting his hands dirty: he had wealthy friends, he got top weight for his journalism and books. He played the market.

We see what we want to see: a drawing room of the kind you might come across in numerous unpretentious rectories, restored cottages, captured farmhouses. Too much furniture: fabric-covered armchairs, baggy sofas, inherited desk, mahogany card table (thought to be rather good, possibly Georgian). Chintz curtains, fading Mahal carpet. There is no nonsense about integrated design. Somewhere for everybody to sit, to sprawl; alcoves shelved, family photographs, paintings by Dad (not Dadd). Look closer. This seemingly commonplace room is hung with eighteenth-century chandeliers that gleam in a vulgar abundance of teardrops. That smudgy view of the Thames, over the desk, is by Claude Monet. A gift from Emery Rose who bought the lucrative foreign rights to Churchill's books, after the Second World War. It's a useful conversational piece among the dozens of loosely Impressionist daubs by the householder.

Punchdrunk with history, blinded by uniforms, medals, presentation cigar boxes in malachite and silver, groups of old folk stick and cluster. They lived it once and now they want it confirmed. In writing. In images. They are reluctant to step outside, into the garden. Which way should they turn? Towards the fish pond? Churchill, after a good lunch, would sit on his chair, dripping maggots for his beloved carp. His 1930s paintings of the pond, in reproduction, have something of late Monet: shallow water, red-gold fish shapes among the lily pads. A mood of retirement and contemplation.

The rain brings out the scent from beds of santolina, dripping lavender. Lady Churchill supervised the planting, with advice from her cousin Venetia Montagu. The terraced rose garden with its heavy-headed excesses, the sheer bulk and weight of petals, is an experience that is quite unlike the tokenism of suburban and municipal patches. Terrace to lawn. Vine-draped pergola to pavilion. A line of canvas-backed chairs, tilted against the wall, to let the rain run off. White oast houses beyond an orchard that is heavy with late fruit. Alcoves for private conversation; benches hidden by tall yew or box hedge, summer houses and rose walks.

It is shocking to admit, but here at last is the paradise garden. Water running from rocks, into ponds and pools and lakes. Fruit. Walks offering varied views of house and park. Domestic felicity (underwritten by blood, connections, power). A small paradise is achieved and, despite the ticket-buying crowds, it is present and accessible in a way that the contrived 'views' of Painshill, the retrievals of Enfield Chase, are not. Churchill, who saw most of his investments wiped out in the Wall Street Crash of 1929, did a Walter Scott, or Jeffrey Archer, he wrote himself (dictated, flogged his researchers) back to prosperity: a torrent of sonorous hackery, jobbing journalism and cardboard history (in sets, volumes, yards). While the garden evolved. Grew, flourished. It's hard to imagine Lady Thatcher, banished from power, having much time for plant catalogues. Her retreat in quasi-pastoral Dulwich was very soon abandoned. The rose, for Tony Blair, is only useful as a symbol, a thornless logo.

Chartwell was well chosen. The absolute Englishness of England (soft and southern) is manifest in every photograph; a dream country of orchards that don't have to be picked, cattle as pets, toy farms, sentimental ecology. The great man bricklaying in a velvet boilersuit, roof tiling in Homburg, gloves, cigar. An old house on the spring line, knocked about, rebuilt by Philip Tilden, to represent no particular place or period. A landscape that is unthreatening, rounded, fertile. A Kentish Arcadia: H.E. Bates's Larkin family (for toffs). A moderately dysfunctional troop who were amateur in every sense (except that of staying afloat, raising the readies). And the certain knowledge, under-writing this bucolic charade, that Westminster was just over the hills. The car was waiting. On every M25 map, among the nine- and eighteen-hole golf courses (five of them between Godstone and Sevenoaks), is the proud red dot for Chartwell. Chartwell means that it's time to swing north, to head for home.

If, by whatever accident, Chartwell is the paradise garden, can Churchill be seen as its painter? Now sodden, dripping, I arrive at the Studio, by way of the Golden Rose Walk. The Studio is no euphemism, tumbledown shed or Portakabin: it would be a substantial house in Islington, a terrace in Hackney. The scale of this building, the views on offer, might suit a Rodin or a Courbet. The stuffed bull's head, provided by Manolete, and hung over the door, doesn't mean that the old man had any truck with Picasso and Iberianism. He painted from a wooden armchair, his back to the landscape.

On either side of the A21, fixed in permanent opposition, are the emanations of Churchill and Samuel Palmer. Churchill is always photographed looking east towards Underriver and Palmer's Golden Valley. These are non-complementary ver-sions of the pastoral. Palmer's innocent shepherds and cowgirls turn agricultural labour into a sacerdotal experience, woods as churches: he was always peeping, surveying, peering short-sightedly through a leafy frame. 'The dream,' he wrote to John Linnell, 'of antepast and proscenium of eternity.' Palmer, an 'old Tory', issued at his own expense a pamphlet denouncing the rick-burning activities of depressed Kentish labourers.

'The English Radical and the Gallic Jacobin are brothers,' he wrote (in *An Address to the Electors of West Kent*). 'Let us rally around once more . . . round the noble standard of Old Kentish loyalty.' So declaimed the Londoner, the harvest moon sentimentalist.

Churchill was a royalist, rogue Liberal, turncoat; he paid lip-service to the established Church (no private chapels at Chartwell). But Palmer was that extraordinary thing: a fanatic for the Church of England. A fundamentalist of the middle ground. The High Weald was that ground; an extension of William Blake's *Virgil* woodcuts.

The walls of Churchill's studio are hung with his back catalogue, crammed like the Royal Academy Summer Show – in the days when Palmer found his paintings perched a few inches from the ceiling. The lakes and springs and orchards of Chartwell, by Churchill's mediation, do not become sites of vision. His canvases are resolutely occasional, holiday memories, overworked postcards from the Med; grace and favour villas and yachts. A Cook's Tour of hobbyism: Marrakech, Venice, Monte Carlo, Jamaica. The Surf Club at Miami. Hot colour generously applied. Lashings of Sickert gravy. There is no attempt to work, by series or season, towards an understanding of this Kentish landscape; no fixation, no obsessive return, under different conditions of light, to the garden and the surrounding countryside.

Churchill didn't look, he sat. He passed the time. The trick of painting, begun 'by accident' (as his daughter Mary Soames explains), 'took the role of a therapy, distracting him from the traumatic debacle of the 1915 Dardanelles campaign'. No such therapy was available to those unfortunates who were there, in the hell of it. The endless views strung around the Chartwell estate become a gloss on dark history; florid rehabilitation, a strategy for elective amnesia. The paintings are never about the situation the painter is confronting, they confirm the position in which he set his stool: lakes and arbours and beaches.

A few palm trees, a distant snow-covered range of mountains.

Churchill took up this practice, as a relief from deep depression, while staying in a rented farmhouse, near Godalming. A tame expert was wheeled in for complimentary advice: society portraitist Sir John Lavery. Then came Sickert, the friend of Degas, frequenter of music halls, murder obsessive: master of varnished darkness, half-drunk pints, the urban condition (boredom). Sickert, not ashamed to use a newspaper photograph as the basis for a composition, taught Churchill to project slides on to canvas, to bypass line-drawing.

If brought to it, if forced, Churchill could be 'paintatious' (his word) about Chartwell. The Weald, under snow, as seen from the drawing-room window. The Honorary Academician Extraordinary, exhibiting under the pseudonym of 'David Winter', had no trouble in being accepted for the summer show. Samuel Palmer sweated on rejection. The Golden Valley of Underriver was his invention, he affected it; the way future generations have come to see it. He imagined – and therefore established – a secret paradise; accessible in a period of innocence, then lost. The Palmer industry is rudimentary, a few walkers, an art school. The only book on Palmer stocked by Tate Britain was not displayed on the shelves, had to be searched out when I requested it. There was a late flurry of interest in Palmer when his works were faked by Tom Keating, the tricks of vision easily duplicated.

Churchill's *Painting as a Pastime* remains in print, along with postcard reproductions, videos, mugs, coasters, key rings. This much-visited, much-admired National Trust property is the ultimate point for the tourist who wants to leave London without leaving London; the paradox of an open asylum in which the demons of history can be drugged with scents, bright colours and a prostituted landscape.

5

After Westerham, we cross the young Darent, and then the M25; heading north. The six-lane section of motorway (naked central reservation, modestly planted soft estate) is balm to our spirits. In the distance, to the east, the road is beginning to curve, anticipating our journey up the Darent Valley. For once the speeding transients are playing it by the book, observing the correct distances between vehicles. There are no jousting heavy-goods lorries travelling in packs. Our river/road is sublimely democratic: it has endured Surrey and Kent, counties that prefer to pretend it's not there, and it is heading home. Of course, an orbital motorway can't have a home, but it can have memory, a starting point: Junction 1a with its toll booths, its sense of being a frontier post. The crossing of the Thames at Dartford. Multiple-choice highways. Essex or the coast. Canterbury, Greenwich. The Bluewater retail pit.

In my mythology, the M25 is born of the Thames: conceived at Runnymede (by Staines), dying at Dartford. In bloody twilight. Echoes of Eliot: 'Burning burning burning burning.' Misbegotten in an upriver canoe. Expiring in oil slicks. Grey to grey: the immense skies of the Thames Estuary. Liquid to light: an Aegyptian temple beneath Runnymede Bridge (with its golden bars, its smoky shadows). Out of these mysteries comes a metalled ribbon of consciousness, that saga of simultaneity: a tidal motorway carrying the psychic freight of all the landmass it contains.

The uplift, after the deadening effect of Westerham, is in finding ourselves on Beggars Lane – which flows into Green Lane, before being absorbed by the Pilgrims Way. It feels as though we have come through some sort of test. The hedges are high and the air is ripe (humming, throbbing) – with slurry. We might be the last humans. Uninhabited lanes and deserted farmhouses (protected by barking dogs) remind us, yet again, of *The War of the Worlds*. Complacency and patriotism, the givens of a great empire, challenged by fanatical aliens, viral invaders, off-screen primitives. It's wafer thin, a membrane, the liberal-democratic consensus: aspirations, dialogue, technological advances. Pyres of dead sheep, smouldering dumps, are always in the next field. The estate, hidden behind a screen of poplars, contains a row of bacteriological research prefabs, where whitecoats are paid to think the unthinkable. To amuse themselves with 'worst case' scenarios.

On a farm, between the M25 and the Pilgrims Way, I take the final photograph that turns out to be something close to what I intended: a mass of tyres holding down a black polythene mound. A long-roofed barn, the kind Samuel Palmer liked to sketch, peeps over the curve of this Michelin dome. Call it: *Death of the Motorway*. A beach of black rubber necklaces. A negative of the Great White Tent on Bugsby's Marshes.

Focus, which had been playing up since we left Merstham, gave way entirely: *into the Valley of Vision*. My spectacles were lost, abandoned, and my camera had a bad case of the Gerhard Richters: Richter pastoral. Snapshots with the shivers. The results, from here on, were truer to the way I felt, the way I *really* saw the road, than all my previous impersonal loggings. Incompetence meant: insight. Inscapes. The photograph of 'Renchi on the Pilgrims Way' is a painterly stew, not an identity card. The abandoned blue shirt, hanging across the white ground of the T-shirt, is a squeeze of Vlaminck.

There is liberation in these soft images. The road sign I recorded, PILGRIMS WAY, is now a long thin shape that defies interpretation; you can't tell if it's stone or tin. But the green that surrounds it, busy with black smears, white floaters, has a wondrous ambiguity. I've never (on our orbital walk) had the courage to let go in this way, the economics of photography require a visible return. I'm only doing it to keep a record of where we've been, the provocative details I'm sure to forget.

There is no detail. Wrecked focal length has pushed me into territory explored and espoused by visionary filmmakers such as Stan Brakhage (friend of the Black Mountain poets). The optics of risk. ('My first instruction, then: if you happen to have a light meter – give it away,' Brakhage wrote. 'We must deal with the light *of* Nature, then with the Nature of Light. And set your science aside, please, as we've no more use for it than what is *of* it as embodied in the camera in hand.')

The blurred images, first, simplify the narrative – then worry me towards a deeper, more considered sense of place. What doesn't matter – script, commentary, hierarchy of significance – vanishes. It seems that the 'faulty' camera is now dictating the terms: I didn't pass it over to anyone met on the road, no such person existed. And yet, here we are, developed print in hand: Renchi and I in the same image. Two figures standing in a gap in the hedge. Distance is realised by bands of colour. The white lines on the road float free – like angelic footsteps. The camera, unprompted, has produced a double portrait.

Notice: a dead hare. Leaping. Flying. A messenger spirit; ears erect, hind legs stretched. With sharp focus, the creature is a roadside casualty, crawling with flies. Roadkill unworthy of the satchel. Now it's a force of nature.

The rest of our walk is recorded on the same terms: soft shapes, ripe colour, more dream than document.

Our way, respecting the lie of the land, was straightforward: in theory, on the map. A footpath through Chevening Wood, across the north-flowing M25, to Otford. It had been a long day, but the early evening light, the North Downs behind us, churches among woods, brought us close to Samuel Palmer and his nocturnal wanderings.

I was delighted to find, in a letter from Palmer to George

Richmond (fellow 'Ancient'), intimations of the appropriate astigmatic vision. Palmer, met in town, was an eccentric figure: short, enveloped at all seasons in a trailing coat, protected by the broad rim of a Mad Hatter's topper. His arms and legs were afterthoughts, vestigial appendages on a stubby torso. He felt the cold. He wore long white mufflers, layers of waistcoat. His coat was a tent. Every stroll through London was an expedition: pockets bulging with spare rations (biscuits, pies, cheese), inkwells, pens, sketch pads and libraries of books. Eyebrows lofted in an expression of perpetual surprise – the world too much in his face – he blinked behind a pair of large round spectacles. He was well aware of his own absurdity, he knew that he set young ladies 'a-giggle'. From Shoreham, on 14 November 1827, he wrote to Richmond:

Tell them that herein is my disadvantage – whereas mine eyes are dim save when I look at a fair lady – and whereas I can only see their lustre thro' my goggles, those said unlucky goggles so scratch'd and spoil'd that all the fire of the love darting artillery of my eyes is lost upon *them* and rebounds not to my advantage, the ladies seeing only two huge misty spheres of light scratchd and scribbled over like the sun in a fog or dirty dish in a dark pantry, as lustre lacking, as leaden and as lifeless as a lad without a lady. But tell them sometimes to think on me, as I very often think of them, as in sullen twilight rambles, sweet visions of lovely bright eyes suddenly sparkle round me, lume my dusky path – double the vigour of my pace, rebuild my manhood and renew my youth.

Our sullen twilight ramble ran straight up against the Chevening Estate; private road, path denied. A considerable detour. Arthur Mee in his guide to Kent writes of 'a beautiful public walk through the park'. A walk that is now off-limits. We strain local hospitality by finding a hosepipe, with which to top up our water bottles, alongside a muck heap in the Home Farm.

'Kent has no lovelier corner so near to London,' gushes Mee. 'It comes at the end of a lane that has no turning.' This is very true. But turn we must, for a weary half-circuit of the park, dropping close to the motorway – before coming back to the village and St Botolph's Church.

Chevening was the home of the Stanhopes. The house, Mee guessed, was 'basically probably Inigo Jones'. Basically probable or not, the version I carried home, a smudge among the trees, would require an Indiana Jones to unravel its secrets: the private chapel, the Tudor and Elizabethan tombs that predated the Stanhopes.

Also buried here was the third earl, Charles Stanhope, politician and experimental scientist, who married William Pitt's sister. Stanhope, aspiring to oblivion, erasure, asked to be interred at Chevening: as 'a man of no account'. As a politician, the third earl acquired the nickname of 'Citizen Stanhope', by proposing to acknowledge the French Revolution. He found himself in a parliamentary minority of one. A medal was struck with that motto.

Mee glosses Citizen Stanhope's scientific achievements: 'He invented means for safe-guarding buildings against fire, took out patents for steam vessels, devised printing appliances which he presented to the public, perfected a process of stereotyping, had original ideas about electricity, shared lightning-conductor experiments with Benjamin Franklin, invented a microscopic lens which bears his name, devised a new way of making cement more durable, and found a way of curing wounds in trees.'

He walked about the village, alone, talking to himself, gesturing violently; a care-in-the-community aristo who brooded on cement overcoats for patching wounds in lightning-struck trees. The sort of free-associating, lateral-thinking boffin who might well have conceived of an orbital motorway – before the invention of the internal combustion engine. Before television existed to feather his pension.

My slanted, out-of-focus church tower (St Botolph's) is a homage to Stanhope. We have to conjure some human presence to revive this latest empty village, this evening set. We're in the claw of the motorway, the volute of Junction 5. From the road, motorists barely notice the hills, parks, spires: Samuel Palmer quotations. They have no sense of what it is to be *in* the village of Chevening at twilight; the golds and the greens, the avenue alongside the burying ground. Such (oppressive) tranquillity can only be achieved by taking land into the custodianship of the MOD, the National Trust, an exclusive golf course. The Pilgrims Way, a clear path from Titsey to Otford, suffers from indignities inflicted by private landlords and estate managers.

Closing on the M25, by Lime Pit Lane, we pass Morant's Court Farm. This was where London carters, coming out of town through Bromley, dropped Samuel Palmer's visitors: the Ancients, John Linnell, William and Catherine Blake. Palmer would send out a boy to meet them, guide them in, by just the way we were walking. Linnell, notoriously careful with his cash, tried to arrange his own transport on carts carrying furniture or farm produce. In 1829, unwell, in need of recuperation, revival of spirits, he arrived with George Richmond at Morant's Court Hill: to be greeted by 'a strangely dressed figure with a wheelbarrow'. He was trundled away, oblivious to the remarks of coachman and passengers, towards the village of Shoreham.

The delusion persists: the Valley of Vision, Earthly Paradise, is a one-day walk from London (Charing Cross or Millennium Dome, according to taste). A few hours, drudging through industrial dereliction, suburbs, captured villages, will carry the walker into Arcadia. Or, at worst, the town dweller's version of it. The dream. Linnell, broken in health, vexed by his large family, wrote to Palmer: 'I have found so much benefit from my short visit to your valley . . . I Dream of being there every night almost and when I wake it is some time before I recollect that I am at Bayswater.'

Sleep channels open. Lost highways matted with grass. City life is made tolerable by the knowledge that a single day's travel will deposit you in this bowl of tranquillity. Waltham Abbey, Shoreham, the Lea and Darent Valleys: paradise reservations. So it seemed. So the Victorian artists (craftsmen, seekers) insisted: selective vision. Varnished and glowing; red and gold and green. William Blake's methods adapted to piety and senti- ment. Rick burning, trade unionism, Luddite outrages: such manifestations of rural discontent were denounced. The Valley of Vision was a Tuscany for weekend runaways in search of the Simple Life (i.e. cheap farmhouse lodgings, cider, music, the romance of hop picking). Palmer loved September. He was always trying to persuade his mates to come down for the hop season; so picturesque, autumnal – exclusive.

The forensic sharpness of Linnell, Palmer – and, in due course, the Pre-Raphaelites – is contradicted by the evidence of my out-of-focus camera. The motorway really could be water. When Blake made his only visit to Shoreham, in a stage wagon (like a pioneer trekking to the American West), drawn by a team of horses, he didn't appear as outlandish as the Ancients – who wandered the countryside declaiming from *Macbeth* and talking talking talking. Blake settled in a smoky chimney-corner with his churchwarden pipe, to discuss (with Palmer's rackety, bookseller father) what they called 'the traverse of sympathy'.

What should have been our golden road, our 'traverse of sympathy', carrying us outside the M25 and down to Otford, was a long-shadowed hell: Palmer's sticky nocturnes invaded by Robert Crumb. Ugly motors eager to do damage. Rage pods caught between hedges. Better to head off, dodging oncoming traffic in the fast lane of the motorway, than stick with the Pilgrims Way. It's a rat run, the revenge of the com- muters. Deserted villages are coming to life: it's madness, so we're told, twice a day. And death-in-life the rest of the time. Lights on, blue TV windows, dogs to walk.

We manage to get off the road – which has no verge – and into the fields, the heavy earth; but we're soon returned. There is no other route. Every third car is a red Jag: either they've been watching too many episodes of *Morse*, or they want to hide the roadkill on the paintwork. Otford, with its quaint High Street, its proudly timbered survivors, its pond and Tudor ruins, is notable, so far as we're concerned, for one feature: the railway station.

Here Offa fought a great battle with the Men of Kent. He has my sympathies. A few more miles of the Pilgrims Way (twinned with Brands Hatch) and I'd be ready for Linnell's wheelbarrow. It's been a long haul, but we've made it to the Darent Valley; now we can head north, back to the Thames.

Our train journeys (reverse commuting) are always unreal. People heading into London are dressed for action, talking compulsively (if in company), unable to sit still if travelling alone. We're slumped, dirty, silent: if we look out of the window at the flashing suburbs, it feels as if we're cheating. Train travel is a film for which we haven't bought a ticket. *Otefort*. Otta's ford. The otter is one of the 'clean' animals of Zoroastrianism; which, with the dog, it is a great sin to kill. Put aside that grim final hour on the road. Let it be. We'll be back before Palmer's hop season is over.

6

We had been standing for ever, outside the station at Otford, the group of us. A hard moon pinging up and down like a table-tennis ball dancing on a fountain. Day/night, day/night: to the end of time. The death of the cosmos in William Hope Hodgson's Wellsian fantasy, *The House on the Borderland*.

We posed for photographs beside the fence: WE'RE WORK-ING ON YOUR STATION/RAILTRACK. We were a self-conscious restatement of Samuel Palmer's gang, the Shoreham Ancients; city folk up for a ramble. Too loud. Too early. Too many.

Time was squeezing, closing us down: 27 September 1999. We had three months – three walks? – to make it back to Waltham Abbey and down the Lea Valley to the Millennium Dome. Before the Big Night.

The Darent Valley brought them out of their pits: Kevin Jackson (who had been in strict training, jogging up library steps, marching to the bar) and Marc Atkins, loping towards the ticket machine at London Bridge, at the finely calculated last moment; the depth of stubble on his cranium precisely dupli-cating that on his chin. Kevin's leather jacket, which dazzled the payroll boys in the station café at Staines, has contracted leprosy. It's been on manoeuvres. It may, unilaterally, have invaded somewhere hot and dusty. Kevin grins, blinks. Hands in pockets (baggy tracksuit trousers). Trainers instead of boots. Big hair, head on the tilt. 'Moose', his friend Peter Carpenter calls him. I can see it, the powerful head as a trophy: nailed to the wall. He's serious about this walk, serious about cutting back on the reference books. He's here to be here. To pick up camera tips from Marc.

We're happy to be heading for the Thames at Dartford. But, even though we'll be travelling within a few fields of the M25, we are losing its acoustic footprints. The chalk hills, covered in beechwood, will act as a baffle. We have to take the continued presence of the motorway on trust; believing that it won't let us down. It'll be there at the finish.

A full moon, analgesic, above a double-camera surveillance pole. Crossed contrails. The pink (of an experimental rabbit's eye) over Sevenoaks and the Weald. Rain has been promised: hence, my golfing umbrella. I picked it up in Middlesex Street for £3. I hate umbrellas, the way they poke at you on narrow pavements; the look of them, mean when furled, dangerous in action. A downpour drove me to it. This umbrella, brought out for the first time, gave a certain bounce to our Otford survey. It was useful for pointing at fancy brickwork, repelling the natives.

The well of St Thomas à Becket is to be found in private grounds. We prowl the boundaries. Renchi attempts conversation with a dog walker who has acquired the full English dog-walking kit: green wellies, shooting jacket (velvet shoulder-patches), Black Forest hat with optional ear flaps. A monster hound, shaggy and sodden, tracks us, barging into our knees, demanding attention.

The town is asleep and therefore as close as it's going to come to being outside time. Otford and the Darent Valley connect with remembrances of pre-industrial Europe; poplars, gardens with statues and fountains, vineyards, grey walls topped with red tiles. Low hills in soft light. The villa. Roman traces that haven't been totally obliterated by road and railway.

The duck pond is listed. And the ducks get a food allowance from the parish council. The greengrocer and the chemist have given up, closed down. Countryside hangs on to anything that can be turned into a postcard, but is uninterested in preserving community (though debating it continually, as a way of keeping out disruptive influences, unsuitable immigrants). It works pretty well if you can afford it; if you shop in the Bluewater quarry.

We touch the walls of buildings to dowse for lost heat. St Bartholomew's Church, with its sharp flints and whitish clunch, ironstone from the Lower Greensand, material cannibalised from Roman middens, is a geological accretion; an expression of place scratched out of the immediate locality. Visitors moon around, in quest of revelation, expecting the unexpected, the previously unnoticed clue. Pevsner descriptions, lists of physical features, dates, methods of construction, don't help. Old superstitions stay with us. The church as a fixture in time, a place of compulsory attendance: christened, confirmed, married, buried. Heritaged grass squeaks with forgotten voices, clumsy boots tramping over dead faces.

We have to accept the version written on the board. A detached tower stands for an ecclesiastical palace, gifted by Cranmer to Henry VIII. An outsider, such as the poet/filmmaker Pier Paolo Pasolini, can take a pile of medieval bricks, an arch or a barn, and give them back to us as an energised version of Chaucer. Riffraff and rentboys supplying the faces. The British have too much respect for antiquity to let it live. We need the strings, the madrigals, the explainers. Superstition draws us to these scars; we circle and poke. Bruce Chatwin quotes Werner Herzog: 'Walking is virtue, tourism deadly sin.'

We're walking tourists. We pass through landscapes on which we have no claim. We spend money in pubs. We visit the obligatory sights: churches, parks, bunkers, villages with literary or painterly associations. We take photographs. But, alongside the convivial agenda, is a ritual purpose: to exorcise the unthinking malignancy of the Dome, to celebrate the sprawl of London. Historical accuracy is less important, Chatwin asserts on Herzog's behalf, than 'authenticity of tone'. The English look ridiculous when they try to do a Kinski, pop-eyed, dirty white suit: the glare of unconsummated narcissism. Marc, who has been known to get his kit off as a performance artist, does his best. Raise your camera and he'll confront it. But the laugh is just a breath away, the ironic snort.

The Darent is high, fast-flowing after recent rain. Our path is clearly marked. We spot a kingfisher. By tall hedges, through fields and golf courses, we track the river to Shoreham. The young Darent clears debris to work a passage through the chalk. What seems to be a random sequence of twists and turns is no such thing. Rivers, so Kit Hart (of Islington's Hart Gallery) tells me, demonstrate a 'fundamental relationship between mathematics and science'. (Kit was quoting from *Fermat's Last Theorem*.) The length of a river (as walked, from source to mouth, following every meander) is three times the distance as the crow flies. 'The ratio is approximately 3.14 . . . the ratio between the circumference of a circle and its diameter.'

Indulging every whim of the Darent, putting in those extra miles, will remind us of the motorway orbit. Whatever we attempt, it will always feel three times as far as we expect. Distance is stretched to achieve a more satisfying sense of time.

It comes as a shock to find Shoreham where it is, so close to London. I suppose, with confused notions of Blake's Felpham (a suburb of Bognor Regis), I'd always assumed that Palmer's Shoreham was hidden among the South Downs: that Shoreham was in fact the Sussex Shoreham, Shoreham-by-Sea. Domesticated, after the Bloomsbury style, with a touch of Eric Gill's community at Ditchling. A morning's drive away. Shoreham was an exportable fable, an idyll; suspect, fraudulent, magical. Fixed at the equinox.

Nothing of the sort. Shoreham rubs shoulders with the Swanley interchange, with Brands Hatch, Orpington. Shoreham is just a wheel-spin off the M25. Staying on the road, you don't notice it. It doesn't register. No theme park, no shopping mall, no imprisoned animals.

Samuel Palmer was more perceptive; as a child, accompanying his father (another Sam), he tramped through Greenwich, Blackheath, Dulwich. Long excursions, hand in hand, by two troubled humans seeking out hinge places, transfiguring experiences. There were no angel trees in Palmer's Dulwich. The golden light was always in the next field. The Palmers knew the area between Greenwich Park and Dulwich as: 'the Gate into the World of Vision'.

The bright, sickly child (asthma, bronchitis) who had to be regularly braced at Margate and the restless man (bribed by his family to give up trade and behave like a pensioned gent) wandered for miles, eager to escape the gravity of London. The Valley of Vision was identified – as a moral landscape out of John Bunyan. Raymond Lister, the Palmer biographer, opens his study with a quote from *Pilgrim's Progress*.

Yea, I think there was a kind of sympathy between that Valley and him. For I never saw him better in all his pilgrimage than when he was in that Valley.

The orthodox account of Palmer is: precocious child, brief period – in the wake of his meeting with William Blake – of achievement at Shoreham (an Eden of light), marriage, visit to Italy, long decline into production-belt pieties.

There is truth in it, but the conventional picture (visionary succumbing to dreary domesticity) has led to the decline in Palmer's reputation: he's tagged as a follower of Blake, a proto-hippie who got religion. But Palmer, as premature psychogeographer, deserves reconsideration. Some of his letters to fellow Ancients, Richmond and Frederick Tatham, are as wild and freewheeling as Neal Cassady. Everything of Palmer's present, his *now*, had to be squeezed on to those pages. The Shoreham postman becomes a messenger of fate, waiting to bear away every compulsive communication before its argument can be concluded. The sheets of paper, so his correspondents felt, must have been torn from Palmer's hands.

He was never prepared, even when his father-in-law John Linnell pressed him, to make an accurate record of natural forms, the scene that stood before him. In his sketchbooks, Palmer allowed forms to become archetypes. He scribbled in the margins, talked to himself:

Note that when you go to Dulwich it is not enough on coming home to make recollections in which shall be united the scattered parts about those sweet fields into a sentimental and Dulwich looking whole No but considering Dulwich as the gate into the world of vision one must try behind the hills to bring up a mystic glimmer.

Shoreham is still a removed place, a cleft between close hills. We felt its shadowy, covert nature – dark cottages, tangled orchards; it was damp, folded in on itself and its history. Otford was more exposed, caught at a sharp angle between two motorways, M25 and M26. Shoreham was hidden. A sudden turn, a drop in the road, and out of nowhere we're up against the church and the river.

The old High Street was dead. Victorian shops kept their shape, but no longer had a purpose. There was nothing to sell. In 1914 there were twenty shops in the village, now there is one. The only active concern is a small house that, from May to September, doubles as an Aircraft Museum. Relics from the Battle of Britain. The operators have a box of leaflets at their door, soliciting 'aircraft parts, uniforms, eye witness accounts of any aircraft shot down over Southern England during World War II'. The Paul Nash moment is always a possibility in the Kentish woods and fields: the shattered fuselage, the opaque cockpit containing a skull in a flying helmet. A wristwatch around bone.

Renchi has found someone to interrogate: a man (with unnaturally black hair) wearing a light blue shirt and dark blue, sleeveless sweater. A uniform of sorts. Renchi, who lives in the country, recognised him as a postman. In Hackney, we've forgotten that such occupations still exist. Even here the post office is a private house, its ancient logo another heritage decoration. The postman points the way to Palmer's cottage.

Although it looks the part, and we invade the grounds to fire off a fusillade of photographs, this is *not* Palmer's cottage: SAMUEL PALMER SCHOOL OF FINE ART. The house, Reedbeds, is where Australian artist Frank White set up his school in 1958. Timber-framed, lead-windowed, with cross beams, panels of blackened flint, the school is altogether too much: Palmer's life as it should have been.

Renchi won't buy it. Usually the first to invade any property that comes our way, he stays in the road. 'Arty,' he growls – when I photograph the heavy, moist apples that hang low in the orchard behind the house. The whole set is a commentary on Palmer, and Palmer's Shoreham, and nothing to do with the man or his work. Teaching was the bane, the anguish of Palmer's married life: it was the only way of generating a small income, hours of drudgery. It saw him banished to West London and Redhill. Letters, from now on, would be about bills, money, American stocks: 'the kind of people we are obliged to associate with – and from whom I get pupils'.

Palmer lived in a dirty and dilapidated cottage known as 'Rat Abbey'. And then at Water House. When he came with Tatham to the Valley of Vision in the spring of 1826, it was an escape, a chance to play at being 'Ancients'. As with Pre-Raphaelites, Arties and Crafties, hippies, the paradigm was lost in the past: medieval, Gothic – without plagues, torture, hunger and ice. Discretionary poverty. Cider. Bread. Cheese. Nuts. Green tea. Optional peasants bringing in the hops. Poverty which, in Palmer's case (as with so many of Notting Hill's countercultural elite of the Sixties), was underwritten by a small private income and a property portfolio. A legacy from his grandfather allowed him 5*s*. 2*d*. a week. His Shoreham holdings included: 'a Dwelling House Two Tenements . . . another

Dwelling House . . . containing Seven Apartments and Pantrys, and Seven Sleeping Rooms above; also sundry Timber Built Sheds and a small Barn and Stabling'. William Yates, a wheelwright, paid a yearly rental of £21 – 'of which Samuel Palmer always returned One Pound, and this in spite of the opening of the London Chatham and Dover Railway in 1860 with possible developments for the Shoreham Valley'.

Coming away from the small room where Blake and his wife lodged, off the Strand, the Ancients took Shoreham as the realisation of a (misunderstood) pastoral idyll. These door-knob kissing sentimentalists tumbled, by accident, through the gilded frame. And entered a Valley of Vision.

Palmer to Richmond, November 1827:

I have beheld as in the spirit, such nooks, caught such glimpses of the perfumed and enchanted twilight – of natural midsummer, as well as, at some other times of day, other scenes, as passed thro' the intense separating transmuting heat of the soul's alchymy, would divinely consist with the severe and stately port of the human, as with the moon thron'd among constellations, and varieties of lesser glories, the regal pomp and glistening brilliance and solemn attendance of her starry train.

This 'intense separating transmuting heat of the soul's alchymy' is what Palmer chased – even when the result was a portfolio of waxy, impacted views and willed visions. The claustrophobic tightness of his compositions reflects the hermetic self-satisfaction of the Darent Valley: moons become blades, elm and beech and oak are pressed into bloodless rituals. Treat the Shoreham paintings as unlocated eclogues and they are revealed as Christmas cards, labels for honey jars; but track them to source, bringing some of Linnell's Calvinistic exactitude to the task, and the window opens.

The Ancients, sneaking about in thunderstorms, hiding in hollows, tramping the woods at night, were suspect.

'Extollagers', the locals called them: conjurers, mountebanks. Their three-legged camp stools were taken for magical instruments. Suspicions were justified. Hymns in cornfields. Shakespeare's witches summoned to Jenkin's Neck Wood.

Parodic fecundity. Plump apples. Legless sheep like cotton-wool maggots. Church spire as pyramid. 'The clouds drop fatness,' Palmer wrote on the mount of *The Valley Thick with Corn*. The yokel in the fields doesn't labour, he reads a book: as if the harvest were to be brought in by the proper order of words, by magic. Such prolix ripeness makes its contrary inevitable: virus, pestilence, burning pits.

Blake's visions were anchored in the ordinary. They happened. Angel trees. Voices. Visitations from the mythic dead. They dropped in, his gods, when it was convenient for the Lambeth artisan to receive them, when the day's work was done. Glistening fleas with bowls of blood. If they made a nuisance of themselves, they could be dismissed.

The walk, the journey out, was Palmer's method. If he pushed hard enough, he would surely arrive at the Valley of Vision. It was there to be found – beyond Forest Hill and Bromley. Visionary tourism. Of the kind we practised; linking place with place, going with the drift, meandering through burial grounds and golf courses.

'It is not enough coming home to make recollections in which shall be united the scattered parts.' I knew that Palmer was right; the uniting of parts was beyond me. What should I make of Palmer's visit to Hackney? He hadn't wanted to go, to stay with a Welshman in Pembroke House, a private asylum. But he was obliged by the overweening pressure of Celtic hospitality – and his hope that 'a day at Hackney from which *I cannot get off* will give me fresh vigour for a new set of work'. Rural Hackney, a suburb of market gardens and madhouses, captured Samuel Palmer – for one night only. He was interrupted, dragged away from a half-finished drawing; brought to sleep in a house of troubled dreamers. Hackney and Shoreham were twinned, in order to promote future pilgrimages. 'Fresh vigour'. The kind of journey that exists only if it is worth recording.

In Palmer's day, as he points out in a letter to John Linnell, it was 'very nearly as cheap' to buy produce in Shoreham as in Borough Market, Southwark. Under the arches, by Southwark Cathedral, hops could be 'got retail at less price than you would have paid for in its own garden'. Villages within a forty-mile circuit of London found themselves buying their own goods back – at a premium. The retail logic of Bluewater was already in place.

The Shoreham produce on which Palmer and his mates glutted themselves was only there because the local farmers supplied the London markets. The Ancients picnicked on loss-leaders, damaged goods; windfall that wasn't required in the city. Tastes that were too unsophisticated for metropolitans.

In September 1999, at Palmer's favourite season, no breakfast was to be had in the village. So the postman informed us. No call for it. We must go out onto the road, the A225, to a coffee stall.

Huge sunflowers sway against the red brick of the church wall. BLESSED ARE THE DEAD. So it says on the lych gate (where the bier was set down, during burial services, to await the coming of the clergyman). Marc Atkins stoops to photograph a sundial. A yew walk leads the eye towards low hills.

We straggle out of town. And there, in a lay-by on the busy Shoreham Road, is Daisy's van: dispenser of monster burgers to the carriage trade. A forlorn cyclist in yellow helmet, rain top and tights is the only other customer. Daisy's cuisine is criminal, the double cheeseburger is obscenely good value. It oozes yolk and tomato sauce and melted goo. Even Marc's veggie burger looks a shovel of squashed hedgehog. His side order of refried potatoes, a coronary indulgence, spills from the plate. Rain drips into our blue-glaze coffee mugs. We settle ourselves around several white plastic tables, munching and mono-loguing, and trying to make ourselves heard above the traffic, the downpour; the commuter trains squealing into Shoreham station.

Nothing much on Palmer remains in print; the connection with Shoreham is kept alive by the tourist industry, by an extension of the blue plaque thesis. Addresses are of interest if a literary or social association can be claimed. The story must be grounded. *The Valley Thick with Corn* is franchised as a Shoreham illustration, even though its location is generic – and it dates from the period immediately before Palmer moved out of London.

The specific was always troublesome. In 1849, long after he left Shoreham, Palmer wrote: 'If I am spared to go again into the country I hope to begin a new plan – not sitting down to local matter, but walking and watching.' Walking and watching defined his art. Fretful movement to discover a landscape win-dow, a boudoir of the picturesque – to be prettied up, peeked at through scratched spectacles.

As a sickly, hypochondriac old man exiled to Redhill, Palmer was ordered by his medical adviser to take some exer-cise. He had managed no more, in months, than an arthritic shuffle around the garden, kicking at weeds. Beyond the limits of his property, two walks were possible: 'he dreaded the ordeal of either route'. The view had been ruined, he spluttered in traditional suburbanite fashion, by developers. Wrapped in an enveloping Inverness cloak, a copy of Virgil's *Bucolics* in his pocket, he dragged himself to a certain five-barred gate.

'Having touched the gate-post,' as his son Herbert reports, 'he returned scowling with anger and disgust much as a member of a chain gang goes back after exercise to prison.'

The business of the gate is pertinent. Gates are handy as des-tinations, somewhere to lean, a framing device: they promote a view. Weekenders walk to gates. Remember the sequence in

Joseph Losey's *Accident*? (Screenplay by Harold Pinter from a novel by Nicholas Mosley.) The unstructured Sunday afternoon (tennis, overlapping meals, booze, boredom): a short country stroll to work up a thirst, a five-barred gate. A few ominously inconsequential remarks: flies, nettles, corrugated earth.

When the M25 circuit had been completed, and much of the first draft written, Renchi and I returned to Kent to find a five-barred gate. Palmer's Valley of Vision, stretching from Dulwich to Shoreham, didn't finish there: it went on with the Darent to Otford, and beyond. A day's walk to the south: to Underriver. The Golden Valley: the 'heat of the soul's infabulous alchymy'. Palmer's nocturnal ramblings took him into the hills above Sevenoaks, where he watched the sun rise over 'the flower of Kentish scenery'.

After marriage and the Italian tour, Palmer settled in London – but made regular excursions to Cornwall and Wales, in search of exploitable scenery. From Tintern Abbey he wrote to George Richmond, begging him to 'come hither'. The sublime in its tamest form appealed to Palmer. He had no taste for the cosmic agitation of Turner. 'After my pastoral has had a month's stretching into epic I feel here a most grateful relaxation and am become once more a pure quaint crinkle-crankle goth,' he gushed.

The quaint and the crinkle-crankle are what he found at Underriver. He lodged at Underriver House – now a private property, unhandsome but very sure of itself. Palmer and Linnell produced reams of five-barred gates, views from an eminence on Rook's Hill: Linnell's 'Underriver', Palmer's *The Golden Valley, or Harvesting with Distant Prospect*. We set out to find this spot. Renchi had his sketchbook, his coloured pens.

The morning was misty: we saw nothing beyond the hawsers as we crossed the Dartford Bridge. At Underriver, the mist lifted. We parked in a pub and set off through the usual empty lanes. The Palmer franchise was everywhere in evidence: unpicked fruit, blackberries in the hedges, orchards, cobwebs on gates. Round the back of Underriver House, at the end of a gravel drive, we spotted something that might have inspired Palmer's pen and ink drawing of 1829, *Ancient Barn*. Except that the barn had enjoyed a tasteful and imaginative make-over (along with every other Kentish oast house): it was now, certainly, a property – with studio windows, bright wood, a managed garden.

A man we met in the lane – affable, alert, in trainers and jogging gear, walking a lean dog (with a pedigree that shamed us) – confirmed the barn's provenance. He was the owner. It was murder, he said, for an hour every morning (ten minutes from the motorway), then peace returned. The Golden Valley was regilded. It seemed an enviable way of life: morning walk, restored barn. If you had the equity.

Past Absaloms, another heritage farm, we climbed Rooks Hill. Remembering the Palmer catalogue – *Near Underriver* (*c.* 1843) and *View from Rooks Hill* (1843) – we felt sure we were on the right track for our five-barred gate (now replaced by a stile). Yes, this was it. The same gap in the trees. The Golden Valley revealed, pretty much as the painters had it. Palmer's red-roof barn is now a corrugated shed. His melancholy cattle are pigs in hooped shelters; industrial swine, pre-bacon lollers in shit. A few goats. From the corrugated shed, a screeching of guinea fowl (who have just had their fortunes told) puts the necessary tremble into the landscape.

As Renchi sketches, the mist clears. A reference book – *Underriver (Samuel Palmer's Golden Valley)* by Griselda Barton and Michael Tong – is open on his lap; the double page of Linnell and Palmer spread out for comparison. A line of poplars interrupts the prospect. Gentle hills to the south, the rim of the Weald. Palmer doesn't do smell or sound (as Breughel does), he's interested in grading light; achieving float, solipsism. A landscape voyeur. A peeper through curtains of foliage. He prospects, he acts as a pimp for estate agents and developers. This place is magic: buy it.

We returned to Shoreham by the back route, avoiding Sevenoaks. It was important, we felt, to make the sideways link with the M25. On the day of that first expedition, with Kevin and Marc, we had walked the Darent Valley like a ditch – seeing trains, but having to imagine the motorway.

Driving out of London towards the coast, you might notice a traffic-monitoring camera on a pole sticking out of woodland, just after Junction 4. That was our marker. To the west of Shoreham you climb steeply; the village tidies itself away, leaving the church spire. You come up alongside the chalk cross, mentioned on the war memorial by the river. After the first ascent, through Meenfield Wood, you hear the chant of the M25. Intimations of civilisation.

Down across fields to Timberden Bottom, then another brief ascent to the tunnel under the motorway. Shivering against a five-barred gate is a dying animal, a sheep covered in flies. There are no shepherds, few farms. Renchi sets off to find a human who might be interested in the loss of his investment. Empty houses, barking dogs: no resolution. A mascara of black insects outlines the sheep's blank stare, the white rubber eyes. They feed on dead sight.

Renchi is being slightly mysterious about our destination: Badger's Mount (which is depicted on the OS map as an enclosure of spiked huts). When we emerge on the west side, the motorway is still with us, visible through the woods. We are back inside the hoop. We circumnavigate Badger's Mount, which is indeed an enigma, coy about its attractions. The perimeter is a wilderness of impenetrable scrub, low fences woven in, piss-off signs (courtesy of MOD).

A fortnight after the World Trade Center attack, paranoia is justified; it sings. Now I remember a postcard Renchi sent, after the first Shoreham walk, that said:

In Cambridge I dug again for anecdotal reference to unblock the blank disguise of the North Downs and discovered there was an Earth Tremor in Westerham in the 18th century that shook buildings and caused more than a ripple on the pond. Sadly the earth did not open quite wide enough to swallow two of their local heroes . . .

Another angle came from a friend's brother's partner's nephew who worked for a defence contract at Fort Halstead (not on the map but near the M25 near Otford) with computer company LOGICA.

The village we were approaching was Halstead, ribbon-development filling a fork in the road. Why should such a place, where you might meet a traffic cop having a tea break, boast of a substantial 'Police Office'? And nothing else: beyond 'Church, remains of', Old Rectory and pub.

Politically sensitive forensic investigations, Renchi had heard. Fragments bagged when the bombers hit the City or Docklands. Badger's Mount to Fort Halstead: the story of the motorway circuit, of England. His instinct about this site was confirmed by the presence of sanctioned woodland (the sort that reminds me of Alfred Hitchcock, sylvan backdrops hovering at the margin of disbelief). Here, once again, was that Epping Forest mix: trails for the disadvantaged, bird cards – and bunkers where the police gun down cut-out terrorists. Check in at the hut, pick up a leaflet: Orchid Walk, Owl Walk, Lizard Walk. ('The Lizard walk is also available in a large printed booklet for the visually impaired.') Obey the rules: 'Continue through the kissing gate, here the woods open up to shrub land. Turn a quarter right towards the bottom of the valley and continue up the other side to a concrete stile.'

Ecology and secrecy. Fort Halstead is a green fort. Tony Sangwine, the motorway horticulturalist, began with the MOD. First, a protective curtain of greenery. Then creative planting to improve the quality of life for the mole people, the Official Secrets mob. Whoever laid out Fort Halstead did a good job. Scrub, thorn and thicket at the rim, then tall trees and low buildings (after the fashion of the Royal Gunpowder Mills at Waltham Abbey). You don't see the barbed wire and the swivelling CCTV cameras – until you make the initial penetration, until it's too late.

An off-road vehicle with official markings tracks us, all the way from the roundabout, keeping its distance. There is only one entrance to the Fort. A long driveway, screened on both sides, leading to a set of gates. The police vehicle parks itself by the gates. No challenge, nothing said. I'm not taking out my Sony DV. I'm not risking an out-of-focus snap. A quick Palmer doodle from Renchi would summon a snatch squad. It's all for our own good, of course. To preserve democracy and the free world. If we've learnt anything on our tramp, it's this: Blake was right. Energy can only be understood as a system of contraries, polarities, oppositions: Fort Halstead mirrored, across the M25, by Samuel Palmer's Shoreham. Palmer at Underriver working in pen and ink to counter Churchill's splashy Chartwell oils. The world is kept in balance, the wheel spins. Blake was wise enough to journey in his imagination: 'over trembling Thames to Shooters' Hill and thence to Blackheath, the dark Woof'. Fort Halstead, surrounded by orchids and lizards and owls, was the kennel of that Woof.

7

After Shoreham, going north, the fields are damp, footpaths puddled. Patterns of mud combed by tyre tracks. Crisscrossing lines: a desert seen from space. Flinty ground between diminishing avenues of herbs. A low, featureless sky. Everything drips and drags. We have to pull our boots from the suck of clay.

Marc and Kevin, allied by height, by philosophies of the camera, drift back: in conversation. Equestrian tackle is hung, drying, from metal gates. Horse-heads nudge over fences. Not a day for riding.

The approved walk is an illustrated book, better read than experienced. The post-Shoreham landscape is Italian, predicated on an assumption of sunlight. Lullingstone, tight to the A225, has its castle, lake and Roman villa. Therefore: kids. Teachers, buses.

The villa is kept, for its own protection, inside a shed. 'Is this a post office?' one of the children asks. Ghost voices inside the hangar come from audio commentaries. Curators enjoy their *Gladiator* moment. The river path colludes; farm, fertile valley – with no visible obstruction to contradict the mood, no unsightly industry.

Wildlife display panels are trailers for shy birds who dip and flutter and disappear. Willow and alder and dark oak guide us through Lullingstone Park (golf and deer). We are experiencing hop country from which the hoppers have been banished (the last London hop trains stopped in 1960). Now hopping is mechanical.

Red brick memory-mansions. The gatehouse of Lullingstone Castle has its Union flag (just like a Barratt estate). A taller standard is topped with a model Spitfire. House and grounds are open to the public (FINAL SEASON!). The parish church of St Botolph's, within the castle grounds, boasts of its noble dead, the landowners: the Peche and Hart Dyke families (with their Tudor pedigrees).

By the village of Eynsford – approaching the mysteries of Junction 3, the Swanley Interchange – walkers are in denial: *there is no M25*. We are outside the circuit, playing at a Kentish country ramble. Looking for kingfishers, appreciating fields where grain and vegetables were produced for export to Derenti Vadum (aka Dartford), Durobrivae (Rochester), Londinium. Nothing happened between the Romans and the Tudors, between Samuel Palmer and Pop Larkin. No TV explainer has appeared with a convincing narrative.

South London villains, economic immigrants (of the better sort), like the pedigree: the bleach and polish of these hamlets. The history. The elbow-room. The motorway at the bottom of the lane. Houses can be any colour you fancy – so long as they're white (black beams permitted on pubs). My golfing umbrella, the only gaudy splash in the landscape, comes into its own. The road at the ford is flooded to the depth of about a foot (according to the measure by the bridge).

Long-horned cattle mope and steam (Landseer-fashion) by the river's threatened banks. The water is rising, the Darent spreading itself – with the ambition of becoming a small lake. On the gates of 'Meadow View' cattle are cloned in wrought iron, all pelt and no legs. Like Scottish comedians who have run out of patter. And taken to Bud Flanagan overcoats. Another high risk property, Bridge House, features a Notre-Dame gargoyle among the hanging baskets; a horned demon on an Ionic column. Two more devils grin from the lintel of the door. Welcome to Eynsford, twinned with Rennes-le-Château.

Atkins is hooded and in dark glasses. As is Moose Jackson. I legitimise them with a flash-photograph. Moose has the cultural reference at his finger tips: Chris Marker's *La Jetée*. Future dead masked against the horror of the past. Against documentary evidence of bent fictions.

The church of St Martin runs with the theme of heads: detached and poking out of walls. As if these gargoyles, shrunken saints, were abandoning Christianity and reverting to paganism. Eynsford, according to Arthur Mee, has claim to 'a straight mile unique on the map of rural England, beginning with the site of a Roman house, passing a Norman castle, and ending at the site of a Saxon settlement'. Fifteen chill faces peek from the plaster, measuring their mile, the lost alignments. Green Men, May Queens. The energy is in the stone, the natives can't compete. They do their best, medieval carvings brought to life (with some reluctance). They move slowly, in case their limbs should crumble into dust. They stare.

We tramp, gratefully, towards the motorway (the M20). At Farningham, on the road's edge, we discover a bookshop of such transcendent obscurity that it has slipped Driffield's net: no listing in *drif's guide* (or in the orthodox directory put out by Skoob). The now-vanished Driffield, more dedicated than Pevsner, went everywhere. The exiled German scholar was, by Drif's reckoning, an amateur: he slept at night, sometimes for as much as three hours. Drif lay awake, lights on, radio blaring, licking his pencil and writing up the day's report, barking at his own witticisms. He succeeded in turning himself into a brand name and then he disappeared. His books, triumphs of crazed scholarship, dedicated misinformation, sledgehammer humour, self-confessed genius, are out of print; treasured by antiquarians who don't want their quests simplified by the Net. No other information-obsessive, so far as I know, has managed a literary form that so nearly duplicates the sound of his own voice: Drif writes at a bellow. He tub-thumps sentences, rivets puns. He moves across the landscape a little faster than the speed of light. Dosed on black coffee, he polishes his putdowns before he sets out; he's bored by what he knows. The inertia, the snobbery,

the incompetence, the petty corruptions of libricides skulking
in their pits. His books are a labour of tough love, the perfect
means of ensuring that he has enemies everywhere. The trade
is masochistic. They wait, quaking, for the appearance of the
grand inquisitor on his annual progress. They can't bribe him
with under-the-counter desiderata, or complimentary mugs
of coffee swill. Lacking all scruples (and proud of it), he is
incorruptible. He will pocket the bunce, but it won't sugar
his report.

Farningham and Drif were made for each other. It was a
charity to step inside this shop; heaped, mounded, treble-
stacked with necrotic paper. Bibliographic scrag ends. The
slurry of the publishing industry. Titles so undesirable that
Oxfam would have left them in a black bag on the steps of Sue
Ryder. I was transfixed. The others panicked. They started, as
civilians will, to pout like goldfish. To mistrust the air: they'd
been landed in an alien environment.

It was a point of honour to walk out of this dump with something, anything. Courteous as a Cossack, I tipped out boxes,
ransacked shelves. The best I could do was Miriam Colwell's
Young, a 'post-Salinger, first-person narrative' from 1955 (which
I tried unsuccessfully to punt to my ageing Juvenile Delin-
quency collectors). 'Intimate story of two American teenage
girls . . . blue jeans, cokes & convertibles.' VG in somewhat
rubbed dust-jacket. Yours for a tenner. Postage included.

Renchi, as I feared, engaged the proprietor in conversation. Like all dealers, I treated this man as a necessary obstacle, a
palsied hand into which to drop a few coins. Never give them
an opening. The only reason the shop existed was to bring
the unwary in from the street, to provide an audience for:
The Story. The Ancient Mariner experience. Simon's tale, I had
to admit, was one of the best. His special needs, I assumed, were
no more extreme than those you'd find in a hundred such
establishments: bookdealers, even if they begin as fun-loving
athletes, soon crumple into melancholia, horseshoe-spine,

life-threatening obesity, shingles, myopia, incipient gangrene, flatulence. Simon had a yarn to pitch that would have subdued a crew with normal human sympathies. His image and his story travelled with us for miles. He became the messenger, the guide for that walk: dead books and a keeper waiting to talk to travellers. The oracle of Farningham.

Simon had been a *Mirror* journalist at Canary Wharf. A near-name. Busy, successful. With prospects. Before, as he explained (haltingly, painfully), he had the accident; and flew out of the shattered back window of a car. Simon wasn't slim or lithe. That's what stayed in my mind, the horror of being sucked from the window, backwards. Squeezed like a bladder of offal through the tight slit of a letterbox.

He recalls that frozen instant of time so vividly. One minute, a career journalist sitting comfortably – then nothing makes sense. Glass re-seals itself behind him, the road unfurls. His unprotected head strikes a lamppost: with the impact of something fired from a cannon. He spends a hundred days in a coma; fed by his mother with a spoon. That period isn't lost, it's always there like a story he's been told. Deleted, mythical. He quits his damaged shell and inhabits another place. He speaks of it now as a 'dream'; erotic, slightly saline. He saw a naked girl on a marble slab. There were pale encounters in a nether world. He remembers the moves he made. When and how he decided to return.

After such an experience, what does the bookshop matter? Other people's words. Cancelled texts. Vanities from which a new life must be forged. The horror and the vision are both replayed: he has to make sense of them. The shop is a cave of random confessions, strangers' voices. He is its curator. In perpetuity. When I give him his 20*p*, he mutters: 'Oh good, now I can have some lunch.'

Eynsford's famous straight mile, the broad valley floor, made it attractive to planners: an east/west road (achieved) and a new airport for London (outflanked by powerful local interests). Metropolitan greed nibbles at this countryside: flour mills, tall chimney stacks. We pass under one motorway and on towards a railway and a viaduct.

As we cross the Darent at Horton Kirby, we meet with a fishing party that would have delighted Izaak Walton. True Kentish men (under the unimpressed eye of a Romany-dark woman) doing something illegitimate, robbing kingfishers of their prey. The poachers have the characteristic pallor of the interhighway settlements: turnip faces, thicker at base than crown, large ears, lank hair curtaining mercury eyes. The juveniles favour a Beckham fuzz, to save the prison barber work. Both types are stubbled, blue-chinned, it's a medical condition. Loose mouths, tugged up at one corner, sneer. The teeth, surprisingly, are big and white and strong: the fisherfolk look like Hollywood actors playing backwoods cannibals.

They're not angling for perch or pike or eel. A spotter crabs his way along a sewage pipe while his mate drops in the bright yellow line: with a large magnet on the end. They're dipping for coin, or scrap; rings, crash helmets, bicycle wheels. The suspicion is: whatever is down there in the murky stream, they know about it. The fishing party is a none-too-subtle method of recovering swag. The booty from the day's work, so far, is one hub cab and an empty tin can. The woman spits.

Shamed that our lives lack such commercial acumen, the spirit of self-help promoted by Lord Tebbit, we sidle off to the pub beneath the viaduct. Which turns out to be what passes on this turf for a sophisticated establishment – run by a female bodybuilder and her white T-shirt, gold bracelet, geezer-in-residence. Showbiz and steroids. Good-hearted folk, affable to damp strangers, happy to do a pie and pint. The pub has a gallery of erased celebrities around the walls: character actors who left *EastEnders*, only to discover that being called a 'character' was a euphemism for unemployed. After the motorway blowjobs and the destroyed septa, the tabloid frenzy, you were condemned to the northern clubs, Raquels in Basildon, sing-alongs under the viaduct. The remembered names, for those who watch daytime TV and do the quizzes, were: Gareth Hunt, Tessa Sanderson and magician Fay Presto.

Seated among this exhibition of the reforgotten, Kevin comes into his own; he's a compulsive list-maker, a print and radio journalist, contriver of profiles, puffer of lost lives. Names, dates, stories. I don't mean that being on the road, in move-ment, hobbles his style, or caps the outpouring of anecdote; but, necessarily, his audience is limited. To whoever is alongside him in boggy field-margin, splashing through fords, quizzing gravestones. The pub is a better forum. The small round table. And, beneath this railway viaduct in South Darenth, at the outer limits of Dartford, he has struck lucky: a fabulous display of the unrecognisable, reverse celebrities, unvarying variety acts, body-sculptors, freaks of withdrawn fame.

I love the innocence of these flock-wallpaper albums as much as he does. By such devices, monochrome gods and god-desses (dressed like bouncers), we can recover memory; who we were when the glamorous ghosts first appeared on the (bought-for-the-coronation) TV goldfish bowls of our child-hood. Thorn EMI multiples of John Dee's crystal. The rogues' gallery in the viaduct pub is a challenge: remember the name and you'll remember some part of yourself you'd rather let go.

Kevin talks of Epsom. The literary references have been stacking up: William Blake, David Gascoyne. Kevin reminds me that Tommy Butts, son of Blake's patron Thomas, men-tions in his diary (14 August 1809) that 'Mr. and Mrs. Blake are very well . . . they intend shortly to pay the promised visit at Epsom.'

Gascoyne, in a memoir called 'Oahspe', unravels an episode that seems in a few pages to contain all the elements that distin-guish his work: magic, derangement, a sleepwalker's courage. An Edgar Allan Poe tale comfortably relocated to the Eng-lish Thirties; polite, grey-brown, lethal. From a dusty shelf in

Watkins Occult Bookshop, Cecil Court, Gascoyne acquires *OAHSPE: A New Bible* – glossed as 'the most astonishing book in the English language'. It will, so he hopes, lead him to information about a cult called Kosmon.

'For some years I continued to speculate intermittently about the possible existence of an underground organization concerned with an aberrant fake book of revelations purporting to expound the secrets of the visible universes and their cosmogonies. A time came when my mental state began to deteriorate to such an extent that eventually I underwent a series of nervous breakdowns.'

He notices: spectral messengers on underground platforms, their cheeks daubed by 'sticks of anthracite'. Conspiracy theories and 'parousial notions' interbreed; the cults of Kosmon and Scientology are linked in Gascoyne's mind. Drawing him towards Surrey, the foothills. As William Burroughs, chasing his own demons, checked into the L. Ron Hubbard franchise at East Grinstead (in the mid-Sixties), so Gascoyne found himself trapped in Epsom.

'The disorder I was suffering from when admitted to a psychiatric establishment near Epsom was accompanied by a number of vehement convictions. I believed myself to be a vessel containing momentous insights that it was my boundless duty to impart . . . I believed intensely that there was a world-wide conspiracy going on, the intent of which was to rob us of our minds and souls. Scientology was allied with the adepts of Kosmon at the heart of the conspiracy.'

The conspiracy was rooted in the London suburbs, in parkland, in the Epsom colony. Madness and vision cooked and simmered. (The madness began with that argument between insight and duty. With being a poet. A condition for which there is no known cure.) Gascoyne was convinced that his fellow inmates would be susceptible to his message. Imagine then his horror when he discovered that the old man in the next bed, a silent, sunken ruin, 'was actually a longstanding

Kosmon initiate and official, and even had a copy of *OAHSPE* in a tin box under his bed'. Gascoyne willed himself to stay awake, to wait until his neighbour was snoring – so that he could liberate this dangerous text. He was, of course, caught in the act and forcibly sedated.

The female bodybuilders, the Magic Circle conjurors, the once-celebrated poets whose works are no longer a part of a shrinking literary consciousness, summoned another Epsom name. Kevin told us about William Hayward, poet, author of a single published novel, *It Never Gets Dark All Night*. Hayward had been a correspondent of David Jones. He had, at some point, been taken into the Epsom gulag. The novel dealt with the experience.

'Should we contact him?' I asked.

'Dead. I think, suicide. Peter Carpenter has the whole story.'

So it was arranged, that when the motorway circuit was completed, Kevin would fix another day in Epsom. His friend Peter Carpenter, poet and publisher, could guide us around town and tell us about William Hayward.

8

'In this town,' Peter Carpenter announced, 'one in ten is mad.'
Our problem, outside Epsom station, was identifying that *one*.
The tour party, assembled on the pavement, you could start
there: twitchy, grinning like foxes, clothed from a dressing-up
basket. Much too old for this foolishness, a walk around Carpenter's childhood and adolescence (schools, pubs, asylums).
The balding, hook-nosed man in the collarless blue shirt
wanted, so badly, to tell his tale: the audience was incidental.
Like all poets, and most schoolteachers, he was used to talking
to himself; this morning's drive down the motorway was just
enough rehearsal to crank him up to speed. Lay out the past in
the right order and it loses its venom.

Wednesday 17 May 2000. Renchi has brought a friend
interested in springs and Surrey subterranea, the art of the
motorway fringes. Kevin has lined up two of his inner circle:
Carpenter (our guide) and Walrus (aka Martin J. Wallen,
Associate Professor of English at OSU, Stillwater, Oklahoma).
Asked how we'll recognise Carpenter, if we arrive first at the
rendezvous, Kevin says: 'So high.' Vague gesture of the arm.
'Bullish. See him coming through a crowd in London, quite
frightening.'

When we steam, mob-handed, down the drive of the old
Horton hospital, we are a pack of the dispersed, looking for
sanctuary. The townscape, in the months since we paid our last
visit, has changed beyond recognition. WELCOME TO HORTON
VIEW AND THE PADDOCKS. Fluttering banners: TAYWOOD.
A SELECTION OF 2, 3, 4 & 5 BEDROOM HOUSES & APART-
MENTS. Three white flag poles mark the border of the captive
estate.

The asylum has been replanted, opened to motor vehicles. There is some evidence for the continuing presence of builders, none of civilians, home owners, new suburbanites. The Epsom colonies have been revised into loops and crescents, so that clients can drive effortlessly in and out. Nobody is trapped, coerced, *detained*. BEAZER HOMES. WAY OUT. THANK YOU FOR OBSERVING SIGNS & DRIVING CAREFULLY.

Behind the improved flagship properties, corrugated sheds hide the last traces of a repressed history. A lick of pink paint on wrinkled tin; recreational facilities with barred windows. The yard where farm produce was once sold still exists, you need a map to find it. Sad vegetables on an unmanned table. WARNING. THESE PREMISES ARE PROTECTED BY A 24HR SECURITY AND CLOSED CIRCUIT TELEVISION SYSTEM. PACKS INFOTEL LTD. Withered beans and knobbly tomatoes covered by CCTV cameras.

Previous inmates wander the new roads, questing for something they recognise. Nobody has found them suitable clothing: one, stiff-backed, twisting as he walks, is barechested; another has a tight white, Sunday-best shirt, buttoned to neck and cuff, inherited jeans. They seem to march, eyes down, where Carpenter's merry men slouch or spring, cameras primed, constantly swivelling.

During what he calls 'The Lost Years' – a period Jackson summarises as 'lager, vodka, unsuitable girlfriends, takeaways, footy, monotony, despair and nights in the Iron Horse' – Peter Carpenter worked in an Epsom bookshop. On Saturday afternoons, paroled patients visited town. (They're called clients now: CLIENTS BACK FOR LUNCH. While there is still lunch, there is still hope.) Horton inmates were given sweetie money to spend. Every week the same kleptos would drift into the bookshop, liberate the same books (Asimov, Heinlein, L. Sprague De Camp); take them home. Without fuss, they would be gathered up and returned. (This may go some way towards explaining the popularity of that school of fiction.)

The visiting academic, Dr Wallen, is getting more of his special subject ('Romanticism') than any reasonable Oklahoma resident has the right to expect. He's got strong teeth and a nice hawky profile that could have been chiselled from the totem pole which now stands in the park behind Long Grove Hospital. He's always grinning: not like Piety Blair (the fear rictus), but like a man who can't believe his luck. Kevin has him pegged as: 'bon viveur, weight-lifter, malcontent, dog lover, former owner of cowboy boots'. He's into Coleridge, Beddoes and Nitrous Oxide: not much use in Stillwater, but useful preparation for a day trip to Epsom.

Wallen's tense watchfulness and proper rectitude (waiting for the pub) plays nicely against the Jackson/Carpenter double act. Ventriloquist and moosehead dummy. Who keep exchanging roles – so that the story can be told, backwards, in every detail. In stereo. There is much talk of Cambridge, Pembroke College, and of the former Epsom inmate and spurned novelist, William Curtis Hayward. Just as Kevin helped to preserve some record of the achievements of Dr Dylan Francis, so Peter Carpenter has obsessively gathered every scrap of information, every published and unpublished word by William Hayward.

What Carpenter wants now is to lead us to St Ebba's, the most easterly of the hospitals, on the far side of Hook Road. St Ebba's is still an active concern. The Italianate tower is in place. (Carpenter tells us that the poet Alan Brownjohn was once, as a child, locked in that tower.) The atmosphere is heavy, time doesn't flow. The estate is like an English village built by Cold War Russians for war games. Such whimsical notions are contradicted by the villagers: a speedfreak in a baseball cap who mimes the rolling of a monster spliff, a scarecrow who calls to the birds, a man perched on a bench who thinks he *is* a bird. Several Down's syndrome adolescents stare at us; they are the only ones to whom we are not invisible.

The point of our (de)tour is to locate a cemetery. Carpenter remembers being here, in a field, with his mother. There were memorials to those who died during the war, when the hospitals were requisitioned; as well as gravestones for the hospital children.

Carpenter was sure this was it, a buttercup field with a view of the Horton tower. We do what we can with potential mounds and bumps, but the cemetery has been swallowed in thorn bushes and sycamore. There is no physical evidence of the memorial. Alongside a bridlepath of loose chippings and small pebbles, Carpenter stands bemused, waving his arms. 'I'm sure it was here.' Either he has been betrayed by an unreliable memory, or memory has been violated in some way.

Renchi asks for numbers. How *many* dead? How *many* unrecorded? He picks up pebbles, counting them, putting them into his knapsack. Fingers raw, pack sagging: he's well into the hundreds.

Local papers were incensed by the developer's sacrilege: WAR HEROES' GRAVE ANGER. They settled on the number 4,000. 'War heroes lie in an overgrown cemetery where 4,000 hospital patients are buried in mass graves.' Owner-developer Michael Heighs refused church groups (backed by Epsom and Ewell Council) permission to erect a memorial cross. The hospitals had housed the shell-shocked casualties of the First War. The developer tried to strike a deal: if he allowed the memorial would he be given clearance to build on the land?

The war dead, the mutilated of Flanders, have their champions; hospital patients, wrapped in sacking, went unrecorded into a mass grave. HELM, a charitable group concerned with those who had been 'returned to the community', lobbied for some kind of memorial to the forgotten generations. Mr Heighs wouldn't budge without his development deal. The site, bought 'for a peppercorn sum from the health authorities', remains in limbo – in the expectation that Green Belt laws will change. 'Would you give someone a piece of your garden for nothing?'

Subsequent correspondents, unwilling to accept developer as scapegoat, concentrate on the original contract. It stank. 'The thing I find most shocking about it all is the fact that the health authorities sold . . . the land in the first place. Why on earth did they do that? Was it a continuation or reflection of their un-caring and irreverent attitude towards the thousands of harmless people unnecessarily sent to grim psychiatric institutions of the Epsom cluster?'

Keeping up a good pace, flogging around town, our guide was due to check in for a hernia operation. This outing, he assured us, justified his discomfort. By green lanes and half-forgotten paths we navigated the Epsom fringes, from Carpenter's school (a brazen march through pee-stink corridors) to Nonsuch Palace (stones in the grass). A hubble-bubble of free-associating anecdotes: inspirational English master Kenneth Curtis taught poet Geoffrey Hill (who dedicated *King Log* to him). Millais used Hogsmill 'as a backdrop for his Ophelia'. John Procter was a school friend . . .

Procter? Musician and polemicist (aka 'I, Ludicrous'). An educated joker who had written and performed an M25 anthem. Spoken voice: 'The M25, London's orbital. Take a ride.' With acoustic interference, throbbing and moaning. More lift-shaft than garage: 'The M25, the M25.' Composed at the start, around 1986, Procter's chant is charmingly antique; sensible and a little crazy. 'The old farms forgotten, except on out of date maps.' Procter admits that he won't be using the road, other than to visit 'relatives in Somerset'. Or: 'cricket in Kent.' For what Kevin Jackson refers to as 'an inconclusive period', Peter Carpenter acted as Procter's manager. 'Sort of.'

The secret agenda of the day, what we're edging towards, as we all recognise, is: The Tunnel. The subterranean network that Renchi and I walked past when we climbed Ashley Road towards the Downs. This time we're going in, Renchi's cemetery pebbles will be used in a giant M25 sand-painting. He hopes to find a suitable cavern or sanctuary.

As a writer (former market trader, parks gardener, ullage man), I have no status to protect. But I wonder about the professional academic and the English master from a public school, how would they look in the local press – as convicted trespassers? Doc Wallen is grinning (Doc Holliday on ether) as he goes over the fence. KEEP OUT. Renchi manages to drag open the heavy metal door. I find the stub of a nightlight. (Evidence of suburban satanism? Drug orgies?)

The brick tunnel drops into darkness. My nightlight gives a feeble glow. Illuminates the veins in my hand. The door, designed to withstand bomb blasts, creaks; threatens to close behind us. The underground complex is rumoured to stretch for miles, with hidden entrances in various parts of town. Fifty or sixty yards in, we hit water. We're really not equipped for this, we'll have to come back on another occasion. The tunnel divides, branches off; there are cell-like sidechambers.

By the dying candleflame, Renchi scratches the outline of his M25 drawing on the damp floor. He'll return, with drummers, sand, chalk – and the pebbles from St Ebba's cemetery. We're quite relieved to have an excuse for a retreat to the pub.

A figure in a suit, standing on the embankment, spots us. He makes no challenge, doesn't move. But when Renchi and his troop pitch up for their shamanic ceremony, the tunnels are definitively sealed. The schematic drawing has to be laid out, over several hours, on the ramp.

The Amato pub, in the early evening, is varnished, brassy; occupied by check-jacket and mustard corduroy equestrians. It's generous of them to let us in. We don't talk horseflesh and we're not cranking up for a serious session. We've walked past mansions with complicated ironwork gates, past stables and fields of cattle with designer coats, cleaner, less ostentatious than Hollywood wives.

Drink in hand, day's ration of Romanticism digested, Doc Wallen recalls *his* childhood: Carpenter hasn't got the monopoly on Wordsworthian soliloquies. Louisiana. Wallen's father was a surveyor for an oil company. In a house by the bayou, dim figures moved at night, circling the bed. A Southern Gothic dreamscape. Faulknerian shadows: grandfather, spurned by the detested son to whom he had left the farm, died where he lay. An unremoved corpse, busy with maggots, in a nest of rat-filth.

Such images infect the pub. Peter Carpenter speaks of William Hayward, a troubled life that brought him, inevitably, to Epsom. If the tale is not properly told, the man fades away; the legend is discredited. We allow ourselves to become identified with those we promote, so that the manufacture of another writer's biography is a gloss on our own. Present neglect supports elective obscurity. The reappraisal of a vanished reputation must initiate a turn in the biographer's fortune. These exercises move between literary archaeology and psychic vampirism.

I listen to Peter's fragmentary account. I read pamphlets of Hayward's poetry and I obtain a copy of the novel, *It Never Gets Dark All Night*. This was published by Heinemann in 1964. He was in good company; other titles promoted (on the back of the dust-wrapper) include Anthony Burgess's *Nothing Like the Sun* and Patricia Highsmith's *The Two Faces of January*.

The cover illustration is a solar disc floating over three very serious bohemians: clean hair and anoraks (male) and trowels of eye-shadow (female). We are revisiting the Lawrentian Spring (CND and rented cottages), before the Summer of Love. Bran Lynch, an uncocky and self-doubting Ginger Man, hanging on to the 1,000-foot contour in the soft limestone country of the Cotswolds, wanders on set 'wearing the overcoat of a literary critic and a pair of army socks'. Hayward's comedy is stoic, melancholy; the world squeezes his heart. He has the pulse of the land: 'Sheepcrunch. The iron blathering of tractors. And the sun aggressing through the cracked window.'

The weekend party sours into its Monday aftermath, spill and chill and mismatched underwear, sticky tea grains in a burnt saucepan. A 'large, genial negro' called Shiner makes an uncomfortable entrance (current sensibilities on red alert): Shiner has possession of a black Jaguar car. Has he 'borrowed' it? 'What you mean, boy? I hired it. Been working on the motorway. An' Roz likes a bit of speed. That so, honey?'

She 'blushes'. We blush. But, if we're old enough, we've lived through such fictions before, seen the period awkwardness drop away, found surviving strengths. Class shapes the narrative, not race. Hayward doesn't like cities, or the transport infrastructure. 'Innumerable family cars were being eased out of congested garages onto congested roads ... There would probably only be a few hundred injured in this rush, and those certainly the least deserving.'

The cold cottage, the bothy, the borrowed lodge: somewhere remote, out of it, to contemplate – what? The impossibility of salaried employment, urban life, relationships? Thin sunlight on barren fields, a dreadful silence: 'It was so quiet she could hear the copulation of flies.' Hayward's characters, like the author, are oppressed by their ability to articulate, explain, use language.

Lynch cracks and is removed to a fictional version of the Epsom hospital in which Hayward himself had once been incarcerated. The hospital has its snobberies, hierarchies of incompetence. Robotic table-tennis and ECT are compulsory. 'Everything was quiet, sunny, calm, but below these obvious suggestions of the air a hint of indescribable horror and violence.'

Within parkland, behind high walls, in an environment policed by burly men in white coats (NCOs left over from recent wars), Lynch encounters 'the burning'. 'With clinical assistance he cut his way back into sanity, but the shadow of the greater reality was never far from his mind.'

The asylum as rite of passage – through brain-shock,

redirected lightning – goes back to Mary Shelley. And to Hayward's contemporaries, Sylvia Plath and Anne Sexton. To Ken Kesey. To Carl Solomon (dedicatee of *Howl*), to Allen Ginsberg's 'starry dynamo'. And Harold Pinter's Aston (in *The Caretaker*): 'Then one day they took me to a hospital, right outside London . . . They used to come round with these . . . I don't know what they were . . . they looked like big pincers, with wires on, the wires were attached to a little machine.' Hayward, shocked in every way, every sense, is closer to the Gloucestershire poet/composer Ivor Gurney (and David Jones) than to the excited Laingian rhetoric of the Sixties. He associates himself with the landscape in which he lives, with forms of traditional knowledge. He fears: love and its loss.

His angst feeds in that dark ditch of the English imagination, the First War: in missing it. The guilt. Edward Thames spending a final, shivering winter in an Epping Forest cottage. Hayward's bland Cotswold escarpment lacks shellholes, blackened tree stumps, bones poking from mud. Hayward faces: 'The dilemma of those who are chosen to speak, but dare not. The trivial escape via sheer sensation, or the terrified plunge into the narrowing corridor of psychosis. With the increasing urgency of the voices on one side, it is scarcely possible not to crack.'

Hayward's sense of place is respectful. Districts are recalled by a few precisely observed details. Epsom is vividly present in the walk that only a patient or hospital visitor would recognise, our green way between gulag and station. Locals, so Peter Carpenter informed us, know these byways as 'The Slips'.

Released from confinement, Bran Lynch 'took a narrow footpath that ran behind the backs of absurd villas towards the centre of town'. His delusions couldn't be contained in a complacent Surrey town. 'His particular kind of illness was a bit much for provincials to cope with. Even his insanity, it appeared, was metropolitan.' City: madness, voices. Country: incubation or denial of visionary experience, silence.

Lynch, the dreamed double, walks Hayward's walk: as we walked it, the same geography.

Tarry pavement soft after much sun. Rigidly fenced little back gardens, nakedly exposed from the sly angle of this path. Like a succession of intricately decorated privies, each revealing the particular crapulous mode of the indwelling imagination. Some with gnomes, goldfish. Some with pampas grass. Some with prize dahlias. One tusked and hummocked with coarse grass and weeds, among which lay jagged tins of Kit-e-Kat. At the end of this one a lithe sumac, already beginning to turn.

The aristocratic countryman's eye falls on the follies and pretensions of suburbia, and exposes its own shame; an awkward passage through a mundane world. The banality of Epsom is eternal: Lynch enters the same cheap clothing store we visited. He buys 'tapered K.D. trousers', and gives his flannels to a charity shop. He takes a train for London.

The nakedness of the relationship between author and avatar possessed Peter Carpenter. Carpenter saw Hayward/Lynch as a significant Epsom figure, a man purged and refined by the hurt he had suffered. He sent me a 'draft biographical outline'. Research materials for a potential 'life'; a story that would, in all probability, never be written.

Born (1931) to an established, landowning Gloucestershire family. Parents separate. A 'peripatetic existence', with his mother, 'moving between various hotels in the South of England and relations in the Isle of Man'. The estate is sold. They retreat to Galloway.

Dartmouth Royal Naval College. Hayward is allowed to leave the Navy to try for Oxford. Labourer on an organic farm. National Service. Merton College, Oxford. Fruit picking, libretto for opera. Oxford literary friendships include: Edward Lucie-Smith, Elizabeth Jennings, Adrian Mitchell. Receives instruction with a view to converting to Roman Catholicism.

'Viva'd for a First but awarded a Second.' Decides against becoming a Catholic, meets David Jones. They correspond.

Publishers' rep for Elek Books, marriage. Honeymoon in Tenby and West Wales. Drives long distances, 'often sleeping in the back of the van'. Sets up his own press. Moves from cottage to cottage. Children. Flat in Cheltenham: 'acquainted with various poets, artists and bohemians, including Lyn Chadwick and W.S. Graham'. Absorbed in a textual commentary on David Jones's *The Anathemata*.

More poetry, more cottages: no electricity. 'A petrol pump brings water from a well.' Takes up woodcarving. Visits Harrow and discusses his commentary with David Jones.

'Meetings with Gerald Yorke in Forthampton, interest in Aleister Crowley and magical rituals.' Attempts novel. A number of extra-marital relationships: 'drinking heavily and feeling trapped in London'. Quits Arrow Books. 'Investigates possible life as a crofter.' Calls on David Jones 'in a distracted state'. Arrested for assault on police officer: 'remanded in custody and subsequently admitted to Horton Hospital in Epsom.' ECT. Released, after six weeks, into wife's care. Teaches Cheltenham Technical College. Depression. Stays at Tibetan Centre. And at the Cistercian Monastery on Caldey Island (as David Jones had done).

It Never Gets Dark All Night accepted by Heinemann. Research into private papers of Ivor Gurney. Affairs on Ibiza: 'manic episodes and feelings of alienation . . . increasingly reliant upon alcohol, tranquillisers and sleeping pills'. Novel published to generally favourable reviews.

Travels through France, Spain, Morocco, Ibiza: 'hearing voices'. Starts work on novel 'dramatizing a conflict between white magicians in Gloucestershire and black magicians in Ibiza'. Plans to set up bookshop in Exeter. Takes overdose, recovers in hospital. Invests in stock market. Travels relentlessly. Visits England, returns to Ibiza. 'On 9th December 1968, he dies at C'an Marias, probably by his own hand. Body flown back to England and buried at Quedgeley in Gloucestershire in an unmarked grave.'

I open Hayward's novel at random: 'An excess of transparency, described by the experts as a "nervous breakdown", had brought him into direct contact with this world. Yet there were no devils.'

The chain of authorship, of promptings, coincidences, is laid bare. In a way that could only be broached in an Epsom pub, after a day touring lost hospitals and sealed tunnels. Carpenter chases Hayward, who chases David Jones, who is a pivotal figure in my own Welsh mythos. Jones is fractured by war, spiritual crisis, the impossibility of knitting together strands, whispers of Celtic, Roman and contemporary history: broken inscriptions, nervous palimpsests of sign and symbol. He convalesced, through long years, in his Harrow cave, his trench; submerged in boarding houses until he passed into the hands of the nuns. Harrow Hill looks west to the motorway. Hayward, like so many other casualties of London, is shipped out to Epsom.

A table of misaligned Ancients, retro-Romantics, in a racing pub, conduct a seance on nominated predecessors; hoping, like the other madmen of the town, to find clues in printed texts. Kevin Jackson takes the prize by dipping into Jones's *The Anathemata* and fixing on 'a weird premonition of your Epsom encounter with my pal Martin Wallen'.

'The Lady of the Pool' (p. 130):

> brighted up old imaged Lud, as some tell is 'balmed 'Wallon,
> high-horsed above Martin miles, what the drovers pray to

We stroll back to the station. Cars, tucked away in the Sainsbury's park (which closes at seven p.m.), now face a £25 pound 'release' fee. We turn out our pockets, scrape it together. And then the lucky ones get themselves on a train for London.

9

Between South Darenth and Junction 2 of the M25, we walk through an area of ponds, small lakes, deer parks, estates associated with St John of Jerusalem: captured Templar lands, as Renchi would have it. The Net keeps him informed about such things. Chat rooms crammed with speculation about the Sinclairs, Rosslyn Chapel, Danbury Hill in Essex. 'It was the St Cleres who dedicated the church to St John, a connection has been made between other parishes held by the family and hill-top sun-worshipping sites. Their name is said to mean "holy light" and they may have been active in the mysterious cult of "The Priory of Zion".' Etc. Etc.

Such housing as there is has made its treaty with Dartford, pebbledash (under a pink wash) decorated with drooping lines of coloured bulbs, carriage lamps. The effect might have been achieved by wet paint, a mound of gravel and a wind-machine. Cars parked, off-highway, on concrete lawns, are for sale. And, if there's room, green tables offer windfall, the bounty of pillaged orchards. Newsagents are plastered with special offers for excursions to the Millennium Dome.

PLEASE PUT ALL LETTERS FOR ST. JOHN'S JERUSALEM IN THE BLACK POSTBOX TO THE RIGHT OF THE 5 BARRED GATE.

Marc Atkins takes a call on his mobile; his connections sense that he's on his way back to town. Kevin looks mildly shocked. Electronic interconnectedness doesn't fit with his preconceptions (shaping nicely as a future essay): skinhead camera-artist as linear successor to Julia Margaret Cameron, Alvin Langdon Coburn. Kevin's footwear is beginning to pinch. The liberties of Shoreham and the Valley of Vision, vineyards and villas,

have given way to suburban drudgery, hedge tunnels of the
kind we have previously encountered in West Drayton and
Enfield Chase.

As Kevin suffers, Marc revives. He's a poet of margins, bad
skies. Fast-moving weather systems suit him: glints in mud
puddles, darkness at noon, early-evening alchemy. He likes
identifying fault lines, indeterminate zones where towns loosen
their grip: unfinished roads, abandoned civil engineering projects, pylons. He avoids humans – who tend to give the game
away, fix the scene in a particular time scale. Marc's work
is theatrical, future archaeology is what he's after; hints of a
capacity to hang around beyond the point of no return. There
is something sinister in the way he swoops on any railway that
we have to cross; he's busking for disaster, willing catastrophe.
He empties the set, so that the furies can advance without
interference.

When he makes portraits, he's dowsing for a late bloom,
evidence of a well-spent (or misspent) life. It's not that he's an
ambulance chaser, but he appreciates experience as a cosmetic
of revelation. He talks to his victims, draws them out. With
that unnerving height (shaved skull, dark glasses), the request
for a photographic session is not always welcome. It's like
collaborating with an obituarist. He might tell you more than
you want to know.

Industrial units replace farms. FRUIT DISTRIBUTION
CENTRE: a white flag pole garlanded with barbed wire. A faded
Union Jack. We're closing on territory where Englishness is a
threat, faces painted with red crosses. The Darent is nudged
aside by the thrust of the M25 – as it races towards the Thames.
Wat Tyler, famously revolting peasant and local hero, lends his
name to profoundly conservative pubs. Top man: the most popular Dartford heritage token. Before the advent of Mick Jagger.

Flooded gravel pits, desultory fishermen, fade into empty
meadows. The scabby planting of the M25 embankment. On
the hard shoulder, we stop to repair Kevin's feet. A true English

gentleman, of the Captain Oates type, Moose has made no complaint. A steady stream of self-mockery yields to clammy browed (but unadmitted) desperation: will this day *ever* end? When he bares the ruined feet, we blanch. 'Last time,' he announces, with a slightly hollow laugh, 'the nails went black and fell off. I squelched when I walked.'

It was fortunate that Renchi (who stayed overnight in Hackney) had helped himself to the various antiquated packages of plaster from our medicine cabinet: waterproof, quilted, smooth and smelling of matron's room. The Quaker carer gets to work. He binds the abused flippers like Christo wrapping the Reichstag. Each foot has twenty short muscles primed to flex, extend, abduct and adduct the spindly toes: all shot, screaming. The horn of the nail is black (the burnt crisps you find at the bottom of the bag). Epithelial tissue oozes pink, no longer capable of securing nail to toe. It's probably time for Kevin to step outside, into the fast lane. Do the decent thing.

Marc's camera hovers, an inch above the insulted flesh. When he's satisfied that he's got the shot, Renchi supplies fresh socks. The rest of us are bearing up quite well; we can live with Kevin's pain. Somebody on these occasions has to take the bolt, pay the ferryman's fee. It's noble of Kevin to volunteer.

But it's not just Moose Jackson who is on his way out, the M25 abdicates at Junction 2; its title is not returned until it manages to cross the Thames. Panic strikes. Roads spin off in every direction. Powder mills, pumping stations, flooded sports fields will have to be negotiated before we reach town. The Darent is no longer a Kentish stream, it's a canal, a dirty ditch between rat-grey banks. A drudge. The force of the river labours to drive cog wheels and grindstones. Dartford is the property of Glaxo-Wellcome, global pharmacists: insulin for diabetes, digoxin. A strong dose of reality to counter pastoral sugar, the saccharine of Samuel Palmer. Speed to whip the heart's tired muscle.

★

It's wet and light is draining from the sky. Kevin locates a phone kiosk, near the splendour of the Dartford Public Library. He has to call a copy-editor in New York. He's flogged out, gone in the feet, and he's arguing commas with Bill Buford. It's a bad day when Kevin doesn't turn in a page for the *Independent*, an interview with some broken spar of cultural flotsam, a radio show. Greasy phone tucked under chin, striped shirt sticking to a heaving chest, he sweats like a broker on Black Monday. Moose has been reduced to writing pieces for the *New Yorker* (the media equivalent of debating doctrine with Torquemada). Obscure (Eurocentric) references are culled, paragraphs ironed out, minor witticisms exorcised. Ten minutes of this treatment and Kevin is ready to confess: he'll do anything for cash.

Dartford is a town that can't be negotiated on foot. Watling Street sweeps through, but the old pilgrim routes have been re-aligned: nobody *walks* to Canterbury, they stick with the Darent Valley Path (as laid out in the Kent County Council guide). Commercially, riverine Kent is Third World, mid-combat Balkan. Bluewater has stolen the action, leaving a rump of charity shops, fast food outlets and aggrieved pubs. Experience teaches: pedestrian walkways are not for pedestrians. They are magnets for car parks, open-air malls. They define themselves in negatives: no motor traffic, no access to the town at large (side streets, canals). Dull flagstone paths are a compulsory shopping experience for people who don't shop; a zombie treadmill furnished with stone benches on which only the most dispirited transients (lager schools, outpatients, the dispersed) ever perch.

But Dartford hasn't thrown in the towel. Lottery Funds have gifted the town with £2.25 million: for the Mick Jagger Performing Arts Centre. Jagger – Jerry Hall, three of the kids and Jagger's octogenarian parents, Joe and Eva – turned out for the dedication. The Duke of Kent pulled the velvet rope, unveiled the plaque; then Mick climbed on stage to read a speech to the assembled dignitaries. The centre is part of Jagger's old school, Dartford Grammar.

Like any other crusty returnee, Mick banged on about combining performing arts with maths, science and Latin, a well-rounded education. He was modest enough to wonder why *he* had been selected for this tribute, rather than other notable Dartforders; such as General Havelock who relieved the siege of Lucknow – or Wat Tyler. Generals, he supposed, were no longer PC. And revolutionaries unacceptable as role models. 'I won the honour by default.' (Nobody considered fellow townsman Keith Richards.) Tyler and Havelock will have to be satisfied with seeing their names on dodgy pubs. Jagger, who had the sense to get out of Dartford, early and often, fronts the overendowed assembly hall.

Finding Dartford station means battling across fenced roads, dropping into pedestrian underpasses, detouring the long way around civic centres, coping with the river. Having got you, they don't want to let you go: but a return to Cambridge, a night of revisions for the *New Yorker*, is suddenly very attractive to Kevin. A bone-deep drenching in torrential rain, as we try to pick up Dartford Creek, to navigate across the marshes to the Thames – by moonlight, if necessary – is an experience he is happy to imagine. As he settles back in a comfortable railway carriage.

We shake him warmly by the hand, wave him off – then spend forty minutes, trekking through dereliction, drifting west towards Crayford, snarled at by yard dogs, blanked by citizens, splashed by motorists; until we reconnect with the swollen and unrecognisable Darent. The river is tidal as far as the town bridge. Industry, on one side, pumping in noxious additives; tough vegetation on the other.

Heads down against the storm: the great moment comes when the last of the town is cleared and we swim out, exposed and ridiculous, into the apocalyptic erasure of Dartford Marshes. Buildings, road, river: revoked. Indistinguishable. We lean into the rain and navigate by touch and smell. My golf umbrella! I set it down to shake hands with Kevin. It's still there, outside the station; a flag stuck in a cairn of stones by some doomed expedition.

On this black night, the loss is meaningless. It would be like hanging on to a parachute. It's too dark to distinguish either of the rivers, Darent or Cray. Or the river gate that stands like the entrance to a forbidden city, turning pedestrians back for a detour of several miles across the marshes.

We live inside our discomfort. In Dartford, poring over the fiction of the map, we were impressed by the scale and structure of a hospital (the Joyce Green) that should be out there, acting as a marker. A double V pivoting on the inevitable water tower: isolation wards for the worst contagions of the East End. A secure colony-estate with a rail link to the Thames, its own jetty.

Renchi and Marc are hooded, rain cuts through the layers. I've picked up a small black umbrella that somebody has chucked out. No sooner opened than stripped to the prongs. We can't see where we're going. We try to follow the eccentricities of the Darent path − from a high bank, somewhere above the river.

The memory of our walk from Shoreham is wiped by weather, the desolation of the salt marshes. From the embankment, we can make out shapeless dunes, mud, the refuse of London, the indestructibles. For the first time (since Runnymede Bridge), our journey has a proper conclusion: the broad Thames. Minor digressions are swept aside. We stand at the river's edge, the point where the Darent is absorbed. Or what we take to be the edge: pipings of redshank, a slurping earth-soup. We don't move. It's uncomfortable, wet, cold; magnificent. The nonsense of journal-keeping and photography is exposed as sheer folly. This is almost as good as being on the river in a small boat, drifting out to sea. It's that kind of abdication of responsibility.

Heading east, along the Thames path, the Dartford Bridge (with its necklace of slow-moving traffic) is our horizon. Smeared headlights spit their short beams into the wet night. The bridge spells civilisation. And spells it loud: FUCK OFF. Liminal graffiti. A mess of letters sprayed on grey stone windbreaks. FUCK OFF.

Soft detonations overhead: bombbombbomb. Of neverending lorries, containers, monster rigs. The motorway streaks the land with sick light. For half a mile, in every direction, there is hard evidence: burnt-out wrecks, torched and rusting husks, solitary tyres. The trash of transit.

The sewage plant hums and seethes. National Power cooks water, fences off territory. A great chimney stack. A perimeter fence. Block buildings that shudder and hiss. Strategies of the margin (the orbital road) that we have come to know and love. In this wilderness, in our sodden wretchedness, a rush of sentiment. We are homesick for London.

If Kevin had stayed with us, we'd be discussing Eddie Constantine in Jean-Luc Godard's *Alphaville*. The Paris peripheral loop as the access ramp to an intergalactic highway. That's what the M25 needs as an interpreter: a sandpaper-skinned American playing a hardboiled detective (faked by an English author) in a French film with a Swiss director.

Exterior. Night. The suburbs of Alphaville, the Capital City of a distant Galaxy. A lone car is being driven along one of the boulevards, ablaze with flashing lights, neon signs . . .

Lemmy (off): It was 24 hours 17 minutes Oceanic Time when I arrived at the suburbs of Alphaville.

Wormholes in the fabric of time. Mythic projections invade an unoptioned landscape, the gloom over Gravesend. The bridge is more metaphor than reality, lorries disappear into the clouds. Marc gets into character. He loops his favourite literary quotation: 'The horror! The horror!'

And he's right. The dominating voice on this reach of the river belongs to Joseph Conrad, out there on the other shore in his house at Stanford le Hope. ('A whisper that seemed to swell menacingly like the first whisper of a rising wind.') Conrad, monocle to eye, beard elevated, stared across at us – and saw a cruising yawl, the *Nellie*, waiting on the tide. He fed us the line they all quote: 'And this also has been one of the dark places of the earth.' He's a master of shifts and swerves, scrupulously weighted paragraphs that allow one river to fade into another. Lost lives are re-narrated, coastal places lose definition. 'Men and sea interpenetrate.'

On this wild night, out on the Dartford Marshes, I was ready to jump ship, go native. The motorway circuit was beyond resolution. The M25 was lost. There was no access to the bridge. We stumbled through ditches, climbed slippery banks, found a road. Off-highway, in the shadow of the bridge, geometry is unbalanced: more concept than actuality. Eddie Constantine's boulevards as dead ends. Warehouses, roundabouts, fountains. Roads peter out into swamp: Clipper Boulevard, Crossways Boulevard, Anchor Boulevard. Headlights sweep the dark. No shops, no pubs, no humans. To advance on the railway line and the Stone Crossing station, we have to navigate a series of crescents that have been designed with the sole aim of frustrating pedestrians. Momentum is directed towards the Bluewater retail quarry, the Radiant City.

Nervous motorists (a woman and her daughters) waved down, put us on track; an old green path to the station. We're told that it's impossible to walk across the Dartford Bridge. Absolutely forbidden. Turn up with a bicycle and they'll transport you in a truck. Otherwise: forget it. Surveillance levels are high. Police cars are on permanent patrol. We've walked 270 degrees of our circuit and now it's over, we're trapped on the wrong shore. We discuss kitting ourselves out in hard hats and overalls, but that's just bravado. The tour, within the acoustic footprints of the M25, is finished.

The Stone Crossing station is deserted: no ticket office, broken machines. Marc, having sat on a bench, isn't sure that he'll be able to stand up – even if a train does arrive, which seems unlikely. The railway is an icy ladder disappearing into the all-enveloping night.

10

Renchi, back in his Hampshire cottage, cruising websites, re-interrogating ground we had already covered, made contact with Dr J.C. Burne. Burne was the honorary archivist of Joyce Green Hospital, the memory man of the Dartford Marshes. His hospital was doomed; it was about to be rationalised (put to the bulldozer), asset-stripped, reconfigured. The usual land-management scam, in which silence (ignorance) assumes consensus. Local rumour favoured another M25 satellite estate, convenient for Dartford Tunnel and Bluewater. Better-informed whispers revised the plan: a refuge (holding pen) for asylum seekers. Bus 'em in, bang 'em up. The prison hulks, romanced by Charles Dickens in *Great Expectations*, were moored here; beyond the knowledge of the metropolis, a land-scape fit for Gothic projection. Casualties of war had always been held on the marshes, wounded Germans, displaced Poles; their names and dates cut into the red brick of the hospital walls. The French, too, from the Second War: PAILLARD, YVES, 1940. OLIVIER, EMILE. 5.6.1940, FRANCE. DEP. 6.10.1940. The scratch of a bent nail recording a memory-prompt lost to everyone except Dr Burne. And soon to be lost entirely.

Burne will give us the tour (27 March 2000). We must sneak through the gates just ahead of the wrecking crew; ahead of Burne's retirement. The hospital library is due to close, the archive will disappear into other archives – except for files which have been destroyed (contagious, pox carrying).

West Hill Hospital closed in 1997. The Accident and Emergency Department transferred to Joyce Green. Many of the West Hill beds had already been removed to Gravesend; and so, as a pamphlet put out by the library points out, 'for the first time since 1840 when the Workhouse authorities built the hospital the site was devoid of all hospital beds'. Now Joyce Green, just short of its centenary, will vanish and a new hospital, 'built under the Private Finance Initiative (PFI) scheme', will be magicked from the grounds of the former Darenth Asylum.

The 'flagship' Darent Valley Hospital won't be in the Darent Valley and it won't be much of a hospital. It's taken a hundred years to shift from prison hulk to plague ship (for smallpox victims) to New Labour ark. But, from its launch, the Darent Valley Hospital generated reams of publicity, all of it bad.

PATIENT THREATENS LEGAL ACTION AFTER 20-HOUR TROLLEY WAIT IN A 'FLAGSHIP' HOSPITAL CORRIDOR (*Evening Standard*, 10 October 2001). Kerrie Williams, 'mother-of-two', is quoted as saying: 'I'm amazed I actually got through it and lived to tell the tale.' While lying on a trolley in a corridor, she was 'intimately examined', but given no food or water for two days. Williams now understood perfectly what the private/public partnership meant: go 'private' and receive swift treatment, while Joe Public expires on an unattended gurney.

'The place,' Kerrie Williams reports, 'was in chaos.' The new hospital cost £177 million and was built under the scheme whereby the private sector (the same contractors we have met, time and again, on our circuit) throws up something fast and glitzy – and rents it to the NHS. A sweetheart deal. Plenty of glass, generous parking bays and very few beds. Consultants (unconsulted) warned that the Darent Valley Hospital would be too small and that there would be long delays in the A & E Department. In other words, inner city conditions would apply to the perimeter, to Kent. You won't find the drug war casualties of Hackney, mercenaries hosed from the forecourts of night petrol stations. You'll have to make do with road rage, the boredom-stompings of Thamesmead, pub brawls. Feuding inbreeds. The BNP Calibans of economic decline. Middle-class families walking across fields attacked by hammer-wielding maniacs.

The Department of Health may not be much use at delivering hospitals that work, but they are very good at charts, projections, tick-the-box quizzes. The flagship Darent Valley Hospital was judged (in September 2001) to be 'one of the worst in the country'. Its rating by the Department's new classification system was: zero. Zilch. The pits of the pits.

We step out of Dartford station into a non-negotiable nexus of underpasses and flyovers. The retail fly-trap with its herring-bone-brick roads and freakishly thin clock tower is known as 'The Orchard'. It is of course barren and treeless. It acts as a reservation of New Commerce, an escape from the declining Spital Street, the deceased High Street. 'Spital', as a signifier, belongs to the era when Watling Street was still an active concern, when positive discrimination invaders (Romans, Vikings) were marching through – bringing leprosy and the 'sekness that men called ye pokkes'. Dartford was an important staging post on the road to Canterbury, a hill to climb. Workhouse became hospital, became asylum. Isolation was the pitch. The desolation of the marshes (liable to flooding) made Dartford a prime site for pox hospitals, tents for contagious diseases.

The Wat Tyler pub offers: PEASANTS REVOLT BITTER. £1-49 PNT. 3.8 PC. WAT TYLER AND SEVERAL OF THE COMMONS CALLED AT THIS ANCIENT TAVERN (SO IT IS SAID) TO QUENCH THEIR THIRST WITH FLAGONS OF ALE.

Negotiating a route to Joyce Green Hospital, we find ourselves on Temple Hill; commercial imperatives overrule travel information. B & Q. CLEARWATER OPEN FOR BUSINESS AS USUAL. A Mercedes dealership with a forest of flags. A walk of 'about twenty minutes' (pitched by the woman in the breakfast caff) stretches into an hour of uncrossable bypass, marsh mud, site-specific rain. My plate of ham and eggs has been sprayed with a silver film. I can't decide whether to eat it or to have it framed.

Dr Burne is waiting in an office in the Postgraduate Building, sucking at a mug of tea, tapping on a tin of biscuits. The hospital estate with its winged design, its outbuildings, open-air corridors, flower beds and shrubberies, is posthumous. We're used to that, we've come to expect it: good-humoured resignation, folk hanging about in warm rooms nibbling through the remaining stock of chocolate digestives. Waiting for the rumble of JCBs, the skips and Portakabins.

'What's your interest?' Burne challenges. He's seen off plenty of time-wasters, professionally bored media casuals, work experience docu-directors asked to knock up three minutes on TB or cholera. The doctor is alert, gold-spectacled, silver-bearded and forward-leaning. 'Trams, plants or smallpox?'

'All,' Renchi says, playing safe.

'And you?' Burne prods his stick at me.

'Poking about anywhere that wants to keep us out.'

That satisfies the archivist. He's on his feet and heading for the door. 'Come *on*. What are you waiting for? There's plenty of ground to cover.'

Long retired from his work as consultant pathologist at Joyce Green, the doctor devotes himself to its history. He could be Renchi, twenty years down the line: wind-scoured, wrinkled, bald on top. He wears a bright red sweater, dark blue, weatherproof jacket and a Russian hat. He moves rapidly and in bursts, a silent movie: Trotsky on the trot. Renchi, in his flapping headgear (yak herdsman), struggles to keep up.

'Swollen toe, not gout,' says Burne, excusing the stick. The glass-roofed, open-sided walkways are suntraps: one long avenue pivoting into another, a true arcade project. With views on a miraculous garden. Here, diseased Londoners could be aired, cobwebs blown off by river breezes. Blended zephyrs: exotic plants, sewage farm and byre.

Joyce Green was a hospital, or series of hospitals, surrounded by farmland. The 1778 map in Hasted's *History of Kent* shows four farms on the Dartford marshes. 'Joyces' stood beside a lane, leading to Long Reach, which was lost in the 1953 floods. Richard Joyce worked a gravel pit on land acquired by the hospital. His farm enjoyed fresh water from a loop of the Darent and gave good grazing, the soil was rich from regular inundations by the Thames.

Some 341 acres of farmland were purchased by the Metropolitan Asylums Board for £24,815: the Joyce Green Smallpox Hospital, opened in 1903, was the final element in the Dartford colony. Dartford, it had been decided, was the ideal distance from London for the treatment (or removal) of Lunatics and the Contaminated: madness and the pox. There were asylums and schools for imbecile children.

Cattle from Joyce Green farm returned from the marshes by a circuitous route that took them through the hospital grounds. Cows peered in at ward windows. Great, slow, curious beasts stared at convalescents in the airing courts. They grazed the hospital lawns where the grass was too tough for hand-mowers.

Dr Ricketts, a medical supervisor of fierce reputation, was granted a vivisection licence in 1904 to experiment on farm animals, to hack them about as part of his investigation into smallpox. The notion that cattle might be affected by East Enders taking their dose of pale sunlight is a nice reversal of Edward Jenner's pioneering research. Jenner discovered that humans could be protected from smallpox by the use of fluid taken from vesicles found on the udders of infected cows.

In the Edward Jenner Museum, near Berkeley Castle in Gloucestershire, are a number of exhibits donated by Joyce Green Hospital. There is a stereoscopic viewer through which the visitor gazes, expecting some example of Victorian or Edwardian topography. Morally uplifting landscapes. Alpine scenery. A Scottish lake. A spa town. The effect is three-dimensional, nicotine-stained sepia. But the stereoscope defies expectation. Dr J.B. Byles, compiling material to illustrate a book by Dr Ricketts, photographed the action of poxes in intimate detail. Skin as a map, a meteorology of infection; flushed and angry (like those charts that divide London into zones of comparative poverty).

Dr Burne is proud of Joyce Green's paradise gardens, contrived and planted against prevailing conditions, on the edge of a salt marsh. He rattles out the Latin names as he swerves through the estate, pointing with his stick, swooping on some previously unnoticed growth. Walnut trees. Juniper bushes thick with strange fruit, cigarette butts (flicked from the staff room window). There are memorials to surgeons and gate-keepers and a seat dedicated to the Joyce Green gardener, Harry Hopkins.

Hopkins carried through the arboretum conceived by the Medical Superintendent Dr A.F. Cameron. Between 1919 and 1935, he transformed rough, windswept grounds into 'a little paradise'; the subject of a glowing testimony by Arthur Hellyer, one-time patient and gardening correspondent of the *Financial Times*. 'A garden filled with as fine a collection of exotic trees and shrubs as you would be likely to find anywhere near London, except in the most renowned places or at the Royal Botanical Gardens, Kew.' A grove of eight *Koelreuteria paniculata*. Sprays of small yellow flowers and the 'curious bladder-like fruit' that follow them. A young paulowinia. Magnolias by the score. A thicket of yuccas.

The three of us sit on Hopkins's bench, a curve of wooden slats, sheltering in a V of weathered bricks. Someone has left wildflowers in a bottle. Beneath the bench, in heavy clusters, are cigarette stubs. It's obvious, standing back, that Harry Hopkins's memorial duplicates the winged design of the hospital. A cabbalistic conceit: outside as inside, a system of magical equivalents. Within this grove, the spirit of the old gardener (picture him in First War uniform, cap and moustache) is present: curated by Doc Burne who never goes anywhere without a pruning knife. If any part of this secret garden is to survive, it will be down to Burne, and whatever he can replant or graft in his own soil.

Time is not on his side. Burne's expedition has to be conducted at a clip; out of the hospital grounds and down, by overgrown tramlines, to the vanished Long Reach Smallpox Hospital. The river-road where plague ships anchored.

A long green lane, straggly hedges; incongruous tarmac. The black skin is worn away, revealing the underlying pattern of bricks. We step over the first chalked graffito: BNP. Horses stick their heads through gaps in the hedge. 'If they've got a blanket,' Burne says, 'riding school. If not, gypsy.'

Chalk signatures, territorial assertions, come at regular intervals. We are walking down what was once a private railway, linking the isolation units with Joyce Green. Long Reach had its own jetty, demolished in the Seventies. Smallpox ships, paddle-steamers such as the *Atlas*, would make regular voyages from Rotherhithe; there were beds for up to 250 patients. Scrubbed deck planks, a hiss of gas, the stink of sulphur. Whole streets, infected warrens and rookeries, could be evacuated. At first guilty housing was sealed like a ghetto, hung with plague flags. And then, with some degree of secrecy, the sick were shipped out.

'She was a short fat town girl,' Burne chuckled. '*Panorama* sent her down. Heels and all.' We were scrambling over rubble mounds, hacking through a thorn wood. 'It was twilight by the time she got here. A terrible scream, an owl. I asked if she'd like to see the Long Reach mortuary cesspit. She ran. When the programme went out, they used one sentence.'

Bushes heavy with white blossom. We find the cesspit, now hidden, lost in the brambles like a holy well. Dr Burne, forging ahead, can only be distinguished from Renchi by the walking stick and the bright yellow gloves.

Bikers love riverside earthworks, the high banks that keep

the Thames out. Burne doesn't disapprove. A burnt-out car is a rusted antiquity, older than the stories the doctor tells. Older than the plague ghosts.

We stand at the river's edge, taking in the whole broad sweep, Queen Elizabeth II Bridge to the oil storage tanks at Purfleet. Myths grew up around the *Atlas*, when she used to anchor off Greenhithe. Children of the time, now elderly patients in the hospital, were interviewed by Dr Burne. They remembered coffin ships which they confused with the Dickensian prison hulks.

In 1980 a thirteen-year-old schoolgirl wrote an essay based on stories told by her grandmother, Clara Couchman. 'All Gran remembered was being carried at the dead of night in a red blanket by her parents through Greenhithe down to the water front. Then she was taken by rowing boat out to a big boat moored off Greenhithe Reach . . . It was dark and filthy. There were rats on board which you could hear scampering about in the night. It smelt of sulphur candles . . . People stayed on that ship for three weeks and if you were still alive a rowing boat was sent by relations out to the hulk. This ferryman was paid, and had to be paid well. He would call out your name for you.'

Nobody could visit Long Reach without passing through a regime of disinfection, carbolic baths. The system fell down, as always, on English notions of caste. Surgeons and doctors strolled around the checkpoints, unhindered. A gate-keeper who waved through Reuben Message, a Dartford meat vendor, lost his job. The delivery man developed smallpox.

Dr Burne fitted his narrative to the landscape we had struggled through in the dark and the rain. He led us around the hospital estate and out on to the marshes, showing how apparently random piles of stones, holes in the ground, bits of rail, broken gates, belonged to a living history.

The drench from the sewage farm came in columns. You didn't smell it, you wore it. It invaded your clothing. Marsh

Lane, so Burne told us, derived its name from Marsh Gas Lane. Huge gulls feasted on the sewage outflow, rode the tide, pecking at submerged delicacies. 'Do you know how old I am?' Burne challenged. 'Eighty.' He chuckled.

How had we missed it? From the chalk mound of Beacon Hill, a stone cairn on the embankment, the old straight track arrowed into the water tower of Joyce Green Hospital. A thin grey line between hefty, untrimmed hedges. What felt, on the night of the storm, like a march through a completely unstructured landscape now made sense. The view arranged itself into discrete elements. Remove the hospital, garden and tower, and balance is lost; orchards grow wild, there is no estate to give focus and meaning to an exploited wilderness.

Entry to Joyce Green, coming from Long Reach and the isolation wards, was by way of a wicket gate; a fever bell had to be rung. The bell was preserved, as Dr Burne would show us, in the hospital library: polished, with the crest of St George. 'You realise,' he said, understanding our reluctance to leave the riverside, 'that the estate – gardens, woods, farm, hospital – has its own microclimate.'

It was true: the rain, soft and steady, had stopped. The suspension bridge hung over the Thames like a solid rainbow. 'Look: Spanish oak, laurel, white daffodils. Bees and butterflies you won't find anywhere else on the marshes. This place is the uniquest of the unique.' He jabbed with his stick at a fallen tree, brought down across our path. 'That proves it. Ivy kills.'

For Burne, 'filthy plumes of smoke' was an endearment. The power station had as much right to its position on the river as the sewage farm and the hospital – even though pollution bleached the leaves. Fuel had been stockpiled here in advance of the miners' strike: Burne saw Thatcher's strategy before it came into play. Know your own small patch and the rest of the world becomes readable.

★

The tour was over and we were about to head back into Dartford, but Dr Burne was reluctant to let us go. He wanted us to see everything. A humped bridge was the only way of crossing the busy bypass. 'Tricky for cripples in wheelchairs,' he said. The man who was too old for euphemisms.

He led us – the rain was back – into a new estate that had swallowed up the superintendent's villa. Bland units. Statistics to satisfy government white papers. Quota-fillers stacked on the road's edge. Visitors to Joyce Green can no longer walk out of town and ambulances are as rare as albatrosses; what we see from the bridge are the gleaming buses. They appear, so Burne tells us, every ten minutes or so. The destination windows spell out the story: HOSPITAL – DARTFORD – BLUEWATER.

The small wasteland also has its microclimate: hail. Rattling off the road, my unprotected head. This abandoned spot, hidden at the back of the estate, was once the hospital's burial ground. It's on the old maps – 'Joyce Green Cemetery' – but will soon be deleted; the designation would be meaningless. Burne slashes at brambles with his stick, looking for a single gravestone.

He came down here, so he told us, from Staffordshire. He remembered picnics, early in his marriage, on Cannock Chase. He was appointed Consultant Pathologist in 1955. His wife's family were Welsh. Two sons dead. One from diphtheria and the other from being sent 'as a precaution' to the diphtheria hospital.

'It's the ultimate stupidity,' he said. 'What they're proposing for Joyce Green and West Hill. The loss will be incalculable. The work done in the elimination of smallpox was one of the most important medical achievements of the century.'

We were drenched. He didn't want to leave that place. It might be his final visit.

'Do you know that smallpox cultures have been stored in Russia and America? Total insanity. If you don't kill them, they'll kill you. One day they'll get out. Sold off to any fanatic with spare change.' When the paradise gardens of Harry Hopkins have returned to marshland, the Joyce Green viruses will be immortal.

With images of bio-terrorism as a parting gift, we thank Dr Burne and walk over Temple Hill to Dartford. The hail stops as soon as we quit the burial ground. There are notices plastered all over town about the Mick Jagger Performing Arts Centre. Jagger has done an Alleyn. Like the Elizabethan actor and theatre promoter, Edward Alleyn, Jagger has manoeuvred himself from lowlife mountebank to man of property and status. Alleyn founded Dulwich College, Jagger got his name on a Millennium project school-hall.

We stopped for lunch in the Wat Tyler, as a way of reading the mood of the Dartforders. WAT BURGER, CHIPS & SALAD. £3.30. 'And a pint of Peasants.'

A chainsmoking woman sat by the door, her nose in a Wilbur Smith. A pensioned skinhead, grey as anthracite, vast belly sagging out of T-shirt, stared at the floor; two inches of warm beer untouched. A Hamlet cigar salesman was practising a stand-up routine at the bar. Two lads, competitively slaughtered, asked if there were any new vodkas that week. On the wall, above our table, was an advert: a man wheeling a manacled mermaid in a lobster trap.

11

Coming off the bridge, in light rain, we're carved up by a biker. He's in a hurry. The message on his vest says: BLOOD. He's probably lost the Darent Valley Hospital, somewhere among the chalk quarries. He's detouring towards Bluewater. One of Dracula's outriders, I reckon. Emergency supplies for retail vampires.

We can't cross back into Essex without making the Bluewater pilgrimage, setting foot in the Wellsian pit. The Martians used laser technology, carpet-bombs, eco-terrorism. Their successors, the planners and promoters of the Bluewater space station ('a non-smoking environment'), are more subtle. Blueness is the right subliminal message: heavenly ceiling, sparkling sea. Bluewater is aspirational. Profoundly conservative. Bluewater is the measure that separates those who belong, who know the rules and the language, from the sweaty, unshaven mob who rush the Channel Tunnel. *Bluewater* is the perfect name for 'the most innovative and exciting shopping and leisure destination in Europe today'. Bluewater is where the Martians of the New Millennium have landed (the Dome business on Bugsby's Marshes was just a rehearsal). They have learnt their lesson: they don't move out from the crater to threaten London, they let London invade *them*. Excursionists arriving at the chalk quarry, to the east of the Queen Elizabeth II Bridge, find themselves in a sort of processing plant, or customs post for asylum seekers. A channel port (on go-slow). Bluewater skulks in the desert like the set for a *Star Wars* sequel. Humans, having negotiated the precipitous descent, are reluctant to get out of their vehicles.

Pausing, on the lip of the pit, I saw the weird beauty of this excavation. Virtual water, glass fountains and imported sand have replaced the tired Kentish shore as the favoured day trip for Cockneys. Bluewater is the new Margate. The sickly London child Samuel Palmer was sent to the Isle of Thanet to convalesce; sea bathing and sermons. T.S. Eliot nursed his soul-sickness at the Albermarle Hotel in Cliftonville. Such indulgences have been suspended: now perfectly healthy urbanites, primed by subtly placed road signs, descend on Junction 2 of the M25. BLUEWATER. No need for further explanation, the name is enough. Retail paradise. No visas required. City of glass in a kaolin bowl. But the effect of this Martian pod cluster, this ecumenical Disneyland of tinsel-Gaudí, is enervating. Arrive in rude health, buzzing with energy, and a few minutes trawling the overheated malls, losing all sense of direction, overwhelmed by excess of consumer opportunity (choice/no choice), will bring you to your knees. Or to one of the many off-mall pit stops. The headache kicks in: *which* coffee from a list of thirty? (They all taste the same.)

Bluewater is the contrary of the sanatorium in Thomas Mann's *The Magic Mountain*. Instead of a high place in which interestingly tubercular eccentrics rehash the great European themes, here is a hole in the ground in which ordinary, unsuspecting citizens crack up, develop the downmarket equivalent of yuppie flu. They wander the levels, under the soft cosh of muzak, feeling the lifeforce drain. These are the Retail Undead. De-blooded victims of the Purfleet kiss. Travellers in limbo. Suspended between life and death (an extension of the Queen Elizabeth II Bridge).

Chris Petit, a longtime stockpiler of business park and off-highway imagery, is persuaded from his bunker by the promise of a run to Bluewater. (He will then accompany Renchi and I on our pedestrian journey to the north bank of the Thames – however that is to be managed.) We get a ride down my favourite road, the A13, a spin over the bridge in the Merc with blue-tinted windows. The world looks better that way, clouds acquire definition. Supporting cables, mad eyelashes, blink against the climbing sun.

Bluewater has parking space for 13,000 cars. Coming into London on a weekend afternoon, between Junctions 4 and 2 of the M25, you know that this isn't enough. The motorway is clogged, costive. Bluewater has no public parking space. Spend or move on. Pedestrians will never make the descent. They are treated like Morlocks. Any unwelcome incursion will show up on a state-of-the-art security system that cost £1.6 million. There are 350 CCTV cameras watching you wherever you go. Silent, deadly, they drain your essence. Miles of fibre-optic cable. Walls of 28″ and 38″ monitors. Follow the winding road down into the quarry and you're in the movie. The release print is CinemaScope, but that's an illusion, a drive-in fantasy; the true spectacle is the rolling wall of monitor screens, drugged shoppers leaving ectoplasmic contrails. The Bluewater complex is linked to the Dartford Interchange, the bridge, the tunnel; 200 cameras pour images on to digital tape that allows thirty-one days of continuous recording. Lift an Olympus Superzoom 120, a Sony DV, and the uniforms will pounce. No souvenirs from this car park. The movie belongs to Bluewater™. Leisure-terror, that's what frightens them. You might walk away with a Polaroid shot of the fountain, a revolving door, the markings in the car park. (Empty bay reserved for sponsors, politicians, quango vermin.)

Bluewater is what is known as a 'car park-led' project; most of the quarry floor is parking space, the strange retro-futurist construction (by a firm of architects called Benoy) is tacked on, a desert camp. Taliban chic: a very expensive (£370 million) hideaway in a deep chalk bunker. Temporary permanence. The shopping centre shares this characteristic with Lord Rogers's Millennium Dome. To gel with restless M25 consciousness, Bluewater has been designed to feel like a one-night stopover, an oasis for migrants. The huge tents that once sheltered London's smallpox cases on Temple Hill are the inspiration for this collision of ribbed domes and curved windows. The American architectural consultant Eric Kuhne, invited to talk up the site, spoke of 'a new kind of city'. A 'resort'. Rest and recreation for vacationers.

A form of petrol-guzzling tourism has evolved: Bluewater is a Ballardian resort (*Vermilion Sands*), shopping is secondary, punters come here to be part of the spectacle. The North Kent quarry is an unanchored destination: nobody is quite sure where it is. It's never in the same place twice. The surrounding road systems are so complex – FOLLOW THE SIGN FOR CAN-TERBURY – trippers can't work out which side of the Thames they're on. They arrive exhausted. They depart half-dead. They've taken part in the experience of travel. They've seen the car park. Too weary to walk, they stumble into the 'leisure village' with its artificial day-for-night lighting. The place is a gigantic upgrade of Margate's Dreamland arcade: glittery cargo behind glass, get-lucky trash you don't want (but try to win), fast food. Bluewater combines slot-machine avenues with fun fair rides: escalators, lifts, cinemas, indoor jungles, pools, boat-ing lakes, climbing walls and even, yes, cycle hire and a 'discov-ery trail'. Your 'hosts' (welcome, campers) are trained in sign language. There are Braille maps and personal guides for the visually impaired.

From above, Bluewater looks fine: sunlight glancing off pas-tiched oast houses. Petit doesn't risk a smile, he uncreases his Jesuitical frown. There is purpose to his expedition, he wants to buy a pair of Y-fronts; but this is no simple commercial transac-tion, he has roamed half the country, from Cribbs Causeway (outside Bristol) to Asda (Eastbourne), to Lakeside (Thurrock). No joy. The man is a perfectionist. One day, so he believes, he will discover the M&S grail: right weight, style, fit. The Look. The correct gear for the proverbial road accident: no shameful moment on the trolley, if he finds himself taken into Darent Valley Hospital.

At first, Bluewater provokes such impulses. It's like arriving at a Channel port; the transit point becomes a destination. Dover, Folkestone. The same grid of cars. The same concern about getting into the right stream. High white cliffs. Visible evidence of wartime activity; tunnels, huts, gun emplacements. Security (discreet but firm). The dizzy sense of impermanence, not being where you are; exhausted from travel and anticipating more of the same. Customs paranoia. Worries about having left your passport, tickets, green forms, in the kitchen drawer.

We set off in search of duty frees, an investigation of this inland port. It's not England and it's not France; it's more like the US without the genetically modified mall addicts, the mutated burger herds. But Bluewater excursionists are not regarded as urban terrorists if they don't buy buy buy. Thank God. Because nobody has the stamina to shop, to make a decision.

You meet trembling humans who have lost their cars: green zone or blue? The Heathrow experience, jet-lagged, combing the ranks, struggling with heavy bags: which terminal was it, which floor? Tilbury, the old port for London, with its many platforms and shuttle of trains, has died; an echoing ghost. Bluewater (no access by river) has sixty buses per hour, 130 trains per day, five taxi ranks and colour-coded car parks without number.

The design is stolen from the Victorian asylums, from Joyce Green Hospital: a broad V, within a box (or Rubik's Cube). The three barbicans that command the points of the V are House of Fraser, John Lewis, Marks & Spencer. There is an upper and a lower mall. The temperature is unnatural; so temperate that it drives you mad. You can't sweat. You're blow-dried. You can't breathe. Air is recycled as in an airliner. You're supposed to make those air-terminal, duty-free, impulse purchases that you come to regret: shirts that never leave the bag, rubber-sealed bottles of cherries in brandy, lighters for those who don't smoke. Airport consumption is reflex superstition: buy and live.

The toilets are too clean for England and they're open; our cities have long since dispensed with such philanthropic frivolities, converting every pissy trench into a wine-bar or body-tanning facility. Bluewater is the only safe way to visit America, it's the post-11 September destination of choice. Heathrow without the hassle. Then take your pick of: Santa Fe ('South Western American restaurant and Cocktail Bar . . . authentic and exciting'), Ed's ('Authentic 50s American diner'), Tootsies ('Authentic American family restaurant in a stylish setting'). Plus: McDonald's, Kentucky Fried Chicken and the multiplex with blockbuster buckets of popcorn and hogsheads of energy-boosting drinks. These days, only the fake is truly authentic.

Rachel Lichtenstein, author of *Rodinsky's Room*, was dragged here to choose a wedding dress. She lived in Hackney, her mother in Southend: Bluewater was the obvious rendezvous. Twenty minutes on the malls and the ceremony was about to be called off, while Rachel fled to a house of study in the desert. A life of abstinence and prayer. Bluewater's anodyne aquarium walkways provoke many such dramas. The Kenneth Baker anthology of uplifting poems, in relief on every wall, incubates rage. I was ready to tear out the tablets with my fingernails and smash them down on the heads of inoffensive mall-grazers.

A Tate Modern gallery of male underwear fails to satisfy Petit; a mournful shrug and he's away through the revolving doors. It's a great cultural event, melancholy as Wim Wenders, watching Petit work a retail outlet. Shopper as aesthete. He tracks, he drifts; he won't stoop to examine a label or a price tag. The nostrils flare. The stern eyebrows twitch. Some hideous vulgarity, in terms of colour or texture, has been enacted. Behind the mask of disdain, this man is supremely alert, sunk into a trance of mesmeric concentration. Indifference as the ultimate accolade. Bluewater fails, Bluewater must be consigned – like some wretched film or novel – to silence, scorn: the heart-rending sigh of a seeker who has reached out and grasped disappointment. A spoonful of volcanic dust. Petit quits the quarry like a vampire hunter promised wolves and fly-eating maniacs, then fobbed off with a drip of born-again vegans.

The displays of underwear, boots, lipstick – kit – have a disembodied sexuality. Palace of consumer fetishism as art gallery isn't a perverse reading. The 'Dalí Universe' at London's decommissioned County Hall is conducting a phone poll (call: 0901 151 0133) to decide on the best site for a 'sculpture based on a Dalí painting'. Should *Profile of Time* be exhibited at Hampton Court Palace, in Kensington Gardens, the Royal Botanical Gardens at Kew – or at Bluewater? No contest. Bluewater, the posthumous dream of Walter Benjamin, is the clear favourite. The Dalí painting from which the sculpture has been concocted was first shown in 1931. Title? *The Persistence of Memory*.

The payback for my trip to Bluewater is Petit's company on our attempt to cross the Thames (22 October 1999). Research has made it abundantly clear: the Queen Elizabeth II Bridge cannot be negotiated on foot. Neither can we rush the Dartford Tunnel (like desperate asylum seekers from the Calais camp). The best option is a long detour, by river path, to Gravesend. A ferry trip. A slog from Tilbury to Grays (returning us to the bridge and the reborn M25).

Marc fails to make the seven a.m. meeting at London Bridge station. He's been here before, walks recorded in his book *Liquid City* (Isle of Grain to Teddington). The novelty has worn off, feet have healed; he discriminates, picks outings worthy of his talent. That's very reasonable, the images have been logged. Greenhithe, Ingress Park (its Capability Brown plantings handed over to Crest Nicholson), Northfleet, Gravesend: they are part of an earlier narrative. I won't peddle an exhausted tale. Better to pick up where the motorway surges into Essex.

The problem is that video-time and shoot-from-the-hip photo-time are not compatible. Renchi and I have learnt to register detail as we walk; a steady and unspectacular progress. Breakfast, pub lunch, chats with folk met at the wayside. Nothing to break the trance. Video is trance. Once Petit's finger starts to stroke the touch-screen, he's gone. He's inside the image.

Temple Hill throws up seductive views of river, motorway, suspension bridge: Petit might take an hour to find the right spot from which to film. Renchi can't rein himself in. Look, look: blue and white POLICE tape in a field, Costa del Sol bungalows with new silver motors too big for the driveway. The Italianate tower of another captured hospital. WELCOME TO THAMESLINK PARK, ARCHERY HOUSE. Temple Hill is an entire landscape of 'Archery', brash and dissimulating. Loud with inaccurate précis, revised biography. Petit loves it, he scowls and he shoots. Renchi, anguished, frantic to be on the move, smiles. Walking and filming won't work. That's why Petit spends so much time on the road. You can't go wrong; one hand rests lightly on the wheel, the other on the button of the Sony DV. *Radio On*. Bruce Gilbert mixes on cassette, news flashes from the radio. Out in the weather, stuck on the marshes in a steady downpour, the film-essayist suffers. He wants a narrative that can be reduced to a list. A shooting script.

1. On a ridge above the Dartford Crossing: the Sakis Hotel. A venue favoured by migrant US evangelists, operated by slot-machines. SUNDAY BRUNCH £16.95. 3 COURSE CARVERY & JAZZ BAND. EAT AS MUCH AS YOU CAN!

2. CROSSWAYS. Giant letters in a retail park. A plantation of pylons.

3. Approved industrial architecture: a windowless box. On an epic scale. The coming, off-highway aesthetic: neutrality. Absence of signature. ASDA BACKS BRITISH BEEF.

4. AMBIENT GOODS INWARD. Dead roads where container-

transporters park. Limbo zones of rubbish in short grass, improvised culinary and sexual transactions.

5. Ingress Abbey as devastated mud, a building site.
6. Graffito on riverside wall: THATCHER OUT!
7. The cranes and hoists of Northfleet under a heavy sky. Petit eating a banana. A snail hanging from a spear of wet grass. A snail on Renchi's shoe.
8. One hoarding: PELICAN FABRICATIONS, SEACON TER-MINALS LIMITED, BRITANNIA REFINED METALS LIMITED, LONDON COACHES, FLAT-OUT KARTING, THAMES TIMBER.
9. The locked stadium of Dartford and Northfleet FC.
10. A Northfleet café with an expressionist mural: industry returned to life in a smoky (yellow/red) apocalypse. The mural as a window on an alternative world.
11. A wall of figs in a Gravesend industrial estate.
12. A chalk quarry (caged walk) not yet converted into another Bluewater. Renchi suffers from mild, Petit from severe, attacks of vertigo.
13. Riverside houses with Belgian roofs, Corinthian capitals (inverted foliations), arched windows, ogee mouldings. Fallen into disrepair.
14. A fibre-optic colony. Guarded by a lighthouse topped with concrete water tank.
15. Graffito on tile wall: EAT THE ESTABLISHMENT.
16. A microphone, on a tripod, set up on a traffic island.
17. A chaplet of sunflowers woven into a chainlink fence. WARNING GUARD DOGS ON PATROL. KEEP OUT.
18 Memorial tablet to Pocahontas (in bell-shaped hat).
19. The Gravesend–Tilbury Ferry: *Princess Pocahontas*.

We're out, at last, on the grey Thames, at the mouth of the estuary. The voyage towards Essex feels like a mistake. The small craft has to push against the tide. Sky and river merge. Our walk through Surrey and Kent dissolves. We are returned to the familiar shabby narratives of Tilbury (dockside, fort,

World's End pub). To piebald horses roaming a Dutch land-scape of irrigation ditches and rifle ranges.

As the light goes, Petit falls further and further behind; he is trying to make a video-record of salient dereliction (high dock walls, weed-strewn railway tracks, hangdog lamp-standards). We tramp towards Grays. There's no river path, we have to stick with the Dock Approach Road. Tower blocks wink across rough heath. Steady traffic. Everything is visible and nothing is revealed. There must have been a reason once for Grays, but it's been forgotten. Subdued, we wait for the Fenchurch Street train.

Blood & Oil

Carfax to Waltham Abbey

1

Film-essayist Patrick Keiller, who knows about such things, says that Grays once had a wonderful cinema, on a par with the Kilburn State. Now the State of Kilburn can sneer at its riverside rival: Grays is beyond resuscitation. A body bag lined with asbestos.

19 October 1999: we stepped on to the platform to a (glove-in-mouth) tannoy babble that sounded like the three-minute warning. At Fenchurch Street the ticket machines were out of order, trains were running late and station security were shaking down a couple of estuarine chancers (trying to slip into town without the necessary paperwork). The woman behind the plexiglass screen couldn't hear what Renchi said, couldn't imagine why anyone, so early in the morning, would want to travel *towards* Grays. The point of Grays is that you leave before first light, return after sunset – avoid all eye-contact.

Don't misunderstand me, I love the place: it's pre-fictional, post-historic. It has slipped out of the guidebook and into the Gothic anthology. Laughable attempts at civic revival – pedestrianised walkways, covered markets upgraded to prolapsed malls – do nothing to diminish the galloping entropy. The Stalinist turret of Keiller's favourite cinema – STATE – is visible from the station. Dirty brown bricks, deeply scored creases: the aspect of a power station, of Bankside before the makeover.

WHO IS THE DISTRICT CONTROLLER???? Graffito on the underpass. Grays is a breakaway republic, the Uzbekistan of the Estuary. Grays has Tattoo Studios ('Over 18's Only Please!') and food so fast that it avoids the mediation of the microwave, travelling directly from slaughterhouse floor to fast-breeding salmonella culture. Retail facilities behave like uninhabited multi-storey car parks. Trade goods are rejects from car boot sales.

But Grays has something that gives it life and pedigree, Grays has the River Thames. The sky to the east, on this damp morning, could be illuminated by searchlights: a pissy-gold cloud base flushing to a raider's dawn. Nautical pubs are imposing but clapped out. The signboard for The Rising Sun has weathered into a Monet Xerox, Tower Bridge drowning in thin syrup.

The essential qualities of this riparian settlement have not been lost. James Thorne, writing in 1876, sketches Grays as: 'old, irregular, and, like all those small Thames ports, lazy-looking and dirty'. Grays lived off chalk: when they'd finished digging it out for conversion into lime and cement, carting it on to the roads of Essex, they moved into retail landfill – Lakeside, Thurrock.

'Of all the accursed roads that ever disgraced this kingdom in the very ages of barbarism,' wrote Arthur Young in 1757, 'none ever equalled that from Billericay to the "King's Head" at Tilbury . . . the ruts are of an incredible depth . . . and to add to all the infamous circumstances which occur to plague a traveller, I must not forget eternally meeting with chalk wagons, themselves frequently stuck fast until a collection of them are in the same situation, so that twenty or thirty horses may be tacked to each to draw them out, one by one.'

The days of the cement factories and the futile attempts to promote Grays as a sailing resort, a marina, are over: river gives way to road. We've taken our hit of nostalgia, hanging about the dock gates, photographing steam stacks, cranes, jetties. It's time to follow the Thames path, west, towards the Queen Elizabeth II Bridge, the motorway.

The path, which begins with a paved promenade, soon declines into a Barratt estate, dressed as an open-air exhibition of 'computer generated impressions'. This is a strikingly schizophrenic effect: you get the Thames as it is, cloacal, rusty, tired – and, at the same time, you are confronted with computer-generated projections (Grays as it ought to be). A blue-river fantasy feeds directly into khaki drift; a young couple, first-time buyers, stride hand in hand down the riverfront parade towards a line of virgin Barratt villas. Future grass for present mud. The magic mirror of the Barratt hoarding works like Prozac, taking the edge from blight. Pink stone, a cloudless sky; toy boats gussying up a dead river.

Barratt World is hallucinogenic: mushroom villages, Noddy in Essex. No hurt. Cohabiting couples in gainful employment. Regency stripe wallpaper. Red sofa – on which a woman in a green dress sprawls, teasing a coffee cup. Her partner, in immaculate blue shirt (two buttons undone), leans forward. He has another (empty) coffee cup. They are fresh, fragrant. Unblemished. If it wasn't for the coffee cups, they'd be rutting like stags. If everything goes well, and they upgrade from the one-bedroom apartment in Block H of Lightermans Quay (at £86,995) to the two-bedroom apartment at £104,995, they'll acquire the two sinister kids who invade their love nest with a breakfast tray (single red rose, refill of imaginary coffee).

Lightermans Quay has its own map, roads like veins flowing into the A13. Only three destinations are admitted: Southend, Lakeside and the M25. The furthest points of reference are Tilbury and Chadwell St Mary (where Daniel Defoe invested in a tile works – and lost £3,000). 'A calm and tranquil setting with appealing riverside walks,' the promoters claim. 'This whole part of the riverfront is steeped in history.' Which the builders are doing their best to disguise. What counts is ease of access to Junction 30/31 of the M25 and the ten-minute drive to 'the huge shopping complex of Lakeside'.

Ten minutes' walk, on the other hand, carries the excursionist into a wilderness of tall chimneys, chainlink fences, partly demolished block buildings, dank ponds, thorn bushes, coarse grass. The latest units of the housing development, frightened Dutch cottages, shelter on the very edge of a soon-to-be-demolished brownfield site. O'Rourke and Associates are swinging their hammers at the garden gate, bulldozing mounds of rubble, coating the 'double-glazed external windows' in fine dust.

We meet a game old boy, sniffing the tide. A weatherbeaten unident in a flat cap who deeply regrets the destruction of the wild orchards that once marked the river path. 'Better than Vicky Park, it was.' He's been in Grays since he came back from the war. His house in Canning Town had been bombed. It wasn't there, nor was his wife. She'd been relocated. But he couldn't reconcile himself to the exile. 'Sod all life. They do what they want with the river. Criminal.'

As for the Barratt hutches . . . 'Kennels,' he spat. 'Hear everything they say next door. Stretch and you put your elbow through the wall.' They don't build these estates, they grow them overnight.

A younger man with a large dog joined us. A reluctant citizen of Chafford Hundred, a former Canvey Island fisherman. 'Lego homes,' he reckoned. 'They come in kits.' He sounded less enthusiastic than Buckminster Fuller for the flatpack lifestyle. Euro regulations had done for his trade. He pointed to the fast-flowing water. 'I can remember when this was a river of soles.' River of Souls! Golden scintillae riding the wavecrests. We saw it: a floodtide of immortals surging to the west. Before we realised what he meant: soles, fish he could no longer net. The river's bounty, his living.

Chafford Hundred – 'The most coveted address in Britain' (*Evening Standard*, 12 September 2001) – was a plague on the landscape. So the sole-fisher reckoned. The future he would have to endure. A bright new 'commuter-belt village' whacked down on a hillock overlooking a defunct port, a highroad whose vitality had been leeched by Lakeside, Thurrock. Patrick Keiller, conducting a personal survey into housing, found much to admire in Chafford Hundred.

'Who lives there?'

Hammered by government statistics, I needed to know.

Who were these putative householders, where did they come from? I rang Keiller.

'Divorce,' Patrick said. 'And extended life expectancy. Single parents. Split families.'

A colony of the disenchanted in a panorama of disenchant- ment. Amnesiaville. It would take more than divorce or death to get me to Chafford Hundred. But one of the Barratt apart- ments at Grays? Riverview, 'audio entryphone system', elective isolation, 'thirty-five minutes by train to Fenchurch Street' – what could be better? As a studio, a writing space. If I could lift myself into the right socio-economic bracket. Grays was aspirational, a spoof balcony on which to contemplate the river of souls.

Chafford Hundred thrives because it is not really there. It's displaced, not placed: 2,000 (and rising) pristine, anti-vernacular units. Scimitar-shaped Draylon-grass carpets. Second cars. An empty-by-day enclave with no centre and no purpose. Chafford Hundred, as English as one of Prince Charles's model villages, is actually bad-weather California: compulsory democracy, the flag (of the developer), total absence of that inner-city ethnic stew. As we walk away, we are overtaken by a white stretch- limo packed with kids on a birthday outing – to Bluewater?

The satellite estates around Grays are as much about re- possession as possession. In the early Nineties' property slump, late-Thatcherite speculators caught a cold. Ready-cash sharpies (from Deep Essex and London) picked up houses for around £80,000. Now, five and six bedroom properties start at £310,000. Journalist Nick Curtis, reporting for the *Standard*, claimed that there was nothing to do in Chafford – except have babies, rent videos, and watch more houses being built.

As we follow the sweep of the broad Thames, the riverbank evolves into what I call: Dracula's Garden. Plants have had the juice sucked out of them, they've swallowed the filth brought in on the tide. They've stood up to wind, acid rain, the noxious perfume of the soap factory. And they've thrived. Mutated. Treated toxic infusions as growth hormones. Teasels look like spiky hand grenades. Lurid mosses lurk between the stone blocks of the embankment. Tyres, left in the mud, become rock pools. A lovely, lapping tidemark of oil, thick as elephant skin. Abandoned shopping trolleys act as trellises for weeds and rubbery marine growths. Couch grass breaks through a tarpaulin topsoil. Oil is the blood of the place. Oil and its antidote, soap.

Dominating the path to the headland, to Stoneness Lightbeacon, is Dracula's Castle (aka Procter & Gamble's bone-boiling detergent factory). You breathe soap, blow bubbles as you walk. Small pale flowers, meadow saxifrages, have been bleached blue. They've taken the additives and bloomed. A vibrant ecology of compromise has developed along the shore, in the shelter of the hot castle walls, under the pall of perfumed steam.

The factory has been assembled from Vorticist limbs, cylinders, chimneys bolted together. It's all about circulation: hiss, rattle, whistle, crunch. Then storage. Windowless units with steel-grey walls. The industrial icebergs of Thurrock drift towards the Queen Elizabeth II Bridge. Thousands of tons of soap powder waiting to be shipped out. The most austere warehouse/tank has been sited so that the rising sun casts the shadow of the Procter & Gamble smokestacks across a colour-graded screen: a cinema of morning. This great downriver art work has been painted in four bands: dark blue (for the river), lighter blue, metallic grey, to the pearly haze of the sky. Meteorological minimalism. Constable's cloud studies revisioned as a child's building block.

It was easy to miss, but the Canning Town veteran, sucking on his single tooth, put us right. Follow the roughcast wall with the product placement graffito – PERSIL WHITE POWER – to the chalked Maltese cross (with inset swastikas); then turn north, pick up the path through the thicket of thorns. The block building is your target, two bands of colour poking above the trees. Ash, elder, bramble. Chickweed, mallow, sorrel. Nettles, wild carrot, ivy. A deep-green abundance through which we hack: towards the restored (by largesse of Procter & Gamble) twelfth-century church of St Clement's, West Thurrock.

The freakish conjunction of church, block warehouse, factory has us spinning. That a building used by Canterbury pilgrims, a river crossing, should have survived. A major portion of the money required for restoration came from an unlikely source: the makers of *Four Weddings and a Funeral*. West Thurrock is not a backdrop I would have associated with Hugh Grant and Simon Callow. I checked the video. There it was. Dead Callow, resurrected Auden. Establishing shots from the high ground, a glimpse of the bridge. A melancholy walk, after the ceremony, to the riverside. Most of the magic of the place, mercifully, was elided. Actorly business, in English films, pulls rank on location. The facility fee was earned without evidence of the director (or the crew) seeing what was here, a strange geometry of unconnected elements. The knowledge that Thurrock had any meaningful existence before the arrival of the catering vans.

We met a Procter & Gamble gardener in the church grounds, a man in overalls who was prepared to let us in. The grave-yard was a sanctuary for wildlife (and lowlife). We did the tour: saw the outsize headstones of the Essex giants and the memorial to the boys from the training ship *Cornwall* – who were buried in a mass grave in 1915, after going down, in a rowing boat disaster, off Purfleet. We admired the Roman brick courses, the evidence of a circular building, discovered on the south side of the present tower.

Renchi pounced: our old friends the Knights Templar. Only four round churches remained in England, so our guide informed us: the Temple Church (off Fleet Street), the Church of the Holy Sepulchre in Cambridge, a church in Northampton and another at Little Maplestead, Essex. We listened to his pitch, nodding over the tiles (Roman sesquipedalia). Hospitallers and Templars guarded pilgrim routes. Without question, they had been active in this area.

The lid of a large tomb was cracked, the gardener lifted one section: junkies kept their gear inside. Kids from Thurrock and Purfleet haunted the burial ground, smacked out of their heads, sleeping against the church walls. Or, if the rain came in from the river, in a convenient sepulchre. Stanley Spencer's *The Resurrection, Cookham* reworked by Wes Craven.

The headstone of Robert Lee commemorated a man 'who died in the accident of a pistol in the twinkling of an eye'. Bram Stoker's Dracula, respectful of vampire lore, took shelter in a suicide's grave.

Alabaster effigies, inside St Clement's, were chilled: chipped profiles, sliced skulls. The pilgrim route was good business. Crossing water called for risk premiums, offerings, prayer. Fear is the surest source of patronage: fragments of medieval glass, illuminated by a press-switch, featured a voyage through Hell's Teeth – from the cult which followed the 1348 outbreak of bubonic plague. The Black Death. A crowned bear rattling a money bag.

St Clement's, West Thurrock, was one of the river's great secrets. Without the old man in Grays, we would have missed it. I *had* missed it on previous walks; climbing the river wall to photograph stacks of Portakabins, then carrying on towards the Queen Elizabeth II Bridge. But gaining access to the church, touching alabaster flesh, experiencing forgotten plagues as brilliantly coloured shards of glass, confirmed my instinct. *A residue of Count Dracula was still earthed in Purfleet.*

Vampire scholars, such as Kim Newman, have always recognised that yesterday's Undead are today's asylum seekers, the Undispersed. The slow-detonating impact of Stoker's 1897 fiction came, not from its novelty, but from the sense of the book as an original rewrite, the recapitulation of a recurring fable.

Beneath the breastbeating Shakespearean echoes (cod-Irving), and the tent-show religiosity, is a considered and accurate geography. Westwards: Transylvania to Whitby. The Gothic imagination invading – and undoing – imperial certainties of trade, law, class. *Dracula* announces the coming age of the estate agent. Nothing in the book works without the Count's ability to purchase, rent, secure property. Like the Moscow Mafia buying into St George's Hill (proximity to Heathrow), Dracula chose Purfleet, alongside the Thames, so that he could ship out for Varna at a moment's notice. Being an immortal, the Count knew that he only had to hang on for a few years and he would have a bridge across the river, a motorway circuit around London: new grazing grounds. The future M25 was a magic circle, a circle in salt. The Vampire couldn't be excluded, he was already inside! Purfleet rather than Thurrock. The motorway was the perfect metaphor for the circulation of blood: Carfax Abbey to Harefield – with attendant asylums. Stoker predicted the M25, made its physical construction tautologous. The Count's fetid breath warmed Thatcher's neck as she cut the ribbon.

Back home, in his coldwater Transylvanian pile – no shaving mirrors, no central heating – Dracula/Ceauşescu plots his exile, his escape to the fleshpots of the west. He fondles maps and guidebooks: 'These . . . have been good friends to me . . . Through them I have come to know your great England . . . I long to go through the crowded streets of your mighty London.'

London gazetteers are a kind of pornography, a lubricious portfolio of future potentialities. The Lakeside Ikea catalogue would have turned him on to the A13 and the chalk quarries. Ikea were sensitive to 'that well-loved essential bit of storage', the patinised pine cupboard like a vertical coffin. Furniture that needn't cost 'an arm and a leg'.

'Come,' says the Count to Jonathan Harker, 'tell me of London and of the house which you have procured for me.'

Dracula is the original psychogeographer, map fetishist, timetable freak.

The lamps were also lit in the study or library, and I found the Count lying on the sofa, reading of all things in the world, an English Bradshaw's Guide . . . He was interested in everything, and asked me a myriad questions about the place and its surroundings. He clearly had studied beforehand all he could get on the subject of the neighbourhood, for he evidently at the end knew very much more than I did.

The Count, doing his own research, located the heritage set needed for his experiment in English country house living. Sunk in reverie, on the couch in that dim library, he resembles Peter Ackroyd, conjuring up mists and miasmas, busy streets and quiet courtyards, passages where time flows as sluggishly as the Exxon oil-seepage on the Thurrock foreshore. Dracula's special subject is: doctored memory, describing the past in the excited prose of a contemporary observer. The body of London solicits his bite. He knows just where skin is tender, where the stitches will part: the alleys and waste lots and riverside chasms where ancient crimes are unappeased.

It takes a person of rare sensitivity to nominate Purfleet as a convenient-for-Fenchurch-Street-and-the-City estate. Carfax Abbey, Stoker called the place. The etymology, as Leonard Wolf (editor of *The Annotated Dracula*) points out, plays back to the 'fourteenth century Anglo-Norman *carfucks*'. Carfucks. An immaculate crossover with J.G. Ballard and *Crash*. Carfucks. The appropriately suggestive subtitle for the A13 and its tributaries (running off into Rainham Marshes). Lay-bys. Portakabin castles. Breakers' yards. Leashed curs howling like the wolves of the Carpathian Mountains.

Stoker, in the trance of composition, becomes Dracula in his study, the connoisseur of maps. I don't imagine that he ever spent time walking the river path from Grays, he didn't need to; he was in the drift. He had his researchers out on the road, doing the legwork. Harker reports:

At Purfleet, on a by-road, I came across just such a place as seemed to be required, and where was displayed a dilapidated notice that the place was for sale. It was surrounded by a high wall, of ancient structure, built of heavy stones, and has not been repaired for a large number of years. The closed gates were of heavy oak and iron, all eaten with rust.

The ebbing of the tide of time drags London, its heat, to the cold east: Soho becomes Clerkenwell, becomes Hoxton, becomes Shoreditch. Dracula's Purfleet, just inside the present M25, is our West Thurrock. The smoking mass of the Procter & Gamble factory is Carfax Abbey – constructed from giant silver bullets: to suppress memory. The neighbouring lunatic asylum, kept by Dr John Seward, is reconvened as a colony of Barratt homes. The church remains. Bram Stoker's description is better than Pevsner, lively as Ian Nairn.

The house is very large and of all periods back, I should say to medieval times, for one part is of stone immensely thick, with only a few windows high up and heavily barred with iron. It looks like part of a keep, and is close to an old chapel or church. I could not enter it, as I had not the key of the door leading to it from the house, but I have taken with my kodak views of it from various points . . . There are but few houses close at hand, one being a very large house only recently added to and formed into a private lunatic asylum.

There is no medieval chapel in Purfleet. This is it, under the bridge and on to Thurrock; the church of St Clement's, hidden among soap factories and storage facilities, a wild garden of mallow and storkbill and sorrel. A refuge for estuarine junkies.

Like Harker, I kept busy with my Kodak. I strung together numerous 'views', knowing that the alignments would shift; by the time I returned the teasel thicket would be cleared for a car park. My casual topographic record mutates into an epic canvas (painted by Jock McFadyen), or a lovely sequence of small panels, crafted from video-pulls, by the artist Emma Matthews. West Thurrock is in danger of becoming another Barbizon, the stalking ground for a school of weekend casuals. With stools and smocks and binoculars.

We moved on towards the bridge. Heavy clouds hugged the shoreline, black at base, blooded as the sun climbed above the Littlebrook Power Station. Backlit dredgers. Two skeletal towers, one on each shore, carrying power lines. They never fail: river, marshland, the pier that looks like a concrete boat. All the sensory buttons are pushed. Space. Flow. Dereliction. New estates springing up. The thick tongue of oil on the shoreline, its ridges and patterns.

At Stoneness Point, we can see the Dartford Crossing; skinny bridge, cloud road. We look across the Thames at what was once Ingress Abbey (and the Nautical School), at Greenhithe. The subtlety of Stoker's geographical revisions becomes suddenly clear: *he works through triangulation*. Three distinct locations. Three addresses for the coffins of Transylvanian earth, Dracula's bolt-holes: Chicksand Street (off Brick Lane in Whitechapel), Jamaica Lane (Bermondsey) and Piccadilly (with a view of Green Park). A thin isosceles triangle. Like that Portland stone dagger, the steeple of Nicholas Hawksmoor's Christ Church, Spitalfields.

How Stoker laid out his plan without standing here, I can't imagine. He must have had Ackroyd's preternatural skill at processing field reports, gutting and filleting obscure publications and coming up with the juice.

Ingress: 'the act of going in or entering; immersion'. Ingress Abbey was the model for Carfax. St Clement's (on the north shore) was the old church. Joyce Green Hospital would do for the asylum. Fiction compresses the picture. Walking gives it room to breathe; topographical elements separate – but are always visible. Paste those Kodak prints to the wall. Work it out for yourself.

Like Stoker's troop of bungling adventurers, vampire hunters, we're always too late; Dracula has escaped. The V of Joyce Green Hospital is destroyed, the site prepared for economic immigrants. The church is taken into the protection of Procter & Gamble. Ingress Abbey is lost (along with its Capability Brown park). We hit the oracular keys and get the inevitable response: *Ingress Denied*.

After a river trip, at the beginning of the last century, the Shah of Persia said: 'The only thing worth mentioning was at Greenhithe, where there was a mansion standing amidst trees on a green carpet extending to the water's edge.' Ingress Abbey is now being refurbished, at a cost of £4 million, for a software company. The park will be developed by Crest – who have promised 850 homes, plus 'amenities and garden features'. The Carfax walls of 'heavy stone' have been replaced by ubiquitous chainlink fences. Another potent landscape has been exposed to daylight, stripped of its shadows. Another reservoir of memory is drained.

'CALMER WATERS. *A riverside lifestyle to enjoy at your leisure.* Imagine living just 45 minutes from the city, yet a million miles away. In the grounds of an ancient Abbey, framed between the River Thames and acres of mature woodland. Ingress Park is the reality. CREST NICHOLSON. *The Hallmark of a Classic Home.*'

This is how good fiction works: by transposition, a code any half-bright idiot can break. Purfleet is not (in absolute terms) where Carfax is – *but where you see it from*. The switch: subject and object. You learn to empty yourself into the view. At privileged viewing points, the observer vanishes: the fictional residue remains, coheres. It's there even when you don't see it.

The Queen Elizabeth II Bridge, curved and minimalist, is highly strung. Hawsers fade into the sky. A long black line splits the cloud, flashes of movement. White tuning forks anchor a structure that can't support the weight. The bridge is free-floating. This is the only place where the orbital motorway lives up to its metaphoric responsibilities: grandeur, lift – *surprise*.

Vampires, according to Stoker's mythology, have problems crossing water. Count Dracula, open-eyed in his coffin, is trapped on board his vessel – until the ship runs aground, or the tide turns. 'He went south from Carfax,' says the vampire hunter Van Helsing, 'that means he went to cross the river, and he could only do so at slack of tide.' The Queen Elizabeth II Bridge, scarlet lights at dawn and dusk, is a ladder for vampires. A ladder on which blood is turned into oil. And back again. A motorcycle outrider with BLOOD on his vest.

We're advancing through a cyclorama of storage tanks, rattling chutes, private jetties, CCTV, razor wire. TANK TERMINAL. POSITIVELY NO ADMITTANCE/EXCEPT ON BUSINESS/SMOKING AND NAKED/LIGHTS FORBIDDEN/WEST THURROCK OIL TERMINAL. Thurrock on the east side of the bridge, Purfleet on the west: oil everywhere. The fiefdom of the Bush boys: Exxon, Esso. (Enron, Energy: an E-scape loud with entropy.) This is where the fuel protesters, farmers and long-distance hauliers staged their protest. Stop the distribution. Barricade the gates.

Rank upon rank of brilliant blue tractors. Waiting for export. A lake of black oil in the place of Carfax Abbey. But Stoker's themes are still active: immigration, storage, distribution. The motorway brings in the container-stacked stowaways who will be stored in empty hospitals and windowless warehouses, while they wait for dispersal. (The Roumanian Dracula smuggles himself on to English soil in the guise of a black dog.)

Storage is the major downriver industry: human, industrial, retail landfill. Petrol stations all over the south-east are supplied from Purfleet, night-tankers roll in convoys from the gate. Dracula laid down the paradigm: fifty heavy coffins of Transylvanian earth to be distributed across London.

Hieroglyphic entries in thick, half-obliterated pencil . . . the destinations of the boxes. There were, he said, six in the cartload which he took from Carfax and left at 197, Chicksand Street, Mile End New Town, and another six which he deposited at Jamaica Lane, Bermondsey. If then the Count meant to scatter these ghastly refuges of his over London, these places were chosen as the first of delivery, so that later he might distribute more fully.

The Count recognises that property speculation, an adequate portfolio, begins in the badlands: Purfleet, Mile End New Town, Bermondsey. Dracula anticipates the boys in braces, Thatcher's bluenosed-sharks, Blair's private/public arrangements. Buy toxic. Buy cheap: madhouses, old chapels, decaying abbeys. Then make your play: storage and distribution.

Blood and oil. Carfax and Esso. S/O: Stoker's Oracle. The politicians, money men and futures traders take their lead from yellow-cover romances of the previous century. 'All that die from the preying of the Un-dead become themselves Un-dead, and prey on their kind. And so the circle goes on ever widening, like as the ripples from a stone thrown in water.' Like the circle known as the M25, the orbital motorway.

We are standing under the bridge, admiring its curves and stanchions; taking our hit of noise, the stink of heavy oil, paper-pulp rotting in rain. Having set ourselves on the river path, we can't get off. We can't break through to the road. We are obliged to track alongside the Esso drums, to wave at cameras. A Chinese security guard barely understands our question: 'Purfleet?' It means nothing to him.

Renchi stops, sits, to copy a dream into his spiralbound notebook. He summons another river, a yellow table: 'a ritual I have forgotten'.

Beyond the Esso compound is a muddy paddock in which bales of yellowing pulp-paper have been stacked. I take the photograph. It's my last, the lithium batteries are gone and there are no replacements to be had – unless we venture into the Lakeside retail park. A light steady drizzle falls as we get away, through a fence, across railway lines and into Purfleet, near the station.

One of the local Undead (fanged and carious) suggests a late-breakfast caff: TC's. TC as in 'Tank Cleaner'. Behind Purfleet station, you can see the chalk. Carved cliffs. Lorry parks. Portakabins. Hangars in which petrol-carrying tankers are hosed down. TC's Diner, servicing this zone, is a good idea. The only alternative would be: STATION SPICE (Closed). A Tudor-beam pavilion, site-specific to the station, promising: 'Authentic Indian Cuisine & Free Delivery'.

The hyper-authentic TC's – net curtains, seaside bungalow fittings – offers shelter, a comfortable booth and a vegan breakfast for Renchi (which arrives without derision from the kitchen or laughter from the company). TC's is Ur-Purfleet. Oil country catering: generous portions, choice of two red-top news comics, room to spread the maps and plot our reunion with the motorway.

With the second mug of coffee – tomato sauce and egg-splash blotted up on the final square of buttered toast – the walk settles. Conversation declines into satisfied burps. The memory of the morning is fresh and the rest of the day lies on the Formica, waiting to be plotted. We stare out at the rain, the black skies. I'm glad that I picked up another golfing umbrella.

Like Stoker's zoophagus madman Renfield (in the Purfleet asylum), we look west. 'It was a shock to me,' Dr Seward wrote, 'to turn from the wonderful smoky beauty of sunset over London, with its lurid lights and inky shadows and all the marvellous tints that come on foul clouds even as on foul water, and to realise all the grim sternness of my own cold stone building, with its wealth of breathing misery, and my own desolate heart to endure it all.'

2

My camera was out of action. From TC's Diner, until I picked up a throwaway job in Aveley, I was relying on Renchi to keep the record. Our afternoon walk into Essex has a very different feel: when reconstructed from photographs that Renchi supplies, his duplicates. When I try to revive the fiction of that journey, I'm lost. I can't go back into territory where I'm not responsible for laying down the markers.

Renchi is following his own undisclosed agenda. He's not interested in signs, hoardings, graffiti: script. His photographs aren't written. They have a fluid attitude to landscape and our movement across it; the odd thumb in the frame, or unexplained smear, is a bonus. An acknowledgement of the presence of the photographer. Renchi chases light: he starts shooting when it doesn't register, the river before dawn. Sunbursts into the lens. The effect is more painterly. His prints have a green tinge.

I see that I was wearing a light green coat, a woollen cap. I'm brandishing that furled golf-umbrella like a magic wand, pointing, talking. Humping an awkward green rucksack, straps slipping from the shoulder. The physicality comes back, the heat of the wool. The steam that Renchi notes: from the Procter & Gamble smokestack, the tank-cleaning sheds. The casual way he lets a finger block off his composition, lets the viewer know he was there.

The topography of these photographs is inscrutable. Working from Renchi's album, it's easy to understand what the day felt like, how it tasted and how the sky looked. But the squabble of road and rail and river is lost; the bleakness of Mar Dyke with its pylons and boggy fields.

We walked along the rim of chalk quarries that hadn't yet been flooded to make a 'water feature' around which a business park could accumulate. We edged closer to the rebirth of the M25. Sound was panoramic, the full Dolby embrace: train-hiss, motorway whisper, planes following the river. Everything is at a distance – until, without warning, you bump against it: step into traffic, dodge hurtling metal, risk the hard shoulder, climb an embankment of newly planted trees in opaque plastic tubes.

Carfax. *Quatre Face*. The crossing of four roads. The traditional burial place for vampires. In psychogeographic terms, Junction 30 of the M25, the point where the motorway resumes its original identity, is the ultimate Carfax. Ten lanes of the M25 (north/south) violated by the rude east/west incursion of the A13. Their marriage mirrors the crossing of Thames and Queen Elizabeth II Bridge. Currents and countercurrents send vortices of energy swirling in every direction. Gangland rumours locate vanished London faces in concrete flyovers. Ginger Marks, Jack the Hat, Frank Mitchell. The vertical and unseeing dead don't know which way to turn. Stage your protest on the gantry at Junction 30 and you'll bring London to a standstill: north, south, east, west. The circulation of blood, the distribution of oil, the interaction of trance and fugue: the world thrown into chaos.

The TV news channels made it their lead item, when John Whomes, brother of Jack (gaoled for the Essex Range Rover Murders), occupied the gantry. To ensure that his demands were heard. (1) That his legal representatives should attend the ten-week hearing, the investigation into a case with many dubious elements. (2) That Jack Straw should 'sit up' and look at the facts laid before him.

Whomes, a softly spoken, meticulous man, stood on the bridge over the M25 in a bright yellow motorway maintenance jacket and gave interviews to hurriedly dispatched media folk on his mobile. The jacket had been painted with a statement of intent: FREE JACK WHOMES. INNOCENT OF RETTENDEN

MURDERS. There was also a banner: FREE THEM NOW. Whomes was sturdy, shaven-headed, determined. His eyes protected by tinted spectacles. He had picked his spot with great care.

When I met him, in a deserted car park behind Rainham station, as part of a film about the M25, this is how he explained his choice of location:

I planned it for a lot of months. I drove up and down the M25, thinking of a position. There are only four positions where you can get up, cause a protest, and they can divert the traffic off the road and divert it back on.

On the morning that we actually went up there, we left home at five o'clock, got down there and had seconds to get up on the gantry – because we knew it was camera'd and the police would be on us.

A family friend, Peter, I've known since we were toddlers at school, he comes with me on all the protests. He'd come with me that morning because I wanted to get up that first twelve foot of the gantry, because the ladders are missing. He was going to help me and then go. And on the morning, we talked and talked about it, and it was a lovely day, he said, 'I'm coming with you.' And he stuck by my brother all the way through and he came up the gantry with me.

The Range Rover killings at Rettenden achieved acres of coverage. A sensational event treated in a sensational manner: bring back the rope for the scum who poisoned Leah Betts (screamed the tabloids). The broadsheets mused on the way that criminals had migrated to the suburbs and beyond. Upwardly mobile South London villains decamped into Kent, Kenny Noye to his estate in West Kingsdowne. Small fry (booze hauliers, pill distributors, doormen with attitude) took a fancy to Eltham, Swanley, the Isle of Sheppey. Customised bungalows. If you couldn't make it to Spain, you could convert your semi into a hacienda: gin-palace motorcruiser parked on the patio. Pebbledash hutches with wall-sized Sony Trinitrons, American fridges, World of Leather sofas.

The M25 was exposed as a class barrier. Supergrass Roy Garner left Tottenham for a stud farm in Hertfordshire. The Krays acquired a substantial property in Suffolk. Chaps from Plaistow headed for Essex. Why not? Villains and cabbies. Getting away from: litter, sink schools, compulsory ethnicity. The motorway opened the whole thing up, rave culture, warehouse clubs (with girly names), cashmoney. Sacks of it. The three men who had their brains spattered over a Range Rover, down a farm track in Rettenden, were seen as necessary sacrifices. The inevitable consequence of adopting the diesel-corridor of the A13/M25 as a lifestyle choice: pills, noise, extreme violence. Transient derangement syndrome.

Crime changed. The job description. Old-timers (retired psychos, compulsive fabulists) said that they would *never ever* touch drugs. Then wolfed a pharmacopoeia of uppers, downers and inbetweens, while they operated their twilight heritage franchises from Maidstone or Parkhurst. Charlie Kray, always a businessman (so far as retro-tailoring could carry him), went down for the last time after being caught up in a £39 million cocaine trafficking scam.

Raquels in Basildon, in the bottleneck of the A127 and the A13, is where the action unfolded. Mention Basildon to Southenders and they'll die of shame before admitting that they've set foot in the town. Even in photographs, Raquels looks like the punishment block of a military prison. Like an estuarine storage unit with crazy-serif calligraphy. Within the microclimate of ecstasy culture, random and restless mobility (Canning Town to Dagenham to Basildon to Billericay), it became apparent that there had been a major power shift: doormen were now the significant players. I don't mean media-friendly performance artists like Dave Courtney (the cigar-infested skinhead from Bermondsey), but working stiffs like Bernard O'Mahoney (ghosted author of *So This Is*

Ecstasy?). O'Mahoney's account, the background story to the Rettenden Murders, was subsequently filmed as *Essex Boys*.

The cover of *Essex Boys*, the film tie-in edition, places O'Mahoney alongside the three dead men: Tony Tucker, Pat Tate and Craig Rolfe. Any sane citizen would drive miles into East Anglia to avoid this quartet. You wouldn't even want to inhabit the same universe. Ecstasy with steroid chasers. Coke to clear the head. Amphetamines to clear the room. O'Mahoney couldn't sleep without his own brand of Night Nurse, a double dose of chlorpromazine.

After the ecstasy-induced death of Leah Betts, known to O'Mahoney from her visits to Raquels, the Basildon scene imploded: prison-toned crazies, with their cartons of loose cash, their runs to Holland, their big nights at the Epping Country Club, started to rip each other apart. Paranoia was the *starting* point. Drug psychosis. Bent associates. Bent cops. Bent landscape. Who did what to whom seemed less important than where they did it. Which motor they were driving. ('Paranoid?' said O'Mahoney. 'I felt fucking quadraphonic.')

Have a good look at the photographs in *Essex Boys*. And think about the circumstances in which they were taken. Compare and contrast with the gangland portfolios that dress Kray-era PR. Not a tie to be seen, shirts worn outside trousers, and even (forgive me, Ron) jeans. The Latino trash look is in part a gesture towards Marbella, in part a convenience: so that the shiv of choice can be easily accessed. O'Mahoney wasn't a weapons freak, a long knife or bayonet usually sufficed. Indoors, his ordnance was pretty much what you'd need for keeping down mice: CS gas ('purchased on a day-trip to France'), ammonia, gun hidden in the kitchen ceiling. He'd come home for a wash and brush up, after Ronnie Kray's funeral, showing his respects, when the Old Bill turned him over. The gun had been acquired from a farmer 'for use in killing vermin'. There were no bullets.

Most of the violence took place at a coffee stall, in the street outside Raquels, after chucking-out time. Or in Barratt homes: victims jumping from windows, forcible injections, limbs amputated with electric carving-knives. ('Another feller, they decided they were going to cut off his left hand and left foot. I don't know why it was his left hand, maybe they were being kind. All because he made a remark about one of their girl-friends.' Bernard O'Mahoney reminiscing. 'There was a DJ, unfortunately called Bernie, and he was married to a girl and they separated and he kept pestering the ex-wife who was now going with another feller, and they told him to leave her alone. "You're separated, just let it be." But he wouldn't. So they invited him to a flat in Ilford, strangled him and separated him from his head, his hands and his feet. They cut his head, hands and feet off. They've never found his head, his hands and his feet. They dumped him, buried him.')

Off-highway. On the marshes. Anywhere within easy reach of the A13. The Disney Corporation was supposed to be inter-ested in the site, London's last wilderness. Bill Oddie and the Twitchers, the Rainham ornithologists, fought the plan. The Ministry of Defence hoped to do a deal for £1.1 million. 'Its destruction,' said Oddie, 'would have been like knocking down St Paul's and building a multistorey car park.' The marshes survive as big sky wetlands, much loved by avian migrants, scrap dealers, freelance morticians.

When the pressure was on – cops, journos, ripped-off con-federates (all confederates) – O'Mahoney took to the road. Bristol, Birmingham, Liverpool. The coast. And always, above all, the A13 into the M25. ('Three more of the firm's couriers were taken out by police as they were on their way from Basildon to make a drop at a London club. They were stopped by the police at Purfleet. Each had a bag tucked inside his boxer shorts containing 100 ecstasy pills.')

The place where we were standing, admiring John Whomes's gantry at Junction 30, gave us an overview of spectacularly corrupted territory. Everyone wanted a piece of it: Lakeside developers, civil engineers, motorway missionaries, global pharmacists, smalltime pill hustlers, doormen deputed to bury heads and hands and feet.

The Essex police, in pursuit, used the motorway ramp as their top spot for pulling dubious vehicles.

'The M25 is an asset for everybody,' O'Mahoney said. 'There is a stretch of elevated road at Thurrock which is a favourite for the police to arrest people on. I got arrested on there myself with a drug dealer – because when they pull you up on that side of the road, unless you're prepared to jump sixty feet over the side, into a field, they know you're not going anywhere. The M25 is useful for all sorts of people. Essex is surrounded by ports, motorways. Essex is well connected for getting stuff shifted around, do you know what I mean?'

I think, by now, we do. The story is visible in the scars on the landscape. The crossing of roads. Recurring vampire imagery. I'm never going to drive through Thurrock again without a garlic necklace.

O'Mahoney recalls a man named Darren Kerr.

Kerr had been in a telephone box in Purfleet when a car had pulled up. He had acid thrown in his face. Then he was bundled into the boot and dumped in Dagenham . . . He was blinded in one eye and the whole side of his face was a mass of angry scars. His injuries were so bad he had to undergo surgery in the specialist burns unit at Billericay Hospital . . . While recovering in hospital he was paid another visit. A man turned up dressed as a clown. He had Dracula teeth, a clown's wig . . . and he was carrying a bunch of flowers . . . When he saw Darren he whipped away the plastic flowers to reveal a shotgun.

Life happens. First as gothic romance, then as dark comedy: plastic fangs and a sawn-off shotgun. I wasn't sure that the meeting we'd arranged with Bernard O'Mahoney was a good idea. O'Mahoney followed by John Whomes. At a quiet railway station that looked over Rainham Marshes. Early on, Whomes thought O'Mahoney was implicated in the Rettenden killings. The former doorman, a business associate of Tony Tucker and Pat Tate, should have gone down instead of his brother Jack. O'Mahoney wasn't the only one in the frame, the victims were about as popular as flesh-eating bugs; but the supposed ill-will between our potential interviewees gave the afternoon a certain edge.

Former villains (ghosted) never turn up unaccompanied for a meet with a journalist. If you can't bring a minder (a witness), dress an unemployed relative as your driver (dark suit, white shirt, sunglasses). Lean on a mate. We're talking status, respect. The media vermin (jumpy) will be mob handed. They'll have cameras and tape-recorders. You need the reassurance, one of your own at your shoulder; a bent brief to give you the nod. To steer you away from self-incrimination.

We're meeting at a station nobody uses in the day, but we've all arrived by car. The researcher who set this up, a man called John Sergeant, likes his grub. He doesn't mind staying on the road for weeks, confirming conspiracies he's dowsed on the Net, but he needs a burger in his hand, a pork pie, a packet of peanuts. Sergeant has shot off to locate a fast-food outlet in Rainham. I'm waiting, alone, on the steps outside the station.

A man in a dark shirt and black jacket is also hanging about. Tight, thinning hair. Ruddy complexion. Deepset eyes. Solid. The short coat is a leisurewear version of a donkey jacket; a nudge towards the haulage industry. You'd guess: former driver with his own fleet, three or four rigs, concerned about fuel tax. There are two small silver badges on his lapel.

'Bernard O'Mahoney?' It can't be him, this person hasn't brought a minder. Before he answers, he signals to a previously unnoticed partner (waiting in the motor). His son. A young lad. Inconspicuous, well behaved.

Mr O'Mahoney is civil, slightly reserved; he frowns and grins. He laughs readily, but not always in synch with circumstance. You'd say, not having read the book: decent fellow, family man. When Sergeant skids in, elbow on wheel, bun in mouth, O'Mahoney cheers up. 'I know you from somewhere.'

Everybody does. Sergeant has that kind of face, reassuring; wide smile, genuine sympathy for the person he's interrogating. They know that he knows the story, all of it, no point in holding anything back. Sergeant is the best kind of spoiled priest, a confessor in a leather jacket. An *On the Waterfront* hybrid of pre-inflatable Brando and Karl Malden. He's a shape-shifter. Put him one-to-one with a Basildon hardman, up against the perimeter fence of a station car park, and he slouches, uses his hands like a New Jersey mafioso. He leans in, narrows his eyes against the sun. Turn him loose on a speedfreak conspiracy theorist in Lakeside and he'll rap, nod, lick his lips – and be invited to the next monster rave at North Woolwich. Have him debate landfill scams with a Green Peace flake and he'll radiate concern, grow invisible tattoos and talk very, very slowly in a stage whisper. He'll lisp on demand.

We drive in two cars, over the railway line, through caverns of brightly coloured containers, under the A13, past breakers' yards and out on to the marshes. Unlisted, this is one of Europe's great roads. Drainage channel on one side, landfill on the other. Filthy lorries, trucks, vans trying to shove you into the ditch. A stench of unbelievable complexity: necrotic, polluted, maggoty, piscine. Magnificent. London, animal vegetable and mineral, rotting in the ground.

We pull up at the gates of the landfill site. Motorway. Bridge. River. Scrawny crows in a dead tree. A phone kiosk. A location so resonant that you've already been there, without knowing it, in dramas about autopsy detectives in unbuttoned Byronic overcoats.

Bernard O'Mahoney is uninterested, incapable of registering surprise. The immediate arrival of a carload of security uniforms is another non-event: O'Mahoney is a proscribed exile. 'I left Essex because the police banned me from every licensed premises in Basildon. They banned me from the Festival Leisure Park (which includes McDonald's, Pizza Hut, and the cinema). They put it in writing: I'm banned for life. They just said: "Take a hike."'

O'Mahoney's career curve is the best account I've come across of M25 psychosis. He got his start working on the crew building the road, evolved into a courier and e-rep at the height of rave culture, and is now in landfill. Labourer, middle management, independent businessman. The living embodiment of the public/private partnership.

I've always been involved in the haulage industry. Although I don't fear members of the underworld who are after me, what I did in those days might worry your readers – 'cause I actually helped build the M25. I worked on it in the south-eastern section when it was first being built. There was a lot of car dealers and scrap dealers and the like. They got involved with drugs in Essex, because they had lots of money they wanted to wash. You know, they deal a lot in cash. There's a lot of money sloshing around that's not accountable. You know what I mean?

Thatcher's orbital motorway was welcomed by ambitious villains. Access to the wide world. Avoid the Thurrock ramp and it was peachy. 'Stolen lorryload of coffee beans to Liverpool for a relative of deceased train robber Buster Edwards . . . Down to Bristol, doing debts. Bash people up in Birmingham. We were always on the move. The more people you reach, the more money you make. Know what I mean?'

Landfill was a sound career move. A lot of the boys were working the old golf course number. A few of them made enough to retire to Spain, play charity events with Sean Connery.

'Every landfill site in the country is dodgy. Except for the one I work on, obviously. The haulage I'm involved with is not running parcels up and down the country, it's tipper lorries which run muck or waste to landfill sites. There'll always be a problem with landfill because you see lorries running in and out, full of black bin liners. Nobody knows what's in the bin liners and nobody's going to take the trouble of going through them. So, inevitably, you will get all sorts of things ending up on the tips. Including people. Particularly in this area.'

There is no break in the stream of lorries, rattling and lurching over the marsh road. Behind the security gate is an apocalyptic landscape; shifting dunes of rubbish. With more being added every minute. That's why the crows maintain their surveillance. That's why flocks of gulls turn an escarpment of black bags into a snowfield.

From the summit of the new mountain range, hot landfill, you can gaze back on Dagenham; what's left of the Ford empire. Bad management, race tension, outdated work practices. The holding pens, which once gleamed with multiples, waiting to be taken away by road and rail, are deserted. Lakes of petrol in Purfleet and nothing to use it on. Dagenham is the off-highway destination at which nobody wants to stop. A picturesque mess to drive through.

Satellite operations keep the docks ticking over. You can buy a container unit for your garden. Or you could go looking for your missing Peugeot 505. All over London, Islington to Dulwich, Peugeot 505s were vanishing: an unauthorised recall. When police, acting on a tip, swooped on a breakers' yard in Dagenham, they discovered the disassembled sections of numerous Peugeot family cars. Cars with a nickname: the 'African taxi'. Cars that had been 'labelled and packed like sardines' were waiting on two vast articulated trailers. Three hundred and fifty-five Peugeots, taken without permission, were ready to be shipped out to Zambia – where there is an insatiable lust for the brand. The immortality of the Zambian taxi, which can carry up to seven people in relative comfort, is guaranteed by a constant supply of spare parts exported from the East London deadlands.

As the journalist David Williams, investigating this trade, wrote: 'If you look at any TV news bulletin from Sierra Leone or Zimbabwe, you will see these veterans of suburban commuter runs belting along dusty pot-holed streets, sometimes chauffeuring a passenger, sometimes overcrowded with local militia.'

So Dagenham is doing its bit for the export trade. Behind padlocked gates, DI Stephen Balding discovered 'the biggest Peugeot flatpack in the world'. The machine-cannibalism operation kept the spirit of enterprise alive, using docks that the Ford Motor Company no longer required. That's the nature of twenty-first-century capitalism, small and smart, lean and mean: steal to order. Target the Third World. Just like Thatcher and Ken Clarke, roving ambassadors of the carcinogenic combines, peddling fags from a suitcase to poverty-stricken backwaters. Who aren't too fussy about planning permission for those nice new factories. Just like the moralist of the right, Dr Roger Scruton, paid a retainer to place pro-smoking propaganda in his broadsheet polemics.

John Whomes shows a lot of arm. You can't read his eyes behind the tinted glasses. The head is razored. But the hands are articulate. An open-necked polo shirt. He's happy to see O'Mahoney, their differences have been forgotten. They both put the Range Rover killings down to the Canning Town mob. They are cynical about the operations of the police and the judiciary. They know how the world works. But Whomes is determined that his brother's story will be told: it's a miscarriage of justice – and occupying a gantry on the M25 was the best way of getting media attention. CCTV road footage of jams, accidents, could be overlaid with a message: JACK WHOMES. INNOCENT OF RETTENDEN MURDERS.

Everything comes back to the motorway. Hauliers, landfill

cowboys, minicabbers, doormen: they all have an M25 story, they all know Kenny Noye.

Whomes and O'Mahoney start yarning. The Rettenden Murders and the road-rage stabbing at the Swanley Interchange, myths of the road, are linked. Nothing was ever as simple as the black and white versions the tabloids peddled. Kenny Noye's victim, the lad in the van, Stephen Cameron – according to O'Mahoney – was often seen at Raquels in Basildon. 'The feller who died was coming back to us quite regularly. The club where Leah Betts's pill was obtained. His girl friend is from the Grays area. I thought he was a bit leery, to be honest.'

The stabbing at the roadside, O'Mahoney insisted, was 'an everyday thing on the M25'. The necessary consequence of travelling in circles in overheated metal pods. 'People are screaming, jumping and boiling. He's jumped out and Noye's jumped out and Noye's not a spring chicken and he's probably getting a hiding, know what I mean? And unfortunately he lashed out with a knife, but he's paying the price now, ain't he? The papers and the police made a meal of it. No disrespect to the kid who's dead, but if it was anyone else but Noye I doubt if it would have made the papers.'

Did O'Mahoney know Noye?

I only met Noye twice. Noye was a very good friend of Pat Tate, he met Pat in prison. Pat was working in the gym and Kenny had a fair bit of money he wanted to invest because he had too much around him at the time, gold.

Pat came out of prison and wanted a bit of capital to get going again and he asked Kenny for thirty grand, which isn't a lot for Kenny. I went down with Pat to meet Ken in a pub near the raceway in Kent, Brands Hatch. He gave Pat the thirty grand and I think Pat never paid him back, true to form. Noye seemed an all right feller to me.

A mild, warm afternoon. An empty car park. Overlooking the A13. Starlings mass on telegraph wires. Whomes and O'Mahoney are in total agreement: the Rettenden killings, as described, are a convenient fiction.

O'Mahoney: 'It's bullshit. It's total bullshit. I'll put my life on it. I know for a fact that Jack Whomes and Steele did not kill those people. Everybody knows that it was the people from Canning Town.'

Whomes: 'Those three men were shot by a marksman, an absolute precise marksman. I've seen every bit of evidence in the case. I've seen all the photographs – and they're horrific, absolutely horrific. You have nightmares about the photographs, but you have to look, because it's your brother there. I look at the photographs and I think they're saying my brother did this. And I know my brother. I've been brought up with him. I've got four brothers, all close together, and there's no way my brother could have carried that out. He wouldn't even kill a sparrow.'

John Whomes understands: it always comes back to photographs and memory. The Rettenden killings are summarised by the image of a Range Rover parked in a country lane. Whomes had to market an alternative clip: the gantry at Junction 30. The white sheet with the painted words: FREE THEM NOW.

'I wanted to cause a protest,' he said. 'They would use the footage of me up on the M25 instead of the Land Rover coming out of the lane. When they want to refer to Rettenden, they'll have to refer back to me on the M25.'

The motorway, he knew, offered maximum visibility; ten lanes of traffic slowing to a standstill. Nothing else to look at. JACK WHOMES. INNOCENT OF RETTENDEN MURDERS. 'People were going past, bleeping their horns, waving, putting their thumbs up. It was brilliant. It worked brilliantly.'

The two protesters stayed on the gantry, as on the bridge of a battleship; they were there from seven a.m. until lunchtime.

The stunt, unlike Bill Drummond's conceptualist scam, his dead cows hung from a pylon, worked: wide coverage, popular support. And there was an unlooked for bonus: seven hours of landscape vision, seven hours of shifting light and weather.

'It was a strange thing, we were up there, and as you know the M25 is up and down, you can hardly hear yourself think . . . We were chaining ourselves up, wrapping tape to protect the gantry – and, all of a sudden, my mate Peter said, "Look what's happened." And it was just . . . you could hear a pin drop. They'd shut the road off and it wasn't a noise at all. It was quiet. And then I thought to myself, well, that's power. That's a little bit of control. Now I'm in the driving seat. Now they've got to listen to me. It was lovely up there. It's a wonderful road.'

Nobody, since Margaret Thatcher cut the ribbon, has known such silence. Gulls on the landfill tip. The tick of cooling engines. A lull during which the ugly ground at the road's edge could reassert its identity.

'You've got eight miles of tailback,' Whomes said, 'right back to the A127.' Nothing moving. A phantom funeral procession for the ghastly Range Rover. A golden day to remember: from buying the chains at B&Q, to standing on the gantry, to being taken away in the police car. The John Whomes protest, the Swanley road rage killing, the cutting of the ribbon. Dominant images by which the memory-theatre of the M25 counters general paralysis, boredom. Iconic episodes that give structure to our amnesiac circuit.

3

Tucked under the neck of the Queen Elizabeth II Bridge is the ibis (lower case) hotel. On closer inspection, the ibis functions as a no-case stopover for French truckers, for migrants who are never comfortable out of reach of the motorway's acoustic footsteps. The ibis is trilingual: French, German and Franglais. Its symbol is a drooping opium poppy. Not the vulgar Remembrance Day badge tacked to the side of the absent Lord Archer's Lambeth penthouse, but something limp and fin-de-siècle.

The romance of trafficking enlivens the franchise. The ibis is a legitimate operation, but its proximity to the road, its slightly suspect Francophile courtesy ('naturally, we remain at your service day and night'), lets it fly a Casablancan flag of convenience. Rick's Café rented out to Little Chef. The restaurant area has more wine than food; you write your selection on a pad, then wait. Customers, in small tight groups, or solitary and watchful, are universally tired. An elevated TV monitor seems to be fixated on winter sports, ski jumps. Without sound. A leap into thin air: Beckton Alp or the Thurrock ramp favoured by police for pulling drug couriers.

There are other ibis hotels at Heathrow and Docklands. The look is Las Vegas-Egyptian, sand-coloured, sharp-edged. The franchise sees the world as a desert. They serve the camel routes, in the shadow of motorway dunes and flight paths. The ibis, in Egyptian mythology, is a symbol of the soul (the soul of the M25). The morning. The ibis is sacred to Thoth. The ibis bird is sometimes depicted with the crescent moon on its head, signalling a connection to the watery element.

West-facing rooms in the Thurrock ibis look straight out on the motorway, the run to the bridge. Nowhere better for that

Dr Seward moment, sunset over the Esso oil tanks, the paddocks of cars; a soul-shuddering epiphany in the cell of a fly-eating lunatic. Rooms in the ibis *are* cells – clean, anonymous, step-in power-showers. Motorway pilgrims are drawn to the site. I visited the heavily pregnant Effie Paleologou when she carried out her twenty-four-hour 'labour', photographing the road from a fixed position, one shot per hour. Random TV (a silent Blair and Hague). A DeLillo ghost story. Snatched sleep.

A Zurich-based architect, Liat Uziyel, undertaking a memory-retrieval project (begun with a battered *London A–Z*, found in Whitechapel), conceived a building that would wrap itself around the road. A self-curating museum of dreams. The walls of Uziyel's house of memory would be of varying thickness; sometimes solid and sometimes thin as paper. Sensors would be triggered by passing traffic. Pilgrims, who had walked to this place from the city, would cleanse themselves, before lying in alcoves; or secreting objects, handwritten messages, in apertures. The M25, Liat decided, was about erasure.

The ibis hotel was the manifestation of her vision. The noise of the road invaded sleep, penetrating the double-glazing, sending a shudder through the spine. In their furnished cells, transients scoured themselves under jets of water, just a few yards from the cabs of long-distance hauliers.

Women were drawn to the ibis, the incubation cubicles. They recognised the underlying agenda, the therapeutic prescription. The ibis dealt in elective amnesia, retreat and renewal. In every room there was a 'Satisfaction Contract', a 'Keep Cool' card that spelt out a three-step programme for the solving of mental or spiritual difficulties. 'If, however, within 15 minutes your problem isn't solved, we will pick up the bill.' The ibis is a Zen centre, a monastery of the motorway. Five minutes in the lotus position, breathing deeply. Five minutes to tone up. Five minutes to relax, knees against chest. That's it. Back to the road, refreshed. Ready to sell.

When Renchi and I walked up the bicycle lane and on to the

bridge, police cars surrounded us. 'You know you can't cross over.' We know. The 50 mph warning lights are flashing. Road spray soaks us. We set off in the direction of Lakeside.

Lakeside is older than Bluewater, but it's based on the same geology: chalk. Quarrying, then defensive structures, tunnels, forts, redoubts. The fear of invasion evolves into invasion-soliciting technology, business parks and retail landfill. Lakeside has been a TV docusoap and now it's an antiquated rehearsal for Bluewater. With its sorry Mississippi riverboat, its puddle of water, Lakeside is Mark Twain in an H.G. Wells culture.

What I like about Lakeside is the sprawl, the impossibility of navigating a path through its convoluted possibilities. They block roads, force you to detour. The retail experience is a kind of treasure hunt, a rally without maps. You get the maps, as prizes, when you achieve your destination. The maps are unreadable: a lake, a riverboat, pink grey green blue areas. House of Fraser, BhS, Bentalls, C&A, Argos, Boots, Marks & Spencer. Nobody knows how it works. You might spot Ikea on the horizon, but you'll never find the secret entrance. Not the first time. (And if you do make it, you need a native guide to explain the system. The sets, mock-up offices and kitchens and bedrooms, which are *not* for sale. The huge, healthy Swedish hike through pine furniture is compulsory, a training regime before you're allowed into the warehouse. What fascinated me were the books: real books in fake rooms, rows and rows and rows of Swedish editions of Patricia Highsmith.)

Lakeside is not for walkers. We don't hang around. It's exhausting, having your ghost-soul stolen by CCTV cameras, stolen and stored, time-coded: to keep you where you are. 'Once you've been to Lakeside, you'll return again and again!' That's the vampire promise. 'Something for all tastes and ages.' Something for 800-year-old, plasma-gorging Transylvanian aristocrats. 'Lakeside at night . . . it's magical!'

★

It was a relief to get back inside the M25, to the lost village of Aveley, the Mardyke Way and the Mardyke Valley. Ground so proud of its obscurity that some comedian felt obliged to erect a noticeboard, pin a map (gouged by Stanley knives), set an agenda. The sodden Mardyke Way was unwritten, forlorn. Eco-bureaucrats smeared it with their feelgood fictions: 'A secret landscape of classically flat flood plains bounded by ancient woodland on all sides.'

Which interprets as: pylons, irrigation ditches, scrub, damp cattle. Bounded by the 'ancient' Purfleet Arterial Road and the 'classically flat' M25, this country was so sad that nobody had the heart to exploit it.

Burnt-out cars form a causeway across the swamp. A man in a yellow jacket is filling in forms. An old bath, with salvageable taps intact, provides a trough for imaginary horses. This is one of those days when the rain comes down steadily and softly, so that you can't quite be bothered to dig your coat out of the rucksack. Then it pours. You stop. And just as you wriggle into the coat (or, in Renchi's case, the waterproof trousers), the sun breaks through. A pale rainbow over drowned Essex. Teasing us, leading us on.

Lakes, dog walks, public golf courses. In theory, on paper, this is a recreational zone: Thames Chase, a 'Community Forest'. Today, the community can't be arsed. Wood gatherers and charcoal burners stay at home with their feet up. A very wet beast, a hairy greyhound thing, a near-lurcher, plunges into one of the lakes and then shakes himself over us. The owner isn't sure where the path goes, nobody has put that question before. Ever.

The next storm blows my umbrella inside-out, rips off the multicoloured canvas. I bury the naked staff in a hedge. I like the idea of golf umbrellas, abandoned around the road, beginning to flower. Like the Glastonbury thorn.

Public golfers, as we have come to expect, are friendly. After they've spent an hour or two hacking lumps out of the Thames

Chase, watching balls fly backwards in a hurricane, they're ready to chat. They dress down, these old boys: as for a DIY session in a garden shed (baggy cardigan, flannels, comfortable shoes). They point out a hut where anyone with loose change can buy coffee and a bun. If we keep going, heads down, in a northerly direction, we'll find a Green Way.

The brochure confirms the tale: 'Greenways link the towns to the forest. Some of them will be parks that you can walk and relax in; others will simply be car parks.' That's the problem, differentiating. 'Arts and crafts, planting trees and hedges, are just some of the things we want to see more of.'

Green Lane, when we achieve it, is a 'Private Road'. An unsanctioned car park for bombed vehicles. A pastoral Beirut. COUNCIL IS AWARE. A yellow notice taped to the wing of a torched Dagenham multiple. Highway carrion have removed the wheels, windows, numberplates and door handles. Welcome to the Empty Quarter of Nicholson's *Greater London Street Atlas*.

At Corbets Tey, we admire the pargeting and think of Marc Atkins. It might be a moulded shield or an entire wall. The iconography of Essex pargeting is a topic we're too wet to debate. Oak trees, stags, horsemen: the confederacy of the forest. Wet plaster ornamentation that proves we're on the right track. The pull now is towards Epping Forest; the motorway, even when it's in full view, is redundant. Thames Chase publicists are frantic to keep you occupied. Birdwatching, orienteering, trim trails, kite flying, crazy golf, windsurfing, jet skiing, karting, sauna-soaking: they've got them all. These activities may be invisible to the untrained eye, but the drowned fields of the Mardyke Valley are the English Yosemite National Park. A forest of conceptual trees that must, one day, carry Epping to Purfleet. Hence the stucco panels, the impressed trefoils and stars. A coded trail for wood fetishists.

The immediate question is: will they let us into the pub? We're not wet; we're soused, deluged, bedraggled. Colour has run. We're blue. We look like something rescued from the North Sea and left floundering on the deck.

No problem. Corbets Tey is twinned with H.P. Lovecraft's Innsmouth ('blasphemous fish-frogs of the nameless design'). Locals with phosphorescent complexions, neck-breathers, welcomed us: as warm-blooded novelties. Give them credit, they didn't flinch when Renchi stripped off his outer layers and wrung out his thick red socks.

We gnaw at very dead plaice and convulsed scampi. Blind-tested, all the varieties of fishmeat on offer would be uniformly flavourless. A grit of breadcrumbs dressing partially de-iced sog. Sachets of salad cream and tomato ketchup add zest to lumpen wedges of saturated potato. The wedges have a metallic aftertaste. Like something you'd spit out in a dentist's surgery.

While Renchi's kit steams on the old-fashioned radiator, we settle on Upminster as our destination. The end of the District Line. And therefore a part, however remote, of London. Termini are mysterious places. You want to see where the rails die. It's like reaching the ultimate fold in the map, the final footprint of the known world.

Renchi, so he says, is reading Gaston Bachelard: *The Poetics of Space*. This is a coincidence of sorts, because I'm not reading *The Poetics of Reverie* (by the same author); even though I have a copy by my bed. The title was appealing. But the print was too tight. I couldn't get past the thicket of green ink annotations left by a previous owner. 'The night has no future.' It's like having a smart aleck digging you in the ribs. 'Reverie is a manifest psychic activity. It contributes documentation on differences in the *tonality of being*.'

Reverie is the best response to Empty Quarter Essex, something less than trance. Landscape floats. It is there to be seen from passing cars, not to be experienced at first hand. Essex is better remembered than known. The book I'm really reading is Roger Deakin's *Waterlog (A Swimmer's Journey through Britain)*. Deakin left out Mar Dyke and the River Ingrebourne. Lido and lock, his own moat, channel and quarry, he dipped and plunged and thrashed. He lay on his back and drifted. But no London circumnavigation (Lea, Colne, Darent, Wey) was attempted. London's watery dreaming is untapped. Nothing ventured at the hinge of town and country. He does enjoy a circuit of pools within the city and the suburbs, but that's not the same.

Bundles of papers, saved from the damp in plastic folders, are produced by Renchi. Who has been tracking the ground we are covering on the Net. He has accessed: 'An Essex Mystery'. Peter Fox of Witham, an enthusiast for 'the truly excellent ales brewed by Mr Ridley', has located three Essex pubs, all called 'The Compasses', in a dead-straight line. 'The 4th pub called The Compasses creates a circle and points to an ancient centre of Templar activity. Other strange coincidences. Geomancy, Masons, Templars and the Peasants Revolt (1381) could all be linked.' And linked, inevitably, to Danbury Hill ('considered as the highest eminence in Essex'). Danbury Church is dedicated to St John the Baptist, 'patron saint of the Templars.' Fox notes, as do all the Net dowsers, that 'there are Saint-Clere (Sinclair) knights buried in the church'.

Renchi has further evidence, photocopies from topo-graphical guides in his father's library. While he digs them out, I run my own alignment triple: Danbury, the Kelvedon Hatch nuclear bunker (captured farmhouse), Tottenham Hotspur FC's football ground at White Hart Lane. That's the real Essex: Templar/Secret State/footy.

The grey sheets – which spookily show Renchi's hand holding the book open – trace the story of the De Sancto Claro family to Danbury, to the opening of a 'leaden coffin' thought to contain 'the body of the Knight templar represented by the effigy'.

On raising the lead coffin, there was discovered an elm coffin in-closed, about one-fourth of an inch thick, very firm and entire. On removing the lid of this coffin, it was found to enclose a shell about three quarters of an inch thick, which was covered with a thick cement, of a dark olive colour, and of a resinous nature. The lid of this shell being carefully taken off, we were presented with a view of the body, lying in a liquor, or pickle, somewhat resembling mushroom catchup, but paler, and of a thicker consistence. The taste was aromatic, though not very pungent, partaking of the flavour of catchup, and of the pickle of Spanish olives. The body was tolerably perfect, no part appearing decayed, but the throat, and part of one arm: the flesh every where, except on the face and throat, appeared exceedingly white and firm. The face and throat were of a dark colour, approaching to black: the throat was much lacerated . . .

The coffin not being half full of the pickle, the face, breast, and belly, were of course not covered with it. The inside of the body seemed to be filled with some substance, which rendered it very hard. There was no hair on the head; nor do I remember any in the liquor; though feathers, flowers, and herbs, in abundance, were floating; the leaves and stalks of which appeared quite perfect, but totally discolored.

Upminster is London-aspirant, but it is also submerged Essex. The Underground finishes, the railway runs east to Basildon and Southend. Suburbia revealed. Those sponsors of community art, Barratt, have been busy with their 'computer generated' Impressionism. Mega-hoardings: 100 PC HOME EXCHANGE AVAILABLE. Pavements white as tropical beaches. Strollers in unseasonal leisurewear.

The reality check is a grey filter, a winter sun dissolving at the road's edge. Landscape dipping towards the distant motorway. A green and white sign: C. LONDON/ROMFORD/A127. Tears in the eyes.

The evening fields dim, there's a luminescence in the sky. Upminster is far enough from Lakeside to retain some retail heft; fewer charity shops than Dartford, more newsagents and dry cleaners. Eventually, tourists will arrive to photograph the station. It's architecturally undistinguished, but definitive: *The End of the Line*. The town, old as it once was, is now an afterthought. You can smell the beginnings of north-east London; bigger houses, better examples of pargeting (oak trees and herons).

We decide to go with the flow of commuter traffic, to stick with the road. Empty heads and tired feet. Upminster to Harold Wood. We're walking a metalled ridge, hedges and villages, golf courses, empty fields. The dawn sky, witnessed over the Thames at Grays, is matched by dusk at Harold Wood. An effect worthy of Luke Howard or John Constable: underlit cloud-bands above black ground, an horizon of jagged roofs.

A final photograph to celebrate Harold Wood, suburb of suburbs. A composition in three bands. (1) Pargeted oak panel. (2) Picture window, with stained-glass roses; in which walkers, road and evening sky are reflected. (3) Twin hebe bushes (bought at one of the Enfield Chase garden centres).

Now that there are destination signs for Epping Forest and the M25, we can look for the railway station. The next walk, with luck, will return us to Waltham Abbey, and close the circuit.

4

7 December 1999. Liverpool Street station: seven a.m. The idea is to muster the full troop for the return to Waltham Abbey. Kevin Jackson is game, the first arrival. He's so frightened of being late, I have to check the back of his flying jacket for benchmarks. Has he slept here? Pale, pouchy, collar up: the holy drinker shakes recognisable by railway postmen. When I worked in Liverpool Street on the night shift, I learnt to spot non-travelling travellers, TV actors in camelhair coats resting their heads on smart leather luggage. The second-time divorced, newly dropped from a series and come, by habit, to witness the departure of the last train for Colchester. Dossing down, moving off early for a shave in the Gents. A black coffee. A call to the agent's answerphone.

Kevin is mustard keen and alarmingly over-bagged. Families have emigrated with less. Moose is burdened by a rucksack *and* an air-miles shoulder satchel. He's going on somewhere, coming back from something: he never spends two nights under the same roof. It's the Cambridge temperament, restlessness, guilt. The unfinished essay. The abandoned thesis. The masterwork that dies in the drawer. Now that Marxism is as respectable as marquetry (and about as relevant), the Cambridge Apostles have been forced to invent a new brand of subversion. A confederacy of reforgotten texts and landscapes. The loop from Harold Wood to Epping Forest should do the trick. Noak Hill, Watton's Green, Passingford Bridge: even people who live there have never heard of them.

Marc Atkins doesn't show. He wanted to. He was definitely up for it. He was going to bring his partner. But then he had to cancel at the last moment, he'd been offered an exhibition at the National Institute for Medical Research at Mill Hill. He had to take the meeting.

Renchi, panting, arrives just in time for the 7.20. He's been on late shift. And battling through commuters, down the Drain, Waterloo to Bank. He grabbed a taxi, then decided it was quicker to run.

There are no cafés in Harold Wood. What would be the point? Everybody is moving in the other direction. By now, Renchi is operating with the most subtle of maps, discriminations of pink and scarlet, bruise-blue to sky-blue: a geological survey. As a work of art, great. Useless for locating sausage rolls. By my reckoning, there'll be nothing but winter cabbage and raw turnips this side of Theydon Bois. We settle for a bacon roll from a baker's shop.

Leaving the station, to cross the A12 and climb towards Dagnam Park, we have to cope with a stream of Harold Wooders rushing downhill, screeching into their cellphones. They are pale, soapy, razor-raw. Underdressed. The rest of the day will be spent in overheated offices, so this brief exposure to the weather has to be tolerated. Heels and halloween slap. The office, in fact, zooms out to meet them. Opening a tele-communications link, they are there before they arrive. Unpaid overtime eats into a period which should be spent in reverie. Jabber jabber jabber. The whole mob look like revenants, let out of the graveyard, being talked through unknown territory by a distant controller. Between bed and train, nothing. A dull blank. A set of Tipp-Ex'd snapshots.

The Saxon King pub, with its signboard portrait of King Harold (crown, sceptre, rock-dinosaur moustache), proves that we are on track for Waltham Abbey, the grave. Name five famous Saxon kings. Kevin Jackson probably could (in alpha-betical order), but those bags are beginning to make themselves felt. If he has to go to ground, like cop-killer Harry Roberts in

Epping Forest, he's equipped for it: toothbrush, clean shirt, a yard of books.

Harold Wood, Harold Hill, the Saxon King. A stucco forest of ancient trees leading to the Royal Oak pub. The houses on Harold Hill have been laid out in crescents and circuses that look from the air like helmets and shields. This, according to Pevsner, was 'one of the largest L.C.C. housing enterprises after the Second World War'. Seven thousand three hundred and eighty units for 20,000 metropolitan emigrants. 'Architecturally not much of special interest can be discovered.' How much time, I wonder, did Pevsner spend here? His wife at the wheel. Was there anything to get him out of the car?

Broad streets. Privet hedges. Hillside adapted into village green. A school with a view. An ambulance, lights winking, is parked at the end of a terrace. One bright window in a lifeless street.

We amble over uncombed heathland. We're close to the M25 at the point where it starts to pull to the east. The road yields to the gravity of Waltham Abbey.

I've remembered my binoculars. With foreshortening, the stalled motorway dazzles. A plantation of dead trees ('The Osiers', it says on the map). Black willows. Low hills. Six lines of stationary traffic: SAFEWAYS, EDDIE STOBART.

Long shadows chase us. The morning path is quilted in brown leaves. We're back with the boarding kennels and catteries. People do things with horses. If they restore a barn or piggery, they're sure to call it: THE FORGE. And to hang a white horse sign from a chain. Real pigs are not much in evidence. They've gone out of fashion, since the Seventies, when the Hosein brothers, Arthur and Nizamodeen, fed their kidnap victim, Mrs Muriel McKay, to the porkers at Rooks Farm in Stocking Pelham. (In an act of Seventies revivalism, Thomas Harris reran the plot device for his novel *Hannibal*, but nobody noticed.)

Rooks Farm was around the corner in Hertfordshire, but these discreet properties, hidden down farm tracks, have the authentic feel of bandit country. Convenient for the East End, Essex or Suffolk coast. They are so visible (from the M25) that nobody sees them. Gravel pits, plantations, private airfields. Barns, ponds, tin sheds. The mingled scents of heavy-duty slurry and diesel.

This walk is a nightmare for my Nicholson, every mile is a new map; we're cutting across the squares, chasing the broad blue band of the M25. After Noak Hill, we find ourselves, unexpectedly, in Havering-atte-Bower (which behaves like a footnote from Chaucer). The path carries us through a mud yard of caged greyhounds. Who shiver, sniff and piss until the concrete steams. Chained guard dogs snarl.

The churches are all closed. St John the Evangelist at Havering-atte-Bower, with its twelfth-century font, is not interested. We have to make do with a rare example of Essex stocks on the village green. A woman puts us right for Hobbs Cross: 'It's a *very* long way.' Not to be walked. 'At least seven or eight miles.' She restrains her air-boxing dogs, astonished that we intend to carry on.

Hob (or Hop) is Old Norse for 'shelter'. Readers of Alan Moore will be aware of a darker etymology. Pigs again: 'big pigs, and long, with one on other's back'. Pigs and pig gods. The first voice summoned by Moore in his linked sequence of Northampton tales, *Voice of the Fire*, is that of 'Hob's Hog'.

The stink of piggeries, pig squit, recycled offal, rendered bone, stays with us – though no pigs, or other animals, are to be seen. If they're here, they lead lives as resolutely 'interior' as the last years of Marcel Proust. Beasts bent to our convenience. Pre-processed food waiting for the short ride down the M25 to Great Warley. And the gun.

Roads are narrow and straight, sparsely hedged. A man in a white Panama hat tools along in an invalid carriage. We overtake him, comfortably. Thick rubber wheels hiss on wet tarmac.

The most exciting find of the morning is a trig point that tells us where we are, where we've gone wrong.

FREE RANGE EGGS. A giant chicken waves punters towards a brick shed. Father Christmas is parked on a red-tiled roof, with sleigh and reindeer, waiting for the big day. The pargeting fetish explodes: entire walls are given over to hunting scenes, a white world from which all colour has been leeched. OAK-WOOD, 1991: announces a Tudorbethan semi, proud of its antiquity. We're tiptoeing through an area of beamed, forest ranger cottages with car ports for his-and-hers vehicles: a fancy jeep and a London cab (with blue wings). We're close enough to Epping Forest to feel ourselves trespassing on reservations exclusive to those who have acquired the Knowledge.

The Royal Oak (crown in tree) features a 'crab and lobster hut', but it's too early for lunch. This is a special interest landscape. SHEDS SHEDS SHEDS. The bits between villages are perpetual car boot sales. They'll peddle anything. LOGS. MAYHEM PAINTBALL GAME. In the car park, outside a pub called the Rabbits, is a red cab with a Union Flag logo: THE ORIGINAL BEN SHERMAN. The A113 sign − (LONDON 18) ABRIDGE 2 − has been customised with an NF symbol.

Passingford Mill is a John Constable photo-op in the slip-stream of the motorway. Frame out the cars. Reed beds and river and English melancholy. 'Few excursionists,' wrote A.R. Hope-Moncrieff in 1909, 'but such as love quiet and go a-fishing find their way from London so far up the Roding Valley.' He commends Passingford Bridge as 'a pleasant halting-place, looking down to a picturesque mill, and up between the parks of Suttons and Albyns'.

The stillness of the bridge, for those who go a-walking, is more to do with the state of the road than with Mother Nature resting from her labours. Junction 27 is a bad one. Roadworks, terrorist alerts at Stansted, motorway pile-ups in fog. Potential suicides. The M11 was blocked in both directions for four hours, while police tried to talk a Chigwell jumper down from a bridge. 'Thousands of drivers were trapped between the M25 and the North Circular.' Angry commuters honked their horns and yelled at the hesitating depressive. One motorist, according to newspaper reports, said: 'Let the bugger jump. It's only 18 feet.'

Burnt-out cars replace milestones. British Telecom have built themselves a cage: BT PREMISES TRESPASS PROHIBITED. Plessy Thorn Electronics have an interest in Stapleford Aerodrome. IDEAL CHRISTMAS GIFT. A TRIAL LESSON. £30. The perfect present for al-Qa'ida sleepers. Customer-friendly airfields on the edge of the city. They are lined up, wing tip to wing tip, two- and four-seaters. From a distance, they look like gulls on the landfill mountain at Rainham.

LEA: London Executive Aviation. AEROMEGA HELICOPTERS. Renchi strides towards the corrugated sheds: THE DREAM LEISURE CLUB. Very accommodating. Fly you anywhere you want around the M25 circuit – with the exception of the Heathrow corridor.

On the far side of the Roding is Bloody Mead, a sewage farm and Hobbs Cross. One final field – PRIVATE PROPERTY – before Junction 27 of the M25; thin brown earth, flints, a few horses. With the soft going, Kevin's decision to experiment with trainer-type footwear is not looking so clever. A no-win situation: in Surrey, his yellow American rough terrain boots were too heavy; in Essex, rubber slippers suck and drag. The weight of the two bags drives him deeper and deeper into wet mud. By the time we reach Hobbs Cross, he's around the same height as the rest of us. Sunk to his knees in slurry.

HOBBS CROSS EQUESTRIAN CENTRE. A white wall decorated with black horses' heads. The place must have been used for a Mafia convention. Traffic flow, at late-morning levels, is visible above a low embankment. Somebody has left an anti-aircraft gun at the bottom of the field – within easy range of the motorway.

What's unusual about the Coppersale Lane bridge, with its

vision of Junction 6 of the M11 (Junction 27 of the M25), is that Kevin isn't carrying out running repairs on his feet. The interwoven, tumbling rush of the junction is a Niagara to motorway tourists. A border. When we step down, dodge around red and white barriers (that keep out motorists), we'll be on the edge of the forest.

We have a good view of one of Tony Sangwine's soft estates, a sand bar between motorways, a sparsely planted slope. Nothing has taken. Grass is rusty, bushes the colour of shredded tobacco. Road rubbish attracts wildlife. Squashed body cases on the hard shoulder. The only thriving crops are lighting poles and surveillance camera masts. Somewhere someone is watching us watching them. Nobody bothers with the turf island, the dead zone.

So far, so good. The Bull at Theydon Bois. Kevin has got his round in, Renchi has shot off to look for a torch. It's getting dark and the walk through the forest is beginning to play on Kevin's mind. The smile is still there, but it's in danger of becoming fixed. Naked panic in his eyes. Because this time, as we move into night, there's no way out, nothing but trees between the pub and Waltham Abbey. Trees and road.

Another pint? Postpone the moment. The pub is warm and dry. Kevin is replaying his visit to the poet Bill Griffiths in Seaham, County Durham. The shock of it. How poets live. Washing in the sink. Two rooms. With a lodger upstairs. Coal-streaked shoreline. Survivalism. And, despite or because of this, Bill produces book after book. He digs into where he is. He addresses the local and discovers coherent arguments, myths and scandals. He finds the words.

Hackney, of late, has also suffered from strange visitations. There must be something about the place I've missed. It's become a second home to the Prince of Wales. Every time you run up against a police cordon, cop cars without sirens blaring, bored camera crews, you know he's back. Showing solidarity at the mosque. He can't keep away. Snipers on the roof of the school. The caretaker in an Italian suit. Charles dropping in on Albion Drive, the Teachers' Centre, to take a gander at a model of Hackney. Much safer, his advisers will have told him, than sampling the real thing.

What was once a school, one of those red brick Victorian monsters (alma mater to Kray footsoldier Tony Lambrianou and a dozen premier league armed robbers), has been rationalised into a 'professional development centre'. Rest and recreation for battle-fatigued teachers. Advice on how to cope with the latest government rethink, post-spin paperwork. There's always a spot for those who teach the teachers, the bureaucrats of education.

In decommissioned classrooms, Hackney has been miniaturised. A bankrupt Lilliput. Papier-mâché estates, systems that work: demonstrations of electricity, machines humming and throbbing. Craftsmen have given their services. School children have carried out projects. There are tower blocks with tiny photographs of inhabitants who volunteered for the scheme; a micro-video monitor loops a sitting room. Ghosts of soon-to-be-demolished Utopian experiments.

Here is the voodoo version, the idealised borough. Without crime and drugs and craziness. Without sound or smell. Drills or dogs. The secret city in which a couple will sit smiling on a sofa: for ever. In which there is no weather, just drawings of weather. A fit principality for a future king.

'Something must be done.' The hereditary mantra. Heard by miners. Bangladeshis in Brick Lane. They know the proper response: a celebrity photograph to stick in the window of the curry house, an unofficial endorsement. HRH and the manager shaking hands. Part of a gallery of clapped-out media Xeroxes, cricketers on the piss. Tourists in search of the most popular English dish of the moment: Chicken Tikka Masala.

Batteries, springs, bulb. Renchi spreads them on the pub table. Puts them back into his SAS 'power torch' (£1.50) – and finds that it still doesn't work. This was the best that Theydon Bois could come up with. It's about as effective as trying to light a stick of celery.

The barman denies the existence of food. They have menus, yes, customers expect them. Visitors from London, forest sophisticates who subscribe to digital channels. But we shouldn't take the PR too seriously. He's pissed off because Kevin is drinking pints of orange juice and lemonade. In the belief that a hit of sugar will get him to the finish.

A woman who hangs about the place is more helpful. It's late of course. You can't expect to wander in from nowhere and be fed, just because there are signs outside punting Essex-Mex specialities. The portions, when they arrive, are Texan. My 'small' plate of Nachos is a challenge: crispy satchels packed with Copydex cheese.

A light rain is misting the windows. We'll take to the forest paths later, but for now we'll stick with the headlights, the deranged traffic on Coppice Row.

The pub sign at the edge of town does nothing to lift our spirits. SIXTEEN STRING JACK. A painting of a man in a green jacket, noose around his neck, waiting for the horse to gallop away. As light fades and the long road stretches ahead, Renchi steps it out; he disappears among the dark trees. Kevin's hair is plastered to his skull. Rain-slicks alleviate the cold sweat of fear. Epping Forest has a master's degree in disorientation, car-swallowing bogs out of *Psycho*. My snapshot of the Cantab essayist, collar up, mouth agape, makes Munch look like Millais. We're walking into the oncoming headlights. Kevin is limping badly. I hope he's not going to jump.

Trapped between M25 and M11, Epping Forest is a motor-way island with overambitious planting. There are paths marked out for riders, paths for hikers, but I've never walked any distance without getting lost; expecting to emerge in Loughton, finding myself returned to Theydon Bois. Don't ask me how it works. The spirit of the primeval forest is still present and it abhors trippers, map fetishists. Step away from the road by a few yards and the road is cancelled. It disappears. This ridge between the rivers Lea and Roding is a very public secret. Plenty of Londoners have been conceived here, in cars, on tartan rugs; plenty have died. Epping Forest is an unlicensed extension of the cemeteries that cluster around Waltham Abbey.

Five roads meet at the Wake Arms roundabout. Walking towards it in the dusk, the rain, wasn't one of the highlights of our circuit. Dazzled, driven on to slippery verges, subject to the occasional drenching, we plodded on, increasingly locked into misery, increasingly separate. Renchi was remorseless. Kevin was brave, but hobbling. I fell back to chat to the straggler, then marched flat out to keep Renchi in sight.

To take Kevin's mind off the horror of his situation, I asked him about writers who had died in cars. Give him a list and he's happy. Albert Camus was an easy one. Nathanael West. John Lodwick, a novel-a-year journeyman: one of my favourites. J.G. Ballard had a front wheel blow-out on the approach to Chiswick Bridge, spun across two carriageways, turned upside-down. But he wasn't hurt. Then we struggled. I couldn't accept Margaret Mitchell, or Robert Lowell – who gave up the ghost after a heart attack in a taxi. The poet Weldon Kees abandoned his car to go over the side of a bridge, but must be scored as: not proven. Ditto for Manic Street Preacher Richey Edwards at the Aust Service Station. Self-mythologising T.E. Lawrence (despite his connection with Pole Hill in the forest) was out. Richard Farina also. Motorbikes were another story. They were asking for it, the Jim Morrisons of road culture. Peter Fuller (of *Modern Painters*) was being chauffeured back to Bath. That left W.G. Sebald, far ahead of us, and still alive. A melancholy walker, landscape fabulist, collector of photographs: what was he doing at the wheel? I stood in a lift with him once. We didn't speak. The saddest face (moustache, glasses) I ever saw. CULT NOVELIST IN CAR ACCIDENT. The only writer I could recall who went off the M25, pranged his BMW and walked away without a scratch. Lord Archer.

The distance to the roundabout was calculable by reading debris left at the side of the road. Single cans of Foster's ('Official Beer of Sydney Olympics'), Stella Artois, Carlsberg Special Brew and Tango. Two packets of Walkers Crisps (Cheese & Onion), one of Salt & Vinegar. Five McDonald's/Coca-Cola cans. One Lambert and Butler (King Size) cigarette packet. Two Marlboro. One Silk Cut. A Coconut Bar. Smilers (Tropical Pastilles). Four cans of Red Bull ('a carbonated taurine drink with caffeine'). Three burger cartons; one milk carton (2pc fat). Diet Cola. Dr Pepper. Orange peel. Knotted condoms. One stainless steel watch (LB417, Japan). One burnt-out car: POLICE AWARE. One motorcycle engine. These are the contour rings of civilisation as they spread out from the Old Orleans ('A Taste of the Deep South') Roadhouse. A midden for future archaeologists. And present forest creatures: one fox, three grey squirrels.

We've had enough of this road; we plunge into the deep woods. And navigate by sound. It's my intention to hit the earthworks of the Amresbury Banks. The ancient camp, excavated by the Essex Field Club (1881 and 1882), under the direction of the redoubtable General Pitt-Rivers, is now promoted as an alternative, off-highway attraction; a rival to the Old Orleans Roadhouse (with its Georgian carriage lamps). AMRESBURY BANKS IS AN ANCIENT EARTHWORK AND CAN BE SERIOUSLY DAMAGED BY CYCLING. PLEASE DO NOT RIDE YOUR MOUNTAIN BICYCLE HERE. The attention of visitors is also drawn to the fact that 'many of the becch trees in the Forest are dead or dying'.

Dog walkers like the mounds. The Amresbury Camp, on its high ridge, was thought by Victorian antiquarians (on very little evidence) to have been occupied by Queen Boadicea, before her overthrow by Suetonius. Any convenient fable can be pressed into service to lend narrative to a resonant location.

Once the storyboard is hammered into the turf, we can all relax.

We crossed busy Epping Road, picked up another Green Lane, and soon found ourselves clear of the forest. The rain had eased, the sky was pink above a layer of deep blue cloud. From a modest eminence we looked down on the spread of Enfield Chase and the lights of Waltham Abbey. For all of us, including Kevin (whose ruined feet were forgotten), this was a great moment. The sun had dipped below the horizon and there was an unsourced glow in the landscape, as if a deep fire were burning within. The woods were black, the Lea Valley an inky blue. The M25 snaked through like a lava stream; red brake-lights, golden beams.

We were on Crown Hill Bridge, the very spot to which Tony Sangwine (the Highways Agency landscaper) had brought us – when he wanted to show the best the motorway could offer. Sangwine's vision is not so far removed from the builders of the Amresbury Camp. 'I think we've done a good job in treating the road here. Not just the planting but also the alignment. The way the earthworks have been blended. A combination of good engineering practice, good landscape architecture, good horticulture.'

The M25, if it is ever to work as archaeology, as a circuit that combines 'good engineering practice' with good faith, will depend on the quiet labours of men like Sangwine, practical transcendentalists. Think of the motorway in terms of Maiden Castle or Avebury, earth engines, machines designed to provoke enlightenment. The hoop of continually moving light is a gigantic crop circle, visible from space. A doughnut of powdered glass. A winking eye.

Renchi, who has treated the walk as a pilgrimage, who carries stones and feathers and lumps of chalk in his pockets, often speaks of the friendship between two families, the Bicknells and the Trevelyans. Sir George Trevelyan wrote about areas where hard science intersected with mysticism.

Discussing the moon landing, he said: 'It becomes clear that a different form of space exploration is possible by crossing the frequency-rates which demarcate different levels of being and thus entering into an expanded dimension of thought. We have to realise that higher worlds are not merely higher in space but are planes of consciousness and "being" existing in a different vibrational band and therefore quite invisible to our five senses and earth-bound consciousness. Nevertheless, human thinking, when strengthened and lifted through meditation, is a universal organ which can blend with the Thinking which is the very stuff of the universe.'

This is what the M25 must do, shift the frequency-rates, access higher levels of consciousness. Liat Uziyel's notion of a building wrapped around a motorway junction (not far from here), the museum of memory, is a theoretical demonstration of the road's potentiality as a device for hitting 'different vibrational bands'. Breaking the trance. Achieving the drift of plural time.

Tony Sangwine saw the bridge on which we were standing as an evolving art work, a performance piece. 'The bridge emerges from the green estate and leaps across the road . . . There was the question of trying to keep away from the various settlements along the route, and finding a path which made use of the topography to mask the road and to help depress the sound.'

As light goes, sound revives and clarifies. Our senses adjust. We follow our feet down the hill. So many of our suspended narratives find resolution near Junction 26 of the M25. Just a few yards off the road, on Skillet Hill, is the Jewish Cemetery where Rachel Lichtenstein discovered the pauper's grave of the Whitechapel hermit David Rodinsky. A rusting metal plaque to mark the burial place of a man whose final journey took him from Epsom to Waltham Abbey. Thanks to the patronage of Artangel, a headstone and a marble book (with blank pages) were erected at a service of dedication. When Rachel brought her young son David out here for the first time, he led the way. 'Why are we taking this path?' he said. Before arranging black stones on the grave.

On the slope above the cemetery, at the forest's edge, Tennyson had a house. He came to High Beach (or Beech) in 1837, for a stay which falls, as might be expected, into the 'silent and morose decade' that followed the death of his friend Arthur Hallam. High Beach does silent and morose very well. The forest and the world-weary poet's beard were in profound sympathy.

'I have been at this place all the year,' he wrote to Emily Sellwood (from Beech Hill House, High Beach), 'with nothing but that muddy pond in prospect, and those two little sharp-barking dogs.'

High Beach incubated melancholy. Tennyson complained of the absence of birdlife in the forest, the horrors of local society: 'frozen, cold, lifeless'. He drudged, he brooded; the only advantage in his situation was the proximity of London. Londoners came to Epping in excursion mood and went home drunk, dirty, scratched, soaked, disorientated. Wandering the forest tracks, the Earl's Path, the earthworks at Loughton and Amresbury, was like losing yourself in a Gothic cathedral; Durham with the roof lifted off. Tree-pillars extended in every direction. They wouldn't release you. They swallowed light.

Tennyson made his way to Dr Allen's madhouse. 'The association,' Essex historian William Addison wrote, 'was calamitous for both.' The poet was persuaded to invest in one of Allen's schemes: mechanical wood-carving. The Patent Decorative Carving and Sculpture Company was formed. Tennyson risked all the money raised by the sale of his small estate at Grasby, Lincolnshire. The company crashed, Allen was declared bankrupt. Tennyson's marriage was 'indefinitely' postponed, he was left with no means of support.

The best of High Beach was its obscurity, views over the

Lea Valley and Waltham Abbey: 'Ring out, wild bells.' The M25 couldn't have happened to a better place, a silver stream bringing light and life.

Dr Matthew Allen, asylum keeper, floater of companies, drank with Tennyson at the Sterling Club (in London); long smoky sessions in the garden. (Anything to postpone the return.) It was after one of these binges that Tennyson experienced the classic High Beach epiphany – and experienced it, characteristically, as a downer. The lights of the city shimmering through forest darkness: 'flaring like a dreary dawn'.

The stress, the poisoned psyches of the city: Allen was a pioneer in mental health relocation. Fee-paying sylvan benevolence. Lunatics hidden in Epping Forest, where they could wander or be put to work. A private enterprise that anticipated late-Victorian asylum colonies. Allen's converted farms were the direct descendants of the madhouses of Hackney and Hoxton. The sort of 'private home' in Bethnal Green to which the visionary poet Christopher Smart had been committed.

It was reported, in a letter from James Spedding, that Tennyson (who spent a fortnight with Allen) was 'delighted with the mad people'. They represented, the poet felt, the only civilised company to be had in the forest. William Addison is convinced that Tennyson met one of Allen's most celebrated patients. This unfortunate had been boarded in High Beach at the expense of his friends. A country lyricist who had been the sensation of the last season. A Fenland yokel lionised by London society: John Clare, Peasant Poet, naturalist. Yesterday's man.

London drew Clare and hurt him. He remembered the funeral procession of Lord Byron, playhouses with 'morts of tumbling'. He saw what Cockney fools failed to recognise, the living ghosts of Chancery Lane. He stayed late, and silent, at every function to which he was brought; so that he might delay the solitary walk back to his lodgings. In Northampton Asylum, he would become an emanation of Byron. As Don

Juan, he ventriloquised a posthumous voice – by an act of occult possession (as Blake revised the 'errors' of Milton).

Clare imagined, so the doctors said, that he was being punished, imprisoned for bigamy – for a first spiritual marriage, unconfirmed by civil ceremony. His phantom bride already buried in Glinton churchyard, Clare did what any sane man would do, he took off on his epic 'Journey Out of Essex'. Three and a half days walking back to Northborough (in Northants). Gnawing grass torn up from the roadside, chewing tobacco. Without drink. Apart from a pint bought with coins thrown to him by migrant farm labourers. 'Foot foundered and broken down', he completed his hallucinatory voyage. Without maps or money, Clare fixed his bearings by sleeping with his head pointing to the north.

We calculated that this journey, which we were determined to repeat, was around 120 miles. Or the distance of the M25 if it were stretched out into a straight line. Fugue as exorcism: Clare's walk successfully performed the ritual we were toying with. He'd been in the forest long enough to understand the peculiarity of its status as a memorial to a featureless and unreachable past, a living stormbreak at the limit of urban projection.

When Clare, reunited with his corporeal wife, came to write up the journal of his escape, he gave it the correct title: 'Journey Out of Essex'. An expulsion. A rejection. The last of London and ambition. The last of healing and mending; digging, crow-scaring, rambling. The acceptance of the dream, the multiple world. His prose is excited, incantatory, essential. He has to rewalk that road in a seizure. He has to remember to remember; to call up details before they fade. The pains. The errors. Extra miles tramped on miscalculation. There is no better, no more implicated account of the necessity of walking. Clare's motivation was so much more powerful than our own. The Great North Road was still a route down which everything and everyone travelled; coaches, gypsies, farmers, the military, masterless workmen. The M25 goes nowhere; it's self-referential, postmodern, ironic. Modestly corrupt. It won't make sense until it's been abandoned, grown over. (Like the airfields of Middle England, the dormitory villages, the concrete bunkers in corn fields, the nuclear shelters disguised as farmhouses.)

Clare's walk was an act of love. But the version he gave the world was already at one remove, a condemned cell confession. A forged diary rapidly assembled to rationalise an ecstatic episode. It went wrong so quickly, his return. Disgruntled wife, too many children. A cold cottage in an alien village. He had seen the enclosures. He had been wandering in the fields when men came to carry out their survey for the railway company. The landscape didn't know him. He would be removed to spend the rest of his life in Northampton Asylum.

He spurned newspaper 'blarney', false obituaries. He had seen his Mary 'alive and well and as young as ever'. But his walk, undertaken in the spirit of Werner Herzog's tramp from Munich to Paris (to rescue a friend from cancer), had failed: he confirmed his love's death, filled her mouth with earth. He brought himself back to reality: 'homeless at home and half gratified to feel that I can be happy any where'.

The story told in a few scribbled pages. An epitaph. Before they took him away. The diary finishes with quotation marks, opened but unclosed.

'and how can I forget

No period. Nothing lachrymose. No pokerwork homily over the fireplace. A technical demand. The point of any journey, any life: how can I forget?

'Foot foundered and broken down.' Moose Jackson, hobbling and groaning through the outskirts of Waltham Abbey, was paying a very direct homage to Clare. 'I then entered a town and some of the chamber windows had candle lights shineing in them – I felt so weak here that I forced to sit down on the ground to rest myself.'

It didn't come to that, not quite, but the road was much further than it looked from the hill. The illuminated tower of the abbey church, appearing over the roofs, kept us going. I walked with Kevin. He was almost done; he understood that it would be more painful to stop than to carry on. There was only one stop left in him.

Church and grounds are painted with searchlight beams. Renchi, at long last, pilgrimage completed, finds an unlocked door. We have to witness the astrological ceiling, the wall-painting in the side chapel (a fifteenth-century Doom mural). Unseen, it predicted our journey. In darkness, we set out. And in darkness we returned.

The side chapel belonged to the townspeople, not the monks. The Doom painting, this M25 Day of Judgement, was a premature motorway dream: a traffic-directing God, angels blowing down upraised traffic cones. Heaven and Hell. The godly, the ratepayers, led by a bishop into the church, while a mob of naked revellers plunge into Hell's mouth (otherwise known as Purfleet). Demons lurk on Rainham Marshes in the form of saw-toothed river creatures who have managed to crawl ashore. The 'London Orbital' is a medieval nightmare.

We expected to find Kevin where we left him, hooked over Harold's stone, sobbing. His hair – which turned grey in the course of the walk from Theydon Bois – was slicked into a dripping caul. He was like something lifted from the Doom painting. The flying jacket, launched with such confidence in Staines, now justified its combat status. A wrinkled body bag. There was a black plinth in the burial ground: NIGHT NIGHT TOM. But Kevin had vanished. Evaporated. Slipped away into the darkness.

We try the pub, the Welsh Harp. Double brandies are lined up on the bar. Better not to look at Kevin's feet. I pull out the plasters, a needle to pop blisters; Renchi provides the red socks.

Lodged at a table, drinks coming at regular intervals, on a nod to the publican, Kevin is returned to life. A story is a story. How long does it take before actuality, blood and pain, is safely registered as memory? Before it is written up.

The Welsh Harp is another hinge. The M25 trance is over, I have to begin a new memory project, a novel set in Wales. Here's to Walter Savage Landor, David Jones, the Vaughan Twins. It's very companionable in the old pub. Another round, a cigar. Colour returning to Kevin's bloodless fingers as they grip the glass.

We leave him where he is. As far as I know, he's there still. He's probably taken out membership at the Waltham Abbey library. Signed up for night classes in runic prophecy and Pataphysics. He'll never make it across the market square to the mini-cab office. And they haven't got any available cabs. He's come to the end of the line, a Captain Bones exile in the 'Admiral Benbow'. ('This is a handy cove,' says he, at length; 'and a pleasant sittyated grog-shop. Much company, mate?')

Red-and-green streamers, Christmas lights, have been strung across the square – in anticipation of the Millennium Eve. Packs of tarot cards, essential oils, Egyptian cats and figurines are waiting in the New Age shop. Renchi and I head off on what now seems like a very short walk to the station.

Millennium Eve

There was a certain amount of discussion about dates: is it really the end of the century, the Millennium? Will the computers go haywire, bringing planes out of the sky? Or are we in for another misjudged English party with damp squibs?

The burghers of Waltham Abbey are very good at getting their hangovers in early, *before* they start on the serious celebrations. The damp town is bilious, yellow-tongued. (Looking forward to the drama of the spring floods.) Anna agreed to run us up the Lea Valley, to drop us, once again, at Harold's grave.

30 December 1999. Renchi is back at work. Kevin has vanished – taken up residence in the Welsh Harp? Our orbital walk might never have happened. Marc Atkins is prepared to reverse that first excursion, out from the Dome. To mend the mistake, his damaged foot. He's dressed for action: woollen commando beanie, tartan scarf, slithery non-combatant jacket. Camera. Film in pocket. No bags. Nothing to carry. A trick Kevin never learnt.

This time, we collect Marc from Limehouse. I don't want there to be any misunderstandings or delays. He is signing on as official war photographer: to witness the final and absolute dissolution of the Millennium Dome.

Unconvinced drizzle. It's still dark. Sky-leakage. No notes to be kept. My photo journal is a reflex indulgence, now that Marc is present. The cold eye of the landscape valuer.

We climb the embankment to the M25. We check out the spot where Bill Drummond kissed tarmac. It's quite emotional, this parting from an old friend. Not much road traffic, nothing on the river. The sound, back in the abbey, was so precise, in the cold early-morning air; reinforcing the status of the church as an island within an island. By the time we reach the Lee, that clarity is lost. A solitary blue hut. Marc fumbles in the dark, changing his film. Then, just as he clicks the back of the camera shut, lights come on. Harsh, white. The lock is wired. The hut lit like a target.

Neck twisted, left eye closed, Marc squats beside the road, resting his Nikon on the crash barrier. With these photographs, the status of the M25 changes: it becomes historic, monumental. Fixed. Previously, in snapshots and sketches, it was family. No obligation to perform. Belt and braces, knotted handkerchief on head. 'Hold that' was neither spoken, nor implied. Marc's concentration, his technique, brings the motorway into the canon, sets it alongside roads in other countries. That's the difference between a packet of colour snaps and a commissioned portrait. You gain dignity, lose accident.

Already, we can see the blinking pyramid at the summit of the Canary Wharf tower, lined up with pylons and the black rule of water. RIFLES pub at Enfield Lock wishes: MERRY CHRISTMAS TO YOU ALL. Santa's head like a trophy, above the Lee Enfield on the awning. Bagged one.

Too wet to dawdle. We push on towards Ponders End. A rose-red wall bellies out in a way that appeals to Marc. It's topped with broken glass and razor wire. To protect a Flour Mill?

Ponders End, I like to think, is the model for Gerald Kersh's *Fowlers End*. The 1958 novel by the prolific Kersh has always been Michael Moorcock's favourite: 'Everything in it is designed to reach the smallest possible audience – unpopular subject – sleazy characters – very funny.' Moorcock wrote a foreword when the book was reissued. *Fowlers End* is the antidote to the whimsy of Peter Sellers, Margaret Rutherford, Bernard Miles, the charming stock company of British character actors in *The Smallest Show on Earth*. Which was released, to indulgent reviews and modest box-office success, in the year that Kersh's 'unpopular' novel was published. Film and book exploit the same theme: the death of an independent cinema. One is sentimental, quirky and comic, while the other is deranged. Kersh is a master of haywire demotic, prose on the charge. At his best, as in *Fowlers End*, he achieves that impossible thing: he comes out as a Jewish Céline.

This is how you find Fowlers End – by going northward, step by step, into the neighbourhoods that most strongly repel you. The compass of your revulsion may flicker for a moment at the end of the Tottenham Court Road, especially on a rainy March morning . . .

Do not be led astray by this; go north to Edmonton and Ponders End. Who Ponder was and how he ended, the merciful God knows. Once upon a time it was a quagmire; now it is a swamp, biding its time. Further yet, bearing northeast, lies a graveyard of broken boilers and rusty wheels . . . where creatures that once were men live in abandoned railway carriages . . .

Here the city gives up the game.

This is it.

Fowlers End is a special kind of tundra that supports nothing gracious in the way of flora and fauna . . . Even the dogs are throwbacks to their yellow-eyed predatory ancestors that slunk in the trail of sub-men and ate filth. There is a High Street about a hundred yards long, and the most woebegone railway terminal on the face of the earth . . .

Flattering but true, Kersh's travelogue needs no revision. Ponders End is a knot in the railway, roadkill returned to life. There's a pub called the Falcon, with a yellow field gun parked outside; presumably 'borrowed' from the Small Arms Factory at Enfield. The gun strikes a sinister note, as it fails to protect a trashed telephone kiosk and a crop of tower blocks. SORRY NO TRAVELLERS. Reasonable advice. But sticking a howitzer on the pavement is excessive.

Rain seeps and slithers. The PONDERS END WORKING

MENS CLUB, for all its pebbledash pretensions, can't have many bona fide members. Who works? Five or six bright windows in a plantation of tower blocks. Recidivists used to perpetual illumination, overhead lights that can't be switched off. Twenty-four-hour dealers. Insomniacs rummaging through medicine cabinets.

SALON SNIPPETS PAITIENT MODELS REQUIRED FOR FOILS/ CUTTING + NAIL EXTENSIONS. Marc of course has experience in hairdressing. He shaves his own skull, cuts the hair of his partner (and anyone else who is up for it). But the deployment of 'foils' is a sophistication he hasn't acquired. Colour pads pressed to the head in a curious rite.

Ponders End is bereft of the 'paitient', models or otherwise. The place is deserted. A Dalmatian picking through a heap of burst bin bags; wolf-red eyes. Noise is a constant: speeding trains, fork-lift trucks which bleep as they reverse, generators, sirens. An industrial soundtrack and no industry.

A trembling refugee, sheltering under the railway bridge, won't admit that the town runs to a café. He shakes his head, astonished at the idea. A security man from the Flour Mill thinks that there might be somewhere 'foreign', ten minutes down the road.

He's right. It is foreign. And schizophrenic. CLOSED CAFE OPEN. The fry-up is excellent ('bubble and bacon'), the tables clean. It must be a front for something. We are the only customers. Marc loves Ponders End. 'I only photograph empty railway lines, empty streets,' he says. 'People – I find a way to keep them out.'

Settled at his Formica desk, he taps messages into his new mobile phone; receives his first calls. He's been given a £20,000 commission to photograph mathematicians. The show at the National Institute for Medical Research is clinched.

The harder the rain comes down, the faster we stride. We're erasing everything we investigated on the original walk. The smoke from the burning stack at the London Waste facility in Edmonton is indistinguishable from river mist, spray from the elevated carriageway. The sky has dropped.

Under the canal bridge, where something aspirational has been attempted with cobbles, we find a pair of abandoned ankleboots. Marc rearranges them, darting about to find the best angle; as if, by the ritual of photography, he could conjure up the presence of the woman who kicked them off. Before vanishing for ever.

The blighted townscape, where North Circular passes over Lee, is unrevised. Carrier bags trapped in thorny thickets. Rubbish infiltrating chainlink fences. Yellow and black barriers. Humps in the road. A retail park. Flooded fields. Marc, on the central reservation, surfs wheel-spray, as he records volatile waves of traffic.

London rushes at us, tightens the cord. Kersh depicts a city swollen with bad gas, a straining belly eager to disgorge itself on unprotected ground: 'Expanding city population, *plus* your expanding heavy industry, *plus*, of course, rising land values in your outlying suburbs. Well, that's what I'm out here for.' Predatory industrialists, compliant politicians. They live to work the margins, unloved land. As do writers and photographers, the thrill of the spurned. New narratives of dereliction.

The grey concrete walls of the sewage beds at Markfield Recreation Ground, South Tottenham, have been blitzed with aerosol colour, image and text. Robots. Androids. Beast-men with zap weaponry. Spike-breasted women in (blood splashed) bikini briefs. Tags. Spurts. Slogans. SHIT VEGAN. A communal album. Any artist is free to revise, improve, distort. Urban pictographs we don't have time to decode.

The Lee is manufacturing *War of the Worlds* fungus; it's kraken-clogged, choked with green scum. A woman is chucking sliced bread from the window of her new flat, straight into the water. Gulls and ducks squabble. Rats dart from canalside undergrowth to carry off spilt crumbs.

The camp under the Eastway bridge has been abandoned, the council have got the travellers out. Wick Wood: another war zone. Padded car seats. Precarious stacks of tyres. Sections of carpet. Washing machines. Gutted cars. Caravans. Bundles of sodden newspapers: POLITIKA.

WHERE ARE YOU? A cancelled map. Filth flung from speeding vehicles spreads over the embankment. Marc poses at the roadside in his once-white shoes.

We're on home turf, Hackney to Thames. No surprises. I can't believe how quickly we've come back. Everything is in suspension, post-Christmas, pre-Millennium. A red-on-red poster, Soviet pastiche, promotes George Michael: SONGS FROM THE LAST CENTURY. The canal is silted, lifeless. Without colour. A sepia negation, it defies the *idea* of colour, the folk memory.

The Lee Valley Media Zone has abdicated, retired to its second home. The picket fence around the Big Breakfast cottage is black with names, the fishing pixie leers like a child molester. A poster for Peter Greenaway's *8½ Women* is peeling from one of the piers of the Bow Flyover. The wine bar in the Three Mills complex is shut.

Rain rattles on the roof of a blue and black tent. What we have, on this muddy canalside paddock, is a replica of the Dome. A circus tent in which acrobats have been rehearsing for the Big Night. NEW YORK!! NEW YORK!! screams red-bulb lettering. We can investigate the virtual Dome for nothing. They've been flooded out, they've gone. Condensation dripping from sodden canvas. The desertion of the circus animals. Rehearsals are over. This tent can be broken, shifted. The misery is finite. Nobody is watching, nobody cares. Nobody will hold them to account.

It's one o'clock and we've made it to the Isle of Dogs. Marc's limping; he's not too bad, a slight thigh strain. Liquid City. We slither, steaming, into the pub: an old favourite, the Gun in Blackwall Way. Traditional riverside hospitality always on offer: no hot food, stale crisps, nobody at the bar, locked balcony. A place so fiction-friendly that I can never remember what happened the last time I dropped in and what happened in my novel *Downriver*.

Such light as this day ever pretended to has abdicated. We carry our drinks to a table. We look out, directly, on the other Dome, the money pit to which all the celebrities in town have been invited. A royal knees-up due to kick off in twenty-four hours. The Gun's spiked, a couple of pickled regulars sniffling into their half-pints, tomorrow it will be heaving. Anything with a view of the river has been booked solid. We'll start the party now. Order the Jamesons, the beers. Drink to the Dome's damnation.

When we arrived at the spot where they'd filmed the *EastEnders* wedding, near the Ibis Hotel, the Dome was an alien form; a spoiler. It ruined the low level riverscape, the dingy mystique of Bugsby's Marshes. It looked like a collapsed birth-day cake from the now-disappeared bakers on Kingsland Road, a special order. Yellow candles in a mound of icing sugar. It sagged. It should never have been left out in the rain. Miss Havisham, back from the Kentish marshes, in all her decayed and inappropriate finery.

Two hours later, our table, dressed with a red Christmas cloth, was filled with glasses. Six of them in front of Marc – and one in his hand. The Nikon is also on the table, along with a box of matches and the mobile phone.

We've dried off, warmed up. I trot through to the bar for another round, ask for doubles. This is it. The moment has finally arrived. At the cusp of a new millennium, I'll do it: make my first cellphone call. Dome-watch is turning into a session. It feels historic. I want to invite Anna to join us (I don't fancy walking home along the Grand Union in the rain).

The professional drinkers are staying with the big screen, the river looks better when it's electronically processed. We're all pals by this time. We get fresh glasses with every round. I study framed river maps while I wait; remember old trips, with Paul Burwell and Brian Catling, to Tilbury, Sheppey, Southend.

When Anna, in coat, sits down 'for a moment' and is still in the chair an hour later, we realise that time is draining faster than we can record it. The vortex is about to reverse, spin counter-clockwise down the plughole. The bride feast on the far bank, fairy lights, beams from helicopters, will turn into a wake.

My binoculars pass hand-to-hand. 'You taking pictures for the papers? We've had 'em coming in all week,' says an old soak, wobbling towards the Gents. Marc grips a cigar between his teeth, as he designs his shot. When he has licked the last granule of dust from his crisp packet, the Limehouse photographer flattens the eviscerated envelope. He smoothes the lining with the back of his hand, alchemises the tablecloth, red to silver.

Security personnel are rehearsing the arrival of the nobs, the royals. Bulbs wink on tent poles, for the benefit of flights into the City Airport at Silvertown. A final run-through for the Millennium show, the loud hurrah. Jeeps, red carpet. Stand-ins for Blair and Mandelson (the former 'single shareholder'), Lord Falconer. The deputed Blair clone hasn't got the walk right. 'A man whose shoes are too small.' (As poet Geoffrey Hill has it.) A yea-saying preacher, arms thrown wide, who pays other people to steer him away from the shit.

This is better than tomorrow. A grandstand view for the price of a few drinks. No crush. No fighting your way on to the Jubilee Line. No hanging about for hours on Stratford station. No arm-wrestling with sour royalty, during a joyless deconstruction of 'Auld Lang Syne'.

The coloured streamers above the bar are reflected in the window. The Dome is an invader crashed into the swamp on Planet Britain. Wrecked on our floating island, the aircraft carrier that Piety Blair has made us. Cod ritual always favours the Thames: the knighting of Francis Chichester at Greenwich,

CIA product-placement dramas filmed (back-to-back with Jane Austen) in the Royal Naval College. Churchill's funeral barge. The Millennium Wheel (the London Eye) which wasn't ready on the night. The bridge that wobbled. The promised 'river of fire'. Ceremonies invented to paper over civic discontent.

One year from now, on Christmas Eve, I would return to the Dome. They'd slashed the entry price to £1. Tourist shops were selling off their souvenir tat at knockdown prices. I filled three Christmas stockings with Dome kitsch for less than £15. It was still raining. At least 101 stuffed Dalmatians were hanging by the neck from deserted sideshow booths. Coke dispensers were empty. A YEAR OF CELEBRATION: THIS MACHINE IS NOT IN SERVICE.

Time spent here shamed the visitor. I've never been anywhere so dispiriting. TUNNEL OF LOVE/KISS ME SUCK. Small groups, mainly Indian or Bangladeshi, ignored the barely functioning zones to asset-strip souvenir shops.

CITY OF LONDON PRESENTS: MONEY. *Due to the incident which took place on Tuesday 7th November, unfortunately the Millennium Jewels Exhibit will not be open to the public until further notice. On behalf of the Dome and De Beers we apologise for any disappointment caused.*

On the glistening path, where we saw the understudies make their entrance on the day before the millennial eve, I ran into the last of the celebrities: Rowan Atkinson and Tony Robinson. In the form of cardboard cut-outs. Punting a specially commissioned *Blackadder* 'special', large-screen TV to make excursionists feel at home.

Antony Gormley's *Quantum Cloud* was the only object that made any attempt to address the reality of this site: metal filings (that alluded to riverside scrap yards) magicked into a man-shaped cloud. Against a grey sky. This figure, the spirit of place, evolves – as you walk, or drift with the tide. It gives form to inherited melancholy.

The Prayer Space is situated in Harrison Building opposite Millennium Jewels. Nobody is praying. The jewels had to be removed, after a bunch of South London chancers tried to ram the tent with a JCB. An operation sold to the cops from the start. The only high attendance day at the Dome — busybusy crowds mugging like crazy — came when plainclothes police were dressed as tourists and workmen, while they waited for the bandits to make their move.

It would get worse. Government (and the usual quangos) hoped we'd forget about the Dome — until the developers arrived. By November 2001, the deserted and unloved site was haemorrhaging an estimated £240,000 a month. In that year, statisticians reckoned, £21.5 million had gone down the tubes: on a skeleton maintenance staff and all those empty car parks. Even in the Bad News flood around 11 September, nobody could devise an 'on message' boost for the Teflon marquee.

Lord Falconer, invisible minder, unenthusiastic scapegoat, kept his own council. Could anything be done? Rumour spoke of the strategy employed on other burnt-out industrial spaces, the conversion of the tent into a club, a rave facility. Send for naughty Dave Courtney. Or perhaps a theme park? An ice rink? A medical charity, the Wellcome Trust, expressed an interest. As did the Meridian Delta consortium. Marc Atkins might well be prepared to stage a major photographic retrospective. Graveyards, reforgotten authors, nudes and obelisks.

The Arthur Daleys of New Labour intended one thing, as had been obvious from the start: a sell-out. Three hundred acres of Greenwich peninsula real estate, cleaned up with lottery funds, brownfield recovery grants and the rest, available for development. New housing. Chafford Hundred comes to town. With multiplex and the eco-friendly Sainsbury's on its doorstep.

One more drink. A last look through the binoculars. They switch the illuminations on and off. Everything checked.

Nothing can go wrong – can it? Will Self, a fan of the M25, said that the mistake with the Dome was that it played safe. It was too modest. It should have spread itself to envelop the whole of London, right out to the motorway. An invisible membrane. A city of zones and freak shows separated from the rest of England. Ford Madox Ford's old fantasy finally activated.

We couldn't get drunk, but we were very mellow. Boneless. It took a long time to lift a glass. Anna had driven us through the Blackwall Tunnel at the start of all this and she was there for the last rites. We hadn't walked around the perimeter of London, we had circumnavigated the Dome. At a safe distance. Away from its poisoned heritage. Its bad will, mendacity. The tent could consider itself exorcised. This was a rare quest for me, one that reached a fitting conclusion. Here at last was the grail. Up-ended on a swamp in East London. Glowing in the dark.

Acknowledgements

To Renchi Bicknell for his company on the walk around the M25; for his sketches, speculations, enthusiasm. To Kevin Jackson for a steady dripfeed of information, asides, bibliographic offprints. And to the hardy occasionals, Marc Atkins, Bill Drummond, Chris Petit.

With thanks to those who took part in the secondary expeditions: Ivan Bicknell, Peter Carpenter (Epsom guide and William Curtis Hayward informant), Chris Darke, Jock McFayden, Lawrence Peskett, Anna Sinclair (and for those early-morning drives), Will Sinclair, Martin J. Wallen.

Material on the history, fabric and mythology of the M25 was supplied by John Sergeant. Pinky Ghundale's good cheer and efficiency made the impossible possible. Thanks to Keith Griffiths for fronting a post-posthumous film on motorway reverie (the tape beyond 'the final commission').

For generously giving time for interviews, thanks to: J.G. Ballard, Dr J.C. Burne, Ken Campbell, Cicely Hadman, Ros Hadman, Jerry Jones, Rachel Lichtenstein, Bernard O'Mahoney, Beth Pedder, Tony Sangwine, John Whomes.

And thanks for gifts and deeds too numerous to specify to: Sara Allen, Julian Bell, Neil Belton, Vanessa Bicknell, Paul Burwell, Brian Catling, Miranda Collinge, Gini Dearden, Paul Devereux, Andrew Aidan Dun, Gareth Evans, Bruce Gilbert, Mike Goldmark, Jane Greenwood, Bill Griffiths, Brian Hinton, Susie Honeyman, Patrick Keiller, Dave McKean, Emma Matthews, Michael Moorcock, Alan Moore, Chris and Haya Oakley, Effie Paleologou, John Richard Parker, John Procter, Joe Rosen, Robin Summers, Jonathan Thomson, Liat Uziyel, Claire Walsh, Patrick Wright.

Extracts from this book, in an earlier form, were published in the *London Review of Books*, *The London Magazine* and *The River*. A short section appears, courtesy of Michael Moorcock, on the website 'Fantastic Metropolis' and can be found on www.fantasticmetropolis.com.

Extended riffs on themes touched on in *London Orbital* were rehearsed in a sequence of books published in 1999. I think of these books as missing chapters of a larger whole, outstations.

(1) *Sorry Meniscus (Excursions to the Millennium Dome)*. Profile Books. (Expeditions to the building site on Bugsby's Marshes.) (2) *Crash (David Cronenberg's Post-mortem on J.G. Ballard's 'Trajectory of Fate')*. British Film Institute. (Interview with Ballard, road speculations.) (3) *Rodinsky's Room*. Granta. (An investigation carried out by Rachel Lichtenstein into the life and mythology of David Rodinsky.) (4) *Dark Lanthorns (David Rodinsky as Psychogeographer)*. Goldmark, Uppingham.

Select Bibliography

Patrick Abercrombie and J.H. Forshaw, *County of London Plan*, London, 1943

William Addison, *Epping Forest (Its Literary and Historical Associations)*, London, 1945

J.G. Ballard, *The Atrocity Exhibition*, London, 1969

—— *Vermilion Sands*, London, 1973

—— *Crash*, London, 1973

—— *Running Wild*, London, 1988

Griselda Barton and Michael Tong, *Underriver (Samuel Palmer's Golden Valley)*, Westerham, 1995

Neil Belton, *The Good Listener (Helen Bamber: A Life against Cruelty)*, London, 1998

Renchi Bicknell, *Relations*, London, 1973

—— *Michael and Mary Dreaming (A Walk along the Michael and Mary Lines . . .)*, Alton, n. d. [1998]

Ian Breakwell and Paul Hammond, *Brought to Book*, London, 1994

Colin Buchanan, T. Dan Smith, Ernest Marples (and others), *Traffic in Towns*, London, 1963

Dr J.C. Burne, *'Bits and Pieces' about Joyce Green Hospital and the Smallpox Ships*, Dartford, 1999

Edward North Buxton, *Epping Forest*, London, 1905

Mary Caine, *The Kingston Zodiac*, Kingston, 1978

Hugh Carey, *Mansfield Forbes and His Cambridge*, Cambridge, 1984

George Tomkyns Chesney, *The Battle of Dorking (Reminiscences of a Volunteer)*, London, 1871

Christopher Chippindale, *A High Way to Heaven (Clarence Bicknell and the 'Vallée Des Marveilles')*, Alpes-Maritimes, 1998

John Clare (eds. Eric Robinson and David Powell), *John Clare by Himself*, Manchester, 1996

Sidney Colvin, *Memories and Notes*, London, 1921

J.C. Cooper, *An Illustrated Encyclopaedia of Traditional Symbols*, London, 1978

Mary Cosh, *The New River*, London, 1988

Catherine Croft (ed.), *On the Road (The Art of Engineering in the Car Age)*, London, 1999

Theo Crosby, *Let's Build a Monument*, London, 1987

Theo Crosby and Michael Sandle, *The Battle of Britain Monument*, London, 1987

Graham Dalling, *Enfield Past*, London, 1999

Roger Deakin, *Waterlog (A Swimmer's Journey through Britain)*, London, 1999

Don DeLillo, *The Body Artist*, London, 2001

Paul Devereux, *Re-Visioning the Earth*, New York, 1996

Charles Dickens, *Our Mutual Friend*, London, 1864–5

Monica Diplock, *The History of Leavesden Hospital*, Leavesden, 1990

Bill Drummond, *Annual Report (to the Mavericks, Writers and Film Festival)*, Aylesbury, 1998

—— *45*, London, 2000

—— Chris Brooks, ed., visuals by Gimpo, *K Foundation Burn a Million Quid*, London, 1997

Maureen Duffy, *Capital*, London, 1975

Raymond Durgnat, *Franju*, London, 1967

Maurice Exwood, *Epsom Wells (A New History of the Epsom Wells and Epsom Salts)*, Epsom, 2000

Robin Fedden, *Churchill and Chartwell*, Oxford, 1968

Allen Fisher, *Place Book One*, London, 1974

—— *Stane, Place Book III*, London, 1977

Michel Foucault, *Madness and Civilization*, London, 1967

Dylan Francis, *The Risk of Being Alive (Writings on Medicine, Poetry and Landscape)*, Cambridge, 1996

W.P. Frith (ed. Nevile Wallis), *A Victorian Canvas (The Memoirs of W.P. Frith)*, London, 1957

Neil Gaiman and Michael Zulli, *Sweeney Todd: The Demon Barber of Fleet Street (Prologue)*, West Brattleboro, Vermont, 1992

Oliver Garnett, *Chartwell*, London, 1992

David Gascoyne, *Selected Prose (1934–1996)*, London, 1998

Bob Gilbert, *The Green London Way*, London, 1991

Jean-Luc Godard (trans. Peter Whitehead), *Alphaville*, London, 1972

John Graham-Leigh, *London's Water Wars*, London, 2000

Philippa Gregory, *Earthly Joys*, London, 1998

Bill Griffiths, *The Book of the Boat*, London, 1988

—— Clive Bush, *Out of Dissent (A Study of Five Contemporary British Poets)*, London, 1997

—— Clive Bush, ed., *Worlds of New Measure (An Anthology of Five Contemporary British Poets)*, London, 1997

Ian Hacking, *Mad Travelers (Reflections on the Reality of Transient Mental Illnesses)*, Charlottesville, Virginia, 1998

P.G. Hall, *The Industries of London*, London, 1962

Joy Hancox, *The Byrom Collection (Renaissance Thought, the Royal Society and the Building of the Globe Theatre)*, London, 1992

William Hayward, *It Never Gets Dark All Night*, London, 1964

—— *Between Two Rivers (Gloucestershire Poems)*, Wotton-under-Edge, 1999

—— David Jones, *Letters to William Hayward*, London, 1979

Joan Hessayon, *Capel Bells*, London, 1995

Bryan Hewitt, *The Crocus King (E.A. Bowles of Myddleton House)*, Ware, 1997

Christopher Hill, *The World Turned Upside Down (Radical Ideas during the English Revolution)*, London, 1972

—— *The Century of Revolution (1603–1714)*, London, 1961

R. Hippisley Cox, *The Green Roads of England*, London, 1914

A.R. Hope-Moncrieff, *Essex*, revised edn, London, 1926

Ford Madox Hueffer, 'The Future in London', from *London Town, Past and Present* by W.W. Hutchings, Vol. II, London, 1909

Stan Jarvis, *Essex: A County History*, Newbury, 1993

David Jones, *The Anathemata*, London, 1952

Patrick Keiller, *Robinson in Space*, London, 1999

Gerald Kersh, *Night and the City*, London, 1938

—— *Fowlers End*, London, 1958

Bernard Kops, *The World is a Wedding*, London, 1963

Adrian Laing, *R.D. Laing: A Bibliography*, London, 1994

David Lawrence, *Always a Welcome (The Glove Compartment History of the Motorway Service Area)*, Twickenham, 1999

David Lewer and Robert Dark, *The Temple Church in London*, London, 1997

Jim Lewis, *London's Lea Valley (Britain's Best Kept Secret)*, Chichester, 1999

Raymond Lister, *Samuel Palmer: A Biography*, London, 1974

—— (ed.), *The Letters of Samuel Palmer*, 2 vols., London, 1974

—— *Samuel Palmer and 'The Ancients'*, Cambridge, 1984

Barry MacSweeney, *Ranter*, Nottingham, 1985

K.E. Maltwood, *A Guide to Glastonbury's Temple of the Stars*, new edn, London, 1964

Arthur Mee, *Kent*, revised edn, London, 1969

Hamish Miller and Paul Broadhurst, *The Sun and the Serpent*, Launceston, 1989

Alan Moore, *Voice of the Fire*, London, 1996

Bernard O'Mahoney, *Essex Boys* (updated edn of *So This Is Ecstasy?*), Edinburgh, 2000

Francine Payne, A *Brief History of the Darenth Hospitals*, Dartford, n.d. [1988]

John Pearson, *The Profession of Violence*, London, 1972

J.H.B. Peel, *Along the Roman Roads of Britain*, London, 1971

Chris Petit, *The Hard Shoulder*, London, 2001

Nikolaus Pevsner, *Essex*, London, 1954

Jennifer Potter, *Secret Gardens*, London, 1998

Alan Powers, *Serge Chermayeff: Designer Architect Teacher*, London, 2001

Charlie Richardson, *My Manor (An Autobiography)*, London, 1991

Hermann Schreiber, *The History of Roads (From Amber Route to Motorway)*, London, 1961

David Sharp, *The London Loop*, London, 2001

Mary P. Shepherd, *Heart of Harefield (The Story of a Hospital)*, London, 1990

Philip Sherwood, *The History of Heathrow*, reviscd edn, Uxbridge, 1993

Clancy Sigal, *Zone of the Interior*, New York, 1976

Arthur Sinclair, *In Tropical Lands (Recent Travels to the Sources of the Amazon, the West Indian Islands and Ceylon)*, Aberdeen, 1895

—— *Planter and Visiting Agent in Ceylon (The Story of His Life and Times as Told by Himself)*, Colombo, 1900

Iain Sinclair, *The Kodak Mantra Diaries*, London, 1971

Bram Stoker, *Dracula*, London, 1897

—— Leonard Wolf, ed., *The Annotated Dracula*, New York, 1975

C.E. Street, *Earthstars*, London, 1990

David Thomas, *London's Green Belt*, London, 1970

Tony Thompson, *Bloggs 19 (The Story of the Essex Range Rover Triple Murders)*, London, 2000

James Thorne, *Handbook to the Environs of London*, reissued Chichester, 1983

Derek Threadgall, *Shepperton Studios*, London, 1994

Marc Edo Tralbaut, *Vincent Van Gogh*, London, 1969

Ruth Valentine, *Asylum, Hospital, Haven (A History of Horton Hospital)*, London, 1996

H.G. Wells, *The War of the Worlds*, London, 1898

John Whatmore (ed.), *The Shell Book of British Walks*, London, 1987

John Talbot White, *Country London*, London, 1984

Patrick Wright, *The River (The Thames in Our Time)*, London, 1999

Index

Abbey Creek, 48
Abbey National Centre of
    Excellence, 15, 108
Abbots Langley, 140, 148, 169, 171,
    172, 175, 180, 212
Abercrombie, Sir Patrick, 42, 85,
    175, 206
Abyndome, Alexander, 131
Accident (film), 421
Ackroyd, Peter, 142, 208, 488,
    490
Ackroyd, Stirling, 94
Addison, William, 532, 533
Admiralty Powder Department, 41
The African Queen (film), 266
air-raid shelters, Epsom, 358–9
Albert, Prince, 362
Aldrich, Robert, 356
Ali G, 241
Allen, Dr Matthew, 532, 533
Alleyn, Edward, 466
Alphaville (film), 453, 454
Alton, Hampshire, 119, 286, 292
Amato pub, Epsom, 440
Amersham, 189
Amresbury Camp, Epping Forest,
    529, 530
The Anathemata (Jones), 445, 446
Anatomiae Amphitheatrum (Fludd),
    255–6
Ancient Barn (Palmer), 422
The Ancients, 405, 407, 410, 417,
    419
Andrew, Prince, 274, 277

The Annotated Dracula (Wolf), 488
Anthony, Dr Francis, 210–11, 255
Arcana Arcanissima (Maier), 211
Arup Associates, 253
Ashmole, Elias, 211
Ashstead, 331
Asylum, Hospital, Haven (Valentine),
    344–5
Atalanta Fugiens (Maier), 211
Atkins, Marc, 29, 34, 36–37, 44, 45,
    47, 49, 57, 59, 60–61, 66, 69,
    103, 106, 109, 110, 118, 213,
    253, 299, 302, 309, 315, 321,
    326, 382, 386, 410,
    412–13 426, 447, 448, 449,
    455, 473, 519–20, 541, 542,
    544, 545, 546, 548, 550
Atlas (paddle-steamer), 462
The Atrocity Exhibition, 169–70,
    170
Aubrey, John, 332, 333
Aveley, 513
Aznavour, Charles, 164
Ayrton, Maxwell, 113

Babbage, Charles, 40
Bachelard, Gaston, 515
Bacon, Francis, 147
Badger's Mount, 423
Baker, Kenneth, 472
Baker, Stanley, 355–7
Balding, DI Stephen, 506
Balfour, Sir Arthur, 41
Balfour, Harold, 235–6

Ballard, J.G., 69, 169–70, 170, 213, 214, 245, 262–9, 311, 349, 470, 528

Barratt estates, Grays, 480–3

Bartholomew Close, 210–11, 255

Barton, Griselda, 422

Basildon, 498

Batchworth, 187

Bateson, Gregory, 263

The Battle of Dorking (Chesney), 328

bears, mystery surrounding, 54–5

Beckham, Victoria, 132

Beckton Alp, 18, 45, 48

Belfast, HMS, 144, 145

Bell, Joseph, 361, 362

The Bell Jar (Plath), 171

Bellau, Stephen, 358

Belton, Neil, 276–7

Benjamin, Walter, 473

Berkhamsted, 188

Bermondsey, 493

Betts, Leah, 497, 499, 507

Bicknell, Clarence, 382–3, 385–7

Bicknell, Elhanan, 383–4

Bicknell, Ivan, 122

Bicknell, Laurence 'Renchi', 120–4, 125, 127, 131, 133 133–4, 137, 138, 139, 140, 148, 149, 150, 157, 158, 160, 162, 165, 175, 180, 181, 185, 188, 191, 198, 208–9, 212, 213, 215, 216, 217, 231, 232, 239, 240, 248, 250, 252, 253, 259, 270, 278, 279, 282, 283, 285, 286, 291, 292, 299, 302, 303–4, 309, 315, 325, 327, 331, 340, 341–2, 343, 364–66, 373, 377, 378, 382, 385, 386, 390, 391, 411, 415–6, 421, 423, 424, 429, 435, 438, 449, 456, 459, 468, 474, 493, 495, 514, 516, 519, 525, 526–7, 528, 530, 536, 541

Bicknell, Peter, 133–4

Billericay, 480

Billingsley, Captain Rupert, 231

Billyard-Leake, Charles Arthur Moresby, 191, 195

Black Death, 486

Black Lion Hill, 154, 160

Blackheath, 82, 425

Blackwall Tunnel, 47, 551

Blair, Tony, 25, 32, 267, 352, 548

Blake, Catherine, 407

Blake, William, 160, 204, 407, 408, 413, 414, 418, 425, 432

Bliss, Tom, 115

Blisworth Tunnel, 223

Bluewater, 11, 450, 467–73

Boadicea, 529

boarding kennels, noise of, 15

The Body Artist (DeLillo), 52, 201

The Book of the Boat (Griffiths), 222–4

Boorman, John, 253

Borough Market, Southwark, 419

Bovis Fairclough, 253

Bow Creek, 39

Bow Lock, 45

Bowles, E.A., 14, 99–102

Bowles, H.C., 96, 100

Bowling Green House, Bulls Cross, 99

Box Hill, 318, 328, 329

Bragg, Billy, 305

Brakhage, Stan, 404

Brave New World (Huxley), 301–2

Breakfast at Chartwell (Nicholson), 396

Bridge, Ann, 153

British Aerospace (BAe), 72, 300, 305

British Telecom, 524
Bromley-by-Bow, 48
Brooklands racetrack, 251, 299–301
Brown, Pete, 121
Browne, Hablot Knight, 384
Brownjohn, Alan, 437
Buckhurst, Charles Sackville, Lord, 332
Buford, Bill, 450
Bull, William, 86
Bulls Cross, 14, 99, 101, 133
Bunting, Basil, 227
Burges, William, 19
Burke, Thomas, 45
Burleigh, Lord *see* Cecil, William
Burne, Dr J.C., 456, 459, 461–6
Burroughs, William, 264, 268
Burwell, Paul, 222, 548
Bush, Clive, 225–6
Butts, Tommy, 432
Buxton, Sir Thomas Fowell, 345
Byers, Stephen, 64
Byles, Dr J.B., 461
The Byrom Collection (Hancox), 211
Byron, Lord, 533

Caine, Mary, 249, 251, 256, 272, 277, 279, 299
Calder, Simon, 6
Callow, Simon, 485
Cambridge, 279–83, 485
Cameron, Dr A.F., 461
Cameron, Julia Margaret, 447
Cameron, Stephen, 12, 507
Campbell, Ken, 56–7
Campbell, Malcolm, 300
Camus, Albert, 528
canals, as places of suicide, 183–4
Canary Wharf, 34, 49, 265, 542
Capel Bells (Hessayon), 97–8, 136
Capel Manor, 14, 87, 91–2, 97, 102

Capital (Duffy), 208
The Caretaker (Pinter), 443
Carey, Hugh, 280, 282
Carfax Abbey (*Dracula*), 488–9, 490, 491 496
Carmichael, Stokely, 263
Carpenter, Peter, 356, 358, 359, 434, 435, 436–7, 439, 441, 444, 446
Carry On films, 193
Case, Dr (of Leavesden Hospital), 178
Cassady, Neal, 414
Cassiobury Park, 183
Catherine the Great, 319
Catling, Brian, 116, 548
Cauty, Jimmy, 66
Cecil, Robert, Earl of Salisbury, 88, 89, 90
Cecil, William, Lord Burleigh, 87–8, 89–90
Cedars Park, 132
Chadwick, Lyn, 445
Chafford Hundred, 482–3
Chalfont St Giles, 188
Chalk Lane, Epsom, 355
Chambers, William, 91
Channelsea, 48, 50–1
Charles II, 89
Charles, Prince, 525–6
Chartwell, 391–2, 393, 395–401
Chatwin, Bruce, 412
Cheape, Sir John, 387
Chermayeff, Barbara, 282
Chermayeff, Serge, 278, 281, 282
Chertsey, 277, 278–9, 283
Chesney, Sir George Tomkyns, 328–9, 360
Chevening, 404, 406–7
Chigwell, 166–7
Chippindale, Christopher, 382

Chiselhurst, 82
Chiswick Bridge, 528
Church of Our Lady and St Peter, Leatherhead, 325–6
Church of the Holy Sepulchre, Cambridge, 485
Churchill, Lady Clementine, 398
Churchill, Winston, 41, 392, 393, 395–401
Churchill and Chartwell (Fedden), 391–2
Cities for a Small Country (Rogers and Power), 343
City Mill river, 48
Clacket Lane Service Station, 328
Clare, John, 68, 533–6
Clarkson, Edward, 209–10
Clay Hill, 87, 111
Claybury Mental Hospital, 167, 340, 346, 350
Clute, John, 302
Cobb, John, 300
Cobbett, William, 235
Cobham Heath, 300, 306, 311
Cobham Tilt, 324
Coburn, Alvin Langdon, 447
Cohen, David, 59
Coldbath Fields, Clerkenwell, 177
Collet, John, 110
Collins, Cecil, 122
Colne, River, 184, 187, 190, 218
Colne Valley, 220–1
Colney Hatch, 177, 190
Colthurst, Edmund, 93–4
Colvin, Sir Sidney, 318
Colwell, Miriam, 429
Connery, Sean, 371, 504
Conrad, Joseph, 454
Cooke, Sir George, 195, 198
Cooper, David, 148, 156
Cooper, J.C., 145

Corbets Tey, 514, 515
Cornmill Meadow, Waltham Abbey, 126
Couchman, Clara, 463
Country Park, Epsom, 344
Country Walks Around London, 368
County of London Plan (1943) 42–3, 175, 206
Course, Richard, 71
Courtney, Dave, 50, 498, 550
Cowley, 219–20, 222, 225
Cowley, Abraham, 283
Coxe, Sir Richard, 153
Craig, Michael, 193
Cranmer, Thomas, 412
Crash (Ballard), 213, 245, 311
Crash! (TV documentary), 169
Craven, Wes, 486
Crawshaw, Steve, 371
Crest Homes, 150, 152, 167–8, 190, 491
Crews Hill, 136, 137
cricket, 197
The Criminal (film), 355
Crosby, Theo, 144–5
Cross Your Heart and Hope to Live (TV documentary), 194
Crossland, William, 270, 287–8
Crow, Arthur, 85
Crowley, Aleister, 445
Crown, Dr Sidney, 338
Crown Hill Bridge, 530
Croydon, 389–90
Cruise, Tom, 152
Cuffley, 113, 138
Curtis, Kenneth, 439
Curtis, Nick, 483
Curtis, W.T., 158

Dadas, Albert, 146, 147
Dadd, Richard, 362

Dagenham, 45, 47
Dagnam Park, 520
Dahl, Roald, 188
Dalí, Salvador, 473
Dalston, 119, 120
Danbury Hill, 576–7
Darent, River, 393, 413, 431, 448, 449, 452
Darent Valley, 409, 410, 411, 417, 423, 450
Darent Valley Hospital, 458
Dark, Robert, 209
Dartford, 402, 447–455, 456–66
Dartford Crossing *see* Queen Elizabeth II Bridge
Dartford Marshes, 452, 454
Dartford Tunnel, 473
Davidson, Emily, 363
Davis, Michael, 314
Dawson, Jennifer, 171
De Burgh family, 231
Deakin, Roger, 515–6
Dearden, Basil, 193
Decabral, Alan, 12–13
Dee, David, 210
Dee, Dr John, 210, 211, 268
Defoe, Daniel, 332
DeLillo, Don, 52, 201
Denham, 181, 212, 215
Denham Studios, 215
Derby Day (Frith), 356, 360, 361–2
Devereux, Paul, 122, 133
Diana, Princess, 34, 185–6
Dickens, Charles, 183–4, 384, 456
Diggers, 299, 306
Disney Corporation, 500
Donne, John 255
Dorking, 328
Dowding, Air Marshal Lord, 218
Downes, Kerry, 161
Downriver (Iain Sinclair), 546

Dracula (Stoker), 486–9, 490, 491, 492–3
Driffield, 428
Drummond, Bill, 29–33, 34, 35, 36–7, 44, 45, 47, 54, 56, 58–9, 60, 66, 69, 76, 103, 106, 108, 110–11, 112, 116–7, 118, 188, 509, 541
Duffy, Maureen, 208
Dulwich, 414, 415
Dun, Aidan Andrew, 144
Durgnat, Raymond, 163, 164

Earthly Joys (Gregory), 88–9
East India Dock Road, 45
East London Cemetery, 49–50
Edge, S.F., 300
Edinburgh, Duke of, 43
Ediswan Company, 41
Edmonton, 61, 545
Edward Jenner Hospital, Gloucestershire, 460
Edward the Confessor, 172
Edwards, Richey, 528
Egg, Augustus, 361
Eggar, Tim, 74
Egham, 258–62, 291
Eleanor of Castile, Queen, 130–1
Eliot, T.S., 468
Elizabeth I, 92, 93
Ely, Alun, 312, 314
Emberton, Joseph, 282
Endfield, Cy, 356
Enfield Chase, 14, 81, 87, 92–3, 530
Enfield Island Village, 68–9, 70, 73
Enfield Lock, 39, 66, 67–8, 70, 71
Enfield Lock Action Group Association, 71
Enfield Sewage Works, 63

Environment Agency, 62
Epping Forest, 10, 87, 519, 527–32
Epsom, 331–3, 340, 352–4, 443
   Downs, 355, 357–9, 359, 363
   mental hospitals, 337–52, 433,
     435–9
   tunnels, 357–9, 439–40
   war graves, 437–8
   well, 331–3
Epstein, Jacob, 282
Essex, Earl of, 182, 183
Essex Boys (film), 498
Essex Field Club, 529
Essex Range Rover Murders,
    496–7, 499, 501, 504
Etchells, Frederick, 282
Evelyn, John, 93
Eynsford, 427–8, 430–1

Fairey Aviation, 236
Fairview New Homes plc, 68, 70,
   71, 72, 74–5
Falconer, Lord, 548, 550
Farina, Richard, 528
Farningham, 429
Fawkes, Guy, 93
Fedden, Robin, 391
Ferguson Radio Corporation
   Limited, 41–2
Fernihough, Eric, 300
The Fighting Temeraire (Turner),
   385
'Finella', Cambridge, 281–3
Fir Wood, 139
Fisher, Allen, 226
Fleming, John Ambrose, 41
Fludd, Robert, 211, 254, 255,
   255–6
Forbes, Bryan, 194
Forbes, Mansfield, 279, 282
foot-and-mouth disease, 10, 81

Ford, Ford Madox, 204–6, 551
Fort Halstead, 424–5
Forty Hall, 87, 96
Foucault, Michel, 163, 165, 172,
   179
Four Weddings and a Funeral (film),
   485
Fowlers End (Kersh), 542–3
Fox, Peter, 516
Francis, Dr Dylan, 254–6, 437
Franju, Georges, 163–4
Franklin, Benjamin, 406
Freeman, Revd Stephen, 40
Friends Bridge, 53
Friends of the Earth, 71
Frith, William Powell, 355,
   360–3
Fry, Maxwell, 282
Fuller, Buckminster, 157, 194
Fuller, Peter, 528
Fulton, Hamish, 148
Furze Hill House, Reigate, 323
'The Future of London' (Ford
   Madox Ford), 205–6

Gade, River, 180, 182
The Gaia Hypothesis (Lovelock),
   115
Gaiman, Neil, 106–7, 108
garden centres, 135–6
Garnault, Michael, 99
Garner, Roy, 498
Gascoyne, David, 432–4
Gaze, Mike, 114
George III, 93
George VI, 115, 357
George and Dragon, Westerham,
   391
Gerz, Jochen, 103, 116–8
Get Carter (film), 272
Gilbert, Bob, 83

Gilbert, Bruce, 217, 474
Gill, Eric, 281–2, 326–7, 413
Gilpin, William, 319
Gimpo, 30–3, 35, 58
Glastonbury, 249, 250
Godard, Jean-Luc, 453
Golden Grove (pub), 278–9
The Golden Valley (Palmer), 421
Golders Green, 104–5
golf courses, 370–2
Good, Dr James, 231
The Good Listener (Belton), 276–7
Goodman Price Demolition Ltd,
    343
Gordon, Elizabeth, 144
Gormley, Antony, 549
Grace, Michael Paul, 154
Grace, W.G., 154
Graham, W.S., 445
Grand Junction Canal Company,
    182
Grand Union Canal, 180, 181–5,
    187, 190, 212, 218, 220,
    221–2, 227, 228
Grant, Angela, 92
Grant, Hugh, 485
Grant, Russell, 193
Gravesend, 473
Grays, 46, 473, 476, 479–80
Great Bookham Common, 325
Great Expectations (Dickens), 456
Great Foster's Hotel, 272
Great Missenden, 188
Great Wood, Epsom, 344
Greater London Plan 1944
    (Abercrombie), 85
green belts, 83–6
The Green London Way (Gilbert), 83,
    368
Green Path, 229, 232, 237, 239,
    241

Greene, Graham, 188, 264
Greenhithe, 463, 473, 490
Greenwich Observatory, 29, 36–7
Gregory, Philippa, 88–90, 97
Griffith, George, 264
Griffiths, Bill, 221–7, 246, 525
Grogan, Emmett, 263
*A Guide to Glastonbury's Temple of
    the Stars* (Maltwood), 249
Guillaume, Emile, 105
The Gun (pub), 546–7
Gurney, Ivor, 443, 445
Gwynn, Nell, 332

The Ha-Ha (Dawson), 171
Hacking, Ian, 146, 164, 203
Hackney, 8, 20, 33, 418–9,
    525–7
Hackney Cut, 55
Hackney Marshes, 52, 56
Haggerston, 8, 10
Hall, Jerry, 450
Hallam, Arthur, 532
Halstead, 424
Hamilton, the Honourable Charles,
    319, 321, 322, 323
Hamilton, Sir Ian, 395
Hanbury, Samuel, 345
Hanbury, Sir Thomas, 100, 312
Hanbury Institute, Genoa, 383
Hancox, Joy, 211
Handbook to the Environs of London
    (Thorne), 96
Hannibal (Harris), 521
Harefield, 191
Harefield Hospital, 190, 191–200,
    202–3
Harefield Park, 195, 196, 204
Harmondsworth, 232, 233, 237
Harold, King of England, 21, 520
Harold Hill, 521

Harold Wood, 518, 519, 520

Harperbury Hospital, 154, 163, 165, 168

Harris, Thomas, 521

Hart, Kit, 413

Harvey, William, 212, 254, 255

Hatfield House, 87, 93

Havelock, General Henry, 451

Havering-atte-Bower, 522

Hawksmoor (Ackroyd), 142

Hawksmoor, Nicholas, 83, 100, 158–61

Haydon, Benjamin, 356

Hayward, William Curtis, 434, 437, 442–6

Heart of Harefield (Shepherd), 196

Heathrow Airport, 228, 233–8

Heeps, Richard, 246

Heighs, Michael, 438

Heller, Otto, 193

Hellyer, Arthur, 461

Henry VIII, 412

Herne Hill, 384

Heron Hospitality Centre, 58

Hertford Union Canal, 48

Herzog, Werner, 412, 535

Hessayon, Joan, 97–9, 136

Hewitt, Bryan, 99, 102

Hiaasen, Carl, 380

High Beach, Epping Forest, 39, 532, 533

High-Rise (Ballard), 265

A High Way to Heaven (Chippindale), 382–3

Hill, Christopher, 306, 307

Hill, Geoffrey, 439

Hine, George Thomas, 346, 349, 351

The History of Heathrow (Sherwood), 233–4, 235

Hobbs Cross, 522–3, 524

Holloway, Jane, 288

Holloway, Thomas, 270, 287–8

Holloway Sanatorium, 272, 287–8

Holy Cross and St Lawrence Church, Waltham Abbey, 19, 21–3, 103, 536

Home, Stewart, 34

Hooke Hill, 139

Hope Inn, Stanwellmoor, 239–40

Hope Moncrieff, A.R., 97–8, 523

Hopkins, Ben, 202, 203

Hopkins, Harry, 461, 466

Horovitz, Michael, 121

Horton Hospital, Epsom, 338, 341, 342, 345–6, 349, 351, 352, 436–7

Horton Kirby, 431

Hosein brothers, 521

Howard, Ebenezer, 343, 84–5

Howard, Luke, 369

Howe, Viscount, 153

Huicks, Dr, 93

Hulton, Sir Edward, 326

Hunt, Holman, 327

Hurburgh, Peter, 313, 314

Huston, John, 266

Huxley, Aldous, 301–2, 349

ibis hotel, Thurrock, 510, 547

Ikea, Lakeside, 512

An Illustrated Encyclopaedia of Traditional Symbols (Cooper), 145

Illustrations and Account of the Temple Church (Clarkson), 209

Ingress Abbey, 490, 491

Ingress Park, 473

It Never Gets Dark All Night (Hayward), 434, 441–4, 446

Iver Heath, 218

Jackson, Kevin, 222, 246–8, 249, 252, 253–4, 255, 258, 270, 272–3, 277, 278–9, 283, 410, 426, 432, 435, 436–7, 446, 447–8, 448–9, 451, 519, 520, 525, 527, 528, 535–7, 541
Jackson, Nigel, 92
Jagger, Mick, 448, 450–1, 466
Jain Estate, 138
James I, 88, 89, 90
Jarvis, Martin, 71
Jefferies, Richard, 349
Jenner, Edward, 460
Jennings, Elizabeth, 444
Jennings, Humphrey, 279
Jervoise, Samuel Clarke, 153
John Giles and Biven, 175–6
Johnson, Lydia, 347
Johnson, Randolph, 314
Jones, David, 434, 443, 444, 446
Jones, Sarah, 168
Jones, Steve, 371
Jones, Tom, 251, 302
Jones, Vinnie, 50
'Journey Out of Essex' (Clare), 534
A Journey Through Ruins (Wright), 345
Joyce Green Hospital, Dartford, 452, 456–7, 458–66, 491

Keating, Tom, 401
Keats, John, 329
Kees, Weldon, 528
Keiller, Patrick, 304–5, 479, 482–3
Kelvedon Hatch, Essex, 330
Kent, Duke of, 450
Kenyatta, Jomo, 266
Kerouac, Jack, 324
Kerr, Darren, 501
Kersh, Gerald, 207, 542–3, 545

Kidman, Nicole, 152
Kiff, Ken, 122
King's Arbour, 234–5
The Kingston Zodiac (Caine), 249
Knaphill, 342
Knights Templar, 485–6, 516–7
Kops, Bernard, 206–7
Korda, Alexander, 215
Korda, Zoltan, 266
Kosmon (cult), 433
Kray, Charlie, 498
Kray, Reg, 348–9, 498
Kray, Ronnie, 347–9, 498
Kubrick, Stanley, 152
Kuhne, Eric, 470

La Disparition (Perec), 262
La Jetée (Marker), 427–8
La Tête contre les murs (Franju), 163–4
Laing, John, 155
Laing, R.D., 14, 148, 156
Lakeside, Thurrock, 11, 46, 481, 512
Lamb, Charles and Mary, 95
Lambert, Percy, 300
Lambrianou, Tony, 526
Lamont, Norman, 275
Langley Park, 218
Lavery, Sir John, 401
Lawrence, T.E., 528
'Le Scale del Paradiso', 385, 388
Lea Valley, 26, 38–44, 59–77, 86
Lea Valley Developments (LVD), 72
Leatherhead, 325–6
Leatherhead Common, 325
Leavesden Hospital, Abbots Langley, 172, 175–80, 212
Lee, Robert, 486
Lee Enfield rifle, 68

Lee Navigation, 47, 52, 54, 55, 60, 66, 69, 545–6
Lee Navigation path, 45, 47
Lee Valley Regional Park, 39, 48, 127
Lee Valley Regional Park Authority, 38–9, 42, 62, 64, 75, 96
Lee Valley Trading Estate, 60
Leeson, Nick, 372
Lennon, John, 251, 302
Levellers, 306
Lewer, David, 209
Lewis, Dr Jim, 40, 42
Lewis, Monk, 321
Lichtenstein, Rachel, 132–3, 202, 338–40, 348, 472, 531–2
Life for Ruth (film), 193
Light of the World (Hunt), 327
Lightermans Quay, Grays, 481
Limehouse Cut, 48
Linnell, John, 399–400, 407–8, 414, 419, 421
Liquid City (Atkins), 473
Lister, Raymond, 323, 414
Littlebrook Power Station, 490
Locke King, Hugh, 300–1
Lodwick, John, 528
Loh, Daniel, 371–2
London, City of, 71
London Colney Aerodrome, 154
London Executive Aviation, 524
London Eye, 6, 18, 549
London Golf Club, 371–2
The London Loop (Sharp), 83, 368
London Stone, 241
London: The Biography (Ackroyd), 208
London Waste Ltd, Edmonton, 61, 63, 63–4, 74, 545
London's Lea Valley (Lewis), 40
The Lonely Tower (Palmer), 323

Long, Richard, 118, 148
Long Grove Hospital, Epsom, 338, 339, 341, 341–2, 343, 347–8, 349
Long Grove Light Railway, Epsom, 353
Long Reach Smallpox Hospital, 463–4
Losey, Joseph, 355, 421
Lovecraft, H.P., 515
Lovelock, James, 115
Lowell, Robert, 528
Lucie-Smith, Edward, 444
Lullingstone, 426–7
Lutyens, Sir Edwin, 253

M25
  driving around, 13–14
  excessive use of, 82–3
  Junction 9, 327, 328, 330
  Junction 15, 233
  Junction 30, 496
  length, 7, 32
  opening (1986), 3–6
  purpose, 10–12
'M25 Three', 313–4
McClean, Lennie, 50
McDowell, Malcolm, 194
McFayden, Jock, 8, 48, 59, 490
McGoohan, Patrick, 193
McGrath, Raymond, 281
Machen, Arthur, 188–9
McKay, Muriel, 521
McKean, Dave, 107
McKenzie, Kelvin, 371
MacSweeney, Barry, 227
McVitie, Jack 'the Hat', 55, 496
Mad Travelers (Hacking), 146
Madness and Civilization (Foucault), 163
The Magic Mountain (Mann), 468

Maier, Michael, 211
malaria, as treatment for the insane, 350–1
Maltwood, Katharine, 249–50
A Man for All Seasons (film), 266
Mann, Thomas, 468
Manning, Mark, 58
The Manor Hospital, Epsom, 338, 342, 349
Mar Dyke, 495, 515
Marconi Wireless Telegraph Company, 41
Mardyke Path, 513
Marker, Chris, 427
Markfield Recreation Ground, South Tottenham, 545
Marks, Ginger, 496
Marsh Lane, Dartford, 463–4
Marshal, William, Earl of Pembroke, 209
Marshgate Recreation Ground, 53
Marx, Karl, 397
Mason, John, 153
Matthews, Emma, 490
Maxwell, Robert, 391
Mayor Treloar's College, 125
Meacher, Michael, 62–3
Medvedev, Zhores, 115
Mee, Arthur, 405–6, 406, 428
Meenfield Wood, 423
Mendelsohn, Erich, 278
Meredith, George, 329
meridian line, 37, 126–7
Merstham, 370, 371–2, 373–4
Message, Reuben, 463
Metropolitan Asylums Board, 460
Metropolitan Water Board, 95
Meux, Sir Henry, 89
Meux, Lady Valerie, 99
Middlesex Filter Beds, 54, 56
Mile End New Town, 493

Mill Hill, 103, 104, 105–6, 113
Millennium Dome, 3, 6, 17, 29, 34, 81, 200, 265, 469, 541, 546, 547, 549–51
Millennium Eve, 17–26, 541–51
Mills, Sir John, 193
Milton, John, 188
Mitchell, Adrian, 444
Mitchell, Frank, 496
Mitchell, Margaret, 528
Monbiot, George, 349
Monck, George, Duke of Albemarle, 89
Monet, Claude, 397, 398
Montagu, Venetia, 398
Moorcock, Michael, 25, 208, 214–5, 542
Moore, Alan, 107, 246, 522
Morant's Court Farm, 407
Morecambe, Eric, 190, 193
Morton, Andrew, 185–6
Moseley, Billy, 55
Mosquito Chamber, 330–1
Mother London (Moorcock), 208
Mottram, Professor Eric, 225, 226,
Mouth & Foot Painting Artists' Gallery, Selborne 120
multi-storey car parks, 169–70
Museo Bicknell, Bordighera, 383
My Manor (Richardson), 357
Myddelton, Sir Hugh, 93–4, 96
Myddelton House, 14, 91, 96–7, 100, 101, 102
Myers, William Joseph, 153
Myriorama, 162

Nairn, Ian, 489
Napsbury Hospital, 163, 166, 179
Nathan, Sir Frederick, 41
National Association for Mental Health, 351

National Institute for Medical
    Research Mill Hill, 103, 106,
    113–5, 118, 519, 544
National Trust, 318
*Natural History and Antiquities of
    Selborne* (White), 119
Near Underriver (Palmer), 422
Nemon, Oscar, 393
Neumann, Eric, 204
New Eltham, 82
New Labour
    Ballard on, 267
    countryside policy, 86
    mental health policy, 179, 352
New River, 93–6
Newman, Kim, 486
Newman, Nanette, 194
Newmarket, 346
Nicholson, William, 396
Nicholson's Gin Distillery, 49
Nicklaus, Jack, 371
Nieuwkoop, Pieter 114
Night and the City (Kersh), 207
The Nine Lives of Tomas Katz (film),
    201–2, 203
Noak Hill, 519, 522
Nonsuch Palace, 439
North Circular Road, 60
North Downs, 369
Northern Sewage Outflow, 48, 49
Northfleet, 473
Noye, Kenneth, 12–13, 372, 497,
    507
Nuttall, Jeff, 225

Oakley, Chris, 148
O'Connell, Sanjida, 380
Octagon (property developers), 288,
    290, 291
Oddie, Bill, 500
Offa, 409

Old Ford Lock, 51
Olson, Charles, 157
O'Mahoney, Bernard, 498–9, 499,
    500–2, 503, 503–5, 506–8
*The Origins and History of
    Consciousness* (Neumann), 204
Otford, 404, 408–9, 410, 411
Our Mutual Friend (Dickens), 183–4
Ove Arup and Partners, 253

Packer, Kerry, 371
Painshill Park, 318–24
Painting as a Pastime (Churchill), 401
Paleologou, Effie, 104, 106, 116,
    201, 511
Palmer, Samuel, vii, 309, 320,
    322–3, 376, 399–400, 401,
    404–5, 407–8, 410, 414–5,
    416–22, 425, 468
Paracelsus, 255
Parker, Ian, 274
Parker Bowles, Andrew, 102
Pasolini, Pier Paolo, 412
Passingford Bridge, 519, 523
Passingford Mill, 523
Paxman, Jeremy, vii
Payne, Stewart, 70
Peake, Mervyn, 287
Pearson, John, 348
Pedder, Beth, 71–75
Penton Mound, Islington, 94
Pepler, G.L., 85
Pepys, Samuel, 332
Perec, Georges, 262
Persia, Shah of, 491
Petit, Chris, 5, 6, 50, 66, 71, 143–4,
    367, 468, 470, 472–3, 474, 476
Peugeot 505s, illegal export to
    Zambia, 505–6
Pevsner, Sir Nikolaus, 521
Pfizer, Walton Oaks, 367–8

pheasants, killed on roads, 379–80
Pickett's Lock, 63–6
Pilgrims Way, 367, 368, 369, 375, 378, 380–1, 387, 403, 408
Pinochet, General Augusto, 274–7
Pinter, Harold, 443
Piper, John, 91
Pitt-Rivers, General Augustus, 529
Planter and Visiting Agent in Ceylon (Arthur Sinclair), 387
Plath, Sylvia, 170–1
Plessy Thorn Electronics, 524
The Poetics of Space (Bachelard), 515
pollution
Enfield Lock, 70–74
   London Waste Ltd, Edmonton, 61, 63, 63–4, 74
   Ponders End, 40–41, 66, 542, 544
Pope, Alexander, 319, 322
Pope, Sir Thomas, 93
Porters Park, Shenley, 153–4, 158
Potter, Jennifer, 322
Potters Bar, 138, 139, 140–4, 171
Powell, Enoch, 351
Powell, Michael, 4
Power, Anne, 343
Prehistoric London: Its Mounds and Circles (Gordon), 144
Prescott Channel, 51
Procter, John, 439
Proctor & Gamble factory, Thurrock, 484
The Profession of Violence (Pearson), 348
The Prospect (Palmer), 323
Prosser, George Frederick, 319, 320
Pugin, E.W. 287
Purfleet, 10, 46, 201, 463, 487–9, 491, 493

Quantum Cloud (Gormley), 549
Quebec House, Westerham, 392, 394–5
Queen Elizabeth II Bridge, Dartford, 5, 6, 11, 31–2, 46, 252, 453, 455, 463, 464, 467, 473, 480, 491–2, 496, 510

racehorses, 360
The Raging Moon (film), 194
Rainham Marshes, 45, 500, 502
Raisman, Geoff, 114
Rammey Marsh, 75
Rank, J. Arthur, 215–6
Ranter (MacSweeney), 227
Ranters, 306, 307
Raphael, Cecil Frank, 154
Raquel's nightclub, Basildon, 498–9, 500, 507
Raynsford, Nick, 63–4
Redway, Father, 326
Reedbeds, Shoreham, 416
Reigate, 369
Relations (Renchi), 281
'Renchi' *see* Bicknell, Laurence
Rendezvous (café), 390
Repton, Humphry, 167, 168
Repton Park, 166–7, 168, 340
The Resurrection (Spencer), 486
Rettenden, 497–8, 498, 508
Re-Visioning the Earth (Devereux), 122
Reynolds, Bruce, 356
Richard, Cliff, 251, 302
Richards, Keith, 451
Richardson, Charlie, 356–7
Richardson, Eddie, 355, 357
Richmond, George, 404–5, 407, 414, 417, 421
Ricketts, Dr, 460
Ridley, Nicholas, 277

ring roads, origin, 4
The Risk of Being Alive (Francis), 254
Ritblat, Conrad, 358
River Improvement Acts (1424 and 1430), 39
Robbery (film), 356
Roberts, David, 384
Roberts, Harry, 520–1
Robertson, Howard, 282
Robeson, Paul, 266
Robins, William 'Budgie', 314
Robinson, William, 91
Robinson in Space (film), 304–5
Roding Valley, 523, 524
Rodinsky, David, 133, 167, 206, 338–40 343, 348, 350, 531–2
Rodinsky's Room (Lichtenstein and Sinclair), 472
Rogers, Richard, 72, 343
Rogers of Riverside, Lord, 72, 343
Rolfe, Craig, 499
Rooks Hill, 422
Rose, Emery, 397
Rosebery, Lord, 346
Rossen, Robert, 356
Rotherhithe, 462
Rowe, Raphael, 314
Roy, General, 234
Royal Alexandra and Albert School, 370
Royal Gunpowder Mills, Waltham Abbey, 38, 127–30, 330
Royal Holloway College, 270, 287, 291–2
Royal Horticultural Society Gardens, Wisley, 312–3
Royal Small Arms Factory, Enfield Lock, 67, 68, 70, 72
Runnymede Bridge, 252–3, 256, 257

Rural Rides (Cobbett), 235
Ruskin, John, 384

Sainsbury's, Cobham, 316–7
St Ann's Hill, 271, 273, 277, 279
St Bartholomew-the-Great Church, 210, 255
St Bartholomew's Church, Otford, 412
St Bartholomew's Hospital, 212, 254
St Botolph's Church, Chevening, 406, 407
St Botolph's Church, Shenley, 159–61
St Clement's Church, West Thurrock, 485–6, 489
St Ebba's Hospital, Epsom, 349, 358, 437
St George's Hill, 251, 284, 300, 302, 307–8, 308
St Katharine's Church, Merstham, 373–4
St Lawrence's Hospital, Caterham, 176
St Martin's Church, West Drayton, 230–2
St Mary's Church, Harmondsworth, 232, 237
St Thomas à Becket's well, Otford, 411
Salisbury, Earl of *see* Cecil, Robert
Salmon, Joseph, 307
Samuel, Theo, 231
Sanders, James Harris, 153
Sanders of the River (film), 266
Sandle, Michael, 144
The Sands of the Kalahari (film) 357
Sangwine, Tony, 5–6, 258, 325, 424, 525, 530
Sara H, 285–6, 293–6

Schellinks, William, 332
Schnabel, Julian, 319
Schrader, Paul, 247
Scott, George Gilbert, 287
Scruton, Roger, 506
Sebald, W.G., 528–9
Secret Gardens (Potter), 322
Selborne, 119
Self, Will, 551
Sellors, Sir Thomas Holmes, 197
Sellwood, Emily, 532
Sergeant, John, 5, 71, 338, 367,
    502–3
Sevenoaks, 421
Sewardstone, 39
Shadwell, Thomas, 332
Sharp, David, 83
Shasbury, 217
Shaw, Beatrice, 197
The Shell Book of British Walks,
    368
Shelley, Mary, 95
Shenley, 146, 148–61, 163
Shenley Hall, 149
Shenley Hospital, 148, 149–50,
    154–6 163, 166
Shenley Manor, 152
Shepherd, Mary, 196
Shepperton, 265–9
Sherman, Lou, 43
Sherwood, Philip, 233–4, 235
Shooters Hill, 82, 425
Shoreditch, 8
Shoreham, 407, 408, 413, 413–23
Sickert, Walter, 401
Siebel, 259, 260–2, 268
Sigal, Clancy, 155–8
Sinclair, Anna, 9, 19, 20, 21–2, 119,
    286, 541, 548, 551
Sinclair, Arthur, 387
Skillet Hill, 531

Sligo, Marchioness of, 153
Slough, 218
The Smallest Show on Earth (film),
    542–3
smallpox, 460–6
Smith, Andrew, 84
Smith, David, 312–3
So This Is Ecstasy (O'Mahoney),
    498–9
Soames, Mary, 400
South Darenth, 447
South Downs, 369
South Mimms service station,
    141–5
Spedding, James, 533
Spencer, Stanley, 486
Spittles, David, 168
Springfield Park, 56
Squerryes Court, Westerham, 394
Staines, 241–2, 248, 252–3
Stanford le Hope, 454
Stanhope, Charles, 406
Stanwellmoor, 239
Stanyon, John, 195
Stapleford Aerodrome, 524
Stephen, Leslie, 329
Stevenson, Robert Louis, 329
Stoke D'Abernon, 324–5
Stoker, Bram, 486–9, 490, 491,
    492, 493
Stokes, Dr Kenneth, 197
Stoneness Point, 484, 490
Straw, Jack, 267, 274, 276
Stukeley, William, 217, 234
The Surgeon of Crowthorne
    (Winchester), 229
Swan, Joseph Watson, 40–41
Swanley, 82
swans, accidents caused by, 10–11
Swedenborg, Emanuel, 54
Sweetser, Wesley D., 188–9

Tate, Pat, 499, 502, 507
Tatham, Frederick 414, 416
Teachers' Centre, Hackney, 526
Temple Bar, 108, 109, 132
Temple Church, 208–10, 486
The Temple Church in London (Lewer and Dark), 209
Temple Hill, 469, 474
Tennyson, Alfred, 532–3
Thames Chase, 513, 514
Thatcher, Denis, 371
Thatcher, Margaret, 3–4, 6, 92, 274, 274–5, 276, 328
Theobalds Park, 6, 15, 88–91, 106, 108
Theydon Bois, 525, 527
Thomson, Jonathan, 379
Thorn, Sir Jules, 41–2
Thorne, James, 96, 480
Thorpe, 251, 270, 271
Three Mills, Bromley-by-Bow, 48, 48–9, 51, 56
Thurrock, 11, 46, 501
Tilbury, 471, 473, 475, 480
Tilden, Philip, 399
Timberden Bottom, 423
Tissie, Philippe, 146, 147
To the Finland Station (Wilson), 396–7
tobacco, as treatment for the insane, 178
Tobin, Mary, 353
Tomorrow: A Peaceful Path to Real Reform (Howard), 84–5
Tong, Michael, 422
Touch of Evil (film), 272
Tradescant, John, 14, 15, 88–9, 90, 108
Trafalgar House, 72
Trent Park, 87, 93, 111
Trevelyan, Sir George, 530–1

Trocchi, Alex, 183
The True Leveller Standard Advanced (Winstanley), 306
Tucker, Tony, 499, 502
Turner, J.M.W., 384–5
Turner Axis, 144–5
Tyler, Wat, 448, 451

The Unabomber Manifesto, 37, 57
Underriver, 421–3
Underriver (Samuel Palmer's Golden Valley) (Barton and Tong), 422–3
Upminster, 515, 517–8
Uxbridge, 216, 218, 219
Uziyel, Liat, 511, 531

Valentine, Ruth, 344, 346, 349, 352
The Valley Thick with Corn (Palmer), 418, 420
Van Gogh, Vincent, 147–8
Vermilion Sands (Ballard), 470
View from Rooks Hill (Palmer), 422
Virginia Park, 288–91
Virginia Water, 271, 273, 287
Voice of the Fire (Moore), 522

Walker, Amanda, 312–3
Wallen, Martin J., 435, 437, 440, 440–1, 446
Walpole, Horace, 321
Walsh, Raoul, 356
Walter, Eugene Victor, 122
Waltham Abbey, 7, 9, 18–26, 76, 77, 103, 126–32, 530, 535–7, 541–2
Waltham Cross, 88, 130–2
Walton Oaks, 366–7
Walton-on-the-Hill, 364
war graves, Epsom, 437–9

The War of the Worlds (Wells),
303–4, 337, 349, 402
Warren, Peter, 64
waste incineration, 61–3
Waterlog (Deakin), 515–6
Watford, 170, 184–7, 189
Watson, Richard, 62
Watton's Green, 519
Wedgwood, Josiah, 319
Weizmann, Dr Chaim, 41
Welch, John, 287
Welles, Orson, 304
Wells, H.G., 264, 303–4, 337, 349
Welsh Harp (pub), 19, 536–7
Wentworth, 273–7
West, Nathanael, 528
West Drayton, 217, 228, 229–32
West Ham, 49
West Hill Hospital, Dartford, 456–7
West Thurrock, 201, 485
Westerham, 389–93, 402–3
Western Jewish Cemetery, 15,
132–3, 531–2
Weston, Jessie, 59
Wey, River, 284
Weybridge, 284, 286, 299
Whalers (Turner), 385
White, Frank, 416
White, Gilbert, 119
White, Colonel Henry, 153
White, Luke, 153
White Webbs Park, 87, 93, 111
Whiteley, William, 310
Whiteley Village, 309–11, 315
Whiteread, Rachel, 54, 112
Whomes, John, 496–7, 500, 506–7,
508
Wick Wood, 546
Wickham, Anna, 346
Williams, David, 505

Williams, Kerrie, 457
Williams, John, 54–5
Williamson, Aaron, 123
Wilson, Claire Francis, 277
Wilson, Edmund, 396
Wilson, George, 312
Winchester, Simon, 229
Winstanley, Gerrard, 251, 299,
306–8
Wisbey, Tommy, 356
Wisley, 305, 311–2
Woburn Park, 284
Wolf, Leonard, 488
Wolfe, James, 390, 392, 393,
394–5
Wood, Derwent, 393
Woodcote Park, Epsom, 332
Woodroffe, Paul, 327
The World Turned Upside Down
(Hill), 305
Worlds of New Measure (Bush), 226
Wren, Sir Christopher, 109–10
Wright, Ian, 390
Wright, Patrick, 345

Xerox building, Uxbridge, 218–9

Yacoub, Magdi, 190, 199
Yates, Peter, 356
Yates, William, 417
Yorke, Gerald, 445
Young, Arthur, 480
Young (Colwell), 429

Zambia, and export of Peugeot
505s, 505–6
Zola, Gianfranco, 371
Zone of the Interior (Sigal), 155
Zulli, Michael, 106, 109
Zulu (film), 356